Lecture Notes in Computer Science 6456

Commenced Publication in 1973
Founding and Former Series Editors:
Gerhard Goos, Juris Hartmanis, and Jan van Leeuwen

Editorial Board

W0192952

Anna Esposito   Antonietta M. Esposito
Raffaele Martone   Vincent C. Müller
Gaetano Scarpetta (Eds.)

Toward Autonomous, Adaptive, and Context-Aware Multimodal Interfaces

Theoretical and Practical Issues

Third COST 2102 International Training School
Caserta, Italy, March 15-19, 2010
Revised Selected Papers

 Springer

Volume Editors

Anna Esposito
Second University of Naples
and IIASS, International Institute for Advanced Scientific Studies
Via Pellegrino 19, 84019 Vietri sul Mare (SA), Italy
E-mail: iiass.annaesp@tin.it

Antonietta M. Esposito
Istituto Nazionale di Geofisica e Vulcanologia, Osservatorio Vesuviano
Via Diocleziano 328, 80124 Napoli, Italy
E-mail: aesposito@ov.ingv.it

Raffaele Martone
Second University of Naples, Department of Engineering and Informatics
Via Roma 29, 81031 Aversa (CE), Italy
E-mail: raffaele.martone@unina2.it

Vincent C. Müller
Anatolia College/ACT, Department of Humanities and Social Sciences
Kennedy Street, 55510 Pylaia, Greece
E-mail: vmueller@act.edu

Gaetano Scarpetta
University of Salerno
and IIASS, International Institute for Advanced Scientific Studies
84081 Baronissi (SA), Italy
E-mail: scarpetta@fisica.unisa.it

ISSN 0302-9743   e-ISSN 1611-3349
ISBN 978-3-642-18183-2   e-ISBN 978-3-642-18184-9
DOI 10.1007/978-3-642-18184-9
Springer Heidelberg Dordrecht London New York

Library of Congress Control Number: 2010941945

CR Subject Classification (1998): H.5, H.5.2, I.2.7, H.3-4, I.2.10, J.1

LNCS Sublibrary: SL 3 – Information Systems and Application, incl. Internet/Web
and HCI

Typesetting: Camera-ready by author, data conversion by Scientific Publishing Services, Chennai, India

Printed on acid-free paper

Springer is part of Springer Science+Business Media (www.springer.com)

This book is dedicated to our needs,
that may overcome our goals and intentions one day,
though we resist.

Preface

This volume brings together the advanced research results obtained by the European COST Action 2102: "Cross Modal Analysis of Verbal and Nonverbal Communication." The research published in this book was discussed at the Third EUCOGII-COST 2102 International Training School entitled "Toward Autonomous, Adaptive, and Context-Aware Multimodal Interfaces: Theoretical and Practical Issues," held in Caserta, Italy, during March 15–19, 2010.

The school was jointly sponsored by:

a) COST (European Cooperation in Science and Technology, www.cost.eu) in the domain of Information and Communication Technologies (ICT) for disseminating the advances of the research activities developed within the COST Action 2102 (cost2102.cs.stir.ac.uk)
b) EUCogII: 2nd European Network for the Advancement of Artificial Cognitive Systems, Interaction and Robotics (http://www.eucognition.org/).

The school afforded a change of perspective in verbal and nonverbal communication, where the research focus moved from "communicative tools" to "communicative instances" and asked for investigations that, in modeling interaction, will take into account not only the verbal and nonverbal signals but also the internal and external environment, the context, and the cultural specificity in which communicative acts take place.

The consequences in information communication technology (ICT) research should result in the development of autonomous, adaptive, and context-aware multimodal interfaces able to act by exploiting instantiated contextual and environmental signals and process them by combining previous experience (memory) adapted to the communicative instance. This new approach will foster artificial cognitive research by creating a bridge between the most recent research in multimodal communication (taking into account gestures, emotions, social signal processing etc.) and computation models that exploit these signals being aware of the context in which these signals are instantiated and of the internal and external environmental background. Human behavior exploits this information and adapts. Artificial cognitive systems must take account of this human ability for implementing a friendly and emotionally colored human machine interaction. In order to do this, investigations in cognitive computation must move from purely data-driven systems to behavioral systems able to "interact with human to achieve their goals," which may require ability to manifest intentions and goals through "resistance" to other intentions and goals (Müller argues in Chap. 1). In summary, cognitive models must be developed such that the current interactive dialogue systems, robots, and intelligent virtual avatars graphically embodied in a 2D and/or 3D interactive virtual world, are able to interact intelligently with the environment, other avatars, and particularly with human users.

The themes of the papers presented in this book emphasize theoretical and practical issues for modelling cognitive behavioral systems, ranging from the attempts to describe brain computer interface (BCI) applications, a context-based approach to the interpretation and generation of dialogue acts, close synchronization among both speakers and listeners, mutual ratification, interaction and resistance, embodiment, language and multimodal cognition, timing effects on perception, action, and behaviors.

The book is arranged in two scientific sections according to a rough thematic classification, even though both sections are closely connected and both provide fundamental insights for the cross-fertilization of different disciplines.

The first section, "Human–Computer Interaction: Cognitive and Computational Issues," deals with conjectural and processing issues of defining models, algorithms, and strategies for implementing cognitive behavioral systems. The second section, "Synchrony Through Verbal and Nonverbal Signals," presents original studies that provide theoretical and practical solutions to the modelling of timing synchronization between linguistic and paralinguistic expressions, actions, body movements, activities in human interaction and on their assistance for an effective communication.

The papers included in this book benefited from the live interactions among the many participants of the successful meeting in Caserta. Over 150 established and apprenticing researchers converged for the event.

The editors would like to thank the Coordination Council of EUCogII and the ESF COST- ICT Programme for the support in the realization of the school and the publication of this volume. Acknowledgements go in particular to the COST Science Officers Matteo Razzanelli, Aranzazu Sanchez, Jamsheed Shorish, and the COST 2102 rapporteur Guntar Balodis for their constant help, guidance, and encouragement. Appreciation goes to the COST Publication Office for supporting and guiding the publication effort. The event owes its success to more individuals than can be named, but notably the members of the local Steering Committee Alida Labella, Olimpia Matarazzo, Nicola Melone, Giovanna Nigro, Augusto Parente, Paolo Pedone, Francesco Piazza, and Luigi Trojano who supported and encouraged the initiative as well as to the staff members Hicham Atassi, Ivana Baldassarre, Domenico Carbone, Vincenzo Capuano, Francesco Alessandro Conventi, Mauro De Vito, Davide Esposito, Paolo Fioretto, Marco Grassi, and Gianluigi Ombrato who were actively involved in the success of the event. Special appreciation goes to the International Institute for Advanced Scientific Studies (IIASS), with a special mention to the memory of Maria Marinaro, and to the IIASS team Tina Marcella Nappi, Michele Donnarumma, and Antonio Natale who provided precious technical support in the organization of the school. The editors are deeply indebted to Maria Teresa Riviello for the wonderful work done in taking care of the local organization.

In addition, the editors are grateful to the contributors for making this book a scientifically stimulating compilation of new and original ideas. Finally, the editors would like to express their greatest appreciation to all the members of the COST 2102 International Scientific Committee for their rigorous and invaluable scientific revisions, their dedication, and their priceless selection process.

Anna Esposito
Antonietta M. Esposito
Raffaele Martone
Vincent C. Müller
Gaetano Scarpetta

Organization

International Steering Committee

Anna Esposito — Second University of Naples and IIASS, Italy
Marcos Faundez-Zanuy — Escola Universitaria Politecnica de Mataro, Spain
Amir Hussain — University of Stirling, UK
Raffaele Martone — Second University of Naples and IIASS, Italy
Nicola Melone — Second University of Naples and IIASS, Italy

COST 2102 International Scientific Committee

Samer Al Moubayed — Royal Institute of Technology, Sweden
Uwe Altmann — Technische Universität Dresden, Germany
Sigrún María Ammendrup — School of Computer Science, Reykjavik, Iceland
Hicham Atassi — Brno University of Technology, Czech Republic
Nikos Avouris — University of Patras, Greece
Ruth Bahr — University of South Florida, USA
Gérard Bailly — GIPSA, GRENOBLE, France
Marena Balinova — University of Applied Sciences, Vienna, Austria
Marian Bartlett — University of California, San Diego, USA
Dominik Bauer — RWTH Aachen University, Germany
Štefan Beňuš — Constantine the Philosopher University, Nitra, Slovakia
Niels Ole Bernsen — University of Southern Denmark, Denmark
Jonas Beskow — Royal Institute of Technology, Sweden
Peter Birkholz — RWTH Aachen University, Germany
Horst Bishof — Technical University Graz, Austria
Jean-Francois Bonastre — Universitè d'Avignon, France
Nikolaos Bourbakis — ITRI, Wright State University, Dayton, USA
Maja Bratanić — University of Zagreb, Croatia
Antonio Calabrese — Istituto di Cibernetica - CNR, Naples, Italy
Erik Cambria — University of Stirling, UK
Paola Campadelli — Università di Milano, Italy
Nick Campbell — University of Dublin, Ireland
Valentín Cardeñoso Payo — Universidad de Valladolid, Spain
Antonio Castro-Fonseca — Universidade de Coimbra, Portugal
Aleksandra Cerekovic — Faculty of Electrical Engineering , Croatia
Josef Chaloupka — Technical University of Liberec, Czech Republic

Mohamed Chetouani	Universitè Pierre et Marie Curie, France
Gérard Chollet	CNRS URA-820, ENST, France
Simone Cifani	Università Politecnica delle Marche, Italy
Muzeyyen Ciyiltepe	Gulhane Askeri Tip Academisi, Ankara, Turkey
Anton Cizmar	Technical University of Kosice, Slovakia
Nicholas Costen	Manchester Metropolitan University, UK
Francesca D'Olimpio	Second University of Naples, Italy
Vlado Delić	University of Novi Sad, Serbia
Giuseppe Di Maio	Second University of Naples, Italy
Marion Dohen	ICP, Grenoble, France
Thierry Dutoit	Faculté Polytechnique de Mons, Belgium
Laila DybkjÆr	University of Southern Denmark, Denmark
Jens Edlund	Royal Institute of Technology, Sweden
Matthias Eichner	Technische Universität Dresden, Germany
Aly El-Bahrawy	Ain Shams University, Cairo, Egypt
Engin Erzin	Koc University, Istanbul, Turkey
Anna Esposito	Second University of Naples, Italy
Joan Fàbregas Peinado	Escola Universitaria de Mataro, Spain
Sascha Fagel	Technische Universität Berlin, Germany
Nikos Fakotakis	University of Patras, Greece
Manuela Farinosi	University of Udine, Italy
Marcos Faúndez-Zanuy	Universidad Politécnica de Cataluña, Spain
Dilek Fidan	Ankara Universitesi, Turkey
Leopoldina Fortunati	Università di Udine, Italy
Todor Ganchev	University of Patras, Greece
Carmen García-Mateo	University of Vigo, Spain
Augusto Gnisci	Second University of Naples, Italy
Milan Gnjatović	University of Novi Sad, Serbia
Bjorn Granstrom	Royal Institute of Technology, Sweden
Marco Grassi	Università Politecnica delle Marche, Italy
Maurice Grinberg	New Bulgarian University, Bulgaria
Jorge Gurlekian	LIS CONICET, Buenos Aires, Argentina
Mohand-Said Hacid	Universite Claude Bernard Lyon 1, France
Jaakko Hakulinen	University of Tampere, Finland
Ioannis Hatzilygeroudis	University of Patras, Greece
Immaculada Hernaez	University of the Basque Country, Spain
Javier Hernando	Technical University of Catalonia, Spain
Wolfgang Hess	Universität Bonn, Germany
Dirk Heylen	University of Twente, The Netherlands
Daniel Hládek	Technical University of Košice, Slovak Republic
Rüdiger Hoffmann	Technische Universität Dresden, Germany
Hendri Hondorp	University of Twente, The Netherlands

David House	Royal Institute of Technology, Sweden
Evgenia Hristova	New Bulgarian University, Sofia, Bulgaria
Stephan Hübler	Dresden University of Technology, Germany
Isabelle Hupont	Aragon Institute of Technology, Zaragoza, Spain
Amir Hussain	University of Stirling, UK
Ewa Jarmolowicz	Adam Mickiewicz University, Poznan, Poland
Kristiina Jokinen	University of Helsinki, Finland
Jozef Juhár	Technical University Košice, Slovak Republic
Zdravko Kacic	University of Maribor, Slovenia
Bridget Kane	Trinity College Dublin, Ireland
Jim Kannampuzha	RWTH Aachen University, Germany
Maciej Karpinski	Adam Mickiewicz University, Poznan, Poland
Eric Keller	Université de Lausanne, Switzeland
Adam Kendon	University of Pennsylvania, USA
Stefan Kopp	University of Bielefeld, Germany
Jacques Koreman	University of Science and Technology, Norway
Theodoros Kostoulas	University of Patras, Greece
Maria Koutsombogera	Inst. for Language and Speech Processing, Greece
Robert Krauss	Columbia University, New York, USA
Bernd Kröger	RWTH Aachen University, Germany
Gernot Kubin	Graz University of Technology, Austria
Olga Kulyk	University of Twente, The Netherlands
Alida Labella	Second University of Naples, Italy
Emilian Lalev	New Bulgarian University, Bulgaria
Yiannis Laouris	Cyprus Neuroscience and Technology Institute, Cyprus
Anne-Maria Laukkanen	University of Tampere, Finland
Borge Lindberg	Aalborg University, Denmark
Saturnino Luz	Trinity College Dublin, Ireland
Wojciech Majewski	Wroclaw University of Technology, Poland
Pantelis Makris	Neuroscience and Technology Institute, Cyprus
Raffaele Martone	Second University of Naples, Italy
Rytis Maskeliunas	Kaunas University of Technology, Lithuania
Dominic Massaro	University of California - Santa Cruz, USA
Olimpia Matarazzo	Second University of Naples, Italy
Christoph Mayer	Technische Universität München, Germany
David McNeill	University of Chicago, USA
Nicola Melone	Second University of Naples, Italy
Katya Mihaylova	University of National and World Economy, Sofia Bulgaria
Michal Mirilovič	Technical University of Košice, Slovakia
Helena Moniz	INESC-ID, Lisbon, Portugal

Peter Reichl	FTW Telecommunications Research Center, Austria
Luigi Maria Ricciardi	Università di Napoli "Federico II", Italy
Maria Teresa Riviello	Second University of Naples and IIASS, Italy
Matej Rojc	University of Maribor, Slovenia
Nicla Rossini	Università del Piemonte Orientale, Italy
Rudi Rotili	Università Politecnica delle Marche, Italy
Algimantas Rudzionis	Kaunas university of Technology, Lithuania
Vytautas Rudzionis	Kaunas University of Technology, Lithuania
Hugo L. Rufiner	Universidad Nacional de Entre Ríos, Argentina
Milan Rusko	Slovak Academy of Sciences, Slovak Republic
Zsófia Ruttkay	Pazmany Peter Catholic University, Hungary
Yoshinori Sagisaka	Waseda University, Tokyo, Japan
Bartolomeo Sapio	Fondazione Ugo Bordoni, Rome, Italy
Mauro Sarrica	University of Padova, Italy
Gaetano Scarpetta	University of Salerno and IIASS, Italy
Silvia Scarpetta	Salerno University, Italy
Ralph Schnitker	Aachen University, Germany
Jean Schoentgen	Université Libre de Bruxelles, Belgium
Milan Sečujski	University of Novi Sad, Serbia
Stefanie Shattuck-Hufnagel	MIT, Research Laboratory of Electronics, USA
Marcin Skowron	Austrian Research Institute for Artificial Intelligence, Austria
Zdenek Smékal	Brno University of Technology, Czech Republic
Stefano Squartini	Università Politecnica delle Marche, Italy
Piotr Staroniewicz	Wroclaw University of Technology, Poland
Vojtěch Stejskal	Brno University of Technology, Czech Republic
Marian Stewart-Bartlett	University of California, San Diego, USA
Jin Su	Trinity College Dublin, Ireland
Dávid Sztahó	Budapest University of Technology and Economics, Hungary
Jianhua Tao	Chinese Academy of Sciences, P. R. China
Jure F. Tasič	University of Ljubljana, Slovenia
Murat Tekalp	Koc University, Istanbul, Turkey
Kristinn Thórisson	Reykjavík University, Iceland
Isabel Trancoso	Spoken Language Systems Laboratory, Portugal
Luigi Trojano	Second University of Naples, Italy
Wolfgang Tschacher	University of Bern, Switzerland
Markku Turunen	University of Tampere, Finland
Henk Van den Heuvel	Radboud University Nijmegen, The Netherlands
Leticia Vicente-Rasoamalala	Alchi Prefectural University, Japan

Sponsors

The following organizations sponsored and supported the International Training School:

- European COST Action 2102 "Cross-Modal Analysis of Verbal and Nonverbal Communication" (cost2102.cs.stir.ac.uk)

COST—the acronym for European Cooperation in Science and Technology—is the oldest and widest European intergovernmental network for cooperation in research. Established by the Ministerial Conference in November 1971, COST is presently used by the scientific communities of 36 European countries to cooperate in common research projects supported by national funds.

The funds provided by COST—less than 1 of the total value of the projects—support the COST cooperation networks (COST Actions) through which, with EUR 30 million per year, more than 30,000 European scientists are involved in research having a total value which exceeds EUR 2 billion per year. This is the financial worth of the European added value which COST achieves.

A "bottom – Up approach" (the initiative of launching a COST Action comes from the European scientists themselves), "à la carte participation" (only countries interested in the Action participate), "equality of access" (participation is open also to the scientific communities of countries not belonging to the European Union) and "flexible structure" (easy implementation and light management of the research initiatives) are the main characteristics of COST.

As precursor of advanced multidisciplinary research, COST has a very important role for the realization of the European Research Area (ERA) anticipating and complementing the activities of the Framework Programmes, constituting a "bridge" towards the scientific communities of emerging countries, increasing the mobility of researchers across Europe and fostering the establishment of "Networks of Excellence" in many key scientific domains such as: biomedicine and molecular biosciences; food and agriculture; forests, their products and services; materials, physical and nanosciences; chemistry and molecular sciences and technologies; earth system science and environmental management; information and communication technologies; transport and urban development; individuals, societies cultures and health. It covers basic and more applied research and also addresses issues of pre-normative nature or of societal importance. Web: http://www.cost.eu

- EUCogII: 2nd European Network for the Advancement of Artificial Cognitive Systems, Interaction and Robotics (http://www.eucognition.org/)
- Second University of Naples (www.unina2.it/), Faculty and Department of Psychology, Faculty of Science, Mathematics, and Physics and Department of Computer Engineering & Informatics, Italy

- International Institute for Advanced Scientific Studies "E.R. Caianiello" (IIASS, www.iiassvietri.it/), Italy
- Società Italiana Reti Neuroniche (SIREN, www.associazionesiren.org/)
- Regione Campania, Italy
- Provincia di Salerno, Italy

 ESF Provide the COST Office through and EC contract

COST is supported by the EU RTD Framework programme

Table of Contents

I - Human-Computer Interaction: Cognitive and Computational Issues

II - Synchrony through Verbal and Nonverbal Signals

Interaction and Resistance: The Recognition of Intentions in New Human-Computer Interaction*

Vincent C. Müller

Anatolia College/ACT, Dept. of Humanities and Social Sciences,
P.O. Box 21021, 55510 Pylaia, Greece
vmueller@act.edu
http://www.typos.de

Abstract. Just as AI has moved away from classical AI, human-computer interaction (HCI) must move away from what I call 'good old fashioned HCI' to 'new HCI' – it must become a part of cognitive systems research where HCI is one case of the interaction of intelligent agents (we now know that interaction is essential for intelligent agents anyway). For such interaction, we cannot just 'analyze the data', but we must assume intentions in the other, and I suggest these are largely recognized through resistance to carrying out one's own intentions. This does not require fully cognitive agents but can start at a very basic level. New HCI integrates into cognitive systems research and designs intentional systems that provide resistance to the human agent.

Keywords: Human-computer interaction, AI, cognitive systems, interaction, intelligence, resistance, systems design.

1 GOFAI and GOHCI

1.1 GOHCI "Good Old HCI"

It seems to me that there is a development in current Human-Computer Interaction research (HCI) that is analogous to developments in AI in the last 25 years or so, and perhaps there is a lesson to be learned there. Good old HCI (GOHCI) proceeded on the basis of the following image: Fairly intelligent humans interact with very stupid computers and the humans are trying to get the computers to do what the humans want – but the computers often don't get the point, so they need better 'interfaces' for the humans to tell them what to do. This is the agenda in classical GOHCI problems like 'text-to-speech' and 'speech-to-text'. These problems are structured in such a

---

* *Nota Bene:* Before we begin, a word of caution is in order: While I am very grateful for the invitation to address an audience on human-computer interaction, this paper is a case of the blind talking about color. In the best case it can provide some theoretical ideas that might be an inspiration for future work in HCI; namely theoretical ideas from a perspective of theoretical work on artificial cognitive systems. I am grateful to the audience at the Caserta summer school on "Autonomous, Adaptive, and Context-Aware Multimodal Interfaces" (March 2010) for its encouraging response to my programmatic remarks.

A. Esposito et al. (Eds.): COST 2102 Int. Training School 2010, LNCS 6456, pp. 1–7, 2011.

way that they cannot be solved completely, but solutions can only be approached – after all, the computers remain too stupid to get the point.

1.2 GOFAI "Good Old Fashioned AI"

In AI, from the founding fathers onwards the basic approach, for which John Hauge-land coined the expression "good old fashioned AI" or GOFAI [1] was that syntactic processing over symbolic representation is sufficient for intelligence – or perhaps even necessary, as some of the first AI theorists had claimed:

> "*The Physical Symbol System Hypothesis.* A physical symbol system has the nec-essary and sufficient means for general intelligent action. By 'necessary' we mean that any system that exhibits general intelligence will prove upon analysis to be a physical symbol system. By 'sufficient' we mean that any physical symbol system of sufficient size can be organized further to exhibit general intelligence." [2, cf. 3]

The physical symbol system hypothesis was very good news for AI since we happen to know a system that can reproduce any syntactic processing: the computer; and we thus know that reproduction in computing machines will result in intelligence, once that reproduction is achieved. What remains are just technical problems. On this un-derstanding, the understanding that cognitive ability in natural systems involves understanding the computational processes carried out in these systems, Cognitive Science and AI are really just two sides of the same coin. As a prominent proponent once put it: "Artificial intelligence is not the study of computers, but of intelligence in thought and action." [4]

1.3 Computing

It might be useful to add a little detail to the notion of 'computing' and 'syntactic' processing just introduced because they provide what I want to suggest is (or should be) the crucial difference between GOFAI and 'new AI' as well as GOHCI and 'new HCI'. The 'new' approach in both cases is the one that is not purely 'computational', not 'just the data'.

Computing in the sense used here is characterized by two features:

- It is digital (discrete-state, all relevant states are tokens of a type – a 'symbol' in the very basic sense of Newell & Simon)
- It is algorithmic (a precisely described and "effective" procedure, i.e. it defi-nitely leads to a result). The system is thus characterized by its syntactical properties.

The Church-Turing thesis [5] adds to this that all and only the effectively computable functions can be computed by some Turing machine. This means, a programmable computer with the necessary resources (time & memory) can compute any algorithm (it is a universal Turing machine); so it is irrelevant how that computer is constructed, physically. Precisely *the same* computation can be carried out on different devices; computing is 'device independent'. Of course, the practical constraints on available resources, especially on the time needed to move through the steps of an algorithm, can mean that a problem that is theoretically computable, remains practically not 'tractable'.[1]

1.4   Three Levels of Description

One might object at this point that a computer is surely not just a syntactical system – after all, a computer has a size and weight, and its symbols can mean something; these are hardly syntactical properties. However, rather than asking what a computer really *is*, I think it is more fruitful to realize that a given computer can be described on several *levels*:

1.   The *physical level* of the actual "realization" of the computer (e.g. electronic circuits on semiconductor devices)
2.   the *syntactic level* of the algorithm computed, and
3.   the *symbolic level* of content (representation), of what is computed

So, yes a computer has a size and weight (on the physical level 1) and, yes, its symbols have meaning (on the symbolic level 3), but the *computation* is on the syntactic level 2, and only there. Level 2 can be realized in various forms of level 1, i.e. the physical level does not determine which algorithm is performed (on several levels of 'algorithm'). Level 3 can be absent and is irrelevant to the function. It can have several sub-levels, e.g. the computing can symbolize sound, which is speech, which is an English sentence, which is Richard Nixon giving orders to pay blackmail money, ... (levels increasing in 'thickness' in the sense to be explained presently).

Having said that, it is important to realize that the symbolic level is something that is not part of the system but attributed to it from the outside, e.g. from humans. Expressions like "The computer classifies this word as an adverb", "The computer understands this as the emotion of anger" or "The computer obeys the program" are strictly speaking nonsense – or at best metaphorical, saying that the computer carries out some program and some user *interprets* that outcome as meaningful (more details on what is only sketched here in [8]).

2   Intelligence and Goals

2.1   Thick Description

The proposed move away from GOHCI would involve moving away from this purely syntactic level, from the 'data' that we normally begin with. To illustrate what that might mean and why it might be necessary for new HCI, allow me a short deviation to social anthropology. Social anthropology analyzes human culture, so one of its concerns is what makes some observational data 'cultural' and thus relevant for the discipline. A famous proposal that Clifford Geertz developed on the basis of ideas by the philosopher Gilbert Ryle is that for humans things must somehow be *meaningful*. As an example, he considers the observational data of a quick closing movement of

---

[1] I use a classical notion of computing here, essentially derived from Turing [5] – this is not the place to defend the position that this is the only unified notion of computing we have, but some arguments in this direction can be found in [6] and [7].

someone's eye. This, he says, may be part of cultural activity just if it is described 'thickly' as "a wink", rather than described 'thinly' as a "the twitch of an eye". One can wink "(1) deliberately, (2) to someone in particular, (3) to impart a particular message, (4) according to a socially established code, (5) without cognizance of the rest of the company" or (6) to parody of someone else's wink, ... and so on [9]. The 'thick' description involves the meaning of the action in the culture.

This distinction between thick and thin description then allows a first characterization of culture: "As interworked system of construable signs ... culture is not a power; ...; it is a context, something within which they can be intelligibly – that is thickly – described." [9]

Description of what humans do and why they do what they do must thus be "thick"; it must involve the meaning of their actions, their goals and their intentions. (It cannot be 'just the data'.) – This was missing from GOFAI and GOHCI.

3   HCI Is Part of Cognitive Systems Research

Thesis I:
HCI research is a special case of cognitive systems research

Painting the picture in a very broad brush, the move away from GOFAI is a move away from the purely syntactic system – we now recognize that physical realization plays a crucial role and that cognitive activity is embedded in bodily, emotional and volitional activity, often in interaction with other agents (the 'embodiment' of cognition).

In the light of this change, it is useful to take a second look at our explanation of HCI above, that it concerns systems that can interact with humans to achieve their goals – actually this is ambiguous: Whose goals are we talking about that of the 'system' or of the human? Since this is just a special case of the interaction that is, as we just said, crucial to cognitive activity (an aspect of embodiment), we can start to see how HCI can be a part of cognitive systems research. This is not to rehash the truism that computer systems will become 'smarter' over time, far from it: If we look at new HCI, as part of general interaction of intelligent agents, we gain a new perspective of 'thick' HCI that is not dependent on achieving 'higher levels of cognition' (whatever that means) in the machine.

4   Interaction Requires Resistance

Interaction of intelligent agents requires the recognition of the other agent *as* intelligent. What does that mean? Beyond a lot of little details, *intelligence* is the ability to flexibly successfully reach goals. For this reason, the recognition of intelligence requires the recognition of the agents' having goals (though not necessarily *which* goals these are). One typical way to recognize the goals of another intelligent agent is their pursuing of their goals, perhaps resisting our pursuing our own goals.

Thesis II:
Successful interaction requires resistance to the other agent.

Take the example of a very familiar situation: Two people walk towards each other in some narrow corridor. In order to figure out what to do, given my own goals, I might wonder: Is the other walking past me? towards me? passing on which side? One can use a rule ('walk on the right'), negotiate, but in any case one must understand the intentions – through resistance, through some force acting against my movements or intentions.

It is actually *easier* to negotiate with someone who has their own intentions than with someone who just wants to do whatever I do. In the corridor, I am more likely to collide with a super-polite person who is trying hard to get out of my way than with a bullish person who clearly indicates where he is going. It is easier to work with pedals and levers that offer resistance (sometimes called 'feedback', often an unfortunate expression); it is easier to drive a car or fly a plane if the vehicle offers a 'feel' of resistance, of 'wanting' to go this way.[2] Kicking a ball requires a certain resistance from the ball; not too much, not too little. (Note I: Even a simple example like that of the corridor always has a context. Note II: In more complex examples, the role of resistance is larger.)

Basic embodiment nicely supplements this view: our bodily actions are the basis and the model for our cognitive structure. Thus: resistance, first to the body, then to the mind. For example, we say "to grasp" when we mean to understand, and grasping requires resistance of what is grasped. In order to interact with something, we need to take it as a being with a body and a goals, accordingly something that moves purposefully.

This is one of the reasons why the notorious "Turing Test" [12], is too limited; why many people have argued that passing that test is not a sufficient condition for intelligence. But notice that it is a test of interaction, so in trying to decide whether we need new HCI or can stick to GOHCI we can take this test as a sample. In GOHCI, we are trying to pass the test without any intelligence in the system. Can this work? In new HCI, are we rejecting the test as insufficient because it offers no full verbal interaction (thus no prosody), no non-verbal interaction, no prior context, …? When we describe a situation in terms of goals and intentions, we describe it as 'meaningful', i.e. we use a 'thick' description. We need more than 'just the data'.

So, I conclude that interaction requires understanding goals and intentions, e.g. through resistance.

5 Resistance for New HCI

Thesis III: Resistance is essential even for non-cognitive HCI systems

Humans are good at interaction with other cognitive agents, like other humans or animals. We have the ability to attribute mental states to others (this is often expressed as saying we have a 'theory of mind'), even mental states that differ from my

---

[2] Caution: It is easier to know what to expect from the inexperienced because novices follow rules, experts break them [10, 11].

own – humans seem to acquire this ability around age four, as the classical 'false belief tasks' suggest. This recognition of the other as having intentional states is typically taken as a hallmark of higher-level intelligence [cf. 13]. On a neurological level, it is associated with 'mirror-neurons', the existence of which is evidence for this ability – 'seeing someone do x' is very closely associated with 'doing x'. But not only that: Humans use the very same behavior even when they know they are interacting with something that has no cognitive structure, no intentions, no goals. We are very ready to attribute 'as if' intentions to objects, to say that the car 'wants' to go left, to attribute intentions to avatars in games, to getting into a personal relation with the voice of our car navigation system – or even with the car itself (Some of this has been exploited in research that shows how humans will bond with certain 'emotional' robots; e.g. by Turkle and Dautenhahn). We assume intentions in the world, we like to use 'thick' description – one might say we are natural-born panpsychists.

This is the feature that I would suggest New HCI should exploit: Even small resistance of a computing system suggests intentions or goals (and thus intelligence) to the human user, who then knows how to interact with that system. This is not to say that New HCI should wait for computers to become sufficiently intelligent, or that they already are – far from it! What we need to do is to search for usable resistance on a basic level, on the levels that we *need* and that *we can handle* technically, at a given point in time.

Even in the long run, the aim of HCI cannot be a resistance-less computational agent. Who wants a collaborator with no aims and no desires? Someone just waiting for orders and carrying them out to the letter (needing a total description), with no desire to do well, with no initiative? The perfect intelligent collaborator has ideas, takes initiative, prevents mistakes, takes pride in their work, thinks of what I forget – she offers resistance.

Think of the small advances that have been made in certain GUI systems where one can scroll through a list by 'accelerating' that list – it is as though one accelerates an object with a weight that then continues to move on in the same direction. It needs to be accelerated against a *resistance* and it is then only slowed down by the *resistance* it encounters. (Unfortunately the cursor movement and standard object manipulation in the common graphical operating systems are not like this.) Our world is a world full of resistance, the world of resistance-less objects on standard computers is not our world.

Having said that, while scrolling down a list, pushing a lever or kicking a ball are only very loosely associated with the 'feel' of intentions through resistance, adding a little complexity to the interaction quickly does wonders. Think of how a 'Braitenberg vehicle' directly connects sensors to motor actions, and yet achieves surprisingly complex behavior [14] that seems purposeful and 'alive'. Think of how little is required for an animal or even a plant to have 'goals'.

We now know that cognitive systems research has to start with basic behavior that can be described in 'thick' terms – not just the data, and not just the human-level intelligence. New HCI would be interaction of humans with artificial agents that pursue goals and offer resistance – this is the path to successful HCI and to integration of HCI into the larger family of cognitive systems research.

References

1. Haugeland, J.: Artificial Intelligence: The Very Idea. MIT Press, Cambridge (1985)
2. Newell, A., Simon, H.: Computer Science as Empirical Enquiry: Symbols and Search. Communications of the Association of Computing Machinery 19, 113–126 (1976)
3. Boden, M.A.: Mind as Machine: A History of Cognitive Science. Oxford University Press, Oxford (2006)
4. Boden, M.A.: Artificial Intelligence and Natural Man. Basic Books, New York (1977)
5. Turing, A.: On Computable Numbers, with an Application to the Entscheidungsproblem. In: Proceedings of the London Mathematical Society, pp. 230–256 (1936)
6. Müller, V.C.: Pancomputationalism: Theory or Metaphor? In: Hagengruber, R. (ed.) Philosophy's Relevance in Information Science. Springer, Berlin (2010)
7. Dodig-Crnkovic, G., Müller, V.C.: A Dialogue Concerning Two World Systems: Info-Computational Vs. Mechanistic. In: Dodig-Crnkovic, G., Burgin, M. (eds.) Information and Computation: Essays on Scientific and Philosophical Understanding of Foundations of Information and Computation. World Scientific, Boston (forthcoming 2011)
8. Müller, V.C.: Symbol Grounding in Computational Systems: A Paradox of Intentions. Minds and Machines 19, 529–541 (2009)
9. Geertz, C.: Thick Description: Toward an Interpretative Theory of Culture. In: The Interpretation of Culture: Selected Essays, pp. 3–30. Basic Books, New York (1973)
10. Fitts, P.M., Posner, M.L.: Human Performance. Brooks/Cole, Pacific Grove (1967)
11. Dreyfus, H.L., Dreyfus, S.E.: From Socrates to Expert Systems: The Limits and Dangers of Calculative Rationality. In: Mitcham, C., Huning, A. (eds.) Philosophy and Technology II: Information Technology and Computers in Theory and Practice. Reidel, Dordrecht (1985)
12. Turing, A.: Computing Machinery and Intelligence. Mind LIX, pp. 433–460 (1950)
13. Allen, C.: Mirror, Mirror in the Brain, What's the Monkey Stand to Gain? Noûs 44, 372–391 (2010)
14. Braitenberg, V.: Vehicles: Experiments in Synthetic Psychology. MIT Press, Cambridge (1984)

Speaking without Thinking: Embodiment, Speech Technology and Social Signal Processing

Tim Rohrer

Colorado Advanced Research Institute, Box 3736, Boulder, Colorado 80307-3736
rohrer@cogsci.ucsd.edu

Abstract. Neuroimaging results and related results from neuroscience have shown that the "multimodal" areas of the brain responsible for sensory integration are fundamental to semantic comprehension and language production. Developmental studies have shown that language comprehension and production involves infants learning by imitation from their caregivers to coordinate multimodal schemas that cross from one perceptual modality to another. Analyzing the both the physiological and socio-cultural constraints of embodiment on language, perception and cognition, I develop a theory of image schemas. As with the Gestalt perceptual structures, image schemas are dynamic perceptual wholes which prompt for 'normal' pattern completions based on our recurrent experiences in interacting with the world. I conclude by describing how both the theory of image schemas and embodied cognitive science generally can bring a fresh perspective to machine-learning problems such as the visual recognition of speech, emotion and gesture.

Keywords: embodiment, social signal processing, image schemas, gestalt, pattern completion, embodied cognitive science, multimodal schemas.

"It can also be maintained that it is best to provide the machine with the best sense organs that money can buy, and then teach it to understand and speak English. That process could follow the normal teaching of a child. Things would be pointed out and named, etc. Again, I do not know what the right answer is, but I think both approaches should be tried." [1]

1 Embodiment

Chances are that if you have ever tried to learn a foreign language as an adult, you have had to struggle to master the pronunciation of it. In 1998, when I was first learning to speak Danish in preparation for a Fulbright year at the University of Aarhus, I was struggling with pronouncing the Danish /r/. This phoneme is often particularly challenging for native English speakers such as myself, due to the fact that it is both close and yet different from the English /r/, requiring a slightly different mouth shape, tongue position, etc. No amount of trial and effort seemed to please my Danish teacher at the University of Oregon; similarly, no amount of verbal coaching as to where to place tongue on my palate worked until Jan told me "to relax my mouth and say it sloppier. Slur the 'r.' Pretend you're drunk!" Naturally, when I arrived in

A. Esposito et al. (Eds.): COST 2102 Int. Training School 2010, LNCS 6456, pp. 8–22, 2011.
© Springer-Verlag Berlin Heidelberg 2011

Denmark, I choose to perpetuate my language-learning challenges by taking an apartment on a street named Ryesgade, which combined that phoneme with the tongue-twisting Danish /y/, /g/ and /d/. This decision quickly became a source of never-ending amusement for my native Danish-speaking colleagues, who fell all over themselves in their eagerness to teach me how to pronounce the name of the street upon which I lived—and many of whom were keen to subject the hypothesis that drinking would aid my pronunciation of Danish to empirical testing. Indeed, the drink seemed to help me marginally by allowing me to unlearn the habits of motor movement that were prompting the wrong mouth movements, tongue positions and ultimately the wrong vocalizations. As Nietzsche once observed, 'forgetting' can be as important to learning as 'remembering.'

Recall, slowly and carefully, your own experiences here. It is only when we try to learn another 'tongue'—and that commonplace metonymy for a 'language' is deeply revealing as to exactly where many of the challenges in language acquisition lie—that we realize the extent to which our native language constrains us. To pronounce words in the new 'tongue', we must unlearn the habits of tongue and mouth movement that have come with years of daily practice in our native 'tongue'; we must broaden our horizons of motor movement, of how to tremor our vocal chords, of the length and cadence and rhythm of sounds. But it is more than a matter of just learning new motor movements—we also have to teach ourselves to hear the foreign sounds, to hear how these slight differences in what others are doing with their mouths makes the new noise, makes the foreign sound that constitutes a distinct and meaningful unit in a new language. It requires expending considerable conscious effort on matters which, when we speak in our native language, come to us automatically and beneath the threshold of consciousness. But that automation comes at a price; to learn a new language, we must unlearn the constraints of our native 'tongue' that enable us to speak without thinking about the mechanics of pronunciation.

Our embodiment constrains us. Habits of speech, habits of motor movement, habits of hearing—all must be unlearned and relearned again for us to become fluent enough to speak without thinking in the new language. But the fact that these are 'habits' serves to show that 'embodiment' is not merely a matter of physiology, not just the simple matter of learning to place our tongue against our teeth in a new location while vibrating our vocal chords lower or higher in the throat than we are used to doing. Instead, the fact that these are 'habits' entails that they are patterns acquired in-and-across time, through years of social practice. There are both social and physiological components to how our bodies constrain and define how we can be in the world. Consider some of the evidence from how infants learn what noises and what motor movements constitute their native language. For example we know that as infants, we once had the capacity to distinguish perceptually the phonemes that we now find so difficult as adults. Bohn [2] found that infants have what appears to be a near-innate ability to distinguish between the full range of human phonemes on a perceptual basis, but between months 10-12 lose that raw perceptual ability. Instead, infants automate and "zoom in on those contrasts which are functionally relevant (i.e. phonemically distinctive)" in their own peculiar linguistic environment [3]. Infants may babble some of the phonemes that are not present in the native tongue, but over the course of first-language acquisition the phonemes present in its environment will prove more useful to imitate, to learn, to speak, to communicate. The practice and repetition that come with our experience as infants learning to associate this facial expression of the caregiver or these motor movements within its own body with that particular sound hardens into an inability to distinguish phonemes except along the lines of perceptual distinction that our language makes; as adults learning to speak a new language we must unlearn something we have learned to do so early in our lives that it is both physiologically instantiated and socially enculturated in our bodies.

This illustrates a fundamental tension in embodied cognitive science. On one hand, the physiological human body, taken species-wide, yields certain constraints that serve to describe the full range of possible human phonemes. It would do my linguistic abilities no good, for example, to learn to whistle at a pitch higher than what the human ear can hear. My dog might respond to such a trick, but my friends will not. There are clear physiological constraints on what sounds can be used as phonemes in communication that stem from what the human body can do qua human. On the other hand, the human body is always socially enculturated; unlike crocodiles, human infants do not come into the world able to feed and fend for themselves. Thus the range of possible phonemes natively distinguished by any particular one human being is also necessarily constrained by the peculiar facts of what linguistic environment or environments in which that person was raised; in other words, the phonemes used in the particular social and cultural milieu into which that person is born. This second type of embodied constraint is perhaps somewhat softer than the former sort of constraint as, rather than being hard limits on the full range of possibility for humankind, it is a pragmatic set of constraints on the range of possibilities for an individual raised in culture c and at a time t. But odd facts of our physiology complicate such rough-and-ready distinctions between the 'hard' and 'soft' constraints; for example, because the perceptual systems of the human brain are not fully mature at birth, exposure to certain types of stimuli during certain developmental windows—such as for phoneme distinctions in the first year of infancy—'hard-wires' certain perceptual distinctions into the physiology of the developing organism at a depth and intensity that is no longer available after that developmental window closes. Time always complicates matters; this is particularly true when it comes to defining how the human body constrains human cognition.

2 Multimodal Schemas – Developmental Evidence

Note that these experiences are not only embodied but are fundamentally multimodal. Consider again the infant engaged in joint attentional episodes with its caregiver. When the infant learns to associate its visual recognition of certain mouth movements on the face of the caregiver with those of its own motor movements, when the infant imitates the sounds the caregiver makes, the infant is engaged in solving cross-modal perceptual problems. The infant visually observes the face of the caregiver as s/he speaks, sings and coos to the infant; when the infant imitates the facial expressions and sounds of the caregiver, those visual and auditory stimuli are translated across into the motor system, and, coupled with the infant's own auditory feedback from its own vocalization, slowly refined into muscular movements that reliably produce the phonemes of the infant's native tongue. These learning loops require coordinating perceptual experiences from the auditory, visual and proprioceptive motor modalities; they are not only social learning loops, but multimodal and cross-modal as well.

We know from developmental research that infants can imitate facial expressions from just minutes after birth, suggesting that some capacity for cross-modal coordination from the visual to the propioceptive motor modality is innate [4][5]. Consider this finding together with another unusual fact about the physiology of human newborns; their heads are unusually large, particularly when considered in proportion to the rest of their bodies.[1] The usual evolutionary explanations for this physiological fact focus on the increased head size as proportionate to that of other primate newborns. Such accounts emphasize that the increased head size is needed for the larger human brain and argue that the mortality risks to the mother that a larger head poses in childbirth are outweighed by the advantage of having an increased brain size. But if we think about the relative largeness of not just the head but the size of the newborn's face, and note also the comparatively well-developed newborn facial musculature as contrasted with the relative underdevelopment of the newborn's leg musculature, it appears evolutionary pressures have equipped us from birth to imitate facial expressions and solving cross-modal problems.

The study of such learning loops suggests that we are both born with and rapidly acquire additional cross-modal 'schemas' that link different perceptual modalities and domains of experience together. In a schema, relevant pieces of information come not as individual discrete 'bits' but packaged together into coherent perceptual 'images' complete with their part-whole structure. For example, biological bodies are organized in a distinctive manner: the human body has a certain schematic structure defined by the part-whole relations of its muscles and joints; a quadreped such as dog or cat would have a different, but not unrelated, bodily schema; birds, yet another. Infant cognition research has shown that at just 3 months infants can differentiate between a point-light display affixed at the joints of people or animals from a biologically incoherent point-light display; similarly they can differentiate point-light displays[2] depicting animal motion from those depicting moving vehicles [8][9]. As with imitating facial expressions, infants can visually recognize a bodily schema defined by the motions of its muscles and joints; this implies the coordination of experience in the visual and propioceptive domains.

Consider another experimental study of infant cognition [10] (see also [5], [11]) that suggests a cross-modal perceptual basis for a smooth-rough schema: A blindfolded baby is given one of two pacifiers. One has a smooth nipple, the other a nubbed one covered with little bumps. The infant is allowed to suck on the nipple long enough to habituate to it, and then the pacifier and the blindfold are removed. When one smooth and one nubbed pacifier are placed on either side of the infant's head, the infant turns its head to stare at the pacifier just sucked about 75% of the

---

[1] The next time you see a newborn, try to look at it through the eyes of an alien. If those body proportions were to remain constant throughout life, at adulthood the head would be nearly 1 meter tall, roughly as big as the legs—which, curiously enough, resembles how aliens are often depicted in the fanciful illustrations that accompany a reported UFO 'sighting'.

[2] Recall that in his original paper on point-light studies of biological motion, Johansson [6] acknowledged that a source of inspiration in Wertheimer's [7] dotted line drawings of Gestalt structures in perception. In the next section of the paper I explicitly discuss the connections between multimodal schemas and Gestalt theory, particularly with respect to their capacity to induce and regulate pattern-completions.

time, suggesting that there is a cross-modal transfer between the tactile and visual modalities within the infant brain. It is as if the bumpy physical contours of the nipple are translated by the infant's tongue into bumpy activation contours in a tactile neural map of the object surface, which is then shared as (or activates a parallel set of) activation contours in a visual neural map of the object surface.

The ability to perform cross-modal schematic tasks is both present in early infancy and improves with age. Infants appear to be able to perform the Meltzoff and Borton [10] pacifier-selection task from a very early age (1 month), and related studies have shown that infants get better at the task with age ([12] [13]). Other cross-modal image schemas are also present in early infancy. For example, Lewcowitz and Turkewitz [14] show that at about three weeks infants can determine what levels of light intensity correspond to what levels of sound intensity (i.e. volume of white noise), suggesting that there is a cross-modal intensity schema already present in early stages of infant development. Similarly, experiments using the point-light methodology mentioned previously suggest that infants also exhibit knowledge of a path schema from early infancy (3 months). During the first year of infancy infants also learn to attend to the path of motion, manner and different locations along that path, resulting in the emergence of a source-path-goal schema of gradually increasing sophistication. At five months infants are able to attend to the goal of the path traced out by a human hand reaching toward an object [15]; then, at nine months they can distinguish between a hand grasping an object and a hand resting upon it [16]; while at twelve months infants are able to attend selectively to objects by following changes in the direction that a caregiver points or looks [17].

3 Multimodal 'Image' Schemas

Schemas are imagistic. It is perhaps a bit metaphorical to speak of them in such a way, because schemas are not simply visual also bodily, kinaesthetic, propioceptive, auditory, multimodal, cross-modal, etc., but the metaphor of an image highlights certain implications about parts and wholes, paths, direction of motion, balance, spatial relations, the containment and differentiation of objects and elements within the image, and so forth. Unfortunately the visual metaphor also does not highlight the dynamic and temporal qualities of schemas; visual images are static.

Or are they? When Wertheimer published his famous gestalt drawings, one of the key problems they raised was how the dots, lines, or squiggles implied a direction of motion along a path. Wertheimer argued that even static images can imply motion along a path:

> "we are dealing now with a new principle which we may call *The Factor of Direction*. That direction may still be unequivocally given even when curved lines are used is of course obvious... Suppose in Fig. 8 [given here in Figure 1] we had only the part designated as A, and suppose any two other lines were to be added. Which of the additional ones would join, A as its continuation and which would appear as an appendage?" [7]

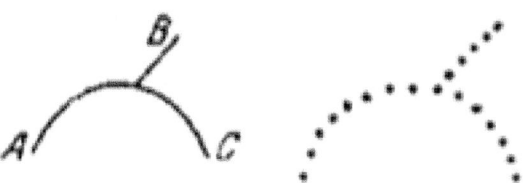

Fig. 1. Wertheimer's Gestalt figures numbered 8 and 9

Static images such as these prompt for pattern-completion—they are dynamic. When we imagine completing the paths specified by the dots in the second figure, we 'know' that segment C is the preferred pattern completion of segment A because we apply a path schema to the direction of segment A. But how do we know this is so? Wertheimer observes: "In designing a pattern, for example, one has a *feeling* how successive parts should follow one another; one knows what a 'good' continuation is, how 'inner coherence' is to be achieved, etc.; one recognizes a resultant 'good Gestalt' simply by its own 'inner necessity'" [7] (italics mine). When we consider the appropriate pattern completion to segment A, we subconsciously imagine what it feels like to draw A, drawing on felt experience from our motoric perceptual modality, and that provides enough impetus for realizing that segment C would be a more 'natural' completion than segment B.

Schemas are imagistic, then, in the sense that they are felt 'Gestalts.' They are perceptual wholes which are both dynamic and encode a myriad of part-whole relations, spatial relations, balance, continuity, and so forth. In *The Body in the Mind*, Johnson [18] first defined an 'image schema' as a recurrent pattern, shape or regularity in, or of, our actions, perceptions and conceptions. He argued that "these patterns emerge primarily as meaningful structures for us chiefly at the level of our bodily movements through space, our manipulation of objects, and our perceptual interactions" (p. 29). His definition was illustrated by several examples of how linguistic and conceptual structure is underlain by image-schematic structure. For instance, the containment schema structures our regular recurring experiences of putting objects into and taking them out of a bounded area. We can experience this pattern in the tactile perceptual modality with physical containers, or we can experience this perceptual pattern visually as we track the movement of some object into or out of some bounded area or container. It is particularly important to see that an image schema can also be experienced cross-modally; for example, we can use the visual modality to guide our tactile and kinesthetic experience when we reach into a container and grasp an object.

Johnson (pp. 30-32) argued that these image-schematic patterns can then be metaphorically extended to structure non-tactile, non-physical, and non-visual experiences. In a particularly striking sequence of examples, he traced many of the habitual notions of containment we might experience during the course of a typical morning routine: We wake up out of a deep sleep, drag ourselves up out of bed and into the bathroom, where we look into the mirror and pull a comb out from inside the cabinet. Later that same morning we might wander into the kitchen, sit in a chair at the breakfast table and open up the newspaper and become lost in an article. Some of these experiences are spatial and physical but do not involve the prototypical containment image schema (as in the example of sitting in a chair) while some of these experiences draw on purely metaphorical extensions of containment (as in the example of getting lost in the newspaper article). Johnson proposed that the containment image schema, or some portion or variation of it, structures all of these experiences.

4 Image Schemas in the Brain

In developing the notion of an image schema then, Johnson and colleagues [18] [19] [20] used the term 'image' in its broad neurocognitive sense of mental imagery and not as exclusively indicating visual imagery.[3] Mental imagery can also be kinesthetic, as in the felt sense of one's own body image. Take another thought experiment as an example. Imagine that I wish to sharpen my pencil. However, the pencil sharpener is located atop a tall four-drawer file cabinet next to my writing desk. Seated, I cannot reach the pencil sharpener by merely moving my arms. It is beyond my immediate grasp, and I will have to get up. What is more, if you were with me in my office, you would immediately grasp my predicament as well.

But how do we 'know' such things as what is within our reach, or are within the reach of others? We know them because we have a coherent body image in our brains – somatotopic neurocortical maps of where our arms and hands are and how they can move, as well as neurocortical maps marking the location of objects in our visual field. We plan motor movements thousands of times each day, constantly re-evaluating the extent of our graspable space given our current bodily position. With a few discontinuities, the body image in the primary sensorimotor cortex is soma-totopic, with adjacent neurons mapping largely contiguous sections of the body:[4] the ankle is next to the lower leg, and that to the knee and upper leg and so on. Similarly, the premotor cortical maps are also fairly somatotopic; e.g. neural arrays mapping hand motions are adjacent to those mapping wrist and arm motions. This topology is highly sensible, given that we need to use our hands and wrists in close co-ordination for tasks such as turning the pencil in the pencil sharpener.

Furthermore, in a series of recent studies on both macaque monkeys and humans, Rizzolatti, Buccino, Gallese and their colleagues have discovered that the sensorimo-tor cortices not only map 'peripersonal' space – i.e., what is within one's own grasp – but also contain 'mirror neurons' with which the premotor cortex simulates the actions being taken by another monkey, or another human [22-27]. When one monkey observes another monkey perform a grasping task with their hands, the mirror neurons will activate the motor-planning regions in the monkey's own hand cortex. The mirror neuron experiments of the Rizzolatti group are cross-modal by design – experience in one modality must cross over into another. In this example, the visual perception of grasping crosses into the somatomotor cortices, activating the same sensorimotor

---

[3] It is important to acknowledge, however, that the term "image schema" also partly emerges from research on visual imagery and mental rotation [21]. The sentence 'the fly walked all over the ceiling', for example, incurs a rotated covering schema [19] (pp. 416-61).

[4] The neural basis for the human body image was mapped by Wilder Penfield and colleagues at the Montreal Neurological Institute [29], where neurosurgeons reported that patients under light anaesthesia either made movements or verbally reported feeling in the regions of their body when the cerebral cortex along the central sulcus was stimulated by the neurosurgeon.

schemas that would be activated by the monkey grasping something on its own. Moreover, other experiments [25] have also shown that the monkey needs only experience a small portion of the motor movement to complete the entire plan. Thus, their experiments also illustrate how the principle of the preservation of the bodily topology in the sensorimotor cortices affords the possibility of image-schematic pattern completion. Similarly, recent findings [27] even suggest that such patterns can serve to integrate sensory input across modalities; a monkey's grasping mirror neurons can fire, for instance, when the monkey hears a sound correlated with the grasping motion, such as tearing open a package. Such findings show that even when triggered from another modality, the brain tends to complete the entire perceptual contour of an image schema in the modality to which it has crossed.

5   Image Schemas and Language Comprehension

Recent research has begun to establish that the sensorimotor cortical regions play a much larger role in such semantic comprehension tasks than previously thought. In the patient-based neurological literature, Suzuki et al. [28] have reported on a brain-damaged patient who has a selective category deficit in body-part knowledge, while Coslett, Saffran and Schwoebel [30] have reported on patients in whom the body-part knowledge has largely been spared. The locations of these lesions suggest that the involvement of premotor and secondary somatosensory regions is functionally critical to the semantic comprehension of body-part terms (see [31]). Similarly, but within experimental cognitive neuroscience, Hauk et al. [32] measured the brain's hemodynamic response to action words involving the face, arm, and leg (i.e. 'smile', 'punch' and 'kick') using functional magnetic resonance imaging (fMRI) techniques. The results show differential responses in the somatomotor cortices, i.e. leg terms primarily activate premotor leg cortex, whereas hand terms activate premotor hand cortex and so on. Their research shows that it is possible to drive the somatomotor neural maps using linguistic – as opposed to perceptual – input.[5] The notion of an image schema may have originated in linguistic and philosophical hypotheses about spatial language, but – given the recent evidence from cognitive neuroscience – is likely to have its neurobiological grounding in the neural maps performing somatomotor and multimodal

---

[5] In a related study by the same group, Pulvermüller et al. [33] used excitatory transcranial magnetic stimulation (TMS), electromyography (EMG) and a lexical-decision task to examine the semantic contribution of the somatomotor cortices. After using EMG to determine exactly where to place the TMS electrode for optimal stimulation of the hand cortex and the optimal amplitude and duration of the TMS pulse, participants viewed linguistic stimuli which consisted of either arm and leg action words or nonsensical psuedowords. The results show that when the left hemispheric cortical region which matched the arm or leg word was excited by TMS, the response time was significantly quicker than in the control condition without TMS. Similar results were obtained using TMS on both hemispheres, but not in the right hemisphere-only condition—as would be expected for right-hand dominant participants. The facilitation in the cortical excitation condition suggests that these somatosensory regions are not only active but functionally implicated in semantic comprehension.

imagery tasks.[6] Parallel experimental results on action sentences from cognitive psychology lend additional credence to the neurological and neuroimaging evidence showing that the mental imagery carried out in the premotor and multimodal somatosensory cortices is functionally critical to semantic comprehension. Numerous experiments assessing the relationship between embodied cognition and language have shown that that there is a facilitatory/inhibitory effect on accuracy and/or response speed that holds for a diverse set of language comprehension tasks.[7] Such experiments suggest that the sensorimotor and somatosensory neural regions implicated by the neuroimaging and the selective-deficits studies are functionally related to language comprehension. The perceptual and motor imagery performed by certain regions of the brain subserve at least some processes of language comprehension: we understand an action sentence because we are subconsciously imagining performing the action.[8] Moreover, cognitive psychologists have shown that the sentence stimuli do not even need to be about literal actions to show the facilitation effects of image-schematic simulations (see [37]).

Using neuroimaging and brain-wave recording techniques, I [38] [34] have developed two cross-methodological lines of experimental evidence showing that the sensorimotor cortex is functionally involved in semantic comprehension. In order to measure whether the same brain areas known to be involved in sensorimotor activity in monkeys and humans would also be activated by literal and metaphoric language about object manipulation, I compared the fMRI neuroimaging results from a hand stroking/grasping task to those from a semantic comprehension task involving literal and metaphoric hand sentences, as well as to a set of non-hand control sentences.[9] The sensorimotor areas active in the tactile task were congruent with previous studies

---

[6] Johnson and I have elsewhere detailed our hypotheses as to the neurobiological grounding of image schemas with respect to both comparative neurophysiological animal models and analogous non-invasive human research [34] [21].

[7] For example, Zwaan et al. [35] found facilitatory effects when the direction of an object's motion implied by a sentence matched a change in the size of the object in two successive visual depictions of a scene; mismatches produced inhibition. Glenberg and Kaschak [36] found similar effects for participants who listened to sentences describing bodily motions either toward or away from the body (e.g. "pull/push") and then responded via a sequence of button presses in a congruent or incongruent direction of movement (toward or away from the body).

[8] For example, Matlock et al. [40] compared the effect of metaphoric motion and no-motion sentences on participants' reasoning in response to an ambiguous temporal question. The motion-sentence group were more likely to choose the response that reflected reasoning using a spatial metaphor for time which was congruent with the spatial metaphor introduced in the motion sentences.

[9] Twelve right-hand dominant subjects participated in a block-design fMRI experiment on a 1.5T Siemens scanner at Thornton Hospital on the UCSD campus, using a small surface coil centered above the sensorimotor cortex with a TR of 4. Participants viewed eight alternating 32-second blocks of hand sentences and control sentences. Three such blocks were averaged together in each semantic comprehension condition. After the semantic data were obtained, one tactile right-hand stimulation block was performed. All data were analyzed using the FreeSurfer fMRI analysis package available from UCSD and MGH [41].

of the somatotopy of the hand cortex [39], and were used to identify regions of interest for the two semantic conditions. As hypothesized, the results in the semantic conditions show that the participants exhibited several overlaps between the somatotopy found for a tactile hand stroking/grasping task and that found for both the literal hand sentence comprehension task and the metaphoric hand sentence comprehension task. These overlaps were concentrated particularly in the hand premotor cortex and in hand sensorimotor regions along both sides of the central sulcus, as well as in a small region of the superior parietal cortex. As expected, the overlaps were larger and more significant for literal than metaphoric sentences, though in most participants these same areas of overlap were observed. Furthermore, many of the cortical areas in which these overlaps were found are similar to those areas active in the hand/arm portion of the action-word experiments by Hauk et al. [32]

As fMRI neuroimaging results are temporally coarse but spatially fine, I also conducted analogous cross-methodological experiments using temporally fine, spatially coarse electro-encephalographic techniques. Participants were presented with a variety of body-part word semantic comprehension tasks, and their brain wave activity measured using event-related potential (ERP) methodologies, and spatially mapped onto the scalp using a current source density technique. The brainwave evidence gathered shows not only a spatial distribution that coarsely and roughly corresponded with the neuroimaging results, but that this occurs during the 400 to 600 millisecond time window generally thought to be crucial for semantic comprehension. In short, this evidence is both spatially and temporally consonant with a functional contribution from image schemas in the sensorimotor cortices to language comprehension.

6 Embodied Image Schemas in Speech Technology and Social Signal Processing

To sum up, image schemas can be characterized more formally as:

1. recurrent patterns of bodily experience,
2. "image"-like in that they preserve the topological structure of the perceptual whole, as evidenced by pattern-completion,
3. operating dynamically in and across time,
4. structures which afford 'normal' pattern completions that can serve as a basis for inference,
5. structures which link sensorimotor experience to conceptualization and language, and;
6. realized as activation patterns (or "contours") in and between topologic neural maps.

Image schemas constitute a preverbal and pre-reflective emergent level of meaning. They are patterns found in the topologic neural maps we share with other animals, though we as humans have particular image schemas that are more or less peculiar to our types of bodies. Even though image schemas typically operate without our conscious awareness of how they structure our experience, it is sometimes possible to become reflectively aware of the image-schematic structure of a certain experience, such as when thinking closely about Wertheimer's depictions of gestalt figures [7], or when one is consciously aware of one's cupped hands as forming a container, or when one feels one's body as being off balance.

At the outset of this paper I began with a consideration of problems of language acquisition and phoneme production in the new language as an example of how our human embodiment constrains our cognition from both a physiological and a socio-cultural standpoint. But I am also quite conscious that many of the researchers I met at COST 2102 were engineers interested in how we might teach computers to speak, to converse, to recognize visual speech elements in video-to-text applications, to process gestures, turn-taking mannerisms and other social signals and to assist those individuals with speech production or comprehension disabilities; in short, engaged with the kind of problems of Turing raised in the quotation that serves a frontispiece to this chapter [1]. What can a massive theory of embodied cognitive science bring to such a table?

One important question embodied cognitive science raises is: What degree of veri-similitude to bodily mechanisms is necessary to solve a particular engineering prob-lem? On one hand, if I am correct in the hypothesis that the various embodied physiological and social constraints shape both the content and form of our cognition and speech, then that would suggest that a very high degree of verisimilitude will be necessary. On the other hand, we have the pragmatic principle of simplicity in engi-neering design, often epigrammatically stated as "Don't design an electric motor by attaching a bathtub." If, for solving a particular problem, we could do without model-ing and simulating multimodal image schemas, or we could solve the problem by some other means, by all means we should consider doing so. Turing and I are in ac-cord here; try all approaches, take whatever works best, keep building.

Two areas, at least, that I see where the theory of image schemas might be helpful are in the areas of visual speech recognition and visual recognition of gesture. In speech technology, computer scientists have coined the term 'viseme' as the rough analog of a phoneme in the visual modality (cf. [42]). But, to my uninitiated eye at least, there seems substantial room to analyze visemes from the perspective of em-bodiment. Several projects spring to mind: investigating the range of the possible im-age-schematic facial, mouth and larynx motor movements from the perspective of the 'hard' physiological embodiment constraints; similarly, and from the from the per-spective of the 'softer' sociocultural constraints, undertaking a comparative linguistic taxonomy of the visemes actually used by speakers of diverse language groups; deriv-ing from such studies sets of image-schematic structures that underlie the visemes in a particular languages or language families; examining the sequence and rate at which these visemes are given to an infant and their effects on phoneme production by the infant; modelling those image schematic structures in visual speech recognition soft-ware and seeing if a computer can use such models to not only aid in the 'guessing' (pattern completion) implicit in speech-to-text transcriptions, but also use them to dis-tinguish between different spoken languages; and so forth. Similarly, a close analysis of the image-schematic range of facial movements might be useful to the studies in both the visual recognition of and the cultural aspects of emotions.

Gesture has been better studied from an embodied cognitive science perspective, or at least in that portion of those fields in which I am well-versed. I regret that I do not have room here to include the analysis of gesture, mental rotation and frames of refer-ence that I touched upon in my oral presentation, but I have given that analysis in considerable detail elsewhere [43] [44]. However, several new ways to look at gesture occurred to me as I listened to the various speakers. For example, we typically regard gesture as something accompanies speech, but it also accompanies listening— something Cummins' time-lapse videos of embodied synchrony in conversation brought out in a humorous and profound way. Yet also, and as I reflected on how we each handled the duties of being session chair, each one of us assuring that the turn-taking politeness requirements of the post-presentation discussion period were being properly upheld, it occurs to me that listener asynchrony is equally as important as synchrony. As I observed the give and take of the questions and answers, patterns of gesture emerged in the interaction; questioners visibly leant forward and hunched their shoulders when listening to the speaker's answers; if the answer were not satis-factory the questioner's forward lean might increase and their tongue might appear at the lips at the slightest pause in the presenter's speech cadence, while if one found satisfaction in the answer there was a clear release of muscle tension and the ques-tioner would recline. There are, in short, a series of gestures which are implicit in the turn-taking decorum of a social encounter, and they go well beyond the raising of the hand and the passing of microphone only present in contrived situations such as an

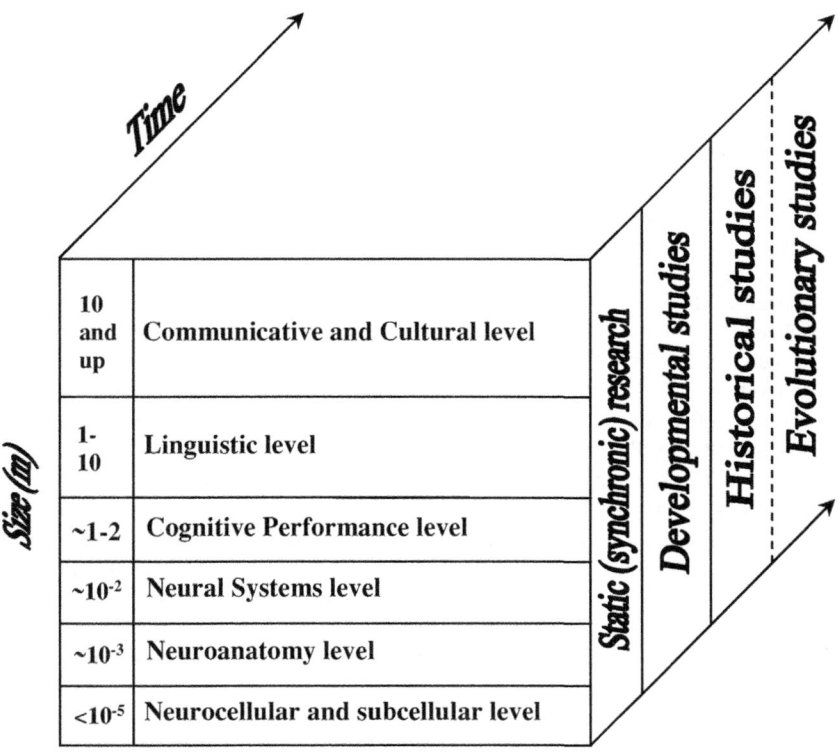

Fig. 2. A theoretic framework for embodied cognitive science considered both spatially (e.g. physical size) and temporally (time)

academic conference. Again, a close analysis of the image-schematic qualities of such turn-taking gestures seems to me to be a fertile field for investigations both naturalistic and experimental.

As a philosophically trained cognitive scientist I will readily acknowledge not being an expert in the fields of speech technology and social signal processing. (And as some of my colleagues are fond of reminding me, being a philosopher and a generalist may very well mean I am not an expert in any field.) But I think there something else important to be gained by stepping back and trying to assess how our individual research projects might be assessed from the general perspective of embodied cognitive science. Scientist and engineers always need to ask certain questions about their research (but often forget): Am I at the appropriate physical scale to address the problem I want to solve? Have I chosen the appropriate time-frame to examine the problem? Which of the synchronic, developmental and evolutionary time frames have I considered? What are the constraints of the methodologies I am using to model or investigate the problem I wish to solve?

In that spirit, I would like to close with a Gestalt figure of my own creation (figure 2). Happy pattern completion.

References

1. Turing, A.M.: Computing machinery and intelligence. Mind 59, 433–460 (1950)
2. Bohn, O.: Linguistic relativity in speech perception: An overview of the influence of language experience on the perception of speech sounds from infancy to adulthood. In: Niemeier, S., Dirven, R. (eds.) Evidence for Linguistic Relativity, pp. 1–12. John Benjamins, Amsterdam (2000)
3. Kristiansen, G.: How to do things with allophones. Linguistic stereotypes as cognitive reference points in social cognition. In: Dirven, R., Frank, R., Pütz, M. (eds.) Cognitive Models in Language and Thought. Ideology, Metaphors and Meaning, pp. 69–120. Mouton de Gruyter, Berlin (2003)
4. Meltzoff, A., Moore, M.K.: Imitation of facial and manual gestures by human neonates. Science 198, 74–78 (1977)
5. Meltzoff, A.: Molyneux's babies: Cross-modal perception, imitation and the mind of the preverbal infant. In: Spatial Representation: Problems in Philosophy and Psychology, pp. 219–235. Blackwell, Cambridge (1993)
6. Johansson, G.: Visual perception of biological motion and a model for its analysis. Perception and Psychophysics 14, 201–211 (1973)
7. Wertheimer, M.: Laws of organization in perceptual forms. In: Ellis, W (ed. & trans.), A source book of Gestalt psychology, pp. 71-88. Routledge & Kegan Paul, London (Original work published in 1923, as Untersuchungen zur Lehre von der Gestalt II, in Psychologische Forschung, 4:301-350) (1923/1938)
8. Arterberry, M.E., Borsnstein, M.H.: Three-month-old infants' categorization of animals and vehicles based on static and dynamic attributes. J. Experimental Child Psychology 80, 333–346 (2001)
9. Bertenthal, B.I.: Infants' perception of biomechanical motions: Intrinsic image and knowledge-based constraints. In: Granrud, C. (ed.) Visual Perception and Cognition in Infancy, pp. 175–214. Routledge, New York (1993)

10. Meltzoff, A., Borton, R.W.: Intermodal matching by human neonates. Nature 282, 403–404 (1979)
11. Stern, D.N.: The interpersonal world of the infant. Basic Books, New York (1985)
12. Rose, S.A., Ruff, H.A.: Cross modal abilities in human infants. In: Osofsky, J.D. (ed.) Handbook of infant development, pp. 318–362. Wiley, New York (1987)
13. Rose, S.A., Blank, M.S., Bridger, W.H.: Intermodal and Intramodal retention of visual and tactual information in young children. Developmental Psychology 6, 482–486 (1972)
14. Lewkowicz, D.J., Turkewitz, G.: Intersensory interaction in newborns: modification of visual preferences following exposure to sound. Child Development 52, 827–832 (1981)
15. Woodward, A.L.: Infants selectively encode the goal object of an actor's reach. Cognition 69, 1–34 (1998)
16. Woodward, A.L.: Infants' ability to distinguish between purposeful and non-purposeful behaviors. Infant Behavior and Development 22, 145–160 (1999)
17. Woodward, A.L., Guajardo, J.J.: Infants' understanding of the point gesture as an object-directed action. Cognitive Development 83, 1–24 (2002)
18. Johnson, M.L.: The Body in the Mind: The Bodily Basis of Meaning, Imagination and Reason. University of Chicago Press, Chicago (1987)
19. Lakoff, G.: Women, Fire and Dangerous Things. University of Chicago Press, Chicago (1987)
20. Lakoff, G., Johnson, M.L.: Philosophy in the Flesh: The Embodied Mind and Its Challenge to Western Thought. Basic Books, New York (1999)
21. Johnson, M.L., Rohrer, T.: We are live creatures: Embodiment, American pragmatism, and the cognitive organism. In: Zlatev, J., Ziemke, T., Frank, R., Dirven, R. (eds.) Body, Language, and Mind, vol. 1, pp. 17–54. Mouton de Gruyter, Berlin (2007)
22. Rizzolatti, G., Craighero, L.: The mirror neuron system. Annual Review of Neuroscience 27, 169–192 (2004)
23. Fogassi, L., Gallese, V., Buccino, G., Craighero, L., Fadiga, L., Rizzolatti, G.: Cortical mechanism for the visual guidance of hand grasping movements in the monkey: A reversible inactivation study. Brain 124, 571–586 (2001)
24. Buccino, G., Binkofski, F., Fink, G.R., Fadiga, L., Fogassi, L., Gallese, V., Seitz, J., Zilles, K., Rizzolatti, G., Freund, H.: Action observation activates premotor and parietal areas in a somatotopic manner: an fMRI study. European Journal of Neuroscience 13, 400–404 (2001)
25. Umiltá, M.A., Kohler, E., Gallese, V., Fogassi, L., Fadiga, L., Keysers, C., Rizzolatti, G.I.: know what you are doing: A neurophysiological study. Neuron 31, 155–165 (2001)
26. Ferrari, P.F., Gallese, V., Rizzolatti, G., Fogassi, L.: Mirror neurons responding to the observation of ingestive and communicative mouth actions in the monkey ventral premotor cortex. European Journal of Neuroscience 17, 1703–1714 (2003)
27. Kohler, E., Keysers, C., Umiltá, M.A., Fogassi, L., Gallese, V., Rizzolatti, G.: Hearing sounds, understanding actions: action representation in mirror neurons. Science 297, 846–848 (2002)
28. Suzuki, K., Yamadori, A., Fujii, T.: Category specific comprehension deficit restricted to body parts. Neurocase 3, 193–200 (1997)
29. Penfield, W.G., Rasmussen, T.B.: The cerebral cortex of man. Macmillan, New York (1950)
30. Coslett, H.B., Saffran, E.M., Schwoebel, J.: Knowledge of the human body: a distinct semantic domain. Neurology 59, 357–363 (2002)
31. Schwoebel, J., Coslett, H.B.: Evidence for multiple, distinct representations of the human body. Journal of Cognitive Neuroscience 4, 543–553 (2005)

32. Hauk, O., Johnsrude, I., Pulvermüller, F.: Somatotopic representation of action words in human motor and premotor cortex. Neuron 41, 301–307 (2004)
33. Pulvermüller, F., Hauk, O., Nikulin, V., Ilmoniemi, R.J.: Functional interaction of language and action processing: A TMS study. MirrorBot: Biometric multimodal learning in a mirror neuron-based robot, Report #8 (2002)
34. Rohrer, T.: Image Schemata in the Brain. In: Hampe, B. (ed.) From Perception to Meaning: Image Schemas in Cognitive Linguistics, pp. 165–196. Mouton de Gruyter, Berlin (2005)
35. Zwaan, R.A., Madden, C.J., Yaxley, R.A., Aveyard, M.A.: Moving words: Dynamic representations in language comprehension. Cognitive Science 28, 611–619 (2004)
36. Glenberg, A.M., Kaschak, M.P.: Grounding language in action. Psychonomic Bulletin & Review 9, 558–565 (2002)
37. Gibbs, R.W.: The psychological status of image schemas. In: Hampe, B. (ed.) From Perception to Meaning: Image Schemas in Cognitive Linguistics, pp. 113–135. Mouton de Gruyter, Berlin (2005)
38. Rohrer, T.: Understanding through the body: fMRI and ERP studies of metaphoric and literal language. Paper presented at the 7th International Cognitive Linguistics Association conference (2001)
39. Moore, C.I., Stern, C.I., Corkin, S., Fischl, B., Gray, A.C., Rosen, B.R., Dale, A.M.: Segregation of somatosensory activation in the human rolandic cortex using fMRI. Journal of Neurophysiology 84, 558–569 (2000)
40. Matlock, T., Ramscar, M., Boroditsky, L.: The experiential link between spatial and temporal language. Cognitive Science 29, 655–664 (2005)
41. Fischl, B., Sereno, M.I., Tootell, R.B.H., Dale, A.M.: High-resolution inter-subject averaging and a coordinate system for the cortical surface. Human Brain Mapping 8, 272–284 (1999)
42. McGurk, H., MacDonald, J.: Hearing lips and seeing voices. Nature, 746–748 (1976)
43. Rohrer, T.: The body in space: Embodiment, experientialism and linguistic conceptualization. In: Zlatev, J., Ziemke, T., Frank, R., Dirven, R. (eds.) Body, Language, and Mind, vol. 2, pp. 339–378. Mouton de Gruyter, Berlin (2007)
44. Rohrer, T.: Pragmatism, ideology and embodiment: William James and the philosophical foundations of cognitive linguistics. In: Dirven, R., Hawkins, B., Sandikcioglu, E. (eds.) Language and Ideology: Cognitive Theoretic Approaches, vol. 1, pp. 49–81. John Benjamins, Amsterdam (2001)

More Than Words: Inference of Socially Relevant Information from Nonverbal Vocal Cues in Speech

Alessandro Vinciarelli[1,2], Hugues Salamin[1],
Gelareh Mohammadi[2,3], and Khiet Truong[4]

[1] University of Glasgow, Sir A.Williams Bldg., G12 8QQ Glasgow, UK
{vincia,hsalamin}@dcs.gla.ac.uk
[2] Idiap Research Institute, CP592, 1920 Martigny, Switzerland
gmohamma@idiap.ch
[3] EPFL, 1015 Lausanne, Switzerland
[4] University of Twente, Drienerlolaan 5, Enschede, The Netherlands
k.p.truong@ewi.utwente.nl

Abstract. This paper presents two examples of how nonverbal communication can be automatically detected and interpreted in terms of social phenomena. In particular, the presented approaches use simple prosodic features to distinguish between journalists and non-journalists in media, and extract social networks from turn-taking to recognize roles in different interaction settings (broadcast data and meetings). Furthermore, the article outlines some of the most interesting perspectives in this line of research.

Keywords: Social Signal Processing, Turn-Taking, Prosody, Nonverbal Behavior, Roles, Personality, Speaking Style.

1 Introduction

There is more than words in human-human interaction. Even if our attention focuses on the verbal content of the messages being exchanged (what people say), we still perceive and interpret the wide spectrum of nonverbal behavioral cues that people display when they talk with others like facial expressions, vocalizations, gestures, postures, etc. These are the signals that help us to understand, beyond the face value of the words we listen to, affective, emotional and social aspects of the interactions we are involved in [14].

Nonverbal communication has been studied mainly by human sciences (psychology, anthropology, sociology, etc.), but recently it has attracted significant attention in the computing community as well. The reason is that nonverbal behavioral cues like those mentioned above are the physical, machine detectable evidence of phenomena non-otherwise observable such as emotions, social attitudes, intentions, etc. This means that the cues, when detected through sensors and interpreted through machine intelligence approaches, can help machines to

A. Esposito et al. (Eds.): COST 2102 Int. Training School 2010, LNCS 6456, pp. 23–33, 2011.

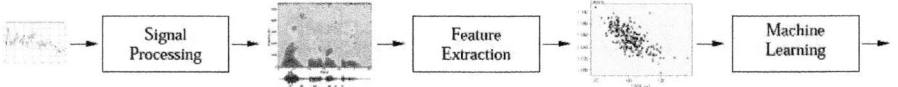

Fig. 1. Journalist / non-journalist recognition approach

become socially and emotionally intelligent, i.e. capable of dealing with human-human interactions like humans do.

This work focuses on two kinds of cues, those related to turn-taking (who talks when, to whom, and how much in a conversation) and the speaking style (the way a person talks). While being only two of the myriads of cues that humans can display, turn-taking and speaking style are important because they are crucial in conversations, the most common and primordial site of human-human interaction.

In particular, this work shows how the turn-taking can be analyzed and modeled to recognize automatically the roles that people play in different interaction settings (broadcast data and meetings), and how the speaking style can be used to discriminate between journalists and non-journalists in broadcast data. In both cases, detection and automatic interpretation of nonverbal cues is shown to be an effective means to extract high level information from spoken data, in accordance to indications coming from human sciences.

The rest of the paper is organized as follows: Section 2 shows how the speaking style heps to distinguish between journalists and non-journalists, Section 3 presents an approach for automatic role recognition based on turn-taking and Social Networks, and the final Section 4 draws some conclusions.

2   Prosody: Spotting Journalists in Broadcast Data

When listening to radio news, it is usually easy to tell whether a speaker is a journalist or not. As journalists are professional speakers who know how to manipulate their voices to keep attention, it is not surprising that their speaking style is peculiar. This difference can come from numerous features, like intonation, pauses, rhythm, harmony and even choice of words. It is still not clear which cues enable the listeners to make a distinction between different styles. Studying on different types of speaking style helps to better understand the process of speech production and perception [4,9,15]. Therefore, areas like speech synthesis, speech recognition and verbal behavior analysis can benefit from speaking style analysis.

There is no taxonomy or dictionary of speaking styles and researchers in the field typically define and compare ad-hoc styles pertinent to their studies, for example spontaneous vs. read speech, slow vs. fast, or stressed vs. non-stressed [10]. The experiments performed in this work focus on the distinction between journalists and non-journalists that can be considered a particular case of the most general distinction between professional and non-professional speaking.

The block diagram of our approach is illustrated in Figure 1. The first stage extracts short-term prosodic features, namely pitch, formants, energy and rhythm: The pitch is the oscillation frequency of the vocal folds, the formants are the frequencies corresponding to the resonance of the vocal tract, the energy is the amplitude of the speech signal, and the rythm is estimated indirectly through the length of voiced and unvoiced segments, the faster the speech rate, the shorter, on average, the segments. All of these features are extracted from 40 ms analysis windows at regular time steps of 10 ms using Praat, one of the most commonly applied speech analysis tools [5].

All of the above features account for short term phenomena because they are extracted from short analysis windows, but the speaking style is a longer term property of speech. Thus, the above features are not used directly, but through functionals that account for their statistical properties. The goal of the second stage in the scheme of Figure 1 is exactly to estimate these properties. In this work, this is done through the entropy of the short-term features. If f is one of the short-term features mentioned above, the entropy is estimated as follows:

$$H(f) = \frac{\sum_{i=1}^{|F|} p(f_i) \log p(f_i)}{\log |F|} \tag{1}$$

where $F = \{f_1, \ldots, f_{|F|}\}$ is the set of f values during an interval of time, and $|F|$ is the cardinality of F. The long-term features are expected to capture the variability of each short-term feature, the higher the entropy, the higher the number of f values represented a large number of times during a long time interval and viceversa.

The third stage of the approach is the classification of the speaking style, represented with a vector including the entropy of the six short term features mentioned at the beginning of this section. The classification is performed with a Support Vector Machine with a Radial Basis Function kernel, an algorithm that uses a set of training samples to identify a discriminant hyperplane expected to separate feature vectors corresponding to different classes.

In the experiments of this work, the SVM is trained with a k-fold approach: The entire dataset is split into k equal size subsets, and $k-1$ parts are used for training the model while the remaining part for testing. This procedure is repeated k times, (each time, one of the subsets is used for testing) and the average error of all k runs will be reported as classification performance measure [2,7], in the experiments of this work, $k = 10$.

The experiments have been performed over a corpus of 686 audio clips including 313 non-journalists and 373 journalists, for a total of 330 identities. The average percentage of clips classified correctly is 88.4. The recognition rate for journalist and non-journalist is 87.3 and 88.4 respectively. In this experiment we have used the total length of all clips which changes for each sample.

In another experiment, we took an interval of equal length from each clip and we analysed the performances for different lengths. Figure 3 shows how the performance changes when the length of the clips increases. The plot shows that the longer clips are better classified. This is not surprising as longer clips allow

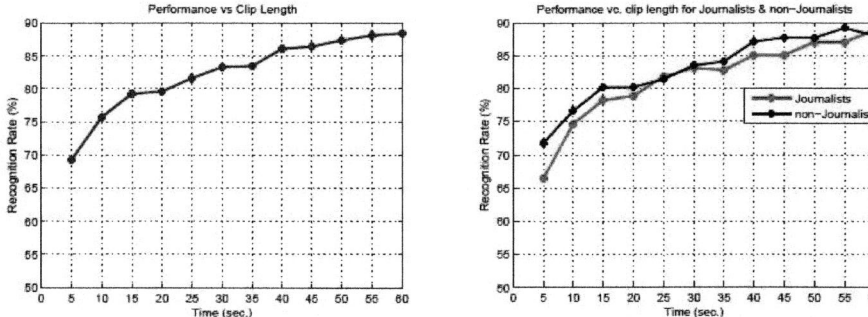

Fig. 2. Recognition performance as a function of the clips length. The right plot shows the results for the two classes separately.

a better estimation of the entropies used as features. Some misclassifications are due to the intrinsic ambiguity of the data: some non-journalist speakers, e.g. politicians and actors that often appear in the media, have the same speaking proficiency as the journalists and, at the same time, some journalists are not as effective as their colleagues in delivering their message. To our knowledge, no other systems performing a similar task have been presented in the literature.

This makes it difficult to say whether the performance of the system is satisfactory or not. For this reason, the performance of the automatic system has been compared with the results obtained by 16 human assessors on a similar task. A set of 30 audio clips were randomly selected from the data corpus. In the set, 17 clips correspond to journalists and 13 to non-journalists. The length of the clips ranges from 3.5 to 75 sec. and it reproduces roughly the length distribution of the data corpus.

The human assessors have listened to the clips and have assigned each one of them to one of the two classes. In order to reduce as much as possible the influence of the content, the assessors do not speak the language of the clips (French), and their mother tongues include English (2 persons), Hindi (5 persons), Chinese (6 persons), Farsi (1 person), Serbian (1 person) and Arabic (1 person). The group of assessors includes 5 women and 11 men.

The total number of judgements made by the assessors is 480 and their overall performance, i.e. the fraction of correct judgements, is 82.3 percent. The women have an overall performance of 88 percent (on average 26.4 correct judgements out of 30), while the men have an overall performance of 79.0 percent (on average 23.7 correct judgements out of 30). On average, each clip has been recognized correctly by 13.2 assessors, but there are two ambiguous clips, recognized by only 2 and 4 assessors respectively, that reduce significantly the average. Without taking into account such clips, the average number of correct classifications per clip is 13.9.

The performance of the automatic system over the same clips submitted to the human assessors is, in the limits of the statistical fluctuations, the same.

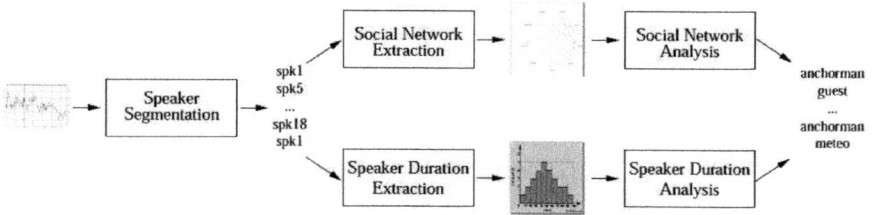

Fig. 3. Role recognition approach

Furthermore, the system and the human assessors tend to make the same decision about the same clip. This seems to suggest that the features proposed in this work actually capture, at least in part, perceptually important aspects of nonverbal vocal behavior, but the dataset is too small for reaching definitive conclusions about this point. Unfortunately, it was not possible to ask the assessors to listen to the whole dataset (more than 7 hours in total) for practical reasons.

3 Turn-Taking: Automatic Role Recognition

Whenever they interact, people play *roles*, i.e. they display predictable behavioral patterns perceived by others as addressing interaction needs fulfilling group functions. This section shows how this phenomenon concerns one of the most salient characteristics of a conversation, namely who talks when, how much and with whom: in a single expression, the turn-taking.

To work on the turn-taking is particularly appealing from a technological point of view because there are many effective techniques for automatically segmenting audio recordings into turns. In general, these give as output a set of triples including a speaker label (a code identifying one of the speakers involved in the conversation), a start time and a duration:

$$S = \{(s_1, t_1, \Delta t_1), \ldots, (s_N, t_N, \Delta t_N)\} \tag{2}$$

where N is the total number of turns and $s_i \in A = \{a_1, \ldots, a_G\}$ (G is the total number of speakers in the conversation and the a_i are the speaker labels). Even if such an information is relatively basic and it seems to miss the richness of a conversation, still it allows one to capture a wide range of social phenomena such as the groups forming around discussion topics [13], the fronts opposing one another in competitive discussions [12], dominant individuals [8], etc. The rest of this section shows how the same information can be used to infer the roles in several interaction settings.

The overall approach is depicted in Figure 3 showing the different steps of the process: first the audio data is split into turns using the speaker clustering approach described in [1], then the turn-taking S is used to extract a Social Affiliation Network (see below for more details) and analyze the duration distribution of the turns. At this point, each person participating in the conversation

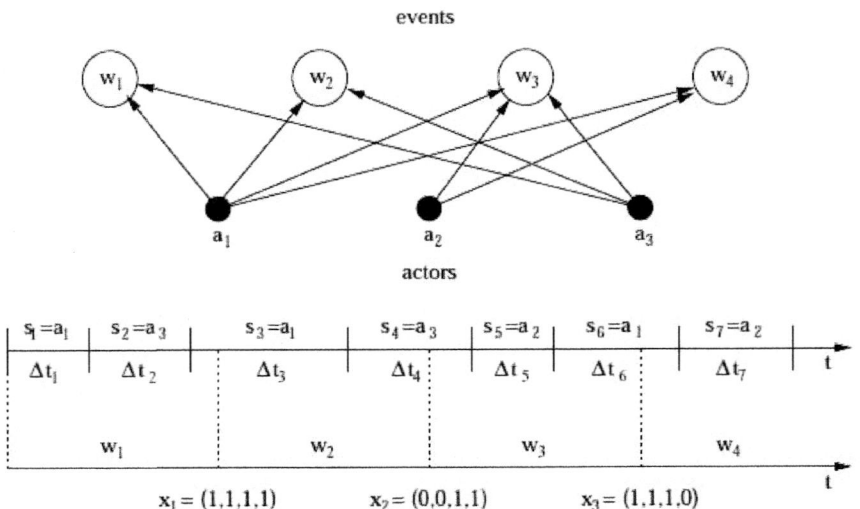

Fig. 4. Social Network Extraction

can be represented with feature vectors and these are mapped into roles using Bayesian classifiers based on discrete distributions.

3.1   Social Network Extraction

The turn-taking S can be used to extract a Social Affiliation Network (SAN) capturing the interaction pattern between people playing different roles. A SAN is a bipartite graph with two kinds of nodes, the *events* and the *actors*. The latter correspond to the people involved in the conversation and the former are defined following the temporal proximity principle: people talking during the same interval of time are likely to interact with one another (see below). Only nodes of different kind can be linked.

Thus, each recording is split into a number D of uniform, non-overlapping intervals w_j that are used as events. Actors are said to participate in event w_j if they talk during it. When an actor a_i participates in an event w_j the corresponding nodes are linked. The main advantage of this represebtation (commonly applied by sociologists to identify social groups) is that each actor can be represented with a tuple $x = (x_1, \ldots, x_D)$, where $x_i = 1$ if the actor participates in the event and 0 otherwise.

The number D of intervals is a hyperparameter of the approach and must be defined via crossvalidation (see below for more details).

3.2   Role Recognition

In mathematical terms, the role recognition step corresponds to finding a mapping $\varphi : A \rightarrow \mathcal{R}$, where A is a set of actors (see above) and $\mathcal{R}$ is a set of roles, such that $\varphi(a)$ is the role of actor a. Each actor is represented with a pair $\mathbf{y}_a = (\tau_a, \mathbf{x}_a)$, where τ_a is the fraction of time during which a talks during a conversation and $\mathbf{x}_a$ is the tuple extracted from the Social Affiliation Network described above.

At this point, the role recognition problem can be thought of as finding the mapping $\hat{\varphi}$ such that:

$$\hat{\varphi} = \arg\max_{\varphi \in \mathcal{R}^A} p(Y|\varphi)p(\varphi). \tag{3}$$

where $Y = \{\mathbf{y}_a\}_{a \in A}$ is the set of pairs $\mathbf{y}$ corresponding to the actors of a given conversation and $\mathcal{R}^A$ is the set of all possible functions mapping actors into roles.

The problem can be simplified by making two assumptions, the first is that the observations are mutually conditionally independent given the roles. The second is that the observation $\mathbf{y}_a$ of actor a only depends on its role $\varphi(a)$ and not on the role of the other actors. Equation 3 can thus be rewritten as:

$$\hat{\varphi} = \arg\max_{\varphi \in \mathcal{R}^A} p(\varphi) \prod_{a \in A} p(\mathbf{y}_a|\varphi(a)). \tag{4}$$

The above expression is further simplified by assuming that the speaking time τ_a and the interaction n-tuples $\mathbf{x}_a$ of actors a are statistically independent given the role $\varphi(a)$, thus the last equation becomes:

$$\hat{\varphi} = \arg\max_{\varphi \in \mathcal{R}^A} p(\varphi) \prod_{a \in A} p(\mathbf{x}_a|\varphi(a))\, p(\tau_a|\varphi(a)). \tag{5}$$

The problem left open is how to estimate the different probabilities appearing in the above equation. As the components of the n-tuple $\mathbf{x}_a$ are binary, i.e. $x_{aj} = 1$ when actor a talks during segment j and 0 otherwise, the most natural way of modeling $\mathbf{x}_a$ is to use independent Bernoulli discrete distributions:

$$p(\mathbf{x}|\mu) = \prod_{j=1}^{D} \mu_j^{x_j} (1 - \mu_j)^{1-x_j}, \tag{6}$$

where D is the number of events in the SAN (see above), and $\mu = (\mu_1, \dots, \mu_D)$ is the parameter vector of the distribution. A different Bernoulli distribution is trained for each role. The maximum likelihood estimates of the parameters μ_r for a given role r are as follows [3]:

$$\mu_{rj} = \frac{1}{|A_r|} \sum_{a \in A_r} x_{aj}, \tag{7}$$

where A_r is the set of actors playing the role r in the training set, and $\mathbf{x}_a$ is the n-tuple representing the actor a.

If the roles are independent, then $p(\varphi)$ corresponds to the following:

$$p(\varphi) = \prod_{a \in A} p(\varphi(a)) \tag{8}$$

Table 1. Role distribution. The table reports the percentage of time each role accounts for in C1, C2 and C3.

Corpus	AM	SA	GT	IP	HR	WM	PM	ME	UI	ID
C1	41.2%	5.5%	34.8%	4.0%	7.1%	6.3%	N/A	N/A	N/A	N/A
C2	17.3%	10.3%	64.9%	0.0%	4.0%	1.7%	N/A	N/A	N/A	N/A
C3	N/A	N/A	N/A	N/A	N/A	N/A	36.6%	22.1%	19.8%	21.5%

and the a-priori probability of observing the role r can be estimated as follows:

$$p(\varphi(a)) = \frac{N_{\varphi(a)}}{N}, \tag{9}$$

where N and $N_{\varphi(a)}$ are the total number of actors and the total number of actors playing role $\varphi(a)$ in the training set.

In this way, Equation 4 becomes as follows:

$$\hat{\varphi} = \arg\max_{\varphi \in \mathcal{R}^A} \prod_{a \in A} p(\mathbf{x}_a|\varphi(a))p(\tau_a|\varphi(a))p(\varphi(a)). \tag{10}$$

and the role recognition process simply consists in assigning each actor the role $\varphi(a)$ that maximizes the probability $p(\mathbf{x}_a|\varphi(a))p(\tau_a|\varphi(a))p(\varphi(a))$.

Finally, the estimation of $p(\tau|r)$ is performed using a Gaussian Distribution $\mathcal{N}(\tau|\mu_r, \sigma_r)$, where μ_r and σ_r are the sample mean and variance respectively:

$$\mu_r = \frac{1}{|A_r|} \sum_{a \in A_r} \tau_a, \tag{11}$$

$$\sigma_r = \frac{1}{|A_r|} \sum_{a \in A_r} (\tau_a - \mu_r)^2. \tag{12}$$

This corresponds to a Maximum Likelihood estimate, where a different Gaussian distribution is obtained for each role.

3.3   Experiments and Results

The experiments of this work have been performed over three different corpora referred to as C1, C2 and C3 in the following. C1 contains all news bulletins (96 in total) broadcasted by *Radio Suisse Romande* (the French speaking Swiss National broadcasting service) during February 2005. C2 contains all talk-shows (27 in total) broadcasted by *Radio Suisse Romande* during February 2005. C3 is the AMI meeting corpus [6], a collection of 138 meeting recordings involving 4 persons each and with an average length of 19 minutes and 50 seconds.

The roles of C1 and C2 share the same names and correspond to similar functions: the *Anchorman* (AM), the *Second Anchorman* (SA), the *Guest* (GT), the *Interview Participant* (IP), the *Headline Reader* (HR), and the *Weather Man*

Table 2. Role recognition performance

Corpus	all (σ)	AM	SA	GT	IP	HR	WM	PM	ME	UI	ID
Automatic Speaker Segmentation											
C1	81.7 (6.9)	98.0	4.0	92.0	5.6	55.9	76.8	N/A	N/A	N/A	N/A
C2	83.2 (6.7)	75.0	88.3	91.5	N/A	29.1	9.0	N/A	N/A	N/A	N/A
C3	46.0 (24.7)	N/A	N/A	N/A	N/A	N/A	N/A	79.6	13.1	41.4	20.3
Manual Speaker Segmentation											
C1	95.1 (4.6)	100	88.5	98.3	13.9	100	97.9	N/A	N/A	N/A	N/A
C2	96.2 (2.6)	96.3	100	96.6	N/A	100	70.4	N/A	N/A	N/A	N/A
C3	51.2 (24.2)	N/A	N/A	N/A	N/A	N/A	N/A	83.3	15.9	42.0	29.0

(WM). In C3, the role set is different and contains the *Project Manager* (PM), the *Marketing Expert* (ME), the *User Interface Expert* (UI), and the *Industrial Designer* (ID). See Table 1 for the distribution of roles in the corpora.

The experiments are based on a k-fold cross-validation approach ($k = 5$) [3]. The only hyperparameter to be set is the number D of segments used as events in the Social Affiliation Network. At each iteration of the k-fold cross-validation, D is varied such that the value giving the highest role recognition results *over the training set* has been retained for testing. The statistical significance of performance differences is assessed with the Kolmogorov-Smirnov test [11].

The performance is measured in terms of *accuracy*, i.e. the percentage of time correctly labeled in terms of role in the test set. Each accuracy value is accompanied by the standard deviation of the accuracies achieved over the different recordings of each corpus.

The results suggest that meeting roles do not result into stable behavioral patterns (at least for what concerns the turn-taking), hence the performance on C3 is lower than the one on the other corpora. The only exception is the *PM* that is actually recognized to a satisfactory extent.

The performance difference when passing from manual to automatic speaker segmentation is always significant for C1 and C2 because the effectiveness of the speaker segmentation is relatively low for these corpora, thus the automatic segmentation is affected by a significant amount of errors. This results, on average, in a 10% accuracy drop.

4 Conclusions

This paper has presented two examples of how nonverbal communication can be used to understand automatically social phenomena like roles or professional activities. These works are part of a much wider range of activities in the computing community that aim at using nonverbal communication as a key towards automatic understanding of social and affective phenomena. An important effort in this sense is done by a European collaboration called Social Signal Processing Network (SSPNet). This project is building a large repository of data, tools, and publications at disposition of the scientific community. The material can be downloaded from the web portal www.sspnet.eu and it covers not only the problems presented in this article, but also a wide spectrum of social phenomena such as group interactions, politeness, competitive discussions, etc.

Technology of nonverbal communication, whether aimed at emotional phenomena like Affective Computing, or at social interactions like Social Signal Processing, promises to bring significant improvement in all technologies where machines are expected to seamlessly integrate human activities, e.g. ambient intelligence, Human Computer Interaction, computer mediated communication, etc.

However, there are significant challenges that must be addressed before these improvements can actually be achieved: while the works presented in this article are based on a single modality (speech), multimodal approaches are likely to be more effective especially when the cues are ambiguous and redundancy can improve robustness. Social interaction is a inherently sequential phenomenon, but most of current approaches do not exploit human behavior dynamics because this is difficult to model. Last, but not least the integration of human sciences findings in computing technologies is not straightforward. All of these challenges open exciting research perspectives that will be addressed in the next years.

References

1. Ajmera, J.: Robust audio segmentation. PhD thesis, Ecole Polytechnique Federale de Lausanne, EPFL (2004)
2. Bishop, C.M.: Pattern recognition and machine learning. Springer, Heidelberg (2006)
3. Bishop, C.M.: Pattern Recognition and Machine Learning. Springer, Heidelberg (2006)
4. Blaauw, E.: The contribution of prosodic boundary markers to the perceptual difference between read and spontaneous speech. Speech Communication 14, 359–375 (1994)
5. Boersma, P.: Accurate short-term analysis of the fundamental frequency and the harmonics-to-noise ratio of a sampled sound. In: Proceedings of the Institute of Phonetic Sciences, Amsterdam, vol. 17, pp. 97–110 (1993)
6. Carletta, J.E., Ashby, S., Bourban, S., Flynn, M., Guillemot, M., Hain, T., Kadlec, J., Karaiskos, V., Kraaij, W., Kronenthal, M., Lathoud, G., Lincoln, M., Lisowska, A., McCowan, I., Post, W., Reidsma, D., Wellner, P.: The AMI meeting corpus: A pre-announcement. In: Renals, S., Bengio, S. (eds.) MLMI 2005. LNCS, vol. 3869, pp. 28–39. Springer, Heidelberg (2006)
7. Cios, K.J., Pedrycz, W., Swiniarski, R.W., Kurgan, L.A.: Data mining: a knowledge discovery approach. Springer, Heidelberg (2007)
8. Jayagopi, D., Hung, H., Yeo, C., Gatica-Perez, D.: Modeling dominance in group conversations from non-verbal activity cues. IEEE Transactions on Audio, Speech and Language Processing 17(3), 501–513 (2009)
9. Laan, G.P.M.: The contribution of intonation, segmental durations, and spectral features to perception of a spontaneous and a read speaking style. Speech Communication 22, 43–65 (1997)

10. Llisterri, J.: Speaking style in speech research. In: ELSNET/ESCA/SALT Workshop on Integrating Speech and Natural Language (1992)
11. Massey Jr. F.J.: The Kolmogorov-Smirnov test for goodness of fit. Journal of the American Statistical Association, 68–78 (1951)
12. Vinciarelli, A.: Capturing order in social interactions. IEEE Signal Processing Magazine 26(5), 133–137 (2009)
13. Vinciarelli, A., Favre, S.: Broadcast news story segmentation using Social Network Analysis and Hidden Markov Models. In: Proceedings of ACM International Conference on Multimedia, pp. 261–264 (2007)
14. Vinciarelli, A., Pantic, M., Bourlard, H.: Social Signal Processing: Survey of an emerging domain. Image and Vision Computing Journal 27(12), 1743–1759 (2009)
15. Weintraub, M., Taussing, K., Hunicke-Smith, K., Snodgrass, A.: Effect of speaking style on LVCSR performance. In: Proceedings of the International Conference on Spoken Language Processing (ICSLP), pp. 16–19 (1996)

A Timely Endeavor: Theoretical, Behavioral, Bioimaging, and Clinical Perspectives on Time Perception

Argiro Vatakis[1] and Georgios Papadelis[2]

[1] Institute for Language and Speech Processing (ILSP),
Research Centers "Athena", Athens, Greece
argiro.vatakis@gmail.com
[2] Department of Music Studies, School of Fine Arts,
Aristotle University of Thessaloniki, Thessaloniki, Greece
papadeli@mus.auth.gr

Abstract. Events and actions evolve over time, making the perception of time one of the most central issues in Cognitive Science. However, to-date many questions remain in regards to time perception and the nature of time. A newly formed network of scientists has recently joined forces in order to advance the human understanding of time though a multidisciplinary approach. This network tackles issues from defining the concept of time to developing rehabilitation techniques and it is fostered by the COST-ESF framework.

Keywords: Time perception, temporal processing, time.

1 Introduction

How do we perceive the timing of all the multisensory events happening around us? And are the physical qualities of time comparable to its perceptual qualities? The discussion about time and time perception (TP) endures through the years in many different disciplines. Time has been viewed as a number, an interval, a movement, a fleeting moment etc. TP, on the other hand, has been quite difficult to characterize and define, thus leading many cognitive scientists to focus on research related to space rather than to time. But the clock is ticking and many questions regarding time and TP remain and require an answer.

1.1 Main Issues on Time and TP

Conceptual analysis and measurement of TP: Time is a concept that has intrigued philosophers, anthropologists, biologists, physicists, and psychologists for quite some time now. Aristotle was the first to ask, in psychological terms, about the way we perceive time. He considered time as "a number of change with respect to the before and after" and posed the question "whether its existence depends on the existence of beings, like ourselves, who can count it" [1]. Since the early days of Psychology, TP has been among the central concerns of scientific investigations in the field and it has been researched worldwide in both behavioral and neuroimaging settings. However, what concept of time is being studied in each laboratory, and what do the findings

A. Esposito et al. (Eds.): COST 2102 Int. Training School 2010, LNCS 6456, pp. 34–38, 2011.

really mean? In the literature, one will find a variety of terms such as time sense, psychological time, temporal reasoning, psychological moment etc. and measures of TP using discrimination, motor tapping, duration, and order judgment tasks, to name just a few. But what conceptual scheme of TP do all these terms and tasks refer to?

Developmental aspects of TP: For years now, researchers have been observing the dynamics of protoconversation in early mother-infant interaction. Human infants, beginning as early as the second month of life, can integrate multisensory events on the basis of time [2]. It is also surprising that rhythmic coordination constitutes a critical feature of caretaker-infant protoconversation and imitates timing patterns similar to that of a friendly adult chat or discussion [3].

Experience of time by infants and young children, however, is quite different from that of adults, since various psychological and neurobiological mechanisms which affect sensitivity to time and shape the timing of motor behavior are not yet fully developed [4]. Experimenting with time developmentally will provide valuable information regarding the time course of TP, but most importantly will influence our knowledge on the association between temporal abilities and the developmental pattern of the neural mechanisms underlying TP early in human development.

Culture, language, and the arts: These domains are major constituents of the sociocultural context which interacts with our experience of time, but their influence on human TP is yet under-researched. We generally perceive time as moving forward and we often express this linguistically using spatial metaphors (e.g., looking "forward" to summer). It has also been demonstrated that people whose native language conceptualizes time with a different directionality (vertical vs. horizontal) interpret statements regarding time differently [5]. Thus, suggesting that our concept of time is modulated by the way a given language associates the concepts of time with nontemporal concepts such as space. What happens in the cases where the concept of time is ambiguously represented in language? For instance, the Hindi language uses only one word "kal" for both "yesterday" and "tomorrow" with the meaning being determined by the context [6]. While the Aymara people appear to have a reverse concept of time by using gestures that place the past ahead and the future behind [7].

But it is not only language that speaks about time. It is also time that constitutes one of the primary structural dimensions of spoken language. Empirical work on speech rhythm has shown that sensitivity to rhythmic properties of language facilitates language acquisition and reading development in children [8], while recent cross-domain studies on the typology of linguistic rhythm have introduced new directions for future research [9].

In the temporal arts –temporal media of the drama and narrative literature, dance, music, and film- the unfolding of events -the succession of sounds in music, or the movements of a dancer- creates an experience of time which differs drastically from that of the ordinary time where one thing is sensed to follow the other in a linear direction. This differential experience of time needs to be explored given its direct links to human cognition and possible application for rehabilitation.

Uncovering the neural correlates of TP: In order to better understand the mechanisms underlying TP, it is essential to investigate the existence of specialized brain systems for representing time and the specific structures involved in these systems. Research to date has provided strong evidence that specific structures in the human brain play a role in the processing of temporal information (e.g., basal ganglia, premotor and motor cortex, superior temporal gyrus, inferior prefrontal cortices). The cerebellum, for example, is argued to be involved in a variety of tasks such as speech perception/production, where the timing of brief intervals is an important component. However, it is not yet clear whether or not the cerebellum is involved only in the short-interval timing, or whether it covers a wide duration range. Recent evidence also showed that the parietal cortex is involved in the processing of temporal intervals. Studies of patients with right parietal stroke have shown decreased temporal order sensitivity for visual stimuli in the contralesional side of space [10]. Such findings, suggest that the right parietal cortex may also play an important role in multisensory integration as a function of time and space.

Understanding TP is also critical in clinical populations. For example, neglect patients mainly show an impairment related to a spatial component of an event, however, neglect can also be observed in the temporal domain [11]. Patients suffering from schizophrenia, depression, or bipolar disorder experience a disorganized TP. Finally, in studies with dyslexic patients, a deficit in the processing of rapidly presented stimuli has been demonstrated [12]. It seems therefore that other disorders (e.g., aphasia) may have a temporal component that has not been explored. Brain functional neuroimaging and animal research should contribute in further elucidating the underlying mechanisms of TP.

TP research extensions to practical, everyday applications: Given the ambiguity surrounding the concept of time, along with the difficulty in understanding TP, the development of time-related applications has been lagging. Even in Artificial Intelligence, the concept of time and its application in Robotics has not yet been explored. The limited time-related applications that have been developed are very successfully and useful. For instance, Tallal and colleagues have developed a therapeutic technique for dyslexics that involve training in temporal processing related tasks. This therapeutic technique was based on research data showing that expanding the transitional element of synthetic syllables (by increasing the formant transition duration from 40 to 100 ms) significantly improved temporal order performance in dyslexics [12].

2 Timely Endeavors

Until now, scientists have been trying to approach these fundamental issues from a single-discipline perspective. It is now clear, however, that multiple disciplines must interact in order to resolve these issues. Recently, one such union has been attempted by a network of researchers in Europe (see Fig. 1). This research network funded by COST-ESF aims (COST ISCH Action TD0904 TIMELY: Time In MEntaL activitY: theoretical, behavioral, bioimaging and clinical perspectives), in four years time, to lay down the foundations for addressing the issues mentioned above. This network seems promising given that it brings together over 120 senior and junior scientists involved in the study of time from different perspectives. This common multidisciplinary effort is unique with the potential to take time-research a step forward.

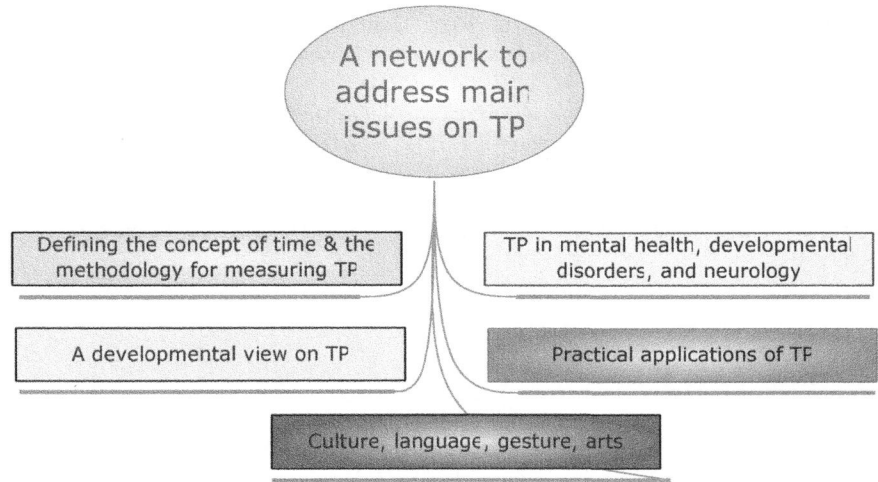

Fig. 1. The main issues targeted by the research network of scientists on TP

Acknowledgments. This work has been supported by the European project COST ISCH Action TD0904 "Time In MEntaL activitY: theoretical, behavioral, bioimaging and clinical perspectives (TIMELY)" (www.timely-cost.eu).

References

1. Coope, U.: Time for Aristotle (Physics IV. 10-14). Oxford Univ. Press, Oxford (2005)
2. Lewkowicz, D.J.: Perception of Auditory-Visual Temporal Synchrony in Human Infants. Journal of Experimental Psychology: Human Perception & Performance 22, 1094–1106 (1996)
3. Trevarthen, C.: Musicality and the Intrinsic Motive Pulse: Evidence from Human Psychobiology and Infant Communication. Musicae Scientiae: Rhythms, musical narrative, and the origins of human communication, 157–213 (1999) (Special Issue 1999-2000)
4. Droit-Volet, S.: Temporal Experience and Timing in Children. In: Meck, W. (ed.) Functional and Neural Mechanisms of Interval Timing, pp. 183–205. CRC Press, Florida (2003)
5. Boroditsky, L.: Does Language Shape Thought? Mandarin and English Speakers' Conceptions of Time. Cognitive Psychology 43, 1–22 (2000)
6. Lemieux, A.: Evidence from Hindi for Proximity as a Consistent Temporal Relation. In: Annual Meeting of the Linguistic Society of America (LSA), January 8-11 (2009)
7. Nuñez, R.E., Sweetser, E.: With the Future Behind them: Convergent Evidence from Language and Gesture in the Crosslinguistic Comparison of Spatial Construals of Time. Cognitive Science 30, 410–450 (2006)
8. Whalley, K., Hansen, J.: The Role of Prosodic Sensitivity in Children's Reading Development. Journal of Research in Reading 29, 288–303 (2006)

9. Patel, A.D.: Music, Language, and the Brain. Oxford Univ. Press, Oxford (2008)
10. Snyder, J.J., Chatterjee, A.: Spatial-Temporal Anisometries Following Right Parietal Damage. Neuropsychologia 42, 1703–1708 (2004)
11. Becchio, C., Bertone, C.: Time and Neglect: Abnormal Temporal Dynamics in Unilateral Spatial Neglect. Neuropsychologia 44, 2775–2782 (2006)
12. Tallal, P., Miller, S.L., Bedi, G., Byma, G., Wang, X., Nagarajan, S.S., Schreiner, C., Jenkins, W.M., Merzenich, M.M.: Language Comprehension in Language-Learning Impaired Children Improved with Acoustically Modified Speech. Science 271, 81–84 (1996)

Instruction and Belief Effects on Sentential Reasoning

Olimpia Matarazzo and Ivana Baldassarre

Second University of Naples - Department of Psychology
olimpia.matarazzo@unina2.it

Abstract. Research in human reasoning has gathered increasing evidence that people tend to reason on the basis of contextualized representations, thus making conclusions compatible with previous knowledge and beliefs, regardless of the logical form of the arguments. This experiment aimed at investigating whether and to what extent sentential reasoning (i.e.reasoning based on compound sentences formed with connectives such as *if/then*, *and*, *or*) was sensitive to the phenomenon of belief effects, under different instruction sets. In a 3x2x2 mixed design (with the last variable as a within-subjects variable), connective sentence (conditional, conjunction and incompatible disjunction), instruction set (logical vs. pragmatic), and statement believability (high vs. low) were varied. Results showed that conjunctions were affected by both instruction set and statement believability, conditionals were affected only by statement believability, whereas no effect of experimental manipulation was found on incompatible disjunctions. Theoretical implications of these findings are discussed.

Keywords: Sentential reasoning, belief effects, instruction set, conditionals, conjunctions, incompatible disjunctions.

1 Introduction

Sentential reasoning is based on compound sentences formed with connectives such as *if/then*, *and*, *or*, *not*, termed, respectively, conditional, conjunctive, disjunctive, negative connectives, as the sentences they generate.

According to propositional logic, there are two different but complementary modes to conceptualize these connectives: a semantic mode, based on the contribution each connective provides to define the truth value of the compound propositions it forms, and a syntactic mode, based on the inference rules that each of them entails. In line with the semantic mode, the connectives are truth-functional, that is the truth-value of the compound propositions formed through them depends uniquely on the truth-value (true vs. false) of the simple component propositions. The pertinence or the consistency between the components is totally irrelevant. The truth tables illustrate (see table 1 for some examples) the meanings of the connectives from the semantic point of view.

In line with syntactic mode (e.g. Gentzen's [1] natural deduction), each connective has two inference rules: one allows to draw a specific inference from the premises containing the connective ("elimination rule for a connective"), the other allows to derive a compound sentence with the connective from two simple sentences ("introduction rule

A. Esposito et al. (Eds.): COST 2102 Int. Training School 2010, LNCS 6456, pp. 39–54, 2011.

Table 1. Conditional, conjunctive, inclusive and incompatible disjunctive connectives truth tables

p	q	p → q (conditional)	p ∧ q (conjunction)	p ∨ q (inclusive disjunction)	p XOR q (exclusive disjunction)	p | q (alternative denial or incompatible disjunction)
T	T	T	T	T	F	F
T	F	F	F	T	T	T
F	T	T	F	T	T	T
F	F	T	F	F	F	T

Note: T= true; F= false; p, q = simple sentence (i.e. a sentence containing a subject and a verb and expressing a complete thought; e.g. It rains; Marco is an excellent student); →, ∧, ∨, XOR, | = logical symbols for the respective connectives indicated in the table. In everyday language the statement form of the five connectives is the following: "if p then q" for conditionals ("If Lucia takes the car, then Marco will walk), "*p* and *q*" for conjunctions ("It rains and it is Monday"), "*p* or *q*, or both" for inclusive disjunctions ("The car has run out of gas or the clutch is broken, or both"), "either *p* or *q* but not both" for exclusive disjunction ("Charles will leave today or tomorrow but not on both days"), "not both *p* and *q*" or "either *p* or *q* but not both" for alternative denial or incompatible disjunction ("It isn't both sunny and cloudy", "Either it is sunny or it is cloudy but not both"). Note that in everyday language exclusive and incompatible disjunctions are expressed in the same way but their meanings are different, as the truth tables show: exclusive disjunction is false when both disjuncts are true or when both disjuncts are false, whereas incompatible disjunction is false only when both disjuncts are true.

for a connective"). For example, given the true premises of the form "If *p* then *q*" and "*p*", the elimination rule for the conditional (or *Modus Ponens*) allows to infer "*q*"; given the two true simple sentences *p*, *q*, the introduction rule for the conjunction allows to infer "*p* ∧ (and) *q*". From the point of view of the syntactic approach, the "meaning" of the connectives is that of the respective inference rules.

Traditionally, the two major approaches to the study of sentential reasoning, mental rules theories [2-8] and mental models theory [9-13], have adopted respectively a syntactic and a semantic perspective. Mental rules theories posit that the human mind is equipped with a basic set of inference schemas akin to the rules for eliminating and for introducing the connectives. By virtue of this correspondence, reasoners are able to capture the formal structure of the arguments containing basic sentential connectives and to draw correct inferences when the form of these arguments matches one or more of the inferences schemas represented in memory. According to syntactic theories, some elementary inferences, such as *Modus Ponens* (henceforth MP), are drawn almost automatically, whereas reasoning difficulties increase as a function of the length and the complexity of the chains of reasoning.

The theory of mental models, which adopts a critical position towards the logical-syntactic account of human reasoning, assumes that sentential reasoning – and, more generally, deductive reasoning – is based on constructing mental models of the possibilities the argument premises refer to and on drawing conclusions consistent with these possibilities. Each model represents a possibility, as well as each row in a truth table represents a possible state of affairs. Nevertheless, the theory postulates that, to minimize the load of working memory, mental models operate in conformity with the principle of truth, that is they tend to represent only the true contingencies and not the false ones. So, for example, in order to represent the conditional "If p then q", people tend to construct only one initial explicit model corresponding to the co-occurrence of p and q, leaving the other two models that constitute the meaning of a true conditional implicit[1]. These models can become fully explicit with tasks demanding a more deliberative reasoning [12,13]. As regards the difficulty of reasoning with sentential connectives, the theory posits that conjunctions – requiring only one model – are the easiest, followed by conditionals – requiring one initial model and three exhaustive models – whereas disjunctions are the most difficult. Inclusive and exclusive disjunctions demand two initial models (indicating that p can occur without q and *vice versa*) and, respectively, two (for exclusive disjunctions) and three (for inclusive disjunctions) exhaustive models; incompatible disjunctions (or alternative denial) always demand three models (indicating that at least one, or both, of the components of the connective sentence is false) [9, 10].

Mental rules theories do not predict differences in reasoning difficulty between the basic connectives as a function of their meaning.

Both theories give a role to pragmatic factors in modulating statements comprehension. According to mental rules theories [5], the interpretative process – taking into account content and context influences on statements understanding – precedes the reasoning process and produces the semantic representations on which the inference schemas act.

According to the mental models theory, the pragmatic modulation of conditionals [11] leads to shape the core interpretation of conditionals as a function of content and contextual cues and prevents to conceive them as truth-functional. Less attention has been devoted to pragmatic factors affecting reasoning with conjunctions and disjunctions.

More generally, not many studies have been dedicated to reasoning with the latter connectives. Except for those carried out to test the competing hypotheses of mental rules and metal models theories [3, 4, 8, 9, 14-19], the studies on disjunctions have been mainly centred on linguistic and pragmatic factors underlining their inclusive or exclusive interpretation [20-24], whereas the studies on conjunctions have been largely focused on their not truth-functional interpretation, in particular on their temporal or causal interpretation [25-27]. Finally, on the basis of the mental models theory, some studies have shown reasoners' tendency to represent conditionals [28-29] and, more generally, sentential connectives [30] in the form of conjunctions.

Most studies on sentential reasoning have focused on conditionals for the central role they play in human cognition, e.g. in hypothetical-deductive thinking, in imagination, in pretence, in making previsions [for a review, see 12, 31-33]. On the whole, performance in conditional reasoning - and, more generally, in deductive reasoning – appears undermined by the complexity of the tasks required (e.g. double negation processing, *Modus Tollens* inference, length of reasoning chains, proliferation of

---

[1] According to the mental models theory, the model falsifying a sentential connective [e.g. the one with the co-occurrence of a true antecedent (p) and a false consequent (*not-q*) for a conditional statement] tends to be built only when reasoners look for a counterexample to evaluate a given conclusion, i.e. a possibility in which the premises hold but the conclusion does not. If the counterexample is found, the conclusion is rejected; otherwise it is maintained.

mental models, etc.) and seems largely affected by pragmatic factors: people are widely sensitive to the content and the context of the arguments and, regardless of their validity, tend to draw conclusions compatible with their own knowledge of the world, even when requested to make only logical deductions.

The latter phenomenon, termed belief bias, is so widespread that it has been considered by Stanovich [34] as an instance of the fundamental computational bias in human cognition, that is the tendency toward automatic contextualization of problems, hindering thinking with abstract representations.

The large empirical evidence of biases in human cognition is taken into account by dual-processing theories of human reasoning [34, 35-39], according to which performance on reasoning tasks is the output of two distinct cognitive systems. One (termed System 1 by Stanovich [34] or Type 1 processes by Evans [37]) is unconscious, fast, automatic, and is based on pragmatic and associative processes; the other (termed System 2 or Type 2 processes) is conscious, slow, deliberative, involves analytic and rule-based processes, and is related to working memory capacity and general intelligence. According to the default-interventionist model - following the term used by Evans [36] to name his own model [35] and that of Stanovich [34] - in everyday reasoning System 1 cues default responses that can be inhibited or modified by the potential subsequent intervention of System 2. According to the parallel-competitive model - following the term used by Evans [36] to name Sloman's associative and rule-based dual process model [38, 39] - the two competing systems function in parallel and the output response is the one produced by the system prevailing in the conflict.

In experimental tasks, instructions demanding to consider arguments' premises to be true and to endorse only necessary conclusions – the so-called logical instructions as opposed to the pragmatic ones, which do not entail those requests – have been assumed to promote the operations of System 2. So, presenting tasks with logical vs. pragmatic instructions can be viewed as a way to test the predictions deriving from dual-processing approach.

The theories considered so far have regarded propositional logic as a normative reference for deductive reasoning, even if some scholars [e.g. 40] advocate a multilogical approach. However, in the last decades the idea that human reasoning has a probabilistic nature – which represents an ecological advantage for living in an uncertain world – has become increasingly widespread. Thus, a number of scholars posit that also "deductive" reasoning would be better conceptualized in Bayesian terms [for a review, see 41] or by means of probabilistic logics [e.g. 42, 43].

As to conditionals, several scholars [41, 44-48] advocate the hypothesis that people understand "if p (antecedent) then q (consequent)" statements in terms of the subjective conditional probability of q given p. The proponents of suppositional theory [47, 48] assume that people evaluate the degree of belief in a conditional adopting a simulative procedure postulated by the logician Frank Ramsey [49]: they suppose p to be true and then compare the number of the co-occurrences of p and q cases with the number of the co-occurrences of p and *not-q* cases, i.e. the number of times where the consequent follows the antecedent with the number of times where the consequent does not follow the antecedent. The higher this ratio, the higher is people's belief in conditional statement. Consequently, the frequency with which an inference such as MP is drawn depends on the believability of conditional.

According to a fully probabilistic approach to human reasoning [41, 43], endorsing a conclusion in function of the believability of the premises cannot be considered a bias anymore, but it should be viewed as people's ecological ability to make predictions, judgements, and decisions in an uncertain world on the basis of their degree of belief in what is expressed by the premises. According to suppositional theory [47, 48], *if* has a suppositional nature and the conclusion of a conditional argument should be expressed in terms of likelihood ratings, reflecting its believability, rather than in terms of bivalent truth values.

Since the proponents of suppositional theory [47, 48] are also among the proponents of dual-processing theories of reasoning [35-37], a clarification should be made as regards conditionals. If one posits that, from a logical point of view, conditionals have a suppositional nature and that a basic inference such as MP reflects the degree of belief in the occurrence of the consequent given the antecedent, then one can no longer consider belief-based conditional inferences to be a bias related to System1. It is only when participants in an experiment persist in basing their reasoning on the believability of the premises, even when instructed to assume them as true, that, according to proponents of both theories, one can speak of belief-bias for conditionals.

The large amount of literature about belief effects on deductive reasoning concerns mainly categorical syllogisms [e.g. 50, 51] and, more recently, conditional inference [52, 53]. To our knowledge, there are no studies investigating the effects of statement believability on conjunctive and disjunctive reasoning.

2   The Experiment

This experiment aimed at investigating whether sentential reasoning varied as a function of the statement believability (high vs. low), of the instructions (logical vs. pragmatic) and of the connective sentence (conditional, conjunction and incompatible disjunction).

As we have said, the effects of statements believability on the conclusion have been investigated essentially with categorical and conditional syllogisms. In literature there is some evidence that logical instructions, requiring to assume the premises as true and to draw only necessary conclusions, enable to reduce belief bias both with categorical [54] and conditional [52] syllogisms. These findings have been seen, in the light of dual-processing theories, as corroborating the hypothesis that the natural tendency to reason on the basis of heuristic and associative processes can be contrasted by instructions allowing to activate reflexive and analytic reasoning processes, based on the formal structure of the arguments.

To our knowledge, this is the first study investigating the effects of beliefs and instructions on conjunctive and disjunctive inferences. More specifically, we chose to compare reasoning with conditionals, conjunctions and incompatible disjunctions in order to examine whether 1) the phenomenon of belief effects would be found in reasoning with the three connective sentences; 2) logical instructions would be able to reduce it. As it will be specified below, we did not emphasize the difference between logical and pragmatic instructions because we were interested to test, among other, the hypothesis that people have at least a basic deductive competence that a few logical instructions suffice to bring out. Note that this hypothesis is compatible with mental rules theories, mental models theory and with the parallel-competitive model of dual-processing accounts of reasoning.

From a theoretical point of view, we expected one of the competing configurations to emerge from our results:

1. an affirmative answer to both the questions, corroborating the predictions of dual-theories of reasoning, in particular those of the parallel-competitive model of dual-processing accounts of reasoning;
2. an affirmative answer only to the first question, corroborating the content- and context-dependent accounts [e.g. 55] or the probabilistic theories [44, 41] of reasoning. Note that, since we used only a weak differentiation between logical and pragmatic instructions, this configuration would be compatible also with the default-interventionist model of dual-processing theories, requiring a strong logical instruction set in order to inhibit the automatic and compelling tendency to produce heuristic and pragmatic responses;
3. belief effects affecting selectively only reasoning with some connective sentences, thus suggesting that the logical meaning of the sentential connectives uninfluenced by this phenomenon was strong enough to contrast the tendency to reason on the basis of contextualised knowledge. These results would be compatible with the parallel-competitive model [38-9] of dual-processing theories, according to which associative and rule-based systems operate in parallel without postulating that the associative system constitutes the basic cognitive functioning on which the rule-based system successively intervenes.

Finally, a fourth configuration, involving propositional logical reasoning in all experimental conditions, in conformity with the predictions of mental rules theories [3,4,8], would be more implausible, given the impressive body of evidence about the people's tendency to reason on the basis of contextualized knowledge. Nevertheless, it is worth noting that in a study investigating the effects of statement probability on conditional inferences by varying the argument structure and the instruction set [56], no difference was found as a function of statement believability and instruction, when the argument structure included the conditional sentence as the major premise.

Two further hypotheses were tested in this study, both related to the mental models theory and both mentioned in the Introduction: 1) the hypothesis of the comparative reasoning difficulty between the three connectives [9, 10]; 2) the hypothesis of the tendency to represent conditionals (or at least their initial model) in the conjunctive form [28-9]. Since in this study we used elementary tasks – requesting to construct only the initial model of each connective sentence to be solved – our rationale was as follows: if the predictions about the connectives difficulty are corroborated, then no difference between the number of conditional and conjunctive inferences should be found, whereas, *ceteris paribus*, incompatible disjunctive inferences should be drawn less frequently than the other two. Otherwise, the predictions of the mental models theory will be disproved and no main effect due to the "connective sentence" variable will emerge from results. Regarding the second hypothesis, if the initial model of both conditional and conjunction is analogous, then no difference between reasoning with the two connective sentences should be found; otherwise their reasoning effects would be different.

We constructed three simple inference tasks, whose premises had the following structure: "if p then q, p" (for conditionals); "p and q, p"(for conjunctions); "either p or q but not both, p" (for incompatible disjunctions). Note that each argument was constituted by a major premise (connective sentence) and by a minor premise (affirmation of the first simple sentence of the connective sentence): for conditionals this corresponds to MP argument. Participants had to choose one of the three conclusions: q *(*corresponding to the correct inference for conditional and conjunctive tasks), *not-q* (corresponding to the correct one for incompatible disjunctive tasks), *no conclusion is certain.*

We chose MP for conditionals because, as we have seen, it represents a hinge inference to test the competing hypotheses deriving from the different theories of deductive reasoning. For conjunctive sentences, instead of presenting a syntactic task, such as the elimination of the conjunction, consisting in presenting only one premise, i.e. the connective sentence, we constructed an inference task similar to MP, with two premises. In order to test the hypothesis of the conjunctive representation of conditionals, we judged more appropriate to present, for both connective sentences, two tasks requiring a similar manipulation of mental models. Among disjunctive connectives, we chose incompatible disjunction, despite its marginality in propositional logic [but see ref. 57 and 58], because it was the most adequate for expressing the manipulation of statement believability, that is for constructing compound sentences where the occurrence of an event was believably vs. unbelievably incompatible with the occurrence of another. In logic, incompatible disjunction is also called alternative denial and both connectives are indicated with the same symbol (|), since their meaning denotes that at least one of the components of the connective sentence is false. From a semantic point of view, the operation of these connectives is to negate a conjunction. In natural language, incompatible disjunction is expressed both through "either p or q but not both" and "not both p and q". Generally, the inference task with this connective is presented as conjunctive syllogism, whose major premise has the form "not both p and q" while the minor can have "p" or "q" form. The conclusion is, respectively, "*not-q*" and "*not-p*". We chose to present inference task with the major premise in disjunctive form, because we were interested in the comparative study of conditionals, conjunctions and disjunctions.

Finally, the instruction set was very reduced. It consisted in the opening sentences that participants were requested to assume as true in logical instructions or merely to read in pragmatic ones. In both types of instructions participants were invited to examine the cases presented following each sentence and to choose the most appropriate conclusion.

2.1 Participants

In this study 180 undergraduates of the Second University of Naples participated as unpaid volunteers: age range from 18 to 41 (M=22,39; SD=4,31). None of the participants had any prior knowledge of logic or reasoning psychology.

2.2 Design

The 3x2x2 mixed design involved the manipulation of three variables: Connective sentence (conditional/conjunctive/disjunctive), Instruction (consider to be true/read the following statements) and Statement believability (high/low). Statement believability was the within-subject variable, the others were between-subject variables.

2.3 Materials and Procedure

Conditional, conjunctive and incompatible disjunctive sentences were selected through a preliminary study in which thirty undergraduates of the Second University of Naples participated as unpaid volunteers. On 100-points scales (none-all), ten participants evaluated the believability of 30 conditional sentences (of the "if p then q" form), 10 participants evaluated the believability of 30 conjunctive sentences (of the "p and q" form), 10 participants evaluated the believability of 30 incompatible disjunctive sentences (of the "either p or q but not both" form). The instructions required to assess the probability that the two simple utterances were connected in the compound proposition, specifying that it meant to assess the probability that the two events described in the compound proposition were connected[2].

More specifically, the instructions for conditionals requested to assess the probability that the first part of the sentence (i.e. the part introduced by "if") entailed the second (i.e. the part following "then"), or, in other terms, the probability that the occurrence of the event introduced by "if" entailed the occurrence of the event following "then". The instructions for conjunctions demanded to assess the probability that the two clauses of the sentence (i.e. the clause preceding and the clause following "and") were connected, or, in other terms, the probability that the two events joined by "and" occurred together. The instructions for incompatible disjunctions requested to assess the probability that the two clauses of the sentence (i.e. the clause following "either" and the clause following "or") were mutually incompatible, or, in other terms, the probability that the two events connected by "either…or" were mutually incompatible.

On the basis of preliminary study results, 7 high believability sentences - with mean between 70 and 90 - and 7 low believability sentences - with mean between 10 and 30 - for each connective sentence were selected. In order to avoid selecting statements that could seem true or false, the probability values above 90 and below 10 were excluded.

It should be noted that the 30 original sentences had been made with the same simple clauses, by varying only the connectives, in order to have compound sentences as similar as possible. Since one of the goals of the study was to test the hypothesis of the conjunctive representation of conditionals, it seemed particularly important to control for the statement content of the conditional and conjunctive sentences. The results of the probability assessment allowed to select eight similar conditional and conjunctive sentences (4 highly probable and 4 scarcely probable) and four similar statements for all three connective sentences (2 highly probable and 2 scarcely probable).

---

[2] As it has been mentioned previously, in the literature the terms the "probability" or the "believability" of a statement are used interchangeably. So, in this article we will do likewise.

Main experiment participants were assigned randomly at the six between conditions and were tested in group sessions. They received a paper and pencil questionnaire, consisting of a three page booklet. Each booklet contained the instructions at the top of the page followed by 14 sentences of the same form (with order randomized across participants). The logical instructions were: "Consider the following statements to be true and, for each of them, examine the case presented, and choose the most appropriate conclusion". The pragmatic instructions were: "Read the following statements and, for each of them, examine the case presented, and choose the most appropriate conclusion in your opinion".

Each sentence was followed by a minor premise (corresponding to p for each of the three sentences "if p then q"; "p and q"; "either p or q but not both" i.e. affirmation of antecedent, affirmation of a conjunct; affirmation of a incompatible disjunct) and three possible conclusions (q, not-q, "no conclusion is certain", where q corresponding to the correct inference for conditional and conjunctive tasks, whilst not-q corresponding to the correct one for incompatible disjunctive tasks).

An example of highly believable conditional task is:
If an animal lives in a house, then it is domestic.
Suppose that an animal lives in a house. What do you have to conclude?
□ *It is domestic*   □ *It is not domestic*   □ *No conclusion is certain*
An example of scarcely believable conjunctive task is:
It is spring and the trees are bare
It is spring. What do you have to conclude?
□ *The trees are bare*   □*The trees are not bare*   □*No conclusion is certain.*
An example of highly believable disjunctive task is:
Either an animal is a bird or it lives in water but not both
An animal is a bird. What do you have to conclude?
□ *It lives in water*   □ *It does not live in water*   □ *No conclusion is certain.*

The presentation order of the 3 conclusions was randomized within each questionnaire.

Once participants completed the inference task, they performed the evaluation task, in which they estimated the level of statements probability through the same instructions than those of the pre-test study. Evaluation task was introduced in order to ascertain whether the participants evaluations of the preliminary study were analogous to those of the participants' main study. The order of the 14 questions was randomized across participants.

2.4 Results

Preliminarily, the means of the evaluation task were computed, in order to check whether these results were conformed to those of preliminary study. Scarcely believable sentences ranged from 10 to 25.71 for conditionals (M=18.57; SD=13.68), from 13.97 to 19.78 for conjunctions (M=17.90; SD=11.12), from 25.46 to 30 for incompatible disjunctions (M=27.85; SD=19.52). High believable sentences ranged from 67.29 to 85.89 for conditionals (M=78.98; SD=13.21), from 69.57 to 92.4 for conjunctions (M=83.44; SD=14.47), from 68.56 to 73.56 for incompatible disjunctions (M=70.40; SD=18.45). So, the preliminary and the experimental evaluations were similar: the manipulation of believability of sentences presented in the experiment was successful.

As regard the inference task, it is worth noting that all participants' responses were of two kinds: correct inferences from the logical point of view (q for conditional and conjunctive tasks; $not\text{-}q$ for disjunctive tasks) or uncertain conclusions. Illogical inferences were never drawn. Consequently, responses were coded as drawn inference (1) or uncertain conclusion (0). On these data a mixed ANOVA, with connective sentence and instruction type as between-subject variables and statement believability as within-subject variable, was performed. Mean percentages of drawn inferences are reported in Table 2.

Results showed two main effects due to *statement believability* ($F_{1,174}=65.204$; p<.001; partial $\eta^2=.273$) and *instruction* ($F_{1,174}=7.002$; p<.05; partial $\eta^2=.039$):participants drew respectively more inferences when statement believability was high (M=.79; SD=.02), than it was low (M=.63; SD=.03), and when the instruction was logical (M=.77; SD=.03) than when it was pragmatic (M=.65; SD=.03). Results also showed four interaction effects: *statement believability* x *connective sentence* ($F_{2,174}=6.618$; p<.01; partial $\eta^2=.071$); *instruction* x *statement believability* ($F_{1,174}=5.450$; p<.05; partial $\eta^2=.030$), *instruction* x *connective sentence* ($F_{2,174}=3.416$; p<.05; partial $\eta^2=.038$), *instruction* x *statement believability* x *connective sentence* ($F_{2,174}=3.789$; p<.05; partial $\eta^2=.042$). Interaction effects were examined by means of simple effects analyses followed by pairwise comparisons, with Bonferroni adjustment for multiple tests: since the three-way interaction includes all two-way interactions, only this will be illustrated. Results showed that conjunctive inferences increased with logical instructions in both high (p<.05) and low (p<.001) statement believability, whereas conditional and disjunctive inferences were never affected by this variable (ps>.05); in both types of instructions conditional (ps<.001) and conjunctive (p<.05 for logical instructions; p<.001 for pragmatic instructions) inferences augmented with high level of statement believability, whilst disjunctive inferences were not affected by this variable (p=.304 for logical instructions; p=.093 for pragmatic instructions).

Further analyses carried out only on conditional and conjunctive tasks in order to test whether participants' responses varied as a function of the similarity vs. difference of the sentences' content (remember that 8 sentences was analogous whilst 6

Table 2. Mean proportions (and standard deviations) of drawn inferences for experimental conditions

Connective sentence	High believability				Low believability			
	Logical instruction		Pragmatic instruction		Logical instruction		Pragmatic instruction	
	Mean	SD	Mean	SD	Mean	SD	Mean	SD
Conditional	.83	.22	.82	.31	.65	.44	.64	.42
Conjunction	.86	.27	.69	.34	.73	.36	.31	.35
Incompatible disjunction	.80	.33	.75	.30	.75	.37	.67	.35

were different) did not show any effect due to this variable and not are reported here. In facts these results paralleled those emerged with all three sentences: probability affected both conditionals and conjunctions whilst instruction set affected only conjunctions. So, regardless of the specific sentence content, conditional and conjunction tasks produced different findings.

3 Discussion

In this study we have investigated the influence of two levels of statement believability and of two types of instructions on inference tasks with conditionals, conjunctions and incompatible disjunctions. Results showed that the patterns of responses were largely moderated by the connective sentence: the believability of the premises and conclusion affected conjunctive and conditional tasks but it did not influence incompatible disjunctions task; only conjunctive task was sensitive to instruction set. Nevertheless no main effect due to the connective sentence emerged from results.

These findings seem quite puzzling because they include some aspects of the three expected configurations, without matching precisely with any of them. On the one hand, they show, in conformity with most literature, that human reasoning tends to be belief-dependent, but on the other they suggest that such a tendency can be contrasted either by instruction set or by linguistic and syntactic constraints entailed in the meaning of the connectives.

It was already noted that only conjunctive inferences varied in accordance to experimental manipulation, i.e. to the level of sentence believability and the type of instructions: from a conjunctive sentence and a conjunct, participants inferred the other conjunct depending on the statement believability, i.e. depending on the associative link they attributed to the two events described by the sentence. However, a large percentage of them were able to put aside their own knowledge and to assume unbelievable sentences as true when invited to do it by logical instructions, thus drawing conclusions based only on the formal structure of the arguments. These results, largely compatible with dual-processing accounts of reasoning, suggest the hypothesis that the connective *and* is represented, at least as regards the sentences presented in this experiment, as a flexible or weak connective, indicating an association of any kind between two events, without attributing a definite truth value to it. As such, its meaning is permeable, on the one hand, to the participants' beliefs about the world and, on the other, to the instructions calling for suspending such beliefs.

So, we conjecture that the difference between logical and pragmatic instructions, at least when containing reduced information such as that utilised in this study, is effective only when it operates upon open and flexible meanings. If this hypothesis is tenable, one can infer that conditionals and incompatible disjunctions have a more defined meaning than conjunctions, so that they have not been sensitive to interpretative changes requested by our instructions. Since we did not drastically differentiate logical from pragmatic instructions in our study, we cannot know whether a more discriminative instruction set would be more effective in increasing logical answers compared with the belief-based ones, in conformity with the predictions of the default-interventionist model of the dual-processing theories. However, the findings that disjunctive inferences were not affected either by instructions or by statement believability, and that in this case logical and not belief-based answers tended to be the most frequent ones in all experimental conditions, seem to undermine the potential objection from the advocates of the default-interventionist model.

In our opinion the permeability of the conditionals, but not of the disjunctions, to the effects of the statement believability not only show that the two connectives have been interpreted differently, but also suggests that the results have been affected by the interaction between the intrinsic level of difficulty of the meanings of the connectives and the task of reasoning they required.

As regards the interpretation of conditionals, our findings support, at a first glance, the suppositional theory [47-8]: MP inferences are influenced by the statements probability, i.e. the degree of belief according to which the antecedent is judged to imply the consequent. Natural logic theories [2-8] and mental models theory [9-13], positing MP respectively as a basic rule of inference and a basic conclusion requiring only a mental model to be drawn, seem scarcely corroborated by our findings: this inference is not ubiquitous even when conditionals are highly believable. However, the percentage of MP inferences was higher than the probability level of sentences, especially when the latter was low: note that on average MP has been drawn by 64.5% of participant in low believability conditions whereas the mean probability of scarcely believable sentences was of 18.57. This means that a number of people drew MP in contrast with their beliefs, and only by virtue of the meaning of the connective, which has been conceived, in these cases, as necessarily involving the consequent given the antecedent, i.e. according to its propositional logical form. We do not address here the logical question [e.g. 59] whether the meaning of a connective is reducible to its inference rules or whether the inference rules reflect the meanings of the connectives. Translating this issue in terms of syntactic and semantic theories of deductive reasoning, our results do not allow to establish whether, in the cases in which MP has been drawn, this has occurred in virtue of the activation of the corresponding rule of inference, given the conditional premises, as the theory of the mental rules posits, or in virtue of the construction of the mental model of the possibilities the conditional refers to, as the theory of the mental models assumes.

However, our findings do not support the hypothesis of the conjunctive representation of conditionals, formulated in the framework of the mental models theory [28-9]. As we said, according to such a theory, in order to draw MP inference it is enough to build the initial model of the conditional, which is similar to that of the conjunction, since both involve the co-occurrence of the two simple clauses constituting the compound sentence. So, the initial representation of conditionals overlaps with that of conjunctions. Consequently, given that our study presented analogous tasks for conditionals and conjunctions, often with the same content for the connective sentences, according to the predictions of the mental models theory no difference would be found in inference tasks with the two connectives. Our results disprove these predictions: their different response to experimental manipulation highlights that the two connectives have been interpreted as having two separate meanings, even when the specific contents of connective sentences were the same.

Concerning the interpretation of incompatible disjunction, we have already specified that it has been the only connective unaffected by experimental manipulation and that logical answers were the most frequent ones in all experimental conditions. This finding represents, in our opinion, the most interesting result emerged from this study.

As already stated, according to the mental models theory, incompatible disjunction is the most difficult connective of the three we have examined, and in this experiment this prediction has been tested. The absence of a main effect due to the "connective sentence" variable seems to have disconfirmed such a prediction. Nevertheless, in our view, the findings indicating a tendency to reason logically with this connective, without a patent difficulty as compared to conjunctions and conditionals, can be attributed to the participants' difficulty to take into account both the type of reasoning required by the disjunction (denying a disjunct when the other is affirmed) and the statement believability. Faced with this difficulty, they evidently focused on the formal aspects of reasoning, putting aside the pragmatic ones, namely the believability of the sentences. So, according to our hypothesis, it is exactly the difficulty of the (incompatible) disjunctive reasoning that increased logical answers.

On the whole, the general hypothesis that emerges from this study, and that needs further empirical evidence to be corroborated, suggests that the tendency to reason on the basis of contextualized representations can be countered by linguistic and syntactic constraints inherent in the kind of reasoning required. We think that this hypothesis is consistent with the parallel-competitive model of dual-processing accounts of reasoning, because it assumes that the associative and the rule-based systems work in parallel and that from time to time one can prevail over the other, depending on the characteristics of the task, the instruction set, the cognitive resources available. In our view, in this study the meanings of the connectives and the type of reasoning they require have led to the composite configuration assumed by our results.

However, other studies should be conducted to support our hypothesis, by modifying experimental design (e.g. alternating between-subjects and within-subjects designs), reasoning tasks (using other inferences, besides those presented in this study), connectives (e.g. using both alternative denial and incompatible disjunction).

We think that if future studies confirm the general hypothesis emerged in this experiment, the widespread idea that human reasoning is fundamentally heuristics-based and can be rectified only by an effortful intervention of logical-analytical processes (i.e. the idea underlying the default-interventionist model of the dual-processing theories) should be at least partially modified.

References

1. Gentzen, G.: Unstersuchungen über das logische Schliessen. Math. Zeitschrift 39, 176–210 (1935); Eng. Tr. Investigations into logical deduction. American Philosophical Quarterly, 1, 288-306 (1964)
2. Braine, M.D.S.: On the relation between the natural logic of reasoning and standard logic. Psychological Review 85, 1–21 (1978)
3. Braine, M.D.S., Reiser, B.J., Rumain, B.: Some empirical justification for a theory of natural prepositional logic. In: Bower, G.H. (ed.) The psychology of learning and motivation: Advances in research and thinking, pp. 317–371. Academic Press, New York (1984)
4. Braine, M.D.S.: The natural logic approach to reasoning. In: Overton, W.F. (ed.) Reasoning, necessity, and logic: Developmental perspectives, pp. 133–157. Erlbaum, Hillsdale (1990)

5. Braine, M.D.S., O'Brien, D.P.: A theory of if: A lexical entry, reasoning program, and pragmatic principles. Psychological Review 98, 182–203 (1991)
6. Osherson, D.N.: Models of logical thinking. In: Falmagne, R. (ed.) Reasoning: Representation and process in children and adults, pp. 81–91. Erlbaum, Hillsdale (1975)
7. Rips, L.J.: Cognitive processes in propositional reasoning. Psychological Review 90, 38–71 (1983)
8. Rips, L.J.: The psychology of proof: Deductive reasoning and human thinking. MIT Press, Cambridge (1994)
9. Johnson-Laird, P.N., Byrne, R.M.J., Schaeken, W.: Propositional reasoning by model. Psychological Review 99, 418–439 (1992)
10. Johnson-Laird, P.N.: Deductive reasoning. Annual Review of Psychology 50, 109–135 (1999)
11. Johnson-Laird, P.N., Byrne, R.M.J.: Conditionals: a theory of meaning, pragmatics, inference. Psychological Review 109, 646–678 (2002)
12. Byrne, R.M.J., Johnson-Laird, P.N.: "If" and the problem of conditional reasoning. Trends in Cognitive Sciences 13, 282–287 (2009)
13. Johnson-Laird, P.: Deductive reasoning. WIREs Cognitive Science 1, 8–17 (2010)
14. O'Brien, D.P., Braine, M.D.S., Yang, Y.: Propositional reasoning by mental models? Simple to refute in principle and in practice. Psychological Review 101, 711–724 (1994)
15. Braine, M.D.S., O'Brien, D.P., Noveck, I.A., Samuels, M.C., Lea, R.B., Fisch, S.M., Yang, Y.: Predicting intermediate and multiple conclusions in propositional logic inference problems: further evidence for a mental logic. Journal of Experimental Psychology 124A, 263–292 (1995)
16. Garcıa-Madruga, J.A., Moreno, S., Carriedo, N., Gutierrez, F., Johnson-Laird, P.N.: Are conjunctive inferences easier than disjunctive inferences? A comparison of rules and models. Quarterly Journal of Experimental Psychology 54A, 613–632 (2001)
17. Garcıa-Madruga, J.A., Gutierrez, F., Carriedo, N., Luzón, J.M., Vila, J.O.: Mental models in propositional reasoning and working memory's central executive. Thinking & Reasoning 13, 370–393 (2007)
18. Van der Henst, J.B., Yang, Y., Johnson-Laird, P.N.: Strategies in sentential reasoning. Cognitive Science 26, 425–468 (2002)
19. Johnson-Laird, P.N., Hasson, U.: Counterexamples in sentential reasoning. Memory and Cognition 31, 1105–1113 (2003)
20. Fillenbaum, S.I.: Or: Some uses. Journal of Experimental Psychology 103, 913–921 (1974)
21. Evans, J.S.B.T., Newstead, S.E.: A study of disjunctive reasoning. Psychological Research 41, 373–388 (1980)
22. Noveck, I.A., Chierchia, G., Chevaux, F., Guelminger, R., Sylvestre, E.: Linguistic-pragmatic factors in interpreting disjunctions. Thinking & Reasoning 8, 297–326 (2002)
23. Newstead, S.E., Griggs, R.A., Chrostowski, J.J.: Reasoning with realistic disjunctives. Quarterly Journal of Experimental Psychology 36A, 611–627 (1984)
24. Paris, S.G.: Comprehension of language connectives and propositional logical relationships. Journal of Experimental Child Psychology 16, 278–291 (1973)
25. Fillenbaum, S.I.: On coping with ordered and unordered conjunctive sentences. Journal of Experimental Psychology 87, 93–98 (1971)
26. Carston, R.: Thoughts and utterances. Blackwell, Oxford (2002)
27. Bott, L., Frisson, S., Murphy, G.L.: Interpreting conjunctions. Quarterly Journal of Experimental Psychology 62, 681–706 (2009)
28. Barrouillet, P., Grosset, N., Lecas, J.F.: Conditional reasoning by mental models: Chronometric and developmental evidence. Cognition 75, 237–266 (2000)

29. Rader, A.W., Sloutsky, V.S.: Processing of logically valid and logically invalid conditional inferences in discourse comprehension. Journal of Experimental Psychology: Learning, Memory, & Cognition 28, 59–68 (2002)
30. Rader, A.W., Sloutsky, V.S.: Conjunctive bias in memory representations of logical connectives. Memory & Cognition 29, 838–849 (2001)
31. Evans, J., Evans, J.S.B.T.: Logic and human reasoning: An assessment of the deduction paradigm. Psychological Bulletin 128, 978–996 (2002)
32. Politzer, G.: Reasoning with conditionals. Topoi 26, 79–95 (2007)
33. Schroyens, W., Schaeken, W., Kristien Dieussaert, K.: The interpretation(s) of conditionals. Experimental Psychology 55, 173–181 (2008)
34. Stanovich, K.E.: Who is rational? Studies of individual differences in reasoning. Erlbaum, Mahwah (1999)
35. Evans, J.S.B.T.: In two minds: Dual process accounts of reasoning. Trends in Cognitive Sciences 7, 454–459 (2003)
36. Evans, J.S.B.T.: On the resolution of conflict in dual process theories of reasoning. Thinking & Reasoning 13, 321–339 (2007)
37. Evans, J.S.B.T.: In two minds: Dual processes and beyond. Oxford University Press, Oxford (2008)
38. Sloman, S.A.: The empirical case for two systems of reasoning. Psychological Bulletin 119, 3–22 (1996)
39. Sloman, S.A.: Two systems of reasoning. In: Gilovich, T., Griffin, D., Kahneman, D. (eds.) Heuristics and biases: The psychology of intuitive judgment, pp. 379–398. Cambridge University Press, Cambridge (2002)
40. Stenning, K., van Lambalgen, M.: Explaining the domain-generality of human cognition. In: Roberts, M.J. (ed.) Integrating the mind, pp. 179–209. Psychology Press, London (2007)
41. Oaksford, M., Chater, N.: Précis of Bayesian rationality: The probabilistic approach to human reasoning. Behavioral and Brain Sciences 32, 69–84 (2009)
42. Jøsang, A.: A logic for uncertain probabilities. International Journal of Uncertainty, Fuzziness and Knowledge-Based Systems 9, 279–311 (2001)
43. Jøsang, A.: Conditional reasoning with subjective logic. Journal of Multiple-Valued Logic and Soft Computing 15, 5–38 (2008)
44. Oaksford, M., Chater, N.: Conditional probability and the cognitive science of conditional reasoning. Mind and Language 18, 359–379 (2003)
45. Oberauer, K., Wilhelm, O.: The meaning(s) of conditionals: Conditional probabilities, mental models and personal utilities. Journal of Experimental Psychology: Learning, Memory, and Cognition 29, 680–693 (2003)
46. Liu, I.M., Lo, K.C., Wu, J.T.: A probabilistic interpretation of "If-Then". The Quarterly Journal of Experimental Psychology 49A, 828–844 (1996)
47. Evans, J.S.B.T., Handley, S.J., Over, D.E.: Conditionals and conditional probability. Journal of Experimental Psychology: Learning, Memory and Cognition 29, 321–355 (2003)
48. Evans, J.S.B.T., Over, D.E.: If. Oxford University Press, Oxford (2004)
49. Ramsey, F.P.: The foundations of mathematics and other logical essays. Routledge and Kegan Paul, London (1931)
50. Evans, J.S.B.T., Barston, J.L., Pollard, P.: On the conflict between logic and belief in syllogistic reasoning. Memory & Cognition 11, 295–306 (1983)
51. Klauer, K.C., Musch, J., Naumer, B.: On belief bias in syllogistic reasoning. Psychological Review, 852–884 (2000)

52. Evans, J., Evans, J.S.B.T., Handley, S.J., Neilens, H., Over, D.: The influence of cognitive ability and instructional set on causal conditional inference. Quarterly Journal of Experimental Psychology 63, 892–909 (2010)
53. Handley, S.J., Newstead, S.E., Trippas, D.: Logic, beliefs and instruction: A test of the default interventionist account of belief bias. Journal of Experimental Psychology: Learning, Memory and Cognition (in press)
54. Evans, J.S.B.T., Allen, J.L., Newstead, S.E., Pollard, P.: Debiasing by instruction: The case of belief bias. European Journal of Cognitive Psychology 6, 263–285 (1994)
55. Hertwig, R., Ortmann, A., Gigerenzer, G.: Deductive competence: A desert devoid of content and context. Current Psychology of Cognition 16, 102–107 (1997)
56. Matarazzo, O., Baldassarre, I.: Probability and instruction effects in syllogistic conditional reasoning. International Journal of Social Sciences 3, 163–171 (2008)
57. Malatesta, M.: An algorithm for deriving tautologies of logic of classes and relations from those of sentential calculus. Metalogicon, XIII 2, 89–123 (2000)
58. Palladino, D.: Corso di logica. Carocci, Roma (2002)
59. Peacocke, C.: Understanding logical constants: A realist's account. Proceedings of the British Academy 73, 153–200 (1987)

Audio-Visual Prosody: Perception, Detection, and Synthesis of Prominence

Samer Al Moubayed, Jonas Beskow, Björn Granström, and David House

Center for Speech Technology, Royal Institute of Technology KTH, Stockholm,
Sweden
sameram@kth.se,beskow@kth.se,bjorn@speech.kth.se,davidh@kth.se
http://www.speech.kth.se

Abstract. In this chapter, we investigate the effects of facial prominence
cues, in terms of gestures, when synthesized on animated talking heads.
In the first study a speech intelligibility experiment is conducted, where
speech quality is acoustically degraded, then the speech is presented to
12 subjects through a lip synchronized talking head carrying head-nods
and eyebrow raising gestures. The experiment shows that perceiving visual prominence as gestures, synchronized with the auditory prominence,
significantly increases speech intelligibility compared to when these gestures are randomly added to speech.

We also present a study examining the perception of the behavior of
the talking heads when gestures are added at pitch movements. Using
eye-gaze tracking technology and questionnaires for 10 moderately hearing impaired subjects, the results of the gaze data show that users look
at the face in a similar fashion to when they look at a natural face when
gestures are coupled with pitch movements opposed to when the face
carries no gestures. From the questionnaires, the results also show that
these gestures significantly increase the naturalness and helpfulness of
the talking head.

Keywords: visual prosody, prominence, stress, multimodal, gaze, head-
nod, eyebrows, visual synthesis, talking heads.

1 Introduction

There is currently considerable interest in developing animated agents to exploit
the inherently multimodal nature of speech communication. As animation becomes more sophisticated in terms of visual realism, the demand for naturalness
in speech and gesture coordination increases.

It has long been recognized that visual speech information is important for
speech perception [1] [2]. There has been an increasing interest in the verbal
and non-verbal interaction between the visual and the acoustic modalities from
production and perception perspectives. Studies have reported possible correlations between acoustic prosody and certain facial movements. In [3] , correlation
between f0 and eye-brows movements is discussed. In [4], correlations between f0
movements and head-movements dimensions are reported and such movements

A. Esposito et al. (Eds.): COST 2102 Int. Training School 2010, LNCS 6456, pp. 55–71, 2011.
© Springer-Verlag Berlin Heidelberg 2011

are found to increase speech-in-noise intelligibility. Such coupling of movements in the acoustic and the visual modalities is usually highly variable, but an understanding of the redundancy of information in these two modalities can greatly help in developing audio-visual human-human and human-machine interfaces to guarantee a maximum amount of interaction. More recently, the contribution of facial prosody to the perception of the auditory signal has been investigated. In [4] it was shown that head movements can be used to enhance speech perception by providing information about the acoustic prosodic counterpart. In [5] and more recently in [6], it is shown that even these movements at the top of the head can aid speech comprehension. Moreover, people can highly discriminate the acoustic prosody of an utterance only by looking at a video showing the top of the head. All these studies suggest a highly shared production and perception of prosody between the acoustic and the facial movements, while knowledge on how to quantize this strong relation, and on how to deploy it in systems is still highly greatly lacking.

2   Audio Visual Prominence

2.1   Acoustic Prominence

Prominence is traditionally defined as when a linguistic segment (a syllable, a word or a phrase) stands out of its context, as defined by [7], others use prominence as the perceptual salience of a linguistic unit [8].

Since the studies in this work are done in Swedish, we present an overview of the acoustic correlates to prominence in the Swedish language. In Swedish, prominence is often categorized with three terms corresponding to increasing levels of prominence: *stressed, accented* and *focused*. Research has reported that the most consistent acoustic correlate of stress in Swedish is segmental duration [9]. In addition, overall intensity differences have also been studied among the correlates of stress, although these differences may not be as consistent as the durational differences [9]. As to *accented* syllables, according to the Swedish intonation model in [10], the most apparent acoustic difference for accented from an unaccented foot is the presence of an f0 fall, referred to as a word accent fall. Thus, accent as a higher prominence level than just stress is signaled mainly by f0, although an accented foot is usually also longer than an unaccented one [11]. Finally, in focal accent, which is the highest level of prominence, the primary acoustic correlates for distinguishing 'focused' from 'accented' words is a tonal one - a focal accent or a sentence accent rise following the word accent fall [10]. However, this f0 movement is usually accompanied by an increased duration of the word in focus, [12], and by moderate increases in overall intensity [13]. In our studies, we deal with prominence as a perceptual continuum, which is separate from its underlying semantic function. Looking at prominence from this stand has been suggested and used previously in [14].

2.2   Visual Prominence

Recently, there has been an increasing focus on the relation between the visual modality (the face) and acoustic prominence [15]. In [16], results on Swedish showed that in all expressive production modes, words which are produced with a focal accent exhibit greater variation in the facial parameters movements (articulators, eyebrows, head, etc.) than when the word is in a non-focused position. In [17], eyebrows movements and head nods, added to a talking head, are found to be a powerful cue to enforce the perception of prominence. In [18] and [19], an investigation on the interaction between the acoustic and the visual cues of prominence is conducted, the results of this study suggest that, during production, when a word is produced with a visual gesture, the word is also produced with a higher acoustic emphasis. The results also suggests that, from a perception perspective, when people see a visual gesture over a word, the acoustic perception of the word's prominence is increased. In [20], it is shown that visual movements do not only enhance the perception of focus, but can even decrease the reaction time in detecting focus; and in [21] it was shown that focus can be detected, not only through head or eyebrow movements, but even through lips movements.

3   Acoustic Detection of Prominence

The detection and quantification of prominence phenomena in speech can play an important role in many applications since it concerns the question of how speech is produced and how segments are contrasted, e.g. decoding in speech recognition, and hence can be used for syntactic parsing [22], speech comprehension [23], and more recently, research is focusing on the audio-visual function of prosody, for example, in [24] it was found that visual prominence can enhance speech comprehension if coupled with the acoustic. Hence, it is important for speech driven avatars to detect prominent segments in the speech signal to drive gestures.

Many studies have investigated the acoustic-prosodic cues to prominence on a syllable or on a word level, some using lexical and higher level linguistic information. This study focuses on estimating prominence using syllable based units, since in some applications, the segmental information words might not be available. This presents a theoretical challenge since such a method requires sufficient information about prominence inside the boundaries of the syllable unit. In addition, some prominence categories (levels) are perceptually based on word level, and hence reliably transcribed data on a syllable or vowel level is not available.

3.1   Prominence Model

In this work, we suggest a linear model for describing syllable prominence, and post integration of the estimated syllable prominence will estimate the underlying word prominence. Linear simple models have already shown good performance, as in [25] on English read and spontaneous speech.

If x is an observation sample from a random parameter X, we define the level of prominence of x as:

$$Prom_x = 1 - f_X(x), f \in [0..1] \tag{1}$$

Where f_x is the normalized likelihood of x in the random distribution of X. If x is a feature vector of n independent features $x = \{x_1, x_2, .., x_n\}$, the prominence level of the observation vector x is:

$$Prom_x = 1/n \sum_{i=1}^{n} w_{x_i} Prom_{x_i} \tag{2}$$

While w_{x_i} is the weighting of x_i.

Since the data has only word level annotations, in the case when x is a syllable level observation, we assume that the syllable with the higher prominence level in the word containing it provides the prominence of the word. In this case, the weights w_{x_i} can be tuned to minimize the error of estimating the word prominence when using only syllable level features.

3.2 Feature Set

As shown in the Swedish prominence model in section 2.1, duration, loudness and F0 movements are major acoustic correlates of prominence. In this study, sets of either syllable level or word level features have been used. Features representing the syllables are taken from the syllable vowel, since vowels represent the nuclei and the acoustically stable part of the syllable: The set of features used include syllable duration, syllable loudness, and syllable F0 features including: average F0, average delta F0, and F0 range.

3.3 Experiments and Results

200 sentences were selected from a corpus containing news texts and literature, read by a professional Swedish actor. The corpus contains high-quality studio recordings for the purpose of voice creation for speech synthesis systems. The speech files from the 200 sentences dataset were phonetically aligned, and the acoustic features, were extracted over all the syllables. Half Gaussian distributions were estimated for each of the features, and the likelihood of each feature was calculated, and hence the prominence level per features. The data in all the tests was split into 4 cross validation folds giving 25% test set size. The baseline in this study was simply taken as the average word prominence for the whole dataset. This gives a fixed prominence value for all the words in the test set.

The weights were estimated by assuming that the syllable which has the highest averaged weighted prominence holds the underlying word prominence, in this case, the weights were optimized using a grid-search optimization to minimize the error on this post-integration function.

The 100% percentage accuracies for estimating word prominence for syllable features are presented in Figure 1, By looking at the results, it is shown that

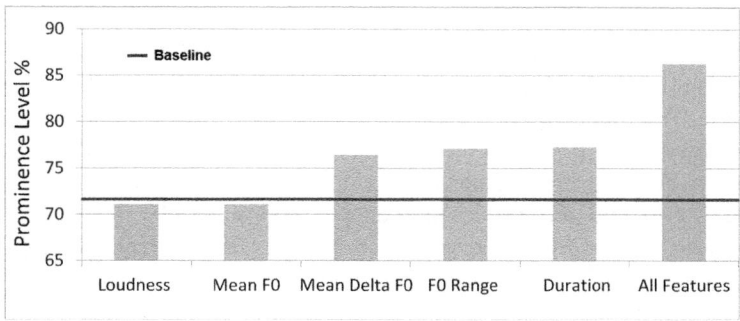

Fig. 1. The prominence detection percentage accuracies for single and multiple features against the baseline. The baseline gives a fixed value of the average prominence of all the words in the dataset.

loudness, and mean F0 are unable to increase the accuracies beyond the baseline; it is good to mention that the distribution of the prominence values per word is highly unbalanced where most words are not prominent, and hence this simple baseline gave an accuracy of 72%. Nonetheless, syllable F0 range performed individually better, and the performance was increased for the syllable duration. The best performance of 86% was reached using all the syllable features combined, with optimized weights equal to: Loudness: 0.13, Duration: 0.52, delta F0: 0.21, F0: 0, and F0 range: 0.14.

As a result, this model allows for detecting the syllables with the highest prominence in an utterance, which then allows the addition of facial gestures on these syllables as visual correlates for prominence. The investigation of effects of such gestures is carried out in the following studies.

4   Visual Prominence and Intelligibility

As mentioned earlier, several studies support the strong relation between the auditory and the visual modalities in perceiving prominence. These studies though, only report that the perception of prominence as a non-verbal prosodic phenomenon is highly aided by certain visual movements, and hence, the visual modality supports the realization of the acoustic prominence which exists in the audio stream.

Since prominence is manifested differently depending on the linguistic segment underlying it, and perceiving prominence aids speech comprehension, an interesting study is whether perceiving cues of prominence through the visual modality can increase speech intelligibility when the acoustic prominence is degraded. And hence, visualizing prominence on the talking head will not only be useful to deliver the function of its acoustic counterpart, but also support speech perception of the acoustic signal.

To investigate such effects, a speech intelligibility experiments was conducted with the help of a lip synchronized animated talking head.

4.1   Method and Setup

In this study, a lip-synchronized talking head was used as the medium for the visual modality; this allows for manipulating the visual modality and keeping the acoustic one unchanged. The talking head used has been shown to provide increased intelligibility in several previous studies [26],[27]. This experiment design deploys the approach of presenting human subjects with a vocoded speech signal, while the subjects are looking at a talking head [28].

40 semantically complete sentences, ranging in length from 6 and 10 words, were selected from the same database used for the detection experiments above.

The speech files of the 40 sentences were force-aligned using an HMM aligner [29] to guide the talking head lips movement generation procedure [30]. The audio was processed using a 4-channel noise excited vocoder [31] to reduce intelligibility. The number of channels was decided after a pilot test to ensure an intelligibility rate between 25% and 75%, that is to avoid any floor or ceiling limit effects.

All the sentences were presented to subjects with an accompanying talking head. The first 10 sentences were presented without any facial gestures, as a training session, to eliminate any quick learning effect for the type of signal vocoding used. The 30 sentences left were divided into 6 groups; every group contained 5 sentences, with a balanced number of words in each group (35-40 words). For each group, 6 different visual stimuli were generated (details in section 4.3). These groups were systematically permuted among 12 normal hearing subjects with a normal or corrected to normal vision, so that every subject listened to all 30 sentences, but with each group containing different visual stimuli. During the experiment, the sentences were randomized for every subject. The subjects had one chance to listen to the sentence, and report what they have perceived as text from the audio visual stimuli.

4.2   Marking Prominence

For the purpose of this study, the gestures which are included in the stimuli are fixed in length and amplitude. And since visual correlates to prominence must be synchronized with their acoustic counterpart, we decided to limit the size of the prominent segment from the whole word to its most prominent syllable, so the gestures are associated with prominent syllables not with words.

To establish that, a native Swedish speech expert had listened to all the 30 test sentences, and marked them temporally for prominence. In this study, the annotation of only one annotators was taken. By investigating the prominence markers, all sentences have received between 1 to 3 prominence marks, and the overall number of marks in the 30 sentences summed to 60.

4.3   Conditions

Following is a detailed description of these variants. It is important to note that, when a sentence received gestures, the number of the gestures that this sentence received was identical in all the conditions (except for the control condition).

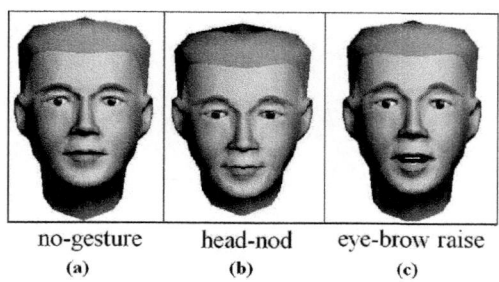

| no-gesture | head-nod | eye-brow raise |
| (a) | (b) | (c) |

Fig. 2. Snapshots of the talking head in different gestural positions (a) neutral parameters (b) lower point of the head-nod gesture (c) peak of the eyebrow raising gesture

- No Gesture (N): The first condition is 'articulators-only' where the face is static, except for the lips-jaw area for the purpose of phonetic articulation. This condition is intended to be a control measurement for the rest of the conditions. Figure 2a displays the talking head in the neutral position.
- Prominence with Head-nods (PH): In this condition, a head-nod was synthesized in synchrony with the place of the prominence markers in each sentence. The design of the headnod gesture was near-arbitrary, consisting of subtle lowering and rising to the original location, the complete motion length was set to 350 ms, which is an estimate of the average length of a stressed syllable in Swedish. Figure 2b shows the talking head at the lower turning point of the head nod.
- Prominence with Eyebrows Raise (PEB): The stimulus in this condition matches the one of the head-nod, except that the gesture in this stimulus is an eyebrow raising, with a matching design in length of trajectories as the head-nod gesture. Figure 2c shows the eyebrow raising gesture at its top turning point.
- Automatically detected prominence with Eyebrows (AP): In this condition, prominent syllables were automatically detected using the automatic prominence detection method explained earlier (section3), and eyebrow raising gesture was coupled with these syllables.
- Pitch Movement (PM): In this condition, eyebrow raise gestures were temporally placed over steep pitch movements. The advantage of this condition is that it is automatically detected, and so it can easily be used for real-time visual speech synchrony in talking agents.
- Random Eyebrows Raise (R): This conditions adds the eyebrow raising gesture randomly on syllables. This condition is made to investigate whether random gestures would benifit or hinder the perception of the acoustic signal.

4.4 Analysis and Results

A string based percentage correct word recognition scoring was manually applied to the answer of each of the sentences of the subjects, and the average recognition rate per sentence was then calculated. As a result, every condition received 60 samples (12 subject * 5 sentences per condition).

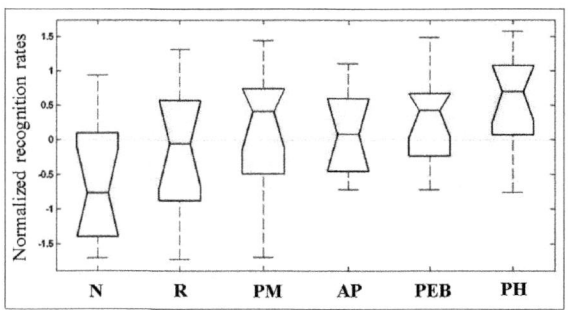

Fig. 3. Box plot of the within subject normalized % correct recognition over conditions

An ANOVA with normalized recognition rates (Z-scored over subjects) as a dependent variable, and Condition (5 levels: No Gesture, Random, Pitch Movements, Prominance Head-nod, and Prominence EyeBrows raise) as an independent variable was applied. Subjects were not included as a factor since per-subject z-score normalization was applied to effectively remove within-subject differences.

Condition gave a significant main effect: $F(4,295)=4.4$, $p <.01$. An LSD post hoc test showed that the conditions: No-Gesture against Prominence Head-nods, No-Gesture against Prominence EyeBrows raise, No-Gesture against Pitch Movements, and Prominence Head-nods against Random eyebrows, are all different using a significance level of .05. It is interesting to notice that the only condition which had significant difference from the random condition (R) was the head-nod (PH) condition, which, in terms of mean recognition rate, had the highest value among all the other conditions (Figure 3). This can be explained by the fact that head-nods actually aid the perception of prominence more than eyebrows, and that more test subjects should be considered to reach a significant difference.

These results mainly indicate that adding head-nods or eyebrow raising on prominent syllables or accented syllables increases speech intelligibility compared to looking at the talking head without gestures at all. On the other hand, adding these gestures randomly over speech, does not increase intelligibility compared to not adding any gestures.

In this study nonetheless, the gestures employed are not optimal or identical to movements employed by humans, but it is still plausible to assume that these movements to some degree carry the same communicative information contained in human gestures.

Gestures and facial movements are a characteristic of audio-visual interaction, and they might have other roles which affect intelligibility and comprehension than indicating prominence. Which might be the reason why there was no significant difference between the random condition and the prominence and pitch movements eyebrows conditions.

Since these facial movements correlate with acoustic prominence, and as concluded in the previous tests, they support speech intelligibility, a natural question to these results is: how will these movements support the interaction between humans and talking heads and in what ways would they affect it.

To study such effects, a follow up study was conducted by using a talking head as a speech synchronized visual support for an audio-based story.

5 Naturalness and Gaze Behavior

To investigate the perceived non-verbal effect of synthesizing the gestures coupled with auditory prominence, an ecological experimental setup was designed by using the SynFace speech driven talking head [27] designed as a visual support for hard of hearing persons [32]. The talking head used in SynFace is the same talking head used in the previous experiment, but SynFace applies a real-time phoneme recognition on the input speech signal to drive the talking head, rather than forced alignment, as was the case in the previous experiment.

The experiment setup is based on presenting an audio novel (audio-book). The audio-book is presented to moderately hearing impaired subjects and the subjects have to evaluate the talking head in different conditions. During listening to the audiobook, the subjects' eye-gaze is tracked using a Tobii T120[1] eye-gaze tracker, which is integrated into the monitor on which the talking head was presented. At the end of listening to each of the audiobook conditions, the subjects were presented with a questionnaire form, Table 1 shows the questions included in the questionnaire form.

5.1 Stimuli and Setup

Subjects firstly had the option to choose one of a long list of audiobooks obtained from the Swedish Library of Audio-and Braille books[2]. The first 15 minutes of each of the audio-books chosen by the subjects were split into 3 parts, each of 5 minutes. The three parts are then randomly manipulated into three conditions: Only audio, audio and talking head (articulatory movements only), and audio and talking head (articulatory movements and gestures). Refer to section 5.2 for a detailed explanation on how the gestures are generated.

After generating the stimuli, 6-speakers stereo babble noise was added to the audio signal to reduce the understanding level of the audiobook. To decide the SNR level of the audio-book, a small speech-in-noise intelligibility experiment was conducted for each subject to calibrate the SNR level.

For the calibration experiments, 15 short Swedish everyday sentences were used, these sentences were between 7-9 syllables in length, and developed specifically for intelligibility testing, based on [2], and used in several previous intelligibility experiments (c.f.[26]), each of these sentences contains three keywords. The SNR was calibrated with a step of 1dB starting initially at an SNR equal to 0dB to reach an approximate 50% keyword intelligibility rate. After calibration, the audio-book SNR level was changed to the calibrated value for each subject

---

[1] http://www.tobii.com/
[2] The Library of Audio-and Braille books: http://www.tpb.se

plus 2dB to allow for an easier understanding of the signal (which in principle should be supported further by viewing the talking head).

A set of 10 moderately hearing impaired male subjects took part in the experiment, with an average age of 71.2 years old. Subjects were seated approximately 60 cm from the screen.

5.2 Gesture Generation

For all the audio-book parts, pitch movements were detected using the method described in section 4.3. Since the automatic detection function showed that it enhances speech intelligibility significantly when coupled with an eyebrow raising, this gives the possibility of automatically detecting pitch movements which allows for a direct implementation in talking heads.

As to what gestures to be synthesized, in [16], all facial parameters seemed to exhibit big variations under prominent words, and in the previous experiment, head-nods and eyebrow raising, have shown to enhance speech comprehension. In addition to these cues, eye blinks have been used as a correlate to stress, and used in talking heads as in [33] based on a model suggested by P. Ekman in [34]. Eye blinks are important biological movements, that have been suggested to synchronize with speech production [35]. They play an important role in the perception of natural facial movement, in speaking, reading and listening situations and are highly correlated with the cognitive state of the speaker [36].

To introduce variability to the facial movements in the talking head, head-nods, eyebrow raising, and eye blinks are coupled with the automatically detected pitch movements. And in order to regulate the amount of gestures and avoid unnatural movement, a maximum of one gesture was allowed to be synthesized inside a moving window of 1 second, that is depending on the steepness the pitch movements detected inside this window (see 4.3). After deciding on the place where the gesture will be added, a uniform random function chooses one of the head-nods, eyebrow raising, or blinks to be added.

5.3 Gaze Analysis

The gaze tracking data of the audiobook sessions was collected for all 10 subjects, and divided into 2 parts for each subject: gaze for a talking head with gestures, and gaze for the talking head without gestures. The first test split the data into two Areas Of Interest (AOI): Face and Not Face, as displayed on the right in Figure 4. The second test split the data into three AOI: Mouth region, Eyes region, and Other. Other represents gaze movements outside the mouth and eyes regions. The left side of Figure 4 shows the location of these AOIs. Two types of visualizations are applied to present the gaze data, the first one is called a Gaze Plot which visualizes the fixations as circles and the saccades as lines between fixations, the size of the circles defines the length of the fixation, so the bigger the circle longer the fixation. The other type is called Gaze Heat Map where the face is cleared in regions where there is higher intensity of gaze and shadowed on less visited areas. Both visualizations are generated from the same data.

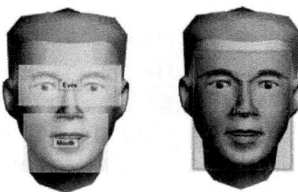

Fig. 4. Left: The eyes and mouth regions of the face Right: The inside and outside regions of the face

Figure 5 shows the Gaze Plot and Heat Map for all the subjects for the two SynFace versions (left: without gestures, right: with gestures). In this figure, it is clear that a wider area of the face was scanned by the subjects in the SynFace with gestures, specially around the eyes, this behavior is more similar to the normal eye-gaze behavior during audio-visual speech perception in noise that is reported in the literature [36] [37]. While in the talking head with no gestures condition (left), the subjects only focused on the mouth, which could be due to the understanding that information about the audio signal is only present in and around the lips and articulators. In the talking head with gestures condition, the subjects browsed the face at all time by fixations and saccades from the mouth to the eyes. It is also clear in the plot, that the saccades into external regions outside the face have been significantly lessened with the use of gestures in the face.

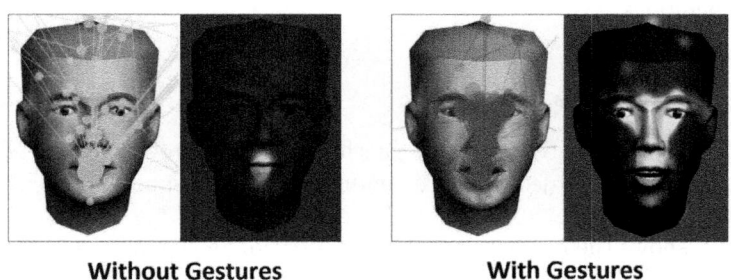

Without Gestures   **With Gestures**

Fig. 5. Gaze tracking results for the ten subjects, showing gaze plot and heat map for both conditions (with and without gestures)

To measure the time the user spent looking at the face during listening to the audio-book, the sum of the fixation length is measured for the areas of interest for all subjects, and for both versions of the face. The left side of Figure 6 presents the average percentage of time in and outside the face for both versions of the face. The figure shows that the time spent by the subjects looking at the face increased from 76% to 96% when gestures are present. And the right side of Figure 6 presents the average percentage of time on the defined regions of the eyes, mouth and the rest of the face. It is interesting to see that the eyes region

has received gaze significantly more in time than the face with no gestures, and
the area outside the face has received significantly less. This can be explained in
that subjects were more engaged with the talking head so that the time spent not
looking at the face was lessened when gestures were present. It is also interesting
to see that the time spent looking at the mouth has lessened when gestures are
present, this means that when gestures are generally present on the face, they
draw the gaze away from the mouth. This, nonetheless, does not mean that
the information extracted from the mouth region is reduced when gestures are
synthesized since peripheral vision can still help perceiving lip movements even
if the eyes are not fixated on the lips, as found in [38].

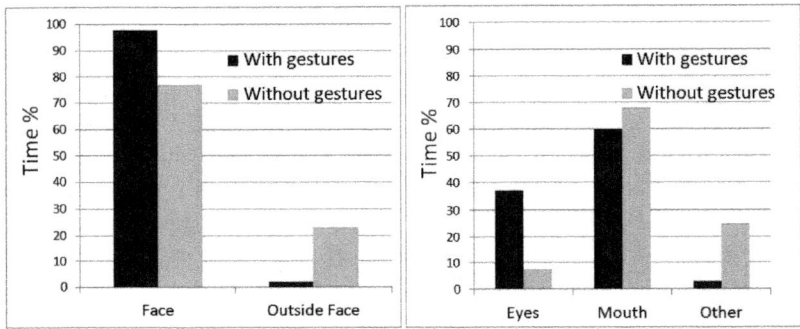

Fig. 6. The percentage of time spent inside and outside the Area Of Interest (AOI) in
the two conditions

5.4   Questionnaires Analysis

Looking at Table 1, the questions in the questionnaire target the subjective
opinions of the test subjects after listening to the audio-book for each version of
the face.

Figure 7 shows the mean and standard deviation of the difference between the
ratings for the *with gestures* face and the *no gestures* face for all the questions,
hence the 0 point represents the rating of the *no gestures* condition for each of
the questions.

An ANOVA was performed with question rating and subject as a dependent
variable, and condition (with gestures, without gestures) as an independent
variable on each of the questions. The results show a significant mean effect
for the Helpfulness (third question), Watching Duration (fourth question) and
Naturalness (fifth question), all at a significance level of .05.

The results of the questionnaires show that subjects spend more time watching the face when gestures are synthesized. This is Consistent with the results
from the gaze analysis. Additionally, the gestures over pitch movements result
in a animated talking face which is significantly more natural, and subjectively
presents a more understandable face than the face with no gestures.

Table 1. The format of the questionnaire form presented to the subjects

Question	Answers [1 .. 5]
1-How much did you understand?	nothing .. everything
2-How much effort did it take to understand?	no effort .. much effort
3-Did the face help?	not at all .. helped me a lot
4-How much did you watch the face?	not at all .. all the time
5-How natural was the face?	unnatural .. very natural

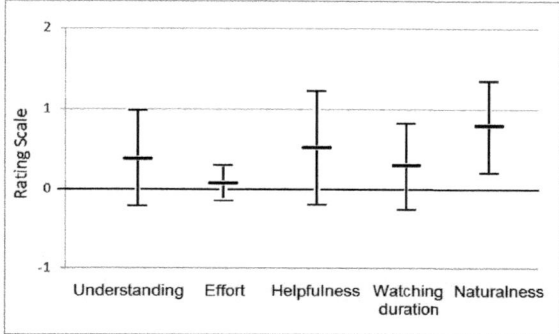

Fig. 7. A plot of the mean and standard deviation of the questionnaire ratings for the face with gestures conditions compared to 0 as the answer for the face with no gestures

6   Discussions and Remarks

The results from the intelligibility experiment indicate that when head-nods and eyebrow raise gestures are visualized during prominent syllables, they can aid speech perception. On the other hand, the results do not present a strong evidence on whether visualizing them during non-prominent syllables may hinder or aid perception.

The speech signal in this test was vocoded, and no pitch information was available to the listener, which may result in a decreased amount of information about the syllabic boundaries in the signal. The visualization of gestures then might be a possible source of voicing information (which aligns with the significant increase of the condition with pitch movements (PM) over the the condition with no gestures (N). We believe that an important function of gestures is temporal resolution and segmentation of the acoustic stream. If gestures during prominence provide information about the syllable boundaries of the prominent syllable, this can, in addition to providing semantic and pragmatic information about the sentence provide segmental information (syllabification) of the underlying acoustic stream.

In Japanese [39], it was found that pitch movement can help in the selection of word candidates. In Swedish, syllables in words are contrasted through lexical stress. It is possible that visual prominence, aligned with prominent syllables, can provide information about the segmental structure of the underlying word, and hence help in shortening the candidate list for the mental lexicon access.

It was shown before that the perception of head movements can increase speech intelligibility [4], and that the motion at only the top of the head can do the same but more reliably in expressive sentences [5]. These studies have used, as stimuli, human recordings of head movements, and hence could not provide quantified information on when these movements communicated their effect. The present experiment, in addition to showing that visual cues of acoustic prominence can aid speech intelligibility, also quantifies this effect through the use of a minimal model of fixed head nods and eye-brows raise movements on well-defined instants in time.

In [40], there is neuro-physiological evidence that matching visual information speeds up the neural processing of auditory information, although where and when the audio-visual representation of the audio-visual signal is created remains unsolved, it is evident that perceiving visual information increases the processing of the auditory stream and hence provides more temporal resolution; from this view, visualizing prominence may also provide information about speech rhythm and syllables boundaries of the underlying linguistic segment.

Going from the verbal effects of visual prominence to the interaction effects, we conducted the audio-book experiment. It has long been recognized now that there is much information present in the face, in addition to the articulators, which provide information about the speech. Animating this visual information makes virtual characters more human-like by exhibiting more variant, complex and human like behavior. In this study, we demonstrated that when gestures are coupled with prominence in acoustically degraded stimuli, the gaze behavior of subjects significantly changed into patterns which closely resemble those used when looking at a real human face; moreover, this also lessened the time the subjects spent looking away from the face. This suggests that the subjects' engagement with the talking head is increased when these gestures are visualized, while these gestures added to the naturalness and helpfulness of the talking face. Many subjects have reported after the experiments that they did not notice that the talking head had embedded gestures in it, which might be a possible indication that the perception of these gestures is realized on a subconscious level; while other subjects have reported that they were excited by perceiving gestures manifested by the face, and that was an indication of some sort of intelligence of the virtual agent.

7   Conclusion

We have investigated whether visual correlates to prominence can increase speech intelligibility. The experimental setup in this study used a lip synchronized talking head. By conducting an audio-visual speech intelligibility test, using facial gestures during prominent syllables, it was found that head-nods and eyebrow raising gestures significantly increased recognition rate. These results reveal new evidence that information about the verbal message is carried by non-verbal visual gestures. The experiment also provides a possibility to deploy these gestures in talking heads which would provide a medium for audio-visual speech perception. We also investigated the effects of synthesizing these gestures over syllables with steep pitch movements on the eye-gaze behavior and on the subjective opinions of moderately hearing impaired subjects; the results show that users' eye gaze extends from only the mouth region in the articulatory only face to the eyes and mouth in the gestural face. In addition to that, the subjects' opinions through questionnaires show an increase in intelligibility of the face when these gestures are added.

This result opens the possibility for talking heads to use visual correlates to prominence to support visual speech perception and aid the communication of prominence through the facial modality. An important application is to synthesize these cues in multimodal speech synthesis and speech synchrony systems, which requires developing real-time automatic prominence detection systems.

While the experiments show the roles of gestures synchronized with prominence, the question of how exactly users parse this audio-visual information and enhance their speech perception using it still need to be investigated. Another interesting question is the study of the rate, design and amplitude of these gestures, and to find what is optimal to provide a more natural and useful animated systems.

Acknowledgments. This work was carried out at the Center for Speech Technology, a competence center at KTH supported by the Swedish research council project #2005-3488. Part of this work is supported by the Swedish national Graduate School for Language Technology GSLT.

References

1. McGurk, H., MacDonald, J.: Hearing lips and seeing voices, vol. 264, pp. 746–748 (1976)
2. Summerfield, Q.: Lipreading and audio-visual speech perception. Philosophical Transactions: Biological Sciences 335(1273), 71–78 (1992)
3. Cave, C., Guaïtella, I., Bertrand, R., Santi, S., Harlay, F., Espesser, R.: About the relationship between eyebrow movements and Fo variations. In: Proc. of the Fourth International Conference on Spoken Language, vol. 4 (1996)
4. Munhall, K., Jones, J., Callan, D., Kuratate, T., Vatikiotis-Bateson, E.: Head Movement Improves Auditory Speech Perception Psychological Science, vol. 15(2), pp. 133–137 (2004)
5. Davis, C., Kim, J.: Audio-visual speech perception off the top of the head. Cognition 100(3), 21–31 (2006)
6. Cvejic, E., Kim, J., Davis, C.: Prosody off the top of the head: Prosodic contrasts can be discriminated by head motion. Speech Communication (2010)
7. Terken, J., Hermes, D.: The perception of prosodic prominence, in Prosody: Theory and Experiment. Studies Presented to Gösta Bruce. pp. 89–127 (2000)
8. Streefkerk, B., Pols, L., Bosch, L.: Acoustical features as predictors for prominence in read aloud Dutch sentences used in ANN's. In: Sixth European Conference on Speech Communication and Technology, Citeseer (1999)

9. Fant, G., Kruckenberg, A., Nord, L.: Durational correlates of stress in Swedish, French, and English. Journal of phonetics 19(3-4), 351–365 (1991)
10. Bruce, G.: Swedish word accents in sentence perspective. LiberLäromedel/Gleerup (1977)
11. Gussenhoven, C., Bruce, G.: Word prosody and intonation.empirical Approaches to Language Typology, 233–272 (1999)
12. Heldner, M., Strangert, E.: Temporal effects of focus in Swedish. Journal of Phonetics 29(3), 329–361 (2001)
13. Fant, G., Kruckenberg, A., Liljencrants, J., Hertegård, S.: Acoustic phonetic studies of prominence in Swedish. KTH TMH-QPSR 2(3), 2000 (2000)
14. Fant, G., Kruckenberg, A.: Notes on stress and word accent in Swedish. In: Proceedings of the International Symposium on Prosody, Yokohama, September 18, pp. 2–3 (1994)
15. Granström, B., House, D.: Audiovisual representation of prosody in expressive speech communication. Speech Communication 46(3-4), 473–484 (2005)
16. Beskow, J., Granström, B., House, D.: Visual correlates to prominence in several expressive modes. In: Proc of the Ninth International Conference on Spoken Language Processing (2006)
17. House, D., Beskow, J., Granström, B.: Timing and interaction of visual cues for prominence in audiovisual speech perception. In: Proc. of the Seventh European Conference on Speech Communication and Technology (2001)
18. Swerts, M., Krahmer, E.: The importance of different facial areas for signalling visual prominence. In: Proc. of the Ninth International Conference on Spoken Language Processing (2006)
19. Krahmer, E., Swerts, M.: The effects of visual beats on prosodic prominence: Acoustic analyses, auditory perception and visual perception. Journal of Memory and Language 57(3), 396–414 (2007)
20. Dohen, M., Lœvenbruck, H.: Interaction of audition and vision for the perception of prosodic contrastive focus. Language and Speech 52(2-3), 177 (2009)
21. Dohen, M., Lcevenbruck, H., Hill, H.: Recognizing Prosody from the Lips: Is It Possible to Extract Prosodic Focus. Visual Speech Recognition: Lip Segmentation and Mapping, 416 (2009)
22. Wang, D., Narayanan, S.: An acoustic measure for word prominence in spontaneous speech. IEEE Transactions on Audio, Speech, and Language Processing 15(2), 690–701 (2007)
23. Grice, M., Savino, M.: Can pitch accent type convey information status in yes-no questions. In: Proc. of the Workshop Sponsored by the Association for Computational Linguistics, pp. 29–38 (1997)
24. Al Moubayed, S., Beskow, J.: Effects of visual prominence cues on speech intelligibility. In: Proceedings of the International Conference on Auditory Visual Speech Processing AVSP 2009, vol. 15, p. 16 (2009)
25. Tamburini, F.: Prosodic prominence detection in speech. In: Proceedings of the Seventh International Symposium on Signal Processing and Its Applications, vol. 1 (2003)
26. Agelfors, E., Beskow, J., Dahlquist, M., Granström, B., Lundeberg, M., Spens, K.-E., Öhman, T.: Synthetic faces as a lipreading support. In: Proceedings of ICSLP 1998 (1998)
27. Salvi, G., Beskow, J., Al Moubayed, S., Granström, B.: Synface - speech-driven facial animation for virtual speech-reading support. Journal on Audio, Speech and Music Processing (2009)

28. Beskow, J.: Rule-based visual speech synthesis. In: Proc. of the Fourth European Conference on Speech Communication and Technology (1995)
29. Sjölander, K.: An HMM-based system for automatic segmentation and alignment of speech. In: Proceedings of Fonetik, pp. 93–96 (2003)
30. Beskow, J.: Trainable articulatory control models for visual speech synthesis. International Journal of Speech Technology 7(4), 335–349 (2004)
31. Shannon, R., Zeng, F., Kamath, V., Wygonski, J., Ekelid, M.: Speech recognition with primarily temporal cues. Science 270(5234), 303 (1995)
32. Al Moubayed, S., Beskow, J., Oster, A.-M., Salvi, G., Granström, B., van Son, N., Ormel, E.: Virtual speech reading support for hard of hearing in a domestic multi-media setting. In: Proceedings of Interspeech 2009 (2009)
33. Poggi, I., Pelachaud, C., De Rosisc, F.: Eye communication in a conversational 3D synthetic agent. AI communications 13(3), 169–181 (2000)
34. Ekman, P.: About brows: Emotional and conversational signals. Human ethology: Claims and limits of a new discipline: contributions to the Colloquium, 169–248 (1979)
35. Cassell, J., Pelachaud, C., Badler, N., Steedman, M., Achorn, B., Becket, T., Douville, B., Prevost, S., Stone, M.: Animated conversation: rule-based generation of facial expression, gesture & spoken intonation for multiple conversational agents. In: Proceedings of the 21st annual conference on Computer graphics and interactive techniques, pp. 413–420 (1994)
36. Raidt, S., Bailly, G., Elisei, F.: Analyzing and modeling gaze during face-to-face interaction. In: Proceedings of the International Conference on Auditory-Visual Speech Processing, AVSP 2007 (2007)
37. Vatikiotis-Bateson, E., Eigsti, I., Yano, S., Munhall, K.: Eye movement of perceivers during audiovisual speech perception. Perception and Psychophysics 60(6), 926–940 (1998)
38. Paré, M., Richler, R., Ten, H., Munhall, K.: Gaze behavior in audiovisual speech perception: The influence of ocular fixations on the McGurk effect. Perception & psychophysics 65(4), 553 (2003)
39. Cutler, A., Otake, T.: Pitch accent in spoken-word recognition in Japanese. The Journal of the Acoustical Society of America 105, 1877 (1999)
40. van Wassenhove, V., Grant, K., Poeppel, D.: Visual speech speeds up the neural processing of auditory speech. Proceedings of the National Academy of Sciences 102(4), 1181 (2005)

Adaptation in Turn-Initiations

Štefan Beňuš

Constantine the Philosopher University, Štefánikova 67, 94074 Nitra, Slovakia
Slovak Academy of Sciences, Institute of Informatics, Dúbravská cesta 9,
84507 Bratislava, Slovakia
sbenus@ukf.sk

Abstract. This study investigates the variability in the temporal alignment of turn initiations and its relationship to the entrainment and power structure between the interlocutors. The data come from spontaneous, task-oriented human-human dialogues in Standard American English, and focus on single-word turn-initial utterances. The descriptive and quantitative analysis of the data show that an emergent asymmetrical dominance relationship is constructed partly through the accommodation (or its absence) to the temporal and rhythmic features of interlocutors' turn-initiations.

Keywords: turn-taking, entrainment, rhythm, affirmative cue words, dominance.

1 Introduction

Building adaptive and context sensitive automated communicative systems requires an understanding of the cognitive systems underlying our communicative competence. One of the relevant cognitive systems that are fundamental for human interaction is the organization of turn-taking. Turn-taking is a dynamically evolving, embodied, cross-modal system that is pervasive in both speech and sign language and is strongly linked to paralinguistic domains such as gaze and gestures; e.g. [1], [2], [3]. In general, this floor-management organization underlies the decisions of 'who speaks when' and must include at least three components: 1) ways of signaling and perceiving the cues for transition-relevant places and turn allocation among interlocutors [4], 2) ways of achieving suitable durations of latencies between the turns, avoiding over-long overlaps or silent pauses, and 3) ways of resolving disruptions in the system [5]. In this paper we focus on the second point.

In current state-of-the-art applications of interactive voice-response systems, turn boundary detection is typically based on silence detection with the threshold between 0.5 and 1 second. Multiple problems arise from this implementation such as the occurrence of false positives or hindrance of cohesion. The primary reason for these problems is that the exchange of turns in human-human spoken interactions is not based on detecting silence. Humans have the ability to detect the projected end of the current turn from multiple prosodic, syntactic, pragmatic and gestural cues; e.g. [6]. But even if we could implement all these human abilities and create systems that reliably predict when the interlocutor is about to finish her turn, we still need a model of when precisely we should start speaking. For this aim, the other feature of human-human interactions is

A. Esposito et al. (Eds.): COST 2102 Int. Training School 2010, LNCS 6456, pp. 72–80, 2011.

crucial: Interlocutors are assumed to be entrained to each other on a number of linguistic and paralinguistic levels, which greatly facilitates communication [7]. This mutual entrainment then provides a basis for meaningfully modeling the timing of turn-initiations as a dynamic incorporation into the rhythmic patterns of the preceding turns [8]. In support of this approach, entrainment has been also found in the metrical features of utterances [9], in intensity characteristics [10], in phonetic and prosodic characteristics of individual words [11], and in accent and other socio-phonetic variables [12]. At the paralinguistic level, conversational partners entrain their body swaying motions [13], and breathing [14].

The aim of this study is to improve our understanding of the adaptation choices human interlocutors make in the temporal initiation of turns, which is a stepping stone to building more natural human-machine dialogue systems. Our focus is on the timing of turn-initial responses in collaborative task dialogues with special attention to single word responses that pragmatically function as agreements, acknowledgments, back-channels, or filled pauses. We will argue that the adaptive behavior can be observed both sequentially in adjacent turns as well as globally over the entire conversation, and that it contributes to the construction of an inter-speaker power relationship.

2   Corpus Description

Data for this study come from a single session of the Columbia Games Corpus [15]. Two female speakers (Spkr1 and Spkr2) played specially designed games without visual contact that involved matching the identity and positions of various objects on their laptop screens. The subjects switched the roles repeatedly. The recordings were then orthographically transcribed, and words were aligned to the source acoustic signal by hand. The analyzed speech in this conversation covers 35.7 minutes and contains 770 turns almost equally distributed between the two speakers (384 for Spkr1 and 386 for Spkr2).

Space restrictions prevent a full description of annotations performed on this corpus but detailed descriptions could be found in [15] or [16]. The prosodic features of the dialogues were labeled using the ToBI annotation scheme [17]. The turn-taking behavior was labeled using a slightly modified scheme from [18] described in [19]. Temporal features such as turn latencies were automatically extracted based on word alignments.

3   Descriptive and Quantitative Observations

In this paper we concentrate on two symptomatic uses of speaker adaptation in the timing of turn-initial single-word utterances. The first type is the sequential local adaptation in adjacent turns. The second is a global adaptation of the timing pattern developed during the entire conversation. We will discuss each of these observations in the following subsections presenting first the descriptive analysis of representative example followed with quantitative tests for the validity and robustness of patterns.

3.1 Local Adaptation: Affirmative Cue Words in Adjacent Turns

Consider the following example in which Spkr1 describes the position of the *iron* on her screen and Spkr2's role is to match the position of this object on her screen with the position of Spkr1's screen. Bold numbers show the turn latencies (i.e. duration of silences across turns). Utterance-final rising, falling and level intonational contours are shown with arrows ↑, ↓, and → respectively; square brackets show overlapped speech.

1. Spkr2: okay, lines up↑ **(0.36)**
2. Spkr1: yeah it's it's almost it's just barely (0.27) like over↓ **(0.45)**
3. Spkr2: o[kay]↑
4. Spkr1: [but] it's basically that same line um so the black part at the bottom of the iron↑ **(0.08)**
5. Spkr2: mmhm↑ **(0.13)**
6. Spkr1: not necessarily like on the same line as the white foot it's just a little bit over↓

The timing of *okay* and *mmhm* in lines 3 and 5 from Spkr2 is different. Two preceding instances of *mmhm* from Spkr2 (not shown in the excerpt) came with the latencies of around 0.2s. Perhaps realizing that her acknowledgment in line 3 was 'too late', Spkr2 avoids another overlap by perfectly aligning her backchannel in line 5 with only a 0.08s latency. Fig. 1 gives a visual representation of this adjustment.

Another type of local adaptation can be observed in the timing of *Adjacency triplets*. In this unit of interaction, the first speaker provides some information or poses a question; the second speaker acknowledges, backchannels, or provides a short answer; and then the first speaker acknowledges this response. In the short excerpt

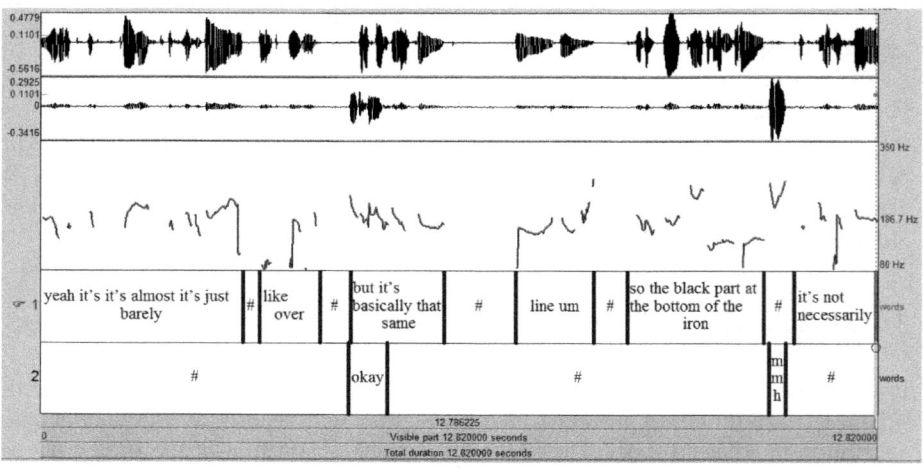

Fig. 1. Adjustment in the temporal alignment of two consecutive turn-initial acknowledgment/backchannels. The top two panels show the sound waves for both speakers, the middle panel fundamental frequency between 80 and 350 Hz, and the bottom two panels show the transcript.

below we see that the length of the silent intervals preceding and following *yeah* from Spkr2 in line 2 are greater than similar intervals surrounding subsequent *no* from the same speaker.

1. Spkr1: basically on the right side of his hat↑ **(0.35)**
2. Spkr2: yeah↓**(0.17)**
3. Spkr1: okay (0.42) and but it's not touching the hat↑**(0.09)**
4. Spkr2: no↑ **(0.12)**
5. Spkr1: okay (0.07) and then the distance →

Adjacency triplets also present suitable material for comparing relative and absolute time in describing the temporal alignment patterns. While the absolute latency duration used in the preceding two examples might be suggestive of temporal entrainment, a much stronger case could be made if these patterns are supported with relative timing as well. This is because relative timing measures are less influenced by the variability in speech rate that is orthogonal to the rhythmical structure of turn-taking. Hence, if the same generalizations can be drawn from both absolute and relative timing measures, the observed rhythmical alignment patterns can be considered robust and general in nature.

One way of relativizing time in turn-taking research is to study the timing of peaks of prosodic prominence in relation to such peaks in the preceding utterance [9], [16], [20]. These prominent syllables, or *P-centers* [8], are assumed to be linked most tightly to the amplitude (loudness) of the syllables [21]. Therefore, we define such prominence peaks as the amplitude peaks of the stressed syllables in all words that received a pitch accent mark in the labeling of the prosodic structure using the ToBI scheme [17]. Fig. 2 illustrates the adaptation of Spkr2 to the rhythmical pattern established by her interlocutor in two consecutive adjacency triplets from the excerpt above. We see that the spacing of the pitch accents in the first question is greater than in the second question, to which Spkr2 adjusts by aligning the prominence peak of the second response more tightly than the first response.

Although the above examples are representative of the analyzed conversation, such context-sensitive descriptive analysis should be complemented with quantitative analyses to assess the validity and robustness of the patterns identified with the examples. Frequent impressionistically-based claims about wide-spread rhythmical entrainment of interlocutors [9] might result from perceptual 'mirage' in which listeners interpret speech as necessarily rhythmical [22], and impressionistic transcriptions of speech may be mis-perceived and unreliable [23].

To test our hypotheses, we employed several quantitative analyses. For example, the distribution of turn types based on the labeling scheme described in section 2 showed that Spkr1 initiated her turns as overlapped with the end of the preceding turn more often than Spkr2; a Pearson chi-square test $r(1, 511) = 6.45$, $p = 0.011$. Spkr2 also produced her turn-initial backchannels, agreements, acknowledgments, and filled pauses with longer latencies than Spkr1; an Anova test $F(1, 397) = 4.6$, $p = 0.032$ with mean latencies 0.33 for Spkr2 and 0.22 for Spkr1. Finally, we tested the correlation between the rate of pitch accents in the last pause-defined unit before the turn-exchange and the latency between the last pitch accent in the turn before the exchange

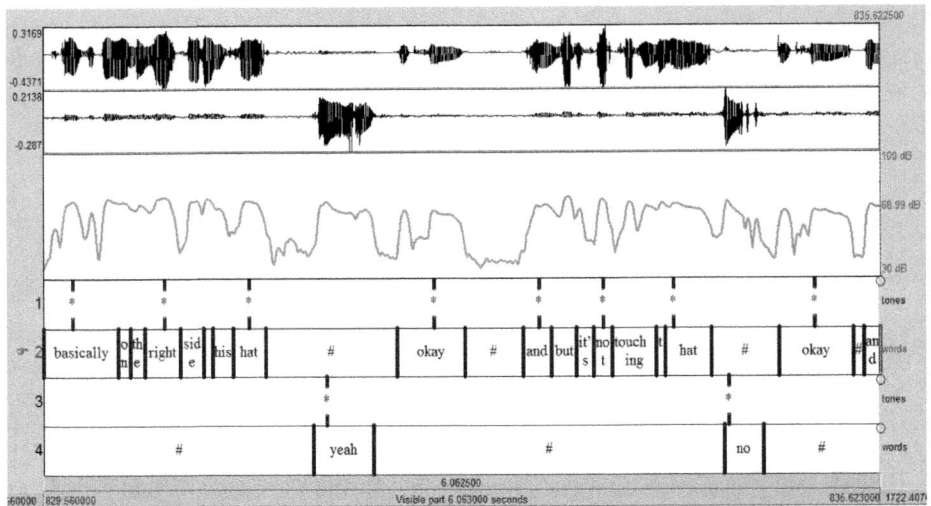

Fig. 2. Adjustment in the rhythmical alignment of two consecutive adjacency triplets. The top two panels shows the sound waves, the middle panel shows intensity between 30 and 100 dB, and the bottom 4 panels show the transcript with pitch accent labels as "*".

and the first pitch accent after the exchange. The rate of pitch accents was calculated as the number of pitch accents divided by the length of the pause-defined unit and represents a rough measure of speech rhythm. If entrainment takes place, we expect shorter latencies following units with faster rate and longer latencies following units with slower rate, hence a significant positive correlation. Despite moderate correlation coefficients, showing a rather low degree of rhythmical entrainment, the values for Spkr2 were consistently significant $r(293) = 0.22$, $p < 0.001$ in all data, and $r(127) = 0.3$, $p = 0.001$ for turn-initial backchannels, agreements and acknowledgments, while significance was never reached for Spkr1.

These findings provide quantitative support for our descriptive analysis that characterized Spkr2 as more accommodating and willing to adapt her turn-taking behavior to her interlocutor.

3.2 Global Adaptation: Timing of Turn-Initial Filled Pauses

Turn-initial filled pauses facilitate both production and perception of linguistic material because they allow speakers to plan their intended message and listeners to prepare to perceive important content [4], they mark discourse and prosodic boundaries [24], and signal planning difficulties associated with cognitive load and the presence of choice [25]. In all those functions, turn-initial filled pauses tend to be produced with significant latencies after the end of the preceding turn. Multiple examples of this default temporal alignment are also present in our corpus. However, we also observed instances of a tight temporal alignment of the filled pauses with the end of the preceding turn. Consider the excerpt below.

1. Spkr1:   okay, how about the little black part, um, where the beak starts, do you see [that]→
2. Spkr2:   **[um]** it's like blinking in and out let me see, um yeah there's like black above the beak righ[t]↑
3. Spkr1:   [o]kay [just a little bit of that]↑
4. Spkr2:   [yeah you can see that]↑
5. Spkr1:   okay and um anything el[se]↑
6. Spkr2:   **[um]** let me think, mm, see
7. Spkr1:   is the tail sticking out from th- b- where the branch is like it's not aligned↑ **(1.18)**
8. Spkr2:   **[um** yeah it's]   not [aligned with the] branch→
9. Spkr1:   [the tail of the lion]↑   [okay]↑
10. Spkr1:   and either is the foot like it's ?-[sticking] out a little bit more↑ **(0.25)**
11. Spkr2:   [the feet]
12. Spkr2:   **um** (2.11) oh the branch on the left side↑

The turn-initial *ums* in lines 2 and 6 overlap the end of the preceding turn. They follow a question, and there is thus no need to hasten to grab the floor, because Spkr1 has explicitly yielded the floor and selected Spkr2 to continue. There is also no need in this context to signal that the interlocutor needs to attend to the speaker, which is another common function of turn-initial filled pauses. This is because Spkr1 is presumably fully attending to Spkr2 as she is expecting an answer to her question. Finally, if these filled pauses signaled planning difficulties, they would be probably preceded by a relatively long silent pause representing cognitive processing, and not temporarily aligned almost perfectly with the end of the preceding turn.

This temporal pattern contrasts with the alignment of *um* in line 8. Here, Spkr2 seems to signal hesitation and aligns her filled pause with the latency longer than one second. Spkr1 seems to detect difficulty in processing her question and adds more information that overlaps with the filled pause from Spkr2. Multiple examples of the contrast in our corpus between this default 'loose' alignment of filled pauses and the 'tight' alignment exemplified in lines 2, 6, and 12 support the analysis that the 'tight' alignment of turn-initiations evolved as a global adaptation of Spkr2 over the entire conversation to avoid the overlaps from Spkr1.

Similarly to section 3.1, we wanted to test the robustness of these observations quantitatively for the whole conversation. First, we observed that 12% of all turns started with a filled pause. Two thirds of these turns (66%) were produced by Spkr2, and this difference between the speakers was significant; $r(1, 770) = 10.51$, $p < 0.001$. Additionally, Spkr2 produced these turn-initial filled pauses with greater normalized mean pitch and tended to produce them also with greater normalized mean intensity than Spkr1; $F(1, 66) = 4.59$, $p = 0.036$ and $F(1, 66) = 3.14$, $p = 0.081$ respectively. This difference signals greater pragmatic importance of turn-initial filled pauses for speaker B than for speaker A.

Finally, Fig. 3 shows the temporal alignment of turn-initial filled pauses for the two speakers. Both speakers have a very clear peak for latencies between 0 and 0.2s, which corresponds to extremely tight temporal alignment. However, Spkr2's histogram also shows wider distribution of latencies and a second discontinuity around the

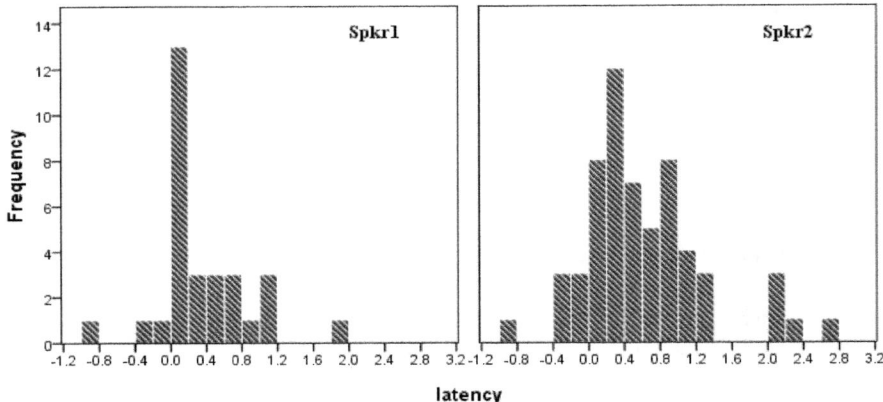

Fig. 3. Latency distributions (between the end of turn-final word and the start of the turn-initial word) in seconds for turn-initial filled pauses separately for two speakers

values of 1 second. We interpret Spkr2's behavior as adapting her default 'loose' temporal alignment of turn-initial filled pauses to a more 'tight' alignment in an effort to secure the floor for her as a reaction to Spkr1's tactics to add more information or take the floor in the absence of such signal. The histograms together with other descriptive and quantitative observations thus support the conclusion that Spkr2 adapted her timing pattern globally during the whole conversation.

An interesting question is how this global adaptation developed over time through the dialogue. Some studies suggest that entrainment to the dialectal features of the speech of the interlocutor happens rapidly at the beginning of the conversation [26]. Yet other results point to continuous entrainment and detrainment of prosodic feature during the course of the dialogue [27]. The temporal evolution of the rhythmical entrainment patterns remains an challenging question for further research.

4   Discussion and Conclusion

We presented two strategies for the adaptation in timing of turn initiations in collaborative tasks. First, speakers used the sequential local adaptations in their adjacent turns to entrain better with the rhythm and turn-taking style of the interlocutor. Second, speakers used a global adaptation of the timing pattern developed during the entire conversation. Both of these adaptations aimed at decreasing the overlap in turn-taking. We also note that the patterns of adaptations discussed above were not automatic since they were prevalent in Spkr2's speech and almost non-existent in Spkr1's speech. Although space limitations prevent a detailed analysis of the two conversations in which the target speakers played the game with different interlocutors, we observed that the patterns we described tend to carry into the other dialogues [28].

Our results lead to the proposal that the temporal patterns in turn-initiations are cognitively meaningful and play a role in constructing an asymmetrical dominance relationship between the speakers. This research shows that future autonomous, adaptive, and context-sensitive dialogue systems should be flexible enough to incorporate both local and global adaptations to the rhythmical and temporal patterns of the interlocutor.

Acknowledgments. This work was supported in part by the Slovak Ministry of Education grant KEGA 3/6399/08 and the Slovak Research and Development Agency project APVV-0369-07, and was done in collaboration with Augustín Gravano and Julia Hirschberg.

References

1. Schegloff, E.: Sequence Organization in Interaction. CUP, Cambridge (2007)
2. Coates, J., Sutton-Spence, R.: Turn-taking patterns in deaf conversation. Journal of Sociolinguistics 5, 507–529 (2001)
3. Goodwin, C.: Transparent vision. In: Ochs, E., Schegloff, E., Thompson, S.A. (eds.) Interaction and Grammar, pp. 370–404. CUP, Cambridge (1996)
4. Sacks, H., Schegloff, E., Jefferson, G.: A simplest systematic for the organization of turn-taking for conversation. Language 50, 696–735 (1974)
5. Schegloff, E.: Overlapping talk and the organization of turn-taking for conversation. Language and Society 19, 1–63 (2000)
6. Ford, C., Thompson, S.: Interactional units in conversation: syntactic, intonational, and pragmatic resources for the management of turns. In: Ochs, E., Schegloff, E., Thompson, S.A. (eds.) Interaction and Grammar, pp. 134–184. CUP, Cambridge (1996)
7. Pickering, M., Garrod, S.: Toward a mechanistic psychology of dialogue. Behavioral and Brain Sciences 27, 169–226 (2004)
8. Couper-Kuhlen, E.: English Speech Rhythm. John Benjamins, Amsterdam (1993)
9. Auer, P., Couper-Kuhlen, E., Müller, F.: Language in Time. OUP, Oxford (1999)
10. Ward, A., Litman, D.: Automatically measuring lexical and acoustic/prosodic convergence in tutorial dialog corpora. In: Proceedings of SLaTE Workshop, Farmington, PA (2007)
11. Pardo, J.: On phonetic convergence during conversational interaction. J. Acoust. Soc. Am. 119(4), 2382–2393 (2006)
12. Aubanel, V., Nguyen, N.: Automatic recognition of regional phonological variation in conversational interaction. Speech Communication (in press)
13. Shockley, K., Santana, M., Fowler, C.: Mutual interpersonal postural constraints are involved in cooperative conversation. Journal of Experimental Psychology: Human Perception & Performance 29, 326–332 (2003)
14. McFarland, D.: Respiratory markers of conversational interaction. Journal of Speech, Language, & Hearing Research 44, 128–143 (2001)
15. Gravano, A.: Turn-Taking and Affirmative Cue Words in Task-Oriented Dialogue. Unpublished Ph.D. thesis, Columbia University, NY (2009)
16. Beňuš, Š.: Are we 'in sync': Turn-taking in collaborative dialogues. In: Proceedings of 10th INTERSPEECH, pp. 2167–2170. ISCA, Brighton, UK (2009)
17. Beckman, M., Hirschberg, J., Shattuck-Hufnagel, S.: The original ToBI system and the evolution of the ToBI framework. In: Jun, S.-A. (ed.) Prosodic Typology: The Phonology of Intonation and Phrasing, pp. 9–54. OUP, Oxford (2004)
18. Beattie, G.: Turn-taking and interruption in political interviews: Margaret Thatcher and Jim Callaghan compared and contrasted. Semiotica 39(1/2), 93–114 (1982)
19. Gravano, A., Hirschberg, J.: Turn-Yielding Cues in Task-Oriented Dialogue. In: Proceedings of SIGDIAL, Association for Computational Linguistics, pp. 253–261 (2009)

20. Bull, M.: An analysis of between-speaker intervals. In: Cleary, J., Moll&aacute-Aliod, D. (eds.) Proceedings of the Edinburgh Linguistic Conference, pp. 18–27 (1996)
21. Cummins, F., Port, R.: Rhythmic constraints on stress-timing in English. Journal of Phonetics 26(2), 145–171 (1998)
22. Laver, J.: Principles of phonetics. CUP, Cambridge (1994)
23. Carpenter, S., O'Connel, D.: More than meets the ear: Some variables affecting pauses. Language & Communication 8(1), 11–27 (1998)
24. Swerts, M.: Filled pauses as markers of discourse structure. J. of Prag. 30, 485–496 (1998)
25. Steward, O., Corley, M.: Hesitation disfluencies in spontaneous speech: The meaning of um. Language and Linguistics Compass 4, 589–602 (2008)
26. Delvaux, V., Soquet, A.: The influence of ambient speech on adult speech productions through unintentional imitation. Phonetica 64, 145–173 (2007)
27. Edlund, J., Heldner, M., Hirschberg, J.: Pause and gap length in face-to-face interaction. In: Proc. of Interspeech 2009, Brighton, UK (2009)
28. Beňuš, Š., Gravano, A., Hirschberg, J.: Pragmatic aspects of temporal alignment in turn-taking. Journal of Pragmatics (submitted)

Sentic Avatar: Multimodal Affective Conversational Agent with Common Sense

Erik Cambria[1], Isabelle Hupont[2],
Amir Hussain[1], Eva Cerezo[3], and Sandra Baldassarri[3]

[1] University of Stirling, Stirling, UK
[2] Aragon Institute of Technology, Zaragoza, Spain
[3] University of Zaragoza, Zaragoza, Spain
{eca,ahu}@cs.stir.ac.uk,ihupont@ita.es,{sandra,ecerezo}@unizar.es
http://cs.stir.ac.uk/~eca/sentics

Abstract. The capability of perceiving and expressing emotions through different modalities is a key issue for the enhancement of human-computer interaction. In this paper we present a novel architecture for the development of intelligent multimodal affective interfaces. It is based on the integration of Sentic Computing, a new opinion mining and sentiment analysis paradigm based on AI and Semantic Web techniques, with a facial emotional classifier and Maxine, a powerful multimodal animation engine for managing virtual agents and 3D scenarios. One of the main distinguishing features of the system is that it does not simply perform emotional classification in terms of a set of discrete emotional labels but it operates in a continuous 2D emotional space, enabling the integration of the different affective extraction modules in a simple and scalable way.

Keywords: AI, Sentic Computing, NLP, Facial Expression Analysis, Sentiment Analysis, Multimodal Affective HCI, Conversational Agents.

1   Introduction

Emotions are a fundamental component in human experience, cognition, perception, learning and communication. A user interface cannot be considered really intelligent unless it is also capable of perceiving and expressing emotions. For this reason, affect sensing and recognition from multiple modalities is getting a more and more popular research field for the enhancement of human-computer interaction (HCI).

In this paper we present a novel architecture for integrating a process for reasoning by analogy over affective knowledge, a facial emotional classifier and a multimodal engine for managing 3D virtual scenarios and characters.

The structure of the paper is the following: Section 2 presents the state of the art of multimodal affective HCI, Section 3 briefly describes the proposed architecture, Section 4 explains in detail how the affect recognition and integration are performed and, eventually, Section 5 comprises concluding remarks and a description of future work.

A. Esposito et al. (Eds.): COST 2102 Int. Training School 2010, LNCS 6456, pp. 81–95, 2011.
© Springer-Verlag Berlin Heidelberg 2011

2   Multimodal Affective HCI

Human computer intelligent interaction is an emerging field aimed at providing natural ways for humans to use computers as aids. It is argued that for a computer to be able to interact with humans it needs to have the communication skills of humans. One of these skills is the affective aspect of communication, which is recognized to be a crucial part of human intelligence and has been argued to be more fundamental in human behaviour and success in social life than intellect [1][2]. Emotions influence cognition, and therefore intelligence, especially when it involves social decision-making and interaction.

The latest scientific findings indicate that emotions play an essential role in decision-making, perception, learning and more. Most of the past research on affect sensing has considered each sense such as vision, hearing and touch in isolation. However, natural human-human interaction is multimodal: we communicate through speech and use body language (posture, facial expressions, gaze) to express emotion, mood, attitude, and attention.

Affect recognition from multiple modalities has a short historical background and is still in its first stage [3]. It was not till 1998 that computer scientists attempted to use multiple modalities for recognition of emotions/affective states [4]. The results were promising: using multiple modalities improved the overall recognition accuracy helping the systems function in a more efficient and reliable way. Following the findings in psychology, which suggested that the most significant channel for judging emotional cues of humans is the visual channel of face and body [5], a number of works combine facial expressions and body gestures for affect sensing [6][7][8]. Other approaches combine different biological information such as brain signals or skin conductivity for affect sensing [9][10].

However this research makes use of a single information channel, i.e. a single type of computer input device, and, therefore, must assume the reliability on this channel. For that reason, the trend in recent works is to consider and combine affective information coming from different channels. That way, eventual changes on the reliability of the different information channels are considered.

Recent literature on multimodal affect sensing is focused on the fusion of data coming from the visual and audio channels. Most of those works make use of the visual channel for body gesture recognition [11] or facial expression classification [12] and the audio channel to analyze non-linguistic audio cues such as laughters [13], coughs [14] or cries [15]. However, very few works fuse information coming from the visual channel with linguistic-based (speech contents) audio affect sensing. With all these new areas of research in affect sensing, a number of challenges have arisen. In particular, the synchronization and fusion of the information coming from different channels is a big problem to solve.

Previous studies fused emotional information either at a decision-level, in which the outputs of the unimodal systems are integrated by the use of suitable expert criteria [16], or at a feature-level, in which the data from both modalities are combined before classification [17]. In any case, the choice of fusion strategy depends on the targeted application.

Accordingly, all available multimodal recognizers have designed and/or used ad-hoc solutions for fusing information coming from multiple modalities but cannot accept new modalities without re-defining the whole system. In summary, there is not a general consensus when fusing multiple modalities and systems' scalability is not possible.

3   Overview of the System

The architecture proposed (illustrated in Fig. 1) is based on the multimodal animation engine Maxine [18], and it consists of four main modules: Perception, Affective Analysis, Deliberative/Generative and Motor module.

The Perception module simply consists of the hardware necessary to gather the multimodal information from the user i.e. keyboard, microphone and webcam. The Affective Analysis module aims to infer the user's affective state from the different inputs and integrate it. The Deliberative/Generative module is in charge of processing the extracted emotional information to manage the virtual agent's decisions and reactions, which are finally generated by the Motor module. In this paper we focus on the presentation of the affective sensing part of the system, explained in detail in Section 4.

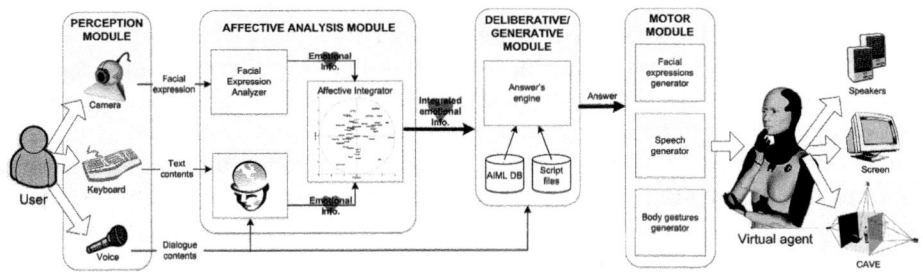

Fig. 1. Sentic Avatar's architecture

4   Affective Analysis Module

The Affective Analysis Module is in charge of extracting emotions from the textual, vocal and video inputs and integrate them.

It consists of three main parts: Sentic Computing, for inferring emotions from typed-in text and speech-to-text converted contents (Section 4.1), Facial Expression Analyzer, for extracting affective information from video (Section 4.2), and Affective Integrator, for integrating the outputs coming from the two previous modules (Section 4.3).

4.1   Sentic Computing

Sentic Computing [19] is a new opinion mining and sentiment analysis paradigm which exploits AI and Semantic Web techniques to better recognize, interpret and process opinions and sentiments in natural language text.

In Sentic Computing, whose term derives from the Latin 'sentire' (the root of words such as sentiment and sensation) and 'sense' (intended as common sense), the analysis of text is not based on statistical learning models but rather on common sense reasoning tools [20] and domain-specific ontologies [21]. Differently from keyword spotting [22][23][24], lexical affinity [25][26] and statistical [27][28][29] approaches, which generally requires large inputs and thus cannot appraise texts with satisfactory granularity, Sentic Computing enables the analysis of documents not only on the page or paragraph-level but also on the sentence-level.

AffectiveSpace. AffectiveSpace [30] is a multi-dimensional vector space built from ConceptNet [31], a semantic network of common sense knowledge, and WordNet-Affect, a linguistic resource for the lexical representation of affective knowledge [32]. The blend [33] of these two resources yields a new dataset in which common sense and affective knowledge coexist i.e. a 14,301 × 117,365 matrix whose rows are concepts (e.g. 'dog' or 'bake cake'), whose columns are either common sense and affective features (e.g. 'isA-pet' or 'hasEmotion-joy'), and whose values indicate truth values of assertions.

In this knowledge base each concept is represented by a vector in the space of possible features whose values are positive for features that produce an assertion of positive valence (e.g. 'a penguin is a bird'), negative for features that produce an assertion of negative valence (e.g. 'a penguin cannot fly') and zero when nothing is known about the assertion. The degree of similarity between two concepts, then, is the dot product between their rows in the blended matrix.

The value of such a dot product increases whenever two concepts are described with the same feature and decreases when features that are negations of each other describe them. When performed on the blended matrix, however, these dot products have very high dimensionality (as many dimensions as there are features) and are difficult to work with. In order to approximate these dot products in a useful way, we project all of the concepts from the space of features into a space with many fewer dimensions i.e. we reduce the dimensionality of the matrix by means of principal component analysis (PCA).

In particular, we perform truncated singular value decomposition (TSVD) [34] in order to obtain a new matrix that forms a low-rank approximation of the original data and represents, for the Eckart–Young theorem [35], the best estimation of the original data in the Frobenius norm sense. By exploiting the information sharing property of truncated SVD, concepts with the same affective valence are likely to have similar features – that is, concepts conveying the same emotion tend to fall near each other in AffectiveSpace. Concept similarity does not depend on their absolute positions in the vector space, but rather on the angle they make with the origin.

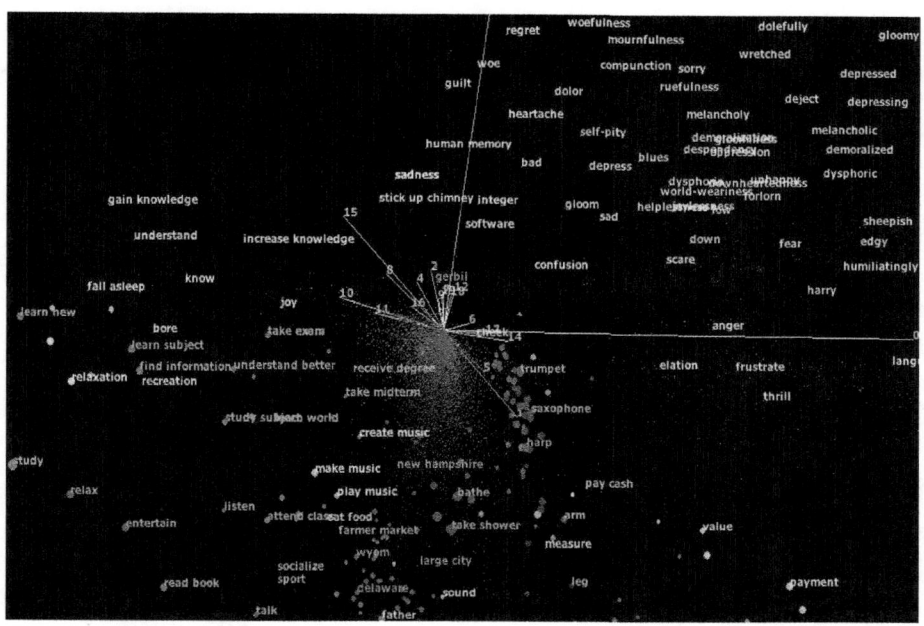

Fig. 2. A sketch of AffectiveSpace

For example we can find concepts such as 'beautiful day', 'birthday party', 'laugh' and 'make person happy' very close in direction in the vector space, while concepts like 'sick', 'feel guilty', 'be laid off' and 'shed tear' are found in a completely different direction (nearly opposite with respect to the center of the space). If we choose to discard all but the first 100 principal components, common sense concepts and emotions are represented by vectors of 100 coordinates: these coordinates can be seen as describing concepts in terms of 'eigenmoods' that form the axes of AffectiveSpace i.e. the basis $e_0,...,e_{99}$ of the vector space. For example, the most significant eigenmood, e_0, represents concepts with positive affective valence. That is, the larger a concept's component in the e_0 direction is, the more affectively positive it is likely to be. Concepts with negative e_0 components, then, are likely to have negative affective valence.

The Hourglass of Emotions. The Hourglass of Emotions is an affective categorization model developed starting from Plutchik's studies on human emotions [36]. In the model (illustrated in Fig. 3) sentiments are reorganized around four independent dimensions whose different levels of activation make up the total emotional state of the mind. The Hourglass of Emotions, in fact, is based on the idea that the mind is made of different independent resources and that emotional states result from turning some set of these resources on and turning another set of them off [37].

The model is particularly useful to recognize, understand and express emotions in the context of human-computer interaction (HCI). In the Hourglass of

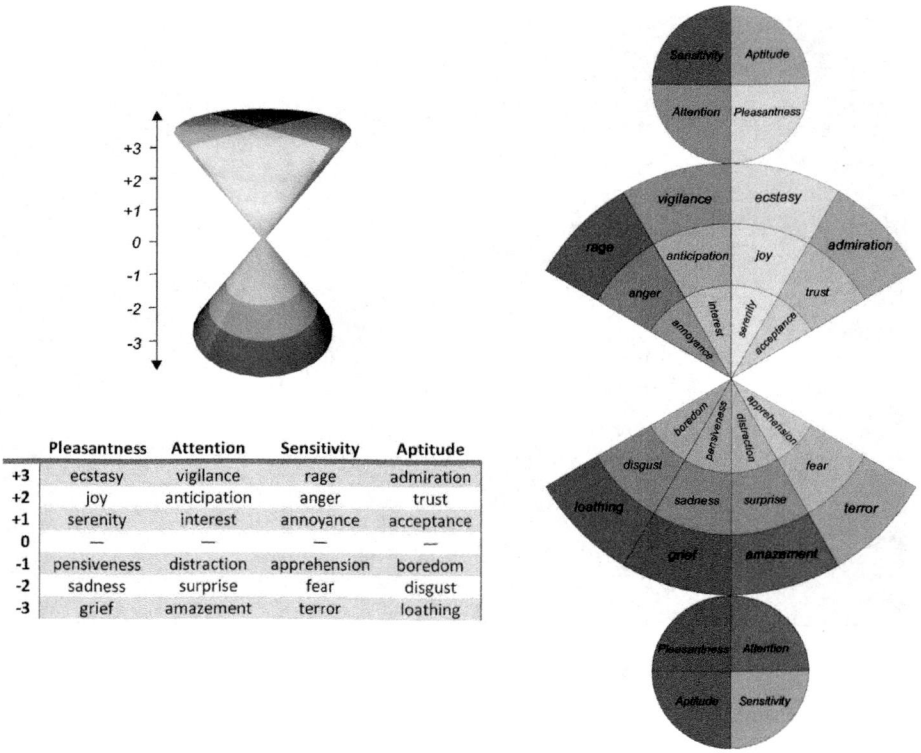

	Pleasantness	Attention	Sensitivity	Aptitude
+3	ecstasy	vigilance	rage	admiration
+2	joy	anticipation	anger	trust
+1	serenity	interest	annoyance	acceptance
0	–	–	–	–
-1	pensiveness	distraction	apprehension	boredom
-2	sadness	surprise	fear	disgust
-3	grief	amazement	terror	loathing

Fig. 3. The Hourglass of Emotions

Emotions, in fact, affective states are not classified, as often happens in the field of emotion analysis, into a few basic categories, but rather into four concomitant but independent dimensions – Pleasantness, Attention, Sensitivity and Aptitude – in order to understand how much respectively:

1. the user is happy with the service provided
2. the user is interested in the information supplied
3. the user is comfortable with the interface
4. the user is disposed to use the application

Each affective dimension is characterized by six levels of activation that determine the intensity of the expressed/perceived emotion, for a total of 24 labels specifying 'elementary emotions'. The concomitance of the different affective dimensions makes possible the generation of 'compound emotions' such as *love*, given by the combination of *joy* and *trust*, or *disappointment*, given by the concomitance of *surprise* and *sadness*.

Sentics Extraction Process. The text contents typed-in by the user and the dialogue contents, traslated into text using Loquendo automatic speech recognition (ASR) [38], go through a Natural Language Processing (NLP) module,

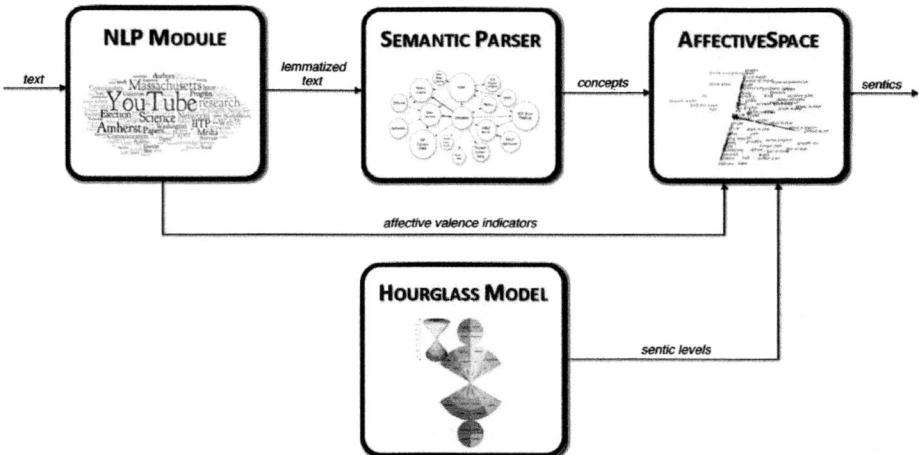

Fig. 4. Sentics Extraction Process

which performs a first skim of the document, a Semantic Parser, whose aim is to extract concepts from the processed text, and eventually AffectiveSpace, for the inference of concepts' affective valence (Fig. 4).

In particular, the NLP module interprets all the affective valence indicators usually contained in text such as special punctuation, complete upper-case words, onomatopoeic repetitions, exclamation words, degree adverbs or emoticons, and it ultimately lemmatizes text.

The Semantic Parser exploits a concept n-gram model extracted from ConceptNet graph structure in order to deconstruct text into common sense concepts. Once concepts are retrieved from the lemmatized text, the parser also provides, for each of these, the relative frequency, valence and status i.e. the concept's occurrence in the text, its positive or negative connotation, and the degree of intensity with which the concept is expressed.

The AffectiveSpace module, eventually, projects the retrieved concepts into the vector space clustered (using a k-means approach) wrt the Hourglass model, and infers the affective valence of these according to the positions they occupy in the multi-dimensional space.

Therefore, the outputs of the Sentics Extraction Process are four dimensional vectors, called 'sentic vectors', which specify the emotional charge carried by each concept in terms of Pleasantness, Attention, Sensitivity and Aptitude. This information is ultimately exploited to produce emotional labels which are given as inputs to the Affective Integrator, as shown in the example below:

Text: Yesterday was a BEAUTIFUL day!
I couldn't find the food I was after and there was pretty bad weather
but I bought a new dress and a lot of Christmas presents.

<Concept: 'yesterday'>
<Concept: 'beautiful day'++>

<Concept: ! 'find food'>
<Concept: 'bad weather'-->
<Concept: 'buy new dress'>
<Concept: 'buy christmas present'++>

Sentics: [1.608, 0.571, 0.0, 2.489]
Moods: joy and interest
Polarity: 0.51

4.2   Facial Expression Analyzer

The Facial Expression Analyzer achieves an automatic classification of the shown facial expressions into discrete emotional categories. It is able to classify the user's emotion in terms of Ekman's six universal emotions (*fear, sadness, joy, disgust, surprise* and *anger*) [39] plus *neutral*, giving a membership confidence value to each emotional category.

The face modeling selected as input for the Facial Expression Analyzer follows a feature-based approach: the inputs are a set of facial distances and angles calculated from feature points of the mouth, eyebrows and eyes. In fact, the inputs are the variations of these angles and distances with respect to the neutral face. The points are obtained thanks to a real-time facial feature tracking program [40].

Fig. 5(a) shows the correspondence of these points with those defined by the MPEG4 standard. The set of parameters obtained from these points is shown in Fig. 5(b). In order to make the distance values consistent (independently of the scale of the image, the distance to the camera, etc.) and independent of the expression, all the distances are normalized with respect to the distance between the eyes i.e. the MPEG4 Facial Animation Parameter Unit (FAPU), also called ESo. The choice of angles provides a size invariant classification and saves the effort of normalization. As regards the classification process itself, the system intelligently combines the outputs of 5 different classifiers simultaneously. In this way, the overall risk of making a poor selection with a given classifier for a given input is reduced.

The classifier combination chosen follows a weighted majority voting strategy, where the voted weights are assigned depending on the performance of each classifier for each emotion. In order to select the best classifiers to combine, the Waikado Environment for Knowledge Analysis (Weka) tool was used [41]. This provides a collection of machine learning algorithms for data mining tasks. From this collection, five classifiers were selected after tuning: RIPPER, Multilayer Perceptron, SVM, Naive Bayes and C4.5.

The selection was based on their widespread use as well as on the individual performance of their Weka implementation. To train the classifiers and evaluate the performance of the system, two different facial emotion databases were used: the FGNET database [42] that provides video sequences of 19 different Caucasian people, and the MMI Facial Expression Database [43] that holds 1280 videos of 43 different subjects from different races (Caucasian, Asian and Arabic). Both databases show Ekman's six universal emotions plus *neutral*.

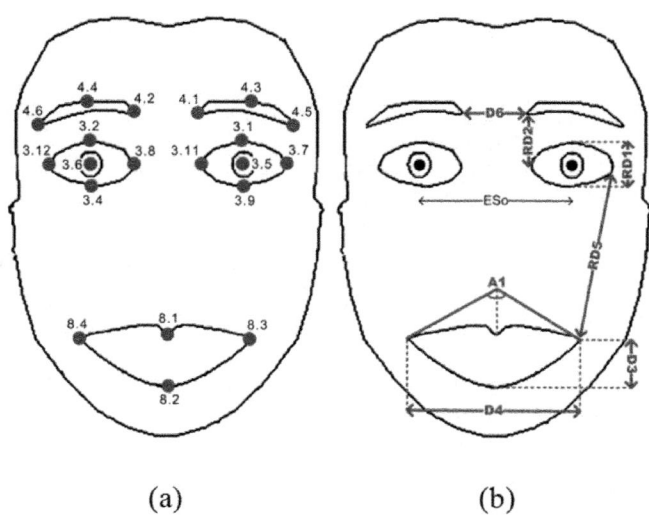

(a)   (b)

Fig. 5. (a) Tracked facial feature points according to MPEG4 standard and (b) corresponding facial parameters

Table 1. Confusion matrix obtained combining the five classifiers

classified as	disgust	joy	anger	fear	sadness	neutral	surprise
disgust	**79.41%**	0%	2.39%	18.20%	0%	0%	0%
joy	4.77%	**95.23%**	0%	0%	0%	0%	0%
anger	19.20%	0%	**74.07%**	0%	3.75%	2.98%	0%
fear	9.05%	0%	0%	**62.96%**	8.53%	0%	19.46%
sadness	0.32%	0.20%	1.68%	0%	**30.00%**	67.80%	0%
neutral	0%	0%	1.00%	2.90%	4.10%	**92.00%**	0%
surprise	0%	0%	0%	11.23%	0%	4.33%	**84.44%**

A new database has been built for testing this work with a total of 1500 static frames carefully selected from the apex of the video sequences from the FG-NET and MMI databases. The results obtained when applying the strategy explained previously to combine the scores of the five classifiers are shown in the form of confusion matrix in Table 1 (results have been obtained with a 10-fold cross-validation test over the 1500 database images).

As can be observed, the success rates for *neutral*, *joy* and *surprise* are very high (84.44%–95.23%). However, the system tends to confuse *disgust* with *fear*, *anger* with *disgust* and *fear* with *surprise*; therefore, the performances for those emotions are slightly worse. The lowest result of our classification is for *sadness*: it is confused with *neutral* on 67.80% of occasions, due to the similarity of the facial expressions. Confusion between these pairs of emotions occurs frequently in the literature and for this reason many classification works do not consider some of them. Nevertheless, the results can be considered positive as two incompatible emotions (such as *sadness* and *joy* or *fear* and *anger*) are confused on less

Table 2. Confusion matrix obtained after considering human assessment

classified as	disgust	joy	anger	fear	sadness	neutral	surprise
disgust	**84.24%**	0%	2.34%	13.42%	0%	0%	0%
joy	4.77%	**95.23%**	0%	0%	0%	0%	0%
anger	15.49%	0%	**77.78%**	0%	3.75%	2.98%	0%
fear	1.12%	0%	0%	**92.59%**	2.06%	0%	4.23%
sadness	0.32%	0.20%	1.68%	0%	**66.67%**	31.13%	0%
neutral	0%	0%	0%	0.88%	1.12%	**98.00%**	0%
surprise	0%	0%	0%	6.86%	0%	2.03%	**91.11%**

than 0.2% of occasions. Another relevant aspect to be taken into account when evaluating the results is human opinion.

The labels provided in the database for training classifiers correspond to the real emotions felt by users although they do not necessarily have to coincide with the perceptions other human beings may have about the facial expressions shown. Undertaking this kind of study is very important when dealing with human-computer interaction, since the system is proved to work in a similar way to the human brain. In order to take into account the human factor in the evaluation of the results, 60 persons were told to classify the 1500 images of the database in terms of emotions. As a result, each one of the frames was classified by 10 different persons in 5 sessions of 50 images.

The Kappa statistic obtained from raters annotations is equal to 0.74 (calculated following the formula proposed in [44]), which indicates an adequate inter-rater agreement in the emotional images annotation. With this information, the evaluation of the results was repeated: the recognition was marked as good if the decision was consistent with that reached by the majority of the human assessors. The results (confusion matrix) of considering users' assessment are shown in Table 2. As can be seen, the success ratios have considerably increased. Therefore, it can be concluded that the confusions of the algorithms go in the same direction as those of the users: our classification strategy is consistent with human classification.

4.3   Affective Integrator

The Sentics Extraction Process outputs a list of sentic vectors which represents an emotional analysis of text and dialogue contents in terms of Pleasantness, Attention, Sensitivity and Aptitude while the Facial Expression Analyzer provides an affective evaluation of video contents in terms of Ekman's six universal emotions. Some researchers, such as Whissell [45] and Plutchik [46], consider emotions as a continuous 2D space whose dimensions are evaluation and activation. The evaluation dimension measures how a human feels, from positive to negative. The activation dimension measures whether humans are more or less likely to take some action under the emotional state, from active to passive. To overcome the problem of the integration of the affective information coming from the Sentic Extraction

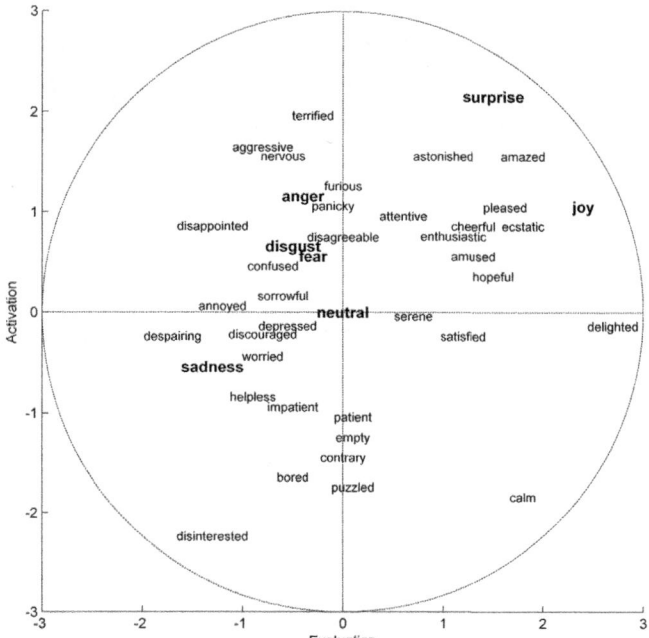

Fig. 6. Whissell's model

Process and the Facial Expression Analyzer, the continuous 2D description of affect is considered.

Bi-dimensional representations of affect are attractive mainly because they provide a way of describing emotional states that is more tractable than using words. This is of particular importance when dealing with naturalistic data, where a wide range of emotional states occurs. Similarly, they are much more able to deal with non discrete emotions and variations in emotional states over time, since in such cases changing from one universal emotion label to another would not make much sense in real life scenarios.

In her study, Cynthia Whissell assigns a pair of values activation-evaluation to each of the approximately 9000 words with affective connotations that make up her Dictionary of Affect in Language. Fig. 6 shows the position of some of these words in the activation-evaluation space.

The emotion-related words corresponding to each one of Ekman's six emotions plus *neutral* and to the levels of Pleasantness, Attention, Sensitivity and Aptitude have a specific location in the Whissell space. Thanks to this, in our work the output information of the Sentic Extraction Process and the labels provided by the Facial Expression Analyzer can be mapped in the Whissell space: a pair of values activation-evaluation can be calculated from the obtained labels, and hence concurrently visualized and compared in the 2D space (Fig. 7).

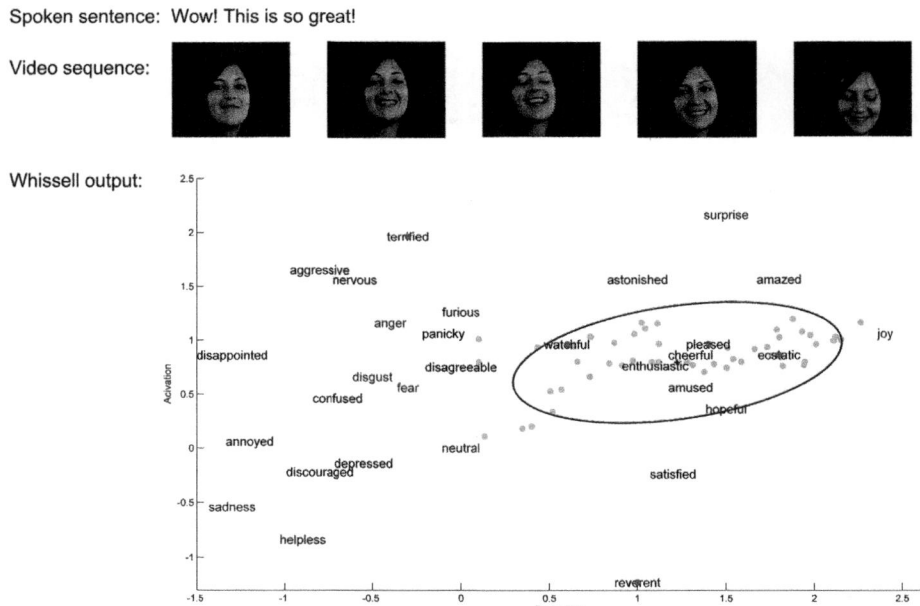

Fig. 7. Example of Affective Analysis Module output: integration of the extracted emotional information (from audio and video) into the Whissell space

In particular, the process of affective integration is achieved through the following three steps:

1. Each one of the emotional labels inferred by the Sentics Extraction Process from the video spoken sentence is mapped as a 2D point on to the Whissell space.

2. In the same way, the Facial Expression Analyzer outputs the user's emotion in terms of Ekman's six universal emotions (plus *neutral*), giving a membership confidence value to each emotional category. The mapping of its output in the Whissell space is carried out considering each of Ekman's six basic emotions plus *neutral* as 2D weighted points in the activation-evaluation space, where the weights are assigned depending on the confidence value obtained for each emotion in the classification process. The final detected emotion is calculated as the centre of mass of the seven weighted points in the Whissell space. That way, the Facial Expression analyzer outputs one emotional location in the Whissell space per frame of the studied video sequence.

3. Finally, the whole set of 2D activation-evaluation points obtained from both the Sentics Extraction Process and the Facial Expression Analyzer is fitted to the Minimum Volume Ellipsoid (MVE) that better covers the shape of the set of extracted points. The MVE is calculated following the algorithm described by Kumar and Yildrim [47]. The final emotional information outputted by affective analysis module for the whole video sequence is given by the x-y coordinates of the centre of that MVE.

5   Conclusion and Future Work

This paper describes a novel architecture for multimodal affective interaction with conversational agents. The proposed system recognizes user's affective state through two different modalities: AffectiveSpace, a process for reasoning by analogy and association over common sense and affective knowledge able to extract affective information in terms of Pleasantness, Attention, Sensitivity and Aptitude from spoken words (dialogue contents), and a Facial Expression Analyzer that classifies the shown user's facial expression in terms of the six Ekman's universal emotions (plus *neutral*).

The emotional information coming from these two different channels is integrated in a simple manner thanks to Whissell's 2D activation-evaluation space, where all the extracted emotional labels are mapped onto x-y locations of that space. The benefits of using Whissell 2D representation are, on the one hand, that the final output of the system does not simply provide a classification in terms of a set of emotionally discrete labels but goes further by extending the emotional information over an infinite range of intermediate emotions and, on the other hand, its capability for improving the overall recognition accuracy helping the system function in a more reliable way.

Furthermore, it opens the door to the integration of new emotional extraction modules in the future (e.g. modules that study user's gestures, gaze, mouse-clicks or keyboard use for affective recognition) in a simple and scalable fashion.

References

1. Vesterinen, E.: Affective Computing. In: Digital Media Research Seminar, Helsinki (2001)
2. Pantic, M.: Affective Computing. Encyclopedia of Multimedia Technology and Networking. Hershy 1, 8–14, Idea Group Reference (2005)
3. Gunes, M., Gunes, H., Piccardi, M., Pantic, M.: From the Lab to the Real World: Affect Recognition Using Multiple Cues and Modalities. In: Affective Computing: Focus on Emotion Expression, Synthesis and Recognition, pp. 185–218 (2008)
4. Riseberg, J., Klein, J., Fernandez, R., Picard, R.: Frustrating the User on Purpose: Using Biosignals in a Pilot Study to Detect the User's Emotional State. In: CHI, Los Angeles (1998)
5. Ambady, N., Rosenthal, R.: Thin Slices of Expressive Behavior as Predictors of Interpersonal Consequences: a Meta-Analysis. Psychological Bulletin 11(2), 256–274 (1992)
6. Camurri, A., Mazzarino, B., Volpe, G.: Analysis of Expressive Gesture: The EyesWeb Expressive Gesture Processing Library. In: Gesture Workshop, Genova (2003)
7. Gunes, H., Piccardi. M.: Bi-Modal Emotion Recognition from Expressive Face and Body Gestures. Network and Computer Applications 30(4), 1334–1345 (2007)
8. Karpouzis, K., Caridakis, G., Kessous, L., Amir, N., Raouzaiou, A., Malatesta, L., Kollias, S.: Modeling Naturalistic Affective States Via Facial, Vocal and Bodily Expressions Recognition. In: Huang, T.S., Nijholt, A., Pantic, M., Pentland, A. (eds.) ICMI/IJCAI Workshops 2007. LNCS (LNAI), vol. 4451, pp. 92–116. Springer, Heidelberg (2007)

9. Pun, T., Alecu, T., Chanel, G., Kronegg, J., Voloshynovskiy, S.: Brain-Computer Interaction Research at the Computer Vision and Multimedia Laboratory. IEEE Trans. on Neural Systems and Rehabilitation Engineering 14(2), 210–213 (2006)

10. Burleson, W., Picard, R., Perlin, K., Lippincott, J.: A Platform for Affective Agent Research. In: International Conference on Autonomous Agents and Multiagent Systems, New York (2004)

11. Petridis, S., Pantic, M.: Audiovisual Discrimination between Laughter and Speech. In: ICASSP, Las Vegas (2008)

12. Valstar, M., Gunes, H., Pantic, M.: How to Distinguish Posed from Spontaneous Smiles Using Geometric Features. In: ICMI, Nagoya (2007)

13. Truong, K., Van Leeuwen, D.: Automatic Discrimination Between Laughter and Speech. Speech Communication 49, 144–158 (2007)

14. Matos, S., Birring, S., Pavord, I., Evans, D.: Detection of Cough Signals in Continuous Audio Recordings Using HMM. IEEE Trans. on Biomedical Engineering 53(6), 1078–1083 (2006)

15. Pal, P., Iyer, A., Yantorno, R.: Emotion Detection from Infant Facial Expressions and Cries. In: Intl Conf. Acoustics, Speech and Signal Processing (2006)

16. Jong-Tae, J., Sang-Wook, S., Kwang-Eun, K., Kwee-Bo, S.: Emotion Recognition Method Based on Multimodal Sensor Fusion Algorithm. In: ISIS, Sokcho-City (2007)

17. Shan, C., Gong, S., McOwan, P.: Beyond Facial Expressions: Learning Human Emotion from Body Gestures. In: BMVC, Warwick (2007)

18. Baldassarri, S., Cerezo, E., Seron, F.: Maxine: a Platform for Embodied Animated Agents. Computers and Graphics 32(4), 430–437 (2008)

19. Cambria, E., Hussain, A., Havasi, C., Eckl, C.: Sentic Computing: Exploitation of Common Sense for the Development of Emotion-Sensitive Systems. In: Esposito, A., Campbell, N., Vogel, C., Hussain, A., Nijholt, A. (eds.) COST 2102. LNCS, vol. 5967, pp. 153–161. Springer, Heidelberg (2010)

20. Cambria, E., Hussain, A., Havasi, C., Eckl, C.: Common Sense Computing: From the Society of Mind to Digital Intuition and Beyond. In: Fierrez, J., Ortega-Garcia, J., Esposito, A., Drygajlo, A., Faundez-Zanuy, M. (eds.) BioID MultiComm 2009. LNCS, vol. 5707, pp. 252–259. Springer, Heidelberg (2009)

21. Cambria, E., Grassi, M., Hussain, A., Havasi, C.: Sentic Computing for Social Media Marketing. In: Multimedia Tools and Applications. Springer, Heidelberg (to appear, 2010)

22. Elliott, C.: The Affective Reasoner: A Process Model of Emotions in a Multi-Agent System. The Institute for the Learning Sciences, Technical Report No. 32 (1992)

23. Ortony, A., Clore, G., Collins, A.: The Cognitive Structure of Emotions. Cambridge University Press, New York (1988)

24. Wiebe, J., Wilson, T., Claire, C.: Annotating Expressions of Opinions and Emotions in Language. Language Resources and Evaluation 39(2), 165–210 (2005)

25. Wilson, T., Wiebe, J., Hoffmann, P.: Recognizing Contextual Polarity in Phrase-Level Sentiment Analysis. In: HLT-EMNLP, Vancouver (2005)

26. Somasundaran, S., Wiebe, J., Ruppenhofer, J.: Discourse Level Opinion Interpretation. In: COLING, Manchester (2008)

27. Hu, M., Liu, B.: Mining Opinion Features in Customer Reviews. In: AAAI, San Jose (2004)

28. Pang, B., Lee, L.: Seeing Stars: Exploiting Class Relationships for Sentiment Categorization with Respect to Rating Scales. In: ACL, Ann Arbor (2005)

29. Abbasi, A., Chen, H., Salem, A.: Sentiment Analysis in Multiple Languages: Feature Selection for Opinion Classification in Web Forums. ACM Transactions on Information Systems 26(3), 1–34 (2008)
30. Cambria, E., Hussain, A., Havasi, C., Eckl, C.: AffectiveSpace: Blending Common Sense and Affective Knowledge to Perform Emotive Reasoning. In: WOMSA at CAEPIA, Seville (2009)
31. Havasi, C., Speer, R., Alonso, J.: ConceptNet 3: a Flexible, Multilingual Semantic Network for Common Sense Knowledge. In: RANLP, Borovets (2007)
32. Strapparava, C., Valitutti, A.: WordNet-Affect: an Affective Extension of WordNet. In: LREC, Lisbon (2004)
33. Havasi, C., Speer, R., Pustejovsky, J., Lieberman, H.: Digital Intuition: Applying Common Sense Using Dimensionality Reduction. IEEE Intelligent Systems 24(4), 24–35 (2009)
34. Wall, M., Rechtsteiner, A., Rocha, L.: Singular Value Decomposition and Principal Component Analysis. In: Berrar, D., et al. (eds.) A Practical Approach to Microarray Data Analysis, pp. 91–109. Kluwer, Norwell (2003)
35. Eckart, C., Young, G.: The Approximation of One Matrix by Another of Lower Rank. Psychometrika 1(3), 211–218 (1936)
36. Plutchik, R.: The Nature of Emotions. American Scientist 89(4), 344–350 (2001)
37. Minsky, M.: The Emotion Machine. Simon and Schuster, New York (2006)
38. Loquendo Audio Speech Recognition, http://www.loquendo.com
39. Ekman, P., Dalgleish, T., Power, M.: Handbook of Cognition and Emotion. Wiley, Chihester (1999)
40. Cerezo, E., Hupont, I., Manresa, C., Varona, J., Baldassarri, S., Perales, F., Seron, F.: Real-Time Facial Expression Recognition for Natural Interaction. In: Martí, J., Benedí, J.M., Mendonça, A.M., Serrat, J. (eds.) IbPRIA 2007. LNCS, vol. 4478, pp. 40–47. Springer, Heidelberg (2007)
41. Witten, I., Frank, E.: Data Mining: Practical Machine Learning Tools and Techniques. Morgan Kaufmann, San Francisco (2005)
42. Wallhoff, F.: Facial Expressions and Emotion Database. Technische Universitat Munchen (2006)
43. Pantic, M., Valstar, M., Rademaker, R., Maat, L.: Web-Based Database for Facial Expression Analysis. In: ICME, Singapore (2005)
44. Siegel, S., Castellan, N.: Nonparametric Statistics for the Social Siences. McGraw-Hill, New York (1988)
45. Whissell, C.: The Dictionary of Affect in Language. Emotion: Theory, Research and Experience, The Measurement of Emotions 4, 113–131 (1989)
46. Plutchik, R.: Emotion: a Psychoevolutionary Synthesis. Harper and Row, New York (1980)
47. Kumar, P., Yildirim, E.: Minimum-Volume Enclosing Ellipsoids and Core Sets. Journal of Optimization Theory and Applications 126, 1–21 (2005)

Patterns of Synchronization of Non-verbal Cues and Speech in ECAs:
Towards a More "Natural" Conversational Agent

Nicla Rossini

Dipartimento di Studi Umanistici
Università del Piemonte Orientale
Li.Co.T.T.- Palazzo Tartara
Via G. Ferraris 109
I-13100 Vercelli, Italy
rossini@lett.unipmn.it

Abstract. This paper presents an analysis of the verbal and non-verbal cues of Conversational Agents, with a special focus on REA and GRETA, in order to allow further research aimed at correcting some traits of their performance still considered unnatural by their final users. Despite the striking performance of new generation ECA, some important features make these conversational agents unreliable to the users, who usually prefer interacting with a classical computer for information retrieval. The users' preference can be due to several factors, such as the quality of speech synthesis, or the inevitable unnaturalness of the graphics animating the avatar. Apart from the unavoidable traits that can render ECAs unnatural to the ultimate users, instances of poor synchronization between verbal and non-verbal behaviour may contribute to unfavourable results. An instance of synchronization patterns between non-verbal cues and speech is here analysed and re-applied to the basic architecture of an ECA in order to improve the ECA's verbal and non-verbal synchronization. A proposal for future inquiry aimed at creating alternative model for the ultimate Mp4 output is also proposed, for further development in this field.

Keywords: Embodied Conversational Agents, Prosody, Non-verbal Communication, Expressions, Gesture-Speech Synchronization.

1 Introduction

This paper presents an analysis of the verbal and non-verbal cues of the most widespread Conversational Agents, GRETA [1], and REA [2, 4] in order to allow for future correction of some traits of their performance still considered to be unnatural by their final users.

Despite the striking performance of new generation ECA, some important features make these conversational agents unreliable to the users, who usually prefer interacting

A. Esposito et al. (Eds.): COST 2102 Int. Training School 2010, LNCS 6456, pp. 96–103, 2011.

with a classical computer for information retrieval (see e.g., [3][1]). The users' preference can be due to several factors, such as the quality of speech synthesis, or the inevitable unnaturalness of the graphics animating the avatar. Apart from the unavoidable traits that can render ECAs unnatural to the ultimate users, instances of poor synchronization between verbal and non-verbal behaviour may contribute to unfavourable results. An instance of synchronization patterns between non-verbal cues and speech is here analysed and re-applied to the basic architecture of an ECA in order to improve the ECA's verbal and non-verbal synchronization. An alternative model for the ultimate Mp4 output is also proposed, for further development in this field.

2 Embodied Conversational Agents: State of the Art

Research into human-computer interaction has led to outstanding results that are particularly advanced, especially in the instances of the M.I.T. MediaLab's Real Estate Agent (REA) [2, 4] and in the IUT de Montreuil's GRETA [1].

Both conversational agents are based on a particularly refined architecture combining input of external sources by means of microphones and webcams, parsing, and output of behavioural and speech segments. The system in question is both intriguing in its capabilities of responding online to a human user and challenging as far as several contrasting issues, such as speed, reliability and "naturalness" of the resulting avatar are concerned.

The software architecture of REA is provided in Fig. 1 ([4]: 526), while Fig. 2 shows the common architecture of an Embodied Conversational Agent as shown in [2]).

As is visible in both figures, a conversational agent's basic structure is a program connecting different modules and sub-modules into a self-organized system.

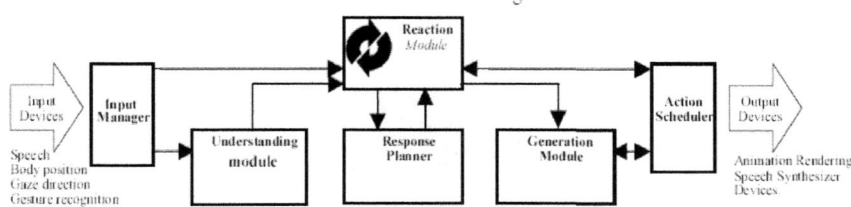

Fig. 1. Software architecture of REA ([4]: 526)

The system in question acquires information from input devices, sends it to a parsing module (In Fig. 1, Understanding Module) and plans an on-line response. A more detailed architecture is presented in Figure 2: as it is visible, the on-line response is obtained by an orchestration of modules such as the language parser, the behaviour generation module, and the behaviour scheduling.

---

[1] GRETA has also been informally tested by the author with 120 B.A. and M.A. students who have judged the agent particularly unnatural without being able to point out completely the reasons of such impression.

In particular, the system acquires data from microphones and input devices, parses them, and generates a multi-modal response by means of a behaviour planner and a speech planner.

Both speech and behaviour are produced in form of synchronized chunks. It is interesting to note that both speech planner and behaviour generator are separate but inter-wired, so that the animation can be synchronized with the speech timing. Both speech and gesture production are selected by means of a constant reference to the encyclopaedia, that is, to an XML tagged database which is also used for the understanding of speech and gesture in input.

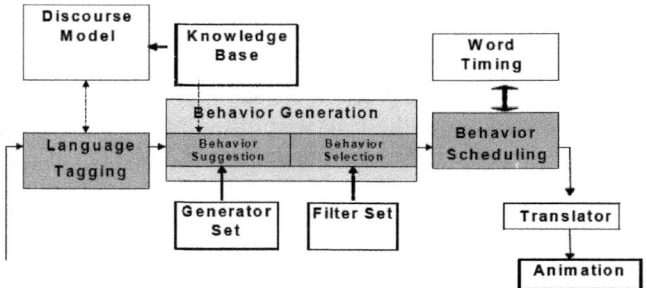

Fig. 2. Architecture of an ECA ([2]: 3). Input arrow on the left side

The animation rendering differs from one Conversational Agent to another, but all of them perform hand gestures and expressions. The most accurate agent for expressions and emotions is probably GRETA, thanks to the work on emotions carried on thus far [7-8]. An instance of GRETA's exceptional facial expressivity is shown in Figure 3.

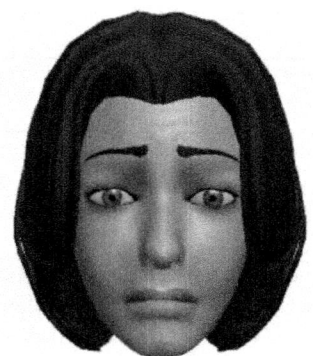

Fig. 3. GRETA's expressivity ([5]: 1839)

REA, on the other hand, has an interesting feature that is not so developed in MAX and GRETA, which is trunk movement in posture shifts [6].

The conversational agent in question is programmed so to allow a posture shift in correspondence with a topic shift in discourse. The occurrence of the posture shift is determined statistically according to a fuzzy logic model [6].

Fig. 4. REA's posture shifts ([6]: 5)

3   Common Problems in ECAs

Despite the interesting architecture and striking responsiveness of Embodied Conversational Agents, whenever these are tested with the intended final users the results are usually discouraging. Participants with no specific knowledge of programming and computational linguistics testing ECAs usually find them unnatural and, if asked [7], strongly prefer to interact with a touch screen.

This negative impressions are most likely to be caused by several factors, such as, on the one hand, the synthesized voice that has usually problems with the imitation of natural prosody and intonation, usually due to chunking generation.

On the other hand, the basic non-verbal traits generated are not natural, both for the graphic quality of the Mpeg video stream, which must be lower than the expectations in order to keep the system running, and for some specific problems of gestural and expressive production. In this section we shall focus on the behaviour of GRETA, as recorded in a state of the art clip of the system available online. The analysis of GRETA's behaviour will be here taken as a starting point for improvements in verbal and non-verbal synthesis.

3.1   Analysis of GRETA's Online Performance

In order to better analyze GRETA's strong and weak points we will here report and analyze a brief segment of GRETA's performance, i.e., the interaction with Mr. Smith in an attempt to simulate the normal doctor-patient interaction. The parameters for gesture analysis here used are explained in detail in a 2001 article addressing the issue [9], while the coding technique is described in [10].

[Good **morning** Mr] Smith///	[I am sorry to tell you] / that you have been dia[gno]sed
Informal salutation S.: 180° e P.A.: s	eyebrows lower in a sad expression	eyebrows' flick (joy, openness to socialization)

Fig. 5. Transcription of a chunk of GRETA's interaction. Square brackets show the part of speech with which non-verbal signals are synchronized.

As can be seen in Fig. 5, GRETA greets her virtual patient with an informal upraising of the hand, palm flat and away from body. This emblem gesture [9] is used in informal and relaxed occasions and can be felt inappropriate in the context given, it being a violation of pragmatic expectations in the human interactant.

Soon after having uttered the chunk "Good morning Mr. Smith" with a synchronized "hello" gesture, GRETA's face adapts to the next chunk and performs a sad expression with a lowering and slight frowning of her eyebrows. The speech chunk that follows contains in fact a keyword for emotion, that is, the adjective "sorry". The sad expression covers the whole chunk "I am sorry to tell you" but disappears after a brief silent pause (the pause in question is also misplaced and due to chunking generation). The rest of the sentence, i.e., "that you have been diagnosed" begins with a neutral expression, while the syllable "gno" of "diagnosed" is synchronized with an eyebrows' flick [11], which is usually a signal of joy or openness to socialization, and thus completely incoherent with the context.

Moreover, a closer look to the hand gestures performed by GRETA (Figure 6) shows a rather unnatural performance due to an excessive rigidity of the hand performing the gesture, which is thus more likely to be comparable to a sign language production, while co-verbal gestures have been found to be performed with a "sloppy hand" [12]. Moreover, the gesture in question is performed at a higher locus [9] than normal and it seems to occupy the zero space for Sign Language.

Fig. 6. Instance of gesture in GRETA

4   Proposal for a More Natural ECA

The problems so far highlighted are basically due to the chunking generation on the one hand and to probabilistic rules based of fuzzy logic for the selection of a synchronized gesture, on the other hand. It seems, in fact, that the "socio-linguistic" variation of gestural use [13] is completely disregarded, probably due to operational problem: a more sophisticated architecture would in fact slow down the system and cause a higher number of breakdowns. Nevertheless, a definite improvement is most likely to be observed with a different architecture relying less on Fuzzy Logic and probabilistic occurrence of gestures and expressions, and a review of the lexicon for the generation of gestures and expressions. The lexicon in question should allow for a more thorough description of context-driven and "socio-linguistic" variation of gestures [13]. More precisely, co-verbal gestures should be marked up according to their normal occurrence in an informal versus formal context and be related to registers in speech, thus shifting from a fuzzy logic program to a mixed system relying on both fuzzy logic and rule based operations. A special focus should also be placed on the commonly disregarded gesture syntax [14-15], or the way gestures combine into kinetic "utterances" [9, 16].

A different problem is the bad synchronization of facial expressions and speech. Because the synchronization between expressions and speech follows a completely different timing if compared to hand gestures and speech synchronization (see e.g., [17]), the latter issue can be resolved by allowing for a distinct behavior planner exclusively devoted to expressions, with its own synchronization timings with respect to speech.

An alternative model is proposed in Figure 7. As can be seen, the ideal architecture for a more natural ECA is based on the separation of *discourse planner*, that is devoted to speech and gesture planning and the word-gesture timing, and *expression planner*, that is exclusively devoted to face expressions. The Expressions Planner is still linked with the discourse planner, but follows a different timing for the synchronization of expressions and speech.

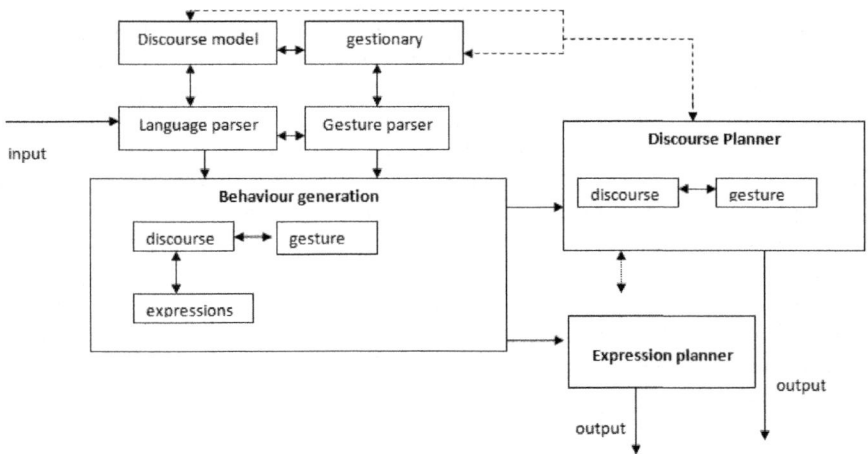

Fig. 7. Proposal for a new ECA architecture

This planner will select the appropriate expressions by means of an analysis of keywords in the discourse planned, if any, and hold the selected expression for the total duration of the utterance. Of course, as the expression planner is not intended to also decode the emotional states of the interlocutor, it will have a separate "vocabulary" of expressions among which the basic one will be selected for output. If in the future the system shall be able to cope with expression decoding, a separate module for emotional appraisal should be linked to the microphone and the camera.

As already stated, the gestures and expressions in the ECA's response should also be planned according to the correct pragmatic rules of social interaction and avoid complete relying on random selection.

Finally, it could also be possible to allow for trunk movements in GRETA: these could be based on a fuzzy logic determination of posture shifts in correspondence with a topic shift, as in REA [6]. Because posture shifts have a lower rate of appearance and are likely to appear with topic shifts in discourse, the introduction of these features is not likely to cause excessive slow-down in the system.

The present proposal does not disregards completely the implied slow-down of such a system, although, in case the modifications proposed here were computationally possible, a higher reliability and usability would certainly result from the modifications.

5   Conclusions

The present article has addressed the most common problems in state of the art ECAs, with special focus on MIT's REA and GRETA. In underlying some common flaws in the state of the art programming and output – such as expressions synchronized with a single sentence chunk, pragmatically wrong gesture types, and an excessive rigidity in the hand performing the gesture – and in suggesting an alternative model, this paper also aims at proposing a more natural ECA, possibly based on pragmatic and sociolinguistic rules in addition and partial substitution of common random rules for the selection of responsive behavior. A different architecture for the ECA is also proposed, for further research: the architecture in question should allow for a separation of the planners for expressions, on the one hand, and the planner for gestures, on the other hand. Such a distinction is motivated by the different synchronization timing and duration of expressions and gestures with respect to speech. The proposal presented here does not disregard completely the implied slow-down of the proposed system but underlines the importance of the modifications proposed here – if computationally possible – for a higher reliability and usability of Embodied Conversational Agents.

Acknowledgments. I am grateful to Dafydd Gibbon and Karl-Erik McCullough for their comments on this article. The responsibility of any errors or inaccuracies remains exclusively with the author.

References

1. Hartmann, B., Mancini, M., Pelachaud, C.: Implementing Expressive Gesture Synthesis for Embodied Conversational Agents. In: Gibet, S., Courty, N., Kamp, J.-F. (eds.) GW 2005. LNCS (LNAI), vol. 3881, pp. 188–199. Springer, Heidelberg (2006)
2. Cassell, J., Stocky, T., Bickmore, T., Gao, Y., Nakano, Y., Ryokai, K., Tversky, D., Vaucelle, C., Vilhjálmsson, H.: MACK: Media lab Autonomous Conversational Kiosk. In: Proceedings of IMAGINA 2002, Monte Carlo, January 12-15 (2002), http://www.media.mit.edu/gnl/pubs/imagina02.pdf
3. Cassell, J.: Trading spaces: Gesture Morphology and Semantics in Humans and Virtual Humans. In: Second ISGS Conference "Interacting bodies". École normale supérieure Lettres et Sciences humaines Lyon - France, June 15-18 (2005)
4. Cassell, J., Bickmore, T., Billinghurst, M., Campbell, L., Chang, K., Vilhjálmsson, Yan, H.: Embodiment in Conversational Interfaces: Rea. In: Proceedings of the CHI 1999 Conference, Pittsburgh, PA, pp. 520–527 (1999)

5. Mancini, M., Bresin, R., Pelachaud, C.: An expressive virtual agent head driven by music performance. IEEE Transactions on Audio, Speech and Language Processing 15(6), 1833–1841 (2007)
6. Cassell, J., Nakano, Y., Bickmore, T., Sidner, C., Rich, C.: Annotating and Generating Posture from Discourse Structure in Embodied Conversational Agents. In: Workshop on Representing, Annotating, and Evaluating Non-Verbal and Verbal Communicative Acts to Achieve Contextual Embodied Agents, Autonomous Agents 2001 Conference, Montreal, Quebec, May 29 (2001),
   http://www.ccs.neu.edu/home/bickmore/publications/
   agents01.pdf
7. Poggi, I., Pelachaud, C.: Performative facial expressions in animated 'faces'. Speech Communication 26, 5–21 (1998)
8. Niewiadomski, R., Ochs, M., Pelachaud, C.: Expressions of Empathy in ECAs. In: Prendinger, H., Lester, J.C., Ishizuka, M. (eds.) IVA 2008. LNCS (LNAI), vol. 5208, pp. 37–44. Springer, Heidelberg (2008)
9. Rossini, N.: The analysis of gesture: Establishing a set of parameters. In: Camurri, A., Volpe, G. (eds.) GW 2003. LNCS (LNAI), vol. 2915, pp. 124–131. Springer, Heidelberg (2004)
10. McNeill, D.: Hand and Mind. What Gestures Reveal about Thought. University of Chicago Press, Chicago (1992)
11. Eibl-Eibesfeldt, I.: Similarities and differences between cultures in expressive movements. In: Hinde, A. (ed.) Non-verbal Communication, pp. 297–312. Cambridge University Press, Cambridge (1972)
12. Kita, S., van Gijn, I., van der Hulst, H.: The non-linguistic status of the Symmetry Condition in signed languages: Evidence from a comparison from signs and speech-accompanying representational gestures (in progress)
13. Rossini, N.: Sociolinguistics in gesture. How about the Mano a Borsa? In: Intercultural Communication Studies, XIII, 3, pp. 144–154; Proceedings of the 9th International Conference on Cross-Cultural Communication (2004)
14. Rossini, N.: Gesture and its cognitive origin: Why do we gesture? Experiments on hearing and deaf people. Università di Pavia Ph.D. thesis (2004)
15. Thies, A.: First the hand, then the word: On gestural displacement in non-native English speech. Universität Bielefeld Ph.D. Thesis (2003)
16. Gibbon, D.: Modelling gesture as speech: a linguistic approach. In: Proceedings of GESPIN 2009, Conference on Gestures and Speech in Interaction, Poznan (September 2009) (to appear)
17. Rossini, N.: Il gesto. Gestualità e tratti non verbali in interazioni diadiche. Bologna, Pitagora (2009)

Top-Down Influences on Eye-Movements during Painting Perception: The Effect of Task and Titles

Evgenia Hristova, Severina Georgieva, and Maurice Grinberg

Central and East European Center for Cognitive Science, New Bulgarian University,
1618 Sofia, Bulgaria
{ehristova,severina.georgieva}@cogs.nbu.bg, mgrinberg@nbu.bg

Abstract. The paper explores the eye-movement patterns while looking at famous paintings belonging to two styles of representational art – surrealist (Dali) and baroque (Caravaggio). Two factors were varied in a factorial design: the task of the viewer and the information about the painting. The two tasks used were 'aesthetic rating' of the painting and 'content description.' For half of the viewers, no information about the paintings was presented, while for the other half the paintings' titles were provided. For baroque paintings, when the titles were presented, the change in eye-movements was small, but the aesthetic ratings showed a dramatic increase. On the other hand, for surrealist paintings, when titles were presented the change in eye-movement patterns was considerable, while no change in the aesthetic ratings was noticed. These results add new information to the exploration of painting perception and the role of top-down effects on eye-movements.

Keywords: art perception, eye-movements, aesthetic judgments.

1 Introduction

Aesthetic experience is a fascinating phenomenon attracting the attention of various scientific approaches. It is believed to combine cognitive processing at different levels and emotional experiences. It has been established in many studies that understanding and aesthetic judgment depend on additional information about the painting, the artist, the style, etc. One of the most promising lines of research is related to experimental methodologies which allow gathering of objective data like eye-movement recordings and biosignals during art work perception. Such studies originate in the now classical works of Buswell [1] and Yarbus [2] which studied the eye-movements patterns while looking at paintings.

In this section, a brief review of the literature related to the role of title and task on eye-movements and aesthetic experience is given. On the basis of this review, the goals and hypothesis of the present study are formulated.

1.1 Influence of the Titles on Aesthetic Experience

It seems generally accepted and even incorporated in some models of art perception (see e.g. [3]) that for aesthetic experience to be positive and pleasurable it is essential

A. Esposito et al. (Eds.): COST 2102 Int. Training School 2010, LNCS 6456, pp. 104–115, 2011.
© Springer-Verlag Berlin Heidelberg 2011

that the viewer has found the meaning of the art work. In this respect, the influence of additional verbal information, allowing for the elaboration of the meaning of art works, on aesthetic rating has been explored in the literature [4], [5]. According to [4] and [5] the availability of titles increases the aesthetic experience when they are not arbitrary and support the understanding and interpretation of the paintings.

The influence of title on painting perception has been investigated in several studies. In two behavioral experiments in [4] the influence of the type of title (descriptive vs. elaborative) on representational and abstract paintings has been explored. Participants were shown paintings and had to rate them using several scales including understanding, liking, interest, etc. The experiment had two phases. In the first phase, the paintings were presented without titles, while in the second phase they were presented without title, with a descriptive and with elaborative titles. For abstract paintings, it was found that elaborative (suggesting a possible interpretation) titles increased the understanding ratings; while descriptive (describing the content of the painting) titles had no effect. However, for short exposure intervals (1 s), the descriptive titles improved understanding more than the elaborative ones. These results were interpreted according to the model presented in [3] which assumes serial information processing and states that more time is required to reach the stages in which elaborative titles could be used in understanding the painting's content. In [4], the liking of the pictures decreased with the presentation of titles.

In similar experimental settings in three experiments Millis [5] found that in general titles influence aesthetic judgment when they are coherent with the content of the picture or when they help the viewers in the elaboration of the meaning of the picture. It was found that metaphorical titles have larger effects than no-titles or descriptive titles, which was attributed to elaboration effects. In this study randomly assigned titles decreased understanding but not aesthetic judgment.

In [6] the role of titles and short descriptions on the evaluation of meaningfulness and hedonic value of paintings has been investigated. The author has found that the effects of the increase in the perceived meaningfulness of the paintings are stable but the expected increase of the hedonic value is found only in a within-participants design. There are strong arguments in [6] that the understanding of the artist's intentions is part of the aesthetic pleasure derived from an artwork (the 'effort after meaning' theory).

The results of the above mentioned studies show that titles play an important role in the understanding and aesthetic evaluation of paintings, although this role is dependent on the type of titles and style of paintings.

1.2   Eye-Movements and Aesthetic Experience

The connection between the viewer's eye-movements and aesthetic experience is another important question considered in several recent studies (e.g. [7], [8], [9]).

Art perception, as perception of objects and scenes, is subject to bottom-up and top-down influences [10], [3]. The gaze is attracted by interesting and informative zones, rich in contours and contrasts. At the same time, the gaze patterns for one and the same painting are different depending on the goal, the experience, and the task of the viewer. There is convincing evidence that fixation positions are highly correlated with the informativeness of a given region in a scene or in a painting (for a review see

[11]). There are also studies, some of which are summarized below, that show that the task of the viewer influences the spatial distribution of the fixations.

In the study of Yarbus [2], mentioned earlier, the influence of the viewer's task on eye movements during looking at a painting was explored. The task was either free viewing or viewing in order to answer specific questions (e.g. what are the ages of the people depicted in the painting). Yarbus showed that the distribution of the fixations on different regions of the painting changes dramatically with the task. Studies on scene perception [12] also demonstrate that task (visual search or memorization) influences the eye movements during viewing of color photographs of natural scenes. They showed that the task had an effect on the number of fixations on specific objects in the scenes.

In other studies, it has been established that the gaze paths of novices and experts differ [13] which indicates a top-down effect. The differences were established on comparisons of the short (< 300 ms) and long fixations (> 400 ms). For instance art-trained viewers used a larger number of long fixations than short ones when viewing a painting as they recognized the overall design and paid more attention to the details.

Some results in the literature [7] claim that no influence of the title of the painting on the eye-movements can be found. According to this study, the eye-movement patterns remain stable despite the manipulation of the information about the paintings which influence other aspects of the aesthetic experience. However, no eye-tracking recordings are used in the study but instead participants are asked to use a pointer to show where they are looking while describing the paintings. Also no quantitative analysis of the pointer's traces was performed (only experts' judgments were used).

1.3   Goals and Hypothesis of the Present Study

As discussed above, the influence of task and additional information on painting viewing and evaluation is a hot topic of research. The studies presented in the previous subsections show that art perception is a highly complex process involving all the stages from low-level visual perception to high-level cognition and conscious experience (e.g. see [14]) and that extensive explorations are needed to fully understand this process.

In line with these studies the present paper explores the influence of task and titles on painting perception and evaluation for two representational styles. Viewers had two tasks – aesthetic judgment or content description – and two conditions with respect to the additional information given – no information or the titles of the art works.

Despite the increasing number of investigations of the influence of the title on the final viewer's evaluation, there is not enough data on how the additional verbal information influences the eye-movement patterns. A hypothesis not tested in the previous research is that titles will provide additional information in the interpretation of the art works and can lead to a change in the eye-movement patterns (fixation positions). The expectation is that the availability of titles will change the gaze patterns during viewing of the painting by focusing the attention of the viewers on zones related or mentioned in the title.

Another main goal is to explore if there is a change in the fixation positions as a result of the task. Based on [2] and [12] it is expected that the task will change the eye-movement patterns of spatial fixation distributions. However, in [2] and [12] the tasks used were visual search for specific objects or answers to specific questions. In the present study more ecologically valid tasks are used – aesthetic rating or content description of the paintings.

Another factor explored is the influence of the artistic style on the viewer's perception and experience. The viewers are presented with famous paintings belonging to two different styles of representational art – surrealist (Dali) and baroque (Caravaggio). The expectation is that the presence of the titles will lead to more substantial changes in the eye-movements and to higher aesthetic ratings for the ambiguous Dali's paintings [15], [16].

2 Method

2.1 Design of the Study

The *task* of the participants and the presence of the *title* were varied in a between-subjects factorial design. The two tasks used were 'aesthetic rating' of the painting and 'content description'. For the aesthetic *rating* task the participants had to rate each painting for liking on a 7-point scale. In the *content* task the participants had to describe the content of each painting after the painting disappears. The second factor varied was the availability of the painting title. For half of the viewers no information about the paintings was presented (in the *no title* condition), while for the other half of the viewers the paintings' titles were provided (*title* condition).

2.2 Stimuli and Procedure

Two Dali's paintings ('Metamorphosis of Narcissus' and 'Swans reflecting elephants') and two Caravaggio's paintings ('Doubting Thomas' and 'The sacrifice of Isaac') were presented among 18 paintings.

Each painting was presented for 10 seconds. In the *rating* task after the painting is no longer shown, the participants had to rate each painting for liking on a 7-point scale (1 = 'I don't like it at all' to 7 = 'I like it very much'). In the *content* task the participants had to describe the content of each painting after the painting disappears. For the *title* condition first the title was presented for 5 seconds and next the painting was presented for 10 seconds. In the *title* condition no other information was presented. In the *no title* condition nothing was presented before each painting.

2.3 Eye-Movements Recordings

Eye movements were recorded using Tobii 1750 remote eye-tracking system with 50 Hz sampling rate, $0.5°$ precision and a 17-inch computer display with resolution 1280x1024 pixels. As the participants viewed the paintings from 60 cm, the screen subtended a visual angle of ~$34°$ horizontally and ~$27°$ vertically. The presentations of the stimuli, the eye-movement recordings, and the rating registration were performed with the specialized software ClearView, developed by Tobii Technology. In the beginning of the experiment a 9-points calibration procedure was conducted for each participant.

2.3.1 Participants

Forty-two participants performed the *aesthetic rating* task (19 in the *title*, 23 in the *no title* condition). 40 participants performed the *content* task (19 in the *title*, 21 in the *no title* condition). All of them were university students participating voluntarily or for course credits. None of the participants had professional art-training or art-related courses. All participants had normal or corrected to normal vision.

3   Results for the Aesthetic Ratings

In the *rating* task participants provided aesthetic ratings on a 7-point scale for each painting (1 = 'I don't like it at all' to 7 = 'I like it very much'). The average ratings for each painting for the *title* and *no-title* conditions are presented in Table 1 and were compared using t-test.

For the Caravaggio's paintings an increase in aesthetic ratings is observed when titles are presented. For 'Sacrifice of Isaac' the rating in the *no title* condition (4.1) increased to 5.5 in the *title* condition (p = 0.036). For 'Doubting Thomas' the rating in the *no title* condition (2.9) increased to 4.5 when *title* was presented (p = 0.015).

For the Dali's paintings the difference in the aesthetic ratings between *title* and *no title* condition is smaller. For 'Swans reflecting elephants' the average rating is 5.5 in the *no title* condition and 5.9 in the *title* condition and the difference is not statistically significant. For 'Metamorphosis of Narcissus' the rating in the *title* condition (5.5) is higher than in the *no title* condition (4.5) but the difference is marginally significant (p = 0.087).

Table 1. Mean aesthetic ratings (standard deviation in parentheses) in the *title* and *no-title* conditions

Author	Painting	No-title	Title
Caravaggio	Sacrifice of Isaac	4.1 (2.0)	5.5 (1.9)
	Doubting Thomas	2.9 (2.0)	4.5 (2.1)
Dali	Swans reflecting elephants	5.5 (1.4)	5.9 (1.0)
	Metamorphosis of Narcissus	4.5 (2.3)	5.5 (1.4)

It was expected that the presence of the titles will increase the liking of the painting as titles give additional information that can help the interpretation and resolving the ambiguities in the paintings' perception. However, the hypothesis is supported only for the Caravaggio's paintings. For the Dali's painting the effect is absent or smaller. This might be due to the fact that these paintings were rated very high even in the no title condition. An additional factor is the difference in style between the two painters. As noted in [17] the influence of additional information (like titles) can vary depending on the style. For the Caravaggio's paintings the titles put the paintings in a very specific religious perspective and this could have influenced favorably the aesthetic ratings.

4   Results for the Eye-Movements Patterns

For each of the four paintings several areas of interest (AOIs) were defined. These are the most salient and informative areas determined on the basis of experts' evaluation and on the basis of the eye-movement data – areas that attracted the most fixations from all the participants.

Fixations were calculated from the raw data using an analysis filter with minimum fixation duration set to 100 ms and maximal allowed variance in the gaze position of 30 pixels. Gaze time for each AOI is calculated as a total fixation time in that area for each participant. Gaze time in each AOI was analyzed in a 2-way ANOVA with **task** (*rating* vs. *content*) and presence of the **title** (*title* vs. *no title*) as between-subjects factors.

4.1 Dali – 'Swans Reflecting Elephants'

For the Dali's painting 'Swans reflecting elephants' 6 AOIs are defined (Fig. 1).

Fig. 1. AOIs (areas of interest) defined on Dali's painting 'Swans reflecting elephants'. The AOIs with a main effect or interaction are numbered.

Gaze time in each area was analyzed as described above. In Table 2 data are presented only for the AOIs in which there was significant main effect and/or interaction.

Table 2. Mean gaze time duration in ms (standard deviation in parentheses) for AOIs in Dali's painting 'Swans reflecting elephants'

AOI	Task	No-title	Title
AOI 1	Rating	897 (939)	2540 (1660)
	Content	943 (875)	2454 (1298)
AOI 2	Rating	878 (655)	600 (783)
	Content	1423 (1003)	958 (835)

There is main effect of the **title** condition on the gaze time in AOI 1 (see Fig. 1). When the title is presented the participants are spending significantly more time (p < 0.001) looking at the elephants (2497 ms) compared to the conditions in which the title is not presented (919 ms). The title helps the viewers to interpret the image and to see the elephants that otherwise are not perceived. This a strong example of how additional verbal information can change the gaze patterns considerably.

For AOI 2 there is also a main effect of the *title*. Participants look longer at this zone when the title is not presented (1138 ms) than when the title is presented (779 ms), p = 0.054. There is also a main effect of the *task* condition on the gaze time in AOI 2. Participants spend less time looking at that AOI in the aesthetic *rating* task (752 ms) than in the *content* task (1202 ms), p = 0.02.

4.2 Dali – 'Metamorphosis of Narcissus'

15 AOIs are defined for the 'Metamorphosis of Narcissus' (Fig. 2). Mean gaze times are presented in Table 3 (again only for the AOIs in which there are significant effects).

Table 3. Mean gaze time duration in ms (standard deviation in parentheses) for AOIs in Dali's painting 'Metamorphosis of Narcissus'

AOI	Task	No-title	Title
AOI 1	Rating	1536 (574)	1471 (626)
	Content	1224 (662)	1880 (841)
AOI 2	Rating	530 (400)	791 (552)
	Content	996 (546)	1014 (386)
Background	Rating	1746 (567)	2152 (768)
	Content	1235 (744)	1202 (864)

In AOI 1 (see Fig. 2) there is a main effect of the *title* condition on the gaze time (p = 0.053): when the title is presented the participants are spending more time looking at the flower (1675 ms) compared to the conditions in which the title is not presented (1387 ms). The interaction between *task* and *title* reveals that in fact such increase is observed only for the *content* task (p = 0.019). When the title is presented in the *content* task the participants spend more time looking at the narcissus.

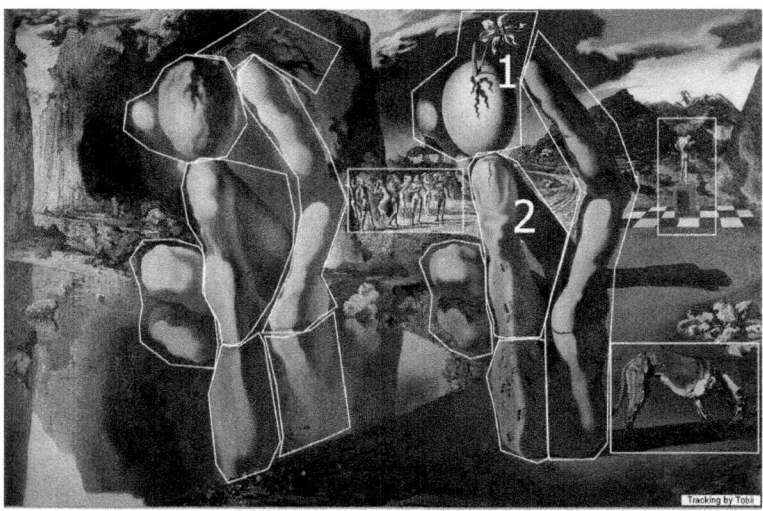

Fig. 2. AOIs (areas of interest) defined on Dali's painting 'Metamorphosis of Narcissus'. The AOIs with a main effect or interaction are numbered.

Main effect of the *task* is observed for AOI 2: when the task is content description it is looked at longer (1105 ms) than when the task is aesthetic rating (648 ms), p = 0.002.

The *task* influences also the time spent looking at the other (**background**) elements that are not included in these 15 AOIs. In the *rating* task participants spend more time looking at these background elements (1929 ms) than in the *content* task (1220 ms), p < 0.001.

4.3 Caravaggio – 'Doubting Thomas'

Gaze time in each zone was analyzed as described above for each of the 6 AOIs defined (Fig. 3). Mean gaze time for 3 of the AOIs is shown in Table 4.

Table 4. Mean gaze time duration in ms (standard deviation in parentheses) for AOIs in Caravaggio's painting 'Doubting Thomas'

AOI	Task	No-title	Title
AOI 1	Rating	1037 (616)	1049 (513)
	Content	1236 (654)	1044 (538)
AOI 2	Rating	3133 (1122)	2282 (1358)
	Content	2650 (833)	3266 (1014)
AOI3	Rating	682 (293)	984 (506)
	Content	1046 (482)	877 (406)

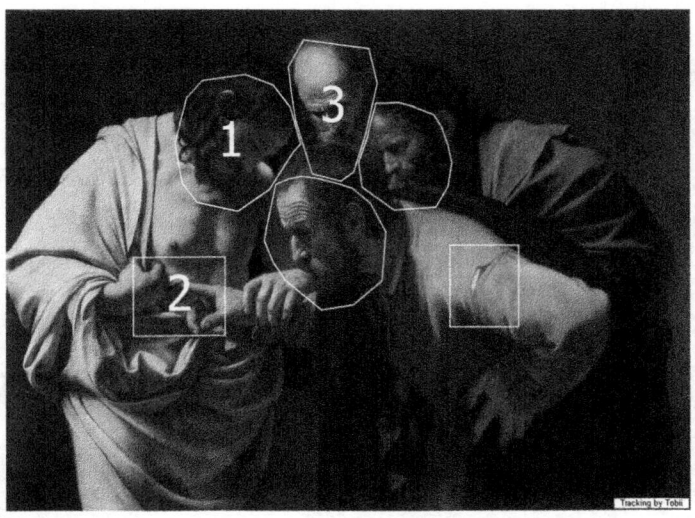

Fig. 3. AOIs (areas of interest) defined on Caravaggio's painting 'Doubting Thomas'. The AOIs with a main effect or interaction are numbered.

In AOI 1 (see Fig. 3) there is main effect of the *task* on the gaze time. In the *content* task participants looked longer at the image of Christ (1320 ms) than in the *rating* task (1042 ms), p = 0.036.

Interaction between *task* and *title* presentation is found in AOI 2 (p = 0.003, see Fig. 4). Participants in the *rating* task looked longer at the wound of Christ when the title was not presented (p = 0.032). While the participants in the *content* task spent more time looking at the wound when the *title* was presented (p = 0.042).

For AOI 3 an interaction between *task* and *title* was also found (p = 0.015, see Fig. 4). Only for the participants in the *rating* task the presentation of the *title* made them look longer at one of the Apostles (p = 0.02).

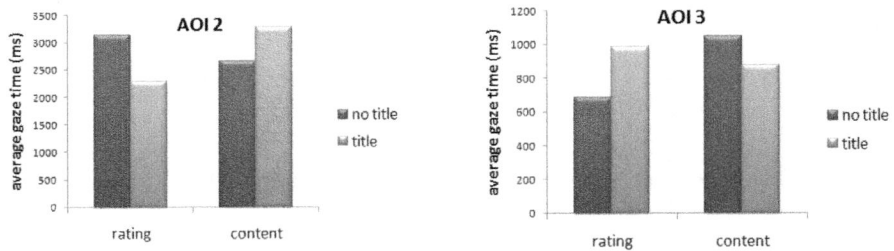

Fig. 4. Average gaze time in AOIs 2 and 3 defined on Caravaggio's painting 'Doubting Thomas' for the *rating* and the *content* task. Black bars – *no title* condition; grey bars – *title* condition.

4.4 Caravaggio – 'Sacrifice of Isaac'

For this painting 10 AOIs are defined (Fig. 5). Gaze time in each zone was analyzed as described above.

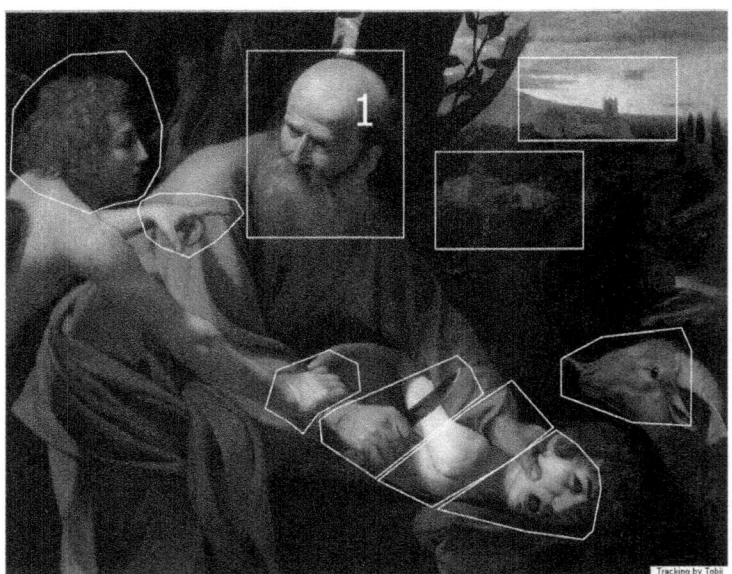

Fig. 5. AOIs (areas of interest) defined on Caravaggio's painting 'Sacrifice of Isaac'. The AOIs with a main effect or interaction are numbered.

For this painting there are very small influences of the **task** and **title** presentation on the eye-movement patterns. In AOI 1 (see Fig. 5) there is an interaction between **task** and **title** condition on the gaze time (p = 0.015). The interaction is shown in Table 5. Only in the *rating* task the participants looked longer at the Abraham when the *title* was presented (p = 0.027). No significant influence of the **title** presentation is found for the *content* task.

Table 5. Mean gaze time duration in ms (standard deviation in parentheses) for AOIs in Caravaggio's painting 'Sacrifice of Isaac

AOI	Task	No-title	Title
AOI 1	Rating	1928 (770)	2534 (944)
	Content	2287 (778)	1988 (783)

4.5 Summary

The analysis for the eye-movements patterns shows that for the Dali's paintings, when the title is presented, the participants' attention is directed to the main elements that are also in the title. The effect is stronger for the painting 'Swans reflecting elephants'). This result is in accordance with the hypothesis of the study. There is also an influence of the task on the fixation patterns.

For the Caravaggio's paintings there are influences of task and title on the eye-movements but they are not so strong and are not related to the persons mentioned in the titles of the paintings. May be the participants in the study are not well acquainted with the biblical stories and thus were not able to identify the characters. This interpretation is also supported by the analysis of the verbal descriptions provided in the content task – participants in the study were not able to describe the correct story depicted even in the *title* condition.

5   General Discussion and Conclusions

The present study aims to study aesthetic judgments and eye-movements during painting viewing. Two types of representational paintings were used – surrealist (Dali) and baroque (Caravaggio). The goal was to explore the role of top-down effects on aesthetic ratings and on eye-movements. In the experiment, two factors related to top-down effects were manipulated – the task and the presentation of the titles.

The expected results were to find the change of the aesthetic judgment and of the eye-movement characteristics related to the experimental manipulation of task and availability of the title. A hypothesis not tested in previous research is that the title presentation will change the eye-movements patterns during viewing of the painting by focusing the attention of the viewers on zones related or mentioned in the title. It was also expected that the presence of the titles will facilitate the interpretation of the paintings and thus will lead to higher aesthetic ratings.

The availability of the titles increased the aesthetic ratings for Caravaggio's paintings but had no effect for Dali's painting. The result contradicts the initial expectations that the presence of the titles will increase the ratings especially for the Dali's paintings. The expectation was based on the assumption that aesthetic experience is increased by the ability to understand the ideas represented in ambiguous paintings such as Dali's works. The absence of the effect for the Dali's paintings might be due to a ceiling effect, as the rating for these painting were already very high in the no-title condition.

On the other hand, there was very small effect on the eye-movement viewing patterns for Caravaggio's painting in all conditions, while there was a significant change for the Dali's paintings. As expected, in Dali's paintings, the viewers' attention was directed to the objects present in the titles. The latter is a top-down effect (not reported previously in the literature) of the type one would expect when ambiguities are present in the painting and which can be resolved based on additional information.

The effect of the task was also observed. However, it was not very prominent for the spatial distribution of the fixations. No drastic changes are found as observed in some of the previous studies (e.g. in [2]). May be this is due to the fact that in contrast to previous research we use two natural tasks for looking at paintings – aesthetic rating and content description. Additional analyses (not presented here) show that the task of the viewer influences the saccades amplitudes. They are considered to be important in studying eye-movements during paintings and scene perception as reflecting global scanning vs. focal processing [12]. Saccade amplitudes are found to be smaller (e.g. the processing is more focal) when the task is content description compared to the aesthetic rating task.

In conclusion, the line of research presented here shows promising results that should be explored in greater detail in future analyses and experiments.

References

1. Buswell, G.: How people look at pictures. University of Chicago Press, Oxford (1935)
2. Yarbus, I.A.: Eye movements and vision. Plenum Press, New York (1967)
3. Leder, H., Belke, B., Oeberst, A., Augustin, D.: A model of aesthetic appreciation and aesthetic judgments. Brit. J. Psychol. 95, 489–508 (2004)
4. Leder, H., Carbon, C., Ripsas, A.: Entitling art: Influence of title information on understanding and appreciation of paintings. Acta Psychol. 121, 176–198 (2006)
5. Millis, K.: Making meaning brings pleasure: The influence of titles on aesthetic experiences. Emotion 1, 320–329 (2001)
6. Russell, P.: Effort after meaning and the hedonic value of paintings. Brit. J. Psychol. 94, 99–110 (2003)
7. Franklin, M.B., Becklen, R.C., Doyle, C.L.: The Influence Of Titles On How Paintings Are Seen. Leonardo 26, 103–108 (1993)
8. Holsanova, J.: Dynamics of picture viewing and picture description. In: Albertazzi, L. (ed.) Visual thought: the depictive space of perception, Benjamins (2006)
9. Wallraven, C., Kaulard, K., Kürner, C., Pepperell, R.: In the Eye of the Beholder - Perception of Indeterminate Art. Leonardo 41, 116–117 (2008)
10. Itti, L., Koch, C.: A saliency-based search mechanism for overt and covert shifts of visual attention. Vision Res. 40, 1489–1506 (2000)
11. Henderson, J., Hollingworth, A.: High-level scene perception. Annu. Rev. Psychol. 50, 243–271 (1999)

12. Catelhano, M., Mack, M., Henderson, J.: Viewing task influences eye movement control during active scene perception. J. Vision 9, 1–15 (2009)
13. Nodine, C.F., Locher, P.J., Krupinski, E.A.: The Role of the Formal Art Training on Perception and Aesthetic Judgment of Art Compositions. Leonardo 26, 219–227 (1993)
14. Myin, E.: Two sciences of perception and visual art: editorial introduction to the Brussels Papers. J. Consciousness Stud. 7, 43–56 (2000)
15. Zeki, S.: The Neural Sources of Salvador Dali's Ambiguity. Leonardo 37, 350–351 (2004)
16. Mamassian, P.: Ambiguities and conventions in the perception of visual art. Vision Res. 48, 2143–2153 (2008)
17. Belke, B., Leder, H., Augustin, D.: Mastering style. Effects of explicit style-related information, art knowledge and affective state on appreciation of abstract paintings. Psychol. Sci. 48, 115–134 (2006)

Visual Sociology in the Classroom: Fostering Interaction Awareness Using Video

Paolo Parmeggiani

Università degli Studi di Udine
Via delle Scienze 208, 33100 Udine, Italia
paolo.parmeggiani@uniud.it

Abstract. In this paper we will present an empirical research about the interactions between teacher and students in a grade three of a secondary school analyzed with video. The methodologies, which shaped our data collection and analysis, are the action research, the conversation analysis of institutional talk within a class, the stimulated recall, and the visual sociology with Computer-Assisted Qualitative Data Analysis Software. We taped some lessons; through the replay of their daily activity we involved students and teacher separately in an auto-observation and video analysis process with the software Transana, highlighting those behaviors which were outstanding for them, eliciting their subjective meanings. Finally we organized a group discussion about the respective interpretative video analysis of the lesson, allowing a reciprocal meta-communication.

This method of group video–analysis forces a re-examination of fixed practices, helping to redefine rigid patterns of interaction and didactic routine.

Keywords: Video-analysis, visual sociology, action research, conversation analysis, stimulated recall, CAQDAS.

1 Introduction

This paper is about a group video–analysis of classroom multimodal communication. We will discuss this issue presenting an empirical research, conducted in a grade three of a secondary high school in Udine, Italy in May 2007, about the interactions between teacher and students.

Our research began when a teacher of philosophy asked for help in improving classroom relations. It is integral for teachers to have good communication with their students. In order to manage the class and to encourage learning, it is important to keep students highly motivated and interested. When students express confusion, chatter, make noise, don't pay attention or whisper to one another, these are often signals that the communication among them and the teacher is deteriorating. At this point it can be difficult to understand what's wrong and therefore hard to change behaviors by applying pedagogic theories that use a top-down approach.

We agreed to help him and the students in this process of changing, involving them in an action research. This approach is particularly suitable when the researcher wants to investigate some events and perceived problems from the "inside" in order to propose

A. Esposito et al. (Eds.): COST 2102 Int. Training School 2010, LNCS 6456, pp. 116–133, 2011.

practical changes. Actually both our teacher and his students did not want just to develop an analysis from an external point of view: they were open to changing their behaviors in order to foster their interactions.

The first part of the researcher's role (as facilitator) has been to guide the class toward questions that accurately represented their real concerns and to help them articulate questions. In a meeting the participants identified the focus, and discuss the method, agreeing to film and analyze a lesson in order to understand the classroom interactions. They were asked to participate in a process of self-observation, using the video to highlight relevant behaviors, to elicit subjective meanings and recognize reciprocal messages of attention or inattention.

Later the researchers facilitated an exchange of information about the teacher's and students' respective interpretations of interactions, which allowed for a reciprocal meta-communication (i. e. communication about communication) [1] [2] regarding the values and emotions underlying participants' classroom behaviors. We used these techniques to promote meta-communication about the class interactions and a discussion of possible improvements that could be made. The rationale is that process of encouraging both the teacher and students' awareness of what happened during the lessons and which were the different meanings could help to improve their relational issues [3].

The second part of the researcher's role (as analyst) has been to apply a conversation analysis of the video footage. This phase of the research helped us to compare the participants' observations with those procedures and structures of the interaction highlighted by conversational analysis of institutional talk in classroom [4].

Finally we conducted an evaluation of the action research with a survey among the participants.

Video recording has been used to observe multimodal communication within the methodological framework of visual sociology, a discipline concerned with the visual dimensions of social life [5]; [6]; [7], but we also incorporated theories and concepts from action research [8], stimulated recall (the role of video as a stimulus for analysis) [9], and conversation analysis (the rules of interaction) [4] [10] [11]. Our research technique employed also the software Transana (Computer-Assisted Qualitative Data Analysis Software) [12].

We believe this method of group video – analysis can become integral part of a collaborative process of change, as it improves the awareness of the events. It forces a re-examination of fixed practices, helping to redefine rigid patterns of interaction and didactic routine.

2 Methodological Issues

Action research and socio-constructionist perspectives define the overall framework of this research.

Why have we decided upon action research? The rationale is that this methodology is a process by which understanding and change can be pursued at one time. The teacher and the students wanted to improve the quality of communication in the class as well as the conditions of teaching and learning; we, as researchers, were interested in analyzing how the class would read and interpret their multimodal communication and wanted to help the process of designing and carrying out this action research project.

According to the socio-constructionist approach [13] we wanted to clarify what and where meanings were embodied in the language and actions of social actors and highlight the process of meaning construction.

Analysis and understanding of interaction requires the ability to interpret the behavior of others. To understand what is going on in the lived social world, we can use our social competence, which is a learned ability. Berger and Luckmann [13] wrote about the sociology of knowledge, analyzing the ways the reality is socially constructed, considered as natural, and taken for granted. For these authors the daily reality is constantly reaffirmed through interaction and conversations. Our subjective reality can only be maintained within a communicative context that we perceive to be plausible. According to this point of view, in our research the teacher's and students' analysis was not a "simple description" of what was seen and heard in the classroom. It was an account of their social construction of reality.

We believe that this meta-communication, through fostering an exchange of opinions about behaviors, aims, and values, was able to improve the didactic setting. Our hypothesis is that meta-communication about the interaction can improve the interaction itself and that this process can be fostered by using the method of collective recall.

Moreover we were interested in comparing the interpretations of the class with concepts and categories coming from the researchers' conversation analysis. In social science triangulation is defined as mixing approaches to get two or three viewpoints upon the things being studied [14]. The underlying assumption is that possible to bring together different modes of analysis (e.g. qualitative and quantitative), seeking convergence across methods [15], to shed light on a social research.

To explain why we choose to compare and combine the points of view of either the insiders and the outsiders of the class (the students, the teacher and the researchers) we need to make some preliminary remarks on the emic/etic concept, developed by the linguist Kenneth L. Pike, who introduced the terms into linguistics and anthropology in 1954 [16]. According to him while the emic perspective focuses on the intrinsic cultural distinctions that are regarded as meaningful and appropriate by the members of the culture or the group under study, the etic perspective relies upon the extrinsic concepts and categories that are appropriate for the community of scientific observers.

Following recent claims [17] [18] we think the two approaches need to be combined to conduct a good qualitative research. To enrich our understanding of interaction dynamics, we made a triangulation of *both* emic and etic perspectives [19] [20]: the insider's subjective one (teachers and students') that relies on the method of stimulated recall, with the outsider's observation and conversation analysis (researchers').

2.1 Action Research

The term "action research" (AR) was coined by the social psychologist Kurt Lewin [8]. He described this method as "a comparative research on the conditions and effects of various forms of social action and research leading to social action" that uses "a spiral of steps, each of which is composed of a circle of planning, action, and fact-finding about the result of the action" [8].

Many scholars point out that AR is research useful in education [21] [22] [23] [24] [25] [26]. David Nunan [27], for example, states that the point of departure for action research in a school setting is the general feeling that the existing praxis could be improved. He suggests asking certain questions to discover whether there is a difference between intents, ideals, and practice and to determine deserving fields of research. Such questions include: is there something that perplexes me, that astounds me, or that irritates me? Is there a difference between what I am thinking of doing and what I am really doing? If so, is there something that I can do to resolve it?

In our view, if a teacher pose these kinds of questions to himself/herself, can start an AR that could improve the quality of education by developing his/her analytical ability. According to John Elliot AR could be considered a form of teacher professional development, in some ways close to a form of 'reflective practice' [28]. Reflectivity is essential for the correction and coherence of the decisions and actions that are undertaken. Reflectivity can lead to a paradigm shift, that is, seeing the event from another point of view. Therefore, improving the didactic praxis relies not only on reflecting on theoretical issues, but also on the interactions in the classrooms and on the effects produced by students' and teachers' actions.

Each person or group can do AR with the aim of improving their strategies, practices, and knowledge of the environments within which they practice. This implies that also students could be considered active actors in this process. Nevertheless AR has also the characteristics of scientific research because it implies a process of reflection, analysis and treatment of the data and is suitable for coping with problematic issues that demand practical, effective and suitable answers [29].

2.2 Stimulated Recall

Stimulated recall is a method in which participants are prompted (here via a video-taped event) to recall thoughts they entertained while taking part in certain events or carrying out certain behaviors. The researcher does not have to give any verbal prompts and the participants do not need to rely only on their memory because they are helped by the images.

The basic idea is that a subject may be able to relive an original situation accurately by using stimuli that were present at the time of that action. Subjects define what is relevant for them while viewing the tape and make comments on what was said or done; for example, the aims, the decisions that were made, significant problems, and recurring behaviors. This procedure allows participants to understand their actions and conduct.

Stimulated recall was originally utilized by Benjamin Bloom as a method to revive the memories of students [9]. This technique has been used with various stimuli (written records, audiotapes, and videotapes) in various ways and settings. For example, it has been used as a research tool for observation analysis of physicians interpersonal interaction [30], to analyze cognitive process used by students in second language learning situations [31], or, more recently, in teaching and learning computer literacy [32].

2.3 Video as a Resource

Video technology has been an important methodological tool for inquiry in classroom research for more than 40 years [33] [34] [35], and now, with digitalization and the help of Computer Assisted Qualitative Data Analysis Software (CAQDAS) [12], it is far more useful, especially for qualitative research and in video feedback [36] [37].

To understand the interaction, a researcher has to observe behaviors and events, focusing on conversation. Observing a classroom is critical to helping teachers better understand their communication and facilitate their students' learning. At the same time, it can be difficult to decide what and how to observe: it is possible to focus on some behaviors, class structure, verbal conversation, and students' levels of engagement or other indicators of process. The use of video and other related data (images of student work or transcripts of dialogues) gives us the opportunity of studying what happens in a class with the advantage of observing the same events repeatedly and more precisely.

Video is used not only to enhance teaching directly, but also in educational development and research. Canning-Wilson [38], for example, emphasizes the role of video as a tool for communication, record-keeping, measuring, and monitoring; it is an evaluation tool, enabling reflection on performance or behavior. Video can improve "teachers' ability to notice and interpret classroom interactions" [39] [40].

A set of observations can arise from the visual information embedded in the video. They concern the deep meaning of the use of the space related to the interactions among participants. As John Prosser states, "proxemics[1] provides important data about individual or group space and relates directly to membership or status: the amount and kind of space accorded to a member of a cultural system reflects status in the structure of that system. Teachers and pupils acquire, mark off, and protect their territory" [41]. Therefore, how teacher and students use the space in the classroom is important because it reveals certain taken-for-granted and hidden behaviors that convey social meanings.

2.4 Conversation Analysis and Institutional Talk

Conversation analysis focuses on talk as situated social practice and interactional organization. It views conversation as sequentially organized through turn-taking and the tacit reasoning procedures people use in the course of everyday talk. This approach was developed by Harvey Sacks, who theorized a turn-taking system of naturally occurring talk. He developed an innovative method of using tape recordings to conduct detailed examination of conversations.

Ervin Goffman and Harold Garfinkel [42] developed the idea that interactional rights and obligations are linked not only to personal identity, but also to macro-social institutions. Studies of institutionalized talk have included, for example, talk in classrooms [4].

While 'ordinary conversation' is a form of interaction that is not confined to specialized settings, in 'institutional talk' the goals of the participants are more limited. Studies of institutional talk focus on restricted environments in which the goals of the participants are institution-specific (for example doctor-patient interactions, the courts

---

[1] Proxemics is concerned with spatial relationship as an indicator of cultural behavior.

of law, schools, etc), restrictions on the nature of interactional contributions are often in force (e.g., in the courts when people are sanctioned for answering when they should not), and institution and activity-specific inferential frameworks are common [43].

The classroom conversation is an institutional talk whose structure is specified by the procedures of interaction between students and teacher [44] [4]. At the beginning of a classroom interaction the teacher can choose two roles: "the role of primary knower of the given information and the manager of the discussion who selects speakers and decides on the direction and pacing of the talk" [45]. He decides who is going to talk, the turn-taking, the length and the subjects of the speeches. He can also give explicit sanctions to students in classrooms for 'shouting out' answers, or talking when he is talking.

The teacher has a basic role in the classroom management: he has to keep the balance between involving everyone in the conversation, and carrying out the planned activities. Students' questions sometimes hold a contradictory meaning. Even though a thoughtful question raised by a student is valued as an indicator of curiosity and understanding, nonetheless it can lead the discourse in an unplanned direction, creating an interruption to the normal flow of the topics in a lesson. If the question is a diversion from the planned classroom discourse, the teacher in a class with many students most often responds by taking back control of the discourse [46].

Turn-taking system in a classroom has some fundamental rules. Mehan and Mc Houl [44] [4] claim that there are two significant features that affect turn-taking during a lesson: there are a large number of potential participants in the interaction whose contributions must be 'rationed' in a formal way, and the talk is designed for an 'overhearing' audience. It is an asymmetric system: the teacher is the only person in charge of the interactions [47]; he plans the aims, he decides the subjects of discussion, and when they have been debated long enough and the class can move on to discuss something else. Antonia Candela [48] argues that power is not an established and acquired right for the teacher: the control of the class is an outcome to gain on a day to day basis.

As Sacks, Schegloff, and Jefferson [49] have noted, interactions with a two-part sequential structure are characteristic of polite everyday conversation.

In contrast, typical classroom discourse initiated by known-information questions has a three-part sequential structure. The same prototypical exchange pattern "IRE" [50] is characterized by a three-part sequence, which involves the teacher producing a question in the first turn (Initiation), a student responding in the second turn (Response), and the teacher giving feedback, or commenting on the student response in the third turn (Evaluation) [51][2].

---

[2] "The presence of an "evaluation", which comments on a replay of a question, seems to be one of the features that distinguishes conversations that take place in a classrooms and other educational settings from those that occur in everyday situations" [52]. These sequences have been given a variety of other labels [51], such as Initiation-Response-Feedback or Initiation-Response-Follow up (IRF) [52], Question-Answer-Comment (QAC) [4], and triadic dialogue [11].

3 Method

After the first meeting in which the participants agreed to start the action research, in order to allow students and teacher to become used to the presence of the camera and other devices, we placed the equipment in full view of everybody and then we filmed some hours of the participants' interactions in class. They soon became used to the presence of the camera and microphone, which did not appear to significantly divert their attention.

The equipment used for the video recording included three small miniDV consumer camcorders, tripods and microphones, selected for their lightness, relative inexpensive and ease of use. No additional lighting was used in the classrooms, as this would have been intrusive. We placed the cameras in three different parts of the room in order to have as much visual data as possible. The cameras (fixed and with automatic controls) were placed in such a way that two videotaped the students and one the teacher. Therefore we filmed two lessons.

We chose to analyze the last lesson, which has the best audio and video quality. All of the dialogue was transcribed. With only three hours of video footage (one hour for each of the three cameras) we were not selective about transcribing the data. Then we edited the video with the software Adobe Premiere, importing our three footage clips and applying the effect "picture in picture" (see Fig.2). This way we got a single split screen video with three synchronized points of view.

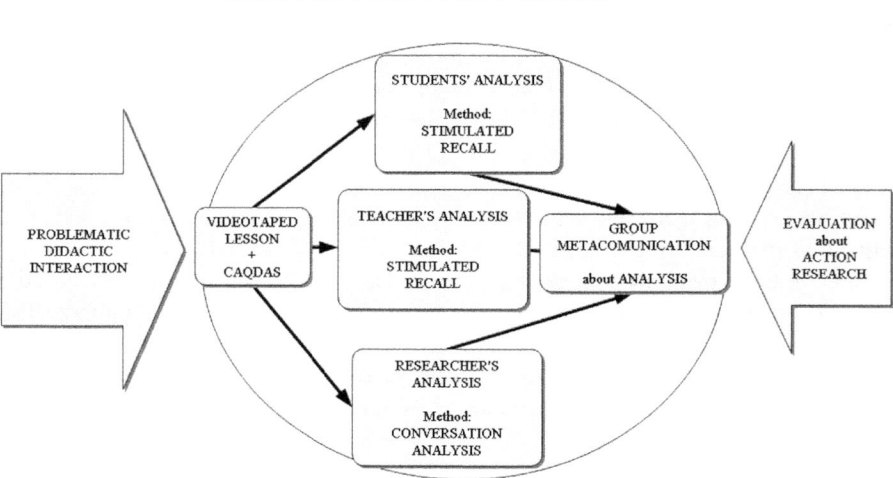

METHODOLOGICAL FRAMEWORK OF ACTION RESEARCH

Fig. 1. Research process flowchart. Students, teacher and researchers have analyzed the videotaped lesson separately. All the subjects shared their different points of view in a group, fostering the comprehension of mutual meanings about that didactic interaction.

Fig. 2. Video recording of the teacher's talk. This picture, taken from video footage, includes the three points of view used to document the lesson. All images are synchronized; in other words, all three scenes are happening at the same moment. In the first one the teacher is talking while standing by his desk, while a researcher is operating the camera close by. In the second frame two students are talking together in low voices, trying to hide from the teacher. In the third a row of students is writing and listening to the teacher. A student with a black shirt is playing with a video game that is kept out of sight (this was pointed out by students in their analysis of the lesson).

A week later we used the videotape-triggered stimulated recall separately in different sessions for the students and the teacher to explore their subjective perspectives of that didactic experience. We asked our subjects to comment retrospectively on videotaped passages of their interactions. The groups watched the video of the lesson using an overhead projector and made comments to the researcher, who took notes and recorded their opinions.

We instructed participants to stop the video whenever they identified some meaningful event or noticed relevant behaviors. This way the playback was interrupted to give the participants an opportunity to discuss the sequence they had just viewed, specifying everything that went through their minds in the situation shown in the playback [53], including beliefs, meanings, thoughts, and feelings about the classroom activity. These relevant moments were collected using a brainstorming technique.

To assist with these analyses we used the software program Transana (Version 2.22) developed for discourse and conversation analysis by researchers at the University of Wisconsin, Madison [54]. This transcription software (see Fig.3) can be used to study observable behavior such as activities, gestures, talks, movements, and social interactions. It facilitates the transcription and analysis of video data and allows annotation and integration of text/transcripts connected to the videotaped events.

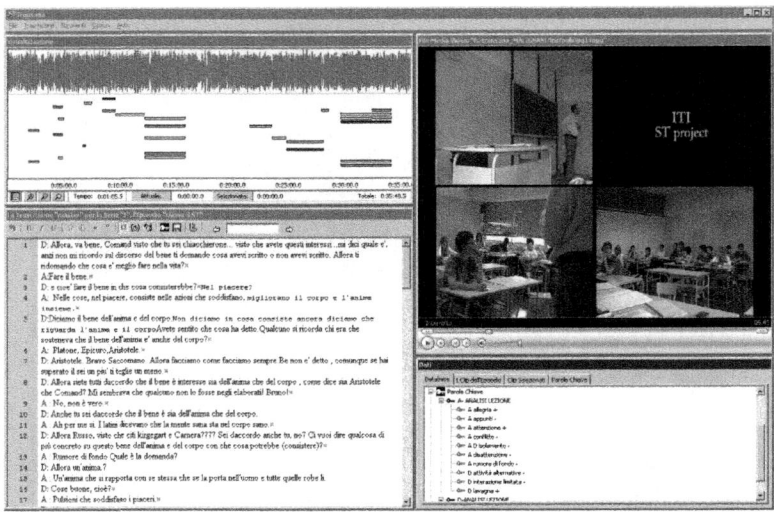

Fig. 3. Interface of Transana software with analysis of the lesson.The software Transana is displayed with its four windows open. From right to left you can see a) the visualization window, which displays visual representations of the data, in the form of a waveform diagram representing the speech and a timeline with a bar chart showing the coding (keywords) that have been applied during the analysis; b) the video window (with three points of view), where the video is displayed; c) the transcript window, where the transcript of the conversation between the teacher and the students is entered and displayed; d) the data window (where you view, organize, and manipulate data) with the keywords used to describe the relevant events.

The user can organize video or audio clips (also from different video files) into meaningful categories, as a procedure for developing and expanding the theoretical understanding of the video. On a single split-screen format, one can view footage in both video and sound waveforms, transcribe the data, view the time line with coded segments, and link specific points in the transcript to individual frames in the video, allowing precise alignment of speech. By placing time codes within the transcript, the software automatically highlights relevant portions of the transcript as the video plays. The greatest advantage of having data accessible in one place is significantly speeding up the transcription and the coding process [55].

During the analysis we used Transana to define specific keywords[3] to identify those events relevant for teacher and students, to record all the keywords linking them to specific points of the transcript, to list the key episodes using coded titles, and to conduct a fast search of digitized audiovisual passages of conversation.

After the students' collective analysis and the teacher's separate observation sessions, the next phase involved a group meeting for openly exchange information, and exploring beliefs to reach a clear consciousness of reciprocal interpretations. Usually focus groups are "a form of qualitative interviewing that uses a researcher-led group discussion to generate data" [56]. We primarily organized this group analysis for a

---

[3] We asked the group of students to name the relevant issues that occurred in the video. The keywords represent what went on among the students and teacher.

reciprocal meta-communication, beginning a social exchange of interpretations of each other's actions, collaborative construction and negotiation of meanings, and opinions about the conversation and interactions of the lessons. We invited everybody back to comment on their participation in videotaped passages of the dialogue that had been selected for analysis, thus permitting juxtaposition with their retrospective comments. The goal was to analyze what was going on during the lesson and invite the participants to share their opinions about their interactions during those events.

When students watched the video recording, they seemingly regarded it as natural and self-evident. Beyond the pleasure or shame of watching themselves talking and acting, it seemed that there wasn't much to explain. But the video also conveyed insights that were unknown to us, as non-members of that specific social group. What was taken for granted by the students wasn't obvious for the teacher, and vice versa.

4   Results

4.1   Students' and Teacher's Analysis

After the student analysis, the teacher analysis and the researcher's analysis sessions, we organized a group discussion about the respective interpretative video analysis of the lesson.

The first result has been that the two points of view (the teacher's and the students' descriptions of the lesson) are different. The teacher made 17 observations, while students made 19, but the 84% of them don't coincide. Only 16 % match.

The main feedback that students had for their teacher contradicted his own view: students didn't think he was too authoritarian (see code T5 in table 1): on the contrary, they believed that he was unable to maintain order (code S4 in table 2). Therefore they outlined many behaviors that they considered improper (from S10 to S19).

Students and teacher talked about all the observations exposed in Table 1 and 2. During the group discussion they admitted that they wouldn't misbehave in such a way during other teachers' lessons, but they did not so because he is "tolerant".

Table 1. Teacher's observations concerning his and students' behavior

	Teacher	Students
Positive	(code T1) The teacher explains complex concepts in an understandable way. (T2) The teacher makes jokes during the lesson.	
Neutral	(T3) The teacher speaks louder in order to overcome the noise. (T4) The teacher stops talking in order to gain the students' attention.	(T10) The students pay more attention than usual because of the cameras.
Negative	(T5) The teacher is authoritarian. (T6) The teacher does not vary students' activities. (T7) The teacher asks rhetorical questions. (T8) The teacher is ironic about the students' answers. (T9) The teacher focuses on having conversations with only the most responsive students.	(T11) The students ask about their grades at the wrong moment.

Table 2. Students' observations

	Teacher	Students
Positive	(S1) The students laugh when the teacher makes a joke, releasing their tension and finally paying attention. (S2) When the teacher writes on the writing board, he makes taking notes easier. (S3) The subject chosen by the teacher makes the difference in the students' participation.	(S9) The class listens and responds in an interested manner.
Neutral		
Negative	(S4) The teacher is not able to maintain order. (S5) The student in the first row is isolated. (S6) The teacher talks to only a few involved students. (S7) The teacher keeps too much distance from the students by standing on a step. (S8) The teacher does not allow a student to talk.	(S10) The students do not take notes. (S11) Noisy groups split the class. (S12) The students do math homework instead listening to the teacher. (S13) Students that are sitting far away do not pay attention. (S14) Students make vulgar signs. (S15) Background noise. (S16) Contrast among the students. (S17) One student stands up without being given permission. (S18) One student is playing a video game. (S19) The students joke around and lack interest in what the teacher says.

Both the students and the teacher mainly focused on their own activities (see Fig. 4 and 5), paying less attention to their counterparts. Both highlighted the negative aspects rather than positive ones, but the students are more polarized in their opinions.

In the students' analysis, they pointed out at least three different facts that are meaningful from the perspective of proxemics. The first is that the teacher was far too distant from them, remaining at his desk most of the time (S7). The second is that he isolated a student by making him sit in the first row, away from others (S5). The third is that the students who were sitting in the last row, far from the teacher, did not pay attention and were more likely to do something else (S13). On the contrary the teacher seems unaware of this dimension of the relation.

Another set of observations arises from the audio information. While the students notice (S11 and S15) that the background noise is a problem for those who want to pay attention, the teacher focus (T3 and T4) on how he tries to gain the attention of the class (see tables 1 and 2).

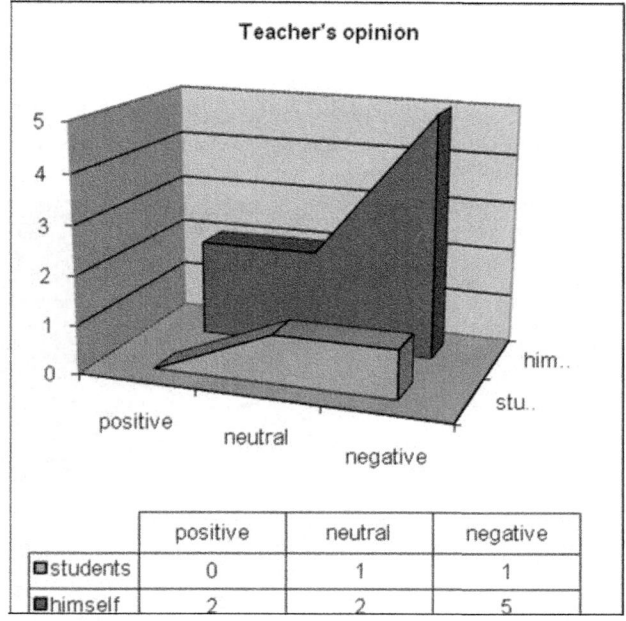

	positive	neutral	negative
□students	0	1	1
■himself	2	2	5

Fig. 4. Teacher's observations about himself and the students

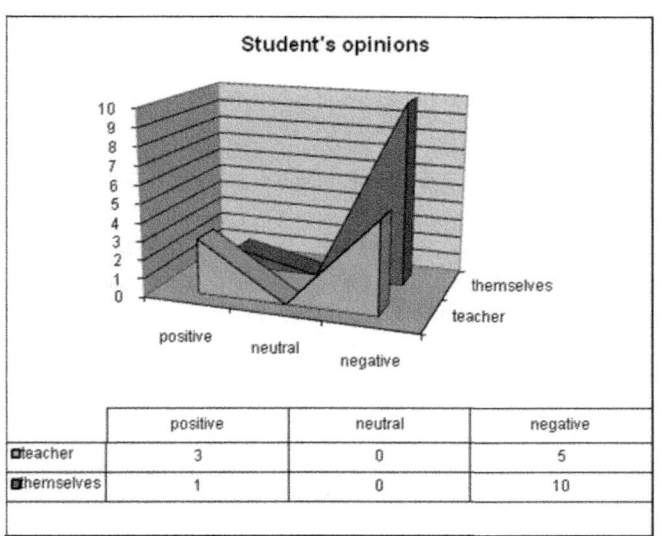

	positive	neutral	negative
□teacher	3	0	5
■themselves	1	0	10

Fig. 5. Students' observations about themselves and the teacher

4.2 Researchers' Conversation Analysis

In addition to students' and teacher's analyses, the conversation analysis (CA) led by researchers, has been an important element of the study. We carried out a detailed examination of recorded conversations, studying the transcripts of the sessions and the gestures of the participants so as to describe the structural organization and social order that they revealed.

The main result has been that the prototypical exchange pattern "IRE" was central not only in CA but also in students' and teacher's observations (see Fig. 6).

Fig. 6. Video recording of the three-part sequence of turn-taking. The teacher is asking a question (IRE). A student in the first row is raising his hand in vain (tired of raising his hand, he supports one arm with the other arm). Another student in the last desk raises his hand and starts to answer the question. Few other students seem interested in the conversation.

Both the teacher and students highlighted problems with turn-taking (T7, T9, T11, S6, S8) in the conversation. According to the students, the teacher made certain mistakes in managing the conversation. He decided to take the first role for the most of the time: some students noticed he talked only with a few students (S6) and he himself complained (T6) about his difficulty to stimulate the students to become more active in the conversation. The students' analysis also pointed out that the teacher, who set the rule of hand-raising before asking a question, didn't respect the rule of giving the student in the first row a turn to talk (S8). All of these events indicate that, to a certain extent, that the teacher had failed in his role of turn-taking control, which disappointed students.

Also in our analysis, students' critiqued how the teacher controlled the topic and flow of discourse, limiting the interactions only to those who knew the answers to his questions. The teacher called this type of interaction "asking rhetorical questions." (T7) As a matter of fact, teacher is often engaged in pedagogical talk with students not to seek information, but just to test their knowledge [57]. If this is a common occurrence, this likely results in the conversation not being interesting enough to maintain the students' attention.

4.3 Students' and Teacher's Evaluation of the Action Research

At the end of this experience we used a survey to determine the students' evaluation about this particular action research. The survey results are based on the responses of twenty students. Most of them think the experience was positive (see Table 3).

Table 3. Students' final evaluation of action research

How was this experience?	Positive: 14	Don't know: 6	Negative: 0
I learned…	A lot: 5	Something: 11	Nothing: 4
I would like that this experience is…	More frequent: 11	More long: 5	More anonymous: 4

Based on our survey results, we think that the length and the number of lessons analyzed were not enough: fifty five percent of students would also like regular analysis sessions.

We also asked the teacher's opinion. In his final report he claimed that the action research was interesting and useful, mostly because it developed in him an attitude to research and reflect on his own behavior.

"The best advantage has been the opportunity to self-evaluate my performance as a teacher, using, thanks to the video, an external point of view. That viewpoint allowed me to observe and to understand which behaviors were effective and convincing during my effort to teach philosophical knowledge to students. I particularly observed how difficult I found it to simultaneously manage:

a) transmission of knowledge,
b) conversation and the logical reasoning with the more clever students
c) whole class' participation, and
d) discipline.

While I was able to handle a) and b), I failed to deal with points c) and d)… I noted some positive effects of this experience even at the beginning of the next school year, as if somebody, unseen, was still observing us and was enabling that process of self-evaluation which is at the core, I think, of the best practice of teaching".

5 Conclusion

In this action research we wanted to foster didactic interaction awareness using video-analysis with CAQDAS. We videotaped a lesson and asked students and teacher to analyze it. They commented and shared their alternative interpretation of relevant events and interpersonal relationships in the classroom.

In conclusion we agree that video analysis of multimodal communication is useful not only for the researcher, but it also can be a powerful tool for professional growth when teachers watch videos of their own teaching, listen to the students' points of view and reflect on behaviors and strategies of the lesson's participants.

Therefore the use of CADQAS could facilitate the transcription, analysis, annotation and comparison of audiovisual data, especially if the same events are interpreted by different actors and there is a lot of information to work with.

We can describe two different approaches in our research: the first was a socio-constructionist approach. In this perspective we explored ideas that emerged from the class itself. We tried to work inductively (bottom-up) rather than deductively (theory-driven). We invited the students and the teacher to freely define what was going on in a lesson, without giving them a theoretical framework or suggesting specific phenomena to search for in the interactions.

The second approach (etic) has been informed by the theoretical principles of conversation analysis. Following this methodology, we analyzed the class interactions, verifying how much their "natural social competence" matched with a more sophisticated and scientific analysis method. We focused on qualities of the talk, including verbal and nonverbal patterns, as well as on power-related behaviors. The goal was to find specific meaningful interaction patterns that would confirm or disconfirm the teacher's and students' elicitations and comments.

The convergence across emic and etic approaches shed light on this social research and conversation analysis supported the class interpretations of interactions.

In most classrooms teachers initiate a question and then evaluate the student's response. This typical questioning style is referred to as IRE and is characterized by teachers choosing the kinds of question to be asked, who may participate in the interaction, and whether to accept or reject the response. In his lessons, as the teacher noted, there were perhaps too many IRE sequences, which made the conversation too predictable and boring. But the more meaningful feedback for the teacher was that students considered him to be lacking in classroom management skills: according to them he wasn't able to keep order and his way of controlling the turn taking during the conversation was inadequate.

Finally, according to participants, the evaluation of practical outcome of this action research was positive

We believe that preliminary findings illustrated in this research demonstrate this methodology is effective, as the process of becoming aware of "problematic" interactions in the didactic relationship is the beginning of their solution. This video analysis can become an integral part of interaction change, as it allows improving the awareness of the events, with a bottom–up approach, which starts from behaviors to explore subjective meanings. Observation and elicitation of the playback are the start for a pluralistic interpretation, a collaborative construction of meaning about those lesson's events. This process also forces a re-examination of established methodological practice and the reciprocal exchange about the alternative interpretations of the interactions within a lesson can give a better insight on the classroom activities, helping to revise teaching practices and change the didactic routine.

This case study is an action research and therefore findings are not generalizable. However, we believe that further research needs to be conducted to verify the results across a greater number of lessons and over a longer period of time.

References

1. Bateson, G.: Steps to ecology of mind. Ballantine Books, New York (1972)
2. Sarangi, S.: Beyond Language, Beyond Awareness: Metacommunication in Instructional Settings. Language Awareness 7, 63–68 (1998)
3. Branco, A.U., Valsiner, J. (eds.): Communication and Metacommunication in Human Development. Information Age Publishing, Charlotte (2004)
4. McHoul, A.W.: The organization of turns at formal talk in the classroom. Language and Society 7, 183–213 (1978)
5. Wagner, J.: Images of Information: Still Photography in the Social Sciences. Sage Publications, London (1979)
6. Becker, H.: Visual Sociology, Documentary Photography and PhotoJournalism: it's Almost All a Matter of Context. Visual Sociology 10, 5–14 (1995)
7. Faccioli, P., Losacco, G.: Nuovo manuale di sociologia visuale. Franco Angeli, Milano (2010)
8. Lewin, K.: Action Research and Minority Problems. Journal of Social Issues 3, 34–46 (1946)
9. Bloom, B.S.: The Thought Process of Students in Discussion. In: French, S.J. (ed.) Accent on Teaching; experiments in general education. Harper & Brothers, New York (1953)
10. Mehan, H.: The Structure of Classroom Discourse. In: Dijk, T.A. (ed.) Handbook of Discourse Analysis, vol. 3, pp. 120–131. Academic Press, New York (1985)
11. Lemke, J.L.: Talking science: Language, learning, and values. Ablex, Norwood (1990)
12. Lewins, A., Silver, C.: Using Software in Qualitative Research. Sage, London (2007)
13. Berger, P.L., Luckmann, T.: The social construction of reality: a treatise in the sociology of knowledge. Anchor Books, Garden City (1966)
14. Denzin, N.K.: The research act in sociology: A theoretical introduction to sociological method. Butterworths, London (1970)
15. Patton, M.Q.: Qualitative Evaluation and Research Methods. Sage, Newbury Park (1990)
16. Pike, K.L.: Language in relation to a unified theory of the structure of human behavior. Summer Institute of Linguistics, Glendale, CA (1954)
17. Helfrich, H.: Beyond the dilemma of cross-cultural psychology: Resolving the tension between etic and emic approaches. Culture & Psychology, 131–153 (1999)
18. Matsumoto, D., Juang, L.: Culture and psychology. Thompson Wadsworth, Belmont (2008)
19. Harris, M.: History and significance of the emic/etic distinction. Annual Review of Anthropology 5, 329–350 (1976)
20. Headland, T.N., Pike, K.L., Harris, M. (eds.): Emics and Etics: The Insider/Outsider Debate. Sage Publications, Newbury Park (1990)
21. Stenhouse, L.: An Introduction to Curriculum Research and Development. Heinemann, London (1975)
22. Carr, W., Kemmis, S.: Becoming Critical: education, knowledge and action research. Falmer, Lewes (1986)
23. McNiff, J.: Action Research: Principles and Practice. Macmillan, Basingstoke (1988)
24. Bogdan, R., Biklen, S.K.: Qualitative Research For Education. Allyn and Bacon, Boston (1992)
25. Usher, R., Bryant, I., Johnston, R.: Adult Education and the Postmodern Challenge. Learning beyond the limits, Routledge, London (1997)
26. Stringer, E.T.: Action Research. Sage Publications, Thousand Oaks (1999)

27. Nunan, D.: Understanding Language Classrooms. A Guide for Teacher-Initiated Research. Prentice Hal, New York (1989)
28. Elliot, J.: Action Research for Educational Change. Open University Press, Buckingham (1991)
29. Eliot, J.: La ricerca - azione: un quadro di riferimento per l'autovalutazione nelle scuole. In: Scurati, C., Giordan, A., Elliot, J. (eds.) La ricerca –azione, Boringhieri, Torino (1983)
30. Kagan, N., Schauble, P., Resinikoff, A., Danish, S.J., Kratwohl, D.R.: Studies in Human Interaction. In: Educational Publishing Services, Michigan State University, East Lansing Michigan (1967)
31. Gass, S.M., Mackey, A.: Stimulated Recall Methodology in Second Language Research. Lawrence Erlbaum, Mahwah (2000)
32. Henderson, L.: Stimulated recall and mental models: tools for teaching and learning computer information literacy. Scarecrow Press, Lanham (2006)
33. Dowrick, P.W., Biggs, S.J. (eds.): Using video. Psychological and Social Applications. John Wiley and Son, New York (1982)
34. Anning, A., Broadhead, P., Busher, H., Clarke, A., Dodgson, H., Taggart, L., White, S., Wilson, R.: Using video-recording for teacher professional development. School of Education, University of Leeds, Leeds (1990)
35. Ulewicz, M., Beatty, A. (eds.): The Power of Video Technology in International Comparative Research in Education. National Academy Press, Washington (2001)
36. Tochon, F.V.: Video study groups for education, professional development, and change. Atwood Publishing, Madison (1999)
37. Tochon, F.V.: Education research: New avenues for video pedagogy and feedback in teacher education. International Journal of Applied Semiotic 2, 9–27 (2001)
38. Canning-Wilson, C.: Role of video in the F/SL classroom. In: Riley, S., Troud, S., Coombe, C. (eds.) Teaching, learning and technology, TESOL, vol. 1, pp. 69–76. United Arab Emirates, Arabia (1999)
39. Sherin, M.G., van Es, E.A.: Using video to support teachers' ability to notice classroom interactions. Journal of Technology and Teacher Education 13, 475–491 (2005)
40. Raingruber, B.: Video-Cued Narrative Reflection: A Research Approach for Articulating Tacit, Relational, and Embodied Understandings. Qualitative Health Research 13, 15 (2003)
41. Prosser, J.: Visual methods and the visual culture of schools. Visual Studies 22, 13–30 (2007)
42. Garfinkel, H.: Ethnomethodology. Polity Press, Cambridge (1967)
43. Drew, P., Heritage, J.: Analyzing Talk at Work: An Introduction. In: Drew, P., Heritage, J. (eds.) Talk at Work, pp. 3–65. Cambridge University Press, Cambridge (1992)
44. Mehan, H.: Structuring school structure. Harvard Educational Review 48, 32–64 (1978)
45. Lee, Y.-A.: Third turn position in teacher talk: Contingency and the work of teaching. Journal of Pragmatics 39, 1204–1230 (2007)
46. Rop, C.J.: The meaning of student inquiry questions: a teacher's beliefs and responses. International Journal of Science Education 24, 717–736 (2002)
47. Fele, G., Paoletti, I.: Interazioni in classe, Il Mulino, Bologna (2003)
48. Candela, A.: Students' power in classroom discourse. Linguistics and Education 10, 139–163 (1998)
49. Sacks, H., Schegloff, E.A., Jefferson, G.: A Simplest Systematics for the Organization of Turn-Taking for Conversation. Language 50, 696–735 (1974)
50. Mehan, H.: Learning lessons: Social organization in the classroom. Harvard University Press, Cambridge (1979)

51. Hauser, E.: Teacher Reformulations of Students. Answers during an Episode of Pedagogical Talk Bulletin of the University of Electro-Communications 19, 93–99 (2006)
52. Sinclair, J.M., Coulthard, R.M.: Towards an analysis of discourse: The English used by teachers and pupils. Oxford University Press, Oxford (1975)
53. Busse, A., Borromeo Ferri, R.: Methodological reflections on a threestep- design combining observation, stimulated recall and interview. ZMD 35 (2003)
54. Woods, D., Fassnacht, C.: Transana The Board of Regents of the University of Wisconsin System, Madison, WI (2007)
55. Greer, T.: Transcription approaches to multilingual discourse analysis. In: 2nd Annual JALT Pan-SIG Conference. Kyoto Institute of Technology, Japan, Kyoto (2003)
56. Given, L.T. (ed.): The Sage encyclopedia of qualitative research methods. Sage, Thousand Oaks (2008)
57. Nassaji, H., Wells, G.: What's the use of 'Triadic dialogue'? an investigation of teacher–student interaction. Applied Linguistics 21, 376–406 (2000)

Analysis of Interrogatives in Different Domains

Helena Moniz[1,2], Fernando Batista[2,3],
Isabel Trancoso[2,4], and Ana Isabel Mata[1]

[1]Faculdade de Letras da Universidade de Lisboa (FLUL), Centro de Linguística da Universidade de Lisboa (CLUL), Alameda da Universidade, 1600-214, Portugal
[2] INESC-ID, Rua Alves Redol, 9, 1000-029, Lisboa, Portugal
[3] ISCTE-IUL - Instituto Universitário de Lisboa, Lisboa, Portugal
[4] Instituto Superior Técnico, Universidade Técnica de Lisboa, Lisboa, Portugal
{helena.moniz,fernando.batista,isabel.trancoso}@inesc-id.pt,
aim@fl.ul.pt

Abstract. The aim of this work is twofold: to quantify the distinct interrogative types in different domains for European Portuguese, and to discuss the weight of the linguistic features that best describe these structures, in order to model interrogatives in speech.

We analyzed spoken dialogue, university lectures, and broadcast news corpora, and, for the sake of comparison, newspaper texts. The statistical analysis confirms that the percentage of the different types of interrogative is highly dependent on the nature of the corpus. Experiments on the automatic detection of interrogatives for European Portuguese, using only lexical cues, show results that are strongly correlated with the detection of a specific type of interrogatives (namely wh- questions). When acoustic and prosodic features (pitch, energy and duration) are added, yes/no and tag questions are then increasingly identified, showing the advantages of combining both lexical, acoustic and prosodic information.

Keywords: Interrogatives, punctuation, prosody.

1 Introduction

In this study we aim at quantifying the distinct interrogative types in different contexts, and discussing the weight of the linguistic features that best describe each of these structures, in order to automatically identify interrogatives in speech.

As in other languages, European Portuguese (EP) has different interrogative types: yes/no questions, alternative questions, wh- and tag questions. A yes/no question requests a yes/no answer (*Estão a ver a diferença?*/Can you see the difference?). In EP, this type of interrogative generally presents the same syntactic order as a statement, contrarily to English that may encode the yes/no interrogative with an auxiliary verb and subject inversion. An alternative question presents two or more hypotheses (*Acha que vai facilitar ou vai ainda tornar mais difícil?*/Do you think that it will make it easier or will it make it even harder?) expressed by the disjunctive conjunction *ou*/or. A wh- question has an

A. Esposito et al. (Eds.): COST 2102 Int. Training School 2010, LNCS 6456, pp. 134–146, 2011.
© Springer-Verlag Berlin Heidelberg 2011

interrogative word, such as *qual*/what, *quem*/who, *quando*/when, *onde*/where, etc., corresponding to what is being asked about (*Qual é a pergunta?*/What is the question?). In a tag question, an interrogative clause is added to the end of a statement (*Isto é fácil, não é?*/This is easy, isn't it?).

This diversity may cause some interrogative types to be easier to detect than others. State-of-the-art studies on sentence boundary detection in general and on detection of interrogatives in particular have discussed the relative weight of different types of feature. [19,20] report that prosodic features are more significant than lexical ones and that better results are achieved when combining both features; [28] claims that results based only on prosodic properties are quite robust; [4], analyzing meetings, states that lexico-syntactic features are the most important ones to identify interrogatives.

These diverging opinions led us to question whether the relative weights of these features should take into account the nature of the corpus, namely the most characteristic types of interrogative in each, and the ways a particular language encodes sentence-type forms. This study addresses that question, using three distinct corpora for European Portuguese: broadcast news, classroom lectures, and map-task dialogues. For comparison sake, we shall also address newspaper text.

The automatic detection of interrogatives may be of particular interest for potential applications, such as the punctuation of automatic speech recognition (ASR) transcripts. Our previous punctuation module aimed only at full stops and commas. One of the objectives of this work is the extension of this module to encompass question marks as well, by combining different types of feature.

Given that the prosodic properties of interrogatives in EP are not equally well studied for all types of interrogative, in particular in what concerns spontaneous speech, the next section reviews these properties, with a particular emphasis on tag questions, which so far have received relative little attention. The different corpora used in this study are briefly outlined in Section 3. The statistical analysis of interrogative types is reported in Section 4. Punctuation experiments with lexical and prosodic features are reported in Section 5. Conclusions and future work are presented in Section 6.

2   Prosodic Analysis of Interrogatives in EP

In EP, declaratives are the most studied sentence type [14,24,6,8,27,9,25]. The intonational contour generally associated to a declarative is a descending one, expressed as a prenuclear H* (in the first accented syllable), H+L* as nuclear tone, and L% as a boundary tone, according to Tones and Break Indices (ToBI) labelling system [21] adapted for Portuguese[1] [25,11]. A similar intonational contour is found in wh- questions[2]. By contrast, the contour associated with a yes/no question is a rising one, expressed either as H* H+L* H% or (H) H+L* LH% (the latter proposed by [10]). [15] also observes descending contours to yes/no questions in

---

[1] http://www.ling.ohio-state.edu/~tobi/

[2] [6] reports ascending contours when the wh- question is polite.

spontaneous speech. As for alternative questions, only [24,15] have described them prosodically. The first intonational unit is described with the contour rising-fall-rising, whereas the second unit exhibits a rising-fall contour. The prosody of tags is still studied too sparsely in EP ([15], for high school lectures, and [6] for laboratory speech). For [6], the tags are described with falling contours, while for [15], these structures are associated with rising ones.

The relative sparse literature on tags led us to analyze them in more detail in our corpora. Tag questions present an idiosyncratic behavior at the lexical, prosodic and segmental levels. Lexically, they are rich, although most of the words/expressions are still not fully studied as tags *certo?*, *correcto?*, *okay?*, *humhum?*, *é isso?*, *inter alia*. Phonetically, they may be produced in various forms (with strong and weak forms, the latter with vowel reduction), and they may also be accented or deaccented.

An analysis of one of the most frequent tags in our corpora (*não é?*/isn't it?) revealed regular trends. The first part (the declarative) behaves as described in general for neutral statements in EP, with H+L* L- or L%. The tag itself is mostly accented and exhibits specific intonational patterns, the most frequent being L*+H L%. When tags are deaccented, they have boundary tones expressed either as L% or LH%. Phonetically, they are mainly produced with weak forms [n'ɛ][3] or [nɐ 'ɛ] *vs.* [nẽw̃'ɛ] and the choice of the form is speaker dependent. When associating both parts (declarative and tag), tags are subordinated relatively to the declarative contour (most frequently with f_0 compression).

3   Corpora

In order to evaluate if the features would be dependent on the nature of the corpus, we analyzed four distinct corpora. The corpus collected within the *Lectra* project [22] aimed at transcribing university lectures for e-learning applications, namely, making the transcribed lectures available for hearing impaired students. The corpus has a total of 75h, corresponding to 7 different courses, of which only 27h were orthographically transcribed (totaling 155k words). *Coral* [26] is a map-task corpus, encompassing 64 dialogues between 32 speakers, and comprehending 7h (61k words). *Alert* is a broadcast news corpus, collected during 2000 and 2001 [18]. The speech recognition subset, used in the experiments described in this paper, includes 61h (449k words). The manual orthographic transcriptions of this corpus were recently revised by an expert linguist, thereby removing many inconsistencies in terms of punctuation marks that affected our previous results. For the sake of comparison, we also used a newspaper text corpus with 148M words. All the corpora were subdivided into train, test and development sets.

4   Statistical Analysis of Interrogatives

Table 1 shows the overall frequency of interrogatives and other punctuation marks in the train sets of the different corpora, taking into account the number

---

[3] Lexicalized in Brazilian Portuguese as *né*.

of sentence-like units (SU). The overall frequency of interrogatives in the data is substantially different: on one hand, the university lectures and the map-task corpora present 20.7% and 23.2%, respectively; on the other hand, the BN and the newspapers corpora have only 2.1% and 1.0%, respectively. The first two corpora have ten times more interrogatives than the latter, a percentage interpretable by the teacher's need to verify if the students are understanding what is being said, and also by the giver's concerns in making his/her follower localize the right path in a map. In broadcast news, interrogatives are almost exclusively found in interviews, and in transitions from anchormen to reporters.

Table 1. Overall punctuation marks frequency in the training sets

	Type	?	!	.	,	:	;	#SUs
Lectra	university lectures	20.7%	0.0%	41.6%	37.6%	0.0%	0.1%	6,524
Coral	map-task dialogues	23.2%	0.4%	66.9%	8.0%	0.0%	1.4%	8,135
Alert	broadcast news	2.1%	0.1%	58.1%	39.1%	0.5%	0.2%	26,467
Newspaper	newspaper text	1.0%	0.2%	30.7%	57.5%	2.4%	0.7%	5,841,273

4.1 Overall Frequency of Interrogative Types in the Training Corpora

The automatic tagging in terms of interrogative types was done for the 4 corpora using the following set of heuristic rules:

1. if the interrogative sentence has one of the following items *quem, qual, quais, quanto(s), quanta(s), quando, quê, a quem, o quê, por que, para que, onde, porque, porquê, o que, como*, then it is classified as a wh- question;
2. if the interrogative sentence has the disjunctive conjunction *ou*, then it is an alternative question;
3. if the interrogative sentence has one of the following items *não é, certo, não, sim, okay, humhum, está bom, está, está bem, não foi, tens, estás a ver, estão a ver, é isso, de acordo, percebido, perceberam, correcto, não é verdade* prior to a question mark, then it is a tag question;
4. otherwise, it is a yes/no question.

This rule set models the lexical expressions that may function as interrogatives, including expressions observed in the training sets that are still not fully described for EP (*e.g.*, tag questions such as *okay?, certo?, correcto?*).

Table 2 shows the overall frequency of interrogative types in the training sets of the four corpora. The table shows that there are different trends in the distribution of interrogative subtypes as well. The university lectures, the broadcast and the newspaper corpora present comparable results for wh- questions. Concerning tag questions, the university lectures corpus has the highest percentage. This may be associated with the teacher need to confirm if the students are understanding what is being taught, and ultimately with styles of lecturing. The map-task also shows a representative amount of tag questions, but yes/no questions are the most expressive type of interrogative in this corpus, mainly due to

Table 2. Overall frequency of interrogative types in training corpora (automatically produced results)

	Wh	Alt	Tags	Y/N	Total SUs
Lectra	42.2%	2.2%	27.0%	28.6%	6,524
Coral	7.5%	3.1%	12.3%	77.1%	8,135
Alert	34.2%	5.5%	10.9%	49.4%	26,467
Newspaper	41.3%	7.8%	1.1%	49.8%	5,841,273

the description of a map made by a giver and the need to ask if the follower is understanding the complete instructions. The Alert corpus shows results that are closest to the newspaper corpus, as expected. As for alternative questions, they are quite residual across these four corpora.

4.2   Building a *Golden Set*

A *golden set* of interrogatives, which constitutes our manual reference, was created by an expert linguist, starting from the automatic annotation of interrogative types of the test sets of the four corpora. Table 3 shows the frequency of each type of interrogative, before and after the manual correction. The agreement between the automatic and the manual classifications was evaluated using Cohen's kappa values [5], and is shown in the last column. In terms of question mark types, the automatic classification performed better for the alternative questions (0.912 Cohen's Kappa), followed by wh- questions (0.874) and yes/no questions with similar results (0.863). The most inconsistent classification, as expected, concerns tag questions (0.782).

Table 3. Automatic and manual classification of interrogative types in the test sets

	#SUs	#?	Automatic				Manual				Cohen's
			Wh	Alt	Tags	Y/N	Wh	Alt	Tags	Y/N	Kappa
Lectra	262	102	39.7%	2.2%	39.0%	19.1%	41.4%	1.0%	40.4%	17.1%	0.922
Coral	3,406	511	9.4%	3.5%	13.5%	73.6%	10.6%	5.1%	18.2%	66.1%	0.849
Alert	2,671	151	42.4%	2.0%	11.2%	44.4%	40.4%	2.6%	10.0%	47.0%	0.895
Newspaper	90,534	2,859	44.9%	7.3%	0.9%	46.9%	43.5%	6.3%	0.8%	49.4%	0.900

The table reveals that rules perform fairly well, the most notorious difference being the classification between tag and yes/no questions in Coral. The low Cohen's Kappa value of this corpus is due to structures that maybe classified as either elliptic yes/no questions (*sim?/yes?* or *é?/is it?*) or tag questions (*declarative + sim?/yes?* or *declarative + é?/is it?*). The Lectra corpus presents the highest Cohen's Kappa value, and differences are mostly due to similar classification errors between tags and yes/no questions. The Alert and the Newspaper corpora contain very complex structures which are hard to disambiguate automatically (*e.g.* embedded subordinate and coordinate clauses) and they are similar in terms of Cohen's Kappa. Thus, we may conclude that, broadcast news and newspaper data are more similar in what concerns the frequency of interrogative subtypes and the nature of the errors, whereas university lectures and map-task dialogues share flexible structures characteristic of spontaneous speech, such as elliptic yes/no questions and tag expressions, which are hard to automatically identify.

Based on language dependency effects (fewer lexical cues in EP than in other languages, such as English) and also on the statistics presented, one can say that ideally around 40% of all interrogatives in broadcast news would be mainly identified by lexical cues – corresponding to wh- questions – while the remaining ones would imply the use of prosodic features to be correctly identified.

5   Punctuation Experiments

This section concerns the automatic detection of question marks in the different corpora, using different combinations of features. This detection will allow the extension of our previous punctuation module which was initially designed to deal only with the two most frequent punctuation marks: *full stop* and *comma* [2]. This module is based on maximum entropy (ME), which provides a clean way of expressing and combining different properties of the information. This is specially useful for the punctuation task, given the broad set of available lexical, acoustic and prosodic features. This approach requires all information to be expressed in terms of features, but the classification is straightforward, making it interesting for on-the-fly usage. All the experiments described in this section follow the same ME-based approach, making use of the MegaM tool [7] for training the maximum entropy models.

The performance results are evaluated using the standard metrics: Precision, Recall, F-measure and SER (Slot Error Rate) [13]. Each slot corresponds to a *question mark*, which means that $Precision = \dfrac{correct}{M}$, $Recall = \dfrac{correct}{N}$, $Fmeasure = \dfrac{2 \times Precision \times Recall}{Precision + Recall}$, and $SER = \dfrac{errors}{N}$, where N is the number of *question marks* in the reference, M is the number of *question marks* in the hypothesis, *correct* are the number of correct *question marks*, and *errors* corresponds to the number of *question mark* errors (misses and false alarms).

In the remaining of this section, we will firstly assess the performance of the module, using only lexical information, learned from a large *corpus* of written data, and then we will study the impact of introducing prosodic features, analyzing the individual contribution of each prosodic feature on spontaneous and prepared speech.

In order to avoid the impact of the recognition errors, all the transcriptions used in these experiments were achieved by means of a forced alignment between the speech and the manual transcriptions, which was performed by the Audimus speech recognition system [1]. The test data of the Alert corpus has about 1% of alignment errors, while the Lectra test corpus has about 5.3% alignment errors. The Coral corpus was not used in this experiment, because of the large percent-

Table 4. Baseline results, achieved with lexical features only

Corpora	#SUs	Correct	Wrong	Missed	Precision	Recall	F	SER
Lectra	1,120	158	32	220	83.2%	41.8%	55.6%	66.7%
Alert	9,552	128	25	287	83.7%	30.8%	45.1%	75.2%
Newspaper	222,127	1100	236	1740	82.3%	38.7%	52.7%	69.6%

age of overlapping speech for which no manually marked time boundaries were available. The reference punctuation concerning the Alert and Lectra corpora was provided by the manual transcriptions of these corpora. The NIST SCLite tool [4] was used for this task, followed by a post-processing step for correcting some SCLite errors.

5.1 Baseline Experiments

The baseline results were achieved by training a discriminative model from the Newspaper corpus containing about 143M words of training data. The following features were used for a given sentence: w_i, w_{i+1}, $2w_{i-2}$, $2w_{i-1}$, $2w_i$, $2w_{i+1}$, $3w_{i-2}$, $3w_{i-1}$, $start\_x$, x_end, len, where: w_i is a word in the sentence, w_{i+1} is the word that follows and $nw_{i\pm x}$ is the n-gram of words that starts x positions after or before the position i. $start\_y$ and y_end features are also used for identifying word n-grams occurring either at the beginning or a the end of the sentence. len corresponds to the number of words in the sentence. The corresponding results are shown in Table 4, where *Correct* is the number of correctly identified sentences, *Wrong* corresponds to false acceptances or insertions, and *Missed* corresponds to the missing slots or deletions. Table 4 reveals a precision around 83% in all corpora, but a small recall. The main conclusion is that the recall percentages using this limited set of features are correlated with the identification of a specific type of interrogative, wh- questions. Recall percentages are comparable to the ones of the wh- question distribution across corpora. As for yes/no and tag questions, they are residually identified.

5.2 Experiments with Lexical and Acoustic Features

The second experiment consisted of re-training the previous model, created from newspaper corpora, with the transcriptions of each training corpus. The ME models were trained on the forced-aligned transcriptions for each speech corpus, bootstrapping from the initial training with newspaper text. As spoken transcriptions contain much more information concerning each word, we have also used all the lexical and acoustic information available. Besides the previous lexical features, the following features were added: *GenderChgs*, *SpeakerChgs*, and *TimeGap*, where *GenderChgs*, and *SpeakerChgs* correspond to changes in speaker gender, and speaker clusters from the current to the next sentence;

---

[4] http://www.itl.nist.gov

Table 5. Results after re-training with transcriptions and adding acoustic features

Corpora	#Correct	#Wrong	#Missed	Precision	Recall	F	SER
Lectra	271	52	107	83.9%	71.7%	77.3%	42.1%
Alert	144	27	271	84.2%	34.7%	49.1%	71.8%

TimeGap corresponds to the time period between the current and following sentence, assuming that sentence boundaries are given by the manual annotation. Lacking a better description for this heterogeneous set, these features will be henceforth designated as *acoustic*. Table 5 illustrates the results achieved with these features, revealing a significant overall performance increase, specially for the Lectra corpus. In this corpus, there are relatively few speaker changes, thus showing the relevance of the *TimeGap* feature.

5.3   Experiments with Prosodic Features

Our next experiments aimed at analyzing the weight and contribution of different prosodic features *per se* and the impact of their combination. Underlying the prosodic feature extraction process are linguistic evidences that nuclear contour, boundary tones, energy slopes, and pauses are crucial to delimit sentence-like units across languages. First, we have tested if the features would perform better on different units of analysis: phones, syllables and/or words. Supported on linguistic findings for EP, *e.g.*, [24,9], we hypothesized that the stressed and post-stressed syllables would be relevant units of analysis to automatically identify punctuation marks. When considering the word as a window of analysis, we are also accounting for the information in the pre-stressed syllables as well.

The feature extraction stage involved several steps. The first step consisted of extracting the pitch and the energy from the speech signal, which was achieved using the Snack Sound Toolkit [5]. Durations of phones, words, and interword-pauses were extracted from the recognizer output [17]. By combining the pitch values with the phone boundaries, we have removed micro-intonation and octave jump effects from the pitch track. Another important step consisted of marking the syllable boundaries as well as the syllable stress. A set of syllabification rules was designed and applied to the lexicon. The rules account fairly well for native words, but still need improvements for words of foreign origin. Finally, we have calculated the maximum, minimum, median and slope values for pitch and energy in each word, syllable, and phone. Duration was also calculated for each one of the previous units.

Features were calculated for each sentence transition, with or without a pause, using the same analysis scope as [20] (last word, last stressed syllable and last voiced phone from the current boundary, and the first word, and first voiced phone from the following boundary). The following set of features has been used: f_0 and energy slopes in the words before and after a silent pause, f_0 and energy differences between these units and also duration of the last syllable and the

---

[5] http://www.speech.kth.se/snack/

Table 6. Recovering the question mark over the Lectra corpus, using prosodic features

Type of Info	Added features	Cor	Wrong	Missed	Prec	Rec	F	SER
Words	Pitch	275	53	103	83.8%	72.8%	77.9%	41.3%
	Energy	266	54	112	83.1%	70.4%	76.2%	43.9%
	Pitch, Energy	273	52	105	84.0%	72.2%	77.7%	41.5%
Syllables	Pitch	269	54	109	83.3%	71.2%	76.7%	43.1%
&	Energy	269	49	109	84.6%	71.2%	77.3%	41.8%
phones	Duration	268	52	110	83.8%	70.9%	76.8%	42.9%
	Pitch, Energy, Duration	268	50	110	84.3%	70.9%	77.0%	42.3%
All Combined		273	50	105	84.5%	72.2%	77.9%	41.0%

Table 7. Recovering the question mark over the Alert corpus, using prosodic features

Type of Info	Added features	Cor	Wrong	Missed	Prec	Rec	F	SER
Words	Pitch	149	27	266	84.7%	35.9%	50.4%	70.6%
	Energy	146	25	269	85.4%	35.2%	49.8%	70.8%
	Pitch, Energy	147	27	268	84.5%	35.4%	49.9%	71.1%
Syllables	Pitch	151	27	264	84.8%	36.4%	50.9%	70.1%
&	Energy	146	24	269	85.9%	35.2%	49.9%	70.6%
phones	Duration	144	28	271	83.7%	34.7%	49.1%	72.0%
	Pitch, Energy, Duration	147	29	268	83.5%	35.4%	49.7%	71.6%
All Combined		146	28	269	83.9%	35.2%	49.6%	71.6%

last phone. With this set of features, we aim at capturing nuclear and boundary tones, amplitude, pitch reset, and final lengthening. This set of prosodic features already proved useful for the detection of the *full stop* and *comma*, showing an improvement of more than 2% SER (absolute) for the Alert corpus [3] relative to the results obtained using only lexical and acoustic features.

The results of recovering question marks over the Lectra and the Alert corpus, using prosodic features, are presented in Tables 6 and 7, respectively. Different combination of features were added to a standard model, which uses lexical and acoustic features, with different impact depending on the corpus. When comparing with the second experiment results, some improvements were achieved, specially for the Lectra corpus, where the combination of all features produced the best results.

Our results partially agree with the ones reported in [20], regarding the contribution of each prosodic parameter, and also the set of discriminative features used, where the most expressive feature turned out to be f_0 slope in the last word of the current boundary and between word transitions (last word of the current boundary and the starting word of the following boundary). As stated by [23], these features are language independent. Language specific properties in our data are related with different durational patterns at the end of an intonational unit and also with different pitch slopes that may be associated with discourse functionalities beyond sentence-form types.

Summing up, when training only with lexical features, wh- questions are expressively identified, whereas tag questions and y/n questions are quite residual,

exception made in the latter case for the bigram *acha que* (do you think). There
are still wh- questions not accounted for, mainly due to very complex structures
hard to disambiguate automatically. When training with all the features, y/n
and tag questions are better identified. We also have verified that prosodic features increase the identification of interrogatives in Alert spontaneous speech
and in the Lectra corpus, *e.g.*, y/n questions with a request to complete a sentence (*e.g.*, *recta das?*) or the tag questions *não é?* in the former corpus, and
certo? in the latter. Even when all the information is combined, we still have
questions that are not well identified, due to the following aspects:

  i) a considerable amount of questions is made in the transition between news-
     reader and reporter with noisy background (such as war scenarios);
 ii) frequent elliptic questions with reduced contexts, *e.g.*, *eu?* (me?) or *José?*;
iii) sequences with disfluencies, *e.g.*, *<é é é> como é que se consegue?*, con-
     trasted with a similar question without disfluencies that was identified: *Como
     é que conseguem isso?* (how do you manage that?);
 iv) sequences starting with the copulative conjunction *e* (and) or the adversative
     conjunction *mas* (but), which usually do not occur at the start of sentences;
  v) false insertions of question marks in sequences with subordinated questions,
     which are not marked with a question mark;
 vi) sequences with more than one consecutive question, randomly chosen, *e.g.*,
     ... nascem duas perguntas: quem? e porquê? (...two questions arise: who?
     and why?);
vii) sequences integrating parenthetical comments or vocatives, *e.g.*, *Foi acidente
     mesmo ou atentado, Noé?* (Was it an accident or an attack, Noé?).

6   Conclusions and Future Work

The availability of different types of corpora with a significantly different percentage of interrogatives amongst them allowed us to verify that the distribution
of interrogative subtypes is also quite distinctive across corpora.

   The set of rules that were specifically created for the automatic identification of interrogative subtypes in EP captures their lexical differences in a fairly
good way. Nevertheless, we extended our analysis in order to discriminate the
problematic structures that were misclassified. For both university lectures and
map-task corpora, tag questions were the most problematic type of interrogative. Due to this fact and also to their frequency in these data, we analyzed
the most frequent pattern of tag questions, *não é?*. We were able to describe
regular phonetic and phonological trends in their production, contributing to
a more substantiated analysis of these structures in spontaneous speech in EP.
We could verify that tag questions are mostly accented, being the most frequent
intonational contour L*+H L%. They are mainly produced with weak forms and
the choice of the form is speaker dependent.

   Reported experiments were performed directly over the forced-aligned data,
using lexical, acoustic and prosodic features. Results pointed out that combining
all the previous features led to the best performance. These experiments also

allowed us to identify pitch related features as the most relevant prosodic features for this task, when used *per se*. These findings compares well with the literature, *e.g.*, [20].

Our efforts in recovering the *question mark* are still in an early stage and can be much improved either by using larger training data or by extending the analysis of pitch slopes with discourse functionalities beyond sentence-form types [16,12]. The extension of these experiments to automatically recognized data is on-going work, integrating extra features such as word confidence measures. However, word error rates are significantly different in the three speech corpora, given that the only in-domain data is currently Alert. The existence of very reduced forms for tag questions also leads us to anticipate many difficulties in correctly identifying them. When working with ASR transcripts, *question mark* detection is performed after automatic sentence boundary detection, which is also achieved using a combination of all features.

To the best of our knowledge, this is the first study for European Portuguese (EP) to quantify the distinct interrogative types and also discuss the weight of lexical and prosodic properties within these structures, based on planned and spontaneous speech data.

Future work directions will encompass similar approaches for other languages, namely, English and Spanish, in order to verify the extend to which our experiments are language-independent.

Acknowledgments. The order of the first two authors was randomly chosen. The authors would like to thank the anonymous reviewers for their helpful comments, and also to Vera Cabarrão for her revision of the Portuguese broadcast news transcripts. This work was funded by FCT projects PTDC/PLP/72404/2006 and CMU-PT/HuMach/0039/2008. The PhD thesis of Helena Moniz is supported by FCT grant SFRH/BD/44671/2008. This work was partially supported by COST Action 2102: "Cross Modal Analysis of Verbal and Non-verbal Communication", by FCT (INESC-ID multiannual funding) through the PIDDAC Program funds, and by DCTI - ISCTE-IUL – Lisbon University Institute.

References

1. Amaral, R., Meinedo, H., Caseiro, D., Trancoso, I., Neto, J.: A prototype system for selective dissemination of broadcast news in European Portuguese. EURASIP. Journal of Advances in Signal Processing 37507 (2007)
2. Batista, F., Caseiro, D., Mamede, N., Trancoso, I.: Recovering capitalization and punctuation marks for automatic speech recognition: Case study for Portuguese broadcast news. Speech Communication 50(10), 847–862 (2008)
3. Batista, F., Moniz, H., Trancoso, I., Meinedo, H., Mata, A.I., Mamede, N.: Extending the punctuation module for European Portuguese. In: Interspeech 2010 (2010)
4. Boakye, K., Favre, B., Hakkani-Tür, D.: Any questions? Automatic question detection in meetings. In: ASRU, Merano, Italy (2009)

5. Carletta, J.: Assessing agreement on classification tasks: The kappa statistic. Computational Linguistics 22, 249–254 (1996)
6. Cruz-Ferreira, M.: Intonation in European Portuguese. In: Hirst, D., Di Cristo, A. (eds.) Intonation systems, pp. 167–178. Cambridge University Press, Cambridge (1965)
7. Daumé III, H.: Notes on CG and LM-BFGS optimization of logistic regression (2004), http://hal3.name/megam/
8. Falé, I.: Fragmento da Prosódia do Português Europeu: as Estruturas Coordenadas. Master's thesis, University of Lisbon (1995)
9. Frota, S.: Prosody and Focus in European Portuguese. Phonological Phrasing and Intonation. Garland Publishing, New York (2000)
10. Frota, S.: Nuclear falls and rises in European Portuguese: a phonological analysis of declarative and question intonation. Probus (14), 113–146 (2002)
11. Frota, S.: The intonational phonology of European Portuguese. In: Sun-uh (ed.) Prosodic Typology II. Oxford University Press, Oxford (2009)
12. Liscombe, J., Venditti, J., Hirschberg, J.: Classifying the form and function of student questions in spoken tutorial dialogs. Elsevier, Amsterdam (submitted)
13. Makhoul, J., Kubala, F., Schwartz, R., Weischedel, R.: Performance measures for information extraction. In: Proc. of the DARPA BN Workshop (1999)
14. Martins, F.: Entoação e organização do enunciado. Master's thesis, University of Lisbon (1986)
15. Mata, A.I.: Questões de entoação e interrogação no Português. Isso é uma pergunta?. Master's thesis, University of Lisbon (1990)
16. Mata, A.I., Santos, A.L.: On the intonation of confirmation-seeking requests in child-directed speech. In: Speech prosody (2010)
17. Moniz, H., Batista, F., Meinedo, H., Abad, A., Trancoso, I., Mata, A.I., Mamede, N.: Prosodically-based automatic segmentation and punctuation. In: Speech Prosody 2010 (2010)
18. Neto, J., Meinedo, H., Amaral, R., Trancoso, I.: The development of an automatic system for selective dissemination of multimedia information. In: International Workshop on Content-Based Multimedia Indexing (2003)
19. Shriberg, E., et al.: Can prosody aid the automatic classification of dialog acts in conversational speech? Language and Speech (41), 439–487 (1998)
20. Shriberg, E., Favre, B., Fung, J., Hakkani-Tur, D., Cuendet, S.: Prosodic similarities of dialog act boundaries across speaking styles. In: Tseng, S.C. (ed.) Linguistic Patterns in Spontaneous Speech, pp. 213–239. Institute of Linguistics, Academia Sinica, Taipei (2009)
21. Silverman, K., Beckman, M., Pitrelli, J., Ostendorf, M., Wightman, C., Price, P., Pierrehumbert, J., Hirschberg, J.: ToBI: a standard for labeling English prosody. In: International Conference on Spoken Language Processing, Banff, Canada (1992)
22. Trancoso, I., Martins, R., Moniz, H., Mata, A.I., Viana, M.C.: The Lectra corpus - classroom lecture transcriptions in European Portuguese. In: LREC 2008 - Language Resources and Evaluation Conference, Marrakesh, Morocco (May 2008)
23. Vassière, J.: Language-independent prosodic features. In: Cutler, A., Ladd, R. (eds.) Prosody: modules and measurements, pp. 55–66. Springer, Heidelberg (1983)
24. Viana, M.C.: Para a Síntese da Entoação do Português. Ph.D. thesis, University of Lisbon (1987)

25. Viana, M.C., Frota, S., Falé, I., Mascarenhas, I., Mata, A.I., Moniz, H., Vigário, M.: Towards a P_ToBI. In: Unpublished Workshop of the Transcription of Intonation in the Ibero-Romance Languages, PaPI 2007 (2007), http://www2.ilch.uminho.pt/eventos/PaPI2007/Extended-Abstract-P-ToBI.PDF
26. Viana, M.C., Trancoso, I., Mascarenhas, I., Duarte, I., Matos, G., Oliveira, L., Campos, H., Correia, C.: Apresentação do projecto Coral - corpus de diálogo etiquetado. In: Workshop de Linguística Computacional, Lisbon, Portugal (April 1998)
27. Vigário, M.: Aspectos da prosódia do Portugês Europeu. Estruturas com advérbios de exclusão e negação frásica. Master's thesis, University of Minho (1995)
28. Wang, D., Narayanan, S.: A multi-pass linear fold algorithm for sentence boundary detection using prosodic cues. In: ICASSP (2004)

Interviewers' Use of Coercive Questioning during a Midterm Period Favorable to the Opposition Party

Angiola Di Conza, Augusto Gnisci, and Angelo Caputo

Department of Psychology, Second University of Naples, Via Vivaldi,
43, 81100, Caserta, Italy
{angiola.diconza,augusto.gnisci}@unina2.it

Abstract. Journalism is generally expected to be objective and neutral—not influenced by political power. Conversely, Italian televised journalism often appears influenced by the distribution of political power. The current study investigates the impact of political changes in Italy on journalistic questioning techniques. Using new software with multimodal and interactive characteristics (Si.Co.D.), we examined the interrogation styles of two interviewers (Vespa and Ferrara), one (Vespa) working for a public television channel (Rai2) and the other (Ferrara) for a private television channel (La7). Specifically, we compared the level of coercion used by these interviewers when questioning politicians from both the center-right and center-left, before and after two elections (2004 European and 2005 Regional elections) that were favorable to the opposition (at the time, center-left). Results showed that the interviewers became more coercive toward the winning coalition (center-left) but in different ways: Vespa reduced his coerciveness toward the governing wing, whereas Ferrara increased his coerciveness toward the opposition. Results are discussed with attention to the political implications of this journalistic bias.

Keywords: Political journalism, Electoral context, Televised interviews, Si.Co.D software.

1 Introduction

Political journalism is considered a worthy instrument for increasing citizens' political sensitivity and awareness. It is of particular importance during the electoral campaigns preceding elections because of its ability to affect voting behavior (particularly in those who are undecided) and, as a consequence, the electoral outcome [1]. In particular, political interviews represent an important mechanism for transmitting information between citizens and their political representatives. Given this role, a collective journalistic style and a common code of journalistic ethics are even more important in today's society.

Researchers have shown interest in analyzing the content and form of political interviews with particular attention to the forces of *coercion* used by the interviewer, or the degree to which an interviewer controls or manipulates the course of the interview through his or her question form. Resting on questions coercion, it is possible to elaborate an index of *toughness* of the interviewer toward one party or another by

A. Esposito et al. (Eds.): COST 2102 Int. Training School 2010, LNCS 6456, pp. 147–154, 2011.
© Springer-Verlag Berlin Heidelberg 2011

computing the bias favoring one political wing over another (general level of coercion of the interviewer toward left-wing and right-wing). It is important to analyze the form and content of both verbal and nonverbal communication. Unfortunately, there is still no instrument able to provide a common way to define and codify the relevant features of language and communication in this way.

Thus, the current study pursues two goals, one methodological and one empirical. First, we propose to test the efficacy of new interactive multimodal software (Si.Co.D., see section 3.2) for categorizing and coding the use of coercive questioning techniques by interviewers. Through this tool, we also propose to compare the differing degrees of coercion used by interviewers with politicians from different political parties at critical political transition points.

To achieve these goals, a study was designed to measure the impact of two elections (European and local elections both unfavorable to the government in charge) on the degree of coercion used by journalists when questioning political candidates in televised interviews. The first journalist selected was a journalist working for a public television channel (Bruno Vespa – Rai1) and the second, a journalist working for a private channel (Giuliano Ferrara – La7). We used a novel coding software, Si.Co.D., to compare two political talk show broadcasts, "Porta a Porta" and "Otto e mezzo" . Bruno Vespa, the anchorman of "Porta a Porta", is considered to be moderate, understandable, gentle and professional but also servile and deferential. In contrast, Giuliano Ferrara, the anchorman of "Otto e mezzo", is known for his aggressive and provocative interviewing style. Even though his strong skills of reasoning and questioning are respected, his verbal arrogance (e.g., interrupting opponents with a combative tone) often causes people to dislike his interviewing style [3].

Italian journalists are often considered too deferential toward the reigning political power and less neutral, independent, objective, impartial, and fair than, for example, their English counterparts [3]. This judgment suggests that journalistic style is, at least partly, a matter of context, and culture is not the only relevant context. If political power is a decisive situational element, the existing distribution of power and the impending changes represent an interesting subject of study. Theoretical considerations and a shared but versatile instrument permit to improve the adaption of the category system to different cultural and situational specificities.

1.1 The Political Context

In 2001, the Italian General Election was unequivocally won by the center-right coalition (with 45.40% support) led by Silvio Berlusconi. However, in the following years, its support declined because of emerging divisions among factions in the coalition and a growing general discontent. The threat of upcoming elections was constant (but did not happen), and the center-right government had to face a difficult test: the coming of the European and local elections. For many Italians and for the government itself, these elections represented a test of the coalition's stability and a measure of electoral trust.

Midway through Berlusconi's leadership (June 2004), Italian citizens were called to vote in the European election and, one year before the end of the legislature, they were called again to vote in local elections (April 2005). The center-left coalition won both elections, the first with a slight margin and the second with a large margin [4] [5].

1.2 Italian Media in 2004–2005

In the last decade, Italian television was composed of both public and private channels. Public channels are Rai1, Rai2 and Rai3 and, historically, are controlled by political factions. Rai1 is a pro-government channel (independent of a specific party, but always linked to the party in power); Rai2 and Rai3 are assigned to the center-right and center-left, respectively. To guarantee impartiality, the governing board of these public channels was appointed by the presidents of the two parliamentary Houses (i.e., Camera and Senato). However, because the Board is typically composed of three experts selected by the majority government and two experts selected by the minority, it often appear strongly affected by political context.

National private channels include the Mediaset group (belonging to Berlusconi's family) and La7 (a channel independent from the government and the Mediaset group). La7 was set up in 2001 in an attempt by the Italian entrepreneur Vittorio Cecchi Gori to create an alternative to Rai and Mediaset. It failed, and in late 2001, the channel was sold again and became a sort of all-news TV targeting only a small audience. However, between 2003 and 2006, the audience of La7 grew (share 3–4%) and, thanks to some programs (such as "Otto e mezzo", considered in this study), captured an even greater proportion of TV viewers (5–6%), although still a smaller number than Rai and Mediaset.

2 Hypotheses

Previous studies have shown that Italian political journalism is less coercive toward the political majority than toward the opposition [1] [3].

We propose to examine differences between Vespa's and Ferrara's journalistic styles and their levels of coerciveness using the Si.Co.D. software designed to allow coding of different linguistic features. We hypothesized that because Rai1 is a public pro-governmental channel, Bruno Vespa would be less coercive with the center-right wing (the current regime) interviewees, whereas Giuliano Ferrara, working for La7 (an independent and more autonomous channel), would be equally coercive toward both the center-right and center-left politicians.

Ferrara's and Vespa's journalistic styles have been compared in a previous study [3]. This study showed that, in general, Ferrara asked more coercive questions than Vespa, but both Ferrara and Vespa asked more coercive questions with center-left representatives (the opposition, at the time) than with center-right representatives (the governing party) regardless of their channel affiliation. The author concluded that even though La7 was more politically independent, both journalists were influenced by the distribution of power and were less coercive with members of the majority coalition.

Based on these results, we were interested in examining whether these same interviewers tended to adapt their behaviors in response to an anticipated shift in Italian politics (from a right-center to a left-center regime), while remaining true to their styles (Ferrara being more coercive and aggressive than Vespa).

We hypothesized that after two significantly positive outcomes for the center-left wing during a center-right governance, journalists would change the focus of their coercive questioning. Specifically, we anticipated an inversion of bias such that journalists would change from being less coercive toward center-right politicians to being less coercive toward center-left representatives because of a journalistic tendency to be more lenient with politicians in power. In other words, we proposed to explore whether journalistic interrogation style would change in advance to favor the anticipated winning party.

3 Method

3.1 Sample

Before (March 2003 – March 2004) and after (April 2005 – April 2006) the 2004 and 2005 elections, we video-recorded 102 broadcasts on Rai1 ("Porta a Porta") and La7 ("Otto e mezzo"). Sixteen politicians were interviewed before and after the two elections. Much of the efforts in the sampling period was devoted to identify the same politicians before and after the two elections. Seven politicians belonged to the left coalition: Piero Fassino (10 broadcasts), Gavino Angius (9), Fausto Bertinotti (8), Luciano Violante (8), Antonio Di Pietro (7), Enrico Boselli (6), and Massimo D'Alema (5). Nine politicians belonged to the right coalition: Renato Schifani (8), Sandro Bondi (6), Fabrizio Cicchitto (6), Marco Follini (6), Carlo Giovanardi (6), Gianfranco Fini (5), Paolo Guzzanti (5), Roberto Castelli (4), and Franco Frattini (4).[1] Once coded, the 102 broadcasts provided 1391 question-answer sequences, 780 asked by Vespa and 611 by Ferrara.

3.2 Si.Co.D.: A New Tool to Code Coercive Questions and Its Observer Reliability

Questions were coded according to a seven-category system, partly based on the literature [6] and partly adapted for cultural differences as guided by a set of structured and unstructured observations conducted by the authors [3]. The coding process was based on the psychological construct of *coercion*, defined as the degree to which a question, by means of its form, imposes its own version of facts on the answer [7] and conveys a set of implicit and explicit assumptions [8, 9]. The final system included the following categories (listed from most to least coercive): Declaration, Tag-question, Yes/no question, Choice, Narrow Wh-question, Broad Wh-question and Indirect. The question form was identified using transcriptions of video-recorded material. Both verbal and nonverbal aspects of the communication were observed, and particular weight was placed on syntactic and intonation criteria. In many languages, the formulation of a sentence is not sufficient to identify it as a question. For example, in Italian, the distinction between a rising and falling intonation is crucial for distinguishing between declarations and yes/no questions.

After categorizing questions into the micro-categories listed above, these micro-categories were then further organized into three macro-categories (Closed, Intermediate and Open coercive question categories) in order to improve cross-cultural comparison

---

[1] For the current statistical analysis, we had to group certain politicians (Follini-Giovanardi, Bondi-Schifani, Frattini-Cicchitto, and Castelli-Guzzanti, all from the right-center) in pairs because of the low number of questions they were asked individually. Therefore, in the current analysis there were actually only five units (politician and politician pairs) from the center-right.

(those used in this contribution).[2] The first three micro-categories (Declaration, Tag-question and Yes/no question) were combined to create the Closed or coercive question macro-category. Choice questions were categorized as Intermediate-level coercive questions. Finally, Narrow and Broad Wh-questions and Indirect questions were categorized as Open or non-coercive questions. The Si.Co.D. software permitted coding of the questions at both a micro- and macro-category level.

To code the questions into micro- and macro-categories, coders were required to complete three phases of multimodal observation (procedures of observation). First, coders had to watch the entire video-recorded interview in an effort to understand the general features of the interview (e.g., duration, names of politicians and of interviewers involved). Next, the coder had to watch the video again, but this time carefully transcribing the question-answer exchange (regarded as the coding unit). In the third phase, they had to watch the video yet again and this time code each of the question-answer exchanges (with the help of the transcripts) into the specified micro- and macro-categories.

However, coding the degree of coercion of a question is complex. To code the question accurately the coder had to attend to multiple linguistic features, including both grammatical form and intonation. Furthermore, the coding always had to be situated within the sequential context of the interview. Third, the coding was multimodal, requiring to observe (watching or listening) audio- or video-recorded materials, transcribe and code them in a computerized format and analyze them through specific software.

The Si.Co.D. software (freeware available at http://osservazione.co.cc/Home/Voci/2010/6/9_Si.co.d..html) is uniquely suited to the types of coding demands present in the current study. For one, it provides a useful tool to simplify the coding process of many category systems, including coercion (micro and macro level); and can be applied to any kind of communication in a question-answer format. It is composed of two sections, the former interactively illustrates the complete category system for coding questions; the latter represents a multimodal catalogue of concrete questions. This catalogue is an interactive database with examples of questions in video or audio format (and their associated transcriptions) from a variety of different sources: political interviews, debates and courtroom examinations (downloaded by radioradicale.it, Creative Commons, 2.5 Italia).

Together with its practical advantages, Si.Co.D. also permits sharing of category systems across authors and across cultures. If cultural differences cannot be reduced due to differences in language, differences among the authors can be reduced through the diffusion of software able to be enriched by the contribution of new theoretical and empirical findings. Si.Co.D. software helps to reduce cross-cultural differences, that might otherwise be problematic, by providing a common coding language. Sharing category systems and specific software can enable comparison not just across studies but across cultures.

In the current study, 80% of the material analyzed was coded by a single observer, 20% was coded by two independent observers and demonstrated high observer reliability, $k = .87$.

---

[2] The macro-categories refer to closure-openness of the questions are less dependent on the grammatical formulation of the question, features that are often language specific. In this way, these macro-categories permit better cross-cultural comparison.

3.3 Procedure and Data Analyses

Once coded, interviewer questions were written into a sequential data file readable by GSEQ 5.0. Then, this data (the probability of coercive questions by each anchorman to each politician before and after the elections) was imported into SPSS.

A mixed 2*2*2 Anchorman*Coalition*Period ANOVA was conducted using the probability of coercive questions as the dependent variable. Anchormen (Vespa vs. Ferrara) and Period (Before vs. After the elections) were within subjects variables, and Coalition (Center-Left vs. Center-Right) was a between subject variable. The V (Pillai's trace) index was used instead of F because it is recommended for small samples. Paired sample t-tests were used for post hoc comparisons. Given the small number of politicians from the right and left parties, we also performed planned comparisons (paired sample t tests), specifically comparing the two anchormen within each coalition before and after the elections.

4   Results

The ANOVA revealed two significant effects. There was a main effect of Anchorman ($F(1, 10)=4.94$, $p=.05$, $\eta^2=.33$). Ferrara (.73, $SD=.02$) was, in general, more coercive than Vespa (.68, $SD=.02$). There was also a significant interaction of Anchorman*Period ($F(1, 10)=20.67$, $p=.001$, $\eta^2=.67$). Post hoc paired sample t-tests showed that before the elections, Vespa and Ferrara asked a similar number of coercive questions ($t(11)=1.71$, $p=.12$), whereas after the elections, Ferrara asked more coercive questions than Vespa ($t(11)=-5.63$, $p<.001$). Before the elections, 72% of Vespa's questions were coercive ($SD=.02$) and 66% of Ferrara's were coercive ($SD=.38$). In contrast, after the elections, 64% of Vespa's questions were coercive ($SD=.03$) whereas 80% of Ferrara's were coercive ($SD=.02$). See Figure 1.

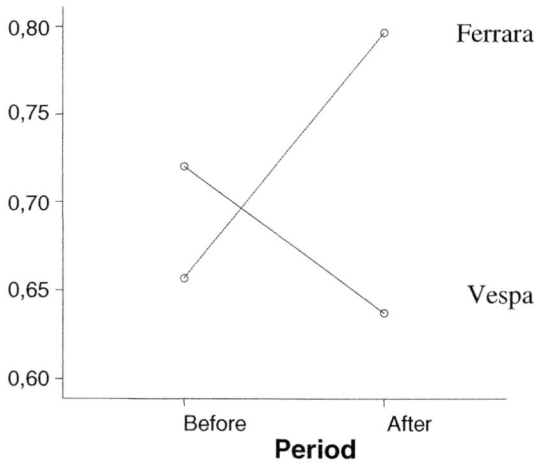

Fig. 1. Average levels of coercion used by each anchorman before and after the elections

We also compared the two anchormen's coercive questioning within each coalition across the two periods. A paired sample t-test showed that Vespa used a similar level of coercive questions with politicians from the left before and after the elections ($t(6)=1.47$, $p=.19$). In contrast, Ferrara increased his coercive questioning with politicians from the left ($t(6)=-3.57$, $p=.01$) from 70% ($SD=.10$) to 81% ($SD=.08$). Furthermore, Ferrara used the same level of coercive questions with politicians from the right before and after the elections ($t(4)=-2.01$, $p=.11$), while Vespa decreased his coercive questioning of politicians from the right from 70% ($SD=.05$) to 59% ($SD=.12$). In conclusion, Ferrara asked politicians from the left more coercive questions, and Vespa asked politicians from the right fewer coercive questions.

5 Discussion and Conclusions

The aim of this study was twofold. First, we wanted to test the efficacy of new software called Si.Co.D. for coding coercive questions in a sample of political interviews.

Si.Co.D. provided good training and calibration of the coders and good inter-observer reliability. It proved to be a powerful tool as it provided a simple and usable way to identify the conceptual definitions for each category and the hierarchical flow in which the questions were organized, using a rich catalogue of examples of each category and their corresponding transcriptions. Sharing this instrument with social scientists may help to identify a common standard for coding the degree of coercion in questions from a variety of contexts and languages, and thereby promote cross-cultural study. Thus, beyond the practical advantages of the Si.Co.D. software (e.g., consistency of training, ease of use, standardization of practice), the software may also contribute to the debate on coercive questioning in journalism and to theoretical advances in general.

The second objective of the current study was to compare the use of coercive questioning by two political TV journalists (Vespa and Ferrara) during a period of political change (from center-right to center-left) by taking advantage of new multimodal software specializing in coding question forms.

We hypothesized that the change in power (from the governing center-right to the center-left) would affect the two journalists' interviewing style. Our results showed that before the elections both journalists used the same level of coercion, but that after the election, Ferrara was more coercive than Vespa. Furthermore, in contrast to our hypothesis, after the center-left won in the European and Regional elections, Vespa did not modify his level of coercion toward the center-left, but actually became less coercive toward the center-right (which had been defeated). Moreover, Ferrara became more coercive toward the center-left and did not change his level of coercion toward the center-right. In short, unlike what we had predicted, neither journalist became more deferential toward the impending, although not yet elected, center-left.

One possible explanation of these results concerns both the indexes of coercion used in this study, and the impending victory that the center-left was going to obtain in the following political elections. Our second sampling was done after the two won-by-the-left elections but before the 2006 General Elections. It is possible that during this particular period, the center-left coalition was considered a valid candidate to win the election in 2006 and consequently to rule the nation. Therefore, approaching the political elections, there could have been a saliency effect that put the center-left politicians at center stage. Coercive journalism is an effective way to obtain precise and pertinent information without losing control of the interview (which is why journalistic style in general is characterized by coercion) [1]. It is possible that coercive questioning was increased toward the center-left to answer key questions as the party was gaining importance. A different index of questioning might have produced different results. Coercive questioning allows the respondent to provide a direct response typically with no negative impact. However, other questioning techniques, such as face-threatening, can have a negative impact if the respondent is not able to provide a good answer to a potentially damaging question. Thus, face-threatening questions might provide a better measure of the interviewer's true partiality [3].

References

1. Gnisci, A., Bonaiuto, M.: Grilling politicians: Politicians' answers to questions in television interviews and legal examinations. J. Lang. Soc. Psychol. 22, 384–413 (2003)
2. Bull, P.: Slipperiness, evasion, and ambiguity. Equivocation and facework in non committal political discourse. J. Lang. Soc. Psychol. 27, 333–344 (2008)
3. Gnisci, A.: Coercive and Face-Threatening Questions to Left-Wing and Right-Wing Politicians During Two Italian Broadcasts: Conversational Indexes of Par Conditio for Democracy Systems. J. Appl. Soc. Psychol. 38, 1179–1210 (2008)
4. Ignazi, P.: Italy. Eur. J. Polit. Res 44, 1063–1070 (2005)
5. Ignazi, P.: Italy. Eur. J. Polit. Res. 45, 1143–1151 (2006)
6. Bull, P., Elliott, J.: Level of threat: Means of assessing interviewer toughness and neutrality. J. Lang. Soc. Psychol. 17, 220–244 (1998)
7. Danet, B., Hoffman, K.B., Kermish, N., Rafn, H.J., Stayman, D.G.: An ethnography of questioning in the courtroom. In: Shuy, R.W., Shnukal, A. (eds.) Language use and the uses of language, pp. 222–234. Georgetown University Press, Washington (1976)
8. Harris, S.: Interviewers' questions in broadcast interviews. Belfast Working Papers in Language and Linguistics 8, 50–85 (1986)
9. Woodbury, H.: The strategic use of questions in court. Semiotica 48, 197–228 (1984)

Emotions and Speech Disorders: Do Developmental Stutters Recognize Emotional Vocal Expressions?

Anna Esposito[1,2] and Alda Troncone[1]

[1] Second University of Naples, Department of Psychology, Caserta, Italy
[2] International Institute for Advanced Scientific Studies (IIASS), Vietri sul Mare, Italy
`iiass.annaesp@tin.it, alda.troncone@unina2.it`

Abstract. This paper intends to evaluate the developmental stutters' ability to recognize emotional vocal expressions. To this aim, a group of diagnosed developmental child stutters and a fluent one are tested on the perception of 5 basic vocal emotional states (anger, fear, happiness, surprise and sadness) extracted from Italian movies and each produced by two actors and two actresses. The results show significant perceptual differences for all the emotional states under examination except for anger and call for further experimental data in assessing the ability of stutters to recognize emotional voices. The reported data are of interest for the development of improved automatic rehabilitation tools for which context specificity must be taken into account for a more friendly and effective human-machine interaction.

Keywords: Emotional vocal expressions of emotion, stuttering disorders.

1 Introduction

The present work starts from the conclusions of [9-10] and attempts to assess them in a more controlled and specifically experimental set up that differs from that proposed by [9-10] in the following features:

1. The subjects are all of the same age both in the control and experimental group;
2. The vocal expressions are produced by male and female voices and all have a different meaning, such that the subject's answers cannot depend on the semantic/grammatical meaning of the sentence (which was the same in [9-10] even though produced with different emotional intonation);
3. The stimuli are extracted from movies and therefore are set in an emotional context ecologically validated by the movie director;
4. Five instead of two among the six basic emotions (happiness, fear, surprise, anger, and sadness) defined by [27] are taken into account allowing to assess the differences independently from the speaker and to extend their conclusions to a larger range of emotional vocal expressions.

The present study therefore, focalizes on the ability of stuttering and fluent children of the same age to recognize emotional vocal expressions in quasi-noisy environmental conditions, and leaves out the possible neuropsychological and neuranatomical correlates. The questions we are trying to answer are: a) Does developmental stuttering

A. Esposito et al. (Eds.): COST 2102 Int. Training School 2010, LNCS 6456, pp. 155–164, 2011.

impair the children' ability to recognize emotional states from speech? b) Is this impairment specific of the type of emotion?

2   Scientific Background

In a daily body-to-body interaction, emotional expressions play a vital role in creating social linkages, producing cultural exchanges, influencing relationships and communicating experiences. Emotional information is transmitted and perceived simultaneously through verbal (the semantic content of a message) and nonverbal (facial expressions, vocal expressions, gestures, paralinguistic information) communicative tools and contacts and interactions are highly affected by the way this information is communicated/perceived by/from the addresser/addressee. Therefore, research devoted to the understanding of the relationship between verbal and non-verbal communication modes, and to investigate the perceptual and cognitive processes involved in the perception of emotional states, as well as the role played by communication impairments in their recognition is particularly relevant in the field of Human-Human and Human-Computer Interaction both for build up and harden human relationships and for developing friendly and emotionally coloured assistive technologies.

In the present paper, consideration is put on stuttering, a mild speech communication disorder. Stuttering may be defined as an involuntary disfluency during speech production and consists in an overt and observable breakdown of the speech fluency which manifests itself with repetitions of sounds, syllables, words or phrases, and/or long interruptions and long pauses between articulated speech sounds [19].

The stuttering phenomena can be observed at any age; nonetheless it is mostly experienced by young children during their development and more precisely during the acquisition of language skills. In fact, it is in 5% of children between 2 and 5 years of age, that the most common form of idiopathic stuttering manifests itself without any apparent physiological cause (such as a cerebral damage and/or an articulatory failure of the motor program for speech production). Generally, the disorder disappears in about 80% of these children leaving only 1% of adult stutters equally distributed per social, economic, cultural and/or ethnical status. Today it is estimated that 3 million people in the USA and 55 million people all over the world stutter [6, 20].

Research investigating the aetiology of developmental stuttering has been conducted for over 30 years in several scientific fields including hearing, linguistics, physiological, psychological and behavioural sciences, nevertheless it remains a phenomenon not completely understood [6] and up to now, no single, exclusive cause of developmental stuttering has been identified. Numerous theories and hypotheses have been advanced in an attempt to provide a rationale and the recent explicative models include psychological, linguistic and neuropsychological factors as well as cognitive abilities, genes, gender and environmental influences [20]. Currently, there is a general consensus to assume that there are several factors contributing to stuttering that call for the adoption of a multi factorial aetiological model [16].

A huge amount of contributions, have compared stutters and fluent subjects providing either empirical or physiological evidence for structural and functional differences in the brains of stutters as well as differences in their cognitive and emotional perception processes [1, 7, 22]. Some of these studies attribute to adult and child stutters compared to typical fluent subjects [23] different cognitive abilities, longer reaction times in cognitive tasks of growing complexity, lower speech performance, poorer verbal expressions and poorer sensory motor responses, due to the increasing difficulties in correctly implementing phonological encoding processes under mounting cognitive stress (caused by stuttering). Recently, Bosshardt [5] has showed that adult stutters compared to typical fluent ones exhibit differences in the activations of the neuronal subsystems involved in the planning of speech and emotions, causing slowness in encoding semantic information (due to the need to dedicate part of their attentional processes to the control of their speech disorder). This latter result is, nevertheless, controversial since such atypical neural activations could be a consequence rather than the cause of the stuttering itself [7, 8, 22]. Support to this hypothesis comes from studies devoted to evaluate emotional, social, and psychological behaviours of stuttering children. In fact, it has been shown that stutters manifest a good self-esteem [2-3] but elevated social anxiety levels [3, 4, 25] and are more at risk of developing phobia [4] or other anxiety disturbs [17] and more reluctant and worried to publicly discuss their disorder [2]. There is also evidence of differences related to the their ability to control and regulate their own emotions since they show a greater emotional reactivity to stressing situations, a minor ability to restore a calm status after an emotional stressing condition, and minor attentive flexibility (intended here as the capacity to move attention and focus when necessary) [8, 26].

Of particular interest is the study of Dimitrieva et al. [9-10] devoted to evaluate the differences between stutter and fluent children in their capacity to recognize emotional vocal expressions under demanding conditions. In this study, 44 stutters aged from 7 to 17 years are compared to 62 typical fluent ones of the same age (grouped into three age groups, namely from 7 to 10, from 11 to 13, and from 14 to 17) to assess their effectiveness in recognizing happy, angry, and neutral emotional vocal expressions produced by an actor both in a quiet and noisy environmental condition. The results reveal a minor ability (in all the three age groups) of the stutters, compared to the fluent children, to recognize such emotional vocal expressions both in the quiet and noisy condition. In addition, the stutter performance improved with increasing age but was always significantly lower than that of normally speaking pears, suggesting a developmental delay of the cognitive processes devoted to the identification of emotions. More in details, the observed differences (considering all together the age, the gender, and the emotions) in the two (quite, noisy) environmental conditions leads the authors to assume a minor activation of the right hemisphere (which is considered to be implied in the processing of emotional information [21]) with respect to the left one that disappears in presence of noise because the functional equilibrium between the two hemispheres is restored. As further support to their speculation, the authors showed that the stutter reaction time, contrarily to what is observed in typical speaking children, was not affected by noise. The authors speculate on these results attributing to stutters different sensorial and processing characteristics of the acoustic signal.

3   Materials and Methods

3.1   Participants

The reported experiment was carried out on two groups of children: 16 stutters, and 30 fluents, both aged between 7 and 8.The 16 stutters were recruited at Phoniatric

Outpatients in Naples, Italy (Azienda Ospedaliera di Rilievo Nazionale Santobono Pausilipon, struttura Dipartimentale di Audiologia e Foniatria; Azienda Universitaria Policlinico, Clinica ORL Ospedale Gesù e Maria, reparto di Foniatria e Audiologia) and at Rehabilitation Centres in the Campania province, Italy. At the time of the present experiment they had all been diagnosed as suffering (during the last previous three years) of a developmental stuttering disorder with different degrees of gravity, and few of them had started a rehabilitation procedure. The control group consisted of 30 children (16 males and 14 females) aged between 7 and 8 recruited at a primary school in Naples, Italy.

3.2 Investigation Tools

In order to evaluate the ability to recognize emotional feelings, both the experimental and control group was asked to participate at an audio test *for the recognition of emotional vocal expressions* – where the subjects listened to 20 emotional vocal stimuli. The *"emotional voices"* were selected by one of the authors from a database of emotional voices already assessed and published in literature [11-12]. In addition, the stimuli were validated by 30 adults obtaining the recognition scores reported in Figure 1. The *"emotional voices"* are Italian sentences of short durations, with a semantic content not related to the expressed emotion. They were selected from famous Italian movies, acted by famous Italian actors/actresses expressing vocal emotional expressions of *happiness*, *sadness*, *fear*, *surprise*, and *anger*. Generally, the stimuli used in these experiments are collected asking an actor/actress to produce a given sentence with different emotional contents (see for example the description of the stimuli in [9, 10]). In this respect, the actor/actress is portraying the requested emotional state from scratch, in a laboratory setting, without an external and internal context of reference that is instead provided when making a movie. The absence of a

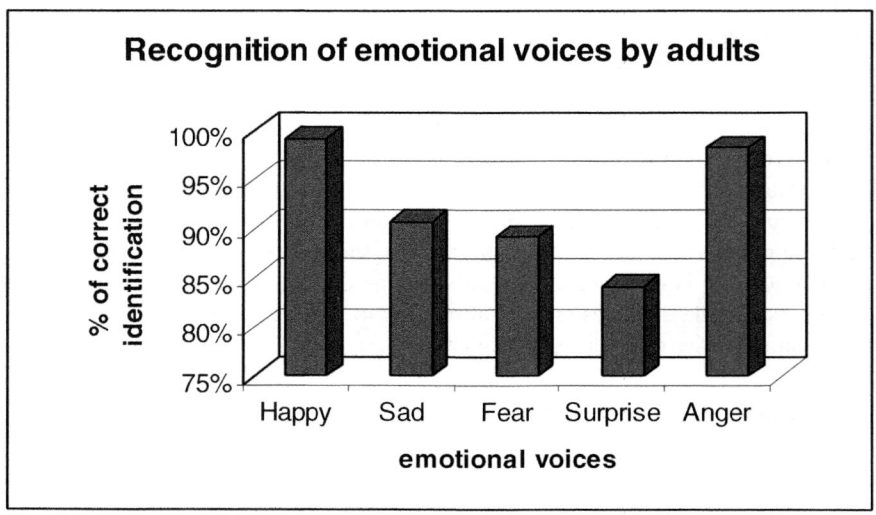

Fig. 1. Adults' percentage of agreement on the five emotional voices under examination

frame of reference may make such stimuli less ecological than those extracted from movies. In fact, being the audio extracted from movies, it was affected by the environmental noise of the scene from which it was extracted. In addition, the actor/actress was not asked to make emotionally coloured a given sentence from scratch, but rather his/her coloured vocal expression was produced in the context of the movie scene and his/her movie performance was assessed by the movie director. More details on the stimuli can be found in [13-15]. Participants from both the experimental and control group were asked to listen to the sentences and label them using either one of the five emotional labels reported above or the label "other".

3.3 Procedures

Only the children satisfying the diagnosis of developmental stuttering were included in the experimental group. Each selected child underwent a speech examination, during which anamnesis information was gathered with particular attention to several factors such as: 1) age when the disorder appeared; 2) presence of the disorder among relatives; 3) linguistic and communication competence, psycho motor abilities, attentional performance and child's hearing abilities. In particular, the children fluency was evaluated through tests on a) spontaneous verbal production (the child was asked some questions about everyday life); b) guided verbal production (reading a text never read before; re-telling of a story previously read); c) verbal production of automatic sequences of days, months, numbers, etc.

The children that passed the above tests and the speech exams were then evaluated in their ability to recognize vocal emotional expressions using the stimuli described above. After creating a suitable *setting* (free of distractions and any disturbing events) and verifying the complete understanding of the task, the 20 emotional vocal expressions were randomly presented to the children through headphones. For each stimulus listened he/she had to choose the emotion he/she thought was being expressed by putting a cross in an answer grid indicating whether the listened emotional vocal expression was one of the five listed above or another not listed for which he/she must provide the appropriate label or no emotion at all. If needed, they were allowed to listen to the stimuli as many times as necessary before choosing the answer.

The subjects of the control group carried out the *test for the recognition of emotional vocal expressions* following the same procedure used for the experimental group.

4   Data Analysis

The percentage of correct identification obtained by the experimental and control group are reported as confusion matrices in Tables 1 and 2 and displayed in Figure 2.

No correlation was found between number of mistakes and current children's age (Pearson correlation coefficient r= 0.15). Similarly, no correlation was found between number of mistakes and the age when the disorder manifested itself (Pearson correlation coefficient $r = 0.065$). These results suggest that the ability of stuttering children to recognize emotional vocal expressions may not be affected by the child's age and the time passed from the onset of the disorder.

Table 1. Confusion matrix for fluent children (N=30)

	Happiness	Sadness	Fear	Surprise	Anger	Other
Happiness	**92.5**	0	1.5	4	1	1
Sadness	1	**83.3**	10.7	1.5	1	2.5
Fear	1	12.5	**73.4**	5.8	5.8	1.5
Surprise	10.7	2.5	13.4	**55**	3.4	15
Anger	0	1	5.7	0	**90**	3.3

Table 2. Confusion matrix for stuttering children (N=16)

	Happiness	Sadness	Fear	Surprise	Anger	Other
Happiness	**65.62**	6.25	3.13	12.5	6.25	6.25
Sadness	1.5	**57.8**	12.5	11	1.6	15.6
Fear	12.5	28.13	**29.69**	6.25	14.1	9.33
Surprise	28.1	6.25	11	**18.75**	23.4	12.5
Anger	3.13	9.32	3.13	3.13	**79.69**	1.6

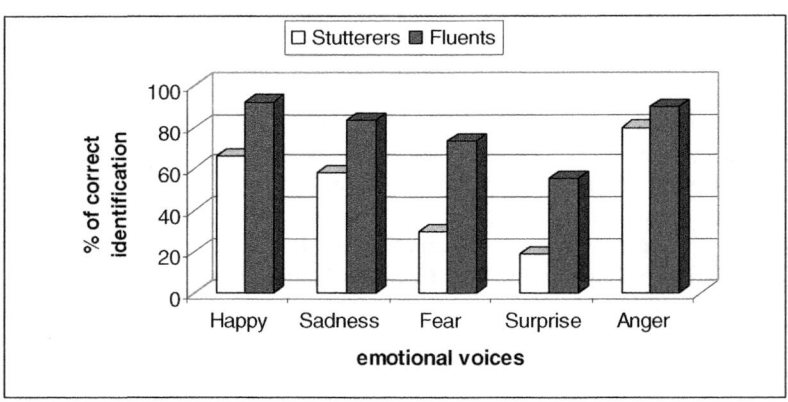

Fig. 2. Percentage of correct identification for the five emotional voices under examination by stuttering (white bars) and fluent (black bars) children

χ^2 statistics, with $\alpha=0.001$, were performed to assess if the answers were significantly different between the experimental and control group. The results are illustrated in Table 3.

The statistics showed that there were significant perceptual differences between stuttering and fluent children for all the emotions except anger.

Table 3. Perceptual significance between agreements provided by stuttering and fluent children

χ^2 Critique= 10.83	
a=0.001	
Anger	3.771
Fear	**32.68**
Surprise	**22.44**
Sadness	**14.28**
Happiness	**21.51**

5 Discussion

The reported data show that there are indeed significant differences in the perception of vocal emotional expressions between developmental stutter and fluent children.

These differences appear to be independent of the child ages and the stuttering duration. This result suggests that stuttering is a disorder related to both speech production and perception and therefore its aetiology cannot only be attributed to a failure of the speech motor program, but it calls for further investigations. We argue that the difference between stuttering and fluent children in recognizing emotional vocal expression can be attributed to the discomfort suffered by the former during social interaction. Interactional circumstances arouse in stuttterers fear, anger, shame, embarrassment, emotional tension, and anxiety and these emotional feelings compromise their ability to recognize the vocal emotional message conveyed by others. This hypothesis is supported by previous studies that find out that there is a discomfort of the subjects' attitudes toward their condition (see [3, 4, 25]).

The present results extend the significant differences found in the work of [9-10] for happiness also to surprise, fear, and sadness, making this impairment specific to these four emotions. Nonetheless, contrarily to what has been reported by [9-10] anger was similarly perceived both by the experimental and the control group. These differences can be attributed to the wide age range used by the authors and/or to their less naturalistic experimental set-up that used the same actor and the same sentence with different emotional intonations. This may have made the stimuli strongly dependent on the actor's voice quality and his ability to simulate a particular emotional intonational contour and may have produced a perceptual confusion in the listeners, particularly for anger. In addition, for this analysis, children were tested on a considerable number of stimuli (120 stimuli, against the 18 proposed in [9-10]) and therefore significant differences show up more consistently. However, given the restricted number of subjects participating to our experiment, more data are necessary in order to assess the difference between our and Dimitrieva et al. [9, 10] results and to determine how stuttering affects the perception and the decoding of emotional states.

The fact that anger was equally well recognized by the control and the experimental group was not unexpected. Previous experiments devoted to assess the amount of emotional information conveyed by the visual and auditory channel using audio alone, video alone and combined audio and video emotional stimuli, extracted from Italian and American English movies and cross culturally assessed on both the languages by Italian and American English subjects revealed that anger was very well recognized independently of the condition and the language [28, 29].

It could be that anger, having a clear functional value for survival entails an easier decoding process than that required to recognize the others basic emotions which prevails over the arousal of stress, emotional tension, and anxiety that stutteres experience in social interactions. We can speculate that identifying anger in the interlocutor may trigger cognitive self-defence mechanisms that are critical for the perceiver's survival, and therefore undergo to a different decoding process that allows its recognition independently of the cultural environment, the communication mode, and the stuttering speech disorder. However, both the present and Esposito et al.'s results on recognition of anger apply to Italian child and to Italian and American adults. More data are needed to verify if the above speculations can be extended to other languages.

6 Conclusions

The present work reports data on the ability of developmental stutters to decode and recognize emotional vocal voices and show that stutters' performance is significantly lower than typical peers for happiness, fear, sadness, and surprise but not for anger suggesting a different perceptual processing of this emotion due probably to its clear survival functional value. The results would be of great utility in the field of human machine interaction, favouring the implementation of more effective and natural speech synthesis and interactive dialog systems devoted to the rehabilitation of this disorder (see [30] for more details).

Acknowledgements

This work has been supported by the European projects: COST 2102 "Cross Modal Analysis of Verbal and Nonverbal Communication", http://cost2102.cs.stir.ac.uk/ and COST ISCH TD0904 "TMELY: Time in MEntal activitY, http://www.timely-cost.eu/ Acknowledgements go to Dr. Maria Teresa Riviello for her useful comments and suggestions, to Miss Tina Marcella Nappi for her editorial help, to Dr. Elvira Tozzi, and Dr. Luisa Villone for their help in recruiting the children participating to the experiment. Acknowledgements go also to Miss Assunta Mazzella for helping in the child assessment.

References

1. Andrews, G., Craig, A., Feyer, A.M., Hoddinott, S., Howie, P., Neilson, M.: Stuttering: a Review of Research Findings and Theories circa 1982. J. Speech. Hear. Disord. 48, 226–246 (1983)
2. Blood, G.W., Blood, I.M., Tellis, G.M., Gabel, R.M.: A Preliminary Study of Self-Esteem, Stigma, and Disclosure in Adolescents who Stutters. J. Fluency Disord. 28, 143–159 (2003)
3. Blood, G.W., Blood, I.M., Maloney, K., Meyer, C., Qualss, C.D.: Anxiety Levels in Adolescents who Stutters. J. Commun. Disord. 40, 452–469 (2007)

4. Blumgart, E., Tran, Y., Craig, A.C.: Social Anxiety Disorder in Adults who Stutter. Depress. Anxiety, 1–6 (2010)
5. Bosshardt, H.-G.: Cognitive Processing Load as a Determinant of Stuttering: Summery of a Research Programme. Clin. Linguist. Phon. 20(5), 371–385 (2006)
6. Büchel, C., Sommer, M.: What Causes Stuttering? PLoS. Biol. 2, 159–163 (2004)
7. Chang, S.E.: Brain Anatomy Differences in Childhood Stuttering. Neuroimage 39(3), 1333–1344 (2008)
8. D'Ambrosio, M.: Balbuzie. Percorsi Teorici e Clinici Integrati. McGraw-Hill, Milano (2005)
9. Dmitrieva, E.S., Gel'man, V.Y., Zaitseva, K.A.: Perception of the Emotional Component of Speech by Stuttering Children against the Background of Noise: I. Analysis of the Efficiency of the Identification of Various Emotions. Hum. Psysiol. 26(3), 258–264 (2000)
10. Dmitrieva, E.S., Gel'man, V.Y.: Perception of the Emotional Speech Component by Stuttering Children Associated with Noise: Communication II. Analysis of the Temporal Characteristics of the Recognition of Different Emotions. Hum. Psysiol. 27(1), 36–41 (2001)
11. Esposito, A., Riviello, M.T.: The New Italian Audio and Video Emotional Database. In: Esposito, A., Campbell, N., Vogel, C., Hussain, A., Nijholt, A. (eds.) COST 2102. LNCS, vol. 5967, pp. 406–422. Springer, Heidelberg (2010)
12. Esposito, A., Riviello, M.T., Di Maio, G.: The COST 2102 Italian Audio and Video Emotional Database. In: Apolloni, B., Bassis, S., Morabito, C.F. (eds.) Neural Nets. WIRN 2009., vol. 204, pp. 51–61. IOSpress, Amsterdam (2009)
13. Esposito, A.: The Amount of Information on Emotional States Conveyed by the Verbal and Nonverbal Channels: Some Perceptual Data. In: Stylianou, Y., Faundez-Zanuy, M., Esposito, A. (eds.) COST 277. LNCS, vol. 4391, pp. 245–268. Springer, Heidelberg (2007)
14. Esposito, A.: Affect in Multimodal Information. In: Tao, J., Tan, T. (eds.) Affective Information Processing, pp. 211–234. Springer, Heidelberg (2008)
15. Esposito, A.: The Perceptual and Cognitive Role of Visual and Auditory Channels in Conveying Emotional Information. Cogn. Comput. J. 1(2), 268–278 (2009)
16. Gordon, N.: Stuttering: Incidence and Causes. Dev. Med. Child Neurol. 44(4), 278–281 (2002)
17. Iverach, L., O'Brien, S., Jones, M., Block, S., Lincoln, M., Harrison, E., Hewat, S., Menzies, R.G., Packman, A., Kraaimaat, F.W., Vanryckeghem, M., Van Dam-Baggen, R.: Stuttering and Social Anxiety. J. Fluency Disord. 27(4), 319–331 (2002)
18. Onslow, M.: Prevalence of Anxiety Disorders among Adults Seeking Speech Therapy for Stuttering. J. Anxiety Disord. 23, 928–934 (2009)
19. Prasse, J.E., Kikano, G.E.: Stuttering: an Overview. Am. Fam. Physician 77(9), 1271–1276 (2008)
20. Packman, A., Onslow, M.: Searching for the Cause of Stuttering. Lancet 360, 355–356 (2002)
21. Saxby, L., Bryden, M.P.: Left-Ear Superiority in Children for Processing Auditory Emotional Material. Dev. Psychol. 20(1), 72–80 (1984)
22. Watkins, K.: Structural and Functional Abnormalities of the Motor System in Developmental Stuttering. Brain 131, 50 (2007)
23. Weber-Fox, C., Spencer, R.M.C., Spruill, J.E., Smith, A.: Phonologic Processing in Adults Who Stutter: Electrophysiological and Behavioral Evidence. J. Speech Lang. Hear. Res. 47, 1244–1258 (2004)
24. Zerneri, L.: Manuale di Foniatria e Compendio di Logopedia. Edizioni Omega, Torino (1989)

25. Kraaimaat, F.W., Vanryckeghem, M., Van Dam-Baggen, R.: Stuttering and Social Anxiety. J. Fluency Disord. 27(4), 319–331 (2002)
26. Karrass, J., Walden, T.A., Conture, E.G., Graham, C.G., Arnold, H.S., Hartfield, K.N., Schwenk, K.A.: Relation of Emotional Reactivity and Regulation to Childhood Stuttering. J. Commun. Disord. 39(6), 402–423 (2006)
27. Ekman, P.: An Argument for Basic Emotions. Cogn. Emot. 6, 169–200 (1992)
28. Esposito, A., Riviello, M.T.: The Cross-Modal and Cross-Cultural Processing of Affective Information. In: Apolloni, B., Bassis, S., Morabito, C.F. (eds.) Neural Nets. WIRN 2010. IOS Press, Amsterdam (in press, 2010)
29. Esposito, A., Riviello, M.T., Bourbakis, N.: Cultural Specific Effects on the Recognition of Basic Emotions: A Study on Italian Subjects. In: Holzinger, A., Miesenberger, K. (eds.) USAB 2009. LNCS, vol. 5889, pp. 135–148. Springer, Heidelberg (2009)
30. Fragopanagos, N., Taylor, J.G.: Emotion recognition in human–computer interaction. Neural Networks 18, 389–405 (2005)

Representing Meaning in Mind:
When Predicate Argument Structures Meet Mental Representations

Rosa Volpe

University of Perpignan Via Domitia
Faculty of Humanities, Department of French
52 Paul Alduy, 66000 Perpignan
rosa.volpe@univ-perp.fr

Abstract. This study has as a central focus the role that pre-linguistic non- verbal information plays in the construction of meaning. More specifically this study explores the role that mental representations - triggered by exposure to "visual sentences" - play on the understanding of written sentences describing them. Ninety-four university graduate and undergraduate students participated in this experimental study characterized by wo modalities (plausible vs. implausible) and four different conditions allowing for the matching up of each visual sentence (Image) with the written sentence (Text) describing it (or not). The results, which are meant to measure (1) the length of time that each participant took to decide whether or not the written sentence described the visual one, and (2) the number of errors that occurred during this decision making process, show that the length of time was shorter when both the visual and the written sentence were plausible. More errors occurred when the written text describing the visual sentence was implausible.

Keywords: Verbal and non-verbal, information, mental representation, sentence comprehension, predicate argument structure, construction of meaning.

1 Introduction

To linguists the structure of meaning depends on the organization of discourse, which provides context; to sociolinguists it depends on social interaction; to psycholinguists it essentially depends on perception as well as on tacit and general knowledge about the world.

This article attempts to reconcile these different perspectives by addressing issues related to both linguistic and non-linguistic information inherent in the process of meaning construction. With this respect, Jackendoff's correspondence rules attempt to explain how 'what we see becomes what we say' (1). Pier Paolo Pasolini approached this same issue by introducing the concept of 'im-sign' (image-sign) to emphasize the role that images, and not only linguistic signs, play in the construction of meaning. In Pasolini's own words, this is what happens to all of us by simply strolling down the street.

A. Esposito et al. (Eds.): COST 2102 Int. Training School 2010, LNCS 6456, pp. 165–179, 2011.
© Springer-Verlag Berlin Heidelberg 2011

By simply walking down the street, we experience the world through images alone: the presence of others all around, theirs expressions, their gestures, their actions, their silence . . . We are inhabited by a world of images (. . .) filled with meaning.

According to this view, our well-organized linguistic productions are nothing but a translation into words of previous cognitive structures that get activated to reproduce the world we live in (2). Because these structures are based on perceptual information, their characteristic is that their nature is extra-linguistic. In discourse they are accounted for by predicate argument structures, also spoken in terms of verbs' thematic roles (3).

1.1 Non-linguistic Information and the Construction of Meaning in Sentences

We experience daily events and live through various situations trying to answer questions of this type: "who, does, what, when, where, how, why . . . ". Such 'tacit knowledge' seems to constitute the 'backbone' of linguistic processing enabling comprehension and production, and it is carried out by each verb's thematic roles. Take for example, the verb *to accuse*: it has been shown that the mental representations it solicits are those of *agent* and *patient* and that they derive from previous experiences such as the witnessing of interactions of people accusing each other, or other people, and/or from various descriptions of such facts. Henceforth, individuals seem to construct world knowledge by organizing for themselves an 'inner' model which includes all of the information each object comes with, as well as all of the situations which it manifests, including the order of events into which it evolves (4).

A study by Cordier and Pariollaud (5) has shown that the understanding of a verb's meaning comes with both general and specific mastery of the meaning of its components. The mental representation of a given situation is thus tied to the structure of the verb. Such representations imply both the semantic components of the verbal core itself and the components associated to its thematic roles (6). On the occasion of an experimental study, subjects were introduced to a particular verb 'out of context,' that is to say without mentioning its thematic roles. Yet, each participant to the data collection spontaneously evoked out loud the verb's thematic role(s) to oneself. Such behavior has been interpreted as indicating that there exists in memory a link between the verb and its thematic roles and it has been concluded that an individual's general knowledge about the world together with his/her mental representations of it play a fundamental role on the structure of meaning. Because verbs carry linguistic information about the syntax of the argument structures they bring about, it can be assumed that verbs give access to the overall structure of the situation and that linguistic competence depends on such knowledge, known as schema (or schemata). If we take the verb *to entertain*, it is not intuitively possible to conceive of a situation of having to entertain without also conceiving of someone who will take advantage of such situation (7).

This being said, would it be possible to conceive of the notion of predicate argument structure as referring to anything else than the sole concepts of agent, patient and instrument of the verb?

1.2 Perception and Language Processes

Le Ny's approach to verb semantics has been said to be 'transcognitive', meaning that it includes notions borrowed from cognitive psychology, linguistics, logics, philosophy, biology and neurobiology (8). According to Le Ny, semantic representations are nothing but "concepts in the mind" which correspond to "realities in the universe," and they constitute what he calls "the individual lexicon". In other words, after having heard (or read) the sentence *Kathy met Sophie in the cafeteria after the break,* what is recalled is a semantic post-representation which would match the perceptual representation one might have experienced had one witnessed such an encounter in reality. Visetti attributes to such 'reconstruction' the name of interpretation and/or synopsis, and introduces the role of action (and of its actor) to explain the process of meaning construction (9). Doing so brings about another element, namely the actor's intention to carry out his/her own 'story.' According to Rosenthal, action comes also with anticipation and all together resorts to experience (10). Immediate experience, whether it is a perception, a thought, an expression, a fantasy, is the result of some sort of development in the present time. Rosenthal identifies it as micro-development since it anticipates what it will allow to perceive, understand, or hear. From this perspective, meaning construction becomes an endless process, and the notion of meaning itself acquires a 'generic shade,' where perception takes the place of 'the original modality of experience,' while the notion of microgenetics implies a psychophysical process involving at the same time both the actual body and the field of experience.

2 Theoretical Background and Experimental Design

Understanding the role that mental representations play in the construction of meaning comes with the understanding of the relationship between verbal semantics and predicate argument structures. While they fulfill a specific linguistic function, predicate argument structures also allow for the organization of more general information of extra-linguistic and perceptual nature (11). Henceforth the development of linguistic competence cannot happen without bringing into play a more general world knowledge. Barsalou has claimed that linguistic symbols and their related perceptive symbols happen simultaneously in each person (12). In other words, a schematic memory of a perceptive event rises at the same time as a schematic memory of a linguistic symbol. This means that linguistic and perceptive symbols share the same dynamics.

Although we forget about the organization of sentence structure while understanding discourse, we keep in mind the conceptual meaning of the sentence. Previous research has shown that propositions allow to link general knowledge to perception thanks to relations identified in terms of type-token, which means that concepts of knowledge get linked to elements of the perceptive world (13). For this to happen, a conceptual system – capable of productively linking types (concepts) to allow for hierarchic structures to develop – is required. These hierarchic structures will then be linked to further elements in the world.

2.1 Perception and Comprehension Processes

This experimental study focuses on the role of visual perception in the construction of mental representations and mental models leading to the construction of meaning. By asking the question: "why is it that language is due to have anchors well beyond a linguistic system?" Glenberg and his colleagues came up with the idea according to which linguistic symbols (such as words and syntactic structures) have meaning only if non-linguistic pieces of experience such as action and perception underlie them (14). Such a hypothesis is confirmed by the results of their studies concluding that language is anchored in the body, thus also confirming Varela's inactive model (15).

As we have seen, Barsalou agrees with the idea of postulating a theory of knowledge construction based on perception, where selective attention allows for the extrapolation of a number of components from perceptive experience in order to build up a number of 'simulators' having the function of concepts. Once established, these simulators will each represent a "type" producing categorical inferences which productively match simultaneously to form complex simulations (conceptualizations) never experienced before; these give birth to propositions building up "elements" in the world. Such a model is not limited to concrete representations as it also extends to abstract concepts (16).

2.2 When Linguistic and Non-linguistic Information Meet to Build Up Meaning

This research studies the role that linguistic and non-linguistic information play in the process of building up meaning. In order to trigger such a process we matched standardized pictures to written sentences which were meant to describe the "visual scenes" represented by these pictures. We organized each set of three pictures, supposedly evoking mental representations of 'daily life events', according to the verb's thematic roles. Our preoccupation was to create the condition for the subjects participating in our study to find themselves in Jackendoff's predicament of having to 'translate all that is seen into what is said.'

In fact, thanks to one's mental representations - the result of background and tacit knowledge, memory, as well as perceptive and body experience - each of us fully contributes at any given moment in time to the process of meaning construction (17). Our study investigates how non-linguistic information (provided by each image-sign picture making up each 'visual sentence' according to its predicate argument structure) influences the construction of meaning of each written sentence describing it. The participants into our experimental research read plausible and implausible written sentences (Text) describing the previously displayed visual sentence (Image). Their task was to say whether the text matched the image, answering YES/NO.

Previous research on the contribution that mental models play on written text comprehension, whether illustrated or not with pictures, has shown that general world knowledge gets organized into mental representations and it contributes to the structure of meaning when it comes to making sense of so to speak, "brand new" situations (18). Henceforth, by taking into account the implicit preexistence, within the mind, of such schemas making up the structure of more general mental representations, our study intends to shed some light on how it contributes to the construction of meaning.

According to the Embedded Construction Grammar model, the understanding of everyday language depends on the triggering of mental simulations of its perceptual and motor content (17). This model predicts that linguistic meanings become the parameters of some aspects of such simulations; thus they behave as an interface between the properties of language on the one hand, and the detailed and encyclopedic knowledge entailed by simulations on the other. Strong evidence exists that during language understanding embodied knowledge is unconsciously and automatically brought to bear (19).

This research aims at (1) finding out whether mental representations affect the construction of meaning, and (2) understanding what kind of relationship mental representations entertain with verbal semantics given that sentence structure is tied to predicate argument structures.

Our choice of pictures, possibly representing daily events, allows us to provide our subjects with what Pasolini calls 'im-signs' (images-signs), thus freeing up 'memory traces' and mental representations of non-linguistic nature. Perception, representing the primary modality of experience, hence shaping up, according to Barsalou, perceptive symbolic systems, and also reflects Rosenthal's idea of anticipation according to which it is also previously anchored in the body (10).

2.3 Method

2.3.1 Participants
Ninety-four university students, both males and females, participated in this study. They were all native French speakers between the age of 19 and 49 years old. 26 students were enrolled in the psychology course at a southern university in France, and 26 other students were enrolled in languages and linguistics courses at a smaller southern university in France; their syllabus of study included: applied foreign languages (mainly English and Spanish), French language teaching, Sociology, History, Modern and Classical languages.

2.3.2 The Experimental Materials
The image-sign pictures
To minimize the uncontrolled effects of non-standardized stimuli, such as film segments or other materials, the choice of our stimuli for this preliminary experimental study had to fall on classic standardized black and white still pictures (image-signs). Overall we created a total of 272 image-text pairs. Out of them 72 pictures belonged to the category 'distractive pairs' which were meant to take the subject "by surprise," thus 'disrupting' the possible learning patterns from being developed for carrying out the task. Compared to the black and white still pictures, the distractive pairs were fully colored very informal, and were chosen randomly from a web database.

From image-sign pictures to "visual sentences"
The whole set of image-sign pictures allowed us to make up a total of 200 "complete visual sentences". These pictures were extracted from existing databases (20), (21). Each visual sentence contained three image-sign pictures, one for each predicate argument structure. Each sentence was meant to "tell a story" and/or represent a "cognitive scene" from daily routine. A horizontal arrow "showed" the order in which the

"visual reading" of these image-signs pictures should occur. We distinguished two types of sentence structures: (A) a two predicate argument structure sentence, and (B) a three predicate argument structure sentence. Let us take for example the following sentence structures:

(A) La jeune fille s'allume une cigarette (English: the young woman lights up a cigarette)
(B) La femme met le bébé dans le landau (English: the woman puts the child in the pram.

Sentences such as (A), a two predicate argument structure sentence, were illustrated with three image-sign pictures, in this case: (1) *a young woman*, (2) *a match* representing the action of *lighting up*, and (3) *a cigarette*. Sentences such as (B), a three predicate argument structure sentence, were also illustrated with three image-signs pictures, in this case: (1) *a woman*, (2) *a child*, and (3) *a carriage*. Notice that visual sentences such as the two predicate argument structure sentence in (A) included also a visual representation for the action of the verb, while visual sentences such as the three predicate argument structure sentence in (B) only contained an image-sign picture for each one of the three predicate argument structures including location. There were a total of 100 sentences of type (A) and a total of 100 sentences of type (B). On the occasion of the treatment, each sentence was prompted randomly. Intending to trigger a pre-linguistic, pre-existent "cognitive scene" representing the meaning in mind, the visual sentence was prompted before the written one.

The choice of our battery of predicate argument structure image-sign pictures stimuli was based on 'recognition values' assigned by graduate and undergraduate students to each image-sign picture on the occasion of a pre-test experiment conducted well before our study.

Experimental modalities: plausible vs. implausible visual representation of meaning
Each predicate argument structure image-sign picture was used to make up both plausible and implausible visual sentences. Take, for example the set of predicate argument structure image-sign pictures for sentence (B) representing each one (1) the woman, (2) the child, and (3) the carriage, this same *plausible* order was followed to "visually retell the story" to trigger a potential pre-existing 'cognitive scene' of the same situation. The same set of predicate argument structure image-sign pictures was also used to make *implausible* visual sentences of the type: (2) the child, (1) the woman, (3) the carriage, thus soliciting meanings such as: the child put the woman in the carriage. In this case, we excluded the possibility that participants might "elaborate passive voice constructions" according to the linguistic passive structures (example: the baby was put by the woman in the carriage) given that, thanks to the prompting of each pair of Image-Text stimuli, the task clearly consisted in having to say whether (yes or not) the written sentences described the visual ones. None of our written sentence stimuli was in the passive form.

Written sentences (Text)
Triggering pre-existing mental representations contributing to the construction of meaning in the mind by simple exposure to visual sentence stimuli, in the first place,

is one of the goals of our experimental study. The second is to assess whether or not each of the written sentences describing the (previous) visual one - this written sentence comes immediately after the exposure to each visual sentence – matches it or not. Hence, in addition to visual sentence stimuli we also created written sentence stimuli describing them to make a pair of *Image-Text* stimuli. The main verbs making up our written sentences were taken from existing databases and from previous experimental studies on predicate argument structures concerned with understanding the role images play in the process of the construction of meaning (22). Namely, the SEMASIT database provided us with those verbs for which the relationship agent/patient within a predicate had been established in a previous study (23).

Experimental modalities: plausible vs. implausible written representation of meaning
Our written sentences are nothing but the description of the visual ones which aim at triggering mental representation. Hence, just as we relied on image-sign pictures to account for predicate argument structure within each sentence, the written sentences were meant to display the agent/patient structure inherent in them, whether their meaning was plausible or not. Take for instance the written sentence (B) *the woman put the child in the carriage* describing the previous visual sentence in the established order (1, 2, 3): this sentence is *plausible*. It becomes *implausible* if the predicate argument structures are arranged in a different order (2, 1, 3) to give: *the child put the woman in the carriage.*

Inter-modality image-text
Having created a battery of visual and written stimuli we paired them up according to the plausible vs. implausible modalities to obtain the following pairs of image-text sentences:

1. The visual sentence (Image) is plausible, and the written sentence (Text) which is also plausible, describes it accordingly. *Image and Text do match*;
2. The visual sentence is implausible, but the written sentence is plausible. The written sentence does not describe the visual sentence accordingly. *Image and Text do not match*;
3. The visual sentence is implausible, as is the written sentence. Neither the visual sentence nor the written sentence make sense. Both sentences are implausible. *Image and Text do match.*
4. The visual sentence is plausible, and the written sentence is implausible. The written sentence makes sense, but the visual sentence does not. *Image and Text do not match.*

2.3.4 The Experimental Treatment
The E-Prime programming of this Image-Text experimental study involved the participants in a training session, followed by the experimental session itself. The training session engaged each individual participating in the data collection to get used to the procedure. Four pairs of Image-Text sentences were delivered on the occasion of the training session.

Having accessed the E-Prime application each participant was immediately prompted to answer a few general questions about their profession (whether or not (s)he was a student), place of origin (whether Nice or Perpignan) and age; (s)he also had to say whether (s)he was right or left handed. At the end of the questionnaire, a black screen appeared announcing the beginning of the data collection session. Directions were then provided indicating what to do to carry out the task. Each participant was informed that (s)he would get engaged in a training session before the data collection itself started, then they were told that the experimental study consisted in having to judge whether, yes or no, the written sentence on the screen well described the visual sentence preceding it. To answer YES/NO, they had to click on the mouse: on the left for YES, on the right for NO. Response time is free. Time being the dependent variable of this experimental study, the amount of time taken to provide each answer gets recorded as soon as the choice is made by clicking on the mouse. In order to begin the data collection each participant is asked to hit the bar.

The first black screen displays the (three, and/or two) predicate argument structure image-sign pictures making up the visual sentence for the entire duration of 100 ms. Immediately after this, another black screen containing a white cross in the middle follows, then a third black screen displaying a written sentence (typed white on black). This sentence describes, or does not describe, depending on the matching modality as explained above, the visual sentence that preceeded. The response time is tied to the subjects' choice. Once the choice is made, the following set of Image-Text stimuli is presented according to the procedure we just described: first comes the black screen portraying, for the entire duration of 100 ms. the (three and/or two) predicate argument structure image-sing pictures representing a visual sentence. At the end of this period of time, a second black screen containing a white cross in the middle follows immediately after. Finally a third black screen containing, this time, a written sentence (in white characters) appears. This goes on until the end of the data collection time, about ten minutes, at the end of which a black screen informs the participant that (s)he has completed the task.

The dependent variables
The dependent variables of this experimental study are both the time taken by each participant to make a choice, and the number of mistakes occurring in deciding whether (yes or no) the written sentence described the visual one or not.

The independent variables
Both the *visual* and the *written* sentences are the independent variables of this study. There were two modalities for each one of these sentence stimuli: plausible and implausible according to whether or not each one represents a real life situation.

The experimental conditions
There are four conditions to this experimental study related with the pairing up of the image-text sentences:

Condition One: the visual sentence is plausible and the written sentence describing it is also plausible. The pair Image-Text matches up nicely. YES, is the subjects' expected answer to the question: does the written sentence describe the visual sentence?

Condition Two: the visual sentence is implausible and the written sentence is plausible. There is no matching up of the Image-Text pair. The expected answer is NO.

Condition three: the visual sentence is implausible, the written sentence is also implausible. The Image-Text pair matches up at the level of implausibility. The expected answer is YES.

Condition Four: the visual sentence is plausible, and the written sentence is implausible. There is no matching up of the Image-Text pair. The expected answer is NO.

The tables here below summarize the modalities and conditions of our experimental study (Table 1) as well as the organization of the stimuli on the occasion of the data collection (Table 2).

Table 1. Modalities and conditions

CONDITIONS	IMAGE visual sentence	TEXT written sentence
1	Plausible	Plausible
2	Implausible	Plausible
3	Implausible	Implausible
4	Plausible	Implausible
MODALITIES	TWO	TWO

Table 2. Organization of the display of the stimuli during data collection

PAS[1]	LIST N. 1		LIST N. 2		LIST N. 3		LIST N. 4	
	Image	Text	Image	Text	Image	Text	Image	Text
3	P	P	I	P	I	I	P	I
3	I	P	I	I	P	I	P	P
3	I	I	P	I	P	P	I	P
3	P	I	P	P	I	P	I	I
2	P	P	I	P	I	I	P	I
2	I	P	I	I	P	I	P	P
2	I	I	P	I	P	P	I	P
2	P	I	P	P	I	P	I	I

2.4 Results and Discussion

The analysis of variance (ANOVA) accounts for values about the length of time participants take to choose whether YES or NO the written sentence describes the preceding visual sentence, and to estimate the recurrence of errors during this decision making process.

---

[1] Predicate Argument Structures

Concerning the incidence of *errors* the results show:

The Image	$F(1,93)=79,881$, p= ,00000
The Text	$F(1,93)=12,956$, p=,00051
The interface Image-Text	$F(1,93)=16,961$, p=, 00008

More specifically, our data collection suggests that when the Image (visual sentence) is Plausible, the incidence of error is stronger when participants have to decide whether or not the Text (written sentence) describing it is Implausible than when it is Plausible.

$$F (1,93) = 27,37 \quad p<.001$$

This result is quite predictable. In fact, if both the Image and the Text are Plausible, then the process of matching up meanings from visual and written input happens smoothly. On the contrary when the Image is Plausible and the Text is Implausible, participants seem to 'cling' more heavily on the structure of the written text rather than being 'facilitated' by the immediate visual input the visual sentence provides. In this respect, the simulation view of language (24) predicts that words in a phrase or in a sentence trigger lexical-level simulations (general word meaning) that encompass the larger phrase or sentence of a situation specific simulation. This being said, it seems that confronted to a written sentence that does not make sense - not only because it does not match with the previous visual sentence preceding it, but because in and by itself, the Implausible sentence is meaningless, no real life situation corresponding to it (for example: the baby put the women in the carriage) - participants pay more attention to comprehending the text than relying on the Image. In other words, when the mental representation of the "who, does, what" that drives the syntactic level of meaning structure in sentence understanding, does not match up with the verb semantics, the Plausible meaning structure of the visual sentence does not help to bridge the gap.

In this respect to the time taken to produce the YES/NO answer, the results show the following:

The Image	$F(1,93)=77,68$ p= 0,000
The Text	$F (1,93)=11,01$ p= 0,001
The interaction Image-Text	$F(1,93)=0 ,1693$ p= 0,6870

In other words, these results suggest that the response time has been longer when the visual sentence is Implausible compared to the Plausible one.

$$F(1,93)= 77,68 \quad p= ,00000$$

This result is also predictable. In fact, Implausible Images (visual sentences) are meant to portray a 'distorted reality.' They represent life situations that could not trigger any mental representations of any sort, as they make little or no sense (example: the child put the woman in the carriage). Having to decide whether the written sentence describes the previous visual one takes longer when the Image (visual sentence) is Implausible. When the Image is Plausible there is no 'meaning matching conflict' at the level of mental representation. The visually represented meaning

Table 3. ANOVA with the dependent variable count of right/wrong answers and the independent variables IMAGE, TEXT, IMAGE*TEXT

	SS	DF	MS	F	P
IMAGE	9,8513	1	9,8513	79,8811	0
Error	11,4891	93	0,1233		
TEXT	0,9855	1	0,9855	12,9565	0,000514
Error	7,0741	93	0,0761		
IMAGE*TEXT	0,7511	1	0,7511	16,9608	0,000083
Error	4,1187	93	0,0443		

Table 4. ANOVA with the dependent variable response time and the independent variables IMAGE, TEXT, IMAGE*TEXT

	SS	DF	MS	F	P
IMAGE	2,099902	1	2,099902	795,6886	0
Error	2,513928	93	2,703148		
TEXT	5,812424	1	5,812424	11,0173	0,0021290
Error	4,906406	93	5,275705		
IMAGE*TEXT	7,8485550	1	7,8485550	0,1633	0,687088
Error	4,470501	93	4,806990		

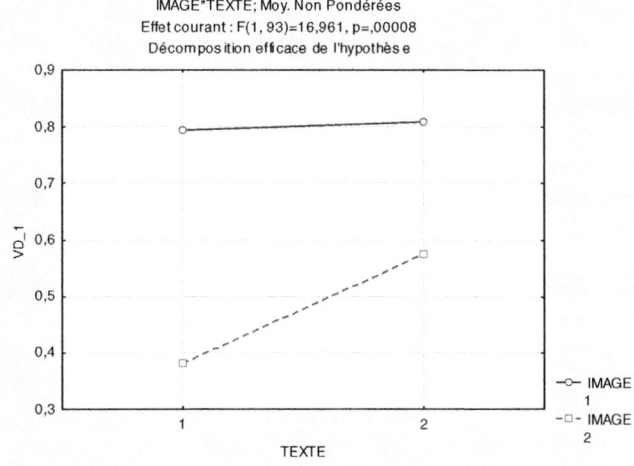

Fig. 1. Incidence of errors: answers for visual (Image) vs. written (Text) sentences according to different modalities: (2) Plausible vs. (1) Implausible

matches with the 'mentally represented reality,' the choice is easily made, and the time it takes to make it is shorter. This does not apply when the visual sentence is Implausible. In fact, it takes longer to attempt to reconstruct and/or elicit meaning in mind that doesn't fit any representation.

General Discussion
We created our Image-Text stimuli and we organized them according to the two modalities Plausible and Implausible, and the four conditions as described above, with the intent to study the role mental representations play in the process of constructing meaning in the mind, and to understand the interplay of linguistic and non linguistic information during the process of sentence comprehension. The results show that mental representation of meaning is triggered both by written and visual sentences. In particular, we acknowledge that when both written and visual sentences represent Plausible meanings, participants perform better compared to when they have Implausible sentences. In other words, they make fewer errors and take less time to construct meaning from visual sentences than from written ones. This tendency is confirmed by the fact that during the decision making process, in answering whether YES/NO Texts (written sentences) describe or not Images (visual sentences), the incidence of errors for Plausible sentences is less important compared to the Implausible ones. The same tendency applies to measures of the span of time participants take to decide whether or not written sentences describe visual ones. We can then conclude that when it comes to Implausible sentences, whether written or visual, the triggering of mental representations becomes problematic. Such behavior can be ascribed to the fact that it takes longer to match one's triggered mental representation of Implausible visual sentences than of Plausible ones given that the meanings evoked by the Implausible sentences is not 'mentally available.' Consequently, we conclude that mental representations contribute to the construction of meaning process.

Recent research consistently supports the idea according to which perceptual information contributes to activation of simulations responsible for language comprehension (12), (25).

More specifically, according to the simulation view of language, when we watch a car, for instance, a process for storing its perceptive symbols gets triggered. Such perceptive information is processed, organized and stored in a coherent system so that it can be used again to simulate similar experiences consistent with the same object. The perceptive symbols related to a specific entity or event situation are integrated in a schema containing perceptive symbols drawn from previous category members. Take our previous example: the schema for a car is made up of a series of multimodal pieces of information representing what it means to have such an experience. A schema is never the result of a direct experience with the 'thing' itself. In fact, compared to the experience from which the schema is issued, both the schema and its simulation contain less information.

To summarize, according to Barsalou, this is what happens: (1) the sequence of a simulated event makes up a concept's schema ; (2) the concept partially represents the simulation, namely those aspects that make the construction of a representation consistent with the situation possible; (3) within the concept the perceptive symbols play a central role, including those making up the perceptive simulation. The latter more particularly represents the process according to which a perceptive simulation is compared to the perceived situation to establish a given relationship. When it succeeds, such a procedure results in a "true" simulator, which means that we learn to simulate the experience of successfully by connecting an internal simulation with a perceived scene. The concept for "false," including negative expressions, is strictly tied to the concept for "true" resulting from having observed the absence of a relationship between the simulator and the simulation. This means that the perceptive symbolic systems can directly represent the most difficult abstract concepts. Such concepts can be of a perceptive nature as they are grounded in temporary simulations, both internal and external.

Acknowledgments. Particular thanks to Prof. Thierry Baccino at the *University of Nice* for supporting this research, as well as to the members of the Cognitive Psychology laboratory for contributing in many different ways to this experimental study. Special thanks also go to Prof. Jerome - UMR 5244 - *Centre de Biologie et D'écologie Tropicale et Méditerranéenne* - CNRS UPVD for his assistance with the statistical analysis, and to Prof. Hélène Guillaume from the *Département d'Etudes Anglaises et Américaines de l'Université de Perpignan Via Domitia* for proofreading my last draft in English.

References

1. Jackendoff, R.: An Argument on the Composition of Conceptual Structures. In: Theoretical Issues in Natural Language Processing, July 25-27, vol. 2, University of Illinois at Urbana-Champaign (1978)
2. Pasolini, P.P.: Emirismo Eretico. Saggi Ed. Garzanti (1972); Colin, M.: Structures Syntaxiques du Message Filmique. Documents de Travail. Centro Internazionale di Semiotica e di Linguistica, Univesità di Urbino (Settembre-Ottobre 1985)
3. Rastier, F.: Sémantique interprétative. PUF, Paris (1987)
4. Ferretti, T.R., McRae, K., Hatherell, A.: Integrating Verbs, Situation Schemas, and Thematic Role Concepts. Journal of Memory and Language 44, 516–547 (2001)
5. Cordier, F., Pariollaud, F.: From the choice of the patients for a transitive verb to its polysemy. Current Psychology Letters 21(1) (2007)
6. Kupersberg, G., Caplan, D., Sitnikova, T.: Neural Correlates of processing syntactic, semantic, and thematic relationships in sentences. Language and cognitive processes 21(5), 489–530 (2006)
7. McRae, K., Spivey-Knowlton, M.J., Tanenhaus, M.K.: Modeling the influente of thematic fit (and other constraints) in on-line sentence comprehension. Journal of Memory and Language 38, 283–312 (1998)
8. Le Ny, J.-F.: La sémantique des verbes et la représentation des situations. Syntaxe 1 Sémantique – Sémantique du lexique verbal 2 (2000)
9. Visetti, Y.-M.: La place de l'action dans les linguistiques cognitives. Texto, 1mars (1998)
10. Rosenthal, V.: Perception comme anticipation: vie perceptive et microgenèse. In: Sock, R., Vaxelaire, B. (eds.) L'Anticipation à l'horizon du Présent, pp. 13–32. Mardaga, Liège (Collection Psychologie et Sciences Humaines) (2004)
11. Valette, M.: Linguistique énonciative et cognitives françaises. Ed. Honoré Champion, Paris (2006)
12. Barsalou, L.W.: Perceptual symbol systems. Behavioral and Brain Sciences 22, 577–660 (1999)

13. Zwaan, R.A., Radvansky, G.A.: Situation Models in Language Comprehension and Memory. Psychological Bulletin 123(2), 167–185 (1998)
14. Glenberg, A.M., Robertson, D.A.: Symbol Grounding and Meaning: A Comparison of High Dimensional and Embodied Theories of Meaning. Journal of Memory and Language 43, 379–401 (2000)
15. Varela, F.: L'inscription corporelle de l'esprit. Seuil, Paris (1993)
16. Zlatev, J.: Intersubjectivity, Mimetic Schemas and the Emergente of Language. Intellectica 2-3, 123-151, 46–48 (2007)
17. Bergen, B.K., Chang, N.: Embodied Construction Grammar in Simulation-Based Language Understanding. In: Östman, J.O., Fried, M. (eds.) Construction Grammar(s): Cognitive and Cross-Language Dimensions, John Benjamin (2003)
18. Gibson, J.J., Gibson, E.J.: Perceptual learning: Differentiation or enrichment? Psychological Review 62, 32–41 (1955)
19. Zwaan, R.A., Taylor, L.J.: Seeing, Acting, Understanding: Motor Resonance in Language Comprehension. Journal of Experimental Psychology: General 135(1), 1–11 (2006)
20. Bonin, P., Peerman, R., Malardier, N., Meot, A., Clalard, M.: A new set of 299 pictures for psycholinguistic studies: French norms for name agreement, image agreement. Journal of Behavior Research Methods, Instruments1 Computers 35(1), 158–167 (2003)
21. Alario, F.-X., Ferrand, L.: A set of 400 pictures standardized for French: Norms for name agreement, image agreement, familiarity, visual complexity, image variability and age of acquisition. Journal of Beahvior, Research, Methods, Instruments & Computers 31, 531–552 (1999)
22. Thompson, C.K.: Neural Corelates of Verb Argument Structure Processing. Journal of Cognitive Neuroscience 19(11), 1753–1767 (2007)
23. Pariollaud, F., Cordier, F., Granjou, L., Ros, C.: (à paraître) Une base de données en sémantique du verbe: SEMASIT. Psychologie Française
24. Madden, C.J., Therriault, D.J.: Verb aspect and perceptual simulations. The Quarterly Journal of Experimental Psychology, 1–10 (2009)
25. Taylor, L.J., Zwaan, R.A.: Action in Cognition: The Case of Language. In: Language and Cognition: A journal of Language and Cognitive Science, available on the web

Appendix

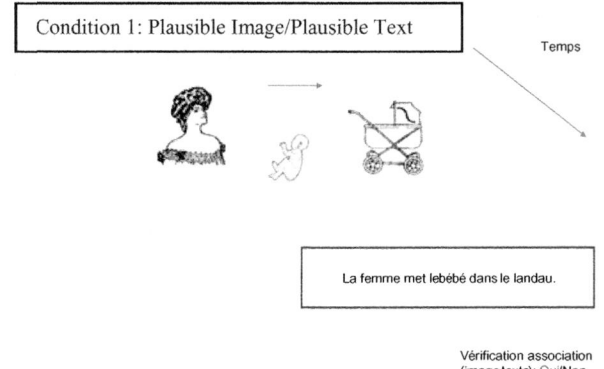

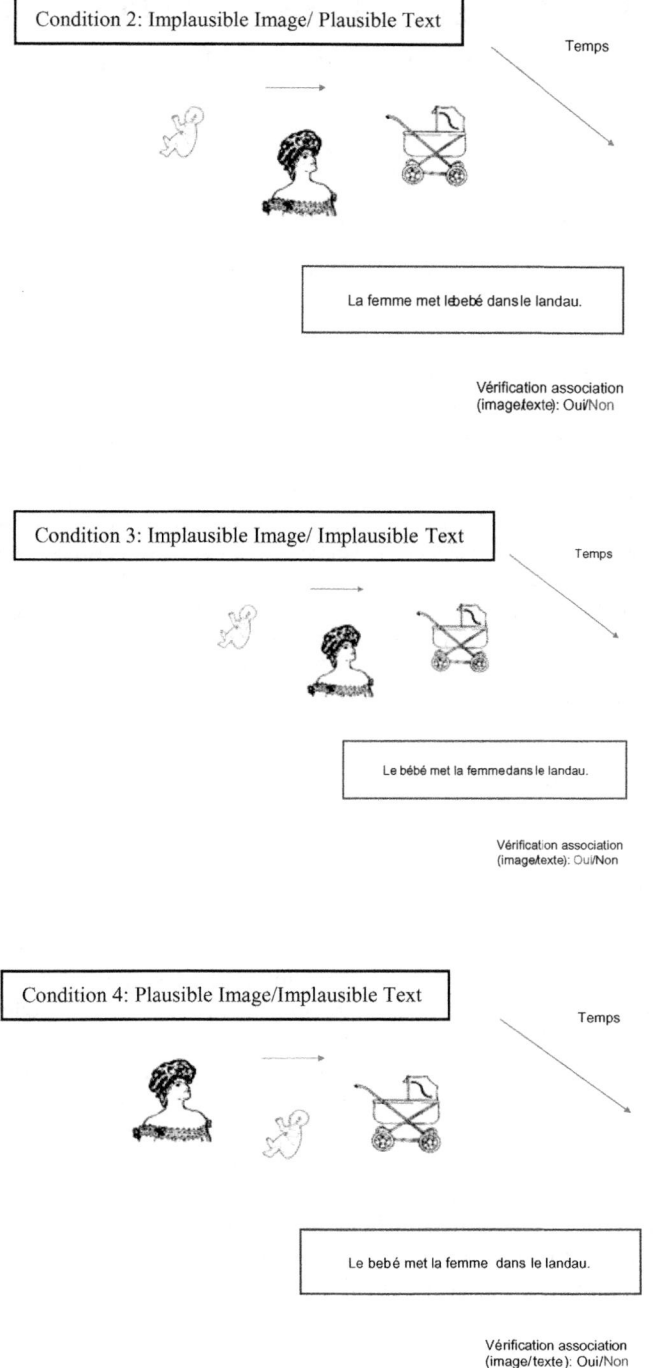

Condition 2: Implausible Image/ Plausible Text

Temps

La femme met le bebé dans le landau.

Vérification association
(image/texte): Oui/Non

Condition 3: Implausible Image/ Implausible Text

Temps

Le bébé met la femme dans le landau.

Vérification association
(image/texte): Oui/Non

Condition 4: Plausible Image/Implausible Text

Temps

Le bebé met la femme dans le landau.

Vérification association
(image/texte): Oui/Non

Beyond the Panopticon Framework: Privacy, Control and User Generated Content

Manuela Farinosi

Department of Economy, Society and Territory, University of Udine,
Via delle Scienze 208, 33100 Udine, Italy
`manuela.farinosi@uniud.it`

Abstract. The overall purpose of this contribution is to explore the meaning and significance of the terms control and privacy in the light of the intensive diffusion of user generated content (UGC). Every day a large number of people all over the world use digital media to share personal details with a vast network of friends and, often, with an unspecified number of strangers producing long lasting digital information. My exploratory analysis is based on 145 compositions written by students from Udine University (aged between 19 and 27). The data from the texts were content-analysed and were then categorized and analysed from a qualitative point of view to understand how young people frame the topic of privacy on the Web. The results show that it is possible to identify ten macrocategories: Privacy, Participation and Sharing, Visibility, Persistence, Replicability and Searchability, Exhibitionism, Risks, Horizontal Control, Invisible Audiences, Vertical Control, Protection, Distrust.

Keywords: Privacy, Control, UGC, social media, interfaces.

1 Introduction

In recent years, the boundary between private life and public life has been blurred. The global diffusion of modern communication networks, the proliferation of human practices using these networks, the development of new digital media that support social relationships, the increasing use of new tools of self-publication on the Internet (such as Facebook[1], YouTube[2], Flickr[3], Wordpress[4]) and the trend toward computerizing and networking everyday objects have exposed a great deal of personal information to intrusive eyes [1] [2] [3] [4] [5] [27]. Thanks to Web 2.0 interactivity and to a new generation of Internet applications (e.g. social network sites, blogs and video or photo sharing sites) a large number of people are now able to use digital media to express themselves, to share personal details with a vast network of friends and, often, with an unspecified number of strangers, to create online profiles, and to produce - in this way – long lasting digital information [2] [6] [7]. This should raise a number of

---

[1] http://www.facebook.com
[2] http://www.youtube.com
[3] http://www.flickr.com/
[4] http://wordpress.com/

A. Esposito et al. (Eds.): COST 2102 Int. Training School 2010, LNCS 6456, pp. 180–189, 2011.

new issues for designers and developers of multimodal interfaces and interactive applications but, unfortunately, the user interfaces very often don't provide people the tools necessary to understand and check the visibility of their personal data. According to Mynatt and Nguyen the real enemy of privacy practices in ubiquitous computing is not Big Brother but "interfaces that do not give people the needed tools of awareness and control to comprehend and shape the behavior of the system" [8:1]. It would be desirable a production of interfaces able to provide to users a sort of feedback by reflecting what the system currently knows about them. To be effective, user interfaces have to be designed to recreate social context online in order to disclose different things to different people and avoid to make visible the same content available to your friends to your boss too.

The current scenario can be considered an important and essential starting point to understand how to develop software architecture and multimodal interfaces more sensitive to personal privacy. As people increasingly live in close contact with the new ICTs it is important to consider the results of this analysis in order to build interfaces based on reflective architectures that reproduce online the same principles of distribution and adequacy that characterize the distribution of content in offline environments.

2   Literature Review

From Youtube to Facebook, a vast amount of personal material is exposed to a mass audience on the Internet and it would seem that very often the desire to put oneself on display is stronger than the fear of being monitored [24] [25] [26]. Social media are dramatically changing not only the way we interact with other people, but also our view of what is a "private" [6] [9] [3] [23]. They mark a move toward a more interactive, social and collaborative web, but also one that is more and more coming under surveillance [10]. In the Web 2.0 environment the traditional panoptic principle of observation has to a certain extent been transformed and the Panopticon [21] [22] [5] itself has come to have a broader meaning [10] [11]. Everyone online can be at the same moment observer and observed. The central tower is changing its meaning, but - as in Bentham's building - the observer is invisible to the observed. The new Internet applications challenge the traditional ideas of surveillance [11] and the new control practices cannot be adequately described within the classical framework of vertical control. Social media seem to introduce a horizontal control as well, which can change the informational dynamics of the space and contribute to privacy violations [12] [17]. Gross and Acquisti note that, "While privacy may be at risk in social networking sites, information is willingly provided. [...] the perceived benefit of selectively revealing data to strangers may appear larger than the perceived costs of possible privacy invasions" [6:3]. Their empirical research conducted on Carnegie

---

[5] The Panopticon is an architectural plan designed by English philosopher Jeremy Bentham at the end of the eighteenth century to impose order on the lives of criminals and madmen. This plan was annular and included a semi-circular building with several individual prison cells visible from a surveillance tower located at the centre of the semicircle. The observation tower allowed all inmates to be visible, while the prisoners never knew whether or not they were being watched or even if there was anyone in the tower [21] [22].

Mellon University students founds no significant correlation between privacy concerns and information revelation.

According to danah boyd[6] it is possible to analyse social network sites (SNS) as "the latest generation of "mediated publics" – environments where people can gather publicity through mediating technology" [13:2]. In some respects mediated publics are like traditional unmediated publics (cafes, shopping centres, parks, etc.), but they differ from them in four characteristics:

- persistence: texts, photos and videos are stored and last for a long time;
- replicability: digital content can be copied and reproduced in another context;
- scalability: online content can potentially have a high level of visibility;
- searchability: information can be easily retrieved by anyone through a simple web search [14] [15].

These environments reflect three of the dynamics that Meyrowitz [16] attributed to broadcasting media:

- invisible audiences: online the potential visibility of content is enormous. The architecture of the tools of Web 2.0 is so designed that users do not know who has looked at their data or at their profile. They are unable to perceive their audience.;
- collapsed contexts: it is almost impossible to maintain distinct social contexts because technical settings are not capable of capturing social complexities and cannot represent the actual social relations between users;
- the blurring of public and private: the boundaries between public sphere and private sphere are becoming even more indiscernible [16] [15] [12].

In the online public space it is impossible for people to tailor their expression to their audience and to maintain "contextual integrity"[7] because almost every aspect of the architecture of web 2.0 directly conflicts with the offline norms of distribution [17] [12]. The way personal information flows through the net is very different from the way personal information flows through offline environments as online everything can be easily recorded, stored and retrieved. People are artificially unaware of who they are performing for. Echoing Goffman's theory on social performance and the presentation of self [18] it is possible to analyse the problem of the loss of privacy as the problem that arises when the walls that usually separate social situations come crashing down. Any content people upload online is automatically broadcast to everyone else at the same time and is equally accessible to everyone without respect for classical social norms of distribution and appropriateness [17] [12] [23]. On the contrary, in everyday life people are in the habit of behaving differently with a different public in different social situations in order to maintain privacy ("selective disclosure") [18] [19].

---

[6] The author has decided to write her name in lower case letters for personal and political reasons. For further information see http://www.danah.org/name.html

[7] "Contextual integrity" is a conceptual framework developed by Helen Nissenbaum for explaining privacy expectations. She analyses privacy in term of norms of transmission of personal information and classifies them in: norms of appropriateness and norms of distribution. These norms govern almost all social spheres and determine roles, behaviors and expectations. Contextual integrity is maintained when both types of norms of information flow are respected, and it is violated when any of the norms is infringed.

As Grimmelmann explains, we "don't say private things when the wrong people are listening in. To know whether they might be, we rely on social and architectural heuristics to help us envision our potential audience." [20:18]. The architectural properties of the majority of web 2.0 applications, however, cause contexts to collapse and spread information in new ways, exposing private content to unwanted gazes [6] [12] [23] [25]. They are not able to capture the real social nuances and to reflect the real complexity of daily reality. They create a "technological fiction" that distorts social relations [12] and that is deeply counterintuitive and counterproductive in the protection of the private sphere. By default, texts, photos or videos uploaded by a user are immediately available to anyone in the world [23]. This is completely opposed to the traditional norms of distribution. The potential and underrated implication of these new forms of exposure is the development of what has been defined as "peer-to-peer privacy violation" [20] or "participatory surveillance" [11]. Unfortunately, as Fuchs has recently pointed out [4], the topic of surveillance on social media have been unstudied. There are only few research focused on this aspect. Tufekci [7] conducted a quantitative survey and found that 94,9% of Facebook users use their real name, 75,6% indicate their relationship status, 72,2% their sexual orientation. Sonia Livingstone [3] conducted qualitative interviews with young social network users and found out that they want to share their personal profile with friends and keep it private from others. Lewis et al. [25] conducted a research on students' SNS profiles and found that students with a lot of friends and a high level of activity tend to have private profiles.

My research aims to contribute to this field, analyzing how young people frame the topics of privacy on the Web. In particular, it explores the main categories of discourse that young people employ when speaking about privacy and control on the Internet.

3   Method

To investigate the social construction of privacy and surveillance issues and to capture perceptions of online privacy concerns I focused my attention on the so-called "Y Generation", the first generation to have grown up with digital technology and that usually spends a lot of time online. My exploratory research is based on the analysis of 145 essays on the topic of "Privacy and UGC" written by a convenience sample of first degree students in Multimedia Science and Technology (aged between 19 and 27 years) of the University of Udine. Firstly, I asked them to write a composition of 3-4 pages as homework describing what they think about this topic and then I analysed the content of their works from a quali-quantitative point of view in order to identify what the most frequent opinions were. Following Marvasti's model, the texts collected were divided into explanatory macrocategories (not mutually exclusive). The definition of the macrocategories arose inductively and was based on an understanding which emerged through interaction with the data available. This means that I approached the data analysis without any preset list of macrocategories and analyzed the information to identify those that theoretically matched the phenomena portrayed in the data set. This method was very useful in organizing the findings related to the topic of my analysis and, as Marvasti points out, this approach offers "convenience [...] in simplifying and reducing large amounts of data into organized segment" [28:91].

The macrocategories were ranked by their frequency of mention and then analysed from a qualitative point of view to understand how young people frame the topic of privacy in the Web 2.0 environments and to reconstruct the most frequent items used to speak about this issue [28] [29].

4   Results and Discussion

From the content analysis of the compositions written by the convenience sample it emerged that it is possible to cluster the texts into ten different - but not mutually exclusive - macrocategories. In this paper will be deeply analyzed only those that occupy more than 10% of the whole discourse of university students.

Table 1. Macrocategories of meaning expressed by students of the considered sample

Macrocategories	% and number of times each macrocategory was used
Privacy	27.5% (133)
Participation and Sharing	17.1% (83)
Visibility, Persistence, Replicability and Searchability	17% (82)
Exhibitionism	11.8% (57)
Risks	10.4% (50)
Horizontal Control	6% (29)
Invisible Audiences	3.6% (17)
Vertical Control	3.6% (17)
Protection	1.6% (7)
Distrust	1.4% (6)
	100%

The most frequent macrocategory which emerged from the analysis of students' compositions is "privacy". This topic is present in 27.5% of the whole discourse of university students and probably this data is affected by the title of the composition itself. Most of the students of the sample write that they are convinced that the best way to protect the private sphere online is self-regulation and self-censorship. In their opinion, users have to establish what can be shown to the world because in this new scenario the traditional privacy laws are not sufficient to protect individuals. A lot of students think that there is no correct recipe for knowing how much personal content people can publish online and for understanding what type of material would be best for showing to other users. According to them it depends on personal aims and personal expectations and concerns personal ethic and moral. Several students criticize the widespread superficiality and shallowness in the content that the average user uploads online, that sometimes leads to a complete lack of awareness of Internet potentiality. But there are also others who believe that this renunciation of personal intimacy is a conscious move and is the price to pay for living online. Many students observe that in the past few years the boundary between the public and private dimensions has been blurred and there has been a gradual trespass of the private sphere in the public one. This perception is even more frequently predominantly based on the realization that nowadays private content is becoming a topic of discussion. Some students of the sample ask for an international law for online privacy protection while some others harshly criticize the ambiguity and the lack of transparency of the SNSs' interfaces. Only a few decry the complete absence of media literacy in most Internet users.

The second relevant macrocategory which emerged from the texts written by the sample is that of "participation and sharing" of digital content on the web. As we can see in Table 1 this topic is present in 17.1% of the whole discourse of university students. This data is significant if we read it in the light of the first macrocategory, that of "Privacy". A higher level of participation and sharing means a greater amount of content published online and available to anyone, everywhere in the world. This content is public, but very often it concerns the private sphere of the users. The attention of the sample is often focused on a generic social participation. Most of the students of Multimedia Science and Technology course speak about Internet participation in enthusiastic terms, describing it as a tool with enormous potentiality in relationships and interconnectivity. Some of them see the Internet as the "world of the young" and SNSs as a safe place, where they can shelter from intrusive eyes. They think that these online pages are familiar places where you can feel at home and upload what you want. This perception is arguably completely wrong and could be deceptive because it might prompt them to believe that SNSs are private spaces. For many students of the sample uploading content online, sharing their life with somebody is a primary factor of online survival. From the compositions it has emerged that there are two relevant ideas:

— the first one considers online participation as a crucial element also in offline life. Very often students use SNSs as a platform to keep in touch with mates or friends and talks opened online continue offline at the bar, or at university. Sometimes the Internet itself becomes a talking point and could be a focus for socializing;

— the second one, instead, considers online participation and sharing as a factor to escape from the loneliness of daily life and to find a refuge space, a relief valve, where you can open up and exchange your views with someone.

In this scenario protection of the private sphere looks like a sort of obstacle to get the whole world involved in your private life.

The third macrocategory that emerged from the compositions of the sample is closely related to the properties of online public spaces, that includes visibility, persistence, replicability and searchability [15]. The topic is present in 17% of the whole discourse of university students. Probably this percentage points to the greater knowledge of digital communication which characterizes university students of Multimedia Science and Technology course. They seem to pay much attention to online service properties, but - according to what they write - this awareness doesn't seem to have direct consequences on the way in which they use SNSs.

In the fourth place on the table above there is the macrocategory of "Exhibitionism". It is present in 11.8% of university students' discourse. When the private sphere becomes the main subject of user generated content, the consciousness that the personal individuality can be expose publicly also begin to evolve. According to some scholars this awareness is spreading the communicative logic of the shop window [30] and is giving birth to new practices based on visibility and exhibitionism [31].

Some people are ready to do anything in exchange for getting themselves noticed or for emerging from anonymity. Showing the private dimension means finding different ways to relate with the online world and developing a new semantics that leads people to describe themselves through links and content shared online. People usually upload their best photos online and try to appear as glamorous as possible. Some students of the sample analyzed this topic from a critical point of view. Others spoke about it in enthusiastic terms. In their compositions very often the concept of fame and exhibitionism is connected with the artistic sector and the wish to become famous. For some students this conceals an hidden desire for social acceptance.

The fifth macrocategory is that of "Risk". This topic takes up 10.4% of the whole discourse of university students. Of the online risk perceived more often by the students and cited more in their essays is violence. When they talk about violence they usually refer to videos on YouTube. Maybe the video content has a stronger impact on them and sticks in their mind more easily. According to the sample YouTube videos are implicated in the more specific risks of bullying and pedophilia. Other risks perceived by the students of the sample are the development of some forms of Internet addiction and the overuse in the use of the web. For some of them Internet addiction can sometimes result in a closure towards others and isolation from offline world. Sometimes the sample also speak about the risks of mistaking virtual life for real life and confusing them. Another possible source of risk that emerged from the students' compositions is the declaration of false personal details or lying about their real age in order to gain more opportunities of making friends with minors. A meaningful category – but scarcely explored by the sample – is the risk of slander and of violation of "personal reputation".

5 Conclusions

In the light of these results we can say that Bentham's Panopticon does not seem to adequately describe the new online environment and the actual practices of online self-publication and mutual control in SNSs. If we want to better analyse practices of SNSs it is necessary to go beyond the Panopticon and challenge the vertical conception of control. Although the classical concept of "vertical" surveillance (from up to down) is still relevant – as in the numerous applications of data mining used for direct marketing purposes or of ubiquitous computing - it has been flanked by "horizontal" surveillance (from peer to peer). Web 2.0 services changes the role of observer and observed and offers new opportunities of participation that - involving users in sharing personal details – empower people to spread information about each other. Online everyone can be both controller and controlled, so even the Panopticon has undergone a process of liquefaction. More than before, using new media and their new tools for self-expression and self-publication means creating a sophisticated portrait of yourself that can be watched by everyone. In this scenario it's necessary that interfaces designers and developers work to provide users the tools necessary to understand and check the visibility of their personal data. It would be desirable the realization of interfaces equipped to give to the people a feedback and to show them what the system currently knows about themselves. Future applications should be designed to be more sensitive to personal privacy. It is to be hoped that the next interfaces recreate online social context in order to disclose different things to different people. We are entered in a post-panoptic phase, a phase of liquidity which involves and crosses important aspects of social life of individuals, such as school, work, family. Everything – also social relations and dynamics control - has become more flexible and has been put into question the principle of the central tower of control. However in the current view it is still possible to track the features underlying the Bentham's project. The first concept that is certainly still present is that of "Visibility": how prisoners living in complete insecurity without knowing if control mechanisms work or less and internalizing gaze of power and behaving as if they were always under observation, now Internet users, particularly those enrolled in social networking sites and platforms for photo or video sharing, are gradually acquiring the same knowledge and are beginning to understand that the online environments frequented by them are in fact places public, in which they must be careful because anytime they should act as if they were always under observation.

A concept closely linked to the "visibility" that exists both in the Panopticon and in Web 2.0 platforms is the lack of perception of the audience: no one can know if and when is viewed and it is impossible to verify the presence or absence of supervisor and therefore he/she must develop all the dynamics related to the concept of "audiences invisible" [16].

Regarding the research question - how young people frame the topics of privacy on the Web and, in particular, what are the main categories of discourse that young people employ when speaking about user-generated content and privacy – the results show that it is possible to identify ten macrocategories: Privacy, Participation and Sharing, Visibility, Persistence, Replicability and Searchability, Exhibitionism, Risks, Horizontal Control, Invisible Audiences, Vertical Control, Protection, Distrust.

It would be interesting a continuation of this exploratory study involving more mature generations, to analyze what are the macrocategories put into play by them and see if there are differences in the dimensions of the concept of "private" than people younger. What emerges by examining the material that people upload on the net, is that today the concept of privacy has decreased over time. Privacy still exists, but is a much narrower concept than before.

Beyond the generational aspect, it must also consider the psychological one. It seems clear, in fact, that on the net, it is possible to find two different approaches: there is who calls for greater protection of his/her privacy and acts trying to expose the bare minimum and there is who instead wants the maximum visibility and does everything to appear and show as many people as possible. The two different approaches reflect two strong aspects of personality. Online as offline, in fact it is possible to identify two macro-classes of individuals: the shy and exhibitionist. Web 2.0 has allowed the most timid to easily interact with their contacts and those more narcissistic to be able to make themselves known to the world.

The most worrying element at present is the widespread and erroneous perception of being among friends, that doesn't allows many individuals to realize the potential of transparency and visibility of the material they publish online. The platforms of Web 2.0 place individuals inside a new system of relations that has to be managed.

Reflecting on the methodology adopted and going to draw a hypothetical table of pros and cons we can see how to conduct the parallel investigation - based on an inductive analysis - both from a standpoint of quality and quantity allowed us to "weigh" the macrocategories. This technique has ensured that the semantic macro-categories emerge automatically from data of the compositions written by the sample, mitigating in this way the effects related to the phenomenon of "social desirability" of responses. A weak point of this methodology can be traced in the fact that often the compositions were scattered, off-center, full of discussion and disorganized. The convenience sample of university students is a non-probability sample so it does not provide an accurate representation of the population and the results themselves cannot be generalized to the "Y Generation" as a whole. Like all exploratory research, more-over, it is almost impossible to identify universal characteristics and formulate guide-lines for wider application.

References

1. Lyon, D.: Surveillance society. Monitoring everyday life. Open University Press, Buckingham (2005)
2. Zwerger, I., Medosch, A.: Goodbye Privacy! Welcome Publicity? In: Stocker, G., Schopf, C. (eds.) Ars Electronica 2007: Goodbye Privacy, pp. 16–25. Hatje Cantz, Ostfildern (2007)
3. Livingstone, S.: Taking risky opportunities in youthful content creation: teenagers' use of social networking sites for intimacy, privacy and self-expression. New Media & Soc. 10(3), 393–411 (2008)
4. Fuchs, C.: StudiVZ: social networking in the surveillance society. Ethics Inf. Technol. 12(2), 171–185 (2010)
5. Fogel, J., Nehmad, E.: Internet social network communities: Risk taking, trust, and privacy concerns. Comp. Hum. Beh. 25(1), 153–160 (2009)
6. Gross, R., Acquisti, A.: Information revelation and privacy in online Social Networks (The Facebook case). In: Proceedings of the 2005 ACM workshop on Privacy in the Electronic Society, pp. 71–80. ACM, New York (2005)
7. Tufekci, Z.: Can you see me now? Audience and disclosure regulation in online Social Network Sites. Bull. Sci. Tech. Soc. 28(1), 20–36 (2008)
8. Mynatt, E.D., Nguyen, D.H.: Making Ubiquitous Computing Visible. In: ACM CHI 2001 Conference Workshop on Building the Ubiquitous Computing User Experience - Position paper (2001), http://www2.parc.com/csl/projects/ubicomp-workshop/positionpapers/mynatt.pdf
9. Rundle, M., Conley, C.: Ethical Implications of Emerging Technologies: A Survey. UNESCO, Paris (2007), http://unesdoc.unesco.org/images/0014/001499/149992E.pdf
10. Cascio, J.: The Rise of the Participatory Panopticon. WorldChanging (2005), http://www.worldchanging.com/archives//002651.html
11. Albrechtslund, A.: Online Social Networking as participatory surveillance. First Monday 13(3) (2008)
12. Peterson, C.: Saving Face: The Privacy Architecture of Facebook. Senior Thesis, University of Massachusetts-Amherst (2009), http://works.bepress.com/cgi/viewcontent.cgi?article=1000&context=cpeterson
13. Boyd, D.: Social Network Sites: Public, private, or what? The Knowledge Tree 13 (2007), http://kt.flexiblelearning.net.au/tkt2007/?page_id=28
14. Manovich, L.: Il linguaggio dei nuovi media. MCF Edizioni Olivares, Milano (2002)

15. Boyd, D.: Taken out of context. American teen sociality in networked publics. PhD dissertation, University of California Berkeley (2008),
    http://www.danah.org/papers/TakenOutOfContext.pdf
16. Meyrowitz, J.: Oltre il senso del luogo: come i media elettronici influenzano il comportamento sociale. Baskerville, Bologna (1985)
17. Nissenbaum, H.: Privacy as contextual integrity. Washington Law Review 79(1), 119–158 (2004)
18. Goffman, E.: The presentation of self in everyday life. Doubleday Anchor Books, New York (1959)
19. Beardsley, E.: Privacy: Autonomy and selective disclosure. In: Pennock, J.R., Chapman, J.W. (eds.) Nomos XIII: Privacy, pp. 56–70. Atherton Press, New York (1971)
20. Grimmelmann, J.: Saving Facebook. Iowa Law Review 94, 1137–1206 (2009)
21. Foucault, M.: Sorvegliare e punire. Nascita della prigione. Einaudi, Torino (1976)
22. Bentham, J.: Panopticon ovvero la casa d'ispezione. Marsilio, Venezia (2002)
23. Lange, P.: Publicly private and privately public: social networking on YouTube. J. of Comp-Med. Comm. 13(1), 361–380 (2007)
24. Sheehan, K.B.: Toward a typology of internet users and online privacy concerns. The Inf. Soc. 19(1), 21–32 (2002)
25. Lewis, K., Kaufman, J., Christakis, N.: The Taste for Privacy: an analysis of college student privacy settings in an online social network. J. Comp-Med. Comm. 14(1), 79–100 (2008)
26. OECD: Participative Web and user-created content Web 2.0, wikis and social networking. SourceOECD, 15(2007), i – 128 (2007)
27. Rouvroy, A.: Privacy, Data Protection, and the Unprecedented Challenges of Ambient Intelligence. Studies in Ethics, Law, and Technology, 2(1), art. 3 (2008)
28. Marvasti, A.: Qualitative Research in Sociology. Sage Publications, London (2004)
29. Given, L.M.: The SAGE Encyclopedia of qualitative research methods. Sage Publications, London (2008)
30. Codeluppi, V.: La vetrinizzazione sociale: il processo di spettacolarizzazione degli individui e della società. Bollati Boringhieri, Torino (2007)
31. Goodings, L., Locke, A., Brown, S.D.: Social networking technology: place and identity in mediated communities. J. Comm. & Appl. Soc. Psychol. 17(6), 463–476 (2007)

Micro and Macro Spatial Dimensions of New Media in Five European Countries

Leopoldina Fortunati and Federico de Luca

leopoldina.fortunati@uniud.it,
fdl1g10@soton.ac.uk

Abstract. The aim of this paper is to investigate how the possession of computers and mobile phones and access to the Internet is influenced by micro and macro spatial dimensions and how Europeans have embedded the possession of these technologies into the spatial dimension of their daily life. We gathered our data from two telephone surveys carried out in five European countries (Italy, France, Spain, the UK and Germany) using a representative sample of their populations (N=6609 in 1996 and N=7255 in 2009). Both surveys were sponsored by Telecom Italia. To accurately represent the spatial dimensions of Europe we focused on four variables: house size, city size, socio-economic macro area and country. These variables were analyzed alongside computer and mobile phone ownership and Internet access. The results have allowed us to obtain new insights into how the spatial dimensions of European societies are related to the diffusion of computers, the Internet and mobile phones.

Keywords: computer ownership, Internet access, mobile phone ownership, spatial dimensions, house size, city size, socio-economic European macro regions, Italy, France, Germany, Spain, the UK.

1 Introduction

The fact that space has always been an extremely significant factor in the process of communication is broadly acknowledged by the scientific community studying communication and information technologies [i.e. Thompson, [32]. However, usually one thinks of the concrete context in which the communication process takes place: sociological research projects in the last two decades have explored the usage of new media in the workplace (Fortunati, [9]; Pica & Sorensen, [26]), religious places (Katz, [20]), restaurants (Ling, [23]), trains (Fortunati, [11]), libraries (Hoeflich & Gebhardt & Rössler, [19]) , bars and cafés (Hoeflich, [16]) and so on. In addition, the context of mobility has been explored in contrast to inactivity (Lasch & Urry, [18]) as well as how ICTs have re-shaped towns (Aurigi, [1]; Hoeflich, [17, 18]; Kopoamaa, [21]; Townsend, [31]). The majority of these studies are however based on qualitative research, and so on data which cannot be generalized.

The focus of many of the studies concerning different spatial contexts is the observation of new explicit and implicit grammar rules that mediate behavior in the public space, by means of:

A. Esposito et al. (Eds.): COST 2102 Int. Training School 2010, LNCS 6456, pp. 190–206, 2011.
© Springer-Verlag Berlin Heidelberg 2011

- new trajectories of micro and macro gestures;
- complexification of prossemics;
- -the co-existence and merging of actual and virtual dimensions in the communication process;
- restructuring good manners.

Taipale [29, 30] has recently put forward an in-depth analysis of the role of space in the communication process. This research contested a trope which often recurs in the current sociological literature concerning the mobile phone, contending that the mobile phone is a metropolitan, urban technology.

In this paper we will focus on the role played by micro and macro spatial variables in the diffusion of new media, with the aim of understanding whether or not they influence the process of the diffusion of ICTs and to what extent. We will examine these variables in a situation in which it is possible to look at them all at once and inside a data set generated using a representative sample of five European populations. Moreover, it may be useful to articulate the following two sub-research questions: 1) are these spatial variables all significant in influencing the diffusion of new media, or are there one or more variables which are significant and others that are not? and 2) do larger spatial dimensions possess an increased strength corresponding to their size when influencing the diffusion of new media?

We will produce, where possible, a comparison between these two series of data (1996 and 2009) with the aim of understanding the main changes which occurred in these thirteen years in terms of the diffusion of these three technologies in Europe and in terms of the relationship between these technologies and European spatial dimensions. This will allow us to gain insights into areas which are important in outlining the communication process, allowing us a better understanding of the complexity of this process.

1.1 Literature Review

In the past, several major social theorists such as Simmel [28] have pointed out the importance of space in the communication process; in particular, he proposed that the social space may be seen as being organized according to different kinds of hierarchies. Moles & Rohmes [24] proposed conceptualizing the space in terms of spatial shells, which are similar to concentric circles of growing spaciousness and which correspond to the different dimensions of space surrounding the individual: the space of the house is the first circle, the space of the neighborhood is the second, that of the town is the third, that of the region is the fourth and so on. These two authors studied the manner in which the spatial shells reduced as the age of the individual increased. The outermost spatial shells (corresponding to the biggest distances) reduce around the elderly, and then, progressively, all the other ones follow. Among contemporary scholars, Castells et al. [2] analyzed the relationship between space and communication, distinguishing the space of places from the space of flows. In terms of the space of places, generally speaking, the concrete context in which communication takes place has been the most explored dimension. In contrast, as regards the space of flows, the context of mobility has been explored in relation to how ICTs re-shaped the towns (Kopomaa, [21]; Townsend, [31]) and finally in relation to how ICTs use reshaped the urban/rural dimension, for example, in China (Fortunati et al., [13]). However the majority of these studies are based on qualitative research and so on data which is not generalizable. At the cross between the notion of space of places and of space of flows is found the analysis proposed by Fortunati [11], which promotes the human body as the place in which a complex system of communications occurs and in which specific practices of convergence of the new (and old) media take place and merge with other systems of communication (such as fashion and good manners). Taipale [30] recently proposed an in-depth analysis of the role of space in the communication process, producing quantitative and qualitative data regarding Finnish society. This shows that the old separation between a rural dimension deprived of technology and an urban dimension well equipped with technology does not exist anymore. But which are the primary issues within the current sociological debate concerning the relationship between space and new media? The main conclusions discussed and elaborated upon in the debate regarding the diffusion of computers, mobile phones and the Internet are as follows. There is a shared understanding that the social use of new media has:

- developed the double register of space-actual and virtual-to describe the increase in the communication space;
- introduced the new concept of absence/presence (Fortunati, [10]; Gergen, [15]) and the notion of imagined co-presence (Urry, [33]);
- deeply influenced the evolution of the human sensorium (Crang & Thrift, [3]).

In 2009, Forlano [7] published an interesting paper in which she stresses the need to develop new spatial categories at a conceptual level. In particular, she uses the concept of "codescapes" in order to describe a new analytical category that integrates both physical and digital spaces. We support this new definition since homes, offices and third places are increasingly layered with digital information networks. Furthermore, this new term "codescapes" allows us to better describe the process of the reconfiguration of people, places and information which is occurring in the contemporary media landscape.

Another useful notion is that of spatial media, proposed by Shin [27]. Shin looks at technological artifacts as media which are able to create spatially differentiated social interactions also through immaterial, symbolic or affective elements. His notion of spatial media is useful, even more so if it is integrated with Sheppard's contribution [4]. Sheppard discusses spatial media in an original way, considering their relational features and seeing them as symbols which connect people and places. Traditionally, space has always been considered as a relational concept in the sense that humans acquire the notion of space through their relationship with other humans (initially, the mother). However, Sheppard argues that spatial organization does not emerge out of a set of preconceived spatial categories such as place, space and territory. Rather, "it is an emergent result of how places are connected together". In addition, the context in which technological artifacts are accessed can help to define the connection between places, rather than the internal attributes of the places themselves. Therefore, spatial media are about how people and places are connected together at the same time.

The studies that we mentioned concerning spaces as contexts were facilitated by the fact that concrete contexts are easier to investigate and that their influence is also more evident. The importance of these studies is undeniable, but they do not tell us to what extent space is important and the weight of spatial dimensions in the communication process. The role of less investigated spatial dimensions, such as the house size or the size of the urban and rural environment in which the mediated communication process takes place, as well as that of the region and of the country, is the object of this study.

The theory that we intend to apply is that of spatial shells as proposed by Moles & Rohmer [24], but read in the light of Forlano's [7], Shin's [27] and Sheppard's [4] contributions. Therefore, this study should be able to support a more complex notion of spatial shells, viewed as digital and physical spaces, characterized by different social interactions (mediated and non mediated) as well as symbolic and affective elements, and connected by multiple networks of relationships.

The structure of this article is as follows: the next section is dedicated to the illustration of the method which has been used, then we will illustrate the results of the two research projects regarding the role of spatial variables –the size of the house, the city, the macro region and the country- on the ownership of new media. Then we will analyze the effects of the four spatial shells considered together. In the final sections, we will discuss the results and draw conclusions.

2 Method

We will present in this paper the results of two surveys carried out in the five most populous and industrialized European countries (France, Germany, Italy, Spain and the UK) in 1996 and 2009. The questionnaires were conducted via a phone survey (CATI), and consisted of 6609 subjects in 1996 and 7255 in 2009, involving in both cases a representative sample of the population. The purpose of these two surveys was very broad, but here we will present and discuss the data relating to the diffusion and adoption of new media (namely the computer, the Internet and the mobile phone). Consequently, we considered four micro and macro spatial variables and several socio-demographic variables. The study which was conducted in 2009 partially replicated the research project carried out in 1996[1] (Fortunati, [8]). A complete replication was not possible due to the fact that in 2009, Europe was faced with a new field of information and communication technology, so the questionnaire had to be restructured. Furthermore, this is not a longitudinal study, since the samples were made up of different respondents. Telecom Italia financed both studies[2].

The demographic variables included in these research projects are gender, age, education, activity, family typology, income, house size (unfortunately only in the first survey), city size, socio-economic macro area and country. Among the respondents in 1996, 3,170 were male (48.0%) and 3,439 were female (52.0%), while in 2009, 3,551 were male (48.9 %) and 3,704 were female (51.1 %). The respondents' age was categorized into five groups (14-17, 18-24, 25-44, 45-64 and 65 years and

---

[1] To simplify the exposition we will use the term Europe and Europeans to indicate these five countries and their populations.

[2] In this study a weighted dataset was used in order to correct some distortions (related to age, education and ownership of the computer and access to the Internet) which affected the correct representation of the various quotas of the sample.

over). Level of education was divided into the following categories: low (primary and secondary school diploma), middle (high school diploma) and high (College/University degree or higher). Respondents' occupational classifications included persons who were employed, unemployed, housewives, students and retired. The typology of families consisted of single people, couples without children, couples with children, single-parent families and mixed families (all the other types of families). Income, with regards to the 1996 survey, was divided into three categories for each different currency, but they were all equivalent to the values adopted in 2009. In 2009 these values corresponded to: 20-30,000 euros per year (low); 30,001-60,000 euros per year (middle) and 60,001 or more euros per year (high). Finally, the spatial variables investigated were the house, the city, the macro region and the country.

The question regarding house size, which was investigated only in 1996, had to be structured in a different way in the UK ("How many living and bedrooms do you have?") and in all the other countries ("What is the surface area of your home?"), since this variable required information which is given in a different way in various cultures. In particular, while in all the continental countries people were accustomed to stating the dimensions of their house in square meters (sqm), in the UK people were accustomed to describing the dimensions of their house using the number of rooms. In order to have a consistent variable, we estimated the dimensions of a room at an average of 16 square meters, so that it was possible to discern a unitary answer for all the respondents. However, this variable must be treated with great caution. Five categories were outlined with respect to city size[3], while the macro regions in the various countries included groups of regions which form a homogeneous socio-economic system[4].

The analyses which are reported here are monovariate (frequencies), bivariate (cross-tabulations) and multivariate (logistic regression analyses). In particular, when

---

[3] In 1996 the categories were as follows: up to 20,000, 20,000-50,000, 50,000-100,000, 100,000-500,000 and 500,000 and more, but the answers did not include British respondents since they found very difficult to answer to this question; in 2009 they were: up to10,000, 10,000-30,000, 30,000-100,000, 100,000-500,000 and 500,000 and more. Thankfully, in 2009 British respondents did not find any difficult in answering to this question (for more information, see the paragraph "The second spatial shell: the city size").

[4] As for the macro regions, in Italy they include the following regions: North West = Piemonte, Lombardia, Val d'Aosta and Liguria; North East = Veneto, Friuli Venezia Giulia, Trentino Alto Adige and Emilia Romagna; Centre = Toscana, Umbria, Marche and Lazio; South = Abbruzzo, Molise, Puglia, Basilicata, Calabria, Campania, Sicilia and Sardegna. In France Centre / North East = Centre East, North, East, BP East; Paris = IDF; South = Mediterannée, South East; North West = West, BP West. In Germany N1 = Schleswig-Holstein, Hamburg, Bremen, Niedersachsen; N2 = Nordrhein-Westfalen; N3A+N3B = Hessen, Rheinland-Pfalz, Saarland, Baden-Württemberg; N4 = Bayern; N5+N6+N7 = Berlin, Brandenburg, Mecklenburg-Vorpommern, Sachsen-Anhalt, Sachsen, Thüringen. In the UK, North = North West, Yorkshire, North East; Scotland / N Ireland= Scotland, Northen Ireland, Border; Midlands = Midlands; South East / Anglia = London, South & South East, East; Wales / South West= Wales & West, South West. In Spain North West = Galicia, Asturias, Cantabria, Pais Basco, Castilla y Leon, La Rioja, Navarra; North East = Catalunia, Aragon; Centre = Madrid, Castilla la Mancha, Extremadura; East = Comunidad Valenciana, Murcia, Baleares; South = Andalucia and Canarias.

the χ^2 test was significant in the bivariate analyses, standardized residuals were considered[5]. In respect to the regression analyses, the Hosmer & Lemeshow test was used to verify the goodness-of-fit of the models. Three dichotomous questions about computer and mobile phone ownership, as well as Internet access, were used as dependent variables.

3 Results

3.1 The First Spatial Shell: House Size

Let us begin the analysis of the spatial shells with house size: the modal class for the size of a house within our five countries was from 50 to 99 sqm, as 42.8% of Europeans in 1996 were living in houses of these dimensions. Only a very limited section of our respondents (9.0%) lived in mini or midi apartments. The UK was the European country with the highest percentage of very small apartments (31.1%). The most common house size –between 50 and 99 sqm– was most frequent in the UK and Germany, where it applied to respectively 60.3% and 47.4% of the respondents. Houses between 100 and 120 sqm were more common in Italy (31.1%), while a significant number of houses from 121 to 199 sqm were concentrated in Germany (18.1%) and again in Italy (14.9%). Finally, houses measuring 200 sqm or more were more widespread in France (30.1%), in Spain (26.4%) and in Italy (19.8%).

Moving on now to analyze how house size was distributed within the socioeconomic macro areas of these five countries, it emerged that the smallest houses were significantly more widespread in all the British macro areas, and also in the French macro area of the Paris region. Houses between 50 and 99 sqm, which we observed to be the most common size in Europe, were concentrated particularly in the German macro areas N2 and N5 and in all the British macro areas. Houses from 100 to 120 sqm were instead prevalent within all the macro areas of Italy and in the German macro area N4. Houses between 121 and 199 sqm were located particularly within all the German macro regions, except the N5+N6+N7, as well as in the South and North West of Italy. Finally, big houses (200 sqm or more) were present particularly in all the French macro areas, in the South of Italy and in all the Spanish macro areas, except the North East.

Looking now at how house size interacted with city size, it emerged that the size of the house was inversely proportional to city size (Spearman's rank correlation coefficient = -0.218, significant at 0.01). In fact, 43.0% of the houses between 100 and 120 sqm and 52.7% of those of 200 sqm or more were present in smaller centers with up to 20,000 inhabitants, while 33.9% of mini apartments up to 49 sqm were found in the big cities with at least 500,000 inhabitants, Finally, 19.1% of midi apartments from 50

---

[5] The analysis of standardized residuals is based on the identification of the cells of a contingency table which are responsible for a significant overall chi square. Values outside of +/-1.96 are considered as statistically significant (e.g. Everett, [5]; Field, [6]). However to simplify the analysis we will read only the positive residuals with the purpose to see in which cell the relation was positive. These residuals are reported in the following tables with an asterisk when their values are more than 1.96.

to 99 sqm appeared in cities of medium size (from 100,000 to 500,000 inhabitants), and 20.4% appeared in big cities with 500,000 inhabitants or more.

In 1996 the diffusion of the internet was not influenced by the size of the house in which the respondent lived; however, computer and mobile phone diffusion was. The computer was much more embedded in everyday life than the mobile phone, which was still in its early stages (33.2% of the population had a computer, versus 15.3% with mobile phones). Moreover, these data show that house size had a significant influence on computer and mobile phone ownership which was predominantly concentrated in large apartments from 121 to 199 sqm.

3.2 The Second Spatial Shell: City Size

It is interesting to report the different dimensions of city size in 1996 and 2009 as they appear from the surveys. Three caveats must be made explicit from the beginning: 1) some of the categories used are different and so the data are not strictly comparable; 2) in the first collection of data, answers from the UK are lacking, since British respondents found it very difficult to answer this question given the different organization of the rural-urban continuum in their country. Thankfully, 13 years later respondents did not experience too many difficulties in answering (886 answers over 1411 respondents); 3) the high number of missing answers to this question should not come as a surprise, as many people do not even have a vague idea of the number of inhabitants who live in their city. Despite these caveats, this data is able to provide a sense of the changes undergone in the organization of the European habitat.

If we analyze city size in the European macro areas, it emerges that in 1996 the highest percentage of respondents lived in rural villages (up to 20,000 inhabitants) was related to the North West of Italy and to the macro areas of France such as the North West, the Center/North East and the South. Respondents living in small centers (20,000–50,000 inhabitants) were located primarily in the Paris area and in Germany, in particular in the areas of N3A+N3B, N4 and N1. Respondents living in small cities (50,000-100,000 inhabitants) were more likely to be found in the South and Center of Italy and in the German areas N2 and N1. Respondents living in middle cities (100,000–500,000 inhabitants) were more likely to live in the German macro area N2 and in all the Spanish macro areas except the North East. Finally, respondents living in big cities (more than 500,000 inhabitants) were more likely to stay in the North East of Italy, in the Paris area, in the German macro areas N2, N5+N6+N7 and N1 and in the Center and North East of Spain.

In 2009, respondents living in rural villages (up to 10,000 inhabitants) were located particularly in the North West, North East and South of Italy, in all the German macro areas except N2, and in the North West and the Center/North East of France. People living in small centers (10,000–30,000 inhabitants) were situated in the South, North East and North West of Italy, followed by the German N4 and N3A+N3B. Respondents living in small cities (30,000-100,000 inhabitants) were more likely to be found in the South, North East and Center of Italy, in the East, South and North West of Spain and in the German area N2. People living in medium cities (100,000-500,000 inhabitants) were particularly present in all the British macro regions. Finally, respondents living in big cities (more than 500,000 inhabitants) were more likely to stay in the Paris area and in the South of France, in the South East/Anglia, and in the centre of Spain.

Finally, at a more macro level, city size in the five countries in 1996 and 2009 demonstrates a change that occurred in Europe because of the general progression of urbanization. In 1996, the rural way of living was more widespread in France and in Italy, and the small provincial cities were more commonly found in Germany. The intermediate size cities were more common in Germany and Italy, while Spain appeared to be grounded in the larger dimensions of urbanity. But if we look at 2009, the highest presence of small centers up to 10,000 and from 10,000 to 30,000 was in Italy and in Germany. The small cities with 30,000 to 100,000 inhabitants were more common in Spain and in Italy. The middle sized city was more common in the UK, while the highest presence of big cities was registered in France, followed by Spain. Germany, which in 1996 was made up primarily of medium sized and big cities, in 2009 appeared to have revised its strategy of the habitat, with a strong concentration of small cities with up to 30,000 inhabitants and medium cities from 100,000 to 500,000 inhabitants. On this last dimension also the UK tends to have a strong concentration of small cities, like Germany, while Spain, which in 1996 was particularly rich in cities with 100,000 inhabitants and over, in 2009 appeared to have more cities with 30,000 to 100,000 inhabitants or more.

Ownership of computers, mobile phones and access to the Internet relate in different ways to the spatial dimensions of the city, both because they are technologies which have a different structural relation with the space surrounding them and because our observations were based in two periods when the diffusion of said technologies was in two very different stages. The computer was more established in Europe at the time of the first survey, while the mobile phone was in the second stage of its diffusion and the Internet was just at its beginning. Let us start with the computer. From this data it is clear how the diffusion of the computer in these five countries has been influenced by city size and continues to be influenced now. In particular, in 1996, computer ownership was significantly lower in the small centers and significantly higher in the cities with 500,000 inhabitants or more. It is well known that in the case of the computer the social learning process was vital, that is, support by friends and colleagues in learning how to deal with the device (see also Williams, Stewart & Slack, [34]). In 2009 there was only a general association between city size and computer ownership.

With regards to the diffusion of the mobile phone, neither in 1996 nor in 2009 was the diffusion of this technology influenced by city size. Perhaps this related to the fact that being an individual, personal tool, mobile phone ownership is less likely to relate to the different spatial dimensions of the social sphere. Furthermore, the fact that a mobile phone is cheaper to buy than a computer, and that the expenses for its use are easily controllable thanks to prepaid cards, has freed it from the spatial characteristics of the rural/urban habitat.

Finally, let us analyze the diffusion of Internet access. As expected, Internet access in 1996 was more concentrated in cities with 500,000 or more inhabitants, while being far less in the small centers. This may be due to infrastructure problems, in addition to social learning problems, and the high costs involved for families. Thirteen years later, a general association between city size and Internet access persists, but without any specific relationship to different sized cities.

3.3 The Third and Fourth Spatial Shells: European Macro Areas and Countries

In this paragraph we will not perform a descriptive analysis of the interactions between all European macro areas and the five countries surveyed in 1996 and 2009 because of length restrictions and because more in-depth analysis of this area was possible through the logistic regression that we will present in the following paragraphs.

With regards to Europe in 1996, the mobile phone was significantly more wide-spread in all the Italian macro areas and in some British macro regions such as South East/Anglia, the North and the Midlands. As regards the computer, this device was more common in the German N2, N3A+N3B, N4, in South East/Anglia and the North East of Spain. Internet access was more widespread in South East/Anglia, the North and the Midlands in the UK, and in the German area N2. With regards to the situation in Europe in 2009, the highest concentration of mobile phones was in the South and the Center of Italy. The computer was significantly more widespread in the North of the UK and Internet access was more widespread in all the macro areas of Germany, except N5+N6+N7.

Regarding the diffusion of the computer, the mobile phone and Internet access in 1996 among the five countries being considered, Italy was the one in which the mobile phone was most widespread, followed by the UK. Germany and the UK had the highest percentage of computer owners, and the UK was at the top for Internet access. In 2009, Italy continued to be at first place in terms of the diffusion of the mobile phone, followed by the UK. France was in top place in terms of computer ownership, while Germany and then France had the highest internet access.

3.4 Analysis of the Effects of the Four Spatial Shells Considered Altogether

Table 1 represents the results of a series of logistic regressions that we conducted with the aim of verifying whether or not in 1996 and 2009 spatial dimensions such as

Table 1. Ownership of computer, Internet and mobile phone in Europe in 1996 and 2009: odds ratios and Hosmer-Lemeshow test significance per each model

	Computer		Internet		Mobile phone	
	1996	2009	1996	2009	1996	2009
Country. ref: Italy						
France	0.402***	1.502	0.756	1.695*	0.379***	0.169***
Germany	1.383	2.434***	0.653	3.720***	0.408**	0.179***
Spain	0.597*	1.019	0.663	1.138	0.467*	0.539
United Kingdom		3.164**		3.228***		0.381*
Age. ref: 25-44						
14-17	0.878	1.476	1.150	1.138	1.820*	0.864
18-24	0.834	1.725**	1.087	1.307*	1.201	1.528
45-64	0.922	0.734**	0.690	0.804**	0.823	0.455***
65+	0.369***	0.366***	1.499	0.410***	0.685	0.374***
Education. ref: Low edu.						
Medium education	1.869***	2.197***	1.185	2.019***	1.129	1.692***
High education	3.708***	3.607***	2.799**	3.296***	1.643***	1.871***
Gender. ref: Females						
Males	1.805***	1.559***	1.471	1.395***	1.217*	1.579***

Table 1. (*Continued*)

Activity. ref: Workers						
Unemployed	0.894	0.378***	0.787	0.492***	0.379***	0.551**
Retired	0.558***	0.297***	0.078**	0.358***	0.357***	0.354***
Student	1.881***	1.433	0.968	1.343	0.610**	1.194
Housewife	1.209	0.624***	1.815	0.686**	0.941	0.452***
Family. ref. Couple with children						
Couple without children	0.562***	0.459***	1.431	0.525***	1.197	1.196
Single	0.445***	0.303***	0.926	0.357***	0.705	0.700**
Single parent family	0.743	0.695*	1.568	0.613**	1.623*	0.946
Mixed family	0.894	0.519***	1.189	0.559***	1.329*	0.708*
City size. ref: Up to 10 or 20.000						
20.000-50.000	1.281*		1.961		1.268	
10.000-30.000		0.989		1.178		0.930
50.000-100.000	1.135		2.475*		1.218	
30.000-100.000		1.114		1.048		0.872
100.000-500.000	1.415**	0.983	2.198	0.958	1.181	0.712**
500.000+	1.297	1.096	2.702*	1.144	0.980	0.966
House size. ref: 50-99 sqm						
From 10 to 49 sqm	*0.586**		*0.565*		*0.767*	
From 100 to 120 sqm	*1.317***		*2.325***		*1.312**	
From 121 to 199 sqm	*2.043****		*2.753***		*1.879****	
200 and more sqm	*1.706****		*2.112**		*1.527***	
Macro regions. ref: NW of Italy						
Italy NE	*0.649**	0.693	0.272	0.820	*1.343*	0.806
Italy Centre	*0.750*	0.715	0.851	0.870	*0.943*	1.625
Italy South	*0.386****	0.585**	0.217	0.586**	*0.931*	0.802
France Paris	*1.457*		1.533		*1.655*	
France NW	*1.171*	1.272	0.577	1.191	*1.411*	1.098
France Centre/NE	*1.251*	1.019	1.929	1.058	*1.420*	0.794
France South		1.141		1.115		1.261
Germany N1	0.689	0.779	2.434	0.767	0.949	0.867
Germany N2	1.068	0.885	2.958	0.854	0.795	1.210
Germany N3A+N3B	1.131	0.820	1.841	0.815	1.060	0.945
Germany N5+N6+N7	0.593*	0.474***	1.156	0.412***	0.641	1.470
UK North		0.834		0.806		1.669
UK Wales/SW		0.703		0.754		1.793
UK Midlands		0.426*		0.495*		0.793
UK SE/Anglia		0.339**		0.385**		0.936
Spain NW		1.154		1.325		0.643
Spain NE	2.234**		1.128		1.790	
Spain East	1.103	1.333	0.640	1.410	0.961	0.542
Spain South	0.960	1.091	0.219	1.097	0.729	0.670
Spain Centre	1.506	1.707	1.927	1.354	0.766	0.476*
Hosmer-Lemeshow test sig.	0.781	>0.000	0.683	>0.000	0.095	0.203

Sig.: * = p<0.05, ** = p<0.01, *** = p < 0.001. The statistical software used for these analyses was STATA.

house size, the size of the city of residence, geographical macro areas, and country, considered altogether, influenced the diffusion of the computer, the Internet and the mobile phone in Europe, once gender, age, education, family typology and activity were controlled.

Results in Table 1 show that in 1996 the computer was the more sensitive technology to spatial variables, since the ownership of this device was influenced by all the spatial variables: house size, city size, macro regions and country. Respondents living in mini apartments possessed a computer in fewer cases than those living in houses from 50 to 99 sqm. For the rest of the respondents, the bigger the surface area of the house, the higher the probability that those living there owned a computer. The exception was those living in houses of 200 or more sqm, who had a lower probability of computer ownership than those living in houses of 121 to 199 sqm. This probably means that back in 1996, the computer still required a considerable space in a house in order to be accommodated .

In addition, the size of the city mattered: the bigger the city, the most likely it was that the inhabitants owned a computer. However, there was not a progressive increase, since cities with between 50,000 and 100,000 inhabitants do not appear to act as attractive, spatial infrastructures for the diffusion of the computer, and nor do the biggest cities. Furthermore, the diffusion of the computer was also sensitive to the macro regions: the Italian North East and South were strongly behind on computer ownership, as well as the German macro area composed of N5+N6+N7, while the North East of Spain was far ahead. However, on the whole, France and Spain had, at that time, fewer computer owners than Italy and the other countries.

Apart from the spatial variables, the structural variables which were significant in the model were gender (more males than females had a computer), age (elderly people from 65+ had fewer computers than the younger respondents), education (the higher the level of education, the more likely were respondents to own a computer), activity (retired people had fewer computers and students had more) and finally the family typology, as respondents living in families composed of couples without children or single families had fewer computers.

The Internet in Europe in 1996 was not reacting to macro spatial variables such as country or macro region but only to the micro ones: house size and city size. As we previously noted for the computer, respondents living in houses of 100 sqm or more were more likely to be able to access the Internet. With regards to city size, the larger concentration of Internet connections was in small cities of 50,000-100,000 inhabitants and in big cities (from 500,000 upwards).

In addition to the spatial variables, only two structural variables were significant: education (a high level of education increased the probability of Internet access) and activity, in the sense that being retired dramatically lowered the likelihood of Internet access.

Mobile phone ownership in Europe in 1996 was influenced by country and house size, but not city size or macro regions. France, Germany and Spain had fewer mobile phones than Italy and, as with computer ownership and Internet access, respondents living in houses of 100 sqm or more had a higher probability of owning a mobile.

Several structural variables were significant: gender (males were more likely to possess a mobile phone than females) and age (the youngest respondents from 14 to 17 years old were more likely to possess a mobile than all the other respondents). A high level of education increased the probability of mobile ownership, and people who were unemployed, retired or students had fewer mobiles than workers. Finally, respondents living in single-parent families and mixed families were more likely to possess a mobile phone than those living in all the other kinds of families.

In 2009 the situation in Europe is quite different; these logistic regressions, according to the Hosmer & Lemeshow test, do not seem to fit the data anymore, at least in terms of providing an explanation for computer ownership or Internet access. Evidently, there are other variables intervening that were not accounted for in the 2009 survey.

Computer ownership is more widespread in Germany and the UK than in Italy. In the South of Italy as well as in the N5+N6+N7 areas of Germany, and in the Midlands and the South East/Anglia of the UK, computer ownership is less widespread than in the North West of Italy.

Young people between 18 and 24 years old are more likely to possess a computer than respondents of age 25-44, while respondents of 45 years old are even less likely to own a computer (the likelihood continues to decrease with age). Males have a higher probability than females of owning a computer, and the more educated a person is, the more likely he/she is to have a computer. Housewives and people who are unemployed or retired are still less likely than workers to possess a computer. Finally, respondents living in all the other different families typologies have a lower probability of having a computer than those living in families composed of a couple with children.

As regards the Internet, Germany, the UK and France are more likely to have Internet access than Italy. The South of Italy, the N5+N6+N7 areas of Germany and the Midlands and the South East/Anglia areas of the UK are less likely to have Internet access than the North West of Italy.

Young respondents between 18 and 24 years have a higher probability of having Internet access than those from 25 to 44 years old, while respondents from 45 years onwards have a lower probability. As the level of education increases, more respondents are found to have access to the Internet. Males have a higher probability than females of having a connection to the Internet. Housewives and people who are unemployed and retired are still less likely to have access to the Internet than workers, and respondents living in all the different families typologies have a lower probability of Internet access than those living in families composed of a couple with children.

In terms of mobile phones, the probability that respondents would own a mobile was lower in Germany, France and the UK than in Italy. The macro region where inhabitants are least likely to have a mobile is the Center of Spain. A city of 100,000-500,000 inhabitants has a lower probability of mobile phone ownership than the smallest town with under 10,000 inhabitants.

Respondents of 45 years and older have a lower probability of owning a mobile than respondents of 25-44, and the elderly are even less likely to do so. The more education a person has received increases the likelihood that they will have a mobile. Males have a higher probability than females of possessing a mobile phone and a higher level of education increases the probability a respondent will have a mobile.

Housewives and people who are unemployed or retired are still less likely to own a mobile than workers. Singles and people living in a mixed family have a lower probability of owning a mobile than respondents living in a family made up of a couple with children.

Table 2 summarizes the influence of spatial variables on computer and mobile phone ownership and Internet access. In the first stage of the diffusion of personal computers, all the spatial variables are important, while for the Internet only the spatial variables at a micro level are relevant, and for the mobile only the very micro and the very macro.

On the whole, however, the spatial variable which is the strongest and which maintains its strength over the course of time is country, followed by macro region and then by city size. Therefore it appears that the larger a space is, the stronger its influence is on the possession of new media.

Table 2. Spatial variables' significance (+) at 95% in Europe in 1996 and 2009

	Computer		Internet		Mobile phone	
	1996	2009	1996	2009	1996	2009
House size	+	Np	+	Np	+	Np
City size	+	-	+	-	-	+
Macro region	+	+	-	+	-	+
Country	+	+	-	+	+	+

NB: The data for house size in 2009 were not collected.

In the second step of the analysis we conducted a series of logistic regressions with the aim of investigating whether, if the spatial variables were considered altogether, they would influence the computer and mobile phone ownership and/or Internet access once the structural variables have been controlled. This has now been completed for each individual country, in order to investigate whether the relations between the variables varied significantly between them. As shown in Table 3, some variables, such as city size, lose strength, while the macro regions maintain their influence. Among the structural variables, the strongest are activity and family typology, then education, followed by gender and age.

Each country reacted in a specific way to the spatial variables. In 1996 the most sensitive countries were Germany and Spain, while the least sensitive was France. In 2009 the impact of spatial variables on the ownership of these three media was much more moderate. France and Spain, for example, do not show any significant relationship between the ownership of new media and the spatial variables, while Germany shows only two significant relationships between computer ownership and Internet access and its macro regions. These countries also react in a specific way to the structural variables; for example, in 2009, Spain did not show any significant relationship between gender and new media ownership, while France did not show any significant relationship between age and new media ownership.

Table 3. Ownership of computer, Internet and mobile phone in the five European countries in 1996 and 2009: spatial and structure variables' significance (+) at 95%, and Hosmer-Lemeshow test significance per each model

	Italy 1996			France 1996			Germany 1996		
	Comp.	Inter.	Mob.	Comp.	Inter.	Mob.	Comp.	Inter.	Mob.
Macro Regions	+						+		
City size	+		+	+			+		
House size							+	+	+
Age				+		+	+		+
Gender				+			+		
Education	+			+			+	+	
Activity	+	+	+			+	+		+
Family typology	+	+	+	+			+		
Hosmer-Lemeshow test significance	0.43	n.s.	0.22	0.87	1.00	n.s.	0.35	n.s.	0.91

	Spain 1996			UK 1996		
	Comp.	Inter.	Mob.	Comp.	Inter.	Mob.
Macro Regions	+		+			+
City size	+	+	+			
House size	+		+	+		+
Age	+	+		+		
Gender	+			+	+	
Education	+		+	+	+	
Activity	+					+
Family typology	+	+		+		+
Hosmer-Lemeshow test significance	0.65	n.s.	n.s.	0.06	0.08	0.42

	Italy 2009			France 2009			Germany 2009		
	Comp.	Inter.	Mob.	Comp.	Inter.	Mob.	Comp.	Inter.	Mob.
Macro Regions	+	+					+	+	
City size		+							
House size									
Age	+	+	+				+	+	+
Gender	+	+		+	+		+	+	+
Education	+	+	+	+	+		+	+	+
Activity	+	+	+		+	+	+	+	+
Family typology	+	+	+	+	+		+	+	+
Hosmer-Lemeshow test significance	n.s.	n.s.	0.78	n.s.	0.12	0.26	n.s.	n.s.	0.40

	Spain 2009			UK 2009		
	Comp.	Inter.	Mob.	Comp.	Inter.	Mob.
Macro Regions				+	+	
City size						+
House size						
Age	+	+	+			+
Gender				+		+
Education	+	+	+		+	
Activity	+	+	+	+	+	+
Family typology	+	+	+	+	+	+
Hosmer-Lemeshow test significance	n.s.	n.s.	n.s.	n.s.	n.s.	0.18

4 Final Discussion and Conclusion

These results tell us various things. First, that spatial variables are very important and have to be considered carefully when designing surveys concerning new media.

Second, each area of information and communication technology has its own particular relationship with space and produces a specific communication space.

Third, it seems that the larger the space is the higher is the probability that it will exert influence upon the possession of new media, even though the spatial variables do not increase in strength automatically as the dimensions increase. Media are spaces themselves, which bring different information and communication projects, procedures, practices and potentialities, and that shape in a particular way the space surrounding them. They in their turn are shaped by this space, which conveys social practices but also the infrastructures which are fundamental for the diffusion of ICT.

Fourth, the relationship that each device has with space changes according to the specific moment of its diffusion For example, at the beginning of the diffusion of all new media, the dimension of the house was a relevant factor. The domestication and integration process of technologies inside the domestic space involves the space of the house. Therefore the more a technology is essential to the running of a house, the easier it is to find a solution to accommodate it in the domestic space. Thirteen years later, the importance of macro regions became vital to understanding the ownership of new media. New media seem to be used to enlarge the physical space in which one lives only when this physical space is already large.

Fifth, each country reacts in a specific way to spatial variables, showing that cultures have the strength to respond in a unique fashion to these spatial variables.

Sixth, in the 2009 survey, the socio-demographic variables were no longer useful in explaining computer ownership or Internet access. This has important implications regarding the debate concerning the relationship between social exclusion and these technologies. In this debate there is a rhetoric which attributes the lack of access to these technologies to socio-economic factors. However, this research shows that other variables are involved in the lack of ownership of new media.

Seventh, ICTs are not automatically connected to the urban dimension anymore, in the sense that this dimension no longer allows us to clearly discriminate in terms of who owns new media. This result confirms those obtained by Taipale in his research projects [29, 30].

The notion of codespaces as we redefined it and as it emerges from this research works well, with this one distinction: a crowded physical space does not automatically correspond to a digital intensity.

References

1. Aurigi, A.: Making the digital city: the early shaping of urban internet space. Ashgate, London (2004)
2. Castells, M., Fernandez-Ardevol, M., Linchuan Qiu, J., Sey, A.: Mobile communication and society: a global perspective. MIT Press, Cambridge (2007)
3. Crang, M., Thrift, N. (eds.): Thinking space (critical geographies). Routledge, London (2000)

4. Ekbia, H.R.: An interview with Eric Sheppard: uneven spatialities–the material, virtual, and cognitive. The Information Society 25(5), 364–369 (2009)
5. Everett, B.E.: The analysis of contingency tables, 2nd edn., pp. 46–48. Chapman & Hall/CRR, Boca Raton (1992)
6. Field, A.: Discovering statistics using SPSS, 3rd edn., pp. 698–700. Sage, London (2009)
7. Forlano, L.: WiFi geographies: when code meets place. The Information Society 25(5), 344–352 (2009)
8. Fortunati, L. (ed.): Telecomunicando in Europa. Angeli, Milano (1998)
9. Fortunati, L.: The mobile phone: an identity on the move. Personal and Ubiquitous Computing 5(2), 85–98 (2001)
10. Fortunati, L.: The mobile phone: towards new categories and social relations. Information, Communication, and Society 5(4), 513–528 (2002)
11. Fortunati, L.: Mobile telephones and the presentation of self. In: Ling, R., Pedersen, P.E. (eds.) Mobile communications: re-negotiation of the social sphere, pp. 203–218. Springer, London (2005)
12. Fortunati, L., Manganelli, A.M.: La comunicazione tecnologica: comportamenti, opinioni ed emozioni degli europei. In: Fortunati, L. (ed.) Telecomunicando in Europa, pp. 125–194. Angeli, Milano (1998)
13. Fortunati, L., Manganelli, A.M., Law, P., Yang, S.: Beijing calling...modernization and the social effects of new media in China. Knowledge, Technology, and Policy 21(1), 19–27 (2008)
14. Gergen, K.J.: The challenge of absent presence. In: Katz, J., Aakhus, M. (eds.) Perpetual contact: mobile communication, private talk, public performance, pp. 227–242. Cambridge University Press, Cambridge (2002)
15. Gergen, K.J.: Mobile communication and the transformation of democratic process. In: Katz, J. (ed.) Handbook of mobile communication studies, pp. 297–310. The MIT Press, Cambridge (2008)
16. Hoeflich, J.: Mobile phone calls and emotional stress. In: Vincent, J., Fortunati, L. (eds.) Electronic emotion: the mediation of emotion via information and communication technologies, pp. 63–84. Peter Lang, Oxford (2009)
17. Höflich, J.R.: Part of two frames: mobile communication and the situational arrangement of communicative behaviour. In: Nyiri, K. (ed.) Mobile democracy: essays on society, self, and politics, pp. 33–52. Passagen Verlag, Vienna (2003)
18. Höflich, J.R.: A certain sense of place: mobile communication and local orientation. In: Nyíri, K. (ed.) A sense of place: the global and the local in mobile communication, pp. 149–168. Passagen Verlag, Vienna (2005)
19. Gebhardt, J., Höflich, J.R., Rössler, P.: Breaking the Silence? The Use of the Mobile Phone in a University Library. In: Hartmann, M., Rössler, P., Höflich, J.R. (eds.) After the Mobile Phone? Social Changes and the Development of Mobile Communication, pp. 203–218. Frank & Timme, Berlin (2008)
20. Katz, J.E.: Magic in the air: spiritual and transcendental aspects of mobiles. In: Nyíri, K. (ed.) Mobile understanding: the epistemology of ubiquitous communication, pp. 201–223. Passagen Verlag, Vienna (2006)
21. Kopomaa, T.: City in your pocket: the birth of the mobile information society. Gaudeamus, Helsinki (2000)
22. Lash, S., Urry, J.: Economies of signs and space. Sage, London (1994)
23. Ling, R.: One can talk about common manners!" The use of mobile telephones in inappropriate situations. In: Haddon, L. (ed.) Communications on the move: the experience of mobile telephony in the 1990s, vol. 248, pp. 97–120. Sweden Cost 248, Farsta (2008)

24. Moles, A., Rohmer, E.: Psychologie de l'espace. Casterman, Paris (1972)
25. Nyiri, K. (ed.): A sense of place: the global and the local in mobile communication. Passagen Verlag, Vienna (2005)
26. Pica, D., Sørensen, C.: On mobile technology in context: exploring police work. Journal of Computing and Information Technology 12(4), 87–295 (2004)
27. Shin, Y.J.: Understanding spatial differentiation of social interaction: suggesting a conceptual framework for spatial mediation. Communication Theory 19(4), 423–444 (2009)
28. Simmel, G.: Soziologie: untersuchungen über die formen der vergesellschaftung. Leipzig: Duncker & Humblot [tr.it. Sociologia. Torino: Edizioni di Comunità (1998)] (1908)
29. Taipale, S.: The mobile phone: Is it an urban phenomenon? In: Pertierra, R. (ed.) The social construction and usage of.communication technologies: Asian and European experiences, pp. 82–99. The University of the Philippines Press, Diliman (2007)
30. Taipale, S.: Does location matter? A comparative study on mobile phone use among young people in Finland. The Journal of New Media and Culture, 6(1) (2009), http://www.ibiblio.org/nmediac/summer2009/ MobileLocation.html (retrieved 16 June, 2010)
31. Townsend, A.M.: Life in the real-time city: mobile telephones and urban metabolism. Journal of Urban Technology 7, 85–104 (2000)
32. Thompson, J.B.: The media and modernity: a social theory of the media. Stanford University Press, Stanford (1995)
33. Urry, J.: Mobility and proximity. Sociology 36(2), 255–274 (2002)
34. Williams, R., Stewart, J., Slack, R.: Social learning in technological innovation: experimenting with information and communication technologies. Edward Elgar, Cheltnham (2005)

Nonverbal Expressions of Turn Management in TV Interviews: A Cross-Cultural Study between Greek and Icelandic

Maria Koutsombogera[1], Sigrún María Ammendrup[2], Hannes Högni Vilhjálmsson[2], and Harris Papageorgiou[1]

[1] Institute for Language & Speech Processing, Artemidos 6&Epidavrou, 15125 Athens, Greece,
{mkouts,xaris}@ilsp.gr
[2] School of Computer Science, Reykjavik University, Menntavegur 1, 101 Reykjavík, Iceland
{sma,hannes}@ru.is

Abstract. In this paper we discuss a cross-cultural analysis of non-verbal expressions (gestures, facial expressions, body posture) that have a turn managing function in the flow of interaction. The study was carried out by analyzing and comparing the features of interest in two samples of institutional interaction, namely face-to-face political interviews, in Greek and Icelandic respectively. The non-verbal behavior of the participants in both interviews was annotated following the same annotation process. The attested turn management instances were compared in order to find similarities and differences in terms of frequency and modality preference.

Keywords: turn management, non-verbal expressions, institutional interaction.

1 Introduction

In this paper we study the multimodal behavior of interview participants in two different languages and cultures, Greek (GR) and Icelandic (IC). We focus on the non-verbal expression of turn taking, i.e. the non verbal expressions employed to regulate the flow of interaction, as attested in representative samples of TV interviews. Specifically, we explore if there are diversities -and to what extent- across two seemingly different cultures in the way participants manage the exchange of their turns non-verbally, in the domain of institutional interaction, namely political interviews.

Media talk in general echoes the tendencies in media discourse and thus may contain indicators of culturally driven relations not only between media and politics [1], but also between discourse practices and the overall multimodal interaction among the participants involved. The non verbal channel is inherently related to speech and discourse/conversational structures [2]; non-verbal features are incorporated in discourse practices and can highlight the speakers' behaviour as well as yield insights into culturally specific cues. So, the discourse representation used in the interactional functions across the two cultures may largely affect the production of the respective non-verbal behaviour. What we expect to find are variations in the semiotics of this behavior, namely the choice/ preference of specific facial, hand or torso movements as well as their frequency.

A. Esposito et al. (Eds.): COST 2102 Int. Training School 2010, LNCS 6456, pp. 207–213, 2011.

Several comparative studies have been conducted in order to explore differences in how non-verbal expressions are related to speech. Some examples involve the study of the gestural behavior of speakers belonging to different ethnic groups [3] social groups [4], native& non-native speakers of a specific language [5], and speakers whose language is of different structure and thus their non-verbal expressions fit aspects of the events that are linguistically expressed [6, 7].

The main points from the aforementioned studies are that differences may be due to the structure of the spoken language or to practices related to the interaction conduct per se. It is worth mentioning that, while the data studied in the literature so far pertain to the discourse types of either everyday interaction or narrations, our data, the political interviews, are a sample of institutional interaction. Even so, our expectations from the present study are that interview participants from different cultures make different non-verbal expressions.

However, according to the literature, the methodological outcome of conducting such comparisons is that the attention should be drawn not only to language differences but also to differences in culture or social classes within the culture and, finally, differences in discourse settings. Keeping in mind the above principles and setting aside the pure linguistic analysis, we will closely keep track of the interplay between cultural differences and discourse setting in order to discover which one of those principles is determinant over the non-verbal turn management behavior of the speakers.

2   Data Collection

In the current study, the comparison is focused on the non-verbal attestations of the communicative dimension of turn taking in political interviews between 2 different languages and cultures (GR-IC). In order to identify possible differences or similarities, we studied data taken from political TV interviews. Data in both languages share a common basis regarding (a) the setting of the interaction, namely live broadcast TV political interviews taking place in a studio and pertaining to an institutional type of interaction, (b) the identity of the interview participants; the hosts in both interviews are professional journalists, while the guests are government representatives, the Minister of Industry in the IC interview and the Minister of Public Order in the GR interview respectively, (c) the duration of the interviews, approx. 17 minutes each. The topic of discussion is different in each interview, namely power plants for aluminum companies in IC and police and public order in GR, both very current and controversial issues.

3   Annotation Process

The data we studied are TV political, face-to-face interviews multimodally annotated. In each interview, the audio signal is transcribed[1]. The subsequent video annotation[2] deals with the labeling of the non-verbal expressions (facial displays, hand gestures and torso movements) co-occurring with speech at two levels: (a) identification and

---

[1] http://trans.sourceforge.net/
[2] http://www.lat-mpi.eu/tools/elan/

boundary annotation on the time axis and, (b) assignment of turn management labels. The levels and labels used in the annotation scheme are mainly inspired by the MUMIN v3.3 coding scheme notation [8]. Both audio and visual signals as well as the annotations are perfectly synchronized; the overall set of annotation levels is distinguished by speaker, and all the annotation metadata are integrated into a single xml file.

Table 1. Annotation scheme used; for each feature of face, gesture and torso movements, a detailed set of labels is used to capture the exact form of the non-verbal expression employed

Facial display	Hand gesture	Body posture	Turn management
Gaze	Handedness	Torso	Turn take
Eyes	Trajectory		Turn accept
Eyebrows			Turn yield
Mouth			Turn offer
Lips			Turn complete
Head			Turn hold

4 Turn Taking in Political Interviews

The turn-taking mechanism enables the speakers to manage the smooth and appropriate exchange of speaking turns in face-to-face interaction. Turn taking organization has been investigated thoroughly in order to discover the detailed rules of conversational behavior [9, 10] and the constraints imposed by the context. Specifically, it has been examined how turns are introduced, the forms they may have and the devices by which they are expressed in terms of prosody, discourse strategies and non-verbal cues.

Turn taking is expressed actively through content (words), intonation, paralanguage, and non-verbal expressions [11]. We believe that the multimodal analysis of such behaviors provides significant information and accurate observations besides the study of speech only. Non-verbal expressions do not simply accompany speech but they are indicators of the degree of success of the speakers' intentions and projections and shed light on the strategies used for the accomplishments of the interaction. They are signals by which each participant indicates his/her state with regard to the speaking turn.

Turn taking in political interviews is largely affected by the situational and conversational constraints that are imposed by the institutional frame in which this genre pertains [12, 13].The interview can be regarded as an institutionalized discourse type, because it appears to be highly controlled and conventionalized, constrained by institutional role-distribution and turn pre-allocation and is less prone to spontaneous interventions. Consequently, the non-verbal behavior should follow the principles of this specific frame.

Situationally, the interview takes place in a particular setting, addressing an overhearing audience and complying with several talk-related restrictions, such as a predetermined agenda, time restrictions which lead to monitored turns, speaker selection restrictions, and turn-taking restrictions; the host is primarily responsible for selecting the next speaker and for coordinating the turn-taking sequences; and finally discursive constraints such as talk-framing patterns.

5 Data Analysis

5.1 Non-verbal Turn Management: Frequency

The study of the annotated interviews, of approx. 17 minutes duration each, shows that speakers in both interviews frequently employ non-verbal expressions (NVEs) throughout their turns. Although the total number of attested NVEs is much bigger for the GR interview (982 instances) compared to the IC interview (511 instances), the NVEs related to turn management communicative function are comparable in both interviews (cf. Table 2).

The remaining NVEs are related to other communicative functions that do not form part of this study, such as feedback, emotions/ attitudes expression, content-related NVEs (e.g. iconic gestures) and so on. We therefore assume that the difference in the overall number of NVEs is attributed to instances which are not related to turn management and that GR speakers are more productive regarding this aspect.

Table 2. Distribution of attested non-verbal expressions; TM: related to turn management, other: not related to turn management, total: overall

	Interviewer				Interviewee			
Language	GR		IC		GR		IC	
		[Per Turn]		[Per Turn]		[Per Turn]		[Per Turn]
TM NVEs	147	1.27	112	1.22	137	1.18	139	1.51
other	193	1.66	42	0.45	505	4.35	218	2.37
total NVEs	340	2.93	154	1.67	642	5.53	357	3.88

In the Greek data the total number of turns amounts to 116 while in the Icelandic data to 92. Both interviews participants use non-verbal expressions to regulate their turns according to their interactional needs and goals. There is roughly the same rate of TM NVE production (i.e. NVEs/turn) by both GR and IC interviewers, namely 1.27 NVEs/turn versus 1.22 NVEs/turn respectively. However, the IC interviewee seems to be producing a few more TM NVEs per turn than the GR one with a rate of 1.51 and 1.18 respectively. Further experimentation and data are needed in order to explore whether this difference is due to cultural traits.

The majority of the turn management NVEs are employed by the GR interviewer to express turn offer (37.4%), by the IC interviewer to express turn take (60.7%), by the GR interviewee to express turn accept (46%) and by the IC interviewee to express turn hold (46%).

5.2 Non-verbal Turn Management: Preferred Modalities

The goal of non-verbal turn management may be achieved by single face, hand or torso movements, or through a combined use of distinct modalities, either in a synchronized or a partly overlapping manner. In this study, all figures refer to unique instances of NVEs performed by a single modality.

Although speakers employ most of their expressive means throughout turn management, they show a certain affinity towards particular modalities, as depicted in Figure 1. Specifically, the GR interview participants clearly prefer the facial displays (50.3% for the interviewer and 73.7% for the interviewee), while in the IC interview the preference is shared between gestures for the interviewer (46.4%) and facial displays for the interviewee (58.3%).

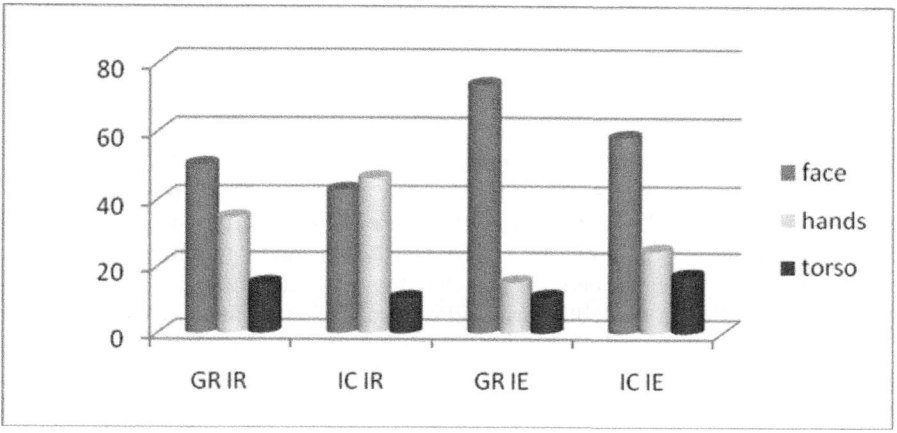

Fig. 1. Percentage distribution of non-verbal expressions of turn management in Greek (GR) and Icelandic (IC) interviewers (IR) and interviewees (IE) respectively

If we go into more detail at the modality subtypes, we attest certain variations regarding the choice of the most appropriate NVE according to the interview participants. Table 3 depicts the preferred modality subtypes. Usually, there is only one

Table 3. Preferred modality subtypes per turn management dimension by the interview participants

Turn Management dimension	GR Interview		IC Interview	
	Interviewer	Interviewee	Interviewer	Interviewee
Turn Take	Head Tilt	Eyebrows raise	Gaze Down	Gaze Down
Turn Accept	Smile	Head Tilt, Gaze Towards	Index Finger	Gaze Down
Turn Yield	Head Nod	Smile	Gaze Down, Gaze Towards	Eyebrows raise
Turn Offer	Head Tilt	—	Gaze Down, Gaze Towards	Eyebrows raise
Turn Complete	Smile, Gaze Towards	Head Nod, Smile	—	—
Turn Hold	—	Head Tilt, Gaze Down	Gaze Down, Gaze Towards, Gaze Sideways	Gaze Down

dominant subtype. In some cases though, some turn management dimensions were highly represented by more than one subtypes, as is the case of turn hold regarding the IC interviewer. Another interesting finding is the fact that the predominant NVE in the Icelandic data is gazing down. Again, more data are needed to interpret this NVE preference and its possible linking to culture-specific behaviour. Finally, the table cells with no entry in them denote that either there were no NVEs catering for the specific turn management dimension, or there was no significant lead of one subtype over another.

6 Discussion

As shown in Section 5, participants in both interviews share roughly the same rate of turn management NVEs. This was not expected, as it is a common belief that the further north you go in Europe, the more reserved and less overtly expressive people become. However, when we examined the most prominent NVEs for each turn management function (Table 3) we realized that there are some differences in the form of turn management between the two interviews. More data is required to substantiate whether the form observed here is characteristic of the culture, but it is interesting to see here how different modalities can serve the exact same function. Further qualitative analysis of non-verbal expression properties such as intensity, complexity and duration will also be the focus of our future work.

Thus, our initial expectations that there should be notable differences between multimodal behaviors among the two languages and cultures were not verified. Instead, non-verbal turn management seems to be coordinated to the discourse strategies that the interviewers use to portray the political situation and its representatives during an interview. The political interview is a strictly framed discourse setting, institutional & conventionalized, different from casual conversation where speakers can express themselves in a more spontaneous and unrestricted manner. Before drawing any general conclusions about the cultural differences regarding non-verbal behavior, it remains to be seen whether switching to another, less restricted interactional domain or setting (like casual conversation) would provide more evidence about culture-specific practices and conventions.

References

1. Lauerbach, G.: Discourse representation in political interviews: The construction of identities and relations through voicing and ventriloquizing. Journal of Pragmatics 38(2), 196–215 (2006)
2. McNeill, D.: Hand and Mind: What Gestures Reveal About Thought. University of Chicago Press, Chicago (1992)
3. Efron, D.: Gesture, Race and Culture. Mouton, The Hague (/1941/1972)
4. Kendon, A.: Geography of gesture. Semiotica 37(1/2), 129–163 (1981a)
5. Kendon, A.: Gesture: Visible Action as Utterance. Cambridge University Press, Cambridge (2004
6. McNeill, D., Duncan, S.: Growth points in thinking-for-speaking. In: McNeill (ed.) Language and Gesture, pp. 141–161. Cambridge University Press, Cambridge (2000)

7. Kita, S., Özyürek, A.: What Does Cross-Linguistic Variation in Semantic Coordination of Speech and Gesture Reveal? Evidence for an Interface Representation of Spatial Thinking and Speaking. Journal of Memory and Language 48, 16–32 (2003)
8. Allwood, J., Cerrato, L., Jokinen, K., Navarretta, C., Paggio, P.: The MUMIN Coding Scheme for the Annotation of Feedback, Turn Management and Sequencing Phenomena. Multimodal Corpora for Modeling Human Multimodal Behaviour. Journal on Language Resources and Evaluation 41(3-4), 273–287 (2007)
9. Sacks, H., Schegloff, E., Jefferson, G.: A simplest systematics for the organization of turn-taking for conversation. Language 30, 696–735 (1974)
10. Ford, C.E., Thompson, S.A.: Interactional Units in Conversation: Syntactic, Intonational, and Pragmatic Resources for the Management of Turns. In: Ochs, E., Schegloff, E.A., Thompson, S.A. (eds.) Interaction and Grammar, pp. 134–184. Cambridge University Press, Cambridge (1996)
11. Duncan Jr., S.: Some Signals and Rules for Taking Speaking Turns in Conversations. Journal of Personality and Social Psychology 23(2), 283–292 (1972)
12. Heritage, J.: Conversation Analysis and Institutional Talk. In: Sanders, R., Fitch, K. (eds.) Handbook of Language and Social Interaction, pp. 103–146. Lawrence Erlbaum, New Jersey (2005)
13. Ilie, C.: Semi-institutional Discourse: The Case of Talk Shows. Journal of Pragmatics 33, 209–254 (2001)

Interpretation and Generation of Dialogue with Multidimensional Context Models

Harry Bunt

Tilburg University
harry.bunt@uvt.nl

Abstract. This paper presents a context-based approach to the analysis and computational modeling of communicative behaviour in dialogue. This approach, known as Dynamic Interpretation Theory (DIT), claims that dialogue behaviour is multifunctional, i.e. functional segments of speech and nonverbal behaviour have more than one communicative function. A 10-dimensional taxonomy of communicative functions has been developed, which has been applied successfully by human annotators and by computer programs in the analysis of spoken and multimodal dialogue; which can be used for the functional markup of ECA behaviour; and which forms the basis of an ISO standard for dialogue act annotation. An analysis of the types of information involved in each of the dimensions leads to a design of compartmented, 'multidimensional' context models, which have been used for multimodal dialogue management and in a computational model of grounding.

Keywords: Multidimensional context modeling, dialogue acts, dialogue semantics, dialogue generation, dialogue act annotation.

1 Introduction

A context-aware dialogue system should base both the determination of its own actions and its interpretation of the user's behaviour on a model of the current context. Every dialogue system is context-aware to some extent, since its operation depends on the dialogue history. For instance, a simple frame-based system for providing public transport information may conduct a dialogue by systematically acquiring a number of parameter values such as the specification of a destination, of a departure place, of a travel date, and an approximate arrival or departure time, and subsequently providing information which results from a data base query with these parameter values. Such a system bases its actions on the current state of the frame, in particular on which parameter values have not yet been found, and interprets user inputs in terms of the parameter values that it is looking for. Such a system has a very limited context-awareness, due to the limited interpretation of 'context' as a set of task-specific parameter values.

In general, the term 'context' refers to the surroundings, circumstances, environment, background or settings of the activity of which the context is considered. In linguistics the term `context' has most often been interpreted as referring to the surrounding text. The context of a spoken dialogue utterance is also often understood in

A. Esposito et al. (Eds.): COST 2102 Int. Training School 2010, LNCS 6456, pp. 214–242, 2011.

this sense, in particular with reference to the preceding dialogue, but the broader interpretation in terms of circumstances, background and settings is important as well, and includes in particular the following:

(1) a. the type of interaction;
   b. the task or activity that motivates the dialogue;
   c. the domain of discourse;
   d. the physical or perceptual conditions;
   e. the information available to the dialogue participants.

Each of these notions of context occur in particular senses of the word `context' in English, as illustrated below:

(2) a. *in the context of a human-computer dialogue*
   b. *in the context of a doctor-patient interview*
   c. *in the context of philosophical discourse*
   d. *in the context of telephone conversation*
   e. *in the context of hardly any shared assumptions*

Each of these notions of context is relevant for the interpretation and generation of dialogue behaviour. Whether one is (a) participating in a dialogue with a computer or in a dialogue with another person may make a great difference, for example, for the interpretation and generation of 'social' dialogue acts like greeting, thanking, apologizing, and saying goodbye. When a human dialogue partner wishes one a good day, at the end of a dialogue, it may be quite appropriate to return the wish, but it seems nonsense to wish a machine a good day[1]. Whether (b) one is being interviewed by a doctor, rather than having a chat with the neighbours, may make a great difference for how much one will say about one's health problems. Similar considerations apply with respect to the other notions of 'context' in (1) and (2).

A definition of context which encompasses all these uses and which is appropriate for the study of dialogue and the design of dialogue systems, is the following:

(3) Context in dialogue is the totality of conditions which influence the interpretation or generation of utterances in dialogue [9].

This definition is rather too broad to be effectively useful. In order to arrive at a more manageable notion of context, we note that, according to this definition, a dialogue context has a proper part formed by those elements that can be influenced by dialogue. Whether one is talking to a computer or to a person (see 2a) is for example typically a permanent feature of a dialogue context, which is not changed by the dialogue. (Although this may happen: the occurrence of a persistent problem in communicating with a computer may cause the user to get connected to a human operator.) Or also, (2b) whether a dialogue takes place in the context of a patient seeing a doctor, or (2c), whether one participates in a philosophical discourse or in a dialogue aiming to know the departure time of a particular train, is not something that changes during a dialogue.

---

[1] We have witnessed inexperienced users of a spoken dialogue system do so, and subsequently be extremely annoyed at their own behaviour.

The consideration of which context information may be changed by a dialogue and which information cannot, leads to the distinction between *local* and *global* context. The global context is formed by the information that is not changed by the dialogue, and is often important in a global sense, having an influence on overall speaking style and use of interaction strategies. The local context contains the information which is changed when an utterance is understood, and is therefore crucial for the semantic interpretation of dialogue utterances.

(4) **Local context** is the totality of conditions which may be changed through the interpretation of dialogue utterances.

Local context information is typically more complex and fine-grained than global context information and requires an articulate form of representation.

In this paper we analyse the question which kinds of information need to be represented in the context model of a sophisticated natural language based dialogue system, taking a context-based approach to the understanding and generation of utterances in spoken and multimodal dialogue. More specifically, we view the meaning of a dialogue utterance in terms of how the context model of a dialogue participant is changed when he understands the utterance as encoding multiple dialogue acts. We summarize the theoretical framework of Dynamic Interpretation Theory (DIT), in which this view has been elaborated, and discuss its consequences for the content and structure of context models for dialogue interpretation and generation. We show how such a context model can be represented by means of typed feature structures, and show how such models can be applied in the study and computational modeling of a range of aspects of spoken and multimodal communication.

2   Context and Dialogue Interpretation in DIT

2.1   Dialogue Semantics

The framework of Dynamic Interpretation Theory owes its name to the observation that communicative behaviour is best understood in a dynamic way, in terms of communicative actions called dialogue acts, which are directed at one or more addressees and which describe what the speaker is trying to achieve as the result of his action being understood by the addressee(s). Upon understanding a dialogue act performed by a speaker (S), an addressee (A) forms certain beliefs about S's intentions and assumptions and other aspects of S's mental state. Consider example (5), showing the effects on A's knowledge about S that occur when A understands a *Check Question* addressed to him.

(5) S, addressing A: *This is the two-forty to Naples, right?*
     (q = this is the two-forty to Naples)
     1. A assumes that S wants to know whether q;
     2. A assumes that S assumes that A knows whether q;
     3. A assumes that S has a weak belief that q.

Note that the latter condition in (5) distinguishes a *Check Question* from a yes-no question. More generally, each type of dialogue act corresponds to a particular effect on an understander's state of information. In DIT, such states of information are called *contexts*, and the description of how context changes capture the understanding of communicative behaviour is called a *context-change semantics* [9]. This approach to utterance meaning is also known as the 'information state update' or `ISU' approach [48].

The application of a context-change approach to utterance meaning can only be successful if the context models that are used contain the kinds of information that can be changed by a dialogue act. For example, the semantic interpretation of a turn-grabbing action, whereby a dialogue participant A tries to take the speaker role from another participant S who currently occupies that role, should involve that S understands that A wants to occupy the speaker role; this can be accommodated in a context-change semantics only if a context model is used which contains information about the allocation of the sender role. (And by the same token, in the case of a multi-party conversation, the understanding of whom the current speaker is addressing requires the modeling of the distribution of the addressee role and other participant roles among the participants in the conversation.) Similarly, the semantic interpretation of a *Stalling* act (*Let me see...*) requires a context model which includes a representation of the estimated time needed by a speaker to construct his next contribution to the dialogue.

More generally, by inspecting the semantic interpretation of the kinds of things that participants in a dialogue say and signal (possibly nonverbally, or partly through language and partly nonverbally) in terms of changes in the context model of an understanding agent, we can obtain a catalogue of the kinds of information that a dialogue context model should include. A crucial step in such a process is constructing a catalogue of "kinds of things that participants in a dialogue say and signal". One of the products of the research in which the DIT framework has been developed is such a catalogue, through the definition of a comprehensive taxonomy of types of dialogue acts, called the DIT^{++} taxonomy[2] (This taxonomy has been designed to include in a systematic and consistent fashion besides the dialogue acts in the original DIT taxonomy [6] also a number of act types from other schemes, such as DAMSL, MRDA, and SLSA, with the aim to define a domain-independent schema for the functional annotation and semantic analysis of multimodal dialogue.

The DIT framework was developed to support the analysis of human dialogue, as well as the design of computer dialogue systems, in particular for system components which are usually called *Dialogue Managers*. Dialogue management is primarily a process of deciding what next to do in a dialogue. The question of what kinds of information should be included in a context model can be approached not only from the perspective of *understanding* dialogue behaviour, but equally from that of the *generation* of dialogue contributions. A Dialogue Manager's task of deciding how to continue a dialogue at a given point, can be formulated as making a choice from the possible things to say, which is a task that presupposes (again) some kind of catalogue of the kinds of things that could possibly and sensibly be said at that point. Or rather, that could be said *given the state of the context that has been brought about by the dialogue up to that point.*

---

[2] See http://dit.uvt.nl

For example, suppose the user has asked the system *Which flights from London are expected this evening after six, and which ones tomorrow morning before twelve?*, to which the answer needs to be looked up by going through a list with tonight's expected arrivals and through the flight schedule of the next morning, a dialogue system could decide that it needs a few seconds to collect this information and that it would therefore be appropriate to perform a *Stalling* act (like *Let me see.., London, this evening,....*) or a *Pausing* act (*Just a minute*). The Dialogue Manager will be able to generate such 'time management acts' only if has an awareness of the time needed by its information processing, in other words, if its context model includes information about the estimated time needed by this processing. More generally, a Dialogue Manager can only generate a given dialogue act if the conditions motivating the performance of that act are represented in its current context model; hence the specification of the functionality of a Dialogue Manager goes hand in hand with a specification of the kinds of information to be represented in its context model. A sophisticated dialogue system would be expected by its users to be able to generate the same classes of dialogue acts as the ones that it can understand, hence the generation perspective on context model requirements and the utterance understanding perspective are two sides of the same medal.

The DIT framework seems especially fruitful for studying the contents of context models because of the detailed taxonomy of dialogue acts that it has defined, which supports a view on communication as consisting of multiple layers of activity, such as the layer of pursuing a particular task or goal, that of taking turns, that of providing feedback, and that of managing the use of time. This multidimensional view posits that dialogue participants are often simultaneously engaged in communicative activities in several of these layers, and that their communicative behaviour is therefore often *multifunctional*. In the rest of this section we summarize the DIT view on multifunctionality in dialogue.

2.2 Multifunctionality and Multidimensionality

Studies of human dialogue indicate that natural dialogue utterances are very often multifunctional. This is due to the fact that participation in a dialogue involves several activities beyond those strictly related to performing the task or activity for which the dialogue is instrumental. As noted by Allwood in [4], in natural conversation, among other things, a participant constantly *"evaluates whether and how he can (and/or wishes to) continue, perceive, understand and react to each other's intentions"*. They share information about the processing of each other's messages, elicit feedback, and manage the use of time and turn allocation, of contact and attention, and of various other aspects. Communication is thus a complex, multi-faceted activity, and for this reason dialogue utterances are often multifunctional. An analysis of this phenomenon [14], [15] shows that functional segments in spoken dialogue on average have 3.6 communicative functions, when functional segments are defined as follows:

(6) A **functional segment** is a minimal stretch of behaviour that has a communicative function (and possibly more than one).

Multidimensional taxonomies support dialogue utterances to be coded with multiple tags and have a relatively large tag set; see e.g. [3], [12], [13], [32], [45]. A large tag set may benefit in several respects from having some internal structure, in particular, a taxonomical structure based on semantic clustering can be searched more systematically and more 'semantically' than an unstructured one, and this can be advantageous for dialogue annotation, interpretation, and generation.

Bunt [12] suggests that a theoretically grounded multidimensional schema should be based on a theoretically grounded notion of dimension, and proposes to define a *set of dimensions* as follows.

(7) Each member of a set of dimensions is a cluster of communicative functions which all address a certain aspect of participating in dialogue, such that:

   1.   dialogue participants can address this aspect through linguistic and/or non-verbal behaviour;
   2.   this aspect of participating in a dialogue can be addressed independently of the other aspects corresponding to elements in the set of dimensions, i.e., an utterance can have a communicative function in one dimension, independent of its functions in other dimensions.

The first of these conditions means that only aspects of communication are considered that can be distinguished according to empirically observable behaviour in dialogue. The second condition requires dimensions to be independent, 'orthogonal'.

Petukhova and Bunt in [40], [41] present test results based on co-occurrence frequencies, phi-statistics, and vectorial distance measures to empirically determine to what extent the dimensions that are found in 18 existing annotation schemas are well-founded. A conclusion from this study is that the 10 dimensions of the DIT^{++} taxonomy, described below, form a well-founded set of dimensions.

2.3 Dimensions

The ten dimensions of DIT^{++} have emerged from an effort to provide a semantics for dialogue utterances across a range of dialogue corpora. Utterances have been identified whose purpose was to address the following aspects of participating in a dialogue:

(8) 1. advancing a task or activity motivating the dialogue;
   2. monitoring of contact and attention;
   3. feedback on understanding and other aspects of processing dialogue utterances;
   4. the allocation of the speaker role;
   5. the timing of contributing to the dialogue;
   6. structuring the dialogue and monitoring the progression of topics;
   7. editing of one's own and one's partner's contributions;
   8. the management of social obligations.

Whether these aspects qualify as proper dimensions can be determined by checking them against definition (7). Take for instance the timing of contributions. Utterances that address this aspect of interacting include those where the speaker wants to gain a little time in order to determine how to continue the dialogue; this function is called

Stalling. Speakers indicate this function by slowing down in their speech and using fillers, as in *Ehm, well, you know,...* The observation that dialogue participants exhibit such behaviour means that the category of functions addressing the timing of contributions (which also includes the act of *Pausing,* realized by means of utterances like *Just a minute, Hold on a second*) satisfies criterion (7.1). Moreover, the devices used to indicate the *Stalling* function can be applied to virtually any kind of utterance, which may have any other function in any other dimension. Timing therefore satisfies criterion (7.2) as well, and hence qualifies as a proper dimension.

A similar analysis can be applied to the other aspects. Of these, the feedback category should be divided into two, depending on whether a speaker gives feedback on his own processing, or whether he gives or elicits feedback on the addressee's processing; we call these dimensions 'Auto-Feedback' and 'Allo-Feedback', respectively [7]. Examples of auto- and allo-feedback are:

(9) Auto-feedback: *Okay, right, m-hm; What?,* nodding, smiling; frowning
    Allo-ffedback: *Okay? all right?; Nonono, Hoho, Wait a minute!*

Similarly, the category of dialogue acts concerned with editing one's own or one's partner's contributions, is better split into those concerned with editing one's own speech, called the Own Communication Management (OCM) dimension (using Allwood's terminology [5], and those concerned with the correction or completion of what the current speaker is saying, which by analogy we call the Partner Communication Management (PCM) dimension. Examples of OCM and PCM acts are (10) and (11), respectively. In (10) the speaker corrects himself; in (11) B corrects A's first utterance (PCM), which is subsequently acknowledged by A.

(10) A: *then we'e going to g-- turn straight back*

(11) A: *back to Avon, drop-*
     B: *pick up the oranges*
     A: *sorry, pick up the oranges*

Dialogue acts with a dimension-specific function are often performed partly or entirely nonverbally, such as positive feedback by nodding, negative feedback by frowning, or turn assignment by direction of gaze. A study by Petukhova [38], performed in the context of the EU project AMI[3], showed that all the communicative functions of the nonverbal behaviour of participants in AMI meetings could be described adequately in terms of the DIT[++] functions, and produced a catalogue of nonverbal means (notably head gestures, facial expressions, and gaze behaviour) for expressing DIT[++] communicative functions, either by themselves or in combination with verbal behaviour.

All in all, this had lead to the distinction of the following 10 dimensions in the DIT[++] taxonomy:

---

[3] Augmented Multi-party Interaction; see http://www.amiproject.org

1. Task/Activity: dialogue acts whose performance contributes to advancing the task or activity underlying the dialogue;
2. Auto-Feedback: dialogue acts that provide information about the speaker's processing of previous utterances. Feedback is 'positive' if the processing was successful at the level that is addressed; negative feedback, by contrast, signals a processing problem;
3. Allo-Feedback: dialogue acts used by the speaker to express opinions about the addressee's processing of previous utterances, or to solicit information about that processing;
4. Contact Management: dialogue acts for establishing and maintaining contact, such as *Hello?*;
5. Turn Management: dialogue acts concerned with grabbing, keeping, giving, or accepting the sender role;
6. Time Management: dialogue acts which signal that the speaker needs a little time to formulate his contribution to the dialogue, or that the interaction has to be suspended for a while;
7. Discourse Structuring: dialogue acts for explicitly structuring the conversation, e.g. announcing the next type of dialogue act, or proposing a change of topic;
8. Own Communication Management: dialogue acts for editing the contribution to the dialogue that the speaker is currently producing;
9. Partner Communication Management: the agent who performs these dialogue acts does not have the speaker role, but assists or corrects the dialogue partner who does have the speaker role in his formulation of a contribution to the dialogue;
10. Social Obligations Management: dialogue acts that take care of social conventions such as welcome greetings, apologies in case of mistakes or inability to help the dialogue partner, and farewell greetings.

Positive and negative feedback acts do not necessarily express only success or problems encountered in processing previous utterances, but may additionally express an *attitude* such as happiness, surprise or regret. For dealing with this phenomenon, DIT makes use of a set of *qualifiers* which can be attached to communicative functions of a responsive nature, indicating a particular emotion or attitude towards the content that is discussed or towards the addressee (see [42]), as illustrated in example (13).

(13) 1. A: Could you please give me the details of that connection?
     2. B: That's flight NY 607, departure eleven twenty a.m., arrival one forty p.m.
     3. A: Perfect! Thanks!

In this example, A's utterance *Perfect!* signals not only that A has processed B's utterance successfully, but also that A is pleased with the information that he received. Using the qualifier attribute `sentiment` with the value `pleased`, this can be represented in the DiAML annotation language[4] as follows:

---

[4] DiAML: Dialogue Act Markup Language, as defined in ISO standard 24617-2 [29].

```
(14) <dialogueAct xml_id="da1" target="#fs3.1"/>
        sender="#a" addressee="#b"
        communicativeFunction="autoPositive"
        dimension="autoFeedback"
        sentiment="pleased"
     </dialogueAct>
```

3 Communicative Functions

Some communicative functions are specific for a particular dimension; for instance *Turn Accept* and *Turn Release* are specific for turn management; and *Stalling* and *Pausing* are specific for time management. Other functions can be applied in any dimension; for instance a *Check Question* can be used with task-related semantic content in the Task dimension, but can also be used for checking correct understanding (feedback). In general, all types of question, statement, and answer can be used in any dimension, and the same is true for commissive and directive functions, such as *Offer, Suggest*, and *Request*. These communicative functions are therefore called *general-purpose* functions, as opposed to *dimension-specific* functions. The use of *Question* acts in different dimensions is illustrated in (15)

(15) 1. Are you open this Sunday. [*Task*]

    2. Did you say Thursday? [*Auto-Feedback*]
    3. Did you hear what I said. [*Allo-Feedback*]
    4. Anyone have anything more to add? [*Discourse Structuring*]
    5. Can you give me a moment to check this? [*Time Management*]
    6. Peter, would you mind to continue? [*Turn Management*]

The DIT⁺⁺ taxonomy of communicative functions therefore consists of two parts:

    1. a set of clusters of **general-purpose functions**;
    2. a set of clusters of **dimension-specific functions**.

Figure 1 shows the taxonomy of general-purpose functions. This taxonomy falls apart into four hierarchies:

  — *information seeking* and *information providing* functions, which seek or provide information, respectively, and which together form the class of *Information Transfer* functions;
  — *commissive and directive* functions, where the speaker commits himself to performing an action, or puts pressure on the addressee to perform or participate in an action; together, these form the class of *Action Discussion*

functions, which bring an action into the discussion that may or should be performed by the speaker, by the addressee, or jointly.

In each of these hierarchies, a mother - child relation between two communicative functions means that the child function is a special case of the mother function, while siblings are alternative, mutually exclusive specializations. The hierarchical structure of the set of general-purpose functions can effectively be used as a decision tree for deciding which communicative function applies to a given dialogue segment.

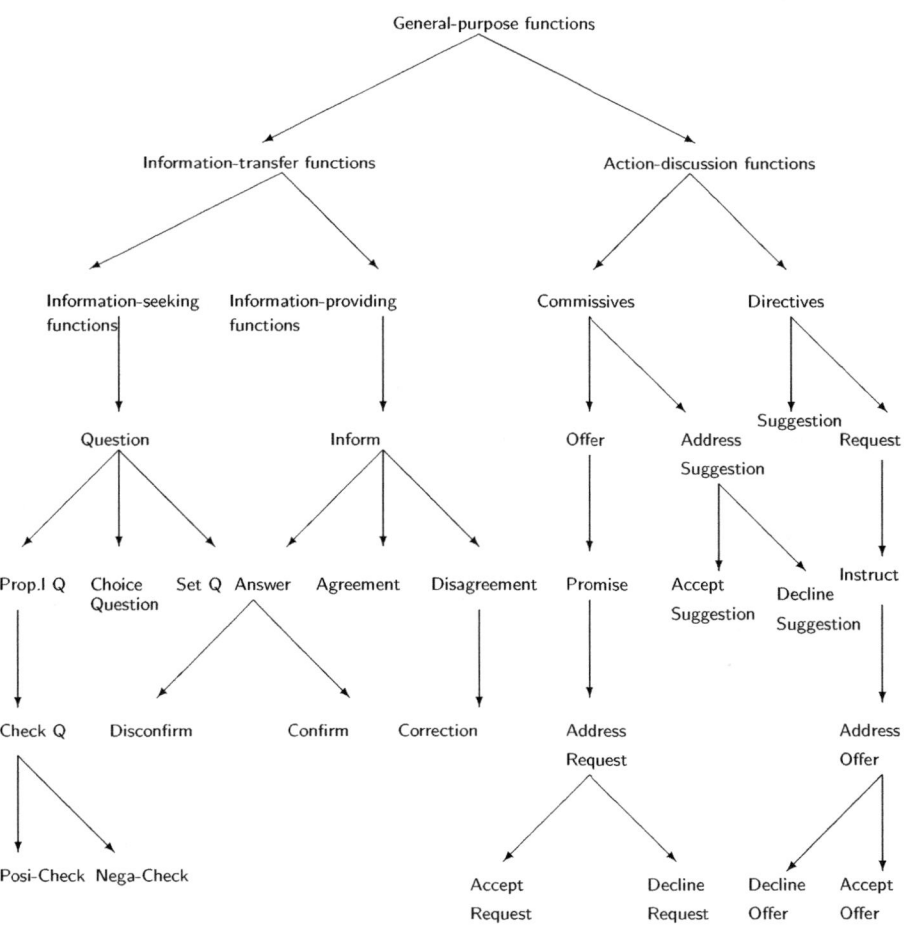

Fig. 1. DIT⁺⁺ general-purpose functions

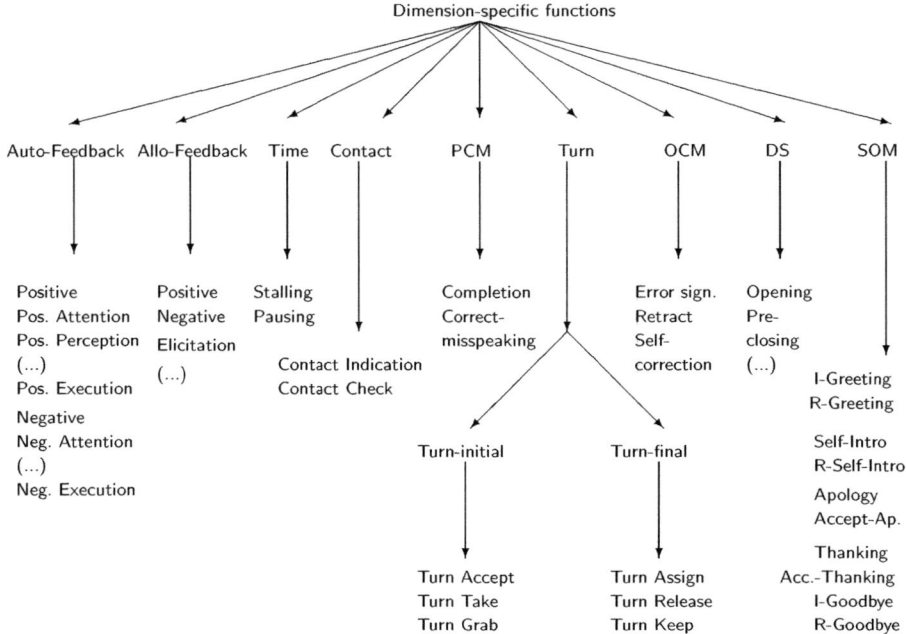

Fig. 2. DIT⁺⁺ dimension-specific functions

4   Content and Structure of a Dialogue Context Model

Considering the content and structure of a context model, it should be kept in mind that a context model by definition is always the context model *of a particular dialogue participant*, since the generation and interpretation of dialogue acts is a separate process for each participant, and it can only be influenced by information about the context as viewed by that participant.

4.1   A Catalogue of Context Information

A well-defined set of dimensions, like those listed in (12), can help us to obtain a catalogue of kinds of information that an adequate dialogue context model should contain, since the communicative activities in each of these dimensions address a different type of information. In this section we examine each of these types of information.

a. Task/Actvity

The dialogue acts in the Task/Activity dimension have information concerning the underlying task or activity as their semantic content, and in order to provide a basis for interpreting and generating such dialogue acts, every context model needs to incorporate this kind of information. We have seen in Section 1 that a very simple, frame-based dialogue system employs a primitive form of this type of information, represented by slots in a frame where certain parameter values can be filled in. More sophisticated dialogue systems, that can accept and generate a variety of dialogue act types, need a more sophisticated representation of task-related information; in particular, they need to take into account that some task-related information is available only to the participant whose context model is considered, some is not available to him but assumed to be available to one or more other participants, and still other information is assumed to be shared. These distinctions are of crucial importance if a dialogue system is to maintain a consistent context model while taking into account that a participant may contribute information that is incompatible with the information in the context model under consideration.

The importance of this point may be appreciated by considering the following example.

(16) 1. A: So the deadline for IWCS passed yesterday, but I didn't submit this time; I wasn't happy with what I'd written so far.
    2. B: But the deadline has been extended, didn't you see?

In this example participant A performs an *Inform* act which provides participant B with certain information; B has reason to believe that A is partly wrong, and expresses that in the second utterance. This illustrates the fact that understanding an *Inform* act with semantic content X, performed by speaker A, does not mean for an addressee B that X is the case, which would be inconsistent with what B knows, but that A *believes that X*. And such a belief is obviously compatible with B believing that X is not the case. More generally, this shows that the representation of task-related information in a context model must be relative to a participant (or to be shared by multiple participants).

An important phenomenon in dialogue is that of establishing a *common ground*, information that each participant assumes to be shared with the other participants. This is for example relevant in the case of a disagreement, like (16); if the participants try to resolve the disagreement, and reach a stage where they believe they have succeeded in doing so, this should be represented in the context model; for this purpose a representation of *assumed common ground* is needed[5].

In sum, the representation of task-related information in the context model of a dialogue participant requires the representation of:

(17) a. information about the task
    b. assumptions about the other participants' information about the task
    c. assumptions about the task-related information that is shared with other participants.

b. Processing Information
b1. Own processing
The dialogue acts in the Auto-Feedback dimension have as their semantic content information about the speaker's own processing of previous dialogue utterances, most often of the last utterance by the previous speaker.

DIT distinguishes five levels of understanding that participants in a dialogue may reach in processing each other's utterances. The lowest level is that of paying *attention*. In a human-computer dialogue this hardly seems a relevant level to take into

---

[5] See [18] for a DIT-based computational model of establishing common ground.

consideration, but it is is quite relevant in human dialogue, especially in multi-party dialogue.

The next higher level, that of *perception*, is particularly important in spoken dialogue systems, where it is associated with problems in speech recognition. Because current ASR systems are far from perfect, there is a tendency in spoken dialogue systems to provide feedback all the time in order to let the user know what the system thinks the speaker said.

The next higher level, that of understanding in the sense of semantic and pragmatic *interpretation*, corresponds to identifying the speaker's intentions, i.e., to recognizing the communicative functions and semantic contents of his dialogue acts, and therefore determining the appropriate context update to perform.

The *evaluation* level is concerned with examining whether the context update, constructed by the successful understanding of a functional dialogue segment, is checked for leading to a consistent state of the context model. If the processing at this level is successful, then the participant's context model is indeed updated. For instance, evaluating a question is deciding whether it can be considered as a genuine request for information, which is worth answering; similarly, evaluating an answer is deciding whether the sender indeed may be assumed to provide information which he (the sender) assumes to be correct.

Reaching the *execution* level means being able to do something with the result of the evaluation. For example, in the case of a question, it consists of finding the requested information; in the case of an answer, successful 'execution' is integrating its content with the context model, leading to a new, consistent state of the model. If an inconsistent state would result, then the integration does not go through, and the execution of the answer fails. Similarly, unsuccessful execution of a question means that the requested information is not found (leading to responses like *I don't know.*)

At each of these levels of processing, a participant may encounter difficulties:

- At the level of attention the problem that may occur is that a participant did not pay attention and therefore did not hear what was said.
- At the level of perception, not only a machine but also a human participant may encounter speech recognition difficulties, e.g. because the speaker spoke unclearly or softly, or because some acoustic disturbance corrupted the communication channel.
- At understanding/interpretation level the participant may be unsuccessful in establishing the communicative function(s) of what was said (e.g. *Is this a question or a statement?*) or may have problems in determining the precise semantic content.
- At evaluation level a difficulty arises when the participant concludes that the speaker said something that is inconsistent with what he said before, or more generally with information that the participant assumed to be shared, for example when an utterance was interpreted as a question which the speaker believes has already been answered. The difficulty is that the context update, determined at the interpretation level, cannot be performed without making the participant's context model inconsistent.
- At execution level a difficulty arises when the participant is unable to perform a certain action which he wants to perform as a result of the other levels

of input processing being successful. For example, the participant has processed an instruction to perform a certain action successfully up to this level, but when actually executing the requested action he runs into an obstacle that prevents him from completing the action.

b2. Partner's processing
In allo-feedback acts the speaker signals his views on the success of the addressee's processing of previous utterances, or he elicits information about that, being uncertain whether the addressee paid attention, correctly heard or understood what was said, or successfully evalutated or executed that. The same levels of processing apply as in the case of auto-feedback.

c. Establishing and Checking Contact
Dialogue participants who cannot see each other have to make their presence and readiness to communicate explicit. Explicit acts for establishing, checking, and maintaining contact are therefore frequently found in dialogues over the telephone or via radio transmission. Especially when communicating over a distance, using communication channels whose reliability is not obvious and/or not instantaneous, a participant's effective presence and readiness are not always evident and are therefore checked (*Hello? Are you there?*).

In face-to-face communication contact is typically not the subject of verbalized dialogue acts, but is indicated and checked nonverbally by means of eye contact and facial expressions.

d. Taking Turns
For understanding and generating turn management acts, a context model needs to represent who currently occupies the speaker role; whether the participant whose context model is considered would like to have it; and if he already has the speaker role whether he wants to keep it, or wants someone else to take over.

e. Time
In order to be in the position to generate a *Stalling* or a *Pausing* act, a dialogue participant must have some information about his own processes involved in the production of a dialogue act. Common causes of *Stalling* are:

- the participant experiences a difficulty in finding or choosing a particular lexical item;
- the participant cannot decide immediately what form to give to the dialogue act that he intends to perform;
- the participant does not immediately have all the information available which is needed for the semantic content of the dialogue act under construction.

A participant's context model should therefore include information about lexical, syntactic, and semantic processes in utterance generation.

f. Discourse Plans
Especially in the case of dialogues with a well-structured underlying task, a participant may have a plan for how to organize the interaction. Professional agents in an

information service, such as operators providing information about telephone numbers and services, or workers in call centers and help desks, often structure the interaction with customers in a fixed manner.

The observation that dialogue participants do not always say explicitly what they mean, using for example indirect questions and conversational implicatures as in example (18), has spawned a certain amount of work which considers as a crucially important task of a dialogue participant to recognize his partner's discourse plan, the so-called *plan-based approach* to dialogue (e.g. [21], [36]).

(18) A: Can you help me, I'm out of petrol.
  B: There's a garage just around the corner.

Elaborate discourse plans include dialogue acts with a fixed form for opening and closing the dialogue, an order in which to address relevant topics, and strategies for providing feedback. A less elaborate discourse plan may consist of only the intention to answer a question, or the plan to interrupt the current speaker and return to a previous topic.

g. Own and Partner Speech Editing
A dialogue participant who edits his own speech, correcting himself or improving his formulation, makes use of information about what he is saying and about what he wants to say.

The performance and interpretation of dialogue acts where a participant edits the speech of the current speaker requires context models to contain essentially the same information relating to the partner's production processes as is needed for editing one's own speech.

h. Social 'Obligations' or 'Pressures'
Social obligations management (SOM) acts reflect the fact that participation in a dialogue is a form of interaction between people (at least originally), and therefore has to follow certain general conventions of human interaction, such as greeting, thanking, and apologizing in certain circumstances. In such circumstances, dialogue participants have to deal with 'interactive pressures' [7] to perform certain actions. For example, before starting a dialogue, in many situations there is a social convention to greet each other - which therefore can occur only at the beginning of a dialogue, and if the dialogue is with an unknown partner, it is often customary to introduce oneself. Such observations can be captured by means of 'interactive pressures' on dialogue participants. For example, when one walks in the street and sees a familiar person approaching, there is a mounting pressure to perform a greeting as one gets closer, questions arising such as: *Does she notice me? Does she recognize me? Can she hear me?*, to which the answers become more certain as you get nearer, until a point is reached where the pressure has become `unbearable', and one performs that greeting – thereby resolving the pressure. The generation of a greeting thus requires context models to contain the representation of such interactive pressures. See also the next section, on the representation of 'Social Context'.

4.2 Representation Structures

In designing an implementation of a context model, two main issues arise: (1) which representation formalisms could be appropriate, and (2) what overall structure should a context model have.

The various kinds of information listed in the previous subsection can be represented in an effective context model in many different ways. here we consider an implementation in terms of typed feature structures, as a computationally attractive an sufficiently expressive representation formalism[6]. Other representation formalisms that have been used for context modeling include discourse representation structures (DRSs, see [44]); the representation structures of Constructive Type Theory (so-called 'contexts', see [1],[9]); and 'modular partial models' [8].

For the overall structure of a context model we can take advantage of the orthogonality of the dimensions listed in (12). The choice of such a set of dimensions has the computationally attractive feature that a multifunctional dialogue segment, when interpreted as a set of dialogue acts in different dimensions, is semantically 'decomposed' into components in orthogonal dimensions, corresponding to independent context update operations. Moreover, in those dimensions where a given dialogue segment does not have a communicative function, we know that its interpretation will not affect the corresponding information in the context model. It therefore seems attractive to structure a context model in the same way as the set of dimensions, in order to maximally 'modularize' the context update processes. However, we will see that there are reasons for partitioning a context model in fewer than 10 compartments.

First, auto- and allo-feedback information are not only very similar in nature, but are also closely intertwined, since an allo-feedback act performed by participant A, and directed at participant B, provides or elicits information about B's processing of something said earlier in the dialogue, and when B responds to that he provides information about *his own processing* of that same something, hence B performs an auto-feedback act. Similarly, a response to an auto-feedback act is often an allo-feedback act. Examples (19) and (20) illustrate this.

(19) 1. A: You see what I mean? [allo-feedback]
     2. B: I see what you mean. [auto-feedback]

(20) 1. A: This Saturday? [auto-feedback]
     2. B: That's right. [allo-feedback]

Second, the information related to time management concerns the progress and time estimate of the speaker's processes involved in utterance interpretation or production, and as such forms an aspect of the information needed for the interpretation or generation of own communication management acts. Hence it seems best to consider time-related information not as a separate compartment in a context model, but rather as part of the information concerning understanding and production processes. This also provides an argument for not separating information about understanding

---

[6] Typed feature structures can also be used for the semantic representation of natural language, hence for the representation of the semantic content of a dialogue act – see [11].

and production processes into separate compartments, but instead to have a single compartment concerning a participant's information processing in general. We call this compartment the **Cognitive Context**; it contains the information needed for the interpretation and generation of auto- and allo-feedback acts, time management acts, and own- and partner communication management acts.

Third, auto- and allo-feedback acts often refer to something that was said before, or to the interpretation of that, as in the following examples:

(21) a. S: Did you say "Thursday"?
   b. S: Could you please repeat that?
   c. S: I meant Saturday this week.

In order to deal with such cases, a dialogue participant needs to have a representation of what was said before, and of how that was perceived and interpreted. This kind of information is commonly called a *Dialogue History*, and next to task-related information, it is the kind of information that is most commonly represented in context models.

When a new contribution to an ongoing dialogue is processed, it is segmented into functional segments, corresponding to dialogue acts (according to definition (6)), which leads to an addition to the context model of the understanding partner that may look as in Figure 3, represented in terms of feature structures.

The segment is defined by a start- and end point, its observable verbal and/or non-verbal form, a sender who produced the segment, one or more addressees, and a set of dialogue acts, each characterized by a dimension, a communicative function, and a semantic content. In addition, if the segment under consideration is nonverbal or a backchannel, like *uh-huh*, it may be produced while another participant is occupying the speaker role, hence this needs to be represented separately.

Since the functional segment is the unit of dialogue act analysis, the representation of a record of what has happened in a dialogue is best structured as a chronologically ordered sequence of functional segments with their interpretation as shown in Fig. 3[7].

$$
\begin{bmatrix}
current\_segment :
\begin{bmatrix}
start : \langle timepoint \rangle \\
end : \langle timepoint \rangle \\
expression : \langle verbatim/nonverbal form \rangle \\
dial\_acts : \{\langle \begin{bmatrix} dimension : \langle dim \rangle \\ comm\_function : \langle cf \rangle \\ sem\_content : \langle content \rangle \end{bmatrix} \rangle\} \\
sender : \langle participant \rangle \\
addressees : \{\langle participant \rangle\} \\
speaker : \langle participant \rangle
\end{bmatrix}
\end{bmatrix}
$$

Fig. 3. Feature structure representation of Dialogue History element

---

[7] The exact chronological organization of the Dialogue History is a nontrivial matter, in view of the occurrence of overlapping and discontinuous functional segments contributed by the same speaker, as well as overlapping segments of (linguistic and/or nonverbal) communicative behaviour by other participants.

Both auto- and allo-feedback need a record of the dialogue history; for own- and partner communication management the current functional segment is needed; and for the generation and interpretation of discourse structuring acts a representation of the planned 'dialogue future' is needed. Moreover, for representing that a participant wants or plans to obtain the speaker role, this should also be represented in the dialogue future component of his context model. The information who currently occupies the speaker role is included in the representation of the current functional segment - so together, *current segment* and *dialogue future* contain the information relevant for generating and interpreting turn management acts; no separate compartment in the context model is needed for this purpose.

All in all, the linguistic context of a stretch of communicative behaviour, i.e. the surrounding dialogue, can be represented in a participant's context model as consisting of three components:

1. the *dialogue history,* i.e. a record of past communicative events;
2. the *current segment,* recording what is currently being contributed to the dialogue;
3. the *dialogue future*, i.e. the discourse plan of the dialogue participant.

This representation of the traditional notion of context in linguistics is one of the compartments in a context model, and we will refer to this compartment as the **Linguistic Context**.

We thus see that the Linguistic Context compartment together with the Cognitive Context contains all the information needed for the generation and interpretation of dialogue acts in the following dimensions: (1) Turn Management; (2) Discourse Structuring; (3) Time Management; (4) Own Communication Management; (5) Partner Communication Management; (6) Auto-Feedback; and (7) Allo-Feedback, i.e., in 7 of the 10 dimensions.

In order to keep the representation structures as simple as possible, we will from now on consider only dialogues with two participants; the generalization to multiple participants is straightforward.

For the task- or activity-related information that needs to be represented in a context model we have seen in (16) that we have to represent a participant's own information about the task, his assumptions about the information that the dialogue partner possesses, and his assumptions concerning the sharing of information. Since task-related information is most often reflected in the semantic content of dialogue acts with general-purpose functions, we will refer to the context model compartment that contains this kind of information as the **Semantic Context**; in terms of feature structures, it can be organized as follows:

$$\left[\ SemContext : \begin{bmatrix} own\_task\_model : \langle beliefs \rangle \\ partner\_task\_model : \langle beliefs \rangle \\ common\_ground : \langle mutual\_beliefs \rangle \end{bmatrix} \right]$$

Fig. 4. Feature structure representation of `Semantic Context'

The representation in a context model of the processing state of the participant who 'owns' the context model, and of his assumptions concerning the partner's processing state, can be represented in a similar way, as consisting of (a) a list of parameters describing the status of each of the processes that are distinguished in utterance understanding and production; (b) a similar list describing assumptions about the status of these processes on the part of the partner; and (c) a description of assumed shared information of this kind. Such shared information plays a crucial role in processes of grounding; in fact, grounding applies not only to information about the underlying task, but also to what was said and how it was understood, as well as to other types of information in the context model. We will therefore see similar three-part structures in all the context model compartments.

The information needed for generating and interpreting dialogue acts in the Contact Management dimension is quite simple and can be characterized with two features, one to indicate whether a participant is present, in the sense of being in a position to use the communicative channels available in the dialogue setting under consideration (such as the telephone, or the computer in an on-line chat); and another to indicate whether a participant is ready to communicate. The compartment containing this information is called the **Perceptual/Physical Context**.[8]

Finally, the context information needed for generating and understanding Social Obligations Management (SOM) acts is somewhat different from that for other dimensions, due to the highly conventional nature of these acts. SOM acts, moreover, come in adjacency pairs. A greeting puts a pressure on the addressee to perform a return greeting. Same for saying goodbye. Introducing oneself puts a pressure on the addressee to also introduce herself. Apologizing puts pressure on the addressee to accept the apology; thanking puts pressure on the addressee to mitigate the cause of the thanking, as in *de rien; pas de quoi* (French); *de nada* (Spanish, Portuguese); *niente* (Italian); *ingen ting at takke for* (Danish). The pressures created by an initial SOM act are called *reactive pressures*. They are similar in nature to interactive pressures (see above, Section 4.1.h); the difference is that interactive pressures are created by properties of the interactive situation, while reactive pressures are created directly by SOM acts.

An interactive pressure can be represented as specification of the dialogue act that one is pressured to perform. This is usually an incomplete specification, for instance only specifying a communicative function. A reactive pressure is typically more detailed, since it is conventional to 'align' with the previous speaker and respond to an initial SOM act with a responsive act of similar form.

All in all, this leads to a context model with five compartments: the Linguistic, Semantic, Cognitive, Perceptual/Physical, and Social Context, which can be implemented in terms of feature structures as shown in Figure 5 (from [43]).

---

[8] This component may also contain information about perceptual context aspects such as the availability of visual information about certain situations in the task domain.

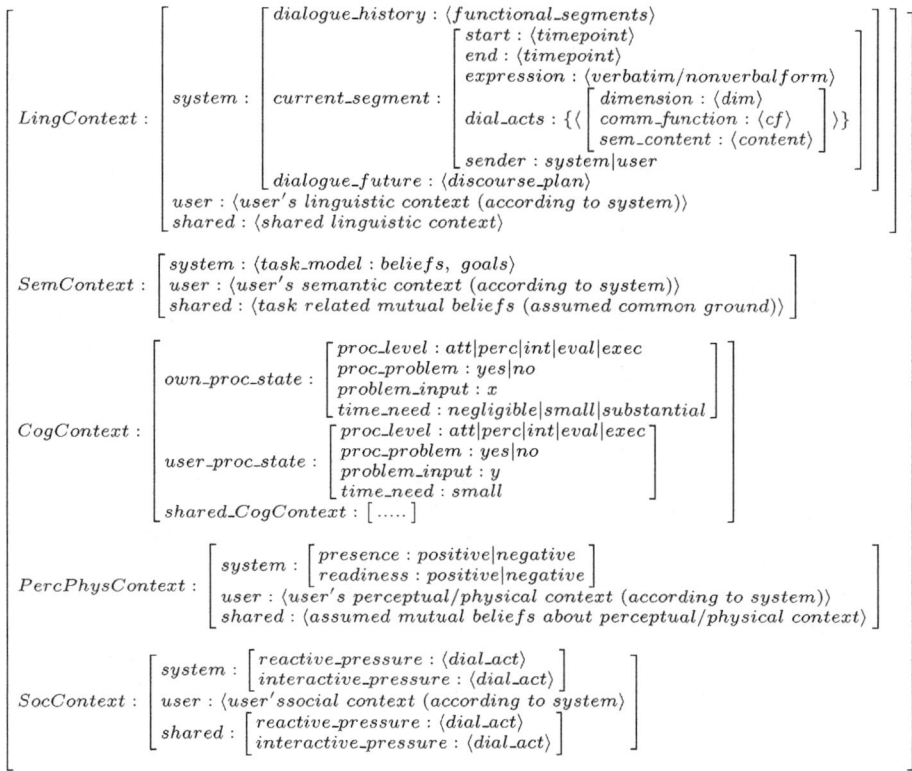

Fig. 5. Feature structure representation of context model in dialogue system

5 Applications

The DIT framework and dialogue act taxonomy have been used successfully in a variety of applications:

- for empirical, theoretical and computational modelling of semantic and pragmatic phenomena in spoken and multimodal dialogue;
- for dialogue annotation, and as the starting point for an ISO effort to define a standard for dialogue act annotation;
- for the design of dialogue system components, in particular for multimodal input interpretation, dialogue management, and the generation of multi-functional utterances in spoken dialogue systems;

In this section we briefly consider each of these applications.

5.1 Semantic and Pragmatic Dialogue Analysis

a. Information flow and grounding. Every communicative function in the DIT[++] taxonomy is formally defined as a particular type of update operation on an addressee's context model. Depending on its dimension, a dialogue act updates a particular context component; a multifunctional utterance leads to the update of several components. This approach provides good instruments for studying and modeling the flow of information between the participants in a dialogue. Fine-grained models of information flow through the understanding of dialogue behaviour in terms of dialogue acts have been developed and analysed in [37], and have resulted in a empirically-based computational model of grounding in dialogue [18].

b. Semantics of discourse markers. Another semantic study based on the multidimensional approach of DIT is that of the semantics of discourse markers; words or phrases that connect the pieces in a dialogue (or in a monologue), like *but, and, so,* and *well.* It was shown that such expressions often perform multiple semantic functions, which are well explained in terms of the dimensions in the DIT^{++} taxonomy (see [39]).

c. Multifunctionality and co-occurrence patterns. To generate multifunctional dialogue behaviour in a sensible way, it is important to have qualitative and quantitative knowledge of this phenomenon, and to know which kinds of multifunctional utterances occur in natural dialogue. It has been shown (see [14], [15]) that, when a fine-grained segmentation is applied to dialogue, with possibly overlapping and interleaved functional segments, the average multifunctionality of a segment in spoken dialogue without visual contact amounts to 1.6 when only explicitly expressed and conversationally implicated functions are taken into account, and 3.6 when entailed functions are also counted.

d. The interpretation of nonverbal dialogue behaviour. An investigation into the applicability of the DIT^{++} taxonomy to nonverbal behaviour in dialogues in the AMI corpus showed that the DIT^{++} functions provided fulll coverage for interpreting the nonverbal activity [38]. The nonverbal behaviour may serve five purposes: (1) emphasizing or articulating the semantic content of dialogue acts; (2) emphasizing or supporting the communicative functions of synchronous verbal behaviour; (3) performing separate dialogue acts in parallel to what is contributed by the current speaker (without turn shifting); (4) expressing an emotion or attitude; or (5) expressing a separate communicative function in parallel to what the same speaker is expressing verbally. The latter occurs relatively rarely, as witnessed by the fact that the multifunctionality of dialogue segments shows only a small increase when synchronous nonverbal behaviour is taken into account.

It may be noted, on the other hand, that with visual contact there is an increase of more than 25% of the number of functional segments, mostly due to participants not in the speaker role providing nonverbal feedback.

5.2 Annotation

a. DIT^{++} annotation. The DIT^{++} taxonomy has been applied in manual annotation of dialogues from various corpora: the DIAMOND corpus of two-party instructional human-human Dutch dialogues (1,408 utterances)[9]; the AMI corpus of task-oriented human-human multi-party English dialogues (3,897 utterances)[10]; the OVIS corpus of task-oriented human-computer Dutch dialogues (3,942 utterances); TRAINS dialogues[11] (in English); and Map Task dialogues[12] both in English and in Dutch. Geertzen et al. [28] report on the consistency with which naive annotators as well as expert annotators were able to annotate, and compares the results. Expert annotators achieve agreement scores of more than 90%; naive annotators achieve scores in the order of 60%.

b. The LIRICS project. In the EU project LIRICS[13] a taxonomy of communicative functions was defined which is a slightly simplified version of the DIT^{++} taxonomy, retaining its dimensions but eliminating the distinction of levels of feedback as well as uncertain variants of information-providing functions, informs with rhetorical functions, and some of the low-frequency functions [34]. The resulting taxonomy has 23 general-purpose functions (where DIT^{++} has 31) and 30 dimension-specific functions (where DIT^{++} has 57, of which 20 fine-grained feedback functions).

The usability of this taxonomy was tested in manual annotation of the LIRICS test suites in Dutch, English, and Italian by three expert annotators. Remarkably high, agreement was found between the annotators; for the general-purpose functions an average κ score was found of 0.98; for the other categories scores ranged from 0.94 for SOM acts to 0.99 for auto-feedback acts (see [35]).

c. Towards an ISO standard for functional dialogue markup

In 2008 the International Organization for Standards started up the project Semantic Annotation Framework, Part 2: Dialogue acts, which aims at developing an international standard for the markup of communicative functions in dialogue. This project builds on the results of an ISO study group on interoperability in linguistic annotation, of which the European project LIRICS was a spin-off.

The ISO project takes the DIT^{++} and LIRICS taxonomies as point of departure for defining a comprehensive open standard for functional dialogue markup. The latest version of the ISO proposal has the status of Draft International Standard (ISO 24617-2:2010). It includes the definition of 26 general-purpose functions and 30 dimension-specific functions, plus three binary-valued qualification attributes (*certainty*, *conditionality*, and *partiality*) and one attribute with an open class of values *sentiment*). These concepts are all defined according to ISO standard 12620 for data category definitions, and will eventually be included in the on-line ISOcat data category registry (http://www.isocat.org)[14].

---

[9] For more information see Geertzen, J., Y. Girard, and R. Morante (2004) The DIAMOND project. Poster at the 8th Workshop on the Semantics and Pragmatics of Dialogue (CATALOG), Barcelona.

[10] http://www.amiproject.org

[11] See [2].

[12] See [22].

[13] Linguistic InfRastructure for Interoperable Resources and Systems; for more information see http://lirics.loria.fr

[14] The data categories are temporarily available at http://semantic-annotation.uvt.nl

In addition to these data category definitions, the standard provides the XML-based annotation language DiAML (Dialogue Act Markup Language), with annotation guidelines and examples of annotated dialogues.[15] See [29] and the summary description in [20].

The DIT++ definitions of communicative functions have been adapted in release 5 (April 2010) so as to be identical to those in the ISO standard for functions which are shared by the two schemes; as a result, the ISO set of concepts is a proper subset of the DIT++ concepts, and DIT++ annotations can make use of the DiAML representation format.

5.3 Dialogue System Design

a. Dialogue management. The DIT++ taxonomy has been used in the design and implementation of the PARADIME dialogue manager, which forms part of the IMIX system for multimodal information extraction (see [30], [31]). The multidimensional dialogue manager generates sets of dialogue acts (in formal representation) that are appropriate in the current dialogue context, and delivers these to a module for expressing a set of dialogue acts in a multifunctional utterance. It makes use of autonomous software agents for each dimension, that generate candidate dialogue acts in that dimension. An evaluation agent examines the set of candidate dialogue acts that is generated in this fashion and decides on sets of candidate acts that can be turned into multifunctional utterances. Figure 6 shows this architecture.

This approach to dialogue utterance generation opens the ppossibiliity to generate multifunctional utterances in a deliberate and controlled fashion.

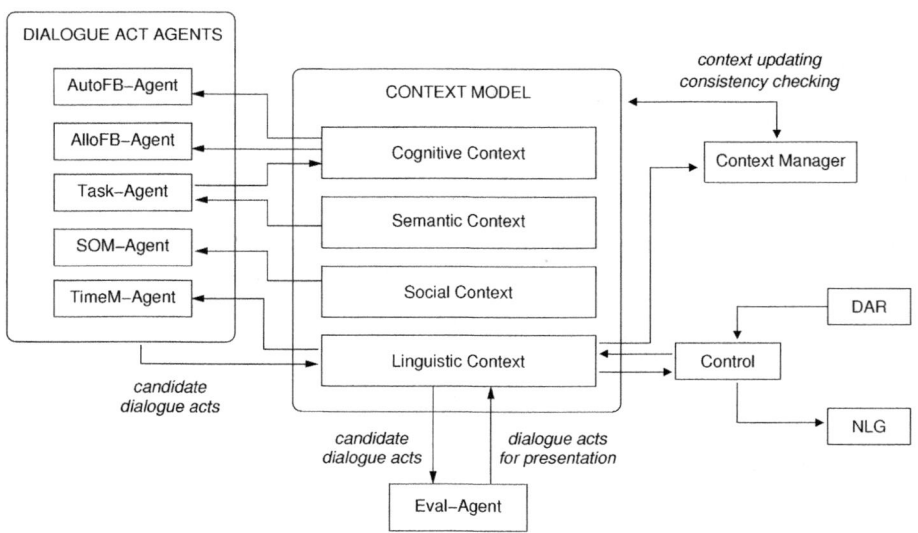

Fig. 6. Multidimensional dialogue manager architecture

---

[15] See also example (14) above.

A more complete implementation of the context model described in Figure 5 has been developed by Petukhova et al. [43] for experimentation with constraints on the generation of multifunctional dialogue utterances.

b. Machine recognition of DIT^{++} functions. A prerequisite for using dialogue acts in a dialogue manager is that the dialogue system is able to recognize dialogue acts with acceptable precision. The automatic recognition of the DIT^{++} dialogue acts (as well as in other taxonomies, such as DAMSL) was investigated for the corpora mentioned above, as well as for dialogues from the Monroe and MRDA corpora. For the various DIT dimensions, F_1 scores were found ranging from 62.6% to 96.6%, without any tweaking of the features used in the machine learning algorithms. This suggests that the recognition of (multiple) functions in the taxonomy is a realistic enterprise. For more information see [27].

5.4 Functional Markup of Embodied Conversational Agents

The DIT^{++} taxonomy has been applied in the analysis of dialogues recorded in a range of different settings involving various combinations of modalities (face-to-face two-person and multiparty conversation, human-computer over the telephone, helpdesk dialogues with visual information on a display,...), and has shown that nonverbal communicative behaviour does not express other types of dialogue acts than those that have been identified in spoken language. The 88 communicative functions in the DIT^{++} taxonomy[16] are sufficient to capture the types of dialogue acts performed not only by verbal communicative behaviour but equally by nonverbal and multimodal behaviour.

This is not to say that nonverbal behaviour does not add anything to the verbal behaviour in multimodal dialogue. Facial expressions, head movements, and hand and shoulder gestures are known to often express certain emotions and attitudes which are added to the speaker's words without changing the communicative function of the verbally expressed dialogue act. Gaze direction, head movements, facial expressions, hand gestures and body posture (in addition to prosody) has also been shown (see [42]) to be used by speakers for expressing their certainty of the correctness of the information that they offer in information-providing acts, or of their commitment in a commissive act; see Table 1 for the main features of nonverbal behaviour that are used to signal certainty.

A variety of taxonomies has been proposed for the classification of emotions and attitudes that dialogue participants may exhibit, from the 6 basic emotions in Ekman's pioneering work [25] to the corpus-based 14 sentiments distinguished by Reidsma et al. [46]; other proposals include those of Craggs and McGee-Wood [24]; Laskowski and Burger [33]; and Ekman's extended taxonomy [26]. For the nonverbal expression of Ekman's basic 6 emotions Petukhova and Bunt [42] found in the AMI multiparty dialogue corpus the features of facial expressions shown in Table 2.

---

[16] DIT^{++} release 5; see http://dit.uvt.nl

Table 1. Nonverbal expressions of certainty

Certainty	Gaze direction	Head movement	Facial expression	Gesture	Posture orientation
Uncertain	aversion redirection involuntary eye movements	waggles	lip-compression; lip-pout; biting/liking; lowering eyebrows; constricting forehead muscles	adaptors, e.g. self-touching; shoulder shrug	posture shift
Certain	direct eye contact;	head nod (for emphasis)	thin lips; pushing up the chin boss; widely open eyes;	beat gestures	leaning forward /to addressee

Phenomena such as the certainty and emotions of a speaker associated with a dialogue act can be modelled with the help of the concept of a *function qualifier* applied to a communicative functions, as mentioned above (see (13) above), and the use of attributes like the sentiment qualifier attribute, used in the corresponding DiAML representation (14)). The findings of Petukhova and Bunt, reported in [42], have been incorporated both in the latest version of the DIT[++] annotation schema and in the ISO Draft International Standard ISO 24617-2[17].

Table 2. Facial expressions corresponding with Ekman's six basic emotions

Emotion	Facial expression					
	Forehead	Eyebrows	Eyes	Cheeks	Lips	Chin
Anger	wrinkled	lower lids; pulled together	lower eyelids tensed and straightened		tensed; pressed together	chin bossf pushed up
Disgust		pulled down down	lower lids tensed upper lids raised; narrowed		upper lip; drawn up; pressed together; mouth open	
Fear		raised straight up	lids raised up		corners pulled; lips stretched; mouth open	jaw dropped
Happy			lids narrowed; eye corners wrinkled	outer, upper area raised	corners raised	
Sad	wrinkled	pulled together raised in center of forehead	narrowed	raised	stretched; corners; turned downt	chin boss pushed up
Surprise	wrinkled	raised straight up	upper lids raised		mouth open; tensed or relaxed	jaw drop

---

[17] For the most recent documentation of this draft ISO standard see
`http://semantic-annotation.uvt.nl`

These observations have given rise to the idea that the DIT⁺⁺ taxonomy and the DiAML language may be useful for the functional markup of the behaviour of embodied conversational agents (ECAs). The use of ECAs in user interface is motivated by the idea that the addition of a face, and possibly more of a body, can help to make the dialogue between a computer and a user more natural, in particular because it may bring emotions and attitudes to the interaction by smiling, bowing, looking happy, sorry, embarrassed, surprised, and so on. But this can only work well if the nonverbal behaviour of the ECA is indeed 'natural' in the sense of expressing the same functions and qualities as the human behaviour that it resembles, and if the behaviour is displayed in the same contexts where a human would display it.

In the ECA community an effort has started to design a standard for the functional markup of ECA behaviour, including a functional markup language. The DiAML language can be the basis of such a markup language, with the elements of the DIT⁺⁺ taxonomy as values of DiAML attributes, and the qualifier attributes and values defined in ISO DIS 24617-2. The latter can be replaced by or supplemented with other or more fine-grained sets of qualifier attributes and values, as appropriate for specific ECA applications.

6 Perspectives and Future Work

In this paper we have presented the DIT framework for context-based dialogue analysis, annotation, interpretation, and generation. We have used the 10 dimensions of the DIT⁺⁺ taxonomy of communicative functions for identifying the types of information that a context model should contain. An analysis of these information types has lead us to design a dialogue participant's context model as consisting of five compartments, called Linguistic, Semantic, Cognitive, Perceptual/Physical, and Social Context, and we have made this design concrete by showing an implementation based on typed feature structures.

We have illustrated the advantages of an articulate context-based approach by its use in a variety of applications, including the detailed modeling of information flow and grounding in dialogue, the semantics of discourse markers, the annotation of spoken and multimodal dialogue (two- and multiparty; human-human and human-computer); the definition of an ISO standard for dialogue annotation; the design of components of a computer dialogue system; and the functional markup of the behaviour of embodied conversational agents.

The DIT⁺⁺ taxonomy of communicative functions has been made fully ISO-compatible, in the sense that:

- the dimensions and the set of communicative functions defined in the ISO standard are proper subsets of those defined in DIT⁺⁺;
- the set of qualifiers defined in the ISO (draft) standard has been adopted;
- the categories of entities and relations underlying the standard is shared with the DIT model, hence the DiAML markup language defined as part of the ISO standard can equally well use the more extended set of concepts defined in DIT⁺⁺. In particular, for the 9 dimensions shared by the two annotation schemes (Contact Management being the only one not shared), every communicative function

defined in DIT⁺⁺ either coincides with a function defined in the ISO standard, or is a specialization of such a function.

Any ISO 24617-2 annotation is therefore also a DIT⁺⁺ annotation, and any DIT⁺⁺ annotation can be converted into a compatible ISO 24617-2 annotation (except for annotations in the Contact Management dimension) by replacing fine-grained DIT⁺⁺-functions by less fine-grained functions where necessary.

The context model described in this paper has been fully implemented for experimentation with dialogue management strategies, but has not yet been incorporated in a dialogue system, where it would offer the possibility to deliberately generate multifunctional utterances; this is an item on the agenda for future work.

Acknowledgements

I thank the members of the Tilburg Dialogue Club for discussions and experiments during which the DIT framework was shaped over the years. This includes Ielka van der Sluis, Simon Keizer, Hans van Dam, Jeroen Geertzen, Yann Girard, Roser Morante, Rintse van der Werf, and especially Volha Petukhova. I thank the members of the ISO 24617-2 project team: Jan Alexandersson, Jean Carletta, Jae-Woong Choe, Alex Fang, Koiti Hasida, Volha Petukhova, Andrei Popescu-Belis, Claudia Soria, and David Traum for discussions on dialogue analysis and dialogue act annotation. The same goes for the members of the Expert Consultancy Group of the ISO project, in particular Jens Allwood, Thierry Declerck, Dirk Heylen, Kristiina Jokinen, Maciej Karpinski, Kiyong Lee, David Novick, Laurent Romary, and Nicla Rossini.

References

1. Ahn, R.: Agents, Objects and Events. A computational approach to knowledge, observation and communication. PhD. Thesis, Eindhoven University of Technology (2001)
2. Allen, J., Schubert, L., Ferguson, G., Heeman, P., Hwang, C.J., Kato, T., Light, M., Martin, N., Miller, B., Poesio, M., Traum, D.: The TRAINS Project: A case study in building a conversational planning agent. Technical Note 94-3, University of Rochester (1994)
3. Allen, J., Core, M.: DAMSL: Dialogue Act Markup in Several Layers (Draft 2.1). Technical Report, Discourse Resource Initiative (1997)
4. Allwood, J.: An activity-based approach to pragmatics. In: Bunt, H., Black, W. (eds.) Abduction, Belief and Context in Dialogue. Studies in Computational Pragmatics, pp. 47–80. Benjamins, Amsterdam (2000)
5. Allwood, J., Nivre, J., Ahlsén, E.: Speech Management or the Non-written Life of Speech. Nordic Journal of Linguistics 13, 1–48 (1990)
6. Bunt, H.: Context and Dialogue Control. Think Quarterly 3(1), 19–31 (1994)
7. Bunt, H.: Dynamic Interpretation and Dialogue Theory. In: Taylor, M., Bouwhuis, D., Néel, F. (eds.) The Structure of Multimodal Dialogue, vol. 2, pp. 139–166. Benjamins, Amsterdam (1995)
8. Bunt, H.: Context Representation for Dialogue Management. In: Bouquet, P., Serafini, L., Brézillon, P., Benerecetti, M., Castellani, F. (eds.) CONTEXT 1999. LNCS (LNAI), vol. 1688, pp. 77–90. Springer, Heidelberg (1999)
9. Bunt, H.: Dialogue pragmatics and context specification. In: Bunt, H., Black, W. (eds.) Abduction, Belief and Context in Dialogue. Studies in Computational Pragmatics, pp. 81–150. Benjamins, Amsterdam (2000)

10. Bunt, H.: A Framework for Dialogue Act Specification. In: 4th Joint ISO-SIGSEM Workshop on the Representation of Multimodal Semantic Information, Tilburg (January 2005), http://let.uvt.nl/research/ti/sigsem/wg
11. Bunt, H.: Quantification and modification represented as Feature Structures. In: 6th International Workshop on Computational Semantics (IWCS-6), pp. 54–65 (2005)
12. Bunt, H.: Dimensions in dialogue annotation. In: LREC 2006, 5th International Conference on Language Resources and Evaluation, pp. 919–924 (2006)
13. Bunt, H.: The DIT^{++} taxonomy for functional dialogue markup. In: AAMAS 2009 Workshop, Towards a Standard Markup Language for Embodied Dialogue Acts, pp. 13–24 (2009)
14. Bunt, H.: Multifunctionality and multidimensional dialogue semantics. In: DiaHolmia, 13th Workshop on the Semantics and Pragmatics of Dialogue, pp. 3–14 (2009)
15. Bunt, H.: Multifunctionality in Dialogue. Computer Speech and Language 25(2011), 222–245 (2010), http://dx.doi.org/10.1016/j.csl.2010.04.006
16. Bunt, H., Girard, Y.: Designing an open, multidimensional dialogue act taxonomy. In: Gardent, C., Gaiffe, B. (eds.) DIALOR 2005, Proceedings of the Ninth Workshop on the Semantics and Pragmatics of Dialogue, pp. 37–44 (2005)
17. Bunt, H., Keizer, S.: Dialogue semantics links annotation for context representation. In: Joint TALK/AMI Workshop on Standards for Multimodal Dialogue Context (2005), http://homepages.inf.ed.ac.uk/olemon/standcon-S01.html
18. Bunt, H., Keizer, S., Morante, R.: An empirically-based computational model of grounding in dialogue. In: 8th Workshop on Discourse and Dialogue (SIGDIAL 2007), pp. 283–290 (2007)
19. Bunt, H., Romary, L.: Standardization in Multimodal Content Representation: Some Methodological Issues. In: 3rd International Conference on Language resources and Evaluation (LREC 2004), pp. 2219–2222 (2004)
20. Bunt, H., Alexandersson, J., Carletta, J., Choe, J.-W., Fang, A., Hasida, K., Lee, K., Petukhova, V., Popescu-Belis, A., Romary, L., Soria, C., Traum, D.: Towards an ISO standard for dialogue act annotation. In: LREC 2010, 8th International Conference on Language Resources and evaluation (2010)
21. Carberry, A.: Plan Recognition in Natural Language Dialogue. MIT Press, Cambridge (1990)
22. Carletta, J., Isard, A., Isard, S., Kowtko, J., Doherty-Sneddon, G.: HCRC dialogue structure coding manual. Technical Report HCRC/TR-82 (1996)
23. Clark, H.: Using Language. Cambridge University Press, Cambridge (1996)
24. Craggs, R., McGee Wood, M.: A categorical annotation scheme for emotion in the linguistic content of dialogue. In: André, E., Dybkjær, L., Minker, W., Heisterkamp, P. (eds.) ADS 2004. LNCS (LNAI), vol. 3068, pp. 89–100. Springer, Heidelberg (2004)
25. Ekman, P.: Universals and cultural differences in facial expressions of emotion. In: Cole, J. (ed.) Nebraska Symposium on Motivation. University of Nebraska Press, Lincoln (1972)
26. Ekman, P.: Basic Emotions. In: Dalgliesh, T., Power, M. (eds.) Handbook of Cognition and Emotion, pp. 207–283. John Wiley, Sussex (1999)
27. Geertzen, J.: The automatic recognition and prediction of dialogue acts. PhD Thesis, Tilburg University (2009)
28. Geertzen, J., Petukhova, V., Bunt, H.: A multidimensional approach to dialogue segmentation and dialogue act classification. In: 8th Workshop on Discourse and Dialogue (SIGDIAL 2007), pp. 140–147 (2007)
29. ISO DIS 24617-2: Language resource management - Semantic Annotation Framework - part 2: dialogue acts, ISO, Geneva (August 2010), http://semantic-annotation.uvt.nl

30. Keizer, S., Bunt, H.: Multidimensional dialogue management. In: 7th Workshop on Discourse and Dialogue (SIGDIAL 2006), pp. 37–45 (2006)
31. Keizer, S., Bunt, H.: Evaluating combinations of dialogue acts for generation. In: 8th Workshop on Discourse and Dialogue (SIGDIAL 2007), pp. 158–165 (2007)
32. Larsson, S.: Coding Schemas for Dialog Moves. Technical report from the S-DIME project (1998), http://www.ling.gu.se/sl
33. Laskowski, K., Burger, S.: Annotation and analysis of emotionally relevant behaviour in the ISL meeting corpus. In: LREC 2006, 5th International Conference on Language Resources and Evaluation (2006)
34. LIRICS D4.3: Documented Set of Semantic Data Categories. EU eContent Project LIRICS Deliverable D4.3. 3 (2007a), http://semantic-annotation.uvt.nl
35. LIRICS D4.4: Multilingual Test Suites for Semantically Annotated Data. EU eContent Project LIRICS Deliverable D4.3 (2007b),
    http://semantic-annotation.uvt.nl
36. Litman, D., Allen, J.: A Plan Recognition Model for Subdialogues in Conversation. Cognitive Science 11(2), 163–200 (1987)
37. Morante, R.: Computing meaning in interaction. PhD Thesis, Tilburg University (2007)
38. Petukhova, V.: Multidimensional interaction of multimodal dialogue acts in meetings. MA thesis, Tilburg University (2005)
39. Petukhova, V., Bunt, H.: Towards a multidimensional semantics of discourse markers in spoken dialogue. In: 8th International Workshop on Computational Semantics (IWCS-8), pp. 157–168 (2009)
40. Petukhova, V., Bunt, H.: Dimensions of Communication: a survey. TiCC Technical Report TR 09-003, Tilburg Center for Cognition and Communication, Tilburg University (2009)
41. Petukhova, V., Bunt, H.: The independence of dimensions in multidimensional dialogue act annotation. In: Human Language Technologies: The 2009 Annual Conference of the North American Chapter of the ACL (NAACL 2009), pp. 197–200 (2009)
42. Petukhova, V., Bunt, H.: Introducing Communicative Function Qualifiers. In: Fang, A., Ide, N., Webster, J. (eds.) Language Resources and Global Interoperability. Proceedings of the Second International Conference on Global Interoperability for Language Resources (ICGL 2010), pp. 123–131. City University of Hong Kong (2010)
43. Petukhova, V., Bunt, H., Malchanau, A.: Empirical and theoretical constraints on dialogue act combinations. In: 14th Workshop on the Semantics and Pragmatics of Dialogue (PozDial), Poznan (2010)
44. Poesio, M., Traum, D.: Towards an Axiomatization of Dialogue Acts. In: Twente Workshop on the Semantics and Pragmatics of Dialogue, pp. 207–222 (1998)
45. Popescu-Belis, A.: Dialogue Acts: One or More Dimensions?. ISSCO Working Paper 62, ISSCO, Geneva (2005)
46. Reidsma, D., Heylen, D., Odelman, R.: Annotating emotion in meetings. In: LREC 2006, 5th International Conference on Language Resources and Evaluation (2006)
47. Traum, D.: A Computational Theory of Grounding in Natural Language Conversation. PhD Thesis, Department of Computer Science, University of Rochester (1994)
48. Traum, D., Larsson, S.: The Information State Approach to Dialogue Management. In: Smith, R., van Kuppevelt, J. (eds.) Current and New Directions in Discourse and Dialogue, pp. 325–353. Kluwer, Dordrecht (2003)

Coordination, Not Control, Is Central to Movement

Fred Cummins

School of Computer Science and Informatics,
University College, Dublin
fred.cummins@ucd.ie
http://pworldrworld.com/fred

Abstract. The notion of the control of action is contrasted with that of coordination. In coordinated action, many parts of the body (or bodies) come together to act as if they served a specific purpose, recognizable as a behavioral goal. Such simpler domains of yoked components are called coordinative structures. Examples are given of the harnessing of components into coordinative structures. In the first case, known as synchronous speech, two speakers are subsumed within a single dyadic domain of organization that exists for as long as the speakers speak in synchrony. In the second case, a time-varying set of articulators work collaboratively in generating natural and fluent movement in accordance with a behavioral goal consisting of a desired utterance. In the latter case, we introduce a new model, extending the venerable task dynamic model familiar to students of articulatory phonology. In the new embodied task dynamic model, precise gestural timing arises, not from computation and control, but from considerations of optimality in movement. A candidate function for optimization combines terms derived from the estimation of articulatory effort, perceptual clarity, and speech rate. Both of these examples illustrate a methodological advantage of dynamical models that demand that the modeler first identify both components and system boundaries as they occur within the context of a specific behavioral goal. This contrasts with many approaches within computational cognitive science.

Keywords: speech production, motor control, coordination, dynamical systems, embodiment, autonomy.

1   Introduction

In the study of human behavior, and its relation to brain activity, misunderstandings abound. The phrase "motor control" invites a particularly pernicious misreading that is likely to trap the unwary into a cartoon vision of the brain as a master puppeteer, simultaneously sending "control signals" down neural wires, that have "motor action" or behavior, as their end product. This interpretation is a grotesque distortion of the role of the brain. It fundamentally mischaracterizes its place in the systematic organization of behavior. The puppeteer that

A. Esposito et al. (Eds.): COST 2102 Int. Training School 2010, LNCS 6456, pp. 243–255, 2011.
© Springer-Verlag Berlin Heidelberg 2011

lurks behind a simplistic interpretation of the notion of "control" is a homuncular invention whose mysterious agency appears to be made manifest through the inert machinery of the body.

Unfortunately, something like this myth informs most accounts of overt behavior, particularly those in which behavior is seen as the output of a system of three parts: *perception*, considered as input, *cognition* as the substantial middle, and *action* or overt behavior as the final product. This is the familiar architecture of conventional cognitive psychology, and it has, for many, the status of orthodoxy. It is perhaps unsurprising that those who regard their inquiry as directed towards the cognitive heart of this hypothetical system should expend little effort in questioning the role of its peripheral twins, perception and action. Yet it seems, to this author, that the study of the origin and form of action has languished disproportionately on the fringes of cognitive science (and cognitive psychology in particular), and that a fundamentally different account of the role of the brain is becoming available within what we might term a post-cognitivist framework [19,14,28,7,6].

An alternative to the notion of *control* in describing movement for goal directed behavior is available, and this is *coordination* [14]. Two brief accounts of coordination during speaking will be presented here. Each of them makes use, not of information processing concepts, but of the vocabulary of Dynamic Systems Theory. The first looks at coordination across multiple individuals, and the second looks at coordination among a constantly changing set of body parts within an individual. In each case there is a system that is understood to constitute a well-formed domain in which the constituent parts exhibit lawful interrelations. In neither case is this system a perception-cognition-action unit, and in neither case is the notion of control of use in teasing out the lawfulness we observe within the system. Both bodies of work may be of interest to speech scientists, for whom the specific tasks involved are of obvious relevance. It is to be hoped that the modeling issues that arise, and the implications of adopting a dynamical perspective in understanding action will be of interest to a wider set of researchers within the emerging post-cognitivist framework.

2   Coordination and Coordinative Structures

As long ago as 1930, the Russian physiologist Nikolai Bernstein observed a curious and telling characteristic of the skilled movements of blacksmiths as they repeatedly hit an anvil with a hammer [1,16] (Fig. 1). He recorded movement at the shoulder, elbow, hand, and at the point of contact between hammer and anvil. Variability from blow to blow was minimized at the point of contact, and not at any of the biomechanical joints. This seems appropriate for skilled action, as the behavioral goal that finds expression here is best expressed at that point, while there are many potential configurations of the limb segments that can give rise to equally accurate hammer blows. But it raises huge problems for any account of the movement as arising from central control directed from brain towards the periphery. If the brain were issuing control signals, and we make the

Fig. 1. Movement variability in this skilled action is minimized at the point where hammer meets anvil, and is greater at the shoulder, elbow, and wrist joints

further not unreasonable assumption that any biological process is attended by some non-zero noise level, then noise or error introduced at the shoulder joint would appear as additive noise at the elbow joint, and error from both shoulder and elbow should appear together with wrist noise at the wrist joint. In short, in a multi-link system, distal errors are predicted to be larger than proximal errors. Even if some error correction were possible at the elbow to compensate for shoulder error, it is inconceivable that the point of minimum variation should be the point of contact between hammer and anvil, where direct intervention by the brain is impossible in principle. This argument holds true whether the controlled variables are taken to be joint angles, torques, muscle lengths, or any other candidate.

This example illustrates a well-known, but perplexing, characteristic of skilled action: although the actor is possessed of a hugely flexible biomechanical system with an innumerable number of potential degrees of freedom, when this system is engaged in the pursuit of a specific behavioral goal, it behaves *as if* it were a much simpler system, with vastly fewer degrees of freedom, in which all the parts work cooperatively towards the attainment of that goal. Perturbation or error at one point of the system is smoothly and rapidly compensated at another part. The rapidity and specificity of compensation appears to rule out any processing architecture that consists of an executive centre that is informed of distal errors and that computes appropriate compensatory changes to control signals. For example, Kelso et al. found that a perturbation to the jaw during production of the final consonant of either /bæz/ or /bæb/ generated compensatory movement that was specific to the articulatory goal currently constraining movement [15]. When the target was /z/, there was an almost immediate response of the tongue, while when the goal was /b/, the response was seen in the movement of the two lips. Crucially, the goal-specific response kicked in approximately 20 ms after the perturbation, which is sufficiently rapid to rule out an account couched in terms of monitoring and error-correcting by an executive controller.

These kind of observations have led to the notion of a *coordinative structure*, which is a task-specific functional linkage of specific body parts, such that they act as a unit in the achievement of the behavioral goal [27]. Another term frequently employed is *synergy* [16]. On this view, parts of the body flexibly partake in a series of organizational forms that are defined by the behavioral goals. We might speak of the emergence, maintenance, and dissolution of special-purpose kicking machines, scratching machines, speaking machines, throwing machines, etc. Skilled action is found to organize the many parts of the body so that they act with common purpose. The effective complexity of the biomechanical system partaking in the action is greatly reduced once a clear and practiced behavioral goal is established.

When body parts become coordinated in this fashion, they constitute a domain of organization within which the component parts are lawfully related. Change in the state of any one component is not entirely independent of change in the state of any other. Components may themselves be complex entities that can be decomposed into sub-constituents that are coordinated to bring about the component-level behavior, and no single level of behavioral description can claim to be privileged. For example, Kelso and colleagues have long studied the form of coordination exhibited when two effectors (fingers, hands, etc) are constrained to oscillate with a common frequency [14]. Given the behavioral goal provided by the task description, only two forms of stable coordination are observed, one in which the effectors oscillate with common phase (synchrony) and one in which they are half a cycle out of step with each other (syncopation). Many features of this system, including rate-dependent multi-stability, phase transitions, critical fluctuations, hysteresis, etc, have been modeled using the Haken-Kelso-Bunz (HKB) model [12]. Details of the model are not relevant here, but the structure of the model provides an insight into how dynamical models might approach the systematic simplification that is evident in skilled action. First, the behavior of individual components is characterized. In the present case, that amounts to describing each effector as a self-sustaining oscillator. Then the behavior of the components in the service of the task is described. The lack of independence between the effectors ensures that this system-level description is simpler (of lower dimension) than a full description of the components and their mutual interactions. In the HKB case, the model then provides a formal account of how the higher dimensional component description collapses to the simpler system-level description.

The system being described here is not a whole person. It is the two effector system, which is considered as a whole—a domain of organization constituted by the coordinated movement of two components. In developing a dynamical account of observed phenomena, the identification of the domain of the model is an important first step, formalized as the definition of the *state* of the system. The selection of appropriate state variables allows the modeler to potentially identify lawful domains of organization that transcend the somewhat arbitrary boundaries separating brains, bodies and environments. This is clearly illustrated in the interpersonal coordination documented in Schmidt, Carello and Turvey (1990). In that study, the task of oscillating two effectors at the same frequency was distributed across two individuals, seated, each wagging their lower leg. The same hallmarks of differential pattern stability were found in this scenario, in that there were two and only two stable patterns of coordination (synchronous/syncopated), there was a greater stability of the synchronous pattern and a strong tendency for the syncopated pattern to transit to the synchronous one in a rate-dependent manner. Of course these two individuals are not obligatorily coordinated. Each is free to stand up and go about their individual lives. But *in the context of the behavioral task*, they behave (or more accurately, the system comprising their two legs behaves) as as a simpler system with few degrees of freedom.

3 Synchronous Speech

Something very similar is seen in the coordination displayed by subjects within the synchronous speech experimental situation. Synchronous speaking is a behavioral task in which a pair of subjects are given a novel text, they familiarize themselves briefly with the text, and then they read the text together, in approximate synchrony, on a cue from the experimenter [8]. It is distinguished from the related notion of choral speaking, in that the text is new and is thus not produced with the exaggerated prosody familiar from the group recitation of oaths, prayers, etc. Typically, subjects are very good at this task, and without any practice, they maintain a tight synchrony with lags (temporal offset between their speech streams) of no more than 40 ms on average [9]. This is comparable to an asynchrony of no more than a single frame of video. Perhaps remarkably, practice does not generate much improvement; the synchronization task appears to tap into a natural facility for synchronization with another person, despite the complexity of the task of speaking.

How should we view the sustained exhibition of very tight synchrony between two speakers (Fig. 2)? One way, and that most readily at hand within most current approaches, is to view each speaker as an independent system. A speech production system within each individual is held responsible for the planning and execution of movement. To this picture, we would have to add a perceptual component that monitors the speech being produced by the other, that compares one production with the other, and that makes corresponding adjustments. This unwieldy picture appears obligatory if we treat the brain as controlling puppeteer, and if we view the people involved as perception-then-cognition-then-action systems. Construing the synchronous speaking situation in this way, we would expect to see evidence of drift between speakers and compensatory error correction at time lags that would allow for re-planning and alteration of control parameters. As that is not what we observe experimentally, one might instead regard one speaker as providing a lead, to which the other

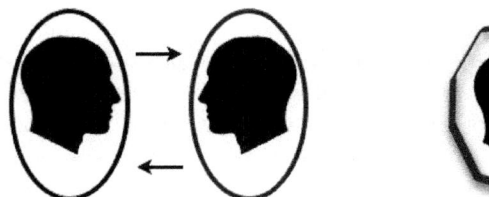

Fig. 2. As modelers, we have the freedom to chose to regard a pair of synchronous speakers as a single system, or as two distinct and interacting systems

responds. This would suggest that somewhat stable performance might be found with a fixed lag between speakers. This is never the case. For each speaker, the inherent variability that attends normal unconstrained speaking would be augmented by the additional requirement of attempting to match the timing of the co-speaker. Variability would therefore be predicted to increase. It does not. The difficulty in adequately describing (modeling) the situation stems from the prior commitment to the locus of control as lying within an individual.

If we instead view the two speakers as enslaved components within a single overarching system, each of them both driven and driving the behavior of the system as a whole, our expectations would be rather different. Where we know speech production to be inherently complex and variable, even within the speech of a single individual, we would expect a simplification, or reduction in variability while the speakers are behaving as components within a superordinate system. This is, indeed, what we find [10,11]. Variability in segment duration, in pitch movement, and in pause behavior are all reliably found to be reduced in synchronous speech, as compared to speech that is not so constrained. If the components of the system are mutually correcting, just as in the coordinated movement of body parts within a skilled individual, we would expect no clear leader-follower behavior, and this is, in fact, what we find.

A blacksmith's arm is perfectly capable of wielding a violin bow, of scratching a blacksmith's chest, or of shaking the hand of the fishmonger. But when the blacksmith pursues a well-defined behavioral goal, demanding skilled (and hence unreflective) action, the arm acts as part of an overall domain of organization that is brought into existence in pursuit of just that goal, and that ceases to exist once the blacksmith turns to other tasks. So too, in speaking synchronously, each speaker temporarily becomes part of a larger organizational domain, and the speaker acts as if he were a component within the larger system. Tellingly, we find that when one speaker makes an error, the usual result is for the entire fragile coordinative system to fall apart, each speaker recovers full autonomy, and the speech of each is immediately and completely decoupled from that of the other. The error destroys the boundary conditions imposed by the common behavioral goal.

If this account of coordination, within and across individuals, appears counter-intuitive, it is probably because the conviction is rooted very firmly that behind every lawful intentional action must lurk a controller. How else, we might reasonably ask, is one possible movement selected out of many alternatives? How, indeed, are we to account for volition in action and our sense of being the authors of our own lives? Such existential qualms are probably not warranted here, and some of the unease may be vanquished by recognizing that the type of model being developed within a dynamical framework is fundamentally different from that within a perception-cognition-action, or cognitivist, framework[1]. The dynamic account of action suggests that the fluid movement typical of skilled coordination derives its form from the lawful constraints operative on the many components that contribute to the overall behavior. An account is then required of the nature of these constraints. Why is that we observe one form of movement and not another? This question is particularly vexing as the behavioral goal that underlies the temporary organization of parts into a single-purpose domain of organization does not, by itself, contain any specification for how that goal is to be achieved. In reaching to scratch my nose, there are many possible trajectories my hand and arm could take, and one of these actually happens, without any sense of pondering, selection, or doubt.

An important part of the answer is to look more closely at the specification of the behavioral goals, and to see to what extent they might serve to differentiate among possible forms of movement. Given specific goals, some forms of movement may be *optimal* in a strict and quantitative sense, and optimality criteria may be the best candidates for formal expression of the constraints that are operative. For example, it has been demonstrated that gait selection in horse locomotion makes sense when considered in light of energetic requirements [13]. For each of the three gaits studied, walking, trotting, and galloping, the metabolic cost varied with rate. This allowed identification of rates for each gait at which energetic costs are minimized. Horses observed in the paddock adopting these gaits spontaneously did so at rates that are, in fact, approximately optimal. Locomotion is a form of action that has been shaped both phylogenetically over many millennia, and ontogenetically through constant practice. It seems highly plausible that the resulting action is constrained to be optimal with respect to many potential criteria. Analysis of bone strain as a function of speed leads to similar conclusions as the analysis of metabolic cost as indexed by oxygen consumption [13,2].

We turn now to another characterization of speech coordination within a model, but framed at quite a different level. We demonstrate that optimality criteria may provide some explanatory power in interpreting the form of observed movement, and may help to bridge the gap between accounts couched in terms of control or in terms of coordination by reducing the need for explicit intervention by a controller.

---

[1] One way of describing the difference between the modeling approaches is available in the Aristotelian distinction between *efficient* cause, which comfortably accommodates the notion of a controller, and *formal* cause, which describes lawful domains of organization without the need to commit to any such central executive.

4   Embodied Task Dynamics

When we speak, the set of goals we embody can be described in many ways: transmission of a sequence of words, effecting a response in the other, making a particular kind of sound, etc. One particularly informative way of describing speech production is as a sequence of articulatory gestures produced in parallel streams, where the gestures correspond to primitive units of combination within a phonology. This is the basic premise of Articulatory Phonology [3], and has provided a powerful explanatory framework for understanding both categorical and gradient features found in articulation [5]. Fig. 3 shows a partial gestural score (by analogy with a musical score) for the utterance /pan/. Each row (or 'tier') is associated with a (vocal) tract variable. These are linguistically significant dimensions of variation. Note that the times of individual gesture onsets and offsets do not necessarily align across tiers, as gestures are not simply co-extensive with phonemes. Thus velum lowering precedes tongue tip movement for the /n/, as is well known from phonetic data. Each tract variable is represented as a simple mass-spring dynamical system for which a target equilibrium position is provided during periods in which the gesture is active, as specified in the score. During periods of activation, tract variables move smoothly towards their targets, and when the associated gesture is no longer active, they relax to a neutral position. It is then necessary to map from the space of tract variables (which are all independent of one another and thus context-free) to the space of articulators, where multiple tract variables may compete for influence over a specific articulator. For example, the jaw is crucially involved in three of the four tract variable movements shown, and for a period, there are conflicting influences on the jaw, pushing it lower for the /a/ target, and raising it for /n/.

The tricky business of mapping from tract variables to articulators within an articulatory synthesis system is provided by the task dynamic model, originally introduced in [21] to account for limb movement, and later extended to the speech domain in [22]. Task dynamics uses techniques from linear algebra to

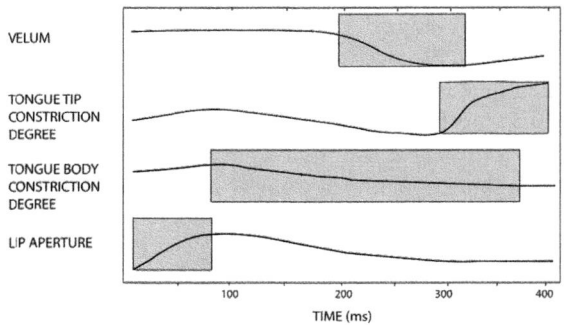

Fig. 3. Partial gestural score for the utterance /pan/. Blocks represent activation intervals. Curves represent tract variable movement.

uncover the optimal mapping from tract variable motions (arising from the mass-spring dynamics) to model articulator motions. In this way, the nice, smooth motion resulting from relatively simple dynamical systems (tract variables) can be manifested in the more complex space of a model vocal tract. Together, articulatory phonology and its task dynamic implementation have been very successful at accounting for a wide range of linguistic phenomena, and at linking observed movement to underlying discrete behavioral goals through a principled and explicit mapping [4,5].

A gestural score contains information about both sequential order, and precise timing. It can thus be interpreted as a sophisticated kind of control algorithm, with task dynamics providing the means by which its control variables are made to do real work. Getting the timing right within the gestural score is thus a difficult problem, and one of fundamental importance. Past approaches have sought to learn appropriate timing from articulatory data using neural networks [22], using an extra layer of planning oscillators [18], and by introducing a degree of flexibility in relative timing through so-called phase windows [20].

In a recent development of the task dynamic model, Simko and Cummins [25] sought to divide the control task represented in the gestural score into two distinct parts. The specification of serial order among gestures is specified independently of the timing among gestures. A modified form of task dynamics then makes it possible to express constraints under which the speech is produced, and these constraints, in turn, allow us to distinguish forms of movement that are more or less efficient, and thus to find an optimal gestural score that satisfies the overt goal (the gesture sequence) and that reflects the constraints under which speech is produced. Fig. 4 shows a simple gestural score before and after optimization. The top panel (before) specifies only the linear order of the sequence /abi/, while precise timings have emerged after a process of automatic optimization in the lower panel. In the radically simplified vocal tract model employed so far, we model only the consonants /p/ and /b/[2] and the vowels /a/ and /i/.

Optimization is based upon a cost function with three weighted components: $C = \alpha_E + \alpha_P + \alpha_D$. Collectively, these express the high-level constraints under

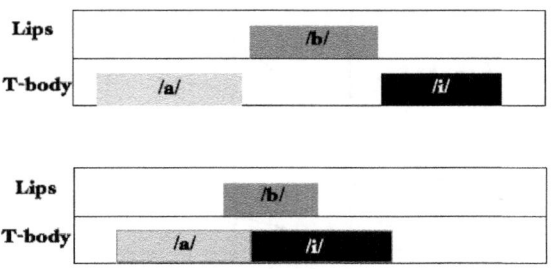

Fig. 4. Gestural score before and after optimization

---

[2] Without a glottal model, there is no meaningful distinction within the model between these stops and their voiced counterparts, /b/ and /d/.

which speech is produced. The first two components, α_E and α_P serve to establish a trade off between ease of articulation and communicative effectiveness. α_E is a quantification of the effort expended in executing a series of movements, while α_P is a cost that rises if articulation is sloppy, or the speech is hard to parse by a listener. Together, the relative magnitude of these weights serves to locate a given production as lying on a specific point on a scale from hypo-articulation to hyper-articulation [17]. The third component, α_D places a relative cost on executing an utterance quickly. Full details of the model are presented in [24,26] and a summary overview can be found in [25].

Fig. 5 illustrates the output of the model. Movement traces are shown for jaw (light solid line), tongue body (heavy solid) and lips (dashed). The vertical lines demarcate the interval of consonant closure. Movement of the lips within that interval arises from soft tissue compression. This score, and the associated movement traces, is derived fully automatically from the sequence specification /abi/ and specific choices of weights for the three elements in the cost function, C. The resulting form of movement is fluent, and to date, has matched published details of articulatory movement with a high degree of accuracy [26]. Further development, including extension to a full vocal tract model, will be guided by precise articulatory data.

The gestural score of the original articulatory phonology/task dynamics model is a form of control algorithm that specifies both sequence and precise timing. In the more recent embodied model, these jobs are separated. The input to the model (the residual control element) comprises just the behavioral goal expressed as a sequence of gestures, without explicit timing information. To these is added the specification of constraint under which speech is produced (the cost function weights), and this collectively allows computation of the optimal form of movement. This is

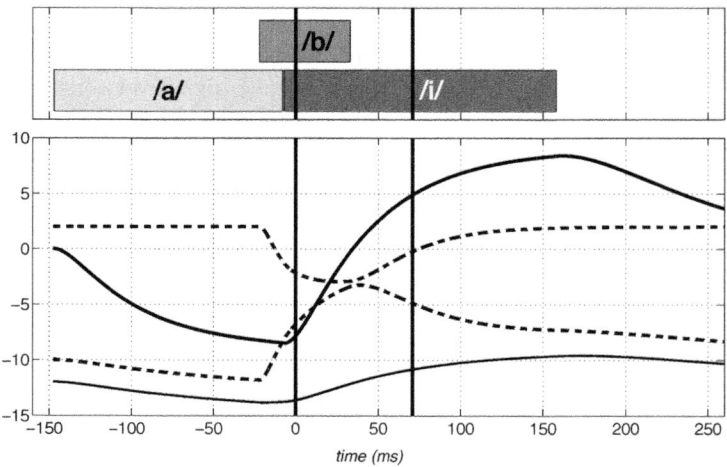

Fig. 5. Sample movement traces after optimization. Heavy solid line: tongue body; Light solid line: jaw; Dashed lines: lips. Vertical lines demarcate the interval of consonant closure.

no longer a control algorithm, but rather an account of the form of observed movement couched in terms of discrete behavioral goals along with high-level intentional constraints (weights).

5   Dynamics and Autonomy

In each of the two examples presented herein, an attempt is made to understand the form of observed behavior, while remaining somewhat agnostic as to the underlying (efficient) causes. We observe tight synchrony among speakers and wish to find the best characterization thereof that can account for reduced variability, sustained synchrony without leaders, and the fragility of the cooperative behavior when errors creep in. The conceptual tools of dynamical systems, and in particularly their application to understanding coordination, provide an appropriate vocabulary and instrumentarium for capturing this regularity. They do so by taking the identification of the system to be modeled as a critical part of scientific inquiry. Rather than assuming that the sole domain of autonomy in behavior is the individual person, the dynamical approach here posits the temporary capture of two subjects within a superordinate dyadic domain.

In the embodied task dynamic model, the set of entities that exhibit mutual coordination changes over time. The boundaries of the set are determined by the gestural score, which in turn arises from a minimal set of discrete behavioral goals, and some context-specific constraints. Collectively, these serve to identify an optimal form of movement, where 'optimality' has a precise and quantifiable meaning. Again, the domain within which lawfulness and constraint operate is not give a priori, but is rather dependent on time-varying behavioral goals and the context within which behavior occurs.

The brief accounts provided here to not do justice to either experiment or model. For those details, the reader is encouraged to seek out the primary publications referenced herein. The goal here has been to show how the adoption of a dynamical perspective can help in understanding the structure and lawfulness of behavior, but that this approach also demands an openness with respect to the system being modeled. Any dynamic modeling must first be explicit about the set of state variables to be considered. This initial choice positively encourages the creation of models that cut across the somewhat arbitrary boundaries that separate brain, body, and environment, and gives the modeler pause for thought about the domain being studied: is it a person, a well-defined subset of the person, a person plus a tool, a set of persons? The right answer will, in all cases, be an empirical issue, and will depend on where lawfulness is observed. This flexibility to identify lawfulness at many different levels may ultimately encourage us to identify time-varying domains within which components exhibit interdependent behavior that is both constitutive of, and constrained by, the system level organization.

A final word is appropriate to fend off an inevitable potential point of confusion. The notion of autonomy within dynamical modeling is clearly separate from the concept of agency. The autonomous domain is precisely that set of variables that exhibits a lawful set of relations among its components. To identify, e.g. a dyad, as an autonomous domain is to make an observation about the structure and form of their collective behavior. It does not say anything at all about the more mysterious notion of agency. Even though individuals may act as relatively simple components within an overall pattern, this does not rob them of their intrinsic autonomy. This is clear when we realize that participants in a Mexican wave are acting as simple components in a collective organization, without any sacrifice of their ability to later leave the game and go buy a hot dog.

References

1. Bernstein, N.A.: A new method of mirror cylographie and its application towards the study of labor movements during work on a workbench. Hygiene, Safety and Pathology lf Labor, 5:3–9, 6:3–11 (1930) (In Russian); Cited in Latash (2008)
2. Biewener, A.A., Taylor, C.R.: Bone strain: a determinant of gait and speed? The Journal of Experimental Biology 123, 383–400 (1986)
3. Browman, C.P., Goldstein, L.: Articulatory phonology: An overview. Phonetica 49, 155–180 (1992)
4. Browman, C.P., Goldstein, L.: Dynamics and articulatory phonology. In: Port, R.F., van Gelder, T. (eds.) Mind as Motion, ch. 7, pp. 175–193. MIT Press, Cambridge (1995)
5. Browman, C.P., Goldstein, L.: Articulatory gestures as phonological units. Phonology 6(02), 201–251 (2008)
6. Calvo, P., Gomila, A.: Handbook of Cognitive Science: An Embodied Approach. Elsevier Science Ltd, Amsterdam (2008)
7. Chemero, A., Silberstein, M.: After the Philosophy of Mind: Replacing Scholasticism with Science. Philosophy of Science 75, 1–27 (2008)
8. Cummins, F.: On synchronous speech. Acoustics Research Letters Online 3(1), 7–11 (2002)
9. Cummins, F.: Practice and performance in speech produced synchronously. Journal of Phonetics 31(2), 139–148 (2003)
10. Cummins, F.: Synchronization among speakers reduces macroscopic temporal variability. In: Proceedings of the 26th Annual Meeting of the Cognitive Science Society, pp. 304–309 (2004)
11. Cummins, F.: Rhythm as entrainment: The case of synchronous speech. Journal of Phonetics 37(1), 16–28 (2009)
12. Haken, H., Kelso, J.A.S., Bunz, H.: A theoretical model of phase transitions in human hand movement. Biological Cybernetics 51, 347–356 (1985)
13. Hoyt, D.F., Taylor, C.R.: Gait and the energetics of locomotion in horses. Nature 292(5820), 239–240 (1981)
14. Scott Kelso, J.A.: Dynamic Patterns. MIT Press, Cambridge (1995)
15. Kelso, J.S., Tuller, B., Vatikiotis-Bateson, E., Fowler, C.A.: Functionally specific articulatory cooperation following jaw perturbations during speech: Evidence for coordinative structures. Journal of Experimental Psychology: Human Perception and Performance 10(6), 812–832 (1984)
16. Latash, M.L.: Synergy. Oxford University Press, USA (2008)

17. Lindblom, B.: Explaining phonetic variation: a sketch of the H&H theory. In: Hardcastle, W.J., Marchal, A. (eds.) Speech Production and Speech Modelling, pp. 403–439. Kluwer Academic, Dordrecht (1990)
18. Nam, H., Saltzman, E.: A competitive, coupled oscillator model of syllable structure. In: International Conference on Phonetic Sciences (2003)
19. Port, R., van Gelder, T. (eds.): Mind as Motion: Explorations in the Dynamics of Cognition. Bradford Books/MIT Press, Cambridge (1995)
20. Saltzman, E., Byrd, D.: Task-dynamics of gestural timing: Phase windows and multifrequency rhythms. Human Movement Science 19(4), 499–526 (2000)
21. Saltzman, E., Kelso, J.A.S.: Skilled actions: A task dynamic approach. Psychological Review 94, 84–106 (1987)
22. Saltzman, E., Munhall, K.: A dynamical approach to gestural patterning in speech production. Ecological Psychology 1, 333–382 (1989)
23. Schmidt, R.C., Carello, C., Turvey, M.T.: Phase transitions and critical fluctuations in the visual coordination of rhythmic movements between people. Journal of Experimental Psychology. Human Perception and Performance 16(2), 227–247 (1990)
24. Simko, J., Cummins, F.: Embodied task dynamics. Psychological Review (2009) (in press)
25. Simko, J., Cummins, F.: Sequencing of articulatory gestures using cost optimization. In: Proceedings of INTERSPEECH 2009, Brighton, U.K. (2009)
26. Simko, J., Cummins, F.: Sequencing and optimization within an embodied task dynamic model. Cognitive Science (in revision 2010)
27. Tuller, B., Turvey, M.T., Fitch, H.L.: The Bernstein perspective: II. The concept of muscle linkage or coordinative structure. Human Motor Behavior: An Introduction, 253–270 (1982)
28. Wallace, B., Ross, A., Davies, J., Anderson, T.: The Mind, the Body and the World. Psychology after Cognitivism. Imprint Academic, Charlottesville, VA (2007)

Speech, Gaze and Head Motion
in a Face-to-Face Collaborative Task

Sascha Fagel and Gérard Bailly

GIPSA-lab, 961 rue de la Houille Blanche, BP 46, 38402 Grenoble, France
sascha.fagel@tu-berlin.de

Abstract. In the present work we observe two subjects interacting in a collaborative task on a shared environment. One goal of the experiment is to measure the change in behavior with respect to gaze when one interactant is wearing
dark glasses and hence his/her gaze is not visible by the other one. The results
show that if one subject wears dark glasses while telling the other subject the
position of a certain object, the other subject needs significantly more time to
locate and move this object. Hence, eye gaze – when visible – of one subject
looking at a certain object speeds up the location of the cube by the other subject. The second goal of the currently ongoing work is to collect data on the
multimodal behavior of one of the subjects by means of audio recording, eye
gaze and head motion tracking in order to build a model that can be used to
control a robot in a comparable scenario in future experiments.

Keywords: eye gaze, eye tracking, collaborative task, face-to-face interaction,
head motion capture.

1 Introduction

Speech is a natural and highly developed means of human communication, i.e. to transmit information between humans. However, while a person speaks there are more
sources of information accessible for the listener than just the spoken words. Along with
the linguistic content of the speech also para-linguistic and extra-linguistic cues contained in the speech signal are interpreted by the listener that together constitute the verbal information. Moreover, when humans communicate not only through an acoustic
channel, e.g. face-to-face, there are also non-verbal cues that accompany speech, appear
simultaneously with speech or appear without the presence of speech at all. Aside from
static features such as the shape of a person's face, clothing etc., non-verbal cues potentially arise from any movements of the body other than speech articulatory movements.
The most obvious non-verbal cues during speech communication originate from movements of the body [5], the face [7], the eyes [1], the hands and arms [14], and the head
[9]. More recent reviews can be found in [10], [18], [11], [16], and [17].

Iconic gestures produced during speech such as nods and shakes for "yes" and "no"
are rare. Non-verbal cues mostly contribute to the conversational structure or add information to speech in form of visual prosody. Hence, head motion can be predicted or
generated for the use in virtual agents by the use of acoustic prosodic features, e.g. by
mapping to head motion primitives [8] [12], or orientation angles [6] [19]. Eye gaze is

A. Esposito et al. (Eds.): COST 2102 Int. Training School 2010, LNCS 6456, pp. 256–264, 2011.
© Springer-Verlag Berlin Heidelberg 2011

linked to the cognitive and emotional state of a person and to the environment. Hence, approaches to eye gaze modeling have to deal with high level information about the communication process [18] [15] [2].

All the aforementioned modalities of communication can be used for deixis, i.e. to point to specific objects or regions in space. In scenarios where humans interact in a shared environment, head movements and eye gaze of a person can relate to objects or locations in that environment and hence deliver information about the person's relation to that environment. Contrastive focus in speech (e.g. blue ball followed by GREEN ball) was shown to provide a processing advantage in the localization of objects [13] and hence can be used for verbal deixis. While hand movements are often explicitly used to point to objects, head motion and eye gaze yield implicit cues to objects (multimodal deixis [2]) that are in a person's focus of attention as the person turns and looks towards the object of interest. The present paper describes an experimental scenario of a face-to-face task-oriented interaction in a shared environment. The accessibility of eye gaze information while referring to an object in the environment is manipulated and it is hypothesized that the task performance decreases when eye gaze cues are prevented or not perceived.

2 Experiment

2.1 Procedure

Two subjects are seated on chairs at opposite sides of a table. The table contains two identical designated areas, one on either side of the middle line between the subjects. An area consists of 9 slots in a row: each slot has one of the symbols {A,I,O}, each three slots (A,I,O) have the same color {red, green, or blue}. 9 cubes are placed in the slots of one of the two areas. Each cube shows a label, a letter from {P,T,B,D,G,M,N,F,S}, on that side facing the subject (informant) who is sitting close to the cubes. The informant has access to the labels of the cubes but only the other subject (manipulator) is allowed to modify the environment, i.e. to move cubes. Each move starts with a quasi-random pause of the control script that aims to establish mutual attention. Then the computer informs the manipulator confidentially by earphones about the label of one cube to be moved. Then the manipulator tells the label to the informant in order to request the position of the cube. The informant searches among the cubes and tells the symbol and color of the slot where the requested cube is located. Then the manipulator takes the cube, places it on the opposite field in the area close to herself and completes the move by pressing a mouse button. See Figure 1 for a snapshot of the game during a move. 72 of these moves are completed, arranged in 12 rounds of 6 moves. The role assignment (who is informant and who is manipulator) is changed during the experiment as well as the condition (with or without dark glasses).

Following the design of the game board, the position of a certain cube is verbally specified by e.g. "A rouge" ("A red"); due to the particular structure of the language – the experiment was carried out in French – the noun (label) naturally precedes the adjective (color). Therefore, the first part of a verbalization specifies the exact position inside one of the three colored areas where the rough position is given last. This is important to note as implicit deixis by head and eye gaze can be assumed to be not

Fig. 1. One subject's view recorded by a head mounted scene camera. This subject's roll is informant: she sees the labels on the cubes and tells the position of the requested cube. The role of the opposite subject (shown in the figure) is manipulator: she requests the position of a cube by telling its label, moves the cube (here the third from six cubes to be moved) and ends the move by a click on the mouse button.

completely unambiguous but to convey information of the approximate position which thus precedes the accordant verbal information.

We monitored four interactions of one person (reference subject) with four different interactants to study the influence of social rapport and interpersonal attunement. All rounds with the same role assignment and condition are grouped to a block. The order of these blocks is counterbalanced across the 4 recordings so that in recordings 1 and 2 the reference subject is manipulator first and in recording 3 and 4 second, and in recordings 1 and 3 the dark glasses are worn first and in recording 2 and 4 second. Two training rounds of three moves were played before the recording (one for each role assignment) and subjects were instructed to play as fast as possible but not overhastily.

3   Technical Setup

During the interaction we recorded the subjects' heads with an HD video camera (both subjects at a time by using a mirror), the subjects' head movements by a motion capture system, the subjects' speech by head mounted microphones, and the eye gaze of the reference subject and a video of what she sees by a head mounted eye tracker. We also monitored the timing of the moves by the log file of the script that controls the experiment. The different data streams are post-synchronized by recording the shutter signal of the motion capture cameras as an audio track along with the microphone signals as well as the audio track of the HD video camera, and by a clapper board that is recorded by the microphones, the scene camera of the eye tracker and the motion capture system simultaneously. Figure 2 shows an overview of the technical setup.

Fig. 2. Technical setup of the experiment comprising head mounted eye tracking, head mounted microphones, video recording, and motion capture of head movements

4   Results

4.1   Analyses

The speech was annotated on utterance level with Praat [4], head orientations are computed and then refined and labeled in ELAN [3]. The timings of the confidential playbacks and mouse clicks that end the moves are imported from the log file of the control script. The timings of the phases of the interaction are inferred from these data, i.e. for the manipulator: wait for confidential instruction, listen to confidential instruction, verbalization of cube request, wait for information, move the cube and complete the move; for the informant: wait for cube request, search the cube, verbalization of its position, observe its relocation.

The duration from the end of the confidential playback of the instruction to the completion of a move by pressing the mouse button (completion time) was calculated for each move. Additionally, this duration was split at the start of the verbalization of the position of right cube by the informant, which provides the time needed by the informant to search the cube (search time) and the time needed by the manipulator to locate and place the cube (location time).The number of (wrong) cubes gazed by the reference subject during the search before she finally gazes at the requested cube is determined by visual inspection of the eye tracking data that is superimposed on the video of the eye tracker's scene camera (see Figure 1: the red cross marks the current gaze, here at the target slot where the cube has to be placed). Correlations between the number of wrong cubes, the number of cubes left in the source area (starting with 9 down to 4 in the 6th move of a round), the search time and the location time are calculated.

The rigid motion of the heads, i.e. translation and rotation, is extracted from the captured motion data of the markers on the head mounts. The rotation data is then analyzed with respect to the angular path the informant's head covered during the search for the right cube. The frame-by-frame angular velocity (Euclidean distance between two subsequent rotation angles) is accumulated over of each of these periods and correlations of this measure of quantity of movement to other measures of the search are computed.

4.2 Completion Time

Task completion time is significantly increased (p<.001) when the informant wears dark glasses compared to not wearing glasses. No significantly different completion times were observed for one subject in recording 1 and for both subjects in recording 2. In all other cases completion times are significantly increased. See Table 1 for details.

Table 1. Completion times with and without dark glasses and the significance level of differences

recording	A manipulator. B no glasses	A manipulator. B with glasses	B manipulator. A no glasses	B manipulator. B with glasses
1	4.39*	4.74*	4.33	4.10
2	3.87	3.75	3.96	4.08
3	3.22**	3.80**	3.82*	4.40*
4	3.47*	3.77*	3.52*	4.04*
all	3.73*	4.02*	3.91*	4.16*
both roles	3.82**	4.09**		

* p<.05, ** p<.001, p>.05 otherwise

4.3 Search Time and Location Time

Over all recordings the search time was not significantly different between with and without dark glasses. This indicates that the dark glasses did not perturb the search of the cube. Location times, however, i.e. the duration from hearing the position of the cube to its completed relocation, are significantly increased in five of eight cases (the two role assignments in each of the four recordings). No significant differences were observed for the same cases where no different completion times were found. Across all four recordings separately for both role assignments as well as across both role assignments the search times are not significantly differing where the location times are significantly increased. See Table 2 for details.

4.4 Number of Cubes

The total number of wrong cubes gazed before the requested cube is found is exactly the same in both conditions. Table 3 shows the correlation between number of wrong cubes gazed at and the number of cubes left as well as their correlation to the search and location times. The location time is negligibly correlated to the number of cubes left and weakly correlated to the number of wrong cubes gazed at. The number of wrong cubes gazed at is moderately correlated to the number of cubes left: there is a tendency to shorter search times when fewer cubes are left (Figure 3). Strong correlation is found between search time and number of wrong cubes gazed at.

Table 2. Search time and location time with and without dark glasses for each recording and across all recordings (same conventions as above)

re-cord-ing	search time				location time			
	A. no glasses	A. w/ glasses	B. no glasses	B. w/ glasses	A. no glasses	A. w/ glasses	B. no glasses	B. w/ glasses
1	1.36	1.27	1.49	1.32	3.03**	3.47**	2.84	2.78
2	1.31	1.27	1.23	1.34	2.55	2.48	2.72	2.74
3	1.15	1.33	1.17	1.22	2.06**	2.47**	2.65**	3.18**
4	1.49	1.47	1.18	1.24	1.98**	2.30**	2.34*	2.80*
all	1.33	1.33	1.27	1.28	2.41*	2.68*	2.64**	2.87**
both roles	1.30	1.31			2.52**	2.78**		

* p<.05, ** p<.001, p>.05 otherwise

Table 3. Correlations between number of wrong cubes gazed at, number of cubes left, search time, and location time

	No. of wrong cubes	*No. of cubes left*
cubes left	0.45	
search time	**0.74**	0.35
location time	0.26	*0.12*

Table 4. Correlation coefficients between the quantity of movement during the search and the number of wrong cubes gazed at, the number of cubes left and the search time. The number of wrong cubes gazed at is only determined for the reference subject.

	No. of wrong cubes gazed (subj A only)	*No. of cubes left*	*search time*
quantity of movement	**0.76**	0.19	0.41

4.5 Head Motion

An ANOVA shows no significant differences between the conditions with and without dark glasses concerning the quantity of movement during the search. However, there is a tendency for the reference subject to more head motion without dark glasses.

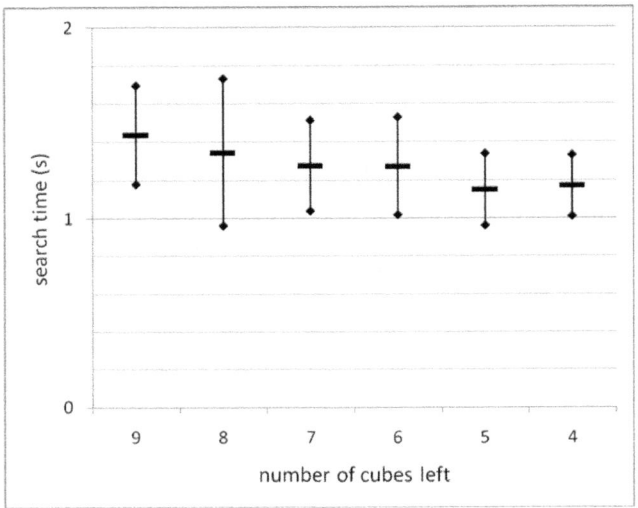

Fig. 3. Mean and standard deviation of search time over the number of cubes left

Correlation coefficients are calculated between the quantity of movement during the search and the number of wrong cubes gazed at, the number of cubes left and the search time. The quantity of movement is only marginally correlated to the number of cubes left to search. The quantity of movement is strongly correlated to the number of wrong cubes gazed at and moderately correlated to search time.

5 Conclusions and Discussion

The present experiment investigates the impact of the visibility versus invisibility of one subjects eye gaze on the performance in a task-oriented human-human interaction. The task completion included the localization of an object, a labeled cube, that was explicitly referenced by speech and implicitly by head motion and eye gaze. This deixis by head and eye gaze can be assumed to be ambiguous to some extend but to provide information – on the approximate position of the object of interest – that is redundant to the final word of the verbalization of the object's position. Hence, the implicit deixis preceded the verbal information and potentially speeds up task completion in case the deictic information is used by the subject to locate the object. It was hypothesized that the task performance will be decreased when dark glasses block the visibility of the eyes of the subject that informs the other one about the position of a certain cube. Task completion time is in fact significantly increased when the informant wears dark glasses compared to not wearing dark glasses. Hence, invisibility of eye gaze decreases task performance measured by completion time. Where the time needed by the informant to find the right cube does not differ with or without dark glasses, the time for the other subject (manipulator) to locate and place the cube is significantly increased generally over the whole experiment and more specifically in all cases where the task completion times were increased. Furthermore, the total number of wrong cubes gazed at before the requested cube is found is exactly the same in both conditions. Consequently, dark glasses did not make the search for the cube by its label more difficult for the informant but only blocked the visibility of the eye gaze to the opposite subject that leads to degraded information for the manipulator to locate the cube. Or put the other way round: visible eye gaze provides an important cue for the location of the object of interest. The availability of the gaze path of the informant through the shared environment is crucial to trigger grasping: the resonance of motor activities during joint visual attention, the mirroring of the quest, favors synchronized analysis and decision.

The quantity of movement shows a non-significant tendency to more head motion without dark glasses for the reference subject. This indicates that the reference subject does not use explicit head deixis or implicitly exaggerated movements to overcome the reduced amount of information caused by invisibility of eye gaze. This matches the subject's informal report after the experiment that she did not feel to behave differently with or without wearing dark glasses.

Visual inspection of the recorded video data suggest that the head is not oriented separately to every object that is gazed by the eyes as the head moves somewhat slower than the eyes and the eyes can subsequently fixate two close objects without a change of the head orientation. Hence, the head orientation provides less accurate as well as delayed information about the position of the object of interest compared to eye gaze. This leads to increased task completion time.

The rounds played in the present experiment comprise an inherent decline of difficulty due to the decreasing number of alternatives left as possible object of interest. However, this difficulty was most obviously existent for the subject that has to find the object of interest by searching among the labels of the cubes left. The time needed by the opposite subject to locate the object of interest – referred to explicitly by speech and implicitly by head motion and, if visible, eye gaze – only marginally depends on the number of alternatives if not at all. Thus the referencing of the object in space can be assumed as nearly optimal and eye gaze is an integral part of the transmitted information.

The main result of the experiment is that visible eye gaze yields important information about the location of objects of joint interest in a face-to-face collaborative task between two humans. This is evident from the present work. It can be assumed that proper display of eye gaze might be an important aspect in human-robot interaction as well as in mediated task-oriented interaction.

6 Future Work

One of the recordings where the reference subject acts as informant and does not wear dark glasses was analyzed in detail. The timing of the reference subject's behavioral cues regarding gaze, head orientation, and verbalization was extracted. Both the timing of the interaction and the reference subject's behavior will be modeled by a probabilistic finite-state machine that is capable to control a robot in a comparable scenario. Further analyses of the behavior and a second experiment where a robot will act as informant on the basis of the state machine will follow.

Acknowledgments

This work was financed by the ANR Amorces. Thanks to Amélie Lelong and Frédéric Elisei for their help during the experiment.

References

1. Argyle, M., Cook, M.: Gaze and Mutual gaze. Cambridge University Press, Cambridge (1976)
2. Bailly, G., Raidt, S., Elisei, F.: Gaze, conversational agents and face-to-face communication. Speech Communication 52(3), 598–612 (2010)
3. Berezm, A.L.: Review of EUDICO Linguistic Annotator (ELAN). Language Documentation & Conservation 1, 2 (2007)
4. Boersma, P., Weenink, D.: Praat: doing phonetics by computer (Version 5.1.05) [Computer program] (2009), http://www.praat.org/ (retrieved May 1, 2009)
5. Bull, P.E., Brown, R.: Body movement and emphasis in speech. Journal of Nonverbal Behavior 16 (1977)
6. Busso, C., Deng, Z., Neumann, U., Narayanan, S.S.: Natural head motion synthesis driven by acoustic prosodic features. Computer Animation and Virtual Worlds 16(3-4), 283–290 (2005)
7. Collier, G.: Emotional Expression. Lawrence Erlbaum Associates, Mahwah (1985)
8. Graf, H.P., Cosatto, E., Strom, V., Huang, F.J.: Visual prosody: Facial movements accompanying speech. In: Proceedings of Automatic Face and Gesture Recognition, pp. 396–401 (2002)
9. Hadar, U., Steiner, T.J., Grant, E.C., Clifford Rose, F.: Kinematics of head movements accompanying speech during conversation. Human Movement Science 2, 35–46 (1983)
10. Heath, C.: Body Movement and Speech in Medical Interaction. Cambridge University Press, Cambridge (2004)
11. Heylen, D.: Head gestures. gaze and the principles of conversational structure. Journal of Humanoid Robotics 3(3), 241–267 (2006)
12. Hofer, G., Shimodaira, H.: Automatic head motion prediction from speech data. In: Proceedings of Interspeech (2007)
13. Ito, K., Speer, S.R.: Anticipatory effects of intonation: Eye movements during instructed visual search. Journal of Memory and Language 58(2), 541–573 (2008)
14. Kendon, A.: Gesture and speech: How they interact. In: Wiemann, J.M., Harrison, R.P. (eds.) Nonverbal Interaction, pp. 13–45. Sage Publications, Beverly Hills CA (1983)
15. Lee, J., Marsella, S., Traum, D., Gratch, J., Lance, B.: The Rickel Gaze Model: A window on the mind of a virtual human. In: Pelachaud, C., Martin, J.-C., André, E., Chollet, G., Karpouzis, K., Pelé, D. (eds.) IVA 2007. LNCS (LNAI), vol. 4722, pp. 296–303. Springer, Heidelberg (2007)
16. Maricchiolo, F., Bonaiuto, M., Gnisci, A.: Hand gestures in speech: Studies of their roles in social interaction. In: Proceedings of the Conference of the International Society for Gesture Studies (2005)
17. McClave, E.Z.: Linguistic functions of head movements in the context of speech. Journal of Pragmatics 32, 855–878 (2000)
18. Pelachaud, C., Badler, N.I., Steedman, M.: Generating facial expressions for speech. Cognitive Science 20(1), 1–46 (1969)
19. Sargin, M.E., Yemez, Y., Erzin, E., Tekalp, A.M.: Analysis of head gesture and prosody patterns for prosody-driven head-gesture animation. IEEE Transactions on Pattern Analysis and Machine Intelligence 30(8), 1330–1345 (2008)

Neuroelectric Methodologies for the Study of the Economic Decisions in Humans

Giovanni Vecchiato[1,2] and Fabio Babiloni[1,2]

[1] Dept. Physiology and Pharmacology, Univ. of Rome Sapienza, 00185, Rome, Italy
[2] IRCCS Fondazione Santa Lucia, via Ardeatina 306, 00179, Rome, Italy
Giovanni.Vecchiato@uniroma1.it

Abstract. In recent years the engagement of the customer with the brand or the company advertised has become the dominant issue in the agenda of marketers and advertisers. The aim of this paper is to elucidate if the remembering of TV commercials elicits particular brain activity and connectivity. Results suggest that the cortical activity and connectivity during the vision of the TV commercials that will be remembered by the analyzed healthy subjects is markedly different from the brain activity elicited during the observation of the TV commercials that will be forgotten. In particular, during the observation of the TV commercials that will be successively remembered the amount of cortical spectral activity from the frontal areas (BA 8 and 9) and from the parietal areas (BA 5, 7 and 40) is higher on when compared with the activity elicited by the observation of TV commercials that will be forgotten. The techniques presented here are also relevant in neuroeconomics and neuromarketing in order to investigate the neural substrates sub-serving other decision-making and recognition tasks.

Keywords: Neuroeconomy, neuromarketing, EEG, functional connectivity.

1 Introduction

In recent years, with the increasing complexity of the media landscape characterized by a proliferation of new media, new channels and new ways to advertise brands that has led to a greater audience fragmentation, a smarter consumer control of its media consumption, a lower interest towards advertising, the engagement of the customer with the brand or the company advertised has become the dominant issue in the agenda of marketers and advertisers [1]. Although in the marketing research the term engagement is a complex concept and rather elusive, it is widely recognized that advertising engagement refers to the ability of the message to go beyond the simple exposure and to trigger in the consumer mind a progression of responses towards the brand advertised leading to a shift of awareness, interest, favorability, preference, purchase and re-purchase. Clearly, the consumer buying process doesn't need to follow this linear progression at least in every market category. In repeated purchase categories brand-purchasing is a low-involvement, automated and habitual process and that much advertising content is not consciously processed: perceptions and emotional reactions to the advertising stimulus are stored in the implicit memory [2-3].

A. Esposito et al. (Eds.): COST 2102 Int. Training School 2010, LNCS 6456, pp. 265–282, 2011.
© Springer-Verlag Berlin Heidelberg 2011

Therefore the key is to recognize that engagement isn't a stage but it's a process involving human behaviors of memorization, recognition and decision-making along the path towards the brand purchase. Hence planning the advertising engagement is the challenge facing today's advertisers in order to maximize the communication efforts of the companies through a deep understanding on a) what message is relevant to the consumer, b) where to place it, c) when to find the potential consumer more favorably disposed towards the brand, and through d) the evaluation of the mental responses (how the ad will affect people) for the definition of the objectives and the creative strategy both in the short and the long term.

With a new advertising marketers need to be reassured that the campaign will work before having aired and that their budget will not be wasted. So they largely rely on advertising pre-testing in order to allow them to decide whether airing or not the campaign. Advertising pre-testing industry is a field of market research based on the analysis of feedback to the submitted adv copy gathered from a small sample of the target audience, namely the focus group, to which asking the likeability, emotional involvement, persuasion, favorability and intention to purchase. Often in order to allow the comparison among several alternatives of copy respondents are asked to express their feedbacks using scores (e.g. ranging from 1 to 10) then collapsed by the research company in a unique number score.

However advertising pre-testing is flawed by the respondents' cognitive processes activated during the interview, being the implicit memory so as feelings and most of the essential insights that would really help the decision-makers often inaccessible to the interviewer that uses traditional techniques [4]. In addition, as previously pointed out [3,5] the interviewer has a great influence on what respondent recalls and on the subjective experiencing of it. The cues the interviewer uses help to form what the respondent recalls (known also as suggestive effect of stimulus material). The fact that advertising pre-tests hide or overestimate the real strength of the campaign is more and more recognized by the marketing community so as the lack of predictive power of the aired commercial versus the pre-tested scores proves the failure of old fashioned theories on how the advertising information is encoded in the human brain. Hence it's not surprising that the Bob Lo Iodice, president of the (American) Association of National Advertisers, had wished that "... going beyond traditional focus groups and consumer surveys, market research will embrace scientific approaches that literally tap consumers' brains to learn how they neurologically respond to commercial messages and make brand choices" [6]. Though living in a enlarged and rapidly changing media environment, television is expected to maintain its leadership in addressing messages to mass target groups as testified by the projections for the very next future of advertising investments worldwide allocated on this medium [7]. So it is natural to investigate deeper this medium as the first brick of a re-foundation of the entire building of advertising research.

The aim of this paper is to elucidate if the remembering of TV commercials elicits particular brain activity and connectivity. Several Authors have investigated in the last decades the capability of subjects to memorize and retrieve sensible "commercials" information viewed from a TV screen [8-13]. It is worth of note that in the past several studies used the electroencephalogram (EEG) as brain imaging tool for the analysis of the brain activity during the observation of TV commercials, despite its limitation in spatial resolution due to an insufficient number of electrodes used as well as to the limitation of the processing capabilities [10,13]. Nowadays, this is not more the case since it is well know that the body of techniques know as high resolution EEG allows to detect brain activities as well brain connectivity on the cortical surface with a spatial resolution of a squared centimeter and the unsurpassed time resolution of milliseconds [14-20].

In the present study we studied the cortical activity and connectivity occurring during the observation of TV commercials by the techniques of high resolution EEG and by the use of the functional connectivity estimates performed with the Partial Directed Coherence (PDC, [21-22]). The extraction of significant descriptors of the estimated brain networks with the PDC was obtained with the use of particular graph theory indexes [23]. In particular, subjects are asked to observe for five days (once per day) different documentaries with a series of TV commercials included while their EEG activity was recorded. After the 10 days from the experiment an interview was performed and the subjects indicated which TV commercials they remembered and which they do not remember. The brain activity and the functional connectivity between the cortical areas was then analyzed when the subjects observed TV commercials that have remembered after 10 days and when they observed clips that they have not remembered after such period of time. The experimental questions of the present study will be the following:

1) In the population analyzed, the cortical activity elicited during the observation of the TV commercials that were forgotten ("EEG data of the forgotten TV commercials"; FRG) is different from the cortical activity observed in subjects that have remembered the same TV commercials ("EEG data of the remembered TV commercials"; RMB)?

2) If some differences in cortical activity arose between the FRG and RMB data set, are they frequency dependent?

3) There exists differences in the cortical connectivity patterns between the FRG and RMB data set?

4) If some differences in the cortical connectivity patterns exist, are they frequency dependent?

2   Material and Methods

High-resolution EEG technologies have been developed to enhance the poor spatial information content of the EEG activity [17-20]. Basically, these techniques involve the use of a large number (64-256) of scalp electrodes. In addition, high-resolution EEG techniques rely on realistic MRI-constructed head models and spatial deconvolution estimations, which are usually computed by solving a linear-inverse problem based on Boundary-Element Mathematics [24-25]. Subjects were comfortably seated on a reclining chair, in an electrically shielded, dimly lit room. A 64-channel EEG system (BrainAmp, Brainproducts GmbH, Germany) was used to record electrical potentials by means of an electrode cap, accordingly to an extension of the 10-20 international system. In the present work, the cortical activity was estimated from scalp EEG recordings by using realistic head models whose cortical surface consisted of about 5000 triangles uniformly disposed. The current density estimation of each one of the triangle, which represents the electrical dipole of the underlying neuronal population, was computed by solving the linear-inverse problem according to the techniques described in previous papers [20,22,23].

Thus, a time-varying waveform relative to the estimated current density activity at each single triangle of the modeled cortical surface was obtained. Such waveform was then subjected to the time-varying spectral analysis by computing the spectral power in the different frequency bands usually employed in EEG analysis, i.e. theta (4-7 Hz), alpha (8-12 Hz), beta (13-24 Hz) and gamma (24-45 Hz).

Although we estimated brain activity in all the described frequency bands, in the following we presented those related to theta and alpha frequency bands. In fact, in the EEG literature, these frequency bands have been suggested to be maximally responsive during the observation and the memorization tasks when compared to the beta and gamma bands [9,10]

In each subject recorded, the statistical significance of the spectral values during the observation of the TV commercials was then measured against the activity evaluated during the observation of the documentary for the same subject. This was obtained by computing a time-varying z-score variable for each subject and for each dipole placed on the cortical mantle in the analyzed frequency band. The mean and the standard deviation for such z-score variable was estimated in the documentary period, while the time-varying values of the spectral power in the theta band during the observation of the TV commercial for each dipole were employed.

In order to present these results relative to the experimental conditions for the entire population, we needed a common cortical representation to map the different activated areas of each subject. For this purpose we used the average brain model available from the McGill University website. In this way we were able to display the cortical areas that are statistically significant activated during different experimental conditions in all subjects analyzed. In fact, we highlighted in yellow a voxel of the average brain model if it was a cortical site in which a statistical significant variation of the spectral power between the experimental conditions was found in all the subjects; if such brain voxel was statistically significant in all but one of the subjects analyzed, we depicted it in red. In all the other cases the voxel was represented with a gray color.

By construction, the analyzed maps are then relative to the evolution of the time-cortical activity of the spectral power in the theta band. However, only the statistical significant variation of such spectral power when compared to the documentary period was highlighted in colour. The use of z-score will allow us to have a variable that can be averaged and can be used to synthesize the results of the entire population investigated.

In order to estimate only the functional connectivity between cortical areas, a segmentation of fourteen Brodmann areas, thought to be of interest for this study, were considered as Regions of Interest (ROIs). Bilateral ROIs were the primary orbitofrontal and prefrontal areas, including the B.A. 8, 9, 10, as well as the Anterior Cingulate Cortex (ACC), the Cingulate Motor Area (CMA) and the parietal areas (B.A. 40, 5, 7). The labels of the cortical areas also have a postfix characterizing the considered hemisphere (R, right; L, left).

2.1 Experiment 1

EEG signals were recorded from ten subjects (mean age 30±4 years) exposed to the observation of a different documentary of thirty minutes for five consecutive days. Intermingled with each documentary, three interruptions were generated, after six minutes, in the middle of the documentary and six minutes before the end of the documentary. Each interruption was composed of six video-TV commercials (clips) of about thirty seconds. Then a total of eighteen clips were shown during the whole documentary. The clips were related to standard international brands of commercial products, like cars, food, etc. and non-profit associations (such as FAO, Greenpeace, etc.). None of the spots were broadcast in the country in which the experiment was performed, in order to remove previous unchecked exposure of the subjects to the proposed material. Each day of the experiment the documentary was changed, as well as the order of the presentation of the commercial spots within the documentary, in random order. The documentaries were also new to the subjects. The eighteen video clips presented throughout these five days remained unchanged.

Subjects were not aware during their observation of the documentaries and the TV commercials that an interview would be held after ten days. They were simply asked to pay attention to the documentaries during the five days and no mention of the importance of the clips was made. After a period of ten days, the subjects were recalled in the laboratory and an interview was generated. In the interview, the subjects were asked to recall spontaneously which clips they remembered. According to this information, their high resolution EEG data during the observation of the TV spots were then separated into two different pools. The first pool was related to the EEG activity collected during the viewing of the commercial clips that the subjects had correctly remembered, and this dataset was named RMB. The second pool was related to the EEG activity collected during the observation of the TV commercials that had been forgotten by the subjects, and this set was named FRG. It must be noted that the dataset of the commercials forgotten (FRG) has all the EEG activity relative to the subjects that failed to remember both the images and brand-names of the commercial clips, while the dataset related to the 'remembered' spots (RMB) always included the spontaneous recall of brand-name and the recall of some sequences of the spots viewed. In addition, the EEG activity during the observation of the documentary was also analyzed, and a third pool of EEG data related to this state was generated with the name REST. This REST period was taken as the period in which the subject looked at the documentary. We caught a sequence of the documentary immediately before the appearance of the spot interruption in order to minimize the variations of the spectral responses owing to fatigue or loss of concentration. The non-stationariness of the spectral responses will be minimized in this way, since the rest period was computed near to the period of spot interruption. The length of the rest period was comparable to the length of the spectral responses obtained from the spot analysis, in order to render the variance of the spectral responses similar. Separate analysis of those EEG datasets (FRG, RMB, REST) was then generated and contrasted by using the techniques described below. The idea is to contrast the cortical activity during the viewing of the TV commercials that were remembered by the subjects (RMB) with the cortical activity estimated during the observation of the TV commercials that were forgotten by the subjects (FRG).

The analysis of 'where' the differences between the analyzed conditions occurred in the brain performed by the statistical mapping of power spectra was corroborated by the investigation on 'how' the different cortical areas are interconnected with the use of Partial Directed Coherence (PDC). In order to achieve our purpose, we analyzed the changes of incoming and outgoing flow for each ROI, according to the connection of the Granger's causality, by means of tools employed in the graph theory [23]. In fact, it is well known that a connectivity pattern can be treated as a weighted graph, where the nodes are the ROIs considered and the weighted arcs between nodes are the estimated connections between ROIs obtained by applying the PDC on the cortical data. It is then possible to apply tools already validated and derived from the graph theory to the estimated connectivity graphs during the task performance. In the following, the graph is described by N nodes (equal to the number of the ROIs considered here), and each arc of the graph from the i-th node toward the j-th node will be labelled with the intensity of the PDC value and will be described as wij. The NxN matrix of the weights between all the nodes of the graph is the connection matrix W. In particular, we would like to use the indices related to the strength of the estimated functional links between the cortical areas to characterize the behaviour of the estimated network during the visualization of the spot. Such indices will be described in the following. The simpler attribute for a graph's node is its degree of connectivity, which is the total number of connections with other points. In a weighted graph, the natural generalization of the degree of a node i is the node strength or node weight. This quantity has to be split into in-strength S-in and out-strength S-out indices, when directed relationships are being considered, as in the present case with the use of the PDC values.

These indexes are define in the following:

$$S_{in}(i) = \sum_j w_{ij} \qquad (1)$$

where j = 1, 2, ... N.

$S_{in}(i)$ represents, then, the amount of all the incoming arcs from the graph toward the node i-th, and it is a measure of the inflow of the graph toward such a node. A similar measure can be derived for the outflow from the i-th node of the graph, according to the following formula where the same conventions for (1) yields:

$$S_{out}(i) = \sum_j w_{ij} \qquad (2)$$

Note that in this case the sum is upon all the outgoing weighted arcs that move from the i-th node towards all the other nodes of the graph.

The analysis of the strength indices has been addressed by means of a statistical procedure. Separate ANOVAs for each frequency band have been performed for the in-strength S_{in} and out-strength S_{out} with a significance level at 5%. In particular, the main factors of the ANOVAs are the within factor TASK with two levels, remembered (RMB) and forgotten (FRG), and the within factor ROI related to the ROIs employed in this study. Such ROIs include the BA 8,9,10, 5,7,40 of both hemispheres along with the cingulated motor area (CMA) and the anterior cingulated cortex (ACC). The Greenhouse and Geisser correction was used for the violation of the sphericity hypothesis [26]. Post-hoc analysis with Duncan's test at the 5% statistical significance level was also performed.

2.2 Experiment 2

The whole dataset is composed by EEG registrations of 13 healthy subjects (mean age 30±4 years) watching a documentary of 30 minutes intermingled by a TV commercial. Each subject is exposed to the observation of a same documentary. The subjects were not aware of the aim of the recording, and they only knew to pay attention to the material showed on the screen during the entire 30 minutes. The TV commercial, whose length was 30 seconds, was inserted at the middle of the documentary. Such commercial was realized for a popular brand of beer in Italy, that was on-air on the national TV channels on the days in which the experiment was realized. After the EEG registration each subject was recalled in laboratory where an interview was performed. In such interview, the subjects were asked if they usually drink beer or light alcohol at least once per week. If yes, subjects were considered within the dataset of "drinkers" in opposition to the dataset of "no drinkers". In order to increase the sensitivity of the analysis performed, only the EEG spectral analysis for the "drinkers" was analyzed and presented here.

The hypothesis was that the TV commercial could be better followed by a class of subjects who usually drink beer instead that from other "non-drinkers" subjects.

3 Results

3.1 Experiment 1

Figure 1 shows the areas of statistically-significant (Bonferroni corrected at 5% level of significance) brain activity occurring in all the analyzed population during the observation of the TV commercials that have been remembered (RMB dataset) against the brain activity elicited by the observation of the documentary (REST).

In all the frequency bands analyzed several cortical areas present a spectral power that largely exceeds that computed during the observation of the documentary. Such statistically-significant increase of the spectral power during the RMB condition is rather larger in the right hemisphere than in the left one. Panel B presents, with the same conventions as panel A, the brain statistically significant activity during the observation of the TV commercials that have been forgotten (FRG dataset) contrasted with the brain activity computed during the observation of the documentary (REST dataset). In this case all the subjects analyzed also presented a large, statistically-significant activation of almost all the brain areas in the FRG condition compared with the REST one. In this case, however, a rather symmetrical activity is observed compared with the statistical maps computed for the RMB vs REST condition presented in Panel A of Fig. 1. A successive analysis was then performed, by contrasting directly the RMB and FRG dataset, in order to depict the areas of the brain in which the entire population eventually differs in the spectral power activity in the different frequency bands during RMB and FRG conditions.

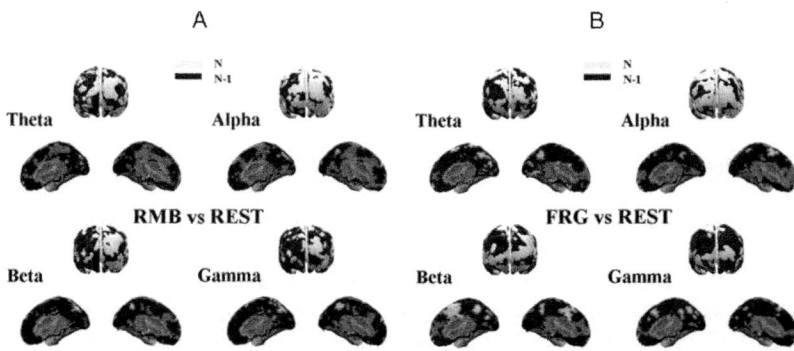

Fig. 1. *Panel A.* Cortical areas of statistically-significant differences between the remembered condition (RMB) against the observation of documentary (REST). There are four groups of statistical maps, generated in the four frequency bands employed, i.e. Theta (upper left quadrant of the figure), Alpha (upper right quadrant), Beta (lower left quadrant) and Gamma (lower right quadrant). In each quadrant three different views of the cortical surface are presented; frontal (upper) and on the lower row a mid-sagittal view from left and right, respectively. On these brain lateral views, the area significantly activated for the RMB dataset when compared with the REST dataset are presented in light gray. These grayscales are relative to the cortical areas that are statistically significantly activated in all the subjects during such comparison (i.e. RMB versus REST). The darker gray represents the areas statistically-significant in all but one subject during the RMB versus REST condition. *Panel B.* Figures present the statistically-significant activity during the observation of the TV commercials that will be forgotten (FRG dataset) contrasted with the brain activity computed during the observation of the documentary (REST dataset). Same conventions as in Panel A.

Panel A of Fig. 2 presents the results of the statistical comparisons between the RMB and the FRG dataset in the Theta and Alpha frequency bands. It is possible to observe that very restricted cortical areas generate statistically-significant differences in all but one of the subjects. In particular, areas of statistically significant differences can be observed in the prefrontal right areas, mainly including BA 8 and 9 (first row), on the Anterior Cingulated Area (second row), and on the right and left parietal areas (third row). Such differences are more evident in the Theta band than in the Alpha band.

In the panel B of the same figure 4 presents the statistically significant activity between the RMB and FRG dataset in the Beta and Gamma frequency bands is presented. It is interesting to note that in this case also frontal and parietal areas differ in the two experimental conditions (RMB and FRG). Larger statistical cortical areas are present in the Gamma band than in the Beta one, as well as a marked activity in the Anterior Cingulated Cortex in the Gamma band. Prefrontal areas (BA 8 and 9) and parietal areas (BAs 5, 7, 40) appeared similar to those already evidenced in Theta and Alpha bands.

The flow analyses related to the observation of commercial advertisements have been performed by means of the PDC values and some indexes of the graph theory according to the methods described in the previous section. For that purpose we analyzed the differences in terms of incoming and outgoing flows of Granger causality

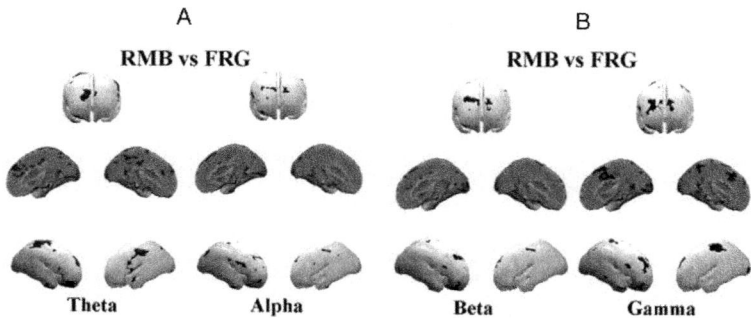

Fig. 2. Figure presents the results of the statistical comparisons between the RMB and the FRG dataset in the Theta and Alpha frequency bands (panel A), and in the Beta and Gamma bands (panel B). In particular, the figure presents three rows; the first row shows the brain in the frontal view, the second row presents the brain in a mid-sagittal view, while the third row (at the bottom) presents the images of the brain's statistically significant activity on the right and left perspective.

connections for each Region of Interest (ROI) analyzed, i.e. the values of S-in and S-out indices previously defined. These indices were computed by use of the values of the statistically significant functional connectivity estimates by PDC, performed at p<0.05, Bonferroni-corrected for multiple comparisons. Details of the estimation procedure for the computation of significant links between cortical areas by PDC are given in a previous publication [22]. The values of S-in and S-out indices were then computed for a selection of the ROIs employed in this study. In particular, the bilateral prefrontal areas (including the BA 8, 9, 10) and the parietal ones (including the BA 40, 5, and 7), with the Anterior Cingulate Cortex (ACC) and the Cingulate Motor Area (CMA).

The analysis of the incoming flow toward each particular ROI described by the S_{in} index was performed by use of the ANOVA with the main factors ROI and TASK. The test returned statistically-significant differences for the main factors ROI and TASK as well as for their interaction (ROI x TASK). The values of the statistical significance for the main factors ROI and TASK were always less than 5% (p<0.05) in all the four frequency bands analyzed. In particular, for the ROI x TASK condition we have p<0.027 in the Theta band, p<0.023 in the Alpha band, p<0.032 in the Beta band and p<0.013 in the Gamma band.

Figure 5 shows the average and standard deviation values of the S_{in} indices computed in the analyzed population for the two datasets computed for each ROI considered. All the four panels present in the Figure (A, B, C, D) present the average values of the S-in index for all the ROIs considered in the different frequency bands. It is possible to see that there is a higher value for the S_{in} index in the RMB than in the FRG condition in the analyzed population. In addition, post hoc analysis performed with Duncan's test at p<0.05 reveals a statistical increase of S_{in} values over the

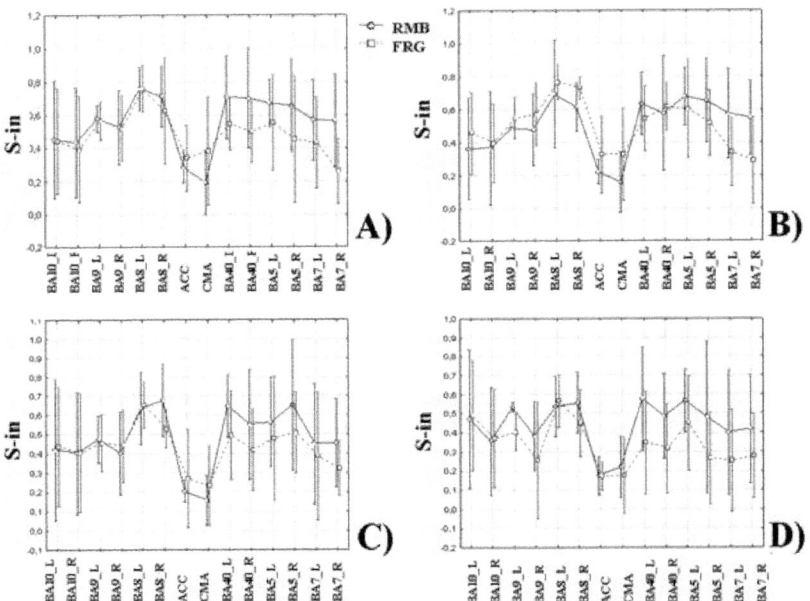

Fig. 3. Figure shows the average and standard deviation values of the S_{in} indices computed in the analyzed population for the two datasets (RMB, circles and continuous line; FRG squares and dotted lines) for each ROI considered. The four panels present in the Figure (A, B, C, D) are relative to the values of the S_{in} index in the four frequency bands considered. In particular, panel A refers to the variation of the S_{in} index across the different ROIs for the Theta band, panel B refers to the Alpha band, panel C to the Beta band and panel D refers to the Gamma band.

parietal areas of both hemispheres for the BA 7 bilaterally in all the frequency bands.In addition, in Theta, Beta and Gamma bands the parietal areas represented by the BA 40 and BA 5 results are statistically-significant bilaterally for the outflow during the RMB condition compared with the FRG condition.

The analysis of the outflow from the different cortical areas, described by the S_{out} index, was also performed by use of the ANOVA. The main factors TASK and ROI results are statistically significant in all the frequency bands analyzed (always under $p<0.05$). For all concerns the statistical interaction between the factors TASK and ROI the tests returned statistically-significant values in all the analyzed frequency bands. In particular, we have $p < 0.012$ for the TASK x ROI factors in the Theta band, $p<0.032$ for the Alpha band, $p<0.042$ for the Beta band and $p<0.016$ for the Gamma band. Despite this significance of the interaction, the Duncan's post hoc tests reveal consistent statistically significant differences between the values of the S-out index in all the frequency bands analyzed only for the ACC and CMA cortical areas, the S-out values being comparable across the ROIs. The computed values of the outflow in the ACC and CMA cortical areas in the RMB condition are significantly greater than the S_{out} index computed in the FRG condition (all the frequency bands are below p<0.03). It must be noted that although high standard deviations are observed in these figures, the ANOVA returns statistically significant differences between the factors used in the analysis. This was because of the superior statistical power of the ANOVA compared with the univariate statistical test.

3.2 Experiment 2

Of the 13 subjects recorded, only seven are "drinkers". Hence, the successive analysis and results are presented for seven of such subjects. We summarized all results for the "drinkers" group in a series of figures showing the statistically significant differences of cortical activation concerning this dataset in the theta frequency band (4-7 Hz). Data regarding the alpha frequency band (8-12 Hz) were equivalent to the theta band and for this reason not shown here. Our figures are formed by a series of subsequent panels each containing two images: the upper one represents a frame of the TV commercial while the lower one displays the corresponding mean brain activity. In particular, the image at the bottom of the panel shows four different views of the average brain model organized in two rows: the upper row comprises the front and left perspective while the lower one the rear and right brain perspective. The temporal axes beat the time of the commercial.

In Fig.4 we present a first series of 7 film segments spanning the whole length of a certain TV spot. Frames are taken each 5 seconds from the beginning of the clip. In such a way panel A represents the first frame of the commercial while panel G shows the last one. By examining this strip it results evident how the temporal evolution of the mean cortical activity changes according to the images viewed by the subjects. In particular, an enhancement of cerebral activity is suggested by the result of the application of the statistic tests at the beginning and at the end of the videoclip presented.

In fact, from the lower row of the figures, it is possible to observe how in the middle film segments very restricted areas provide statistically significant differences when compared to the ones watched at the beginning and at the end of the commercial. This drastic change of activity is more evident in Fig. 5. The present figure is composed by 3 panels representing the first (panel A), the middle (B) and the last (C) frame of the TV spot respectively. The corresponding mean cortical activity completes each panel of the figure. By observing these three images is clear how the middle part of the commercial is characterized by cerebral zones displaying no statistical differences across ROIs, while there are two peaks of activity at the beginning and at the end of the clip.

The analysis of the temporal evolution of the cerebral activity has been performed on shorter time intervals too, aiming at tracking even its variations in closer time instants. These examples show how it is possible to capture significant differences in the cerebral activity, from a statistical point of view, among cortical areas activated, even by reducing the time interval of interest.

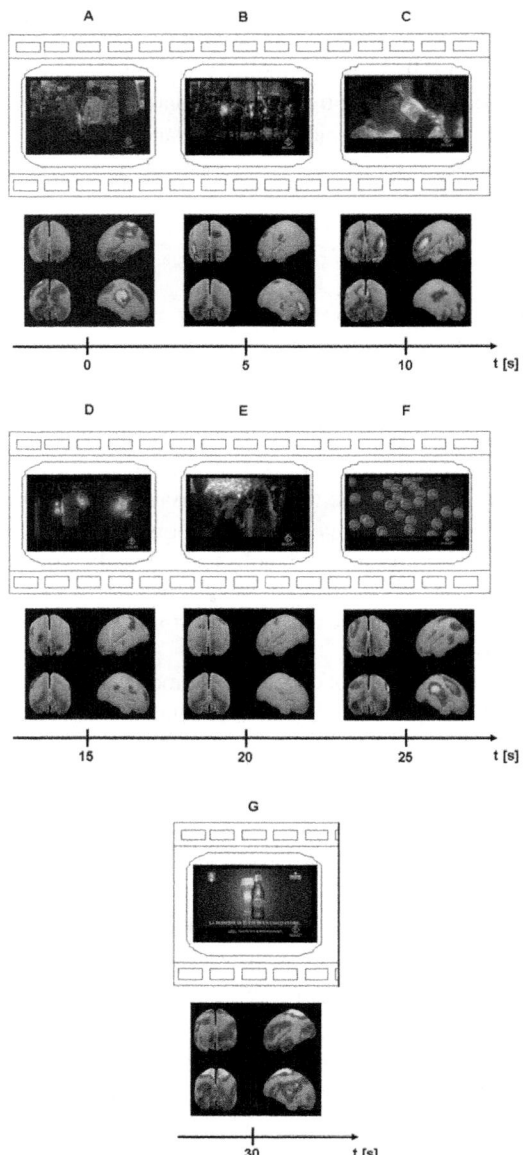

Fig. 4. Tracking of the mean cortical activity of the group of "drinkers" in the theta frequency band spot. The statistical significant activity in this population is shown in seven panels (A-G), each representing subsequent film segments of a TV spot with corresponding brain activity. Temporal axes beats the spot time every 5 seconds: in this way panel A represents the first frame of the commercial while panel G shows the last one. This example illustrates how is possible to track human cortical activity by means of the High-Resolution EEG technique.

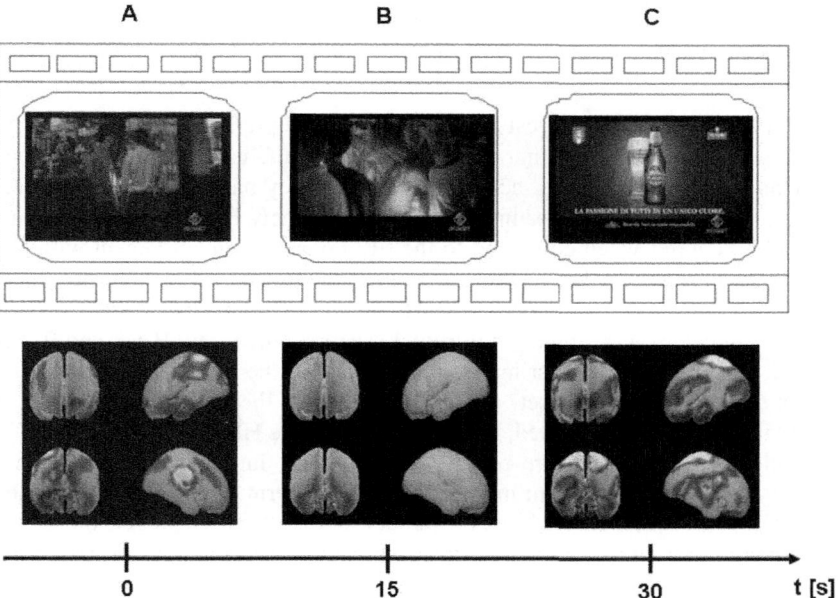

Fig. 5. Tracking of the mean cortical activity of the group of "drinkers" in the theta frequency band spot. The statistical significant activity in this population is shown in 3 panels (A-C), each representing subsequent film segments of a TV spot with corresponding brain activity. Temporal axes beats the spot in correspondence of the beginning (A), the middle (B) and the end (C) of the entire film sequence.

4   Discussion

The results of the study suggested the following answers to the questions elicited in the Introduction:

1) In the population analyzed, the cortical activity elicited during the observation of the TV commercials that were forgotten (FRG) is different from the cortical activity observed in subjects that have remembered the same TV commercials (RMB). In fact, the principal areas of statistical differences in power spectra between such conditions are located almost bilaterally in the prefrontal BAs 8, 9 as well as in the parietal BAs 7. The spectral amplitude in the RMB condition was always higher than the power spectra in the FRG conditions over the BAs 8, 9 and 7.

2) The differences in the cortical power spectra between the RMB and FRG conditions are relatively insensitive to the particular frequency bands considered.

3) The cortical connectivity patterns between the RMB and FRG differs. In particular, in the RMB condition the outflow from the Anterior Cingulate Cortex (ACC) and Cingulate Motor Area (CMA) are statistically significant higher than in the FRG condition. In addition, the bilateral parietal areas linked to the BAs 5, 7 and 40 received an amount of inflow in the RMB condition from the other cortical areas higher than in the FRG condition, statistically significant.

4)   Such significant increase of cortical inflow from all the cortical areas toward the parietal ones has been observed in all the frequency bands investigated, as well as the increase of cortical outflow from the ACC and CMA.

The observed phenomena suggest an active role of the prefrontal and parietal areas in the coding of the information that will be retained by the users from the TV commercials. This role was maintained across all the frequency bands analyzed. A statistical increase of EEG spectral power in the prefrontal (namely BA 8, 9) and parietal areas for the RMB dataset when compared to the FRG one, it is in agreement with the role of these regions that have been advocated during the transfer of sensory percepts from the short term memory toward the long-term memory storage. The results suggested a strong prevalence of a "common" prefrontal bilateral (involving BA 8 and 9) activity in all the subjects analyzed during the observation of the TV commercials that have been remembered (RMB dataset) although in many of them a stronger engage of the left frontal areas have been noted, in agreement with the HERA model [30]. In fact, in such model the left hemisphere plays a decisive role during the encoding phase of information from the short term memory to the long term memory, whereas the right hemisphere plays a role in the retrieval of such information. However, the aim of the analysis here reported for the statistical mapping of the EEG spectral power was to describe the cortical areas engaged in all the population analyzed in the RMB and FRG dataset. This procedure could have reduced the extension of the dominance of the left prefrontal hemisphere due to the presence of some outlier in the population. It must be noted, however, that the role of the right cortices in the storing images has been also underlined since many years in neuroscience [31-32].

   The EEG spectral as well as the cortical network analysis performed in this study suggest a key role of the parietal areas as target of the incoming information flow from all the other cortical areas. A strong involvement of parietal areas during the observation of the TV commercials was also noted in a previous study, performed by using sophisticated MEG recordings [9]. In that study, parietal activations are found by exposing the subjects to advertisements with a marked cognitive content in contrast with the brain activations observed during the observation of "affective" advertisements, located in orbitofrontal cortices [9]. It is likely that also in our case the TV commercials presented to the subjects had no particular "emotive" contents, as they reported in the performed interviews. The engage of parietal cortices as a sign of the fact that the TV commercials will be remembered after 10 days the first observation by the subjects is a robust evidence of this study since it was suggested separately by two different procedures: the estimation of cortical activity and the estimation of the cortical connectivity by using the PDC technique. It can be speculated that the area of differences elicited in the theta band between the RMB and FRG condition belongs to the temporo-parietal junction (TPJ) region. In fact, it has been demonstrated by using BOLD signals that a TPJ enhance was generated when a stimulus change occurs in the modality that is relevant to the current behavior [33]. In addition to the apparent sensitivity to relevant stimuli, the TPJ is also activated in response to potentially novel (unexpected or infrequent) events when an organism is engaged in a neutral behavioral context (i.e. not performing a specific task) [34]. This activation occurs independent of the modality (auditory, tactile, visual) in which the input is delivered, which reflects the multisensory attentional role played by the TPJ. In this case the multisensory attentional role could be related to the encoding of "interesting" part of the TV commercials in the Long Term Memory storage.

Other observations performed with the use of fMRI could support the activity elicited in the superior part of the parietal lobe (SPL) obtained during this study. In particular, the differences in spectral activity between RMB and FRG conditions observed in theta, gamma and in a less extend in alpha and beta frequency bands are relative to the SPL. Previously, it was observed that the time course of the BOLD signal in the right SPL exhibited transient activity when attention was shifted between spatial locations. The transient nature of the signal elicited by the SPL suggests that this area of the parietal cortex is the source of a brief attentional control signal to shift attentive states, and is not the source of a continuous signal to actively maintain the new attentive state. SPL activation is not apparently restricted to spatial shifts alone and this region is activated when subjects shift their attention between any two dimensions of the input; for example, shifts between superimposed houses and faces [35,36], shifts between two different features of an object [37] or shifts between two different sensory modalities all activate SPL. It may be speculated in the present case the high spectral activity in the SPL cortical areas for the RMB data set could be then related to the particular processing of the TV commercials that instead lacks in the FRG case. However, it must be noted that the attention is a necessary requisite for the subsequent recognition of scenes from TV commercials, but it is not per se sufficient to generate a shift from the short term memory storage to the long term memory storage in the brain. However, it has been also suggested as the choose of familiar items is associated with activation of right parietal cortices, indicating outcomes consistent with some form of intention based on previous experience [38], and that the activity of the right parietal cortices could be associated with brand equity [39].

The results suggested an active involvement of the Anterior Cingulate Cortex (ACC) and the Cingulate Motor Area (CMA) as sources of links towards all the other cortical areas during the observation of the TV commercials that will be remembered after 10 days. This result is consistent with several observations performed mainly by using the brain hemodynamic responses that indicated as the ACC region could be involved together some other regions in the process of mentalizing, i.e. generate a representation of the others in our minds [40-42] also in a economic context [43]. In this case the increase activity signalled by the increase of the outflow of PDC links from ACC and CMA towards other cortical regions could be taken as a sign of increased "emotive" attention towards the stories proposed by the different TV commercials that significantly aid the successive memorization. Such "emotional" attention could be hypothesized in the sense of a particular "identification" of the subject with the subjects presented in the TV commercials, at least for those that belong to the RMB dataset.

Summarizing the main results of the present study, a sign of the memorization of a particular set of TV commercials have been found in a group of 10 subjects with the aid of advanced modern tools for the acquisition and the processing of EEG data. The cerebral processes involved during the observation of TV commercials that were remembered successively by the population examined (RMB dataset) are generated by the posterior parietal cortices and the prefrontal areas, rather bilaterally and are irrespective of the frequency bands analyzed. In addition, the parietal areas (BA 5,7,40) are the preferred targets of a transfer of information from all the other cortical areas during the observation of TV commercials that were remembered. Such results are compatible with previously results obtained from EEG recordings with superficial electrodes as well as with the brain activations observed with the use of MEG and fMRI devices. However, it must be noted that high resolution EEG is nowadays a modality that presents high spatial and temporal resolution and it will be able to summarize, with the use of graph theory indexes, the behaviour of the estimated cortical networks subserving the proposed tasks. It is likely that such tool could play a role in the next future for the investigation of the neural substrates of the human behaviour in decision-making and recognition tasks.

References

[1] Cappo, J.: The Future of Advertising: New Media, New Clients, New Consumers in the Post-Television Age. McGraw-Hill, New York (2005)

[2] Heath, R.: The Hidden Power of Advertising. World Advertising Research Center, Henley-on-Thames (2001)

[3] McDonald, C.: Is your advertising working? World Advertising Center, Henley-on-Thames (2003)

[4] Zaltman, G.: How Customer Think. Harvard Business School Press, Boston (2003)

[5] Giep, F., Margot, B.: The Mental World of Brands. World Advertising Center, Henley-on-Thames (2001)

[6] Lo Iodice, B.: Trends to Watch in 2008, Adage website (2007), http://adage.com/article?article_id=122609

[7] Zenith Optimedia (media services agency), Global ad market to accelerate in 2008 despite credit squeeze (2007), http://www.zenithoptimedia.com/about/news/pdf/Adspend%20forecasts%20December%202007.pdf

[8] Krugman, H.E.: Brain wave measures of media involvement. J. Advert. Res. 11, 3–10 (1971)

[9] Ioannides, L., Theofilou, D., Burne, T., Ambler, T., Rose, S.: Real time processing of affective and cognitive stimuli in the human brain extracted from MEG signals. Brain Top. 13, 11–19 (2000)

[10] Ambler, T., Burne, T.: The Impact of Affect on Memory of Advertising. Journal of Advertising Research 39(2), 25–34 (1999)

[11] Rotschild, M., Hyun, J.: Predicting Memory for Components of TV Commercials from EEC. Journal of Consumer Research 472–478 (1989)

[12] Rossiter, J.R., Silberstein, R.B., Harris, P.G., Nield, G.A.: Brain imaging detection of visual scene encoding in long-term memory for TV commercials. J. Advert. Res. 41, 13–21 (2001)

[13] Young, C.: Brain waves, picture sorts®, and branding moments. J. Advert. Res. 42, 42–53 (2002)

[14] Nunez, P.L.: Neocortical dynamics and human EEG rhythms. Oxford University Press, New York (1995)

[15] Bai, X., Towle, V.L., He, E.J., He, B.: Evaluation of cortical current density imaging methods using intracranial electrocorticograms and functional MRI. Neuroimage 35(2), 598–608 (2006)

[16] He, B., Wang, Y., Wu, D.: "Estimating cortical potentials from scalp EEG's in a realistically shaped inhomogeneous head model by means of the boundary element method. IEEE Trans. Biomed. Eng. 46, 1264–1268 (1999)

[17] He, B., Hori, J., Babiloni, F.: EEG Inverse Problems. In: Akay, M. (ed.) Wiley Encyclopedia in Biomedical Engineering, pp. 1355–1363. John Wiley & Sons, Inc., Chichester (2006)

[18] Ding, L., Lai, Y., He, B.: Low resolution brain electromagnetic tomography in a realistic geometry head model: a simulation study. Physics in Medicine and Biology 50, 45–56 (2005)

[19] Ding, L., Worrell, G.A., Lagerlund, T.D., He, B.: Ictal Source Analysis: Localization and Imaging of Causal Interactions in Humans. NeuroImage 34, 575–586 (2007)

[20] Babiloni, F., Cincotti, F., Babiloni, C., Carducci, F., Basilisco, A., Rossini, P.M., Mattia, D., Astolfi, L., Ding, L., Ni, Y., Cheng, K., Christine, K., Sweeney, J., He, B.: Estimation of the cortical functional connectivity with the multimodal integration of high resolution EEG and fMRI data by Directed Transfer Function. Neuroimage 24(1), 118–131 (2005)

[21] Baccalà, L.A., Sameshima, K.: Partial Directed Coherence: a new concept in neural structure determination. Biol.Cybern. 84, 463–474 (2001)

[22] Astolfi, L., Cincotti, F., Mattia, D., Marciani, M.G., Baccala, L., de Vico Fallani, F., Salinari, S., Ursino, M., Zavaglia, M., Ding, L., Edgar, J.C., Miller, G.A., He, B., Babiloni, F.: Comparison of different cortical connectivity estimators for high-resolution EEG recordings. Hum. Brain Mapp. 28(2), 143–157 (2007)

[23] De Vico Fallani, F., Astolfi, L., Cincotti, F., Mattia, D., Marciani, M.G., Salinari, S., Kurths, J., Cichocki, A., Gao, S., Colosimo, A., Babiloni, F.: Cortical Functional Connectivity Networks In Normal And Spinal Cord Injured Patients: Evaluation by Graph Analysis. In: Human Brain Mapping, February 21 (2007) (Epub ahead of print)

[24] Grave de Peralta Menendez, R., Gonzalez Andino, S.L.: Distributed source models: standard solutions and new developments. In: Uhl, C. (ed.) Analysis of neurophysiological brain functioning, pp. 176–201. Springer, Heidelberg (1999)

[25] Dale, A., Liu, A., Fischl, B., Buckner, R., Belliveau, J.W., Lewine, J., Halgren, E.: Dynamic Statistical Parametric Mapping: Combining fMRI and MEG for High-Resolution Imaging of Cortical Activity. Neuron 26, 55–67 (2000)

[26] Zar, J.: Biostatistical analysis. Prentice-Hall, Englewood Cliffs (1984)

[27] Nowinski, W.L., Belov, D.: The Cerefy Neuroradiology Atlas: a Talairach-Tournoux atlas-based tool for analysis of neuroimages available over the internet. Neuroimage 20(1), 50–57 (2003)

[28] Granger, C.W.J.: Investigating causal relations by econometric models and cross-spectral methods. Econometrica 37p, 424–428 (1969)

[29] Yook, S.H., Jeong, H., Barabási, A., Tu, Y.: Weighted Evolving Networks. Phys.Rev.Lett. 86(25), 5835–5838 (2001)

[30] Tulving, E., Kapur, S., Craik, F.I., Moscovitch, M., Houle, S.: Hemispheric encoding/retrieval asymmetry in episodic memory: positron emission tomography findings. Proc. Natl. Acad. Sci. USA 91(6), 2016–2020 (1994)

[31] Braeutigam, S., Rose, S.P.R., Swithenby, S.J., Ambler, T.: The distributed neuronal systems supporting choice-making in real-life situations: differences between men and women when choosing groceries detected using magnetoencephalography. Eur. J. Neurosci. 20, 293–302 (2004)

[32] Braeutigam, S.: Neuroeconomics–from neural systems to economic behaviour. Brain Res.Bull. 67(5), 355–360 (2005)

[33] Downar, J., Crawley, A.P., Mikulis, D.J., Davis, K.D.: The effect of task relevance on the cortical response to changes in visual and auditory stimuli: An event-related fMRI study. Neuroimage 14, 1256–1267 (2001)

[34] Downar, J., Crawley, A.P., Mikulis, D.J., Davis, K.D.: A cortical network sensitive to stimulus salience in a neutral behavioral context across multiple sensory modalities. J. Neurophysiol. 87, 615–620 (2002)

[35] Yantis, S., Schwarzbach, J., Serences, J.T., Carlson, R.L., Steinmetz, M.A., Pekar, J.J., Courtney, S.M.: Transient neural activity in human parietal cortex during spatial attention shifts. Nat. Neurosci. 5, 995–1002 (2002)

[36] Yantis, S., Serences, J.T.: Cortical mechanisms of space-based and object-based attentional control. Curr. Opin. Neurobiol. 13, 187–193 (2003)

[37] Liu, T., Slotnick, S.D., Serences, J.T., Yantis, S.: Cortical mechanisms of feature-based attentional control. Cereb Cortex 13, 1334–1343 (2003)

[38] Ambler, T., Braeutigam, S., Stins, J., Rose, S.P.R., Swithenby, S.J.: Salience and choice: neural correlates of shopping decisions Psychology & Marketing, vol. 21, pp. 247–261 (2004)

[39] Plassmann, H., Ambler, T., Braeutigam, S., Kenning, P.: Kenning What can advertisers learn from neuroscience? International Journal of Advertising 26(2), 151–175 (2007)

[40] Gallagher, H.L., Frith, C.D.: Functional imaging of 'Theory of Mind'. Trends Cogn. Sci. 7, 77–83 (2003)

[41] Gallagher, H.L., Jack, A.I., Roepstorff, A., Frith, C.D.: Imaging the intentional stance in a competitive game. Neuroimage 16, 814–821 (2002)

[42] Walter, H., Adenzato, M., Ciaramidaro, A., Enrici, I., Pia, L., Bara, B.G.: Understanding intentions in social interaction: The role of the anterior paracingulate cortex. J. Cogn. Neurosci. 16, 1854–1863 (2004)

[43] Bruce, K., Rick, S., Elliott Wimmer, G., Prelec, D., Loewenstein, G.: Neural Predictors of Purchases. Neuron 53, 147–156 (2007)

An Evaluation Study on Speech Feature Densities for Bayesian Estimation in Robust ASR

Simone Cifani, Emanuele Principi, Rudy Rotili,
Stefano Squartini, and Francesco Piazza

3MediaLabs, DIBET, Università Politecnica delle Marche, Ancona, Italy
{s.cifani,e.principi,r.rotili,s.squartini,f.piazza}@univpm.it
http://www.a3lab.dibet.univpm.it/

Abstract. Bayesian estimators, especially the Minimum Mean Square Error (MMSE) and the Maximum A Posteriori (MAP), are very popular in estimating the clean speech STFT coefficients. Recently, a similar trend has been successfully applied to speech feature enhancement for robust Automatic Speech/Speaker Recognition (ASR) applications either in the Mel, log-Mel or in the cepstral domain. It is a matter of fact that the goodness of the estimate directly depends on the assumptions made about the noise and speech coefficients densities. Nevertheless, while this latter has been exhaustively studied in the case of STFT coefficients, not equivalent attention has been paid to the case of speech features. In this paper, we study the distribution of Mel, log-Mel as well as MFCC coefficients obtained from speech segments. The histograms of the speech features are first fitted into several pdf models by means of the Chi-Square Goodness-of-Fit test, then they are modeled using a Gaussian Mixture Model (GMM). Performed computer simulations show that the choice of log-Mel and MFCC coefficients is more convenient w.r.t. the Mel one from this perspective.

Keywords: Speech Feature Densities Estimation, Speech Enhancement, Automatic Speech Recognition.

1 Introduction

Speech-based Human-Machine interfaces have been gaining an increasing interest among the related scientific community and technology market. One of the key task to be faced within this architectures is automatic speech recognition (ASR), for which a certain degree of understanding has been already reached in the literature. Despite this, ASR systems still suffer poor performance in presence of acoustic non-idealities, like additive noise. For this reason, environment robustness is one of the most challenging problems in ASR research today. Because it is well known that recognition rates of ASR systems drop considerably when there is a mismatch between training and testing conditions, modifications to the system are necessary to compensate for the effects of interfering signals.

A. Esposito et al. (Eds.): COST 2102 Int. Training School 2010, LNCS 6456, pp. 283–297, 2011.

As a result, a profuse literature of environment-robust ASR techniques has been registered. The following classification can be proposed therein, as highlighted in [1]: feature-enhancement (FE) and model-based (MB) algorithms. The latter class encompass all methodologies aimed to adapt the acoustic model (HMM) parameters in order to maximize the system matching to the distorted environment. Related contributions propose bayesian compensation frameworks [2], and most of them typically rely on Vector Taylor Series approximation for compensating parameter estimation [1].

In the FE approach, the features are enhanced before they are fed into the recognizer, trying to make them as close as possible to the clean-speech environment condition. This means that some extra-cleaning steps are performed into or after the feature extraction module. As shown in Fig. 1, the feature extraction pipeline has three possible insertion points, each one being related to different classes of enhancement algorithms. Traditional speech enhancement in the discrete-time Fourier transform (DFT) domain [3], [4], should be performed at point 1, Mel-frequency domain algorithms [5], [6], should be located at point 2 and Log-Mel or Mel-Frequency Cepstral Coefficients (MFCC) domain algorithms [7], [8], take place at point 3. Since the focus of traditional speech enhancement is on the perceptual quality of the enhanced signal, the performance of the former class is typically lower than the other two classes. Moreover, the DFT domain has a much higher dimensionality than Mel or MFCC domains, which leads to an higher computational cost of the enhancement process.

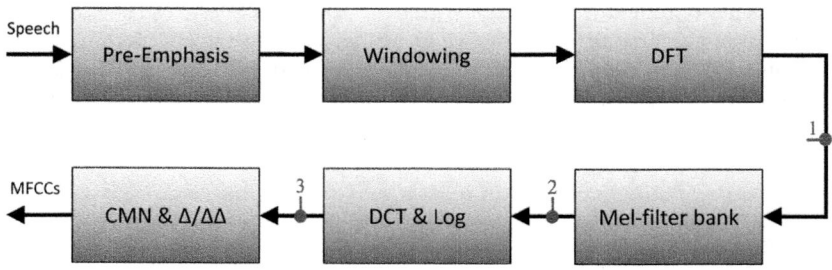

Fig. 1. Feature extraction pipeline

Nevertheless, the three aforementioned classes have close links to a common approach, namely the Bayesian estimation framework. Feature enhancement within this framework requires explicit knowledge of a convenient cost function on the error of the estimate and the joint statistics of the clean signal and of the noise process. For speech signals which have been degraded by statistically independent noise, the marginal distributions of the clean signal and the noise process must be explicitly known, but they are not available in practice. The typical solution is to employ a parametric model based upon a priori theoretical knowledge about the nature of the source as well as empirical observations obtained from that source. The source may represent either the clean signal or the noise process. The Gaussian statistical model has been used in several enhancement algorithms, especially in the DFT domain [3], [4]. As the frame length increases, the pdf of coefficients tends to converge to a Gaussian distribution. However, for the typical DFT frame sizes used in practice (10-30 ms), this assumption is not well fulfilled. For this reason, several researchers have studied the distribution of speech coefficients in the DFT domain and have proposed the use of non-Gaussian distributions, in particular the Gamma or Laplacian pdfs [9], [10], [11], [12], [13], [14], [15], [16]. Nevertheless, while this profuse literature exists in the case of DFT domain algorithms, not equivalent attention has been given to the Mel, Log-Mel or MFCC domains.

In this contribution we investigate the clean speech distribution not only to fill the gap in the Mel, Log-Mel and MFCC domains, but also to offer new possibilities of development of estimators leaning on different models in these domains. The next section gives the mathematical background while section 3 presents the statistical analysis, which is the main objective of the paper. Section 4 proposes a brief overview of some FE algorithms in different domains, in order to show how speech prior densities are employed within the robust ASR schemes. Section 5 concludes the paper.

2   Mathematical Background

Let $x(n)$ and $d(n)$ denote speech and uncorrelated additive noise signals respectively, where n is a discrete-time index. The observed noisy signal $y(n)$ is given by $y(n) = x(n) + d(n)$. According to Fig. 1, the input signal $y(t)$ is firstly pre-emphasized and windowed with a Hamming window. Then, the FFT of the signal is computed and the square of the magnitude is filtered with a bank of triangular filters equally spaced in the MEL scale. After that, the energy of each band is computed and transformed with a logarithm operation. Finally, the inverse discrete cosine transform stage yields the static MFCC coefficients, and the $\Delta/\Delta\Delta$ stage compute the first and second derivatives.

Given the additive noise assumption, in the DFT domain we have

$$Y(k,l) = X(k,l) + D(k,l) \tag{1}$$

where $X(k,l)$, $Y(k,l)$ and $D(k,l)$ denote the short-time Fourier transforms of $x(n)$, $y(n)$ and $d(n)$ respectively, where k is the frequency bin index and l is the time frame index.

The Mel-frequency filter banks output power for noisy speech is

$$m_y(b,l) = \sum_k w_b(k)|Y(k,l)|^2 \tag{2}$$

where $w_b(k)$ is the b-th Mel-frequency filters weight for the frequency bin k. A similar relationship holds for the clean speech and the noise. The j-th dimension of MFCC is calculated as

$$c_y(j,l) = \sum_b a_{j,b} \log m_y(b,l) \tag{3}$$

where $a_{j,b} = \cos((\pi b/B)(j - 0.5))$ are the discrete cosine transform (DCT) coefficients.

The output of equation (1) denotes the input of the enhancement algorithms belonging to class 1 (DFT domain), that of equation (2) the input of class 2 (Mel-frequency domain) and that of equation (3) the input of class 3 (MFCC domain) algorithms. Our purpose is to find an estimate of the clean MFCC $c_x(j, l)$, denoted with $\hat{c}_x(j, l)$, given the noisy signal $y(n)$.

2.1   The Bayes Estimation Framework

As stated above, we want to estimate a speech feature x given its noisy observation y. Because of the generality of this framework, x and y may represent DFT coefficients, Mel-frequency filter banks outputs or MFCCs. Applying the standard assumption that clean speech and noise are statistically independent across time and frequency as well as from each other leads to estimators that are independent of time and frequency.

Let $\epsilon = x - \hat{x}$ denote the error of the estimate and let $C(\epsilon) \triangleq C(x, \hat{x})$ denote a non-negative function of ϵ. The average cost, i.e., $E[C(x, \hat{x})]$, is known as *Bayes risk* $\mathcal{R}$ [17], and is given by

$$\mathcal{R} \triangleq E[C(x, \hat{x})] = \int \int C(x, \hat{x}) p(x, y) dx dy$$
$$= \int p(y) dy \int C(x, \hat{x}) p(x|y) dx$$

in which Bayes rule has been used to separate the role of the observation y and the a priori knowledge.

Minimizing the *Bayes risk* $\mathcal{R}$ with respect to $\hat{x}$ for a given cost function results in a variety of estimators. The traditional *mean-square error* (MSE) cost function, $C^{MSE}(x, \hat{x}) = |x - \hat{x}|^2$, gives:

$$\mathcal{R}^{MSE} = \int p(y) dy \int |x - \hat{x}|^2 p(x|y) dx \qquad (4)$$

$\mathcal{R}^{MSE}$ can be minimized by minimizing the inner integral, yielding the MMSE estimate:

$$\hat{x}^{MMSE} = \int x p(x|y) dx = E[x|y] \qquad (5)$$

The log-MMSE estimator can be obtained by means of the following cost function $C^{log-MSE}(x, \hat{x}) = (\log x - \log \hat{x})^2$, thus yielding:

$$\hat{x}^{log-MMSE} = \exp \{E[\ln x|y]\} \qquad (6)$$

By using the *uniform cost function*, $C^{MAP}(x, \hat{x}) = \begin{cases} 0, & |x - \hat{x}| \le \Delta/2 \\ 1, & |x - \hat{x}| > \Delta/2 \end{cases}$, we get the maximum a posteriori (MAP) estimate:

$$\hat{x}^{MAP} = \operatorname*{argmax}_{x} p(x|y) \tag{7}$$

3 Statistical Analysis of Speech Feature Densities

The previous section highlighted the fact that statistical modeling of the process under consideration is a fundamental aspect of the Bayesian framework. Considering DFT-domain estimators, huge efforts have been spent in order to find better signal models. Earlier works [3], [18], assumed a Gaussian model from a theoretical point of view, by invoking the central limit theorem, stating that the distribution of the DFT coefficients will converge towards a Gaussian PDF regardless of the PDF of the time samples, if successive samples are statistically independent or the correlation is short compared to the analysis frame size. Although this assumption holds for many relevant acoustic noises, it may fail for speech where the span of correlation is comparable to the typical frame sizes (10-30 ms). Spurred by this issue, several researchers investigated the speech probability distribution in the DFT domain [19], [20], and proposed new estimators leaning on different models, i.e., Laplacian, Gamma and Chi, [9], [10], [11], [12], [13], [14], [15], [16].

Although several algorithms already exist, not equivalent attention has been given to the Mel-frequency and MFCC domains revealing the lack of a statistical characterization of such domains in literature. Our aim is to study the speech probability distribution in the DFT, Mel-frequency and MFCC domains, so as to provide the scientific community with a statistical characterization consistent with the same set of speech data for all the domains under consideration. This may possibly open the way to the development of estimators leaning on different models in these domains as well. The analysis has been performed on the TiDigits and the Wall Street Journal (WSJ) database, where clean speech segments of one hour have been built by concatenation of random utterances at a sampling rate of 16kHz. The coefficients used to compute the histograms has been generated by means of the feature extraction pipeline of Fig. 1, using a 32 ms hamming window with 50% overlap, a 23-channel Mel-frequency filterbank and a 12-channel DCT. The histograms of STSA and Mel-frequency coefficients are then fitted by means of a nonlinear least-squares (NLLS) technique to six different pdfs, listed in Table 1. Instead, the modeling of LogMel-frequency coefficients and MFCCs is accomplished using multimodal models, as further explained in the following. The goodness-of-fit has been evaluated by means of the Kullback-Leibler (KL) divergence, which is a measure that quantifies how close a probability distribution is to a model (or candidate) distribution. Choosing p as the N bins histogram and q as the analytic function that approximates the real pdf, the KL divergence is given by:

$$D_{KL} = \sum_{n=1}^{N} (p(n) - q(n)) \log \frac{p(n)}{q(n)} \tag{8}$$

D_{KL} is non-negative (≥ 0), not symmetric in p and q, zero if the distributions match exactly and can potentially equal infinity.

3.1   Non-linear Least Squares

Least squares is a mathematical procedure for finding the best-fitting curve to a given set of m observations by minimizing the sum of the squares of the "residuals", that is the distance of the observed data point from the assumed model. When the model is a non-linear function of n unknown parameters ($m > n$) non-linear least squares procedures are employed. Consider a set of m data-points (x_i, y_i), $i = 1, \ldots, m$, and a model function $y = f(x, \Theta)$ depending on n parameters, $\Theta = (\theta_1, \ldots, \theta_n)$. It is desired to find the vector Θ of parameters such that the curve fits best the given data in the least squares sense, that is, the sum of squares

$$S = \sum_{i=1}^{m} r_i^2 = \sum_{i=1}^{m} y_i - f(x_i, \Theta) \tag{9}$$

The minimization is accomplished by setting $\nabla S = 0$. Since the derivatives $\frac{\partial r_i}{\partial \theta_j}$ are functions of both the independent variable and the parameters, the gradient equations do not have a closed solution. Therefore, initial values must be chosen for the parameters, which are then refined iteratively

$$\theta_j \approx \theta_j^{k+1} = \theta_j^k + \Delta \theta_j \tag{10}$$

where k is the iteration and $\Delta \theta_j$ is the shift vector. At each iteration the model is linearized by approximation to a first-order Taylor series expansion about Θ^k and the local minimum is found by means of a least squares algorithm, i.e. Gauss-Newton.

3.2   Estimation Results

The Gaussian assumption models the real and imaginary part of the clean speech DFT coefficient by means of a Gaussian pdf. Because of the relative importance of short-time spectral amplitude (STSA) rather than phase, the spectral estimation problem is usually reformulated in terms of the former quantity and the probability distribution of the STSA coefficients has been investigated here. The reason is that amplitude and phase are statistically less dependent than real and imaginary parts, resulting in a more tractable problem. Furthermore, it can be shown that phase is well modeled by means of a uniform distribution $p(\alpha) = 1/2\pi$ for $\alpha \in [-\pi, \pi)$.

Table 2 shows the KL divergence between measured data and model functions. The divergences have been normalized to that of the Rayleigh PDF, that is, the Gaussian model. The curves in Fig. 2 represent the fitting results, while the gray area represents the STSA histogram averaged over the DFT channels. As the KL divergence highlights, the Gamma pdf provides the best model, being capable of adequately fit the histogram tail as well.

Table 1. Modeling probability density functions

$$Rayleigh:\ p = \frac{x}{\sigma} \exp\left(\frac{-x^2}{2\sigma}\right)$$

$$Laplace:\ p = \frac{1}{2\sigma} \exp\left(\frac{-|x-a|}{\sigma}\right)$$

$$Gamma:\ p = \frac{1}{\theta^k \Gamma(k)} |x|^{k-1} \exp\left(\frac{-|x|}{\theta}\right)$$

$$Chi:\ p = \frac{2}{\theta^k \Gamma(k/2)} |x|^{k-1} \exp\left(\left(\frac{-|x|}{\theta}\right)^2\right)$$

$$Approximated\ Laplace:\ p = \frac{\mu^{\nu+1}}{\Gamma(\nu+1)} |x|^{\nu} \exp\left(\frac{-\mu|x|}{\sigma}\right),\ \mu = 2.5\ \text{and}\ \nu = 1$$

$$Approximated\ Gamma:\ p = \frac{\mu^{\nu+1}}{\Gamma(\nu+1)} |x|^{\nu} \exp\left(\frac{-\mu|x|}{\sigma}\right),\ \mu = 1.5\ \text{and}\ \nu = 0.01$$

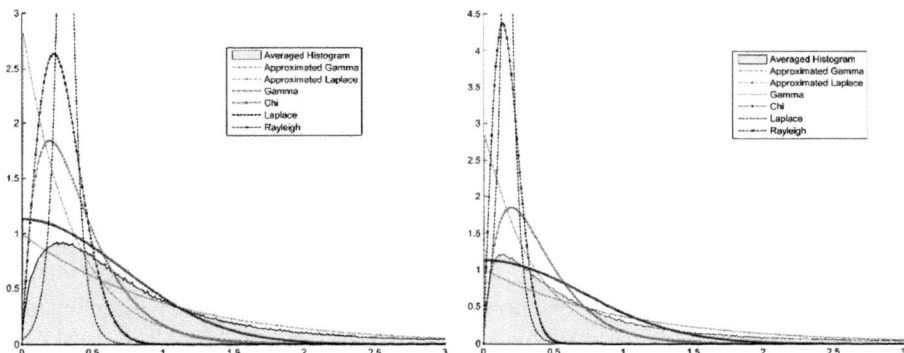

Fig. 2. Averaged Histogram and NLLS fits of STSA coefficients for the TiDigits (left) and WSJ database (right)

Table 2. KL divergence between measured data and model functions

Statistical Model	STSA		MEL	
	TiDigits	WSJ	TiDigits	WSJ
Laplace	0.15	0.17	0.21	0.29
Gamma	0.04	0.04	0.08	0.07
Chi	0.23	0.02	0.16	0.16
Approximated Laplace	0.34	0.24	0.21	0.22
Approximated Gamma	0.31	0.20	0.12	0.12

The Mel-frequency coefficients has been fitted against the same modeling pdfs of the STSA coefficients. The KL divergences, normalized to that of the Rayleigh PDF, have been reported in Table 2.

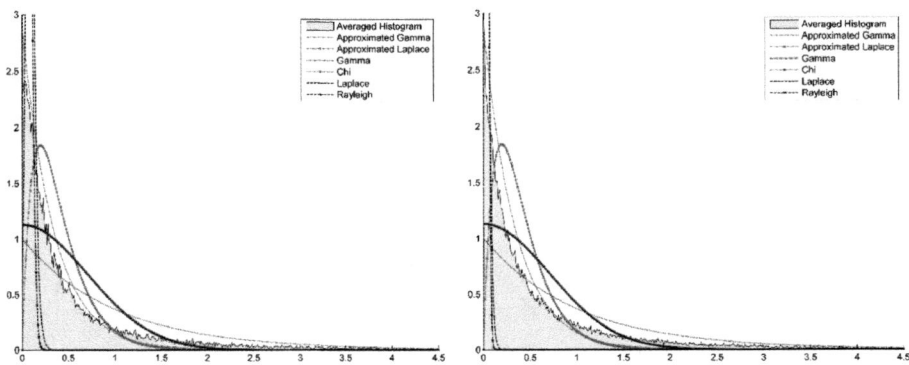

Fig. 3. Averaged Histogram and NLLS fits of Mel-Frequency coefficients for the TiDigits (left) and WSJ database (right)

Fig. 3 represents the fitting results and the Mel-frequency coefficient histogram averaged over the filterbank channels. The Gamma pdf still provides the best model, even if the difference with other pdfs are more modest.

The modeling of LogMel-frequency coefficients and MFCCs cannot be performed using the same technique employed above. In fact, the histograms of these coefficients, depicted in Fig. 4 and 5, reveal that their distributions are multimodal and cannot be modeled by means of unimodal distributions. Therefore, multimodal models, such as Gaussian Mixture Models (GMM) [21] are more appropriate in this task: finite mixture models and their typical parameter estimation methods can approximate a wide variety of pdf's and are thus attractive solutions for cases where single function forms fail. The GMM probability density function can be designed as a weighted sum of Gaussians:

$$p(x) = \sum_{c=1}^{C} \alpha_c \mathcal{N}(x; \mu_c, \Sigma_c), \quad \text{with } \alpha_c \in [0,1], \quad \sum_{c=1}^{C} \alpha_c = 1 \qquad (11)$$

where α_c is the weight of the c-th component. The weight can be interpreted as *a priori* probability that a value of the random variable is generated by the c-th source. Hence, a GMM pdf is completely defined by a parameter list $\theta = \{\alpha_1, \mu_1, \Sigma_1, \ldots, \alpha_C, \mu_C, \Sigma_C\}$.

A vital question with GMM pdf's is how to estimate the model parameters θ. In literature exists two principal approaches: maximum-likelihood estimation and Bayesian estimation. While the latter has strong theoretical basis, the former is simpler and widely used in practice. Expectation-Maximization (EM) algorithm is an iterative technique for calculating maximum-likelihood distribution parameter estimates from incomplete data. The Figuredo-Jain (FJ) algorithm [22] represents an extension of the EM which allows not to specify the number of components C and for this reason it has been adopted in this work. GMM pdf's obtained after FJ parameter estimation are shown in Fig. 4 and 5.

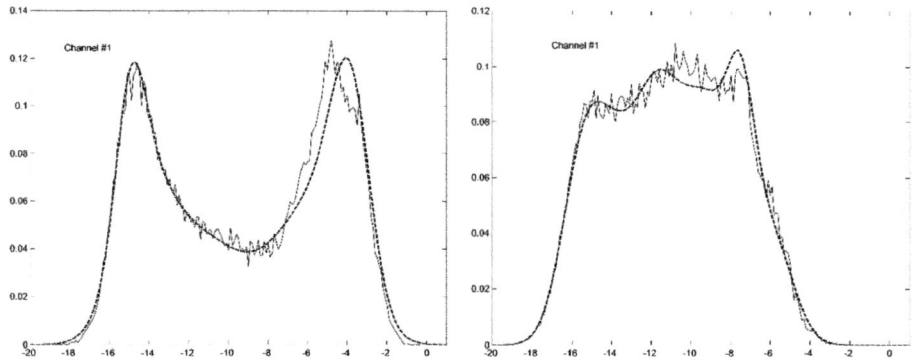

Fig. 4. Histogram (solid) and GMM fit (dashed) of the first channel of LogMel coefficients for TiDigits (left) and WSJ database (right)

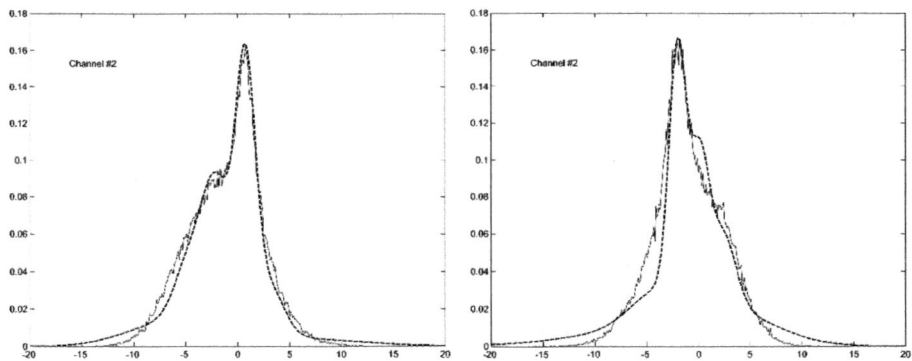

Fig. 5. Histogram (solid) and GMM fit (dashed) of the second channel of MFCC coefficients for TiDigits (left) and WSJ database (right)

4   Enhancement Algorithms

This section proposes an overview of some FE algorithms in the considered domains, in order to show how speech prior densities are employed within the robust ASR schemes. Finally, the performance of the described algorithms, previously evaluated in other works [7], [8], [25], are briefly reported to summarize their behavior in the ASR task.

4.1   Short-Time Spectral Amplitude Approaches

Assuming that the real and imaginary part of the clean speech DFT coefficient are Gaussian distributed, it follows that the clean speech STSA is Rayleigh distributed. Let $X \triangleq A \exp(j\alpha)$ and $Y \triangleq R \exp(j\theta)$, we have

$$p(a, \alpha) = \frac{a}{\pi \lambda_x} \exp\left\{-\frac{a^2}{\lambda_x}\right\} \tag{12}$$

$$p(Y|a, \alpha) = \frac{1}{\pi \lambda_d} \exp\left\{-\frac{1}{\lambda_d}|Y - ae^{j\alpha}|^2\right\} \tag{13}$$

where $\lambda_x \triangleq E\{|X|^2\}$, and $\lambda_d \triangleq E\{|D|^2\}$ are the variances of a spectral coefficient of the speech and the noise, respectively. Substituting (12) and (13) into (5) gives [3]:

$$\hat{A}^{MMSE} = \Gamma(1.5)\frac{\sqrt{v}}{\gamma} \exp\left(-\frac{v}{2}\right) \left[(1+v)I_0\left(\frac{v}{2}\right) + vI_1\left(\frac{v}{2}\right)\right] R \tag{14}$$

where $\Gamma(\cdot)$ denotes the gamma function, $I_0(\cdot)$ and $I_1(\cdot)$ denote the modified Bessel functions of zero and first order, respectively. v is defined for each coefficient as $v \triangleq \frac{\xi}{1+\xi}\gamma$, where ξ and γ represent the *a priori* and *a posteriori* signal-to-noise ratios (SNR), respectively, and are defined as $\xi \triangleq \frac{\lambda_x}{\lambda_d}$ and $\gamma \triangleq \frac{R^2}{\lambda_d}$.

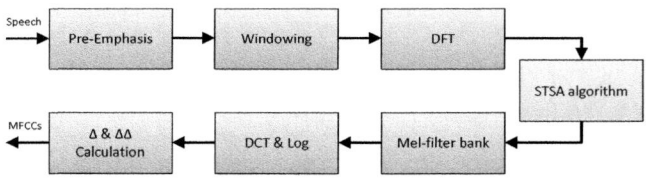

Fig. 6. STSA pipeline

Since both λ_x and λ_d are unavailable, they must be estimated from noisy observations as well. The simplest method to estimate the noise variance λ_d is to update its value during speech pauses by means of a voice activity detector. More sophisticated techniques have been presented in [23]. Instead of estimating λ_x, ξ is frequently estimated using the *decision-directed* approach [3]. Furthermore, it is shown in [3] that the optimal phase estimator is the noisy phase itself, $\hat{\alpha} = \theta$.

Recalling (6), the log-MMSE spectral amplitude estimator is given by:

$$\hat{A}^{log-MMSE} = \exp\left\{E\left[\ln A|Y\right]\right\} \tag{15}$$

The evaluation of (15) for the Gaussian model is conveniently done by utilizing the moment generating function of $\ln A$ given Y [24]. This leads to:

$$\hat{A}^{log-MMSE} = \frac{\xi}{1+\xi} \exp\left\{\frac{1}{2}\int_v^\infty \frac{e^{-t}}{t}dt\right\} R \tag{16}$$

Similarly, applying Bayes rule to equation (7), the computationally simpler MAP spectral amplitude estimator can be found [4]:

$$\hat{A}^{MAP} = \underset{A}{\mathrm{argmax}}\, \frac{p(R|a)p(a)}{p(R)} \qquad (17)$$

Under the Gaussian statistical model, a Rice pdf is obtained for the density of the noisy amplitude given the speech amplitude after polar integration of (13) [18]:

$$p(R|a) = \frac{2R}{\lambda_d} \exp\left\{-\frac{R^2 + a^2}{\lambda_d}\right\} I_0\left(\frac{2aR}{\lambda_d}\right) \qquad (18)$$

Note that it is sufficient to maximize only $p(R|a)\cdot p(a)$, since $p(R)$ is independent of a. A closed form solution can be found if the modified Bessel function $I_0(x)$ is asymptotically approximated by $e^x/\sqrt{2\pi x}$ and is given by:

$$\hat{A}^{MAP} = \frac{\xi + \sqrt{\xi^2 + (1+\xi)\frac{\xi}{\gamma}}}{2\,(1+\xi)}R \qquad (19)$$

The inaccuracy introduced by the aforementioned approximation may become unacceptable when using different statistical models, i.e., Gamma model. To overcome this problem, a joint MAP (JMAP) estimator of the amplitude and phase may be found [4]:

$$\begin{aligned}
\hat{A}^{JMAP} &= \underset{A}{\mathrm{argmax}}\, \frac{p(Y|a,\alpha)p(a,\alpha)}{p(Y)} \\
\hat{\alpha}^{JMAP} &= \underset{\alpha}{\mathrm{argmax}}\, \frac{p(Y|a,\alpha)p(a,\alpha)}{p(Y)}
\end{aligned} \qquad (20)$$

The JMAP estimator of the amplitude is given by

$$\hat{A}^{JMAP} = \frac{\xi + \sqrt{\xi^2 + 2\,(1+\xi)\frac{\xi}{\gamma}}}{2\,(1+\xi)}R \qquad (21)$$

while the JMAP estimator of the phase is again the noisy phase, $\hat{\alpha} = \theta$.

4.2   Mel-frequency Domain Approaches

In [5] a log-MMSE estimator of the Mel-frequency filter bank's output in power for the clean speech has been presented and is given by:

$$\hat{m}_x^{log-MMSE} = \exp\left\{E\left[\ln m_x | m_y\right]\right\} \qquad (22)$$

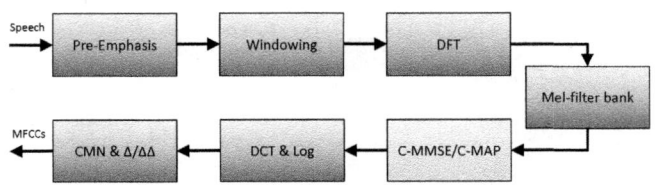

Fig. 7. Mel-frequency Domain pipeline

The equivalent JMAP estimator has been proposed in [6] and is given by:

$$\hat{c}_x^{JMAP} = \underset{c_x}{\text{argmax}} \ln \left[p(c_x | m_y) \right] \tag{23}$$

Under the Gaussian statistical model the estimators have the same form of (16) and (21), respectively, except for the definitions of the *a priori* and *a posteriori* SNRs, which are defined as $\xi \triangleq \frac{\lambda_x}{\lambda_n}$ and $\gamma \triangleq \frac{m_y^2}{\lambda_n}$, where $\lambda_n \approx \lambda_d + \lambda_\phi$, with $\lambda_x \triangleq E\left\{ m_x^2 \right\}$, $\lambda_d \triangleq E\left\{ m_d^2 \right\}$, and

$$\lambda_\phi \triangleq E\left\{ \left(\sum_k 2|X(k,l)||D(k,l)| \cos \phi(k,l) w_b(k) \right)^2 \right\} \approx 2 \frac{\sum_k w_b^2(k)}{(\sum_k w_b(k))^2} \sqrt{\frac{\lambda_x}{\lambda_d}} \lambda_d$$

ξ is again estimated using the *decision-directed* approach [3].

4.3   Log-Mel and MFCC Domain Approaches

In [8] an MMSE estimator in the log-Mel domain has been presented. Moving from the problem formulation of section 2, the authors developed a statistical model for the log-spectral domain acoustic distortion, which allows the computation of the conditional likelihood for the noisy speech observation in the same domain. The model has the following expression:

$$\ln m_y = \ln m_x + g(\ln m_d - \ln m_x) + r \tag{24}$$

where r represents an error term which can be modeled as a Gaussian random vector and $g(z) = \ln(1 + e^z)$. This assumption allows straightforward computation of the likelihood for the noisy speech observation which, combined with a GMM for the speech prior and a deterministic prior noise model, leads to a closed-form MMSE estimator.

A further MMSE estimator in the MFCC domain has been recently presented in [7]. Recasting the problem in terms of a statistical distortion model, they consider the clean speech Mel-frequency filter bank's output coefficient m_x as a function of the distorted counterpart m_y and a gain g:

$$m_x = g \cdot m_y \tag{25}$$

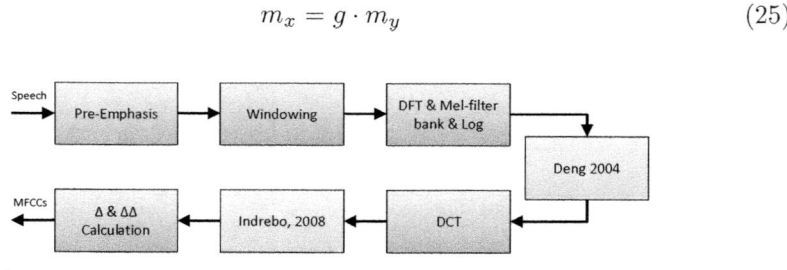

Fig. 8. MFCC Domain pipeline

Therefore, the j-th MFCC dimension of the noisy speech can be represented as:

$$c_y(j) = c_x(j) - \left(\sum_b a_{j,b} \cdot \ln g(b) \right) \qquad (26)$$

The MMSE estimator of the clean speech MFCC, $\hat{c}_x = E[c_x|c_y]$, is found using a GMM to represent the prior distribution, $p(c_x)$ and assuming the conditional distribution $p(c_y|c_x)$ to be Gaussian, with mean and variance given by:

$$\mu_{c_x|c_y} = c_x - E\left[\sum_b a_{j,b} \cdot \ln g(b) \right]$$
$$\Sigma_{c_x|c_y} = E\left[\left(\sum_b a_{j,b} \cdot \ln g(b) \right)^2 \right] - E\left[\sum_b a_{j,b} \cdot \ln g(b) \right]^2 \qquad (27)$$

The gain parameters may be estimated by assuming g to be beta distributed.

4.4   ASR Results

The aforementioned estimators have been evaluated on the Aurora-2 noisy speech database using the Hidden Markov Model Toolkit (HTK). Input signals were divided in frames of 200 samples with an overlap of 60% and an FFT of 256 bins. The number of Mel-spaced triangular filters was 23, and pre-emphasis and cepstral mean normalization were included in the feature extraction pipeline. Feature vectors are composed of 13 MFCCs (including C0) and their first and second derivatives.

Table 3. ASR Results

Enhancement domain	Algorithm	C	M
STSA	Ephraim & Malah, (16)	77.62	86.91
	Wolfe & Godsill, (21)	76.66	85.72
Mel-frequency	Yu et al., (22)	76.56	87.97
	Rotili et al., (23)	75.69	89.58
Log-Mel	Deng et al., [8]	85.15	/
MFCC	Indrebo et al., [7]	82.24	89.74
Baseline	(No enhancement)	66.92	88.79

Results, reported in Table 3, are expressed as word accuracy percentage, averaged on the 0–20 dB SNR range in step of 5 dB. Recognition has been performed using both clean (C) and multicondition (M) acoustic models. It can be noted that Mel-frequency domain results are comparable to STSA domain ones, though there is a slight drop using the clean acoustic model and a slight rise using the multicondition one. A most comprehensive presentation of these and the previous results can be found in [25]. Despite log-Mel and MFCC domain estimators have not been directly evaluated, for the sake of completeness Table 3 reports the results appeared in literature which have been obtained under conditions similar to the ones used in this work.

5   Conclusions

Bayesian framework is the base of a number of algorithms for clean speech estimation in noise robust ASR and the choice of the speech prior is of crucial importance for the success of the estimate. In this contribution the clean speech distribution has been investigated under several domains: analysis performed on the clean speech DFT magnitude showed that Laplacian, Gamma and Chi distribution best represent the underlying distribution. The same analysis conducted on Mel-frequency coefficients showed that the Gamma distribution provides the best fit. Finally, the analysis on LogMel and MFCC coefficients showed the multimodal nature of their respective distributions, and demonstrated how the use of GMM is able to represents the effective distribution. Future contributions will address the development of Bayesian estimators exploiting the findings of this work.

References

1. Li, J., Deng, L., Yu, D., Gong, Y., Acero, A.: A unified framework of HMM adaptation with joint compensation of additive and convolutive distortions. Computer Speech & Language 23(3), 389–405 (2009)
2. Wang, X., O'Shaughnessy, D.: Environmental Independent ASR Model Adaptation/Compensation by Bayesian Parametric Representation. IEEE Trans. Audio, Speech, and Lang. Process 15(4), 1204–1217 (2007)
3. Ephraim, Y., Malah, D.: Speech enhancement using a minimum-mean square error short-time spectral amplitude estimator. IEEE Trans. Acoust., Speech, Signal Process 32(6), 1109–1121 (1984)
4. Wolfe, P.J., Godsill, S.J.: Efficient alternatives to the Ephraim and Malah suppression rule for audio signal enhancement. EURASIP J. Appl. Signal Process 2003, 1043–1051 (2003)
5. Yu, D., Deng, L., Droppo, J., Wu, J., Gong, Y., Acero, A.: Robust speech recognition using a cepstral minimum-mean-square-error-motivated noise suppressor. IEEE Trans. Audio, Speech, and Lang. Process 16(5), 1061–1070 (2008)
6. Rotili, R., Principi, E., Cifani, S., Squartini, S., Piazza, F.: Robust speech recognition using MAP based noise suppression rules in the feature domain. In: Proc. of the 19th Czech-German Workshop on Speech Processing, Prague, Czech Republic, pp. 35–41 (September 2009)
7. Indrebo, K.M., Povinelli, R.J., Johnson, M.T.: Minimum Mean-Squared Error Estimation of Mel-Frequency Cepstral Coefficients Using a Novel Distortion Model. IEEE Trans. on Audio, Speech & Lang. Proc. 16(8), 1654–1661 (2008)
8. Li Deng, J., Droppo, J., Acero, A.: Estimating cepstrum of speech under the presence of noise using a joint prior of static and dynamic features. IEEE Trans. on Speech & Audio Proc. 12(3) (2004)
9. Breithaupt, C., Martin, R.: MMSE estimation of magnitude-squared DFT coefficients with SuperGaussian priors. In: Proc. IEEE ICASSP 2003, vol. I, pp. 896–899 (2003)
10. Lotter, T., Vary, P.: Speech Enhancement by MAP Spectral Amplitude Estimation using a Super-Gaussian Speech Model. EURASIP Journal on Applied Signal Processing 7, 1110–1126 (2005)

11. Martin, R.: Speech enhancement based on Minimum Mean-Square Error Estimation and Supergaussian Priors. IEEE Trans. Speech and Audio Process 13(5), 845–856 (2005)
12. Andrianakis, Y., White, P.R.: Speech spectral amplitude estimators using optimally shaped Gamma and Chi priors. Speech Communication (51), 1–14 (2009)
13. Erkelens, J.S., Hendriks, R.C., Heusdens, R., Jensen, J.: Minimum Mean-Square Error Estimation of Discrete Fourier Coefficients with Generalized Gamma Priors. IEEE Trans. Audio, Speech, and Lang. Process 15(6), 1741–1752 (2005)
14. Hendriks, R.C., Martin, R.: MAP Estimators for Speech Enhancement Under Normal and Rayleigh Inverse Gaussian Distributions. IEEE Trans. Audio, Speech, and Lang. Process 15(3), 918–927 (2007)
15. Chen, B., Loizou, P.C.: A Laplacian-based MMSE estimator for speech enhancement. Speech Communication (49), 134–143 (2007)
16. Dat, T.H., Takeda, K., Itakura, F.: Generalized Gamma modeling of speech and its online estimation for speech enhancement. In: Proc. of ICASSP 2005, pp. 181–184 (2005)
17. Van Trees, H.L.: Detection, Estimation, and Modulation Theory. Wiley, New York (1968)
18. McAulay, R.J., Malpass, M.L.: Speech enhancement using a soft-decision noise suppression filter. IEEE Trans. Acoust., Speech, Signal Process 28(2), 137–145 (1980)
19. Gazor, S., Zhang, W.: Speech Probability Distribution. IEEE Signal Processing Letters 10(7) (July 2003)
20. Jensen, J., Batina, I., Hendriks, R.C., Heusdens, R.: A study of the distribution of time-domain speech samples and discrete Fourier coefficients. In: Proc. of IEEE SPS-DARTS, pp. 155–158 (2005)
21. Redner, R.A., Walker, H.F.: Mixture densities, maximum likelihood, and the EM algorithm. SIAM Rev. 26(2), 195–239 (1984)
22. Figueredo, M.A.T., Jain, A.K.: Unsupervised learning of finite mixture models. IEEE Trans. on Pattern Analysis and Machine Intelligence 24(3), 381–396 (2002)
23. Cohen, I.: Noise estimation in adverse environments: improved minima controlled recursive averaging. IEEE Trans. Speech Audio Proc., 466–475 (September 2003)
24. Ephraim, Y., Malah, D.: Speech enhancement using a minimum-mean square error log-spectral amplitude estimator. IEEE Trans. Acoust., Speech, Signal Process 23(2), 443–445 (1985)
25. Principi, E., Cifani, S., Rotili, R., Squartini, S., Piazza, F.: Comparative Evaluation of Single-Channel MMSE-Based Noise Reduction Schemes for Speech Recognition. Journal of Electrical and Computer Engineering 2010, Article ID 962103, 6pages (2010)

Naturalness, Adaptation and Cooperativeness in Spoken Dialogue Systems

Milan Gnjatović, Darko Pekar, and Vlado Delić

Faculty of Technical Sciences, University of Novi Sad,
Trg Dositeja Obradovića 6, 21000 Novi Sad, Serbia
milan.gnjatovic@alfanum.co.rs, darko.pekar@alfanum.co.rs, vdelic@uns.ac.rs
http://www.ftn.uns.ac.rs/

Abstract. In this paper, we consider three distinct but interacting "cognitive" features of spoken dialogue systems that may contribute to better acceptance by users: naturalness of the interaction, adaptation and cooperativeness. In order to achieve them, we particularly concentrate on the dialogue management functionalities of modeling contextual information and of dynamical adapting both analytical and generative aspects of the system's behavior according to the current state of the interaction. Finally, we illustrate the introduced design concepts for the spoken dialogue system Contact.

Keywords: cognitive technical systems, context modeling, adaptive dialogue strategies.

1 Introduction

The importance of increasing the level of acceptance of spoken dialogue systems by users is widely recognized. Adaptive dialogue management is a promising research direction to address this question. Although considerable research effort in the field is already to be noticed (an overview is available in [7]), its possibilities are by no means sufficiently explored. In this paper, we particularly concentrate on the dialogue management functionalities of modeling contextual information and of dynamical adapting both analytical and generative aspects of the system's behavior according to the current state of the interaction. We discuss how they can be used to achieve three distinct but interacting "cognitive" features of spoken dialogue systems that may contribute to better acceptance by users: naturalness of the interaction, adaptation and cooperativeness. This paper also illustrates these design concepts for the spoken dialogue system Contact [2], [6]. The system Contact is primarily intended to be used by blind and visually impaired people—it reads aloud textual contents (e.g., news, articles, etc.) from various newspapers and websites over the telephone line. We report the development of the dialogue management module in this system.

A. Esposito et al. (Eds.): COST 2102 Int. Training School 2010, LNCS 6456, pp. 298–304, 2011.

2   Naturalness of Interface Language

An important aspect of naturalness of the interaction is certainly naturalness of the interface language. The essence of naturalness of the interface language is that users can express themselves without conscious effort to follow rules of a predefined grammar while producing their utterances. This implies that a language interface should be able to cope with various dialogue phenomena related to the users' language, such as different syntactic forms of users' utterances, high frequency of ungrammaticalities, context dependent utterances, etc. To achieve this, we introduced a model of attentional information on the level of a user's command (cf. [3], [4]). Based on general observations on the structure of spoken language made in [1] and on the theory of discourse structure introduced in [5], this model underlies our approach to processing flexibly formulated user's utterances in human-machine interaction. For the purpose of this contribution, we illustrate our model of attentional state—the focus tree.

After inspection of spontaneously uttered subjects' commands from the domain-specific corpus FirstContact[1], we differentiate among three *focus classes* whose instances form attentional information. They are given in the following list, starting from the most general focus class and ending with the most specific:

- *Newspaper focus*—Focus instances contained in this class relate to the newspapers and websites whose content is available in the system Contact.
- *Section focus*—Focus instances contained in this class relate to sections (e.g., News, Weather, Sport, etc.) in newspapers.
- *Article focus*—Focus instances contained in this class relate to articles in sections.

To give an example: the command "read latest news from the Limes" contains two phrases that determine two focus instances. The phrase "latest news" relates to the section focus class, while the phrase "the Limes" relates to the newspaper focus class. These three focus classes are interrelated—an instance of a more specific focus class is a sub-focus of an instance of the immediately preceding more general focus class. We map focus instances onto the focus tree. An example of the focus tree[2] for the system Contact is given in Figure 1. At every moment of interaction, the current focus of attention is represented by exactly one node in the focus tree. During the processing of a user's command, focus instances comprised in it are automatically extracted and mapped onto the focus tree with respect to the position of the current focus of attention. Also, the user's command may change the focus of attention.

---

[1] The corpus FirstContact contains audio and video recordings of strictly system-guided dialogues—i.e., without adaptive dialogue management—between the naïve users and the system Contact.

[2] For the purpose of easier representation, in this example we reduce the number of newspapers to two ("The Limes" and "Most"), each of them being divided into two sections (one relating to news, the other to weather) that contain one or two articles. It means that we show only a part of the "wider" focus tree including more newspapers, sections and articles. However, this reduced representation implies by no means a reduction of complexity of the observed dialogue domain.

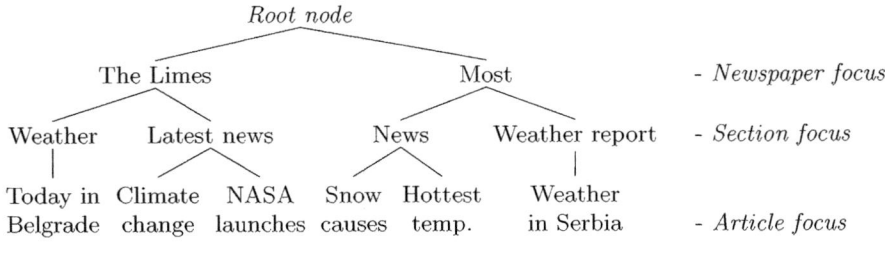

Fig. 1. The simplified focus tree for the system Contact

3   Adaptive Dialogue Strategies

As mentioned above, one of the central guidelines in our approach is that the dialogue manager should dynamically adapt its dialogue strategy according to the actual state of the interaction. This idea can be considered to be of general nature. Here, we illustrate it for the system Contact. In the following subsections, we describe three main steps in defining an adaptive dialogue strategy.

3.1   Step 1: Modeling the State of Interaction

After the inspection of dialogues from the corpus FirstContact, we model the state of the interaction as a composite of four interaction features:

- **The command status:** When a command uttered by the user is processed[3], it is assigned to one of the following classes: "valid" command, "unrecognized" command, "help" command, or "system" command.
- **The focus of attention:** Represents the current focus of attention, i.e., a node in the focus tree that carries the focus of attention. The possible values are: "onInnerNode", when the focus of attention is placed on an inner or the root node in the focus tree, and "onTerminalNode", otherwise.
- **The number of focus candidates:** Represents the number of nodes in the focus tree that are candidates to carry the focus of attention after performing the user's command. Possible values are: "zero", "one", and "more".
- **The support intensity:** Represents intensity of support provided by the system. Possible values are: "high", in potentially critical phases of the interaction, and "low", otherwise.

We briefly comment the support intensity. The user may experience various problems in the interaction with the system. The manner of providing support to the user should be tailored to meet the user's needs. To illustrate, let us assume that the user instructed an illegal command for the first time in the course of the interaction. In this case, support with low intensity would be appropriate, e.g., just a warning given by the system might be enough. But, if the user repeatedly

---

[3] Note that the speech recognizer returns also confidence scores for recognized words.

utters illegal commands, the system should probably provide support with high intensity, e.g., it may guide the user to formulate a valid command by stating iterative questions, etc.

3.2   Step 2: Defining Dialogue Strategy Components

In our approach, a dialogue strategy is a composite of predefined, discrete dialogue strategy components. At each time the system applies its dialogue strategy, it should decide which dialogue strategy components to apply and in which chronological order. Some of the dialogue strategy components defined for the system Contact are given and explained in the following list:

- **read:** If the current focus of attention is placed on a node representing an article, the system reads the article. Otherwise, the system behaves as in the strategy component **offerTopics**.
- **offerTopics:** If the current focus of attention is placed on an inner node or the root node (for example, a node representing a newspaper), the system reads names of its children nodes (in our example, sections in that newspaper) and asks the user to select one of them.
- **reportIllegalCommand:** The system informs the user that there is no such an article, a section or a newspaper that would satisfy criteria from his command.
- **reportUnrecognizedCommand:** The system informs the user that his command was not recognized.
- **reformulate:** The system asks the user to reformulate his command.
- **setSupportIntensity:** The system increases the intensity of support.
- **clearSupportIntensity:** The system decreases the intensity of support.

3.3   Step 3: Defining Dialogue Strategies

The essence of an adaptive dialogue strategy is that the dialogue manager takes into account the current state of the interaction in order to decide which dialogue strategy components to apply and in which chronological order. Here, we discuss how such an adaptive dialogue strategy could be defined. It is important to note that a dialogue strategy is not hard-coded in the source code of the dialogue management module. Instead, it is defined in an external textual file that is loaded, interpreted and evaluated at run time. When loading a file containing a definition of a dialogue strategy, the parser within the dialogue management module interprets the dialogue strategy and, thereafter, the dialogue management module applies it. This makes two levels of adaptation possible: the dialogue strategy is not only dynamically adapted according to the current state of the interaction, but also the dialogue strategy itself can be redefined at run time (just by loading another external file containing a new definition). A more detailed description of the syntax for defining a dialogue strategy is outside of the scope of this paper and will be discussed in other paper. Here, Figure 2

```
if _commandStatus is unrecognized and _supportIntensity is low
    then reportUnrecognizedCommand setSupportIntensity
if _commandStatus is unrecognized and _supportIntensity is high
    then offerTopics
if _numberOfFocusCandidates is zero and _supportIntensity is low
    then reportIllegalCommand reformulate setSupportIntensity
if _numberOfFocusCandidates is zero and _supportIntensity is high
    then reportIllegalCommand offerTopics clearSupportIntensity
if _numberOfFocusCandidates is one and _currrentFocus is onInnerNode
    then offerTopics clearSupportIntensity
if _numberOfFocusCandidates is one and _currrentFocus is onTerminalNode
    then read clearSupportIntensity
```

Fig. 2. An example of an adaptive dialogue strategy for the system Contact

shows a part of the external textual file defining an adaptive dialogue strategy for the system Contact.

In our approach, an adaptive dialogue strategy is a sequence of if-statements. In this example, the conditions in the if-statements are logical expressions that contain variables (whose names start with underscore) representing the interaction features defined in Section 3.1. The syntax of the logical expressions is close to natural language and has a clear intuitive meaning. Each time the system applies its dialogue strategy, these conditions are evaluated in a top-down manner—only the if-statement containing the first condition evaluated to true is executed. The body of an if-statement is a sequence of dialogue strategy components defined in Section 3.2.

4   An Example

We briefly illustrate the dialogue strategy introduced in the previous section. We give an analysis of an actual dialogue between the user and the system Contact that took place during the testing of the system. Because we were particularly concentrated on demonstrating functionalities of the dialogue management module, both the user and the system used typed text to communicate in this dialogue in order to exclude side effects related to speech recognition and speech synthesis. The observed dialogue fragment is given in Figure 3.

In the command User$_1$, the user asks for a specific article in the newspaper Limes. Although there is such an article in the knowledge base of the system (cf. Figure 1), it is not contained in the newspaper Limes. Therefore, the third if-statement in the dialogue strategy defined in Section 3.3 is executed. Following the dialogue strategy, the system (in System$_2$) informs the user that there is no such an article that would satisfy the criterium in his command, advices him to reformulate the command and increases the intensity of the support. In his turn User$_3$, the user reformulates slightly the command, however not enough to change the criterium in the command. But in this moment, since the intensity of support is increased, the fourth if-statement in the dialogue strategy is executed.

User₁: *Give me that article from Limes about the hottest temperature.*
System₂: *Sorry, I didn't find anything that satisfies the criteria in your command.*
          Could you please reformulate your last command?
User₃: *From Limes. The article about the hottest temperature.*
System₄: *Sorry, I didn't find anything that satisfies the criteria in your command.*
          Which newspaper do you want to read: The Limes, Most?
User₅: *I said Limes.*
System₆: *Which section do you want to read from: Weather, Latest news?*
User₇: *Please find the hottest temperature article.*
System₈: *I'm reading: Hottest Temperature ever heads science to Big Bang ...*

Fig. 3. Dialogue between the user and the system Contact

So, again following the defined dialogue strategy, the system takes the initiative to prevent further negative developments. It states iterative questions (starting with System₄) in order to guide the user towards more specific focus instances. At first, the user accepts the system's guidance. In the command User₅, he specifies the newspaper (note that the user specifies the wrong newspaper again). The fifth if-statement is executed and the system states the next iterative question System₆. But in the command User₇, the user decides not to follow the guided dialogue, but to ask again for the article. Still, he does not specify explicitly the newspaper and, thus, he relaxes the command's criterium, so the system's search is not limited to the content of the newspaper Limes only (as it was in the command User₁). Now, the sixth if-statement is executed and the system reads the specified article that was previously found in the other newspaper.

It is clear that we could define a more optimized dialogue strategy for this particular user information need. However, it should be noted that the aim of this example was not to evaluate the dialogue strategy introduced in Figure 2, but just to illustrate how an adaptive dialogue strategy may be specified by means of a set of rules and how it was applied in the observed dialogue fragment.

5   Conclusion

In this paper, we discussed some design concepts aimed to increase the level of naturalness, adaptation and cooperativeness in spoken dialogue systems and illustrated them for the system Contact. The functionality of the dialogue manager can be summarized in the following points:

(1) For a given vocabulary of words and phrases that are recognized by the speech recognition module, we allow flexible formulation of users' commands, instead of predefining a grammar for accepted commands. Processing of commands is independent of the predefined grammar used in the speech recognition module. The model of attentional state was demonstrated to function well for different syntactic forms of users' commands both in Serbian and English.

(2) We described the method for designing adaptive dialogue strategies and implemented it for the system Contact. Two levels of adaptation are provided. First, the dialogue strategy is dynamically adapted according to the current state

of the interaction. Secondly, it should be noted that the system's dialogue strategy is defined in an external textual file—independently of the implementation of the dialogue management module. Thus, the dialogue strategy itself can be redefined, even at run-time, just by loading a file containing a new definition—no recompilation of the program's source code is necessary. The syntax for defining a dialogue strategy is close to natural language and has a clear intuitive meaning, so a non-technical user (i.e., with no programming knowledge) may define a non-trivial adaptive dialogue strategy.

(3) Finally, with respect to generalizability of this approach, both the model of attentional state and the method for designing adaptive dialogue strategies described in this paper are intended to be task-independent. As a small illustration: they have been already successfully implemented in two crucially different interaction domains. In [3], they are applied for a prototype dialogue system for supporting users while they solve a graphical task. The graphical display that is involved in that interaction represents an additional non-linguistic context shared between the user and the system and, thus, significantly influences the language of the user. At the other hand, the same models are applied for the system Contact that is primarily intended to be used by the visually impaired and does not include a graphical interface or task solving activities.

Acknowledgments. The work described in this paper was supported in part by the Ministry for Science and Technological Development of the Republic of Serbia, within the project TR1101: "Human-Machine Speech Communication".

References

1. Campbell, N.: On the Structure of Spoken Language. In: Proceedings of the 3rd International Conference on Speech Prosody 2006, Dresden, Germany (2006)
2. Delić, V.: A Review of R&D of Speech Technologies in Serbian and their Applications in Western Balkan Countries. In: Keynote Lecture at 12th SPECOM (Speech and Computer), Moscow, Russia, pp. 64–83 (2007) ISBN 6-7452-0110-x
3. Gnjatović, M.: Adaptive Dialogue Management in Human-Machine Interaction. Verlag Dr. Hut, München (2009) ISBN 978-3-86853-189-3
4. Gnjatović, M., Rösner, D.: An approach to processing of user's commands in human-machine interaction. In: Proceedings of the 3rd Language and Technology Conference, LTC 2007, pp. 152–156. Adam Mickiewicz University, Poznan, Poland (2007)
5. Grosz, B., Sidner, C.: Attention, Intentions, and the Structure of Discourse. Computational Linguistics 12(3), 175–204 (1986)
6. Ronto, R., Pekar, D.: Developing a Telephone Voice Portal with ASR and TTS Capability. In: Proceedings of 49th ETRAN, Tom II. Society for ERAN, Budva, Montenegro, pp.392–395 (2005) (in Serbian) ISBN 86-80509-54-X
7. Wilks, Y., Catizone, R., Turunen, M.: Dialogue Management. In: COMPANIONS Consortium: State of the Art Papers (2006) (Public report)

Towards Semantic Multimodal Video Annotation

Marco Grassi, Christian Morbidoni, and Francesco Piazza

Department of Biomedical, Electronic and Telecommunication Engineering
Università Politecnica delle Marche - Ancona, 60131, Italy
{m.grassi,c.morbidoni,f.piazza}@univpm.it
http://www.semedia.dibet.univpm.it

Abstract. Nowadays Semantic Web techniques are finding applications
in several research fields. We believe that they can be beneficial also in
multimodal video annotation to enhance the annotations management
and to promote an effective sharing of collected multimodal data and
annotations. To have an insight about how the task of video annotation
is commonly performed and the created annotations are managed and to
evaluate how to improve these tasks using semantic web techniques, we
set up a publically available survey. In this paper, we discuss the results
of the survey and trace a roadmap towards the application of semantic
web techniques for the management of multimodal video annotations.

Keywords: Multimodal video annotation, semantic web, ontology,
survey, faceted browsing.

1 Introduction

Recent studies have revealed how human communication is an highly multimodal
process in which elements such as human language, speech, gesture, gaze, and
facial expression actively participate together and in synchrony to convey the
full informative content of the communication [1]. To fully understand the underlying mechanisms of human communication and of emotions, a cross-modal
analysis of all these channels it's necessary. The starting point in this study is
the collection of experimental data, through different elicitation techniques for
generating spontaneous dialogues, recorded in the form of multimedia objects as
images, speech, video and audio-video segments. All these data have to be later
carefully labeled and analyzed from a wide spectrum of disciplines in a structured
manner to determinate the most relevant features and their correlations. Apart
from its intrinsic difficulty, a big issue of multimodal video annotation is due the
lack of a unique standardization of the descriptors used for the annotations and
of a web architecture for the sharing and the management of the encoded data
that deeply limits the diffusion of labeled multimodal video datasets.

To have an insight about how the task of video annotation is commonly performed, how the created annotations are managed and to evaluate how to improve these tasks using semantic web techniques, we set up a publically available
survey. In this paper, on the base of the interesting results of the survey, we trace
a roadmap towards the application of semantic web techniques for the management of multimodal video annotations.

A. Esposito et al. (Eds.): COST 2102 Int. Training School 2010, LNCS 6456, pp. 305–316, 2011.
© Springer-Verlag Berlin Heidelberg 2011

2   Multimodal Video Annotation

Multimodal video annotation is an highly time-consuming - more than one hour work can be required for labeling one minute of video - and complex task, particularly expensive and error prone. A wide set of relevant information needs in fact to be encoded not only about speech, facial displays, gestures but also relative to the emotional state of the speaker, turn taking management and sequencing in the conversation.

2.1   Video Annotation Tools

Several specialized software applications have been developed in recent years to provide support to the annotation task [2]. Anvil[3] software gives support for hierarchical multi-layered annotations, visualization of waveform and pitch contour and offers an intuitive annotation board that shows color-coded elements on multiple tracks in time-alignment. ELAN [4] is a free linguistic annotation tool for the creation of text annotations for audio and video files. The annotations can be grouped on multiple layers or tiers that are part of tier hierarchies. Each level of description is represented in ELAN on a tier. OntoELAN [5] inherits all ELAN's features and extends the tool with an ontology-based annotation approach. It can open and display ontology specified in OWL (Ontology Web Language) other to create language profile and ontological tier. The EXMAR-aLDA [6] system consists of a data model, a set of corresponding XML formats and a number of software tools for the creation, management and analysis of spoken language corpora. The TASX Annotator enables an XML-based annotation of multimodal data on multiple tiers which facilitates a parallel annotation as well as an immediate comparison across the different modalities of interest. MacVisSTA is a software program, for Mac OS, developed to code different aspects of behavior (speech, gaze, gesture, etc.). Most of these software also allow to perform complex searches based on temporal and/or structural relations in the single generated annotation files and some of them also simple text searches across multiple files. By the way, all these software, being conceived as desktop applications, perform search queries only locally in the user PC. In addition there is no handling for different users permissions and everyone can modify, read or create new annotations.

2.2   Annotation Schemas

Different schemas have been developed to supply standardized vocabularies for the annotation, indicating the features that have to be described and the terminology to use in the description. Such schemas have been encoded in XML to provide machine processability and to be used by the video annotation tools. The MUMIN multimodal coding scheme [7] is intended to be a general instrument for the study of gestures and facial displays in interpersonal communication, in particular the role played by multimodal expressions for feedback, turn taking management and sequencing. Inside the HUMAINE project, EARL (Emotion

Annotation and Representation Language) [8] has been developed for the annotation of audio-video databases and used with Anvil software. EARL is encoded in XML Schema and offers a powerful structure for describing emotion, by dimensions, intensity and appraisals. Recently also the Emotion Markup Language Incubator Group, The W3C (World Wide Web Consortium), which operates for the definition of standards and guidelines for Web development, has published a working draft that specifies Emotion Markup Language (EmotionML) 1.0 [9]. This markup language is designed to be usable in a broad variety of technological contexts while reflecting concepts from the affective sciences. The BML (Behavior Markup Language) [10] has been developed inside the SAIBA project, to describe human nonverbal and verbal behavior in a manner independent of the particular used animation method. The ISO 24617-2 is currently under development to provide an international standard for annotating dialogue with semantic information, in particular concerning the communicative functions of the utterances, the kind of content they address, and the dependency relations to what was said and done earlier in the dialogue [11].

The existence of a wide number of descriptors for video annotation, encoded in several different annotation schema, it's the unavoidable consequence of the variety of the purposes for which the multimodal video annotation is designated, of the kind of media that is annotated and of the tools used for the annotation. This makes impossible the definition of a unique standard annotation schema that could grant at the same time flexibility (possibility to use a large set of descriptor adapt to every kind of description) and interoperability (possibility to share understandable information between different users). By the way, between the different schemas there are often similarities in the used descriptors. Unfortunately, most of the available annotation schemas are expressed in XML Schema, which is a powerful language for defining the structure of XML documents with a syntax that is based on XML itself. Anyway XML Schema that does not supply enough expressiveness to encode the semantic of the information in a machine processable language and does not allow the mapping between similar concepts expressed in different annotation schemas, which would be highly beneficial to promote interoperability.

3 Semantic Web

The Semantic Web is an initiative that aims to improve the current state of the World Wide Web, most of whose content is today perfectly suitable for human consumption, but it remains completely inaccessible to machines. Semantic web tackle tackles this problem through an appropriate representation of information in the web-page, able to univocally identify resources and encode the meaning of their description. Even if originally created for the Web, Semantic Web techniques are suitable for application in all the scenarios that require advanced data-integration, to link data coming from multiple sources without preexisting schema, and powerful data-modeling to represent expressive semantic descriptions of application domains and to provide inferencing power for applications that need a knowledge base, as it's the case of multimodal video annotation. Multimodal video annotation task generates in fact a huge quantity of metadata relative to relevant information regarding several facets of human communication as language, speech, gesture, facial expression, etc. Complex models and annotation schemas are required to encode and manage such information. In addition the lack of standardization in the description models and of the lack of machine interpretable semantics in the annotation schemas prevent an effective sharing of the annotations.

The Semantic Web uses uniform resource identifiers (URIs) to univocally identify entities and the resource description framework (RDF) to express the information in an univocally interpretable format, whose basic building block is an object-attribute-value triple i.e. a statement. To provide machine-accessible and machine-processable representations, RDF triples are encoded using a XML syntax. To define the semantics of the encoded data Semantic Web makes use of ontologies, formal explicit descriptions of concepts and properties of a represented domain. Ontologies make possible the sharing of common understanding about the structure of information among people or software agents. Once that relevant information have been encoded in a semantic aware language on the base of specific domain ontologies, expressed in machine accessible language like OWL and stored in a triplestore, a purpose-built database for the storage and retrieval of RDF triples, such information become available as an interconnected knowledge base. Advanced search queries can be performed on such knowledge base and the results can be displayed and explored using innovative data visualization paradigms like faceted browsing.

3.1   Human Emotion Ontology

The Human Emotion Ontology (HEO) [13] is an high level ontology for the description of human emotions. It provides a set of high level features that can be further refined using lower level concepts and properties related to more specific descriptions or linked to other more specialized ontologies. Heo is currently used to encode affective information extracted from web pages using Sentic Computing, a novel artificial intelligence tool for sentimental analysis [14]. HEO provides a wide set of properties that allows to describe emotions in many different way, by category, dimension, action tendency, appraisal and more (Fig.1). It represents a remarkable example of how an ontology can be used to create a description framework that could grant at the same time enough flexibility, by allowing the use of a wide and extensible set of descriptors to represent all the main features of an emotion, and interoperability, by mapping different description models. In fact, HEO has been developed in OWL-DL to take advantage of its expressiveness and its inference power in order to map the different models used for emotions description. Using OWL-DL, in fact, HEO provides a taxonomical organization of emotions categories and properties restrictions that link emotions descriptions made by category and dimension.

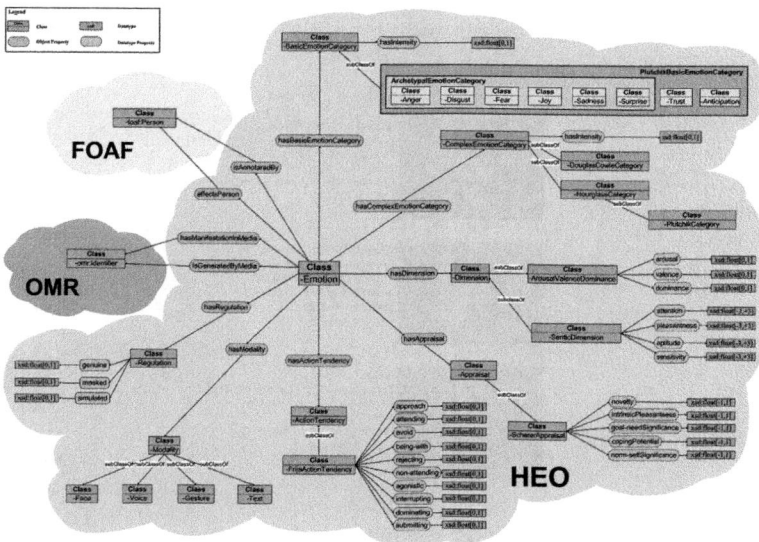

Fig. 1. The Human Emotion Ontology

3.2   Faceted Browsing Paradigm

Faceted classification allows the assignment of multiple categories to an object, enabling the classifications to be ordered in multiple ways, rather than in a single, pre-determined, taxonomic order. This makes possible to perform searches combining the textual approach with the navigational approach. Faceted search, in fact, enables users to navigate a multidimensional information space by concurrently writing queries in a text box and progressively narrowing choices in each dimension. Several tools are today available for implementing faceted browsing. The SIMILE Exhibit API [15], in particular, constitutes a set of Javascript files that allows to easily create rich interactive web-pages including maps, timelines, and galleries with very detailed client-side filtering.

3.3   Semantic Video Annotation Tools

A part from OntoELAN, there are several semantic video annotation tools, although not designed for multimodal annotation, that provide interesting features for the annotation. M-OntoMat-Annotizer (M stands for Multimedia) [16] is a user-friendly tool that supplies a graphical interface for loading and processing of visual content (images and videos), extraction of visual features and association with domain ontology concepts. VIA (Video Image Annotation Tool) [17] allows users to import its descriptors from predefined OWL ontology files and to perform the annotation of specific video regions and enable the captivation of movement trajectories. SVAT (Semantic Video Annotation Tool) [18] enables film analysts to efficiently annotate video footage. SVAT also support a plug in

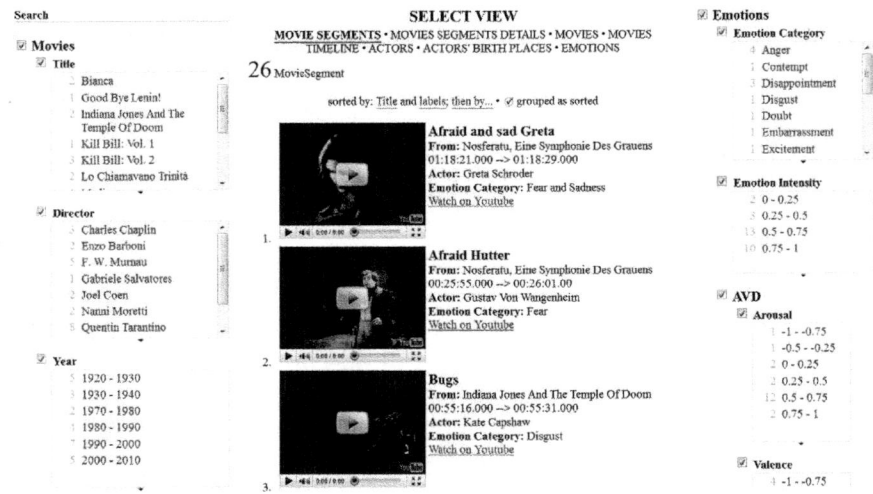

Fig. 2. Exhibit demo webst

for object recognition and search tool based on Difference-of-Gaussian local key points and computed SIFT descriptors as local low-level features for every frame in the video. Project Pad [19] is a web-based system for collaborative media annotation for teaching, learning and scholarly applications. The system offers an easy to use direct manipulation interface and allows users to browse and work with audio, video and images from digital repositories and to create their own online notebooks.

4   Video Annotation Survey

The survey was divided into 5 sections. The first one was about the used multi-modal video annotation tools. The purpose was to inquire about the users level of satisfaction and to determine which existing features should be modified or improved and what additional features should be added to enhance the annotation process. The second part was about the schemas used for the annotations creation and the modalities used in the annotations sharing. The purpose of the third and fourth part was to inquire about the level of knowledge of about the Semantic Web and of the existing semantic video annotation tool that we mentioned above and to evaluate the applicability of Semantic Web technique to support the process of multimodal video annotation. In the last section of the survey we also presented a simple demonstrative web site based on the faceted browsing paradigm, as proof of concept of our ideas, in order to receive feedbacks about their soundness and feasibility. The web site (Fig.2), developed exploiting the Exhibit API, contains several fragments of movies whose affective content was annotated according the HEO ontology and encoding the metadata in a semantic aware language. Different views are available to display such information organized in different fashion, from a detailed tabular representation of all the encoded information, to a timeline of movies release date and a map view of the actors places of birth. The faceted menus allows to easily browse the encoded information and to intuitively perform advances queries adding or removing constrains in the faceted properties.

We spread our survey through the members of COST 2102, a research action about the Cross-Modal Analysis of Verbal and Non-Verbal Communication, and sixteen participants with experience in multimodal annotation applied to the survey. The survey and its complete results are publically available at www.semedia.dibet.univpm.it/survey/videoannotation.

4.1   Results Discussion

Rather than comparing in detail the performances of the existing tools and annotation schemas, the main purpose of the survey was to inquire about the actual state of the art in multimodal video annotation and its possible enhancements, particularly through the application of Semantic Web techniques. In the following we discuss the main conclusions that can be inferred from results analysis.

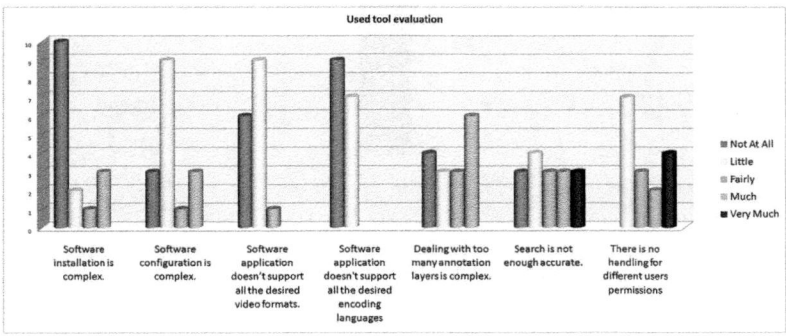

Fig. 3. Tools evaluation

Survey shows a remarkable satisfaction of the participants about the software that they use (12 people use ELAN and 4 people use Anvil). This is not surprising considering that these tools are the result of a long and continuous development process. As shown from the results Fig.3, most of the users do not encounter particular problems in installing and configuring the software and are satisfied with its support for different video formats and different encoding languages. Some difficulties emerge in dealing with many annotation layers but they are hardly avoidable being intrinsic on the complexity of multimodal video annotation task. What appears not completely satisfactory is instead the search functionalities whose accuracy could be improved and the management of different user permission, a functionality which is missing in the actual video annotation software and that could be useful for cooperative video annotation.

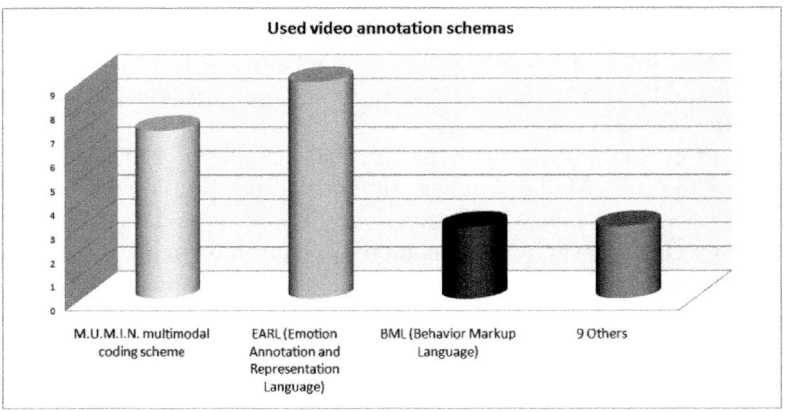

Fig. 4. Used video annotation schemas

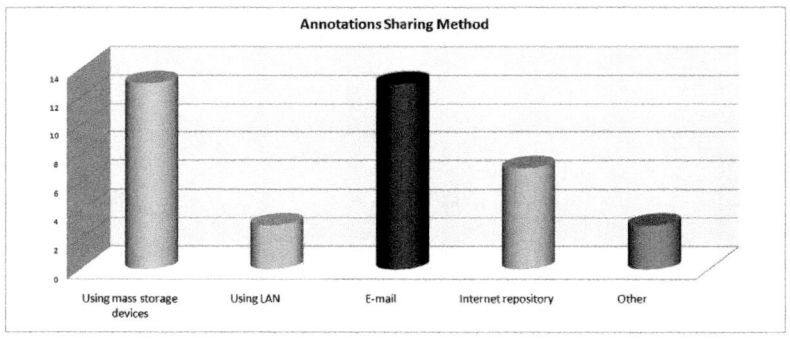

Fig. 5. Annotation sharing methods

Several different annotation schemas are used in the annotation. All of the schemas proposed in the survey (MUMIN, EARL, BML) are used by at least one participant and many of them also use more than one schema (Fig.4).

It's worth to notice how while the annotation tools have evolved in the course of the year to become more and more mature and sophisticated, the techniques used for annotation and video sharing are still very basic. Most of the data transfer is done by mass storage or e-mail exchange rather than exploiting web repositories (Fig.5). The use of video sharing services, which have become very common internet services, if only we think to Youtube, is completely ignored.

Most of the participant had just a limited knowledge of the Semantic Web and apart from OntoELAN they didn't know the proposed semantic video annotation tools. By the way, all of them agreed that the application of semantic web techniques would be beneficial in the field of multimodal video annotation (Fig.6). They also find the proposed exhibit demo web site an interesting way to display and manage the annotated video segments (Fig.7).

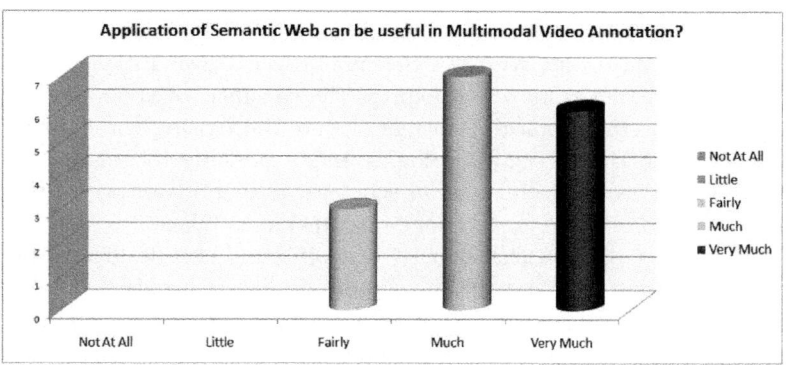

Fig. 6. Semantic Web applicability

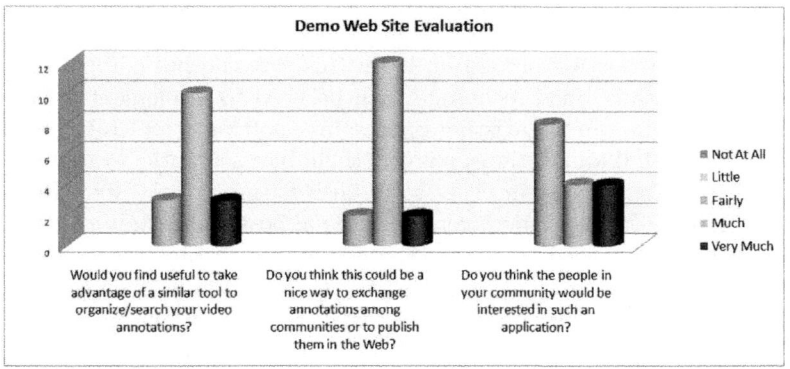

Fig. 7. Demo web site evaluation

5   A Roadmap towards Semantic Multimodal Annotation

Survey results indicate that multimodal video annotation doesn't require big improvements regarding the creation of the annotations. Sophisticated tools already exist to support users in this task. They offer a wide set of advanced features for creating annotations but also require a considerable learning time for the users to familiarize with the GUI and to fully exploit the offered functionalities. The efforts to improve multimodal video annotation should rather focus in the encoding and the management of the created annotations in order to enhance the effectiveness of the search queries, which at the moment appear not fully satisfactory, and to promote a larger annotation sharing, exploiting the possibilities offered by Web.

The application of Semantic Web techniques is particularly suitable for this purpose to enable what we define "semantic multimodal video annotation", which means a more powerful annotation encoding that can be exploited to implement an efficient web based architecture for annotation management and sharing. Evolving from the actual data encoding mostly based on XML document structured according to XML Schemas towards semantic data encoding based on RDF instances allows to express the semantic of the annotation in a univocally interpretable machine format. In addition rising the existing annotation schemas to the level of ontologies makes possible to create a mapping between different existing multimodal schemas, taking advantage of the higher expressiveness of language for ontology description as OWL.

To such purpose it's not necessary to develop brand new desktop applications for video annotation, which would be something like reinventing the wheel but only to provide tools to convert the annotations and the annotations schemas in a semantic aware format. Several techniques and tools have been developed in recent years that allow to operate such transformation. Most of them perform the conversion using standard XML technology XSLT (Extensible Stylesheet Language Transformations) [20] which is an XML-based language used for the transformation of XML documents into other XML documents. Using XSLT the original document is not changed; rather, a new document is created based on the content of an existing one, granting in this way the full compatibility with the existing software. Such techniques can be used to implement a standalone application or a plug-in for existing open source software, as ELAN, capable of selecting the created annotations, convert them in a semantic aware format and store them in a triple store in order to publish it through the web. In this way the introduction of a semantic layer it's made almost completely transparent to the users, that don't need to change the way in which they create the annotation, using their usual annotation tools and the annotation schemas, but just to perform a very simple additional step to make the annotations available through the Web. Also the annotated videos can be published online, exploiting existing video sharing services as Youtube or setting up an on purpose video streaming server.

Once that the annotations are encoded in a semantic aware format and published on the Web jointly with the videos, a web application can be developed using the faceted browsing paradigm to display and browse the videos and the annotations and to perform advanced queries over the entire knowledge base stored into the triple store. For each video the Web application should display all the created annotations, providing different views to organize the annotations, for example using timelines or tabular representations. Faceted menus, automatically created based on the properties of the ontologies used for the annotation, can be used to intuitively filter the annotations adding or removing constrains on the faceted properties. The Web interface should also provide to the common functionalities of the desktop video annotation tools. Users should be able to play the videos and visualize the time aligned annotation during its reproduction or to select single annotations and to play the corresponding video segments. Also at least some basic video annotation functionalities should be provided to the users to delete, modify and add annotations.

User and group management is a de facto standard feature of today web application, which is very well supported by the web architecture. On the contrary

this functionality is completely missing in common desktop applications for multimodal video annotation. An effective handling for different users and groups
permissions for the management of the published video annotation can therefore
be easily implemented for the Web application. This can constitutes an important feature for improving video annotation sharing and promoting collaborative
video annotation. In this way, in fact every user can set different levels of protection for the visualization, modification or deletion of her annotations for different
users or group of users. For example a user can allow everyone to display her
annotations but authorize only the users belonging to her own research group
to modify them.

6   Conclusions

Multimodal video annotation is a complex task, which is at the base of many
different researches regarding several fields as human communication, emotions,
gesture research. We believe that the application of Semantic Web techniques
in this field can represent a key factor enhance the task of multimodal video
annotation.

In this paper, on the base of the results of our survey, we traced a roadmap
toward the implementation of semantic multimodal video annotation, individu-
ating the techniques and the tools that can be used to implement a novel system
for a more efficient management and sharing of the created annotations exploiting the potentialities offered by the Web. The purpose is to push forward the
productivity of multimodal video annotation task, enhancing the accessibility of
videos and annotations and promoting their sharing between the researches, by
making all these data available on the web as an interconnected knowledge base.

References

1. Sebe, N., Cohen, I., Gevers, T., Huang, T.S.: Multimodal Approaches for Emotion
   Recognition: A Survey. In: Proc. Of SPIE-IST Electronic Imaging. SPIE, vol. 5670,
   pp. 56–67 (2005)
2. Rohlfing, K., et al.: Comparison of multimodal annotation tools - workshop report.
   Gesprachsforschung-OnlineZeitschrift zur verbalen Interaktion 7, vol. 7(7), pp. 99–
   123 (2006)
3. Kipp, M.: Anvil - A generic annotation tool for multimodal dialogue. In: Proceedings of the 7th European Conference on Speech Communication and Technology
   (Eurospeech), Aalborg, pp. 1367–1370 (2001)
4. Wittenburg, P., et al.: ELAN: a professional framework for multimodality research.
   In: Proceedings of the 5th International Conference on Language Resources and
   Evaluation (LREC 2006), pp. 1556–1559 (2006)
5. Chebotko, A., et al.: OntoELAN: an ontology-based linguistic multimedia annotator. In: Proceedings of IEEE Sixth International Symposium on Multimedia Software Engineering, 2004, December 13-15, pp. 329–336 (2004)
6. Schmidt, T.: Transcribing and annotating spoken language with EXMARaLDA.
   In: Proceedings of the LREC-Workshop on XML Based Richly Annotated Corpora,
   Lisbon. ELRA, Paris (2004)

7. Allwood, J., Cerrato, L., Dybkjaer, L., et al.: The MUMIN Multimodal Coding Scheme. NorFA yearbook (2005)
8. Schrder, M., Pirker, H., Lamolle, M.: First suggestions for an emotion annotation and representation language. In: Proceedings of LREC 2006 Workshop on Corpora for Research on Emotion and Affect, Genoa, Italy, pp. 88–92 (2006)
9. Paolo, B., et al.: Emotion Markup Language (EmotionML) 1.0 - W3C Working Draft (October 29, 2009),
   http://www.w3.org/TR/2009/WD-emotionml-20091029/
10. Kopp, S., Krenn, B., Marsella, S.C., Marshall, A.N., Pelachaud, C., Pirker, H., Thórisson, K.R., Vilhjálmsson, H.H.: Towards a Common Framework for Multimodal Generation: The Behavior Markup Language. In: Gratch, J., Young, M., Aylett, R.S., Ballin, D., Olivier, P. (eds.) IVA 2006. LNCS (LNAI), vol. 4133, pp. 205–217. Springer, Heidelberg (2006)
11. Bunt, H., et al.: Towards an ISO Standard for Dialogue Act Annotation'. In: Proceedings of the Seventh conference on International Language Resources and Evaluation, LREC 2010 (2010)
12. Antoniou, V.H.: A Semantic Web Primer. MIT Press, Cambridge (2004)
13. Grassi, M.: Developing HEO Human Emotion Ontology. In: Fierrez, J., Ortega-Garcia, J., Esposito, A., Drygajlo, A., Faundez-Zanuy, M. (eds.) BioID MultiComm 2009. LNCS, vol. 5707, pp. 244–251. Springer, Heidelberg (2009),
   http://www.semedia.dibet.univpm.it/heo
14. Cambria, E., Hussain, A., Havasi, C., Eckl, C.: Sentic Computing: Exploitation of Common Sense for the Development of Emotion-Sensitive Systems. In: Esposito, A., Campbell, N., Vogel, C., Hussain, A., Nijholt, A. (eds.) COST 2102. LNCS, vol. 5967, pp. 148–156. Springer, Heidelberg (2010),
   http://cs.stir.ac.uk/~eca/sentics
15. Simile Exhibit API, http://simile-widgets.org/exhibit
16. Petridis, K., Anastasopoulos, D., Saathoff, C., Timmermann, N., Kompatsiaris, Y., Staab, S.: M-ontoMat-annotizer: Image annotation linking ontologies and multimedia low-level features. In: Gabrys, B., Howlett, R.J., Jain, L.C. (eds.) KES 2006. LNCS (LNAI), vol. 4253, pp. 633–640. Springer, Heidelberg (2006)
17. Video Image Annotiation (VIA), Informatics and Telematics Insitute (CERTH-ITI),
   http://mklab.iti.gr/via/
18. SVAT Semantic Video Annotation Tool by JOANNEUM RESEARCH,
   http://www.joanneum.at/en/fb2.html
19. Project Pad by Northwestern University,
   http://dewey.at.northwestern.edu/ppad2/index.html
20. Van Deursen, D., et al.: XML to RDF conversion: a generic approach. In: 4th International Conference on Automated Solutions for Cross Media Content and Multi-Channel Distribution (2008)

The Effect of Subharmonic Stimuli on Singing Voices

Marena Balinova[1], Peter Reichl[1,2], Inma Hernáez Rioja[2,3], and Ibon Saratxaga[3]

[1] University of Applied Sciences Technikum Wien,
Höchstädtplatz 5, A-1200 Vienna, Austria
[2] FTW Telecommunications Research Center Vienna,
Donaucitystr. 1, A-1220 Vienna, Austria
[3] AHOLAB, University of the Basque Country,
Alda. Urquijo, s/n, E-48013 Bilbao, Spain
balinova@technikum-wien.at,
{inma.hernaez,ibon.saratxaga}@ehu.es, reichl@ftw.at

Abstract. Unlike harmonics, which play a central role in the spectral analysis of voice signals, the equivalent concept of subharmonics is traditionally considered to be a rather theoretical one. In this paper, we introduce an approach for using them as stimuli in the context of voice teaching for opera singers. Starting from the observation that faulty vocal technique may be perceived by specifically trained listeners as lack of certain subharmonics in the vocal structure, we are interested in adaptation phenomena on the singer's side which are triggered by playing low notes (potentially corresponding to those subharmonics) on a piano immediately prior to the execution of certain musical phrases. As a first step, we report on some initial experiments on the impact of such stimuli on the observed harmonic spectrum, and thus explore how such a novel voice formation approach could benefit from adequate signal processing support.

Keywords: Singing voice, harmonic spectrum, subharmonics, voice teaching.

1 Introduction

Undisputedly, using the human voice as an efficient instrument for verbal communication in front of large audiences highly benefits from a solid technical foundation. Achieving a conscious and sensible mastery of the individual vocal material in a stable and controlled manner often needs years of intensive training and formation, as is perhaps most evident in the fields of music and theatre. Practical experience with voice teaching, on the other hand, usually boils down to a somewhat enigmatic process where the teacher tries to improve the vocal quality of the student using a broad spectrum of approaches, ranging from complex physical exercises over pictorial descriptions to simply mimicking examples of more or less correct vocal technique. Thus, vocal formation tends to stay at an associative and abstract level, and moreover is highly dependent on a successfully working relationship between teacher and student. Hence, to develop a method of voice teaching which is based on facts rather than association, and as such is also accessible to scientific evaluation, may safely be considered quite a challenge.

A. Esposito et al. (Eds.): COST 2102 Int. Training School 2010, LNCS 6456, pp. 317–323, 2011.

In our work, we aim at contributing to this task by addressing the effects of external triggers on perceived vocal quality. We are focussing on the singing voice for different reasons. First of all, it realizes the potential of the human vocal apparatus most comprehensively. Vocal faults are more obvious and more easily to detect than with the speaking voice, while their correction requires a precise technical approach. Last not least, the consequences of erroneous voice technique are immediate and potentially fatal, up to threatening the careers of even highly celebrated singers.

In this paper, we address the potential of "subharmonic stimuli" (provided as very low tones played on a piano) for changing and correcting wrongly produced vocal sounds, and aim at providing initial evidence for their impact on the harmonic spectrum, as a first step towards a more objective perception of vocal quality. The remainder of the paper is structured as follows: In section 2, we discuss related work on harmonics and subharmonics, especially from the perspective of professional opera singers. Section 3 describes our approach for determining the potential impact of subharmonics in voice teaching, and presents and discusses initial experimental results. Section 4 concludes the paper with a brief summary and outlook.

2   The Relationship between Subharmonics and Voice Quality from the Point of View of Opera Singers and Voice Coaches

Whereas the idea of using subharmonic triggers in a voice teaching context is new and original, and to the best of our knowledge has not yet been mentioned even in the pedagogical literature, the concept of subharmonics itself is well-known, however mostly considered as a theoretical one. In general, subharmonics are defined as frequencies which are unit fractions of a fundamental frequency f_0 (i.e. $f_{1/n} = f_0/n$), pretty much in the same way in which harmonics are defined as multiples of f_0 (i.e. $f_n = n \cdot f_0$). Based on mathematical methods like, e.g., Fourier transforms, harmonics have since a long time played an essential role in characterizing sound spectra both in speech and music. To this end, usually a sinusoidal model is applied, assuming that a signal is purely periodic and can thus be treated as a linear combination of weighted cosine functions, whose frequencies are multiples of the fundamental frequency f_0, while their phase shifts can be arbitrary. If the power spectrum of sounds contains significant energy around these harmonics (which is especially the case for musical sounds), they are also perceivable directly by the listener, most clearly for instance in the case of so-called overtone singers who have developed special vocal techniques to produce sounds which are dominated by certain specific harmonics.

However, in reality the sound perception abilities of the human auditory system are much more sophisticated and complex. For instance, the phenomenon of difference tones (Tartini tones), i.e. phantom pitches whose frequency corresponds to the frequency difference between two tones actually played at the same time, has been discovered by violinists already in the 18th century, see e.g. Mozart [1] for details. Houtsma and Goldstein [2] have provided extensive experimental evidence for the ability of identifying missing fundamentals which correspond to two concurrently perceived harmonics, up to harmonics of orders around 10. Terhard's [3] investigation of more complex sounds has led to the concept of a virtual pitch which is extracted by the human ear from a sound or a group of sounds, without being part of the corresponding Fourier spectrum. Finally, Schneider et al. [4] have as well investigated the perception of complex sounds, but from a neurological point of view. They argue that human listeners in general can be divided into two classes, i.e. fundamental hearers (determining the pitch from the fundamental frequency) and overtone hearers (determining the pitch from an immanent overtone analysis).

We mention these few examples of related work in order to support our claim that the human auditory system, especially if trained appropriately, is able to process also very complex sound spectra by reducing them to the perception/extraction of one (or maybe a few) basic frequencies which may or may not be represented in the energy distribution of the frequency spectrum. Therefore, we do not follow Hindemith's assertion [5] that assuming the physical existence of subharmonics is more or less absurd, representing purely theoretical constructs which may merely serve as a framework for analyzing fundamental harmonic structures in musical composition. Instead, during our discussions with professional opera singers and voice coaches, we have came across a much more concrete perception (and application) of the concepts of subharmonics in the context of correct vs. faulty voice technique. In the rest of this section, we would like to briefly introduce this somewhat unusual perspective.

Without going too much into details, singers describe their experience while producing a correct sound as being without limitations, pain, or shortage of breath. The vocal tract is perceived as an instrument which is able to modulate the tone, change dynamics from piano to forte and v.v., and simply make music in a comfortable and agreeable manner. The tone is perceived to be centred in the body. In contrast, if a tone is out of balance, it becomes shrill, sharp or low-pitched, stiff, without resonance, too much in the back or in the front, metallic or dull. In these cases, the tone is perceived as "positionally sharp" or "positionally low", respectively (even if the physical pitch is correct!), and the singer can hardly embark anything upon it.

It is now interesting to observe that singers and/or experienced listeners sometimes refer to the perceptional difference between correct and faulty vocal sounds in terms of wrong or lacking subharmonics. For example, a "positionally sharp" sound is described as too less anchored in the body, equivalent to employing a wrong subharmonic which is too high and thus causes a wrong spectrum of harmonics. Dull tones, on the other hand, are attributed to subharmonics which are too low. If a tone is described as too broad, this is alleged to the parallel perception of two or three subharmonics, while tones based on more than two subharmonics are described as static and causing specific limitations for the singer's voice (breaking tones, lack of legato, no dynamic evolution, sometimes even pain). As a reaction, the singer tends to forcefully push the tone (away from the wrong subharmonic as perceived by the "inner ear" of the singer and/or her body kinesthetics), leading to further vocal difficulties.

Based on these observations, in our work we aim at a more precise description of the laws between perceived vocal quality and corresponding subharmonics, and explore the potential support coming from signal processing analysis. As a first step, in this paper we report on some experiments which aim at demonstrating that subharmonic stimuli have an impact on the harmonic spectrum of a singing voice at all. Based on that, later on we will aim at correlating these effects to the presence of flaws in the vocal technique, thus allowing the identification of "good" and "bad" stimuli and finally their systematic usage for improving the quality of singing voices.

3   Experiments and Initial Results

3.1   Trial Setup and Signal Processing Analysis

We have started our experiments with focus on a specific problem of the tenor voice, the so-called passage ("passaggio") between the middle and the top register. Without going too much into detail, tenors handle the so-called middle register up to d' or e' very differently from the top register starting around f', where larynx and tongue are placed into a low position and the soft palate/velum is lifted up (like with yawning). It is generally agreed that the solution of this passaggio problem is fundamental for any tenor, and there are many examples of singers who did not pay sufficient attention to it and consequently experienced considerable vocal damage (Giuseppe di Stefano being just a particularly well-known and tragic one among many cases).

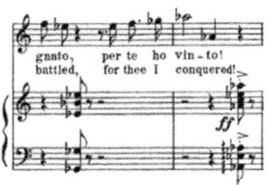 

Fig. 1. Sample phrases: Aida, Aria Radames (left) vs Trovatore, Stretta Manrico (right)

Our trials have been set up as follows: after some general warm-up exercises, an advanced voice student has been asked to sing one of the benchmark phrases depicted in Fig. 1, which have been taken from two Verdi operas and represent typical examples for the passaggio problem sketched above. Then, a voice coach plays some (arbitrary) low tone (subharmonic) on the piano, usually in the Contra register. The student listens carefully, and repeats the phrase as soon as the piano has become silent. This procedure is repeated several times, each time a different low note is played on the piano, and each time the student repeats the phrase once.

The entire experiment is recorded with a portable digital stereo recording device (Zoom H2, 120° cardioid) in standard CD quality (44.1kHz, 16bit linear PCM), with the microphone placed at a constant distance of 20cm in front of the student's face, in order to reduce reverberation effects (unfortunately, during the experiments no anechoic chamber with a piano in it has been available). For reasons of algorithmic complexity, later the signals were downsampled to 16kHz.

While, as sketched in the related work section, it is very well possible for a trained ear to identify subharmonics (or at least lack of them), by definition those cannot be detected in the spectrum of a vocal sound, not even by sophisticated signal processing algorithms. Therefore, we have to develop an indirect approach, starting from what is accessible to signal processing algorithms.

Traditionally, harmonic models have been used for the analysis of the singing voices (see for example [6]), while vibrato issues have been addressed by other approaches [7]. However we have chosen the harmonic model because it provides general information about the partials without making any additional assumption on the produced vibrato.

For our purposes, we have adopted a standard sinusoidal model for calculating the harmonics spectrum. The estimation of the amplitudes is based on the method described in [8]. The analysis is performed in a pitch-asynchronous way, using a window length of at least three pitch periods. The fundamental frequency is calculated with a cepstrum-based pitch determination algorithm [9], followed by a pitch refinement algorithm to improve precision. This refinement calculates an interpolated value in the spectrum, in the surroundings of the initial pitch estimate. Further details on the algorithms are described in [10]. Note that the amplitudes of each harmonic are estimated with fixed frame rate. For our experiments, we have chosen a rate to provide around 4 estimates every period. As we focus on fundamental frequencies of 400–500 Hz (i.e. periods of around 2.0–2.5 ms) the final chosen frame length has been 0.25 ms.

The analyzed signals have durations of 1–2 sec, showing vibrato at different degrees. After carefully evaluating several alternatives for a compact data representation which allows to compare the different available samples, we have chosen a boxplot representation of the data distribution (including the median value of the data at the centre of the box, and the 25th and 75th percentiles at the lower and upper ends) for the first twelve relative harmonic amplitudes, normalized with respect to the amplitude of the fundamental frequency f_0.

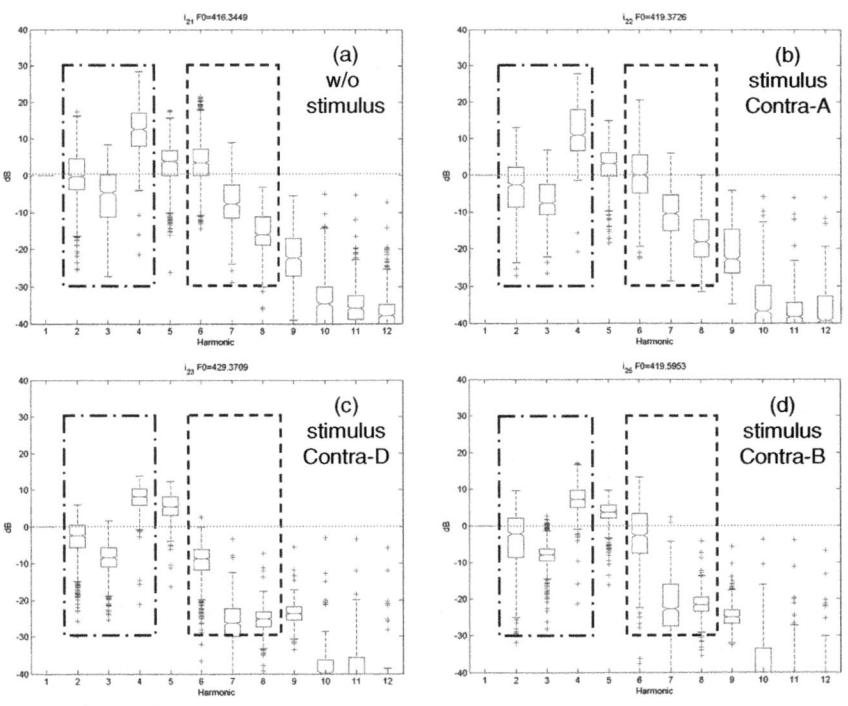

Fig. 2. Box plots vowel /i/ (Aida), student's versions (a) – (d)

3.2   Example Results

Figure 2 depicts four harmonic fingerprints of a typical trial series for the "Aida" phrase, without stimulus (a) and with stimuli as indicated, (b)–(d). For better comparison, the 2nd–4th and the 6th–8th harmonics have been framed in blue, while the green dotted line refers to the null line. We observe that stimuli may have very different effects, ranging from almost no difference between (a) and (b) to rather different levels if compared to (c) or (d), which are most significant around the 7th harmonic, i.e. roughly corresponding to the so-called singer's formant (around 2.8 kHz for tenor voices). Note that an additional expert evaluation has determined pronounced differences between the samples from the perspective of a voice coach: (b) is judged as technically correct, whereas (a), (c) and (d) represent cases of technical deficiencies.

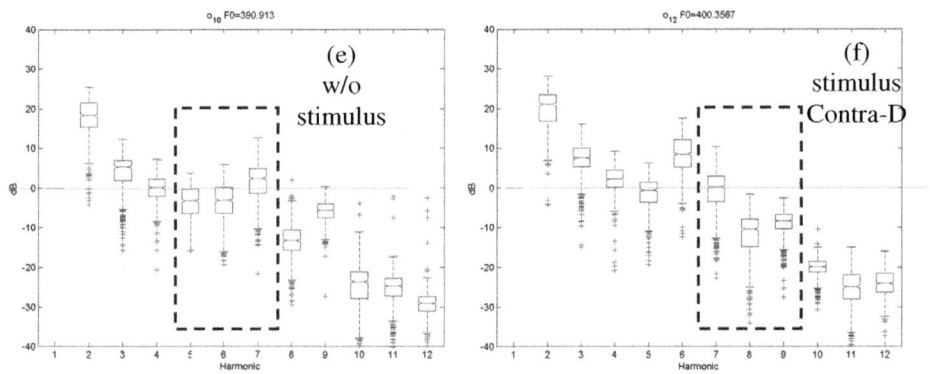

Fig. 3. Box plots vowel /o/ (Trovatore), student's versions (e) – (f)

Fig. 3 depicts two further examples for the "Trovatore" phrase, where (f) corresponds to a stimulus which has been found to lead to technical improvement. In general, for /o/ the spectral changes are less obvious than for /i/, but again around the singer's formant, the stimulus triggers significant deviations (cf. 6th and 7th harmonic).

3.3   Discussion

From our trial results (which are part of a much more comprehensive body of data), we may first of all conclude that external stimuli are indeed able to trigger significant changes in the composition of a voice sound. This is confirmed both by subjective expert analysis, where different degrees of the singer's technical correctness are perceived, and on a signal processing level, where, depending on the vowel, statistically significant deviations can be observed, e.g. close to the singer's formant. From our discussions with the singers it is apparent that they perceive an adaptation of the vocal tract as main cause, such that a sort of resonance space for the stimulus frequency is created. On the other hand, from a vocal coach perspective, vocal faults can be related to lacking subharmonics, which, used as stimuli, lead to improved results. Putting these things together opens the door for a rather new voice teaching approach as soon as the question of the precise correlation between stimulus and result has been solved.

4 Summary and Conclusions

As main original contribution, this paper discusses a novel voice teaching concept which employs subharmonics for the correction of faulty voice technique, and explores how to support this approach from a signal processing point of view. To this end, based on a series of experimental trials, initial evidence on the impact of external stimuli (in the form of low notes played on a piano) on the spectral envelope is presented, and the relationship with a subjective vocal coach perspective is described.

We are fully aware of the fact that the presented material may serve only as starting point for a much broader investigation of this idea. Important issues like the determination of the true envelope (as discussed e.g. by Wolfe or Henrich) as well as the corresponding mapping towards articulation has been deliberately considered out of scope of this work. In addition, current and future work focuses on a broad systematic analysis of the impact of subharmonics on voice tone production, for instance by exploring the behaviour of additional parameters such as the phases of the harmonics. Altogether, this will provide the prerequisites for identifying "good" stimuli and, more generally, determining potential laws behind subharmonic stimulation, which, together with the proper support from corresponding signal processing tools, eventually will allow making this new voice teaching approach generally accessible.

Acknowledgements

Part of this research has been funded by the Austrian Government and the City of Vienna within the COMET program. Additional support from the European COST Action 2102 and from Télécom Bretagne Rennes, France, is gratefully acknowledged.

References

1. Mozart, L.: Versuch einer gründlichen Violinschule (A Treatise on the Fundamental Principles of Violin Playing), 8. Hauptstück, 3. Abschnitt, §20. Augsburg (1756)
2. Houtsma, A., Goldstein, J.: Perception of Musical Intervals: Evidence for the Central Origin of the Pitch of Complex Tones. Technical report, MIT Lab of Electronics (1971)
3. Terhard, E.: Pitch, Consonance, and Harmony. J. Acoustical. Soc. of America 55(5), 1061–1066 (1974)
4. Schneider, P., Sluming, V., et al.: Structural and Functional Asymmetry of Lateral Heschl's Gyrus Reflects Pitch Perception Preference. Nature Neuroscience 8, 1241–1247 (2005)
5. Hindemith, P.: Unterweisung im Tonsatz (The Craft of Musical Composition), Schott, Mainz (1937)
6. Serra, X.: Musical Sound Modelling with Sinusoids Plus Noise. In: Roads, C., et al. (eds.) Musical Signal Processing Swets & Zeitlinger, Lisse, The Netherlands (1997)
7. Arroabarrena, I., Carlossena, A.: Vibrato in Singing voice: The Link between Source-Filter and Sinusoidal Models. EURASIP J. Appl. Sign. Proc. 7, 1007–1020 (2004)
8. Griffin, D., Lim, J.: Multiband Excitation Vocoder. IEEE Trans. Acoust., Speech, Signal Processing 36, 1223–1235 (1988)
9. Luengo, I., Saratxaga, I., et al.: Evaluation of pitch detection algorithms under real conditions. In: IEEE ICASSP 2007, pp. 1057–1060 (2007)
10. Saratxaga, I., Hernáez, I., et al.: AhoTransf: A tool for Multiband Excitation based speech analysis and modification. In: LREC 2010, Malta (2010)

Speech Modeling Using the Complex Cepstrum

Martin Vondra and Robert Vích

Institute of Photonics and Electronics, Academy of Sciences of the Czech Republic
Chaberska 57, CZ 18251 Prague 8, Czech Republic
{vondra,vich}@ufe.cz

Abstract. Conventional cepstral speech modeling is based on the minimum phase parametric speech production model with infinite impulse response. In that approach only the logarithmic magnitude frequency response of the corresponding speech frame is approximated. In this contribution the principle of the cepstral speech modeling using the complex cepstrum is described. The obtained mixed-phase vocal tract model with finite impulse response contains also the information about the phase properties of the modeled speech frame. This model approximates the speech signal with higher accuracy than the model based on the real cepstrum, the numerical complexity and the memory requirements are at least twice greater.

1 Introduction

Parametric speech modeling is again in the centre of attention particularly in the context with statistical parametric speech synthesis realized e.g. by hidden Markov models [1]. The main issue is the quality of the speech reconstruction from the speech parameters. Reconstructed or vocoded speech suffers especially from a buzzy sounding effect. This is given particularly in the case of voiced sounds by a simple periodic impulse train excitation of the vocal tract model, which is mostly a minimum phase system [2]. Such systems are characterized by having maximum energy at the beginning of the impulse response, which together with an impulse train excitation causes buzzy sounding speech. This can be reduced by the residual signal excitation, which can be obtained by inverse filtering [3]. However this requires more computational power and also coding of the residual signal.

Another approach to suppress the buzzy sounding of vocoded speech can be achieved by mixed phase synthesis, which is based on complex cepstrum [4]. A similar approach is described in this paper, but we use different speech segmentation and windowing, which is inspired by the new observation in the complex cepstrum speech deconvolution [5]. The vocal tract model is based on the windowed complex cepstrum of the original speech. The complex cepstrum contains information (besides the logarithmic spectrum magnitude) also about the phase properties of the speech signal, which is mostly not a minimum-phase signal. The complex cepstrum also allows the decompositions of the speech signal into the minimum- and maximum-phase parts, which can be useful for voice or emotion transformation.

The principle of speech modeling using the complex cepstrum will be described using a speech vocoder based on the complex cepstrum. The individual components of the vocoder will be explained step by step and finally the speech reconstructed using the complex and the real cepstrum will be compared.

A. Esposito et al. (Eds.): COST 2102 Int. Training School 2010, LNCS 6456, pp. 324–330, 2011.
© Springer-Verlag Berlin Heidelberg 2011

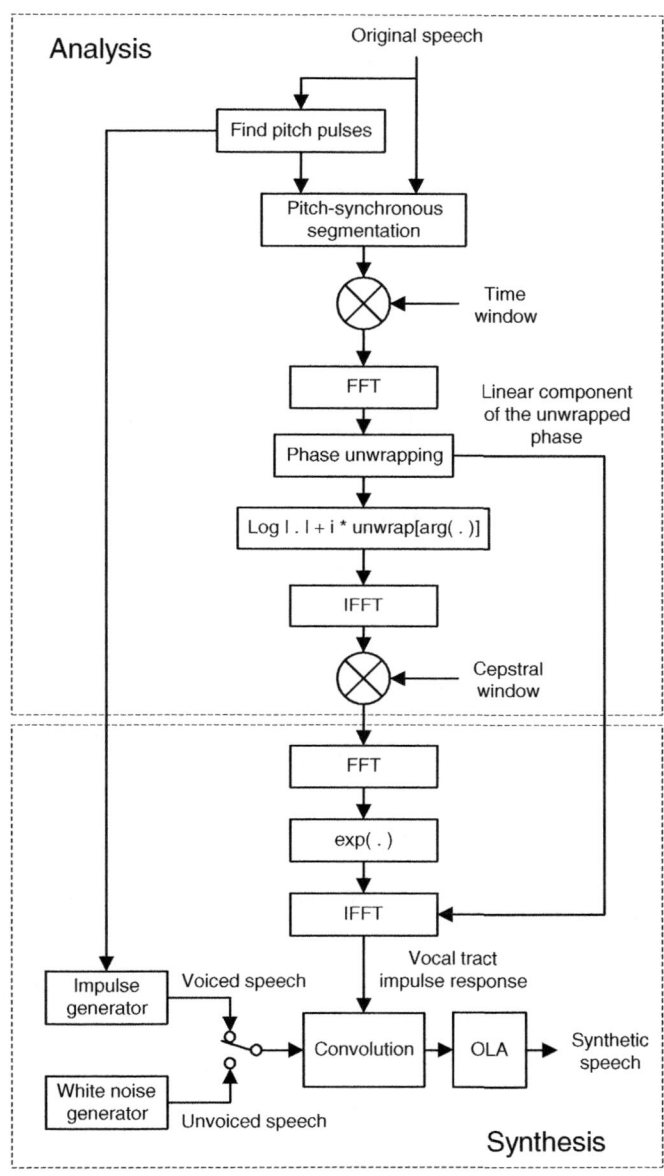

Fig. 1. Speech vocoder based on the complex cepstrum

2   Speech Vocoder Based on the Complex Cepstrum

The term vocoder originated from words voice and coder. A vocoder consists of two main blocks – analysis and synthesis (Fig. 1). The analysis block converts speech into a set of parameters and the synthesis part reconstructs speech from these parameters.

The vocoder is used e.g. in mobile phones to suppress the redundancy of the speech signal.

2.1 Segmentation

For complex cepstral speech analysis we use pitch synchronous segmentation which has to be preceded by pitch pulses localization (glottal closure instants). One frame consists of two pitch periods where the pitch pulse is in the middle of the frame. Frame shift is set to one pitch period. Then a weighting window is applied on the frame. The type of the weighting window has an impact on the spectrum and also on the cepstrum of the speech frame. The widely used Hamming window is in this case not suitable, because it does not suppress the periodicity of the frame completely and for this reason the spectrum of the frame is harmonic and the cepstrum also contains periodic peaks. A better choice is the Hann or Blackman window. Some information about appropriate time windows for cepstrum analysis can be found in [5].

2.2 Complex Spectrum Speech Analysis

Let s_n be the windowed speech frame of the length N, sampled with the sampling frequency F_S. The corresponding complex cepstrum $\hat{s}_n$ is a two sided real, in general asymmetric sequence, which can be estimated using the fast Fourier transform (FFT). In this case we obtain a time aliased version of the complex cepstrum, but using a sufficient high dimension of the FFT, $M > N$, the aliasing can be reduced.

$$\hat{s}_n = \frac{1}{M} \sum_{k=0}^{M-1} \hat{S}_k e^{j2\pi kn/M} \quad , \quad \hat{S}_k = \ln S_k = \ln|S_k| + j \arg S_k , \quad S_k = \sum_{n=0}^{M-1} s_n e^{-j2\pi kn/M} \qquad (1)$$

The sequence S_k is the complex spectrum of the speech frame. The imaginary part of the logarithmic spectrum $\hat{S}_k$, i.e. $\arg S_k$, is the unwrapped phase sequence [6,7]. The linear component from the phase unwrapping is an important parameter for the synthesis part of the vocoder. The part of the complex cepstrum $\hat{s}_n$ for $0 \leq n$ will be called causal cepstrum, the part of $\hat{s}_n$ for $n < 0$ anticipative cepstrum.

As an example of the cepstral speech analysis we use the stationary part of the vowel a. The sampling frequency is 8 kHz, the fundamental frequency 118 Hz, the pitch synchronously windowed speech frame is equal to two fundamental periods in the case of a voiced signal and the dimension of the FFT $M = 1024$. In the example the Blackman window centered on the glottal closure instant is used. The signal, the window, the magnitude and phase spectra and the complex cepstrum are shown in Fig 2.

Separation of the complex cepstrum into the causal and anticipative parts can be also used for speech decompositions into the minimum- and maximum-phase speech components, see Fig. 3. According to [5] the maximum-phase speech component can be considered as the glottal pulse, which can be useful in voice modification (voice or emotion conversion).

For the following comparison of speech reconstructions from the real and complex cepstra let us introduce the real cepstrum. The real cepstrum can be computed similarly to (1) with the difference that we use only the logarithm of the speech spectrum magnitude

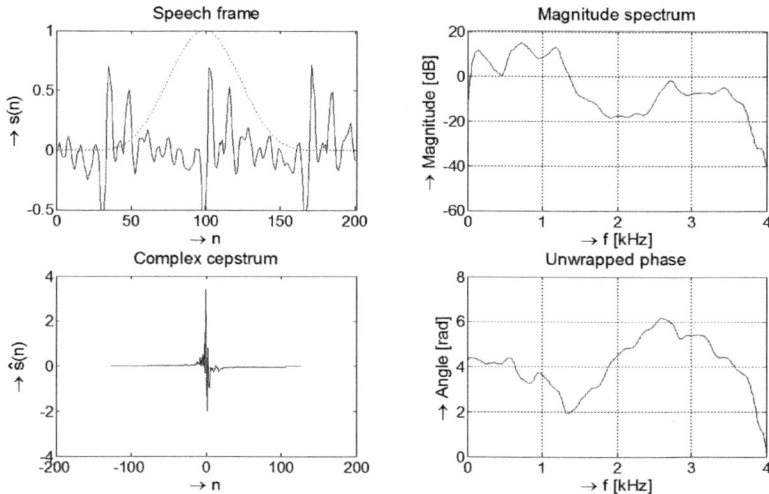

Fig. 2. Signal, spectra and complex cepstrum of the stationary part of the vowel *a*

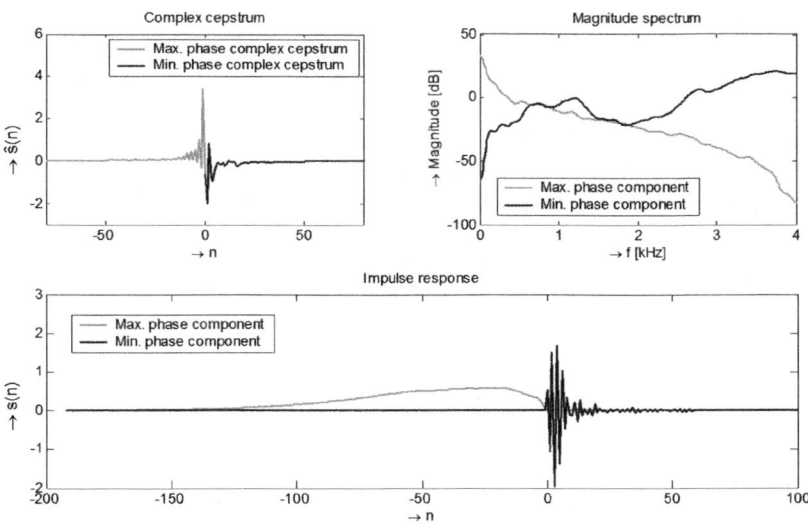

Fig. 3. Complex cepstrum decomposition into maximum- and minimum-phase speech components

$$c_n = \frac{1}{M} \sum_{k=0}^{M-1} \ln|S_k| e^{j2\pi kn/M} \ . \tag{2}$$

The phase is omitted in the real cepstrum computation. The real cepstrum can be also computed from the complex cepstrum by the formula

$$c_n = \frac{\hat{s}_n + \hat{s}_{-n}}{2}, \qquad n > 0, \qquad c_0 = \hat{s}_0 \ . \tag{3}$$

The real cepstrum is also a two sided, but symmetrical sequence. The comparison of the real and complex cepstra is shown in Fig. 4.

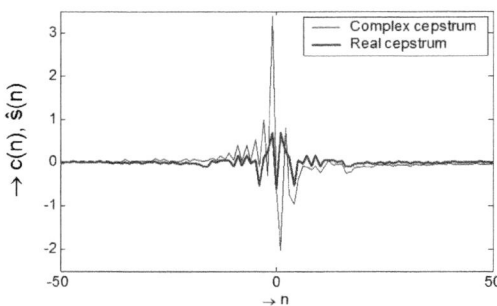

Fig. 4. Real and complex cepstra of the stationary part of vowel *a*

2.3 Vocal Tract Model

The vocal tract model is designed as a finite impulse response (FIR) filter and realizes the convolution of the excitation and the impulse response, which is computed as the inverse cepstral transformation of the windowed complex cepstrum into the time domain. The used cepstral window is rectangular and selects only relevant cepstral coefficients near $n = 0$. These cepstral coefficients correspond to slow changes in the spectrum magnitude – the fast changes can be caused by the fundamental frequency or by other disturbance. The length of the cepstral window must be chosen with regard to the accuracy of the vocal tract model and the sampling frequency. For $F_S = 16$ kHz we use a cepstral window of the length 100, which is centered on $n = 0$. The comparison of the vocal tract impulse responses computed by inverse cepstral transformation of the windowed complex and real cepstra is shown in Fig. 5.

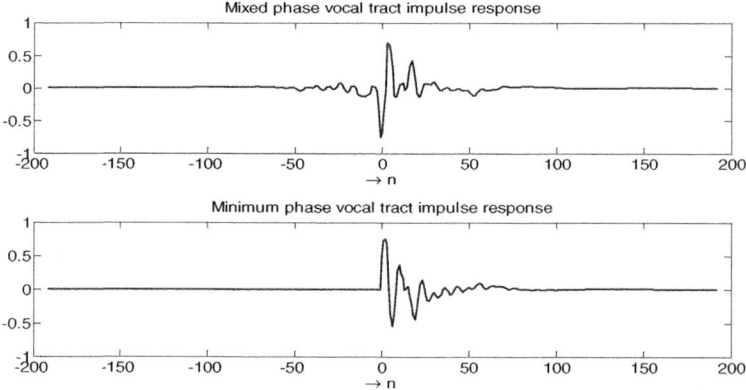

Fig. 5. Impulse responses of the vocal tract models computed from complex and real cepstra

2.4 Speech Synthesis

Speech is synthesized by a parametric model. Voiced speech is generated by excitation of the vocal tract model by the Dirac impulse. Unvoiced speech is generated by excitation of the vocal tract by a white noise generator. Because the convolution of the Dirac impulse and the impulse response of the vocal tract model is trivial, the convolution for voiced speech can be omitted. After the convolution we must use the overlap and add algorithm to fold up the resulting speech, because the analysis segmentation is realized also with overlapping.

It is important to use in the inverse cepstral transformation the linear component from the phase unwrapping, which can be also interpreted as a signal delay. If we omit this term, the successive impulse responses can have different time shifts, which results in rough quality of the synthetic speech. The comparison of the original and vocoded speech from real and complex cepstra is shown in Fig. 6. From this figure it can be seen that the speech signal reconstruction based on the complex cepstrum preserves the shape of the original speech signal. The speech reconstructed from the complex cepstrum has also much higher perceptual audio quality than the resynthesis from the real cepstrum, which sounds a little buzzy.

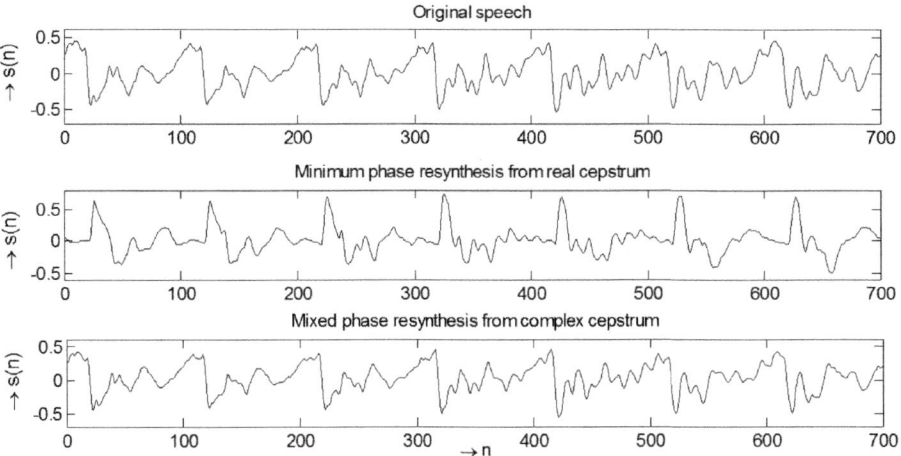

Fig. 6. Original speech and minimum and mixed phase synthesis

3 Conclusion

The main part of speech modeling using the complex cepstrum is the vocal tract model, which is an FIR filter the impulse response of which is computed from the windowed complex cepstrum. The construction of the mixed phase FIR vocal tract model based on the complex cepstrum is straightforward and results in more natural speech synthesis than the minimum-phase approach. This results from the fact that also the information of the phase properties of the modeled speech frame is respected, or in other words that the true spectral properties of the glottal signal are incorporated into the modeling approach. The memory requirements and the numerical complexity are in consequence of the calculation and application of the complex cepstrum at least twice higher than for the real cepstrum.

Acknowledgment

This paper has been supported within the framework of COST2102 by the Ministry of Education, Youth and Sports of the Czech Republic, project number OC08010.

References

1. Zen, H., Tokuda, K., Black, A.W.: Statistical Parametric Speech Synthesis. Speech Communication 51, 1039–1064 (2009)
2. Vích, R.: Cepstral Speech Model, Padé Approximation, Excitation and Gain Matching in Cepstral Speech Synthesis. In: Jan, J. (ed.) BIOSIGNAL 2000, pp. 77–82. VUTIUM, Brno (2000)
3. Drugman, T., Moinet, A., Dutoit, T., Wilfart, G.: Using a Pitch-Synchronous Residual Codebook for Hybrid HMM/Frame Selection Speech Synthesis. In: IEEE ICASSP, Taipei, Taiwan, pp. 3793–3796 (2009)
4. Quatieri, T.F.: Discrete-Time Speech Signal Processing, pp. 253–308. Prentice-Hall, Englewood Cliffs (2002)
5. Drugman, T., Bozkurt, B.T., Dutoit, T.: Complex Cepstrum-based Decomposition of Speech for Glottal Source Estimation. In: Interspeech 2009, Brighton, U.K, pp. 116–119 (2009)
6. Oppenheim, A.V., Schafer, R.W.: Discrete-Time Signal Processing, pp. 768–825. Prentice-Hall, Englewood Cliffs (1989)
7. Vích, R.: Z-transform Theory and Application, pp. 207–216. D. Reidel Publ. Comp., Dordrecht (1987)

Problems of the Automatic Emotion Recognitions in Spontaneous Speech; An Example for the Recognition in a Dispatcher Center

Klára Vicsi and Dávid Sztahó

Laboratory of Speech Acoustics, Budapest University of Technology and Economics,
Department of Telecommunication and Media Informatics,
Stoczek u. 2, 1111 Budapest, Hungary
{vicsi,sztaho}@tmit.bme.hu

Abstract. Numerous difficulties, in the examination of emotions occurring in continuous spontaneous speech, are discussed in this paper, than different emotion recognition experiments are presented, using clauses as the recognition unit. In a testing experiment it was examined that what kind of acoustical features are the most important for the characterization of emotions, using spontaneous speech database. An SVM classifier was built for the classification of 4 most frequent emotions. It was found that fundamental frequency, energy, and its dynamics in a clause are the main characteristic parameters for the emotions, and the average spectral information, as MFCC and harmonicity are also very important. In a real life experiment automatic recognition system was prepared for a telecommunication call center. Summing up the results of these experiments, we can say, that clauses can be an optimal unit of the recognition of emotions in continuous speech.

Keywords: speech emotion recognition, telephone speech, prosodic recognizer, speech emotion database.

1 Introduction

Two channels have been distinguished in human speech interaction. One conveys messages with a specific semantic content (verbal channel); the other (the non-verbal channel) conveys information related to both the image content of a message and to the general feeling and emotional state of the speaker [1]. Enormous efforts have been made in the past to understand the verbal channel, whereas the role of the non-verbal channel is less well understood.

People show affect in many ways in speech, changes in speaking style, tone-of-voice, and intonation are commonly used to express personal feelings, emotions often at the same time as imparting information.

Research on various aspects of paralinguistic and extra linguistic speech has gained considerable importance in recent years.

There are results about emotion characterization in speech and emotional recognition in the literature, but those results were obtained in clear lab speech [2, 3, 4, 5]. Most of

A. Esposito et al. (Eds.): COST 2102 Int. Training School 2010, LNCS 6456, pp. 331–339, 2011.
© Springer-Verlag Berlin Heidelberg 2011

them usually used simulated emotional speech, more frequently produced by artists. On the bases of these imitated databases researchers could find answers to many scientific questions in connection with the perception of the emotional information [7].

But the real word data differ much from acted speech, and in the application of speech technology, real word data processing is necessary. In the last years some works were published dealing with examination [8] and recognition [9] of emotion in spontaneous everyday conversations.

The other big problem of the emotion research is the categorization of the emotion itself.

Group of emotional categorization is the one commonly used in psychology, linguistics and speech technology, also described in the MPEG-4 standard [6]: happiness, sadness, anger, surprise, and scorn/disgust.

The emotions in MPEG-4 standard were originally created to describe facial animation parameters (FAPs) of virtual characters. But these 5 emotion categories do not mask the emotions in the spontaneous speech, and generally the type and frequency of usage of emotions is different in different selection of real world data.

This paper describes an emotion recognition experiment on a corpus of spontaneous everyday conversations between telephone dispatchers and customers, through telephone line. The acoustical pre-processing was prepared on the base of our former experiment on acted speech [10].

Not only the acoustical parameters of emotions were examined and classified, but word and word connection statistics of different emotional text is planned to prepare on the base of the corpus, as well.

2   System Description

During a speech conversation, especially if it is a long one, the speaker's emotional states are changing. If we want to follow the states of the speakers we have to divide the continuous speech flow into segments, and thus we can examine how the emotional state of a speaker change segment by segment through the conversation. The clause was selected as a segmentation unit in our system, on the base of the experiences of our earlier study [10].

The segmentation of the clause sized units was done by our prosodic segmenter [11]. (This segmenter was developed for semantic processing of input speech in ASR, which is used to perform clause and sentence boundary detection and modality (sentence type) recognition. The classification is carried out by HMMs, which model the prosodic contour for each clause and/or sentence modality type. Clause (and hence also sentence) boundary detection is based on HMM's excellent capacity in aligning dynamically the reference prosodic structure to the utterance coming from ASR input. The method also allows placing punctuation marks automatically.)

After the acoustic pre-processing these clause-sized segments were classified according to its emotional content, using support vector machine (SVM) classifier. The block diagram of our system is presented in Fig. 1.

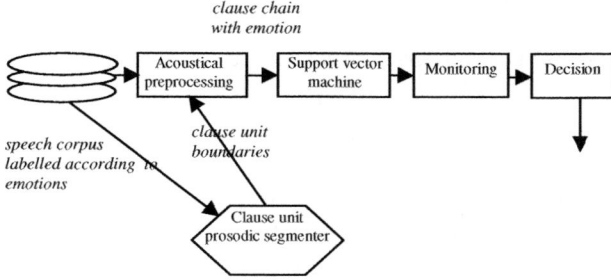

Fig. 1. Recognition system of our speech emotion classifier

In the beginning four different emotional states were differentiated in the recorded dialogues: neutral (N), nervous (I), querulous (P), and others (E). In the later experiments these emotions were grouped. Then the classified clauses were monitored through a time window, much longer than the clause's duration, to give a more certain decision about the speaker's emotional states.

2.1 Acoustical Pre-processing

In general, fundamental frequency and intensity time courses were the most commonly used features for the expression of emotions, both in the field of speech recognition and synthesis. In our earlier automatic emotion recognition experiments, it was found, that adding spectral information greatly improves the recognition results [10]. Accordingly, the fundamental frequencies (F_{0i}), the intensity values (E_i), 12 MFCC and their deltas were measured, using 150 ms time window, in 10 ms time frames, all together 28 feature vectors in every 10 ms. Then the clause unit prosodic segmenter marks the boundaries of clauses in the speech, resulting clause unit chain. On the base of the feature vectors in every 10 ms, statistical data were calculated characterizing each clause unit by multidimensional statistical feature vector, as it is presented on Fig. 2. These statistical feature vectors were calculated as follows: F_{0i} values were

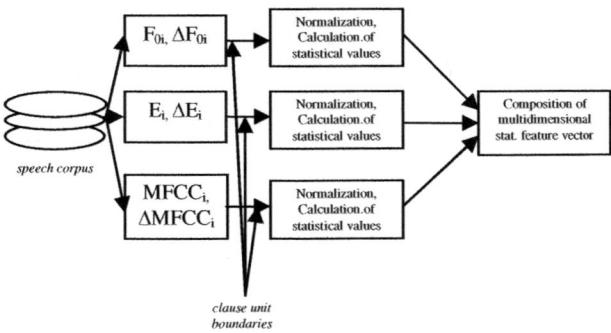

Fig. 2. Acoustical preprocessing

normalized by the F_{01} value of the first time frame and E values were normalized to the max value of E in each clauses. The following statistical data were calculated from these normalized parameters for each clause:

- max, min, mean, median values of F_{0i}
- max, min, median, skew values of ΔF_{0i}
- mean, median of E_i
- max, min, mean, median, skew values of ΔE_i
- maxima, minima, mean values of $MFCC_i$
- maxima minima, mean values of $\Delta MFCC_i$

Thus each clause was characterized by an 87 dimensional vector.

2.2 Speech Corpora

The speech corpora, a collection of customer's service dialogues, were recorded through telephone line, from 250 Hz-3500 Hz, by 8000 Hz and 16 bit sampling rate. 1000 calls were recorded. The duration of dialogs between the dispatchers and customers differed between 1 and 30 minutes.

The "Transcriber" [13] tool was used for the segmentation and labeling while it is appropriate for parallel processing. We wanted to know the linguistic content, the place of clauses in the speech, the emotional content of a clauses, moreover who is speaking, the gender of speakers, etc. Thus the linguistic contents, the boundary of clauses, the emotion, and the speakers with gender were marked in the acoustical signal.

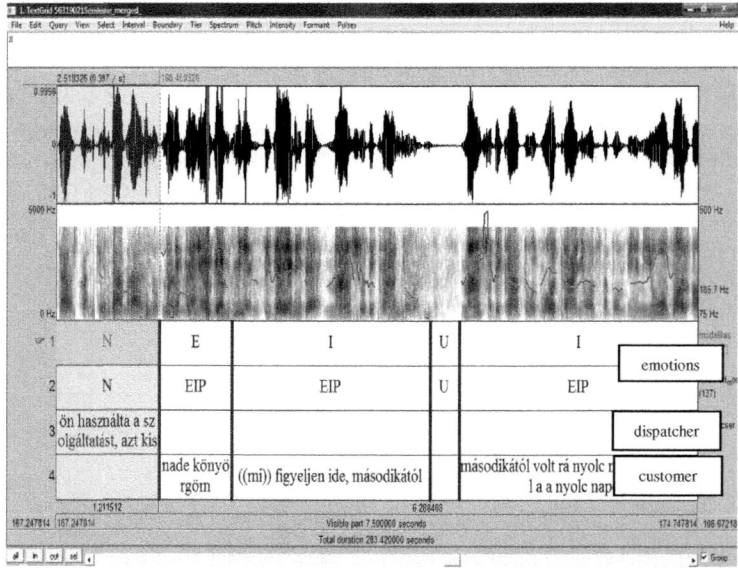

Fig. 3. An example of the segmented and labeled conversation. U:silent period, N:neutral, I:nervous, P: querulous emotion and E: else.

Our prosodic recognizer and segmenter [11] were used to mark the clause boundaries in the recorded speech. Then experts labeled the clause segments by hand according to its emotional contents. Four different emotional states were differentiated in the recorded dialogues: neutral (N), nervous (I), querulous (P), and others (E). Practically there was no more emotion type in the 1000 calls only these 4. Unfortunately in many cases, the customer's speech was neutral. Altogether there were 346 nervous clauses, 603 querulous, and 225 others in the customer's speech and 603 typical neutral clauses were selected from the neutral ones for the classification experiment.

An example of segmentation and labeling of the dialogues is presented on Fig. 3. The handmade segmentation and labeling is presented at the third line, and the labeling result of our classifier is presented below.

The text of the customer and the dispatcher speech were marked in parallel with speech and its emotion.

2.3 Testing of the System

2.3.1 Classification of Clauses According to Its Emotion
For the training and testing of our emotion classifier the so called leave-one-out cross-validation (LOOCV) was used [12], that is, using a single clause from a call as the validation data, and the remaining clauses in the calls as the training data. This is repeated such that each clause in the calls is used once as the validation data. The error matrix in case of the four emotions is to be seen on Table 1.

Table 1. *E, I, P, N* emotions are classified into separate classes

	E	I	N	P	Correct
E	**49**	26	62	88	22%
I	9	**153**	60	124	44%
N	14	38	**398**	153	66%
P	11	70	157	**365**	60%
				average	54%

The I and P emotions are hardly differentiated not only by the classifier, but by the humans too. Thus I and P and E classes were closed up into one class, denominated as the "discontent" emotion. This class of "discontent" and the class of neutral emotions were differentiated and trained. The testing results are shown in Table 2.

Table 2. This **(E, I, P), (N)** emotions are classified into two separate classes as discontent and neutral

	EIP	N	Correct
EIP	**887**	287	76%
N	335	**839**	71%
		average	**73%**

2.3.2 Monitoring of the Emotional State of the Customer

The aim of this research work is to find out a way how it is possible to detect the emotional state of the customer automatically, through a conversation. With this object a 15 sec long monitoring window was selected, and the clauses, which were automatically classified as "discontent" emotion, were counted in this window. Then, the window was moved forward, by 10 sec time steps. On the Fig. 4, some examples are presented, how the automatic monitoring detects the degree of the discontentment of the customer through the conversation. (Discontentment was 100% when all clauses in the monitoring window were detected as discontent.) The results obtained automatically are compared with the results on the hand labeled ones.

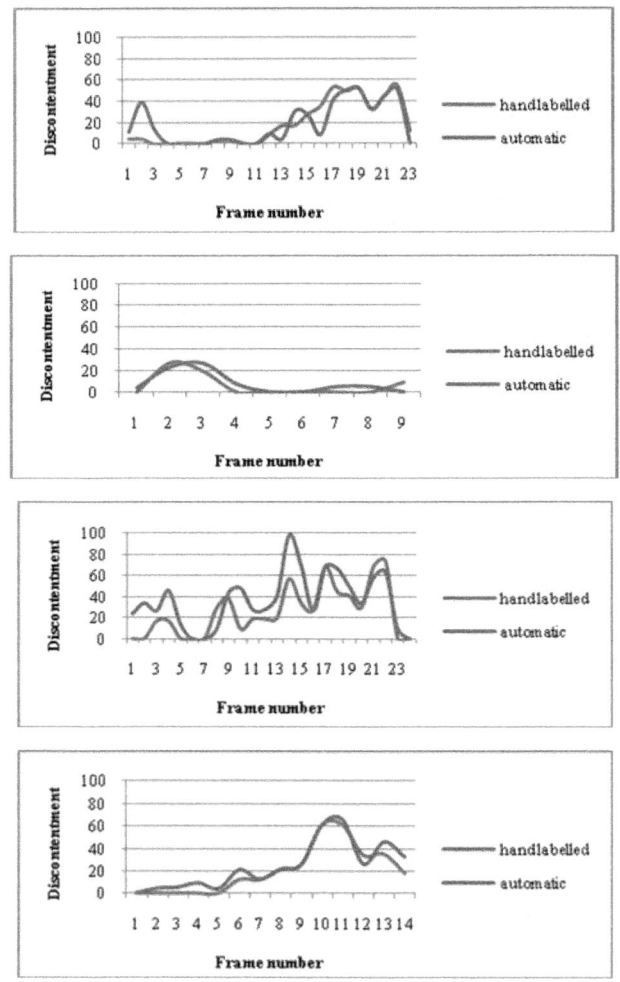

Fig. 4. The degree of the discontentment of the customer through a conversation. (Discontentment was 100% when all clauses were detected as discontent in the 15 sec monitoring window). The results obtained automatically are compared with the results on the hand labeled ones.

On the whole, in case of continuous monitoring, the average distance between the results obtained automatically and on the hand labeled ones is 11.3%, by comparing the monitored values in every 10 sec time steps, and averaged the obtained differences for the full database.

In real usage the main goal of the automatic recognition system is to signal when the discontentment level has reached a critical level. We call it as an "alarm level". This "alarm level" has to be set manually. For example, setting this "alarm level" to 30 percent (that is, if discontentment is above 30%), it was marked when the hand-made value was over this 30% alarm level, and when the automatic value was over this level. Then comparison was done frame-by-frame.

The differences were considered as alarm detection errors. Thus the average detection error was 20.8%. The main reason of the errors is a small shift between the data of automatic recognition and hand labeling at some places. It is illustrated on Fig. 5.

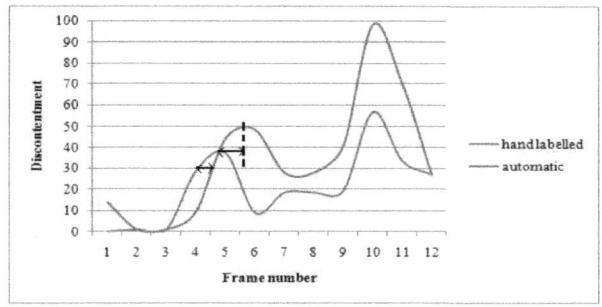

Fig. 5. The enlarged part of the 3rd diagram in Fig. 4. as an example for small shifts in curves of hand labeling and automatic recognition

3 Discussion

The semantic content (verbal channel) and the general feeling and emotional state of the speaker (the non-verbal channel) are expressed at the same time in speech, and the semantic content contributes to the emotion recognition of human.

In our experiments, discussed here, only the nonverbal parameters were used for the training and for the classification, without any linguistic information.

In our second experiment, in section 2.3.2., the classified clauses were monitored through a time window, much longer than the clause's duration, to give a more specified decision about the speaker's emotional states. This monitoring technique seems to be capable to give an alarm if the discontentment of the customer exceeds a threshold, without the usage of verbal channel.

It is clear that much better result can be obtained, if some information of verbal channel would be integrated to the system. This is why we recorded the linguistic content too, through the database processing, as it was described in session 2.2. In the future, we plan to process some linguistic information too, and we are going to integrate the information of the two channel.

4 Conclusions

The aim of this research work was to find out a way how it is possible to detect the emotional state of the customer automatically, through a spontaneous conversation, and to signal when the discontentment level of a customer has reached a critical level.

The simple classification of four emotions (neutral, nervous, querulous, and others) was not very useful. The reason of this fact would be that the separation of the nervous and querulous emotions was not a good decision, because those are hardly differentiated by the humans too, especially without linguistic content.

Thus I and P and E classes were closed up into one class, denominated as the "discontent" emotion. In this case the two classes, the discontent and neutral were correctly classified in 73% in average.

By using our automatic monitoring techniques for the detection of the degree of the discontentment of the customer, (in 15 sec long monitoring window, in 10 sec time step), the average distance between the discontentment obtained automatically and on the hand labeled material is 11.3%.

On the base of this monitoring technique it is possible to sign when the discontentment level has reached a critical "alarm level", in our case it is at 30% of discontentment. The average alarm detection error was 20.8% but the reason of this error, in most cases, is only a small shift between the data of automatic recognition and hand labeling, resulting only a delay or foregoing of an alarm period.

Accordingly the described decision technique can be useful in dispatcher centers, in spite of the fact, that only the nonverbal content of the speech was used for the decision. Of course in the future we are going to process the linguistic content too, parallel with the nonverbal one, hopefully serving so far better result.

Acknowledgements

The research was prepared within the confines of TÁMOP-4.2.2-08/1/KMR-2008-0007 project.

We would like to thank the leader of the SPSS Hungary Ltd. and INVITEL Telecom Zrt. to give free run of the recorded 1000 dialogues for us.

References

[1] Campbell, N.: Getting to the heart of the matter. Keynote Speech. In: Proc. Language resources and Evaluation Conference (LREC 2004), Lisabon, Portugal (2004)
[2] Hozjan, V., Kacic, Z.: A rule-based emotion-dependent feature extraction method for emotion analysis from speech. The Journal of the Acoustical Society of America 119(5), 3109–3120 (2006)
[3] Douglas-Cowie, E., Campbell, N., Cowie, R., Roach, P.: Emotional speech: towards a new generation of databases. Speech Communication 40, 33–60 (2003)
[4] Burkhardt, F., Paeschke, A., et al.: A database of German Emotional Speech. In: N:Proc. of Interspeech 2005, pp. 1517–1520 (2005)

[5] Navas, E., Hernáez, I., Luengo, I.: An Objective and Subjective Study of the Role of Semantics and Prosodic Features in Building Corpora for Emotional TTS. IEEE Transactions On Audio, Speech, And Language Processing 14(4) (July 2006)

[6] MPEG-4: ISO/IEC 14496 standard (1999), http://www.iec.ch

[7] Esposito, A.: The Perceptual and Cognitive Role of Visual and Auditory Channels in Conveying Emotional Information. In: Cogn. Comput. Springer Science+Business Media, LLC (2009), doi:10.1007/s12559-009-9017-8

[8] Campbell, N: Individual Traits of Speaking Style and Speech Rhythm in a Spoken Discourse. COST Action 2102 International Conference on Verbal and Nonverbal Features.... Patras, Greece, October 2007, pp. 107–120. (2007)

[9] Kostoulas, T., Ganchev, T., Fakotakis, N.: Study on Speaker-Independent Emotion Recognition from Speech on Real-World Data, COST Action 2102. In: International Conference on Verbal and Nonverbal Features, Patras, Greece, pp. 235–242 (October 2007)

[10] Tóth, S.L., Sztahó, D., Vicsi, K.: Speech Emotion Perception by Human and Machine. In: Esposito, A., Bourbakis, N.G., Avouris, N., Hatzilygeroudis, I. (eds.) HH and HM Interaction. LNCS (LNAI), vol. 5042, pp. 213–224. Springer, Heidelberg (2008)

[11] Vicsi, K., Szaszák, G.y.: Using Prosody for the Improvement of ASR: Sentence Modality Recognition. In: Interspeech 2008, Brisbane, Ausztrália (2008), ISCA Archive, http://www.isca-speech.org/archive (September 23-26, 2008)

[12] Kohavi, R.: A study of cross-validation and bootstrap for accuracy estimation and model selection. In: Proceedings of the Fourteenth International Joint Conference on Artificial Intelligence, vol. 2(12), pp. 1137–1143 (1995)

[13] Transcriber, http://trans.sourceforge.net/en/presentation.php

Slovak Language Model from Internet Text Data

Ján Staš, Daniel Hládek, Matúš Pleva, and Jozef Juhár

Technical University of Košice, Faculty of Electrical Engineering and Informatics,
Laboratory of Advanced Speech Technologies, Letná 9/A, Košice, Slovakia
{jan.stas,daniel.hladek,matus.pleva,jozef.juhar}@tuke.sk
http://kemt.fei.tuke.sk

Abstract. Automatic speech recognition system is one of the parts of
the multimodal dialogue system. It is necessary to create correct vocabulary and to generate suitable language model for this purpose. The main
aim of this article is to describe a process of building statistical models
of the Slovak language with large vocabulary trained on the text data
gathered mainly from Internet sources. Several smoothing techniques for
different sizes of vocabulary have been used in order to obtain an optimal
model of the Slovak language. We have also employed pruning technique
based on relative entropy for size reduction of a language model to find
the maximum threshold of pruning with minimum degradation in recognition accuracy. Tests were performed by the decoder based on the HTK
Toolkit.

Keywords: Language model, n-grams, speech recognition, spellchecking, text normalization, vocabulary.

1   Introduction

The multimodal dialogue system (MMDS) introduces an interaction between
the human and computer by various inputs such as speech, writing, face-play,
lip movements, etc. For example, the input interface of the module of automatic
speech recognition (ASR) in the MMDS analyses the user voice and transforms
it into a sequence of words in text format. Further, the module of natural language processing (NLP), analyses the sequence of words in order to obtain its
meaning. Other input interfaces in the MMDS are usually the face location and
tracking module, the gaze tracking module, the module of lip-reading or gesture
recognition and hand-writing recognition [1].

State-of-the-art technology and development in the field of ASR are making
possible to use the large vocabulary continuous speech recognition (LVCSR) in
MMDS. Besides acoustic data, text data are necessary for training of a language
model for creation of the LVCSR system. The natural and best available source
of electronic data is Internet or news articles in the electronic form.

Language model determines the probability of a sequence of words, as well
as the word itself, this consequently helps to find the most probable sequence
of words for ASR system, which corresponds to the acoustic information pronounced by the user. The most frequently used models for ASR systems are the

A. Esposito et al. (Eds.): COST 2102 Int. Training School 2010, LNCS 6456, pp. 340–346, 2011.
© Springer-Verlag Berlin Heidelberg 2011

n-gram stochastic language models (SLMs). These models mainly consider the statistical dependency between n individual words [2].

Because every training set is finite and cannot include all word combinations, it might happen that such events can lead to the zero conditional probability. Speaker can also pronounce a sentence that does not appear in the training set. Moreover, zero probabilities lead to errors in recognition. The problem of these events resolves *smoothing* [3] by more uniform redistribution of parts of probabilities of observed n-grams among n-grams that do not occur in training set. Using smoothing has not only better effect in recognition but also increases accuracy of the SLM itself.

It is also necessary to limit the size of vocabulary that participates in the process of generating a SLM. The size of vocabulary also increases the number of n-grams. Most of the high-level n-grams occur in training sets just once. Therefore, the size of these SLMs need to be reduced that can be done using one of the *pruning* techniques [4].

This article is connecting to the work presented in [5] and is organized as follows. First, the fundamental proposed model of building SLMs for Slovak LVCSR is presented. Then, a short overview about every block of the proposed system is described. In following sections, experimental results evaluated on HTK decoder for basic, smoothed and pruned SLMs are summarized. At the end of this paper, future intentions in Slovak language modeling are indicated.

2   Process of Text Gathering and Building SLMs

Process of building SLMs in Slovak language consists of several steps, illustrated in Fig. 1. First, it is necessary to collect a large amount of text data by automatic text gathering systems. These texts in uniform encoding and as raw text are stored. Then all texts are passed through the block of text normalization. In this step, some additional text improvements are performed. For example, all numbers, abbreviations, symbols are transcribed into verbal form. Then each of transcribed documents with description of their title, author, source, etc., is stored in the relational database. The text corpora are created by selecting texts from database and then prepared for training SLMs. Generating of the text corpus for training SLMs includes operations of counting words, selection of vocabulary and spellchecking. Finally, consequential evaluations of SLMs are performed. In the following subsections, each of these steps for building SLMs will be explained in detail.

Text Gathering. In the process of creating the LVCSR system, it is necessary to collect a large amount of text data in order to get an efficient SLM of the given language. Texts are gathered usually from electronic documents such as MS Word (DOC) or Portable Document Format (PDF), etc. Another way is to gather text data from web pages (HTML). We use two automatic systems for text gathering designed in our laboratory. The first system, called *RSS Downloader*, retrieves text data from HTML pages using RSS channels, which are manually

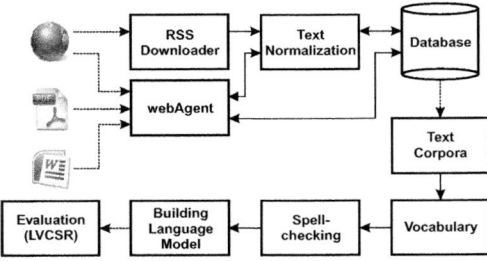

Fig. 1. Block scheme of the process of text gathering and building language model

predefined by user in configuration file. The system automatically downloads every link in RSS channel and extracts text from every gathered web page, written in Slovak language [5]. The second system, called *webAgent*, retrieves text data from various web pages that are written in Slovak language. Besides text data, the system also collects links to other web pages. Moreover, the system is able to detect encoding of the given web page and retrieves text data from PDF and DOC documents. Both automatic systems have implemented methods for duplicity verification, spellchecking and amount of various constraints for incorrect text exclusion, etc.

Text Normalization. This preprocessing step includes additional modifications of text data. All text data must be meeting following conditions: *a.* every sentence has to be in exactly one line; *b.* text data must be tokenized into separate words; *c.* every word should be mapped to lowercase; *d.* numerals, dates, other numbers and special symbols must be replaced by their pronunciation; *e.* abbreviations and monetary units must be expanded; *f.* all punctuation marks must be deleted; *g.* grammatically incorrect words should be filtered.

Relational Database. Each normalized document is stored in database (based on PostgreSQL) with its title, URI of web page and name of the source where article was published. The database is closely associated with systems for text gathering. In the process of insertion text data into database the duplicity verification is performed.

Text Corpora. Selecting the set of articles from database in form of plain text generates the text corpora. Usually, corpora are divided by the theme, for example the corpus of news articles, collection of laws, etc. Such corpora are known as domain-specific corpora.

Vocabulary. It includes a list of unique words that are obtained by counting words in the training corpus. Because the number of unique words is usually too high (it could contain grammatically incorrect words, etc.), the number of words in vocabulary is specified by the number of the most frequent words in the modeled language (for LVCSR usually 100k–300k unique words).

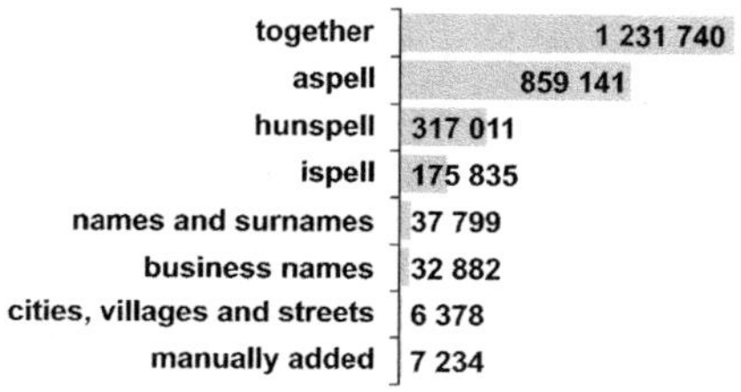

together	1 231 740
aspell	859 141
hunspell	317 011
ispell	175 835
names and surnames	37 799
business names	32 882
cities, villages and streets	6 378
manually added	7 234

Fig. 2. The size of particular dictionaries for spellchecking [number of unique words]

Spellchecking. While grammatically incorrect words or words without diacritics can occur in vocabulary, the spellchecking is often needed. Spellchecking is performed by separation of all words that are not found in lexicon, which contains only grammatically correct words. In our case, the lexicon for spellchecking is created by merging available Open Source lexicons such as *aspell*, *hunspell* and *ispell* with lexicons of proper nouns available on the Internet such as list of frequent names and surnames, cities, towns and villages, names of streets, geographic terms, names of companies, etc. The size of individual lists of unique words in lexicon for spellchecking is illustrated in the Fig. 2. Remaining incorrect words are manually checked, corrected and added back to the lexicon.

Building Language Models. Various types of language models (smoothed, pruned, interpolated, etc.) in the standard ARPA format [2] are generated with the vocabulary by using SRI Language Modeling Toolkit [6].

Evaluation. Used for evaluation of SLM usually are two standard measures: extrinsic evaluation using *word error rate* (WER) and intrinsic evaluation using *perplexity* (PPL). WER is a common extrinsic measure of the performance of a speech recognition, which is defined as

$$WER = \frac{N_{INS} + N_{DEL} + N_{SUB}}{N}. \tag{1}$$

It is computed by comparing reference text read by some person against the recognized result, where N_{INS} is the number of false inserted words in recognized text, N_{DEL} is the number of false deleted words, N_{SUB} is the number of badly recognized words and N is the number of words in reference text [7]. For evaluation of the WER, a working ASR system is necessary.

Another measure is perplexity, which is defined as the reciprocal of the (geometric) average probability assigned by the language model to each word in the test set and is related to cross-entropy $H(W)$ by equation [2]

$$PPL = 2^{H(W)}. \tag{2}$$

Perplexity does not necessarily ensure increase in the accuracy of recognition itself, but usually highly correlates with it. Therefore, perplexity is often used if there is no ASR system available.

3   Speech Recognition Setup

LVCSR System. The setup for decoding was built on HTK Toolkit [8] using the phone list from MobilDat-SK [9], [10] database.

Language Model. The tested language models were built on two text corpora, which consist of articles gathered from various web pages written in Slovak language with the help of our automatic systems for text gathering. The first training corpus size of 225MB consists only of domain-specific newspaper articles. It contains about 2.5 million sentences with 30,820,506 Slovak words, when 546,715 of them are unique words. The second training corpus size of 3.5GB contains about 30 million sentences obtained from various web pages with 435,059,968 of Slovak words, when 1,286,689 of them are unique words. Three different sizes of vocabulary for building trigram language models using SRILM Toolkit [6] were used: 100k, 200k and 300k with 100,347, 201,971 and 300,417 unique word forms respectively.

Acoustic Model. The acoustic model is made of tied triphone hidden Markov models (HMM) having 32 numbers of Gaussian mixtures on state. The HMM acoustic models were built using feature vectors created by 39 *mel-frequency cepstral* (MFC) coefficients. It has been trained using about 75 hours of annotated speech recordings of the parliament speech (downsampled to 16kHz and 16bit PCM). All crossword triphones were constructed from the parliament speech training set and involved no additional noise events except silence and short-pause models.

Test Set. The test data are represented by 75 minutes of parliament speech and contain 8,778 words. The test vocabulary has 3,187 different Slovak words.

4   Experimental Results

Table 1 shows results of WER and the perplexity for trigram language models with large vocabulary of three different sizes trained on two text corpora. Tested have been also two smoothing methods using SRILM Toolkit in the training process: *the Witten-Bell model* and *the modified Kneser-Ney model*. As we can see, the modified Kneser-Ney algorithm moderately outperforms the Witten-Bell and base model on larger corpus, both in case of WER and PPL. The results further show that the use of about fifteen-times larger training corpus for modeling improves WER until 3.35%.

Table 2 shows language model perplexity and WER results as well as the number of bigrams and trigrams evaluated on the test set for different pruning thresholds. We used *relative entropy-based pruning* [4] for the trigram model with modified Kneser-Ney smoothing; size of vocabulary 200k. As it is shown, pruning is highly effective in model size reduction. For the threshold equals 10^{-7} and training corpus size of 225MB we have obtained a model that is 35% of the

Table 1. Effect of smoothing trigram language models

Model	Vocab	WER [%]		PPL	
		225MB	3.5GB	225MB	3.5GB
	100k	18.44	16.06	977.70	633.7
Base	200k	17.17	14.51	1075.8	684.6
	300k	16.67	14.29	1108.2	695.8
	100k	18.44	16.05	977.40	606.7
Witten-Bell	200k	17.19	14.50	1075.3	656.8
	300k	16.68	14.29	1107.5	668.9
	100k	18.24	15.95	963.70	548.9
Modified	200k	17.03	14.52	1059.5	586.2
Kneser-Ney	300k	16.48	14.26	1091.3	597.3

Table 2. Effect of pruning trigram language models

Prune threshold	Training corpus 225MB				Training corpus 3.5GB			
	WER [%]	Number of bigrams	Number of trigrams	Size [MB]	WER [%]	Number of bigrams	Number of trigrams	Size [MB]
no prune	17.03	7,900,077	3,297,936	314	15.15	32,414,672	29,597,353	1795
1e-8	17.28	6,772,688	1,898,237	243	15.81	17,283,483	11,517,916	718
5e-8	17.62	4,728,816	891,631	160	16.84	6,891,775	4,129,588	214
10e-8	17.94	3,308,302	506,700	110	17.56	4,174,825	2,302,159	126

size of the original model with negligible degradation in recognition accuracy. For the language model that was trained on larger training set we observed slightly higher WER when increasing of the pruning threshold.

5 Discussion

Creating an effective language model for the ASR system of highly inflectional language such as Slovak language is not a simple task. First, it is necessary to resolve what size of vocabulary is sufficient for covering conversational Slovak language. It is also important which words this vocabulary can contain. Slovak language has the problem with word likeness of several words as well, which should have been included in the vocabulary with phonetic transcription. For efficient building of a language model is necessary to choose the one optimal or a combination of several smoothing techniques. For using language model in real LVCSR applications which works in real-time, the final model must be compact too, which is achieved by choosing the appropriate pruning threshold. Additional improvements in language modeling are usually given by adaptation of a model to the specific theme, by suitable modeling the unknown words, etc. This knowledge will be the subject of further research that consequently should be lead to decreasing WER of the LVCSR system for highly inflectional Slovak language and using such language model for real task of the ASR.

6   Conclusions

In this article a building process of stochastic language models for the Slovak language have been presented. It includes the process of text gathering, text normalization and generation of the language models. For efficient language modeling, both smoothing and pruning techniques were utilized. These experimental results lead to finding of the optimum ratio between using one of the smoothing techniques and an appropriate pruning threshold.

In future work, we want to focus on the training of stochastic language models on larger training text set with optimal size of vocabulary, appropriate smoothing technique and pruning threshold. Further research should be also focused on the adaptation of language model to the concrete LVCSR task.

Acknowledgments. The research presented in this paper was supported by the Slovak Research and Development Agency and Ministry of Education under research project APVV-0369-07, VMSP-P-0004-09 and VEGA-1/0065/10.

References

1. Chollet, G., Esposito, A., Gentes, A., Horain, P., Karam, W., Li, Z., Pelachaud, C., Perrot, P., Petrovska-Delacrétaz, D., Zhou, D., Zouari, L.: Multimodal Human Machine Interactions in Virtual and Augmented Reality. In: Esposito, A., Hussain, A., Marinaro, M., Martone, R. (eds.) COST Action 2102. LNCS(LNAI), vol. 5398, pp. 1–23. Springer, Heidelberg (2009)
2. Jurafsky, D., Martin, J.H.: Speech and Language Processing: An Introduction to Natural Language Processing, Computational Linguistics, and Speech Recognition, 2nd edn., p. 998. Prentice Hall, Englewood Cliffs (2009) ISBN-13 978-0-13-504196-3
3. Chen, S.F., Goodman, J.: An Empirical Study of Smoothing Techniques for Language Modeling. Technical Report TR-10-98, p. 63 (1998)
4. Stolcke, A.: Entropy-based Pruning of Backoff Language Models. In: Proc. DARPA Broadcast News Transcription and Understanding Workshop, pp. 270–274 (1998)
5. Mirilovič, M., Juhár, J., Čižmár, A.: Large Vocabulary Continuous Speech Recognition in Slovak. In: Proc. of International Conference on Applied Electrical Engineering and Informatics, Athens, Greece, pp. 73–77 (2008) ISBN 978-80-553-0066-5
6. Stolcke, A.: SRILM - An Extensible Language Modeling Toolkit. In: Proc. of the 7th International Conference on Spoken Language Processing, Denver, Colorado, pp. 901–904 (2002)
7. Cowan, I.A., Moore, D., Dines, J., Gatiza-Perez, D., Flynn, M., Wellner, P., Bourlard, H.: On the Use of Information Retrieval Measures for Speech Recognition Evaluation. In: IDIAP-RR-73, Martigny, Switzerland, p. 15 (2005)
8. Young, S., Odell, J., Ollason, D., Valtchev, V., Woodland, P., Evermann, G., Hain, T., Kershaw, D., Moore, G.: The HTK Book (v3.4). Cambridge University, Cambridge (2009)
9. Rusko, M., Trnka, M., Daržagín, S.: MobilDat-SK - A Mobile Telephone Extension to the SpeechDat-E SK Telephone Speech Database in Slovak. In: Proc. of the 11th International Conference Speech and Computer, SPECOM 2006, pp. 485–488 (2006)
10. Mirilovič, M., Juhár, J., Čižmár, A.: Comparison of Grapheme and Phoneme Based Acoustic Modeling in LVCSR Task in Slovak. In: Proc. of the 7th International Conference on Spoken Language Processing, Denver, Colorado, pp. 901–904 (2002)

Automatic Recognition of Emotional State in Polish Speech

Piotr Staroniewicz

Wroclaw University of Technology
Institute of Telecommunications, Teleinformatics and Acoustics
Wybrzeze Wyspianskiego 27, 50-370 Wroclaw, Poland
piotr.staroniewicz@pwr.wroc.pl

Abstract. The paper presents the comparison of scores for emotional state automatic recognition tests. The database of Polish emotional speech used during tests includes recordings of six acted emotional states (anger, sadness, happiness, fear, disgust, surprise) and the neutral state of 13 amateur speakers (2118 utterances). The features based on F0, intensity, formants and LPC coefficients were applied in seven chosen classifiers. The highest scores were reached for SVM, ANN and DTC classifiers.

Keywords: emotional speech, emotional state recognition.

1 Introduction

Emotion recognition in speech is an important aspect of speech-computer communication (i.e. speech and speaker recognition, speech synthesis), which is a reason for trials to develop efficient algorithms for emotion speech recognition in recent years.

The main source of complication during that task is no strict definition of emotions and their classification rules. The literature describes them as emotion-dimensions (i.e. potency, activation, etc.) or discrete concepts (i.e. anger, fear etc.) (Fig.1) [1,2,3,4]. Distinct terms which are easily understood by speakers are usually chosen in acted emotions. In order to be able to compare the results with older studies and because they are generally considered as the most common ones, it was decided to use six basic emotional states plus the neutral state. Despite the fact that there is no definitive list of basic emotions, there exists a general agreement on so-called "the big six" [1,2]: anger, sadness, happiness, fear, disgust, surprise and neutral state. Another problem can be the variability of emotional categories among languages or cultures, considering the fact that most work has been done on Germanic languages.

The paper presents the results of experiments carried out on the Polish speech emotional database (presented earlier in [5,6,7]). The automatic emotion recognition tests were carried out for the same conditions (features, learning, testing sets) to allow the comparison of the effectiveness of tested classifiers.

A. Esposito et al. (Eds.): COST 2102 Int. Training School 2010, LNCS 6456, pp. 347–353, 2011.

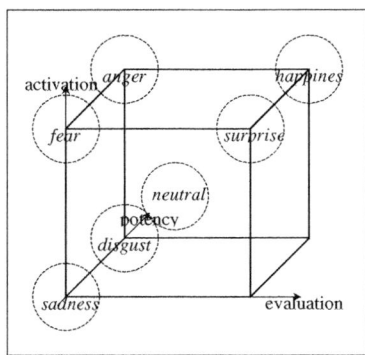

Fig. 1. Six basic emotional states and neutral state on three dimensions of emotional space

2 Database

Despite all disadvantages of acted emotions in comparison to natural and elicited ones (which means recordings of spontaneous speech), only recording simulated (or semi-natural) emotions can guarantee the control of recordings which fulfils [8,9]:

- reasonable number of subjects to act all emotions to enable the generalization over a target group,
- all subjects uttering the same verbal content to allow the comparison across emotions and speakers,
- high quality recordings to enable later proper speech features extraction,
- unambiguous emotional states (only one emotion per utterance).

The amateur speakers who took part in the recordings were sex balanced. All the subjects were recorded in separate sessions to prevent their influencing each other's speaking styles. The speakers were asked to use their own every day way of express-ing emotional states, not from stage acting. The decision of selecting simulated emo-tional states enabled a free choice of utterances to be recorded. The most important condition was that all selected texts should be interpretable according to emotions and not containing an emotional bias. The everyday life speech was used which have some important advantages:

- it is the natural form of speech under emotional arousal,
- lectors can immediately speak it from memory,
- no need for memorising and reading it, which could lead to a lecturing style.

The group of speakers consisted of 13 subjects, 6 women and 7 men each recorded 10 sentences in 7 emotional states in several repetitions. Altogether 2351 utterances were recorded, 1168 with female and 1183 with male voices. An average duration of a single utterance was around 1 second. After a preliminary validation, some doubtful emotional states and recordings with poor acoustical quality were rejected. The Final number of 2118 utterances was then divided into training and testing sets for a later automatic recognition of emotional states (described earlier in [5]). The database was validated with the subjective human recognition tests (presented in [5]).

3 Automatic Recognition

3.1 Feature Extraction

In automatic recognition the following speech features were chosen:

- F0,
- intensity,
- first four formant frequencies (F1, F2, F3, F4),
- 12 LPC coefficients.

For the F0 the following parameters were determined: minimum, maximum, median, mean, range, standard deviation and the mean absolute slope which is the measure of the mean local variability of the F0. For the intensity the minimum, maximum, median, mean, range and standard deviation were calculated. Similarly for formant frequencies the minimum, maximum, median, mean, median of frequency range, range and the standard deviation were determined. Altogether 53 parameters were obtained.

3.2 Classification Algorithms

In the presented tests the following classification methods were applied to the data:

- Bayes algorithm,
- k-Nearest Neighbors (k-NN) classifier,
- Nearest Neighbor (NN) classifier,
- Support Vector Machine (SVM) clasifier,
- Linear Discriminant Analysis (LDA),
- Artificial Neural Networks (ANN),
- Decision Tree Classifiers (DTC).

The k-NN is a classifier which first approximates the local posterior probability of each class by averaging over the k nearest neighbors. Classifying the class by k-NN is performed by voting the majority vote over those neighbors. The $k=5$ was set experimentally. Nearest Neighbor algorithm is a special case of k-NN when $k=1$.

The SVM is the classification method worked out by Vladimir Vapnik [10]. Support Vector Machines were successfully applied in speech emotions recognition and in many cases appear to be superior to other classifiers [11,12,13]. The best classification algorithm and its kernel function was set experimentally. The C-SVC algorithm (penalty parameter $C = 256$) with the Gaussian Radial Basis Function (kernel parameter $\gamma = 0.6$) was applied [14,15,16].

The LDA is a method used to find a linear combination of features which characterize or separate two or more classes of objects or events. The resulting combination may be used as a linear classifier.

As a Neural Network classifier, the conventional multilayer feed-forward network with backwards propagation of errors and one hidden layer was applied (53 neurons).

The DTC classification trees method is not widespread in the field of statistical pattern recognition, however, it is very adept at revealing complex interactions between variables. A popular algorithm used for learning random forest [17,18] builds a randomized decision tree. Random forest algorithm proposed by Leo Breiman [17] provides for many datasets highly accurate results and handle with a very large number of input variables and at the same time learning is quite fast comparing to other methods.

4   Experimental Results

The confusion matrix for all seven tested classifiers, including recognition scores of six basic emotional states plus the neutral one are presented in Tables 1-7. The mean emotional state recognition scores are presented in Fig.2.

Table 1. Confusion matrix for Bayes' algorithm

	Happiness	Anger	Fear	Sadness	Surprise	Disgust	Neutral state
Happiness	**58.5%**	8.2%	7.5%	6.8%	6.1%	5.4%	7.5%
Anger	26.8%	**33.8%**	15.3%	0.0%	7.0%	7.0%	10.2%
Fear	15.7%	11.0%	**38.6%**	5.5%	11.8%	3.1%	14.2%
Sadness	4.0%	1.3%	4.7%	**35.6%**	8.1%	11.4%	34.9%
Surprise	22.1%	2.1%	9.3%	5.7%	**47.9%**	6.4%	6.4%
Disgust	13.2%	6.3%	6.9%	12.5%	7.6%	**32.6%**	20.8%
Neutral state	5.2%	0.6%	3.2%	22.6%	1.9%	18.1%	**48.4%**

Table 2. Confusion matrix for k-NN algorithm

	Happiness	Anger	Fear	Sadness	Surprise	Disgust	Neutral state
Happiness	**73.5%**	9.5%	0.7%	2.0%	8.2%	2.0%	4.1%
Anger	12.1%	**70.1%**	3.8%	1.3%	4.5%	3.2%	5.1%
Fear	12.6%	18.9%	**34.6%**	2.4%	12.6%	7.1%	11.8%
Sadness	2.7%	1.3%	6.7%	**46.3%**	1.3%	14.1%	27.5%
Surprise	9.3%	10.7%	5.7%	5.7%	**63.6%**	2.9%	2.1%
Disgust	6.9%	18.1%	3.5%	10.4%	8.3%	**43.8%**	9.0%
Neutral state	4.5%	7.1%	1.9%	13.5%	2.6%	12.3%	**58.1%**

Table 3. Confusion matrix for NN algorithm

	Happiness	Anger	Fear	Sadness	Surprise	Disgust	Neutral state
Happiness	**39.5%**	20.4%	2.7%	3.4%	11.6%	3.4%	19.0%
Anger	13.4%	**45.9%**	3.2%	1.3%	12.1%	8.9%	15.3%
Fear	6.3%	17.3%	**24.4%**	3.1%	18.1%	3.9%	26.8%
Sadness	0.0%	3.4%	2.0%	**22.8%**	6.7%	14.8%	50.3%
Surprise	12.1%	5.7%	2.9%	6.4%	**61.4%**	3.6%	7.9%
Disgust	5.6%	10.4%	2.1%	6.9%	9.7%	**23.6%**	41.7%
Neutral state	0.6%	1.3%	0.0%	5.2%	0.6%	13.5%	**78.7%**

Table 4. Confusion matrix for SVM algorithm

	Happiness	Anger	Fear	Sadness	Surprise	Disgust	Neutral state
Happiness	**61.2%**	12.2%	2.7%	3.4%	9.5%	4.8%	6.1%
Anger	3.8%	**68.8%**	4.5%	1.3%	8.9%	7.6%	5.1%
Fear	10.2%	15.0%	**36.2%**	5.5%	16.5%	11.0%	5.5%
Sadness	0.0%	2.7%	1.3%	**65.1%**	2.0%	13.4%	15.4%
Surprise	2.1%	5.0%	3.6%	5.0%	**77.1%**	6.4%	0.7%
Disgust	2.1%	11.1%	1.4%	14.6%	6.9%	**55.6%**	8.3%
Neutral state	0.0%	1.3%	0.6%	16.1%	2.6%	16.8%	**62.6%**

Table 5. Confusion matrix for LDA algorithm

	Happiness	Anger	Fear	Sadness	Surprise	Disgust	Neutral state
Happiness	**40.1%**	17.0%	1.4%	8.8%	14.3%	13.6%	4.8%
Anger	12.7%	**61.8%**	1.3%	2.5%	12.1%	5.7%	3.8%
Fear	16.5%	16.5%	**15.7%**	4.7%	33.9%	3.9%	8.7%
Sadness	4.0%	0.7%	0.0%	**55.0%**	2.0%	18.1%	20.1%
Surprise	4.3%	4.3%	0.7%	4.3%	**77.9%**	5.0%	3.6%
Disgust	4.2%	6.3%	0.7%	16.7%	17.4%	**38.2%**	16.7%
Neutral state	1.3%	5.8%	0.0%	21.3%	3.2%	18.7%	**49.7%**

Table 6. Confusion matrix for ANN algorithm

	Happiness	Anger	Fear	Sadness	Surprise	Disgust	Neutral state
Happiness	**55.1%**	15.6%	5.4%	4.1%	10.2%	4.8%	4.8%
Anger	5.7%	**73.9%**	7.0%	2.5%	3.2%	3.8%	3.8%
Fear	14.2%	16.5%	**34.6%**	11.8%	11.8%	4.7%	6.3%
Sadness	1.3%	1.3%	1.3%	**70.5%**	2.0%	8.1%	15.4%
Surprise	6.4%	3.6%	3.6%	5.0%	**75.7%**	2.1%	3.6%
Disgust	2.8%	9.0%	2.1%	21.5%	10.4%	**45.1%**	9.0%
Neutral state	0.6%	3.2%	1.9%	18.1%	3.2%	10.3%	**62.6%**

Table 7. Confusion matrix for DTC algorithm

	Happiness	Anger	Fear	Sadness	Surprise	Disgust	Neutral state
Happiness	**51.0%**	19.0%	1.4%	3.4%	7.5%	6.8%	10.9%
Anger	6.4%	**65.0%**	7.0%	1.3%	7.6%	5.7%	7.0%
Fear	7.1%	21.3%	**33.9%**	10.2%	11.0%	10.2%	6.3%
Sadness	0.0%	0.7%	2.7%	**69.1%**	0.7%	14.8%	12.1%
Surprise	7.1%	4.3%	2.9%	7.1%	**67.9%**	9.3%	1.4%
Disgust	3.5%	9.0%	1.4%	13.9%	5.6%	**56.9%**	9.7%
Neutral state	0.0%	2.6%	0.0%	21.3%	1.3%	20.6%	**54.2%**

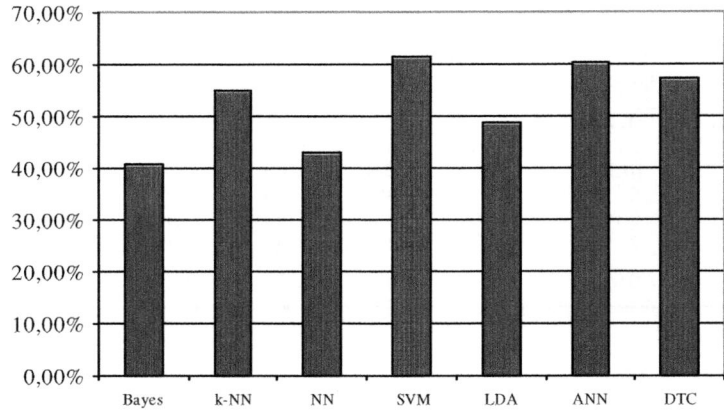

Fig. 2. Mean emotional state recognition scores for all tested classifiers

5 Conclusions

All seven classifiers were tested for the same conditions (same feature vectors, learning and testing sets). Best results obtained for SVM (61.43%) are not much higher than ANN (60.25%) or DTC (57.31%). The considerably high result for the classification trees is noteworthy since this method has not often been applied in similar cases. Lower results were obtained for less complex classifiers (i.e. NN). High scores obtained for SVM confirm its usefulness for the automatic emotion recognition problem [11,12,13]. Since the database contains simulated emotions, *Fear* and *Disgust* as the most difficult to simulate for the speaker had the lowest recognition scores and had the greatest impact on the low mean recognition scores. It is also confirmed by the results of the listeners tests carried out on the same data (mean recognition score of 57.25%), presented earlier [7]. It could be caused by the fact that the speakers found it extremely difficult to express *Disgust* naturally and of course sometimes this emotional state can be better expressed by face than by voice.*Fear* also caused troubles in a proper identification for similar reasons.The listeners were confusing *Sadness* with the neutral state quite often [7] and the same can be noticed for automatic classifiers as well (Tables 1-7) but with the strongest effect for Bayes (Table 1), k-NN (Table 2) and NN (Table 3) classifiers. Confusing Sadness and the neutral state can be partially explained by their near location in the emotional space (Fig.1). The mean scores would be substantially higher for a case with fewer classes of emotions (omitting emotional states most difficult for simulation or classifying them into smaller subsets, like: negative, non-negative etc.). The tested algorithms are only the except of a range of possible classification methods, apart from that, future work could be focused also on acoustic features. Another, more complex way of improving automatic emotion recognition scores would also be integrating other information in the recognition system (i.e. linguistic or dialog).

Acknowledgments. This work was partially supported by COST Action 2102 "Crossmodal Analysis of Verbal and Non-verbal Communication" [19] and by the grant from the Polish Minister of Science and Higher Education (nr 115/N-COST/2008/0).

References

1. Cowie, R.: Describing the Emotional States Expressed in Speech. In: Proc. of ISCA, Belfast 2000, pp. 11–18 (2000)
2. Scherer, K.R.: Vocal communications of emotion: A review of research paradigms. Speech Communication 40, 227–256 (2003)
3. Burkhard, F., Paeschkhe, A., Rolfes, M., Sendlmeier, W., Weiss, B.: A Database of German Emotional Speech. In: Proc. of Interspeech 2005, Lissabon, Portugal (2005)
4. Lugger, M., Yang, B.: The Relevance of Voice Quality Features in Speaker Independent Emotion Recognition. In: IEEE ICASSP 2007, USA, IV, pp. 17–20 (2007)
5. Staroniewicz, P., Majewski, W.: Polish Emotional Speech Database – Recording and Preliminary Validation. In: Esposito, A., Vích, R. (eds.) Cross-Modal Analysis of Speech, Gestures, Gaze and Facial Expressions. LNCS(LNAI), vol. 5641, pp. 42–49. Springer, Heidelberg (2009)
6. Staroniewicz, P.: Polish emotional speech database–design. In: Proc. of 55th Open Seminar on Acoustics, Wroclaw, Poland, pp. 373–378 (2008)
7. Staroniewicz, P.: Recognition of Emotional State in Polish Speech – Comparison between Human and Automatic Efficiency. In: Fierrez, J., Ortega-Garcia, J., Esposito, A., Drygajlo, A., Faundez-Zanuy, M. (eds.) BioID MultiComm 2009. LNCS, vol. 5707, pp. 33–40. Springer, Heidelberg (2009)
8. Douglas-Cowie, E., Campbell, N., Cowie, R., Roach, P.: Emotional speech: Towards a new generation of databases. Speech Communication 40, 33–60 (2003)
9. Ververdis, D., Kotropoulos, C.: A State of the Art on Emotional Speech Databases. In: Proc. of 1st Richmedia Conf., Laussane, Switzerland, pp. 109–119 (October 2003)
10. Vapnik, V.N.: Statistical Learning Theory. Wiley, Chichester (1998)
11. Kwon, O., Chan, K., Hao, J., Lee, T.: Emotion Recognition by Speech Signals. In: Eurospeech, Geneva, Switzerland, Septmeber 1-3 (2003)
12. Zhou, J., Wang, G., Yang, Y., Chen, P.: Speech emotion recognition based on rough set and SVM. In: 5th IEEE International Conference on Cognitive Informatics, ICCI 2006, Beijing, July 2006, vol. 1, pp. 53–61 (2006)
13. Lee, C.M., Narayanam, S.S., Pieraccini, R.: Classifuing Emotions in Human-Machine Spoken Dialogs. In: Proc. Int. Conf., on Multimedia Expo. (2002)
14. Hsu, Ch.W., Chang, Ch.-Ch., Lin, Ch.-J.: A Practical Guide to Support Vector Classification. Department of Computer Science, National Taiwan University (2008), http://www.csie.ntu.edu.tw/~cjlin (last updated: May 21, 2008)
15. Chang, Ch.-Ch., Lin, Ch.-J.: LIBSVM: a Library for Support Vector Machines (2001), http://www.csie.ntu.edu.tw/~cjlin/libsvm/
16. Witten, I.H., Frank, E.: Data Mining: Practical machine learning tools and techniques, 2nd edn. Morgan Kauffmann, San Francisco (2005)
17. Breiman, L.: Random Forests. Machine Learning 45, 5–32 (2001)
18. Witten, I.H., Frank, E.: Data Mining. Practical Machine Learning Tools and Techniques. Elsevier, Amsterdam (2005)
19. COST Action 2102, Cross -Modal Analysis of Verbal and Non-verbal Communication, Memorandum of Understanding, Brussels (July 11, 2006)

Categorical Perception of Consonants and Vowels: Evidence from a Neurophonetic Model of Speech Production and Perception

Bernd J. Kröger, Peter Birkholz, Jim Kannampuzha,
and Christiane Neuschaefer-Rube

Department of Phoniatrics, Pedaudiology, and Communication Disorders,
University Hospital Aachen and RWTH Aachen University, Aachen, Germany
{bkroeger,pbirkholz,jkannampuzha,cneuschaefer}@ukaachen.de

Abstract. While the behavioral side of categorical perception in speech is already well investigated, little is known concerning its underlying neural mechanisms. In this study, a computer-implemented neurophonetic model of speech production and perception is used in order to elucidate the functional neural mechanisms responsible for categorical perception. 20 instances of the model ("virtual listeners/speakers") underwent a speech acquisition training procedure and then performed behavioral tests, i.e. identification and discrimination experiments based on vocalic and CV-syllabic speech stimuli. These virtual listeners showed the expected behavioral results. The inspection of the neural organization of virtual listeners indicated clustering in the case of categorical perception and no clustering in the case of non-categorical (continuous) perception for neurons representing the stimuli. These results highlight a possible neural organization underlying categorical and continuous perception.

Keywords: speech perception, categorical perception, identification, discrimination, neural model of speech production.

1 Introduction

Categorical perception is an important feature of speech, needed for successfully differentiating and identifying sounds, syllables, or words. Categorical speech perception enables humans to map different realizations of one speech sound into one category. This is important in order to achieve a robust discrimination of different speech items, even if these items are realized by different speakers or by different articulations of the same speaker. A quantitative definition of categorical perception, based on identification and discrimination experiments, was given decades ago [1]. Based on this definition it was shown that a consonantal stimulus continuum covering the /ba/-/da/-/ga/-range is perceived more categorically than a vocalic stimulus continuum covering the /i/-/e/-/a/-range [2]. It is unclear whether pure continuous perception occurs at all since even non-speech acoustic stimulus continua like e.g. single tone stimulus continua (pitch perception) indicate a tendency to categorical perception

A. Esposito et al. (Eds.): COST 2102 Int. Training School 2010, LNCS 6456, pp. 354–361, 2011.

(for a discussion of non-speech continuous or categorical perception see [3], [4], [5], and [6]). Currently, the interest in categorical versus continuous perception again increases, because the underlying neural mechanisms of continuous and categorical perception are not yet resolved (see [7] and [8]) and because categorical perception algorithms are needed for the construction of artificial agents [9].

On the basis of computer simulation experiments a neural mechanism will be identified in this study, which could be responsible for categorical vs. continuous perception of acoustic stimulus continua. These experiments are based on a neurophonetic model of speech production and speech perception, which is capable to reproduce the quantitative results of behavioral identification and discrimination experiments occurring for consonantal /ba/-/da/-/ga/- and vocalic /i/-/e/-/a/-stimulus continua [10].

2   The Neurophonetic Model

Our neurophonetic model (Fig. 1) can be divided in a motor feed forward part (from phonemic map via phonetic map or motor planning module to articulatory states) and a sensory feedback part (from sensory preprocessing via sensory-phonetic processing to syllabic auditory map SAM and to syllabic somatosensory map SSM).

In the case of the production (motor feed forward part) of frequent syllables (i.e. already acquired syllables), each syllable is coded by one model neuron on the level of the phonemic map. Activation of that phonemic state (e.g. /ba/) leads to a co-activation of one or more neurons within the phonetic map further co-activating a motor plan, syllabic auditory and somatosensory state for that syllable. At the motor plan level, a gesture score is activated for that syllable, i.e. a high level motor description of all vocal tract actions and their temporal coordination needed for producing that syllable; i.e. consonantal bilabial closing action, vocalic tongue lowering action, and glottal closing action for phonation and the temporal coordination of these vocal tract actions in the case of /ba/ [11]. This motor plan state leads to an activation of specific primary motor states (i.e. articulator positions and movements; cp. [12]) for each time instant during the execution of the syllable.

Within the sensory feedback part, a current somatosensory and auditory state (sensory state) is passed from the periphery (receptor neurons and preprocessing modules) towards the somatosensory and auditoy map for each time instant. The sensory state is stored at the level of the syllabic auditory and syllabic somatosensory map (SAM and SSM as part of the working or short-term memory). Auditory preprocessing is implemented currently by extracting the formant frequency of the first three formants with a time step of 10 ms. Thus the trajectories of the first three formants F1, F2, and F3 over time are stored for a whole syllable within the SAM (syllable formant pattern). In the same way tactile information (i.e. contact area of lips, hard and soft palate) and somatosensory information (i.e. current position and movement velocity of upper and lower lips, tongue tip, tongue body and lower jaw) is updated each 10 ms and stored temporarily in the SSM for produced and currently perceived syllables.

In order to provide the model with speech knowledge, a babbling training and afterwards an imitation training is performed. During babbling training syllabic sensory states related to syllabic motor states were generated for an amount of 2158 random proto-V and 2079 random proto-CV training items (V = vocalic; C = consonant). 1000 training steps were calculated per training item. The babbling training leads to an adjustment of neural link weights between the phonetic map (i.e. a a self-organizing map or SOM) and the motor plan, syllabic auditory, and syllabic somato-sensory map [13]. Currently, two separate 15x15 SOM's were trained for V- and CV-items, i.e. the V-part and the CV-part of the phonetic map. After language-independent babbling training the same SOM's and their neural association to motor map, sensory maps and now also to the phonemic map were further trained now by imitating language specific 6125 V- and 6255 CV-stimuli. This was done for a "model language" comprising five vowels (/i/, /e/, /a/, /o/, /u/), three consonants (/b/, /d/, /g/), and all 15 CV-combinations (C = consonant, V = vowel) of these speech sounds. Again, 1000 training steps were calculated per training item. After babbling and imitation training the model was capable to produce and to perceive these 5 trained vowels and the 15 trained syllables.

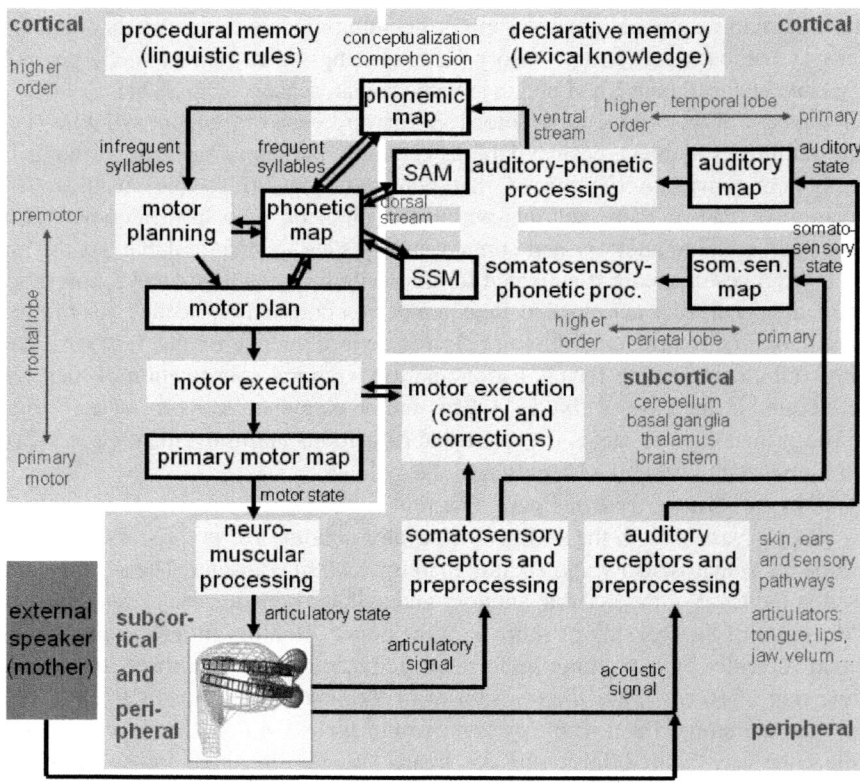

Fig. 1. Organization of the neurophonetic model of speech production and perception. Framed boxes indicate neural maps, arrows indicate neural mappings or processing paths, non-framed boxes indicate processing modules (see also text).

3 Method

20 instances of the model (i.e. "virtual listeners/speakers") were trained using a different initialization of the phonetic to phonemic, sensory, and motor plan map. The knowledge which is acquired for each instance of the model during the babbling and imitation phase (i.e. during the earliest phases of speech acquisition) is stored within the bidirectional neural associations of phonetic to other maps as described above. Thus a phonetic state, which is represented by a neuron within the phonetic map, represents (i) a realization of a phonemic state /V/ or /CV/, (ii) a motor plan state, (iii) an auditory state, and (iv) a somatosensory state. Consequently, the activation of a phonetic state via the phonemic map – as it occurs during production – means that the speaker knows, how to produce that speech item (motor plan), what that speech item sounds like (auditory map), and what the production of that speech item "feels" like (somatosensory map). Moreover, the activation of a phonetic state via the auditory path (i.e. via activation of a syllabic auditory state) – as it occurs during perception – means that the listener is capable to identify its phonemic state via most strongly co-activated neuron within the phonemic map. We tried to visualize this complex information associated with each neuron of the phonetic map in Fig. 2 for the V-part and in Fig. 3 for the CV-part of the phonetic map. 15x15 maps were chosen for the V- as well as for the CV-part (C=/b, d, g/) of the phonetic map (see section 4 of this paper).

After speech acquisition training (i.e. babbling and imitation), the 20 instances of the model as virtual listeners can perform identification and discrimination experiments for a vocalic /i/-/e/-/a/- stimulus continuum (13 stimuli) and for a consonantal /ba/-/da/-/ga/-stimulus continuum (13 stimuli as well, see Kröger et al. 2009). Listening to each of these acoustic stimuli leads to a specific neural activation pattern at the syllabic auditory state level (SAM, Fig. 1) and subsequently to a specific co-activation at the level of the phonetic map. Thus within the phonetic map for each of the 13 V- and 13 CV-stimuli one (winner) neuron can be identified, which exhibits the highest activation and thus represents the phonetic state of that stimulus. These "stimulus neurons" are indicted in Fig. 2 and 3 by bold outlined boxes for the V- and the CV-part of the phonetic map for a sample virtual listener (i.e. model instance 11).

4 Results

Fig. 2 and 3 display the V- and the CV-part of a phonetic map including the visualization of link weights (i.e. strength of connection of neurons) between phonetic and auditory and phonetic and motor plan map for a typical virtual listener (listener 11). A first inspection of this phonetic map indicates that the winner neurons representing the phonetic states of the 13 V-stimuli (also called V-stimulus neurons) are distributed nearly continuously while the CV-stimulus neurons are clustered into 3 groups. And it can be seen that this clustering is related to phoneme regions, i.e. to the /ba/-, /da/-, and /ga/-region (Fig. 3).

We tested the hypothesis that the tendency for clustering of states is higher for the CV- than for the V-case by analyzing the location of all test stimulus neurons within the phonetic maps for all 20 instances of the model. For this analysis two criteria were set for identifying a stimulus neuron cluster: (i) Neighboring neurons within a cluster

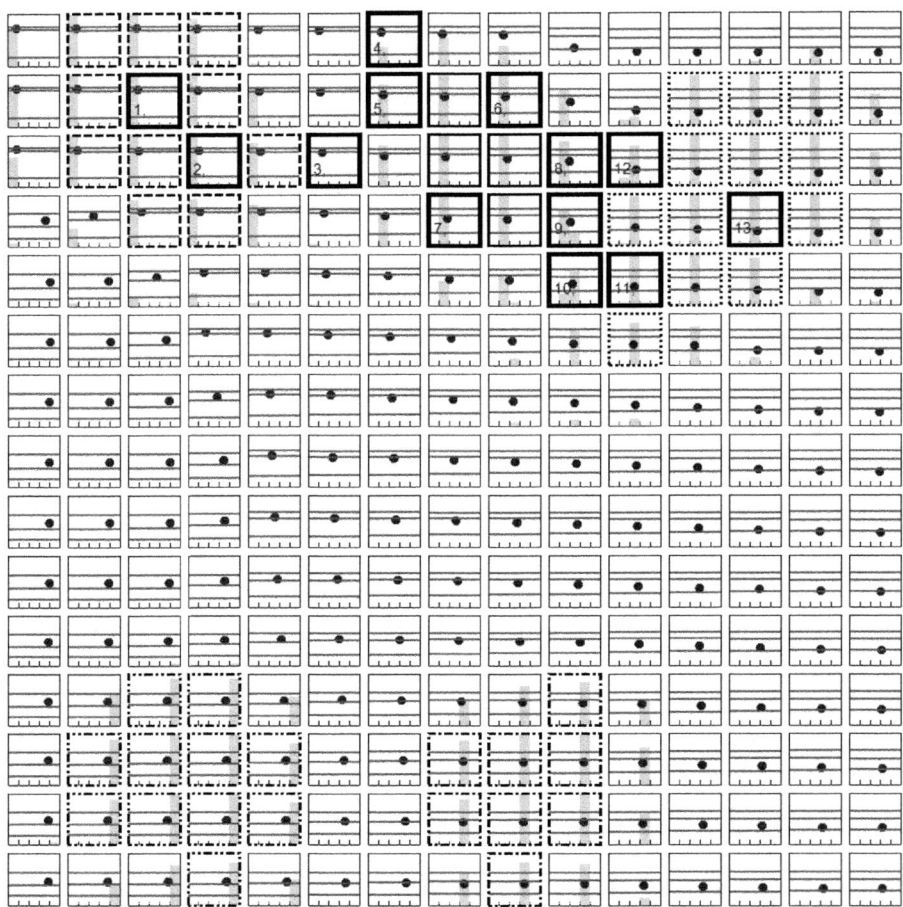

Fig. 2. Phonemic, motor, and sensory states represented by each neuron of the phonetic map for vowels (model instance 11). Each box represents a neuron of the phonetic map for vowels. Light grey bars represent the degree of activation of a phonemic state (from left to right: degree of /i/-, /e/-, /a/-, /o/-, /u/-activation. The dashed and small solid outlined boxes indicate phoneme regions, i.e. an activation of one phonemic state above 80% (dashed = /i/; solid = /e/; dotted = /a/; dash-dotted = /o/; dash-dott-dotted = /u/). The horizontal grey lines indicate the bark-scaled value of the first three formants representing the vocalic auditory state (bottom = 3 bark; top = 15 bark). The dark grey dot indicates the motor and proprioceptive representation of the vocalic tongue position (vertical = front – back; horizontal = low – high). The bold outlined boxes represent neurons which were activated by the vocalic stimulus continuum ("stimulus neurons"). The numbers within these boxes equals the stimulus number within the vocalic stimulus continuum.

need to be at least in a "next but one" relation, i.e. a maximum distance of one intermediate (non-stimulus) neuron is allowed between two neighboring neurons within a cluster. If the distance is greater than that, these two neurons are not members of the same cluster. (ii) A cluster needs to comprise at least 3 neurons.

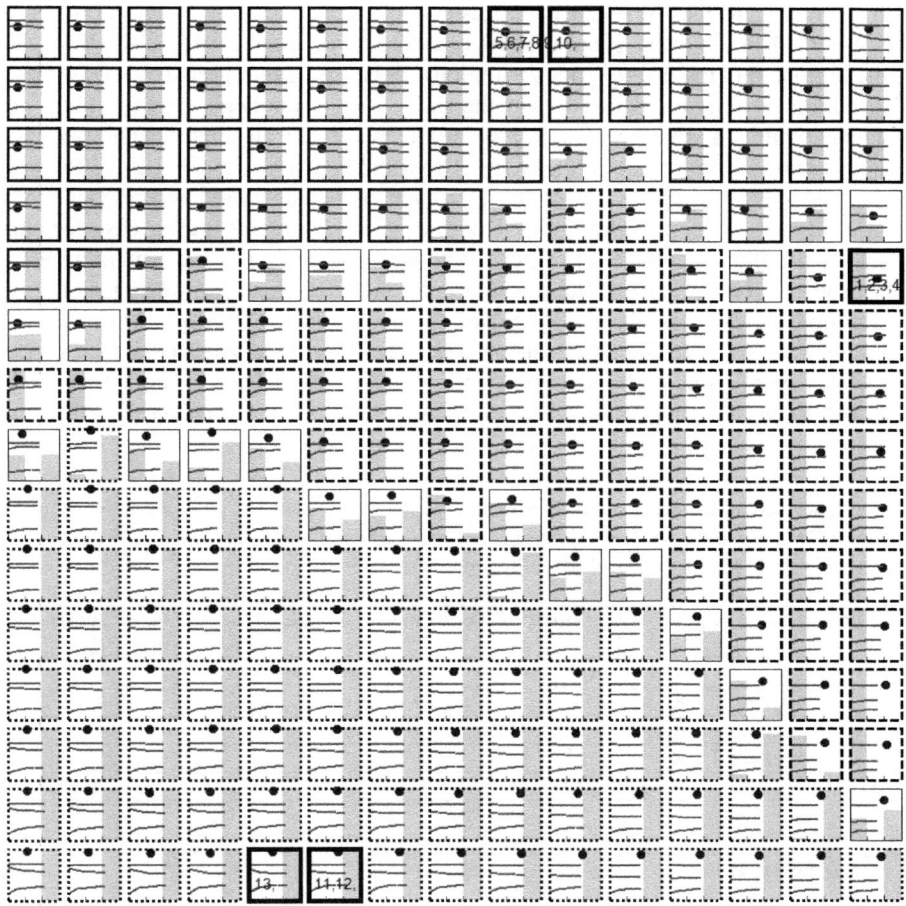

Fig. 3. Phonemic, motor, and sensory states represented by each neuron of the phonetic map for CV-syllables (model instance 11). Each box represents a neuron of the phonetic map for CV-syllables. Light grey bars represent the degree of activation of a phonemic state (from left to right: degree of /b/-, /d/-, /g/-activation. The dashed and small solid outlined boxes indicate phoneme regions, i.e. an activation of one phonemic state above 80% (dashed = /b/; solid = /d/; dotted = /g/). The horizontal grey trajectories indicate the bark-scaled value of the first three formants representing the auditory state of the syllable (bottom = 3 bark; top = 15 bark). The dark grey dot indicates the motor and proprioceptive representation of the final vocalic tongue position within the CV syllable (vertical = front – back; horizontal = low – high). Motor states can only be produced by those neurons which reach a phonemic activation above 80%. In these cases the bar represents the primary consonantal articulator (i.e. labial, apical or dorsal). The bold outlined boxes represent neurons which were activated by the consonantal stimulus continuum ("stimulus neurons"). The numbers within these boxes represent the stimulus number within the consonantal stimulus continuum.

The cluster analysis of all 20 virtual listeners indicates that for 19 virtual listeners, the V-part of the phonetic map exhibits one stimulus cluster covering all three phoneme regions (i.e. the /i/-, /e/-, and /a/-region). This can be interpreted as a continuous distribution of stimulus neurons over the three vocalic phoneme regions. Only one instance exhibits a stimulus cluster, which does not cover all three vocalic phoneme regions (Tab. 1). Furthermore for 11 (of 20) virtual listeners, the CV-part of the phonetic map clearly displays three clusters, each associated with a single phoneme region (i.e. /b/-, /d/-, and /g/-region). This can be interpreted as a clear case for clustering of stimulus neurons with respect to phoneme regions. For the remaining 9 virtual listeners, the CV-part of the phonetic map includes clusters covering more than one phoneme region (Tab. 1). Moreover in the CV-part of the phonetic map, 33 stimulus clusters were identified in total over all 20 virtual listeners, which can be associated with a single phoneme region. In contrast in the case of the V-part of the phonetic maps this only occurs for one stimulus cluster in total over all 20 virtual listeners (see Tab. 1).

Table 1. Results of a cluster analysis for the CV- and V-parts of the phonetic maps of all 20 virtual listeners (instances). The amount of instances, which exhibit the expected clustering, are indicated by bold letters. (CL = cluster; PR = phoneme region)

Type of instance	amount of instances		amount of CL's associated with a single PR	
	/CV/	/V/	/CV/	/V/
1 CL covering 3 PR	1	**19**	0	0
1 CL covering 2 PR	8	0	0	0
1 CL covering 1 PR	**11**	1	33	1
Total	20	20	**33**	**1**

5   Discussion

Our results indicate a stronger tendency towards a clustering of stimulus neurons in the case of the CV-part of phonetic maps than in the V-part. This result underlines that CV-stimuli (/C/ = /b/, /d/, or /g/) are perceived categorically while V-stimuli are perceived less categorically (more continuously) and this result is in accordance with the results of behavioral identification and discrimination experiments done by these virtual listeners [10]. It would be important now to create brain imaging experiments which support (or contradict) these results. But cortical phoneme regions seem to be very small, which makes these experiments very difficult [14].

In accordance with other approaches for modeling categorical perception [15, 9] our approach stresses the importance of *learning* and *neural self-organization* in order to reach typical features of categorical perception. But beyond other approaches our model stresses the importance of a supramodal "phonetic" level of self-organization which – beside linguistic information – takes into account sensory *and* motor information in parallel. We will demonstrate in further experiments that in the case of perception for place of articulation (labial – apical – dorsal) categories may emerge directly from anatomical facts and thus, infants just need (self-)babbling training in order to reach categorical perception of place of articulation. Since articulators (i.e. our hardware) developed during evolution our model also delivers arguments for an evolution of categorical perception [16] at least for the perception of place of articulation.

Acknowledgments. This work was supported in part by the German Research Council DFG grant Kr 1439/13-1 and grant Kr 1439/15-1.

References

[1] Liberman, A.M., Harris, K.S., Hoffman, H.S., Griffith, B.C.: The discrimination of speech sounds within and across phoneme boundaries. Journal of Experimental Psychology 54, 358–368 (1957)

[2] Fry, D.B., Abramson, A.S., Eimas, P.D., Liberman, A.M.: The identification and discrimination of synthetic vowels. Language and Speech 5, 171–189 (1962)

[3] Eimas, P.D.: The relation between identification and discrimination along speech and non-speech continua. Language and Speech 6, 206–217 (1963)

[4] Mattingly, I.G., Liberman, A.M., Syrdal, A.K., Halves, T.: Discrimination in speech and nonspeech modes. Cognitive Psychology 2, 131–157 (1971)

[5] Burns, E.M., Campbell, S.L.: Frequency and frequency-ration resolution by possessors of absolute and relative pitch: Examplex of categorical perception? Journal of the Acoustical Society of America 96, 2704–2719 (1994)

[6] Mirman, D., Holt, L.L., McClelland, J.L.: Categorization and discrimination of non-speech sounds: differences between steady-state and rapidly-changing acoustic cues. Journal of the Acoustical Society of America 116, 1198–1207 (2004)

[7] Poeppel, D., Guillemin, A., Thompson, J., Fritz, J., Bavelier, D., Braun, A.R.: Auditory lexical decision, categorical perception, and FM direction discrimination differentially engage left and right auditory cortex. Neuropsychologia 42, 183–200 (2004)

[8] Liebenthal, E., Binder, J.R., Spitzer, S.M., Possing, E.T., Medler, D.A.: Neural substrates of phonemic perception, vol. 15, pp. 1621–1631 (2005)

[9] Beer, R.D.: The dynamics of active categorical perception in an evolved model agent. Adaptive Behavior 11, 209–243 (2003)

[10] Kröger, B.J., Kannampuzha, J., Neuschaefer-Rube, C.: Towards a neurocomputational model of speech production and perception. Speech Communication 51, 793–809 (2009)

[11] Kröger, B.J., Birkholz, P.: A gesture-based concept for speech movement control in articulatory speech synthesis. In: Esposito, A., Faundez-Zanuy, M., Keller, E., Marinaro, M. (eds.) COST Action 2102. LNCS (LNAI), vol. 4775, pp. 174–189. Springer, Heidelberg (2007)

[12] Guenther, F.H., Ghosh, S.S., Tourville, J.A.: Neural modeling and imaging of the cortical interactions underlying syllable production. Brain and Language 96, 280–301 (2006)

[13] Kohonen, T.: Self-Organizing Maps. Springer, Berlin (2001)

[14] Obleser, J., Boecker, H., Drzezga, A., Haslinger, B., Hennenlotter, A., Roettinger, M., Eulitz, C., Rauschecker, J.P.: Vowel sound extraction in anterior superior temporal cortex. Human Brain Mapping 27, 562–571 (2006)

[15] Damper, R.I., Harnad, S.R.: Neural network models of categorical perception. Perception and Psychophysics 62, 843–867 (2000)

[16] Kuhl, P.K.: Early language acquisition: cracking the speech code. Nature Reviews Neuroscience 5, 831–843 (2004)

The MultiLis Corpus – Dealing with Individual Differences in Nonverbal Listening Behavior

Iwan de Kok and Dirk Heylen

Human Media Interaction
University of Twente
{koki,heylen}@ewi.utwente.nl

Abstract. Computational models that attempt to predict when a virtual human should backchannel are often based on the analysis of recordings of face-to-face conversations between humans. Building a model based on a corpus brings with it the problem that people differ in the way they behave. The data provides examples of responses of a single person in a particular context but in the same context another person might not have provided a response. Vice versa, the corpus will contain contexts in which the particular listener recorded did not produce a backchannel response, where another person would have responded. Listeners can differ in the amount, the timing and the type of backchannels they provide to the speaker, because of individual differences - related to personality, gender, or culture, for instance. To gain more insight in this variation we have collected data in which we record the behaviors of three listeners interacting with one speaker. All listeners think they are having a one-on-one conversation with the speaker, while the speaker actually only sees one of the listeners. The context, in this case the speaker's actions, is for all three listeners the same and they respond to it individually. This way we have created data on cases in which different persons show similar behaviors and cases in which they behave differently. With the recordings of this data collection study we can start building our model of backchannel behavior for virtual humans that takes into account similarities and differences between persons.

Keywords: Multimodal corpus, listeners, task-oriented.

1 Introduction

In the field of embodied conversational agents a lot of effort is put into making the interaction between humans and the agent as natural as possible. Models of interaction behavior can be based on insights from theoretical studies, rules of thumb or they can be based on machine analysis of multimodal corpora of human-human interactions. The problem with using multimodal corpora to analyze and model human behavior is that in the recorded face-to-face conversation only one example of an appropriate way to act in a certain context is recorded even though there may be other appropriate responses to that context than the

A. Esposito et al. (Eds.): COST 2102 Int. Training School 2010, LNCS 6456, pp. 362–375, 2011.
© Springer-Verlag Berlin Heidelberg 2011

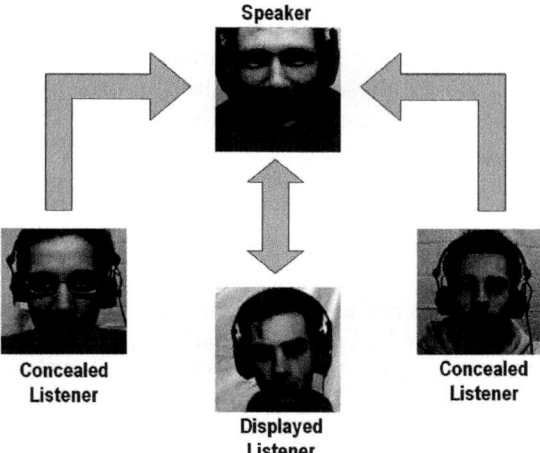

Fig. 1. Schematic overview of the setup for this corpus. Each interaction is between a speaker and three listeners. The *speaker* sees only one of the listeners (the *displayed listener*). The other two listeners, the *concealed listeners*, can see the speaker, but the speaker is unaware of their participation to the conversation. All listeners believe to be the only listener in the interaction.

one recorded. This certainly holds true for backchannel responses. In most situations, there is nothing wrong with missing a backchannel opportunity. When one is using a multimodal corpus to train a model for predicting the timing of backchannel continuers, as was done in [7], this optionality of behaviour provides a problem for evaluation. The issue of variability and optionality of behaviours show bot in training and in evaluation. First, not all the contexts in which a backchannel is possible are used for analysis and modeling, only the contexts in which the listener recorded actually provided a backchannel response are included. Second, the issue also shows during evaluation of the model. Evaluation usually involves comparing the output of the backchannel model trained on the corpus to the actual responses recorded. There might be many cases in which the model predicts a possible backchannel which one might consider correct, but where the actual listener in the corpus did not produce one. These should not be counted as false positives but with most evaluations methods they will.

Besides in timing a backchannel listeners may differ in the type of backchannels they provide. Variation may be related to personality, gender, culture, or the time of day, concentration or attention levels, etcetera. To gain more insight in these differences and to help in training more accurate computational models, we have collected a new set of recordings that shows individual differences between multiple listeners that believe they are interacting face-to-face with the speaker. Each listener thinks he is the only one listening to the speaker and the speaker also thinks there is only one listener (see Figure 1). We will describe the MultiLis corpus in this paper.

Before we present the data collection proper, we will discuss related work which has attempted to deal with the same problem as stated above, in Section 2. The method of data collection we have performed in Section 3. In Section 4 the recordings of the corpus are presented and the annotations made are described in Section 5. The individual differences we captured in this corpus are shown in Section 6. Finally our plans for using this data are discussed in Section 7.

2   Related Work

We are not the first to identify this problem of optionality and to offer a solution. In their effort to create a predictive rule for backchannels based on prosodic cues, Ward and Tsukahara [10] define backchannel feedback as follows: "Backchannel feedback responds directly to the content of an utterance of the other, is *optional* [our emphasis], and does not require acknowledgement by the other." When analyzing the performance of their predictive rule they conclude that 44% of the incorrect predictions were cases where a backchannel could naturally have appeared according to the judgement of one of the authors, whereas in the corpus there was silence or, more rarely, the start of a turn. Listeners might have given a nonverbal backchannel (e.g., a head nod), which is not recorded, but the listeners may also have chosen not to produce a backchannel at all at that opportunity.

Cathcart et al. [2] identified the same problem as well. In their shallow model of backchannel continuers based on pause duration and n-gram part -of-speech tags they remark that human listener differ markedly in their own backchanneling behavior and pass up opportunities to provide a backchannel. Their attempt at dealing with this is to test their model on high backchannel rate data which is based on the assumption that the more backchannels an individual produces, the fewer opportunities they are likely to have passed up.

Both the papers attempt to solve the problem after the data is collected and the model has been produced. This gives them a better insight into the actual qualitative performance of the model by taking the variation into account, but it does not solve the issue at its root, namely the way in which ground truth is established for the contexts in which backchannels are appropriate.

Noguchi and Den [8] look at an alternative way to collect data. In their machine learning approach to modelling back-channel behavior based on prosodic features they need a collection of positive and negative examples of appropiate contexts for backchannels. Because providing backchannels is almost always optional, they also argue that it is not appropiate to consider only those contexts where backchannels are found in the corpus as positive examples and contexts where no backchannels are found as negative examples. As a solution to this they collected backchannels responses from participants in a study, in which the participants looked at a video of a speaker and were asked to hit the space bar on a keyboard at times where they thought a backchannel response was appropiate. The stimuli consisted of several pause-bounded phrases which constitute a single conversational move. Each stimulus was shown to 9 participants. By counting the number of participants that responded positively to the stimuli they classified each one as either an appropiate context for a backchannel, an inappropiate context for a backchannel or as indecisive.

The same approach was also used by Huang et al. [4] where it was dubbed Parasocial Consensus Sampling (PCS). The authors used the annotation thus obtained directly to generate backchannel responses of a virtual human in a simulated conversation with the original speaker. In a subsequent evaluation study, participants rated these conversations and compared them to conversations between the human speaker and a virtual agent that was copying the original listener behavior. Participants thought the agent that used the consensus-based algorithm was more believable and showed higher rapport with the speaker than the agent that copied the original listener.

The Parasocial Consensus Sampling method is particularly useful for analyzing the timing of backchannels, however, there are many more dimensions of human listening behavior that should be accounted for. People also vary in the selection of the type of backchannel they choose (e.g., only a head nod, a head nod accompanied by 'yeah', a head nod accompanied by 'mm-hmm', etc.), or their gaze behavior and body posture. Using the PCS method to annotate these features as well is very time consuming, if not impossible for some behaviors (e.g., body posture). Therefore we propose another way of collecting a corpus for the analysis of (non-)verbal listening behavior which accounts for variation between listeners.

3   Data Collection

The goal of this data collection is to record multiple listeners in parallel in interaction with the same speaker. The corpus consists of interactions between one speaker and three listeners in which each of the listeners sees the speaker on a monitor and the speaker sees only one of the listeners. The listeners are made to believe they have a one-on-one conversation with the speaker and also the speaker is unaware of the special setup How this illusion is created is discussed in Section 3.1. The procedure during recording is discussed in Section 3.2, the tasks are discussed in Section 3.3 and the measures we used can be found in Section 3.4.

3.1   Setup

Each of the participants sat in a separate cubicle. The digital camcorders which recorded the interaction, were placed behind a one-way mirror onto which the interlocutor was projected (see Figure 2). This ensured that the participants got the illusion of eye contact with their interlocutor. In Figure 3 one can see that the listeners appear to be looking into the camera which was behind the mirror. This video was also what the participants saw during the interaction. All participants wore a headphone through which they could hear their interlocutor. The microphone was placed at the bottom of the autocue set up and was connected to the camcorder for recording.

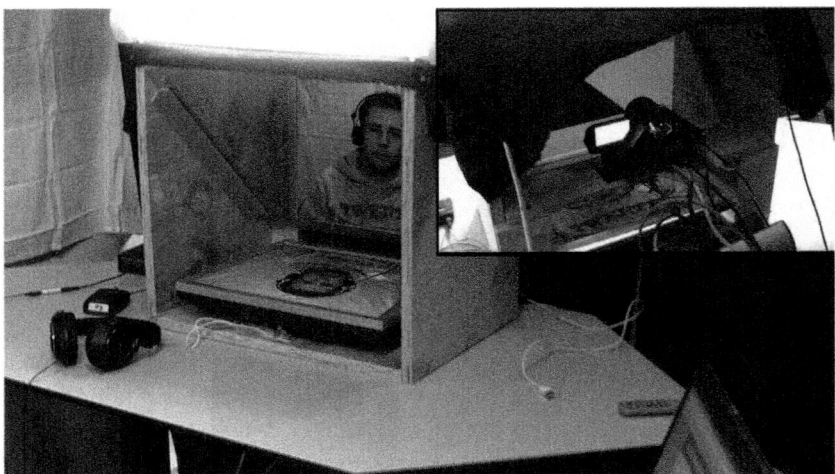

Fig. 2. Picture of the cubicle in which each participant was seated. It illustrates the interrogation mirror and the placement of the camera behind it which ensures eye contact.

During the interaction speakers were shown one of the listeners (the *displayed listener*) and could not see the other two listeners (the *concealed listeners*). All three listeners saw the recording of the same speaker and all three believed to be the only one involved in a one-to-one interaction with that speaker. Distribution of the different audio and video signals was done with a Magenta Mondo Matrix III, which is a UTP switch board for HD-video, stereo audio and serial signals. Participants remained in the same cubicle during the whole experiment. The Magenta Mondo Matrix III enabled us to switch between distributions remotely.

3.2   Procedure

In total eight sessions were recorded. For each session there were four participants invited (in total there were 29 male and 3 female participants, with a mean age of 25). At each session, four interactions were recorded. The participants were told that in each interaction they would have a one-on-one conversation with one other participant and that they would either be a speaker or a listener. However, during each interaction only one participant was assigned the role of speaker and the other three were assigned the role of listeners. Within a session, every participant was a speaker in one interaction, was once a displayed listener and appeared twice as concealed listener.

In order to be able to create this illusion of one-on-one conversations we needed to limit the interactivity of the conversation because as soon as the displayed listener would ask a question or start speaking, the concealed listeners would notice this in the behavior of the speaker and the illusion would be broken. Therefore the listeners were instructed not to ask questions or take over the role of speaker in any other way. However we did encourage them to provide short feedback to the speaker.

3.3 Tasks

The participants were given tasks. There were two different type of tasks the participants needed to perform during the interaction, either retelling a video clip or giving the instruction for a cooking recipe. For the retelling of the video speakers were instructed to watch the video carefully and to remember as many details as possible, since the listener would be asked questions about the video after the summary of the speaker. To give the speakers an idea of the questions which were going to be asked, they received a subset of 8 open questions before watching the video. After watching the video they had to give the questions back so that they would not have something to distract them. After the retelling both the speaker and the listeners filled out a questionnaire with 16 multiple choice questions about the video. Each question had four alternative answers plus the option "I do not know" and for the listener the extra option "The speaker did not tell this". As stimuli the 1950 Warner Bros. Tweety and Sylvester cartoon "Canary Row" and the 1998 animated short "More" by Mark Osborne were used[1].

For the second task the speaker was given 10 minutes to study a cooking recipe. Both the listener and the speaker needed to reproduce the recipe as completely as possible in the questionnaire afterwards. As stimuli a tea smoked salmon recipe and a mushroom risotto recipe were used.

We chose to use two different tasks to be able to see the influence of the task on listening behavior. The retelling of the video is more entertaining and narrative in nature, while the recipe task is more procedural.

3.4 Measures

Before the experiment we asked participants to fill out their age and gender and we had them fill out personality and mood questionnaires. For personality we used the validated Dutch translation of the 44 item version of the Big Five Inventory [6]. For mood we used seven out of eleven subscales from Positive and Negative Affect Schedule - Expanded Form (PANAS-X, 41 items) [11] and the two general positive and negative affect scales. Furthermore we used the Profile of Mood States for Adults (POMS-A, 24 items) [9]. For both PANAS-X and POMS-A we used unvalidated Dutch translations made by the authors. Subjects were instructed to assess their mood of "today".

After each interaction speakers filled out the Inventory of Conversational Satisfaction (ICS, 16 items) [12], questions about their task performance (5 items) and questions about their goals during the interaction (3 items). The listeners filled out an adapted version of the rapport measure [3] with additional questions from the ICS (10 items in total, e.g. "There was a connection between the

---

[1] Canary   Row   (1950):   http://www.imdb.com/title/tt0042304/;   More   (1998): http://www.imdb.com/title/tt0188913/

Fig. 3. Screenshot of a combined video of the four participants in an interaction

speaker and me."). Some questions of the 16 items ICS relate to talking, which the listener does not do in our experiment, so they were left out. Furthermore the listeners answered six questions about the task performance of the speaker, such as "The speaker was entertaining" or "The speaker was interested in what he told". All questions were 5-point Likert Scale.

After the complete session, with all four interactions were finished subjects were debriefed and were asked which interaction they preferred; whether they had believed the illusion of always having one-on-one interaction, and if not, at which moment they had noticed this; in which interaction they thought the speaker could see them; about the delay of the mediated communication, audio and video quality (3 items).

4   MultiLis Corpus

In total 32 conversations were recorded (8 for each task), totalling in 131 minutes of data (mean length of 4:06 minutes). All the conversations were in Dutch.

Audio and video for each participant was recorded in synchrony by the digital camcorders. Synchronisation of the four different sources was done by identifying the time of a loud noise which was made during recording and could be heard on all audio signals.

Videos are available in high quality (1024x576, 25fps, FFDS compression) and low quality (640x360, 25fps, XviD compression). Audio files are available in high quality (48kHz sampling rate) and low quality (16kHz sampling rate). Furthermore a combined video (1280x720, 25fps, XviD compression) of all four participants in a conversation is available (for a screenshot, see Figure 3).

5   Annotations

Speakers were annotated on eye gaze and mouth movements other than speech. Listeners were annotated on head, eyebrow and mouth movements and any speech they produced was transcribed as well. For this annotation we used the ELAN annotation tool [1].

For the listeners the annotations were made in a three step process. First the interesting regions with listener responses were identified. This was done by looking at the video of the listener with sound of the speaker and marking moments in which a response of the listener to the speaker is noticed. In the second step these regions were annotated more precisely on head, brows and mouth movements. Speech of the listener was also transcribed by hand. In the third and final step the onset of the response was determined.

In the following subsections the annotation scheme for each modality will be explained in more detail. In each annotation scheme left and right are defined from the perspective of the annotator.

EYE GAZE. Annotation of the speakers' gaze provides information about whether they were looking into the camera (and therefore looking at the listener) or not and whether there was blinking. For each of these two features a binary tier was created. Annotations were done by two annotators who each annotated half of the sessions. One session was annotated by both. Agreement (calculated by overlap / duration) for gaze was 0.88 and for blink 0.66.

HEAD. For listeners the shape of the head movements. An annotation scheme of 12 categories was developed. The 12 categories and the amount of annotations in each category are given below. Several movements had a lingering variant. Lingering head movements are movements where one there is one clear stroke identifiable followed with a few more strokes that clearly decrease in intensity. If during this lingering phase the intensity or frequency of the movement increases again a new annotation is started.

- **Nod** (681 & 766 lingering) - The main stroke of the vertical head movement is downwards.
- **Backnod** (428 & 290 lingering) - The main stroke of the vertical head movement is upwards.
- **Double nod** (154 & 4 lingering) - Two repeated head nods of the same intensity.
- **Shake** (17) - Repeated horizontal head movement.
- **Upstroke** (156) - Single vertical movement upwards. This can either occur independently or just before a nod.
- **Downstroke** (43) - Single vertical movement downwards. This can either occur independently or just before a backnod.
- **Tilt** (24 left & 15 right) - Rotation of the head, leaning to the left or right.
- **Turn** (8 left & 11 right) - Turning of the head into left or right direction.
- **Waggle** (7) - Repeated nods accompanied by multiple head tilts.

- **Sidenod** (9 & 2 lingering) - Nod accompanied by a turn into one direction (6 left & 5 right).
- **Backswipe** (18 & 2 lingering) - Backnod which is not only performed with the neck, but also the body moves backwards.
- **Sideswipe** (3 left & 5 right) - Sidenod which is not only performed with the neck, but also the body moves into that direction.

Keep in mind that head movements are annotated only in areas where a listener response was identified in the first step of the annotation process. Especially turns and tilts occur more often than reflected in these numbers, but the others are not categorized as listener responses.

EYEBROWS. For the listeners eyebrow raises and frowns were annotated. It was indicated whether the movement concerned one or both eyebrows. When one eyebrow was raised or frowned, it is indicated which eyebrow (left or right) made the movement. In total this layer contains 200 annotations, 131 raises and 69 frowns. These numbers include the annotations in which only one eyebrow was raised or frowning occurred with one eyebrow.

MOUTH. The movements of the mouth are annotated with the following labels (457 in total): smile (396), lowered mouth corners (31), pressed lips (22) and six other small categories (8). Especially with smiles the end time is hard to determine. If the person is smiling, but increases the intensity of the smile, a new annotation is created.

SPEECH. For the speakers we collected the results of the automatic speech recognition software SHoUT [5]. For listeners the speech was transcribed. In total 186 utterances were transcribed. The most common utterances were "uh-huh" (76), "okay" (42) and "ja" (29).

RESPONSES. This annotation layer was created in the third step of the annotation process of the listener. What we refer to as a listener response can be any combination of these various behaviors, for instance, a head nod accompanied by a smile, raised eyebrows accompanied by a smile or the vocalization of uh-huh, occurring at about the same time. For each of these responses we have marked the so-called onset (start time). The onset of a listener response is either the stroke of a head movement, the start of a vocalization, the start of eyebrow movement or the start of a mouth movement. When different behaviors combine into one listener response, either the head movement or vocalization was chosen as onset (whichever came first). If there was no head movement or vocalization present, either the eyebrow or mouth movement was chosen as onset (whichever came first). In total 2796 responses are in the corpus.

Given these annotations, we can start to look at the distribution of the various responses of one listener, both in relation to the speaker's behaviours and in relation to the responses of the other listeners.

Table 1. The table shows the reported answers to questions in the post-questionnaire regarding the manipulation. 14 out of 31 participants reported that they noticed that they were not always seen. In total 11 out of 31 participants could correctly identify the interaction in which they were seen by the speaker.

Noticed illusion?		Seen by speaker?		
		Correct	No Idea	Wrong
Yes	14	6	3	5
No	17	5	1	11
All	31	11	4	16

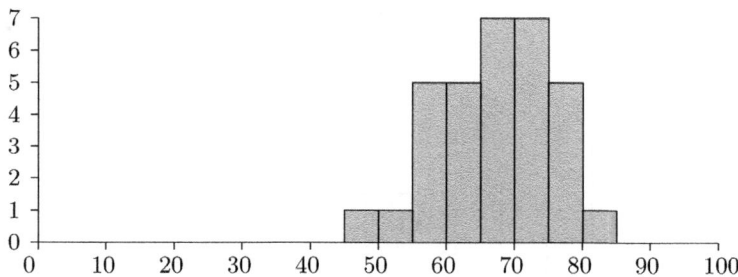

Fig. 4. Histogram showing the distribution of speakers in percentage of speaking time

6   Individual Differences in the MultiLis Corpus

The reason for collecting this corpus was to identify and be able to analyze the differences and similarities between individuals in their listening behavior. In this section we show that we were successful in capturing these differences and similarities in the corpus. We start with a manipulation check to see whether our illusion of one-on-one conversation instead of parallel conversation worked. After this we show results illustrating the differences between the speaker and the listeners captured in the corpus.

Table 1 shows the results of the manipulation check. During the post-questionnaire 14 out of 31 participants reported that they noticed that they were not always seen (1 participant failed to fill out the post-questionnaire). Out of those 14 only 6 could correctly identify in which conversation they were seen by the speaker. In total 11 out of 31 participants correctly identified this conversation. This is hardly above chance (= 33%). So, even when they noticed something was off, they could still not identify the correct conversation. If we look at the amount of responses the displayed listeners (1007) and the concealed listeners (895) gave we see that concealed listeners give on average 12% less responses, but according to a paired-sample t-test between the amount of responses per minute per session of displayed listeners and concealed listeners this difference is not significant ($p = 0.33$).

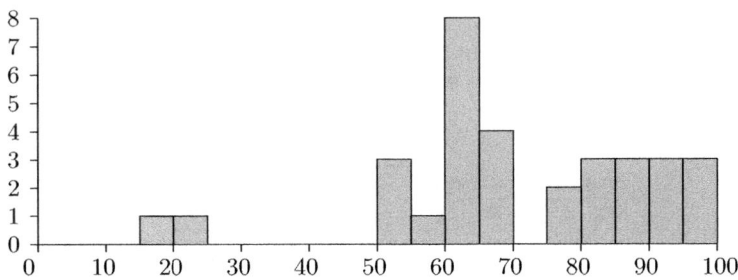

Fig. 5. Histogram showing the distribution of speakers in percentage of gaze directed at the listener

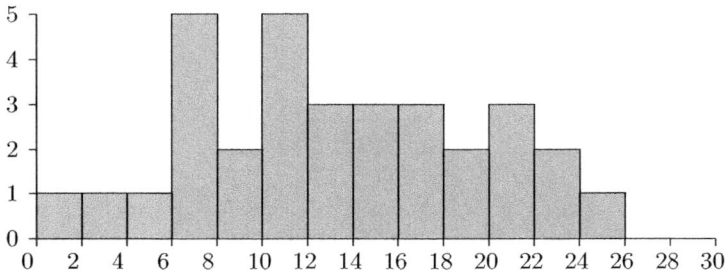

Fig. 6. Histogram showing the distribution of speakers in gaze shifts per minute

An analysis of the speakers' annotations tells us that speakers differ in the amount of time they spoke Figure 4), the amount of time they directed their gaze towards the listener (Figure 5) and the amount of gaze shifts (Figure 6). Speaking time varied between speaking 46.8 % to 83.1% of the time (mean 67.9%). The variation in gaze directed at the listeners is bigger with percentages ranging from 16.3% to 97.0% (mean 67.3%). Also the amount of gaze shifts differs a lot between speakers, from 1.6 to 24.7 gaze shift per minute (mean 13.3 per minute).

Figure 7 shows the amount of responses the listeners gave. For this histogram the average amount of responses of the three interactions of each listener is used. The amount of responses varied between 2.5 and 15.9 responses per minute (mean is 7.5 responses per minute).

Each listener was involved in three interactions. When the amount of responses the listener provides was solely caused by the choices and preferences of the listener, independently of the speaker, the listener would provide on average the same amount of responses in each of these three interactions. Figure 8 shows that this is not the case. We have grouped the interactions with the least amount of responses of each listener, the interactions with the most responses and the ones in between and calculated the mean responses per minute for each group.

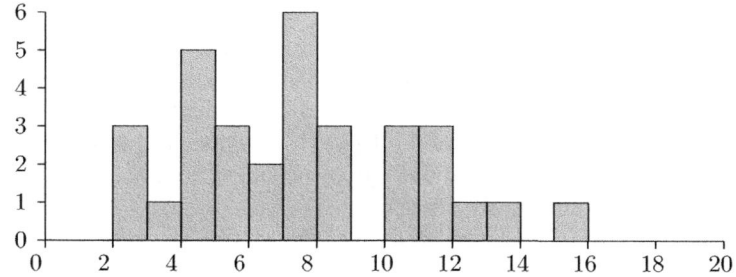

Fig. 7. Histogram showing the distribution of listeners in responses per minute

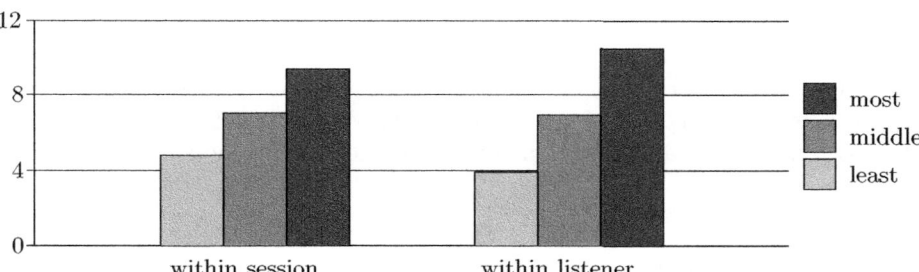

Fig. 8. The left figure shows the average amount of responses per minute grouping together the three listener *within a session* into a group of listeners with the least responses, the listeners with the most responses and the listeners in between. This illustrates that within the three listeners the amount of responses varies quite a lot. The right figure shows the average amount of responses per minute when looking at the three sessions of *each individual listener* and when grouping them into the sessions with the least responses, the listeners with the most responses and the listener in between. This illustrates that the response behavior of each listener is highly influenced by the actions of the speaker.

The right graph in Figure 8 shows that for the group the amount of the interactions with the least responses is 3.9 responses per minute, for the middle group 6.9 responses and the group with the most response, 10.5 responses per minute. So, there is a significant variation within the behavior of the listener, caused by the speaker ($p < 0.001$ on a paired-sample t-test between all groups).

The speaker is not the sole factor here as well. Figure 8 also shows that there is a variation between the three listeners within a session. Calculating the mean responses per minute for each group of the listeners of each session with the least responses per minute ($= 4.8$), most responses ($= 9.4$) and the group in between ($= 7.0$), we get the left graph in Figure 8. The variation is not as big, but still significant ($p < 0.001$ on a paired-sample t-test between all groups). This suggests that the combination of speaker and listener determines the amount of responses the listener gives, where the speaker has a little more influence on this.

To get an indication about the times that multiple listeners produced a response at about the same time, we clustered together the responses of the three listeners. Leaving out smiles and brow movements we identified 1735 clusters. In 128 cases, all three listeners produced a listener response and in 456 cases there were two listeners responding at about the same time. In 1142 of the cases only one of the listeners produced a response.

7   Conclusions and Future Work

With this data set we have created a rich source for researching various aspects of listener behavior. The corpus especially provides more insight into individual differences and similarities in nonverbal listening behavior than previous data sets, because of its unique setup. The setup deals with the limitation of previous corpora of only recording one example of an appropriate way to act in a certain context, by recording three listeners in parallel. With this data intend to improve the learning and evaluation of prediction or generation models for nonverbal listening behavior.

Acknowledgments

We would like to thank Khiet Truong, Ronald Poppe and Alfred de Vries for giving a helping hand during the collection of the corpus, Hendri Hondorp for his help in synchronizing all recordings and Arie Timmermans for his help annotating the data. The research leading to these results has received funding from the European Community's Seventh Framework Programme (FP7/2007-2013) under grant agreement n° 211486 (SEMAINE).

References

1. Brugman, H., Russel, A.: Annotating multimedia/multi-modal resources with ELAN. In: Proceedings of the Fourth International Conference on Language Resources and Evaluation, Citeseer, pp. 2065–2068 (2004)
2. Cathcart, N., Carletta, J., Klein, E.: A shallow model of backchannel continuers in spoken dialogue. In: European ACL, pp. 51–58 (2003)
3. Gratch, J., Wang, N., Gerten, J., Fast, E., Duffy, R.: Creating rapport with virtual agents. In: Pelachaud, C., Martin, J.-C., André, E., Chollet, G., Karpouzis, K., Pelé, D. (eds.) IVA 2007. LNCS (LNAI), vol. 4722, pp. 125–138. Springer, Heidelberg (2007)
4. Huang, L., Morency, L.-P., Gratch, J.: Parasocial Consensus Sampling: Combining Multiple Perspectives to Learn Virtual Human Behavior. In: Proceedings of Autonomous Agents and Multi-Agent Systems, Toronto, Canada (2010)
5. Huijbregts, M.: Segmentation, Diarization and Speech Transcription: Surprise Data Unraveled. Phd thesis, University of Twente (2008)

6. John, O.P., Naumann, L.P., Soto, C.J.: Paradigm shift to the integrative Big-Five trait taxonomy: History, measurement, and conceptual issues, 3rd edn., ch. 4, pp. 114–158. Guilford Press, New York (2008)
7. Morency, L.P., de Kok, I., Gratch, J.: A probabilistic multimodal approach for predicting listener backchannels. Autonomous Agents and Multi-Agent Systems 20(1), 70–84 (2010)
8. Noguchi, H., Den, Y.: Prosody-based detection of the context of backchannel responses. In: Fifth International Conference on Spoken Language Processing (1998)
9. Terry, P.C., Lane, A.M., Fogarty, G.J.: Construct validity of the Profile of Mood States-Adolescents for use with adults. Psychology of Sport and Exercise 4(2), 125–139 (2003)
10. Ward, N., Tsukahara, W.: Prosodic features which cue back-channel responses in English and Japanese. Journal of Pragmatics 32(8), 1177–1207 (2000)
11. Watson, D., Clark, L.A.: The PANAS-X (1994)
12. White, S.: Backchannels across cultures: A study of Americans and Japanese. Language in Society 18(1), 59–76 (1989)

Comparing the Rhythmical Characteristics of Speech and Music – Theoretical and Practical Issues

Stephan Hübler and Rüdiger Hoffmann

Laboratory of Acoustics and Speech Communication,
Technische Universität Dresden, 01062 Dresden, Germany

Abstract. By comparing the features of music and speech in intelligent audio signal processing, both related research fields might benefit from each other. Music and speech serve as a way for humans to express themselves. The aim of this study is to show similarities and differences between music and speech by comparing the hierarchical structures with an emphasis on rhythm. Especially examining the temporal structure of music and speech could lead to new interesting features that improve existing technology. For example utilizing rhythm in synthetic speech is still an open issue as well as rhythmic features have to be improved for music in the fields of semantic search and music similarity retrieval. Theoretical aspects of rhythm in speech and music are discussed as well as practical issues in speech and music research. To show that common approaches are inherently feasible, an algorithm for onset detection is applied to speech and musical signals.

1 Introduction

This short and preliminary report has two roots, both connected to the development of the Dresden UASR system. UASR means *unified approach for signal analysis and recognition* and includes a hierarchical analysis-synthesis framework which serves as a platform for the development of intelligent solutions in the processing of speech and non-speech signals [13]. One of the most challenging aspects in the development of intelligent signal processing systems arises from the question, to what extent temporal aspects are considered to improve the performance and completeness of the analysis or the synthesis process, respectively.

Let us consider this question at first from the viewpoint of speech signal processing. In technical systems, the development of the speech signal vs. time is normally mapped to a sequence of symbols which appear with certain duration. This is a rather simple approach with respect to the temporal structure because it does not take into account that the temporal structure of speech is governed by a hierarchy of events like accents, which can be measured by intensity and time, which is finally expressed by the speech rhythm.

Although the phonetic sciences are highly engaged in discovering the prosodic and especially the time-related properties of the different languages for a long

A. Esposito et al. (Eds.): COST 2102 Int. Training School 2010, LNCS 6456, pp. 376–386, 2011.

time (remember that the first symposion on *intonology* was held in Prague in 1970), the influence on speech technology is restricted to rather simple algorithms for calculating pitch, intensity, and duration of synthesized sounds. This is not satisfactory because prosodic features (especially the more complex ones like rhythm) are potentially suited to improve the performance of speech technology essentially.

The prediction of speech prosody is absolutely necessary for *speech synthesis* systems, to achieve an acceptable level of naturalness. The intonation and sound duration are calculated from the input text by established models. However, a higher organization of timing is normally not considered. There are attempts to improve the prediction by including more levels of the speech hierarchy (e. g. the language model in [28]). Keller discussed in [14,15] the potential role of speech rhythm in synthetic speech. However, the introduction of rhythm in synthetic speech remains an open issue.

The situation in *speech recognition* is even less satisfactory. Although the role of prosody is recognized since a long time (e. g. from the Verbmobil project [19]), the benefits of including prosodic features in an explicit way are rarely demonstrated (e. g. in an UASR-based dialogue application [17]). It is expected that the inclusion of features which describe the temporal hierarchy can essentially improve the recognition of noisy and/or simultaneous speech [6].

There is very much movement in psycholinguistics and phonetics to study speech rhythm and its function. Different systems for quantitative description of rhythm have been discussed (e. g. [12]), but it is not completely clear which of them are suited for an application in technical systems like UASR. In this situation, a look at musical signals where the role of rhythm is clearly recognized could be helpful. This leads us to the second root of this paper.

As we pointed out earlier [13], UASR is applied not only to speech but also to a variety of human and non-human signals, among them also musical signals. A recent project deals with the role of the musical rhythm in automatic systems for music retrieval [11]. It suggested itself to ask whether the speech technology can learn from methods which are established in music processing, and vice versa. This approach is satisfied by neurobiological findings which show a surprising similarity of human speech and music processing [1].

This paper describes first results of our comparative study. The temporal structure of music and speech is examined in Sect. 2 including a literature review. Due to analogies between speech and music Sect. 3 has a look on parallels for common research tasks. The common task of finding onsets in signals is examined as an example more closely in Sect. 4, showing that a common approach is in principle feasible, but has to be adapted to the signal.

2   Rhythmical Composition of Music and Speech

Music and language involve organizing perceptually discrete elements into hierarchically structured sequences [26]. Those discrete elements are at one hand musical tones and on the other hand phonemes or words. The combination of those elements follows principles at multiple levels. Besides different tones and pitches music and speech production involves a second crucial element: time. We can observe different durations, accentuations, natures and patterns of the basic elements. It is quite common to use the term rhythm to describe temporal phenomenas even though no precise definition exists. Londons starting point for example is rhythm as a "movement marked by regulated successions of strong or weak elements" [25]. Cummins in contrast links rhythm to a physiological phenomenon. In speech, rhythm is related to the coordination of the limbs [5], whereas in music it is related to the motoric skills of the musician. When speaking about rhythm, a precise explanation of how the term is used becomes necessary.

Music: Rhythm in music here is restricted to the metrical system. An abstract view at the structural properties that serve to organize the acoustic events. The placement of notes in western music is not arbitrary, it follows certain rules organizing them into a hierarchical metrical structure [23]. Lehrdal points out that though all music groups into units of various kinds, some music does not have a metrical structure at all, but that this theory is applicable for most of the tonal western music. This structure deals with points in time neglecting the duration of the notes. Therefore it is of interest when the musical event takes place. The metrical structure allows certain points in time for the occurring of an event. These points are equally spaced and the duration between them implies the metrical level. Several levels coexist, from the shortest duration (tatum), to longer ones like bar length. The beat is the metrical level at which a human would tap along. Most of the time this is the level of quarter notes which also express the time signature of a song. Figure 1 shows metrical levels with their musical equivalent from eight notes as the tatum up to bar length. Every event on a higher level has to appear in the lower metrical levels. The rhythm according to that framework is the pattern of the actual used possible event positions. Timing represents the actual placement of expressive played events which can and will be imprecise according to the metrical structure [9]. The tempo of the music defines the duration of the events at the metrical levels.

Speech: Human speech is perceived with a certain regularity, which creates a perceived speech rhythm [15]. The timing of speech is changed through contradictions and expansions, accelerations and decelerations [14] where the perceived

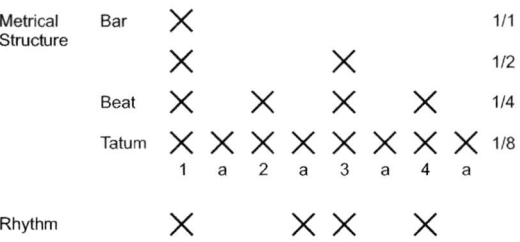

Fig. 1. Metrical hierarchy of western music

rhythm is also based on accents and the character, duration and number of speech components varying between different languages. For ASR systems it is required to find some kind of rhythm characterization that is based on the signal or some kind of systematic representation.

One of the first approaches to rhythm in speech is isochrony, the idea that language divides time rhythmically into equal portions. This leads to the categorization of languages into syllable-, stress- or mora-timed. However Ilse Lehiste claims in 1977 that there are no simple acoustic parameters to describe isochrony, but considers it a perceptual phenomenon of temporal, intonational and motor parameters [22]. No empirical evidence could be found in other studies [7].

Even though Lehiste neglects to find rhythmic properties in the speech signal, latest research is also concerned with metrics [12,27] and beats of the acoustical signal [15]. Beats are rapid onsets of sonorous parts, which are used by Keller to show that strong voice onsets are used as anchor points, which helps the listener to orient within speech. Other approaches to rhythm in speech are in the field of chaotic representation, oscillator systems, neuropsychological expectancy and mathematical statistical prediction of speech events [16].

3 Comparing Research Tasks

Since there are similarities between music and speech, one could try to us techniques across the analysis off these different signals [29]. Krishna draws analogies between following tasks [21]:

- Automatic speech recognition - Automatic music transcription
- Language identification - Music genre recognition
- Speaker identification - Music instrument recognition.

Some languages could be distinguished based on the onsets and durations as done in [12,27]. Music genre recognition, especially ballroomdancestyle recognition, could be utilized based on the onsets of music as well [10]. This is not the most popular way of dealing with language or genre recognition, but quite an interesting approach coming from the rhythmical point of view. For both kinds of signals onset detection plays an important role within the mentioned research tasks. Therefore a common approach for onset detection is applied to speech and music signals in the next section to examine whether the same algorithm could be used for both kind of signals.

4 Onset Detection as Example

Music: Onset detection in music could serve as starting point for features that describe the rhythm of music. For example one could build a beat histogram (on the distances between onsets) representing the strength of the different metrical levels as done for classifying ballroom dances by Dixon [8]. Onsets also divide music into meaningful units where the acoustical features like chords are mostly constant.

Speech: The detection of voiced onsets in speech are useful for evaluating smaller units concerning acoustical features [24]. Rhythmical studies were done among others by Keller [15] and Volin [27]. The following analysis considers the beginning of voiced speech parts.

4.1   Database

For the evaluation procedure, music and speech is needed as audio material with annotated onsets. Pablo Bello kindly provided the database used in [2], making a comparison of the results possible. The database consists of different kinds of musical onsets, namely pitched non percussive (pnp), pitched percussive (pp), non pitched percussive (npp) and polyphonic music (mix). Altogether there are 1060 onsets. The speech database consists of German sentences annotated and recorded by the speech-language pathologist Joan Ma at TU-Dresden in the year 2010. 825 voiced onsets are labeled in total. Table 1 summarizes the composition of the used databases.

Table 1. Onset databases

Database	Onsets	pnp	pp	npp	mix	speech
Bello2005	1060	93	484	212	271	
Ma2010	825					825

4.2   Onset Detection

The principal flow of detecting onsets and evaluating them can be seen in Fig. 2. Starting with the audio a detection function is built to emphasize the onsets of the signal having a lower sampling rate as the audio at the same time. The utilized detection functions are based on the energy of the signal. A peak picker defines the onsets of a signal which can then be evaluated with the annotated reference. The evaluation process involves the generation of receiver operating curves (ROC) explained in Sect. 4.3.

Comparable algorithms in the field of speech processing have a slightly different approach. There goal is to divide speech signals into segments of silence, voiced and unvoiced parts. Basic algorithms rely on simple parameters such as energy contours and zero crossing rates with a classification based on threshold comparison [3]. More extensive algorithms make use of statistical classifiers and

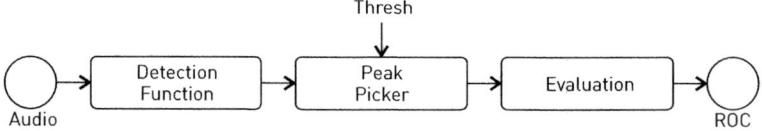

Fig. 2. Onset detection and evaluation

features like MFCCs and LSFs [20]. Also the evaluation process considers the correct assignment of the segments (evaluating every sample) instead of comparing the position of the labels as done in this work. A quantitative comparison with state of the art speech labeling algorithms is therefore not possible.

Detection Function. At first a detection function is build from the audio signal with a lower sampling rate representing the onsets of the audio signal with high peaks. Three different algorithms were used to examine which is most applicable. Klapuri utilized band-wise processing and a psychoacoustic model leading to a detection function that is suitable for a wide variety of input signals [18]. The implementation of the mirtoolbox is used[1]. Examining different detection functions Bello also uses a function based on spectral difference (SVBello-SD) [2]. The used implementation from the Queen Mary University in London is publicly available within the Vamp Plugins[2]. The last algorithm is based on an mpeg-7 feature, the audio spectrum envelope. The specific configuration leads to the energy of 14 bands with a time resolution of 10 ms. For the detection function MSE-Baseline (MSE-BL) the bands are simply summed. An example of the three used detection functions can be seen in Fig. 3.

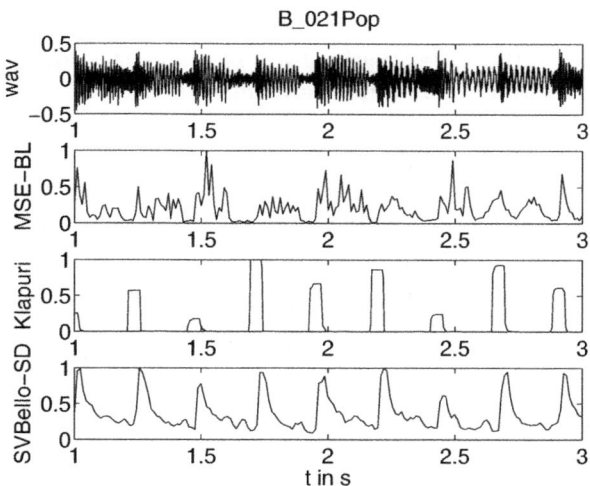

Fig. 3. Two seconds of the musical signal B_021Pop (jaxx.wav in original database from Bello2005) and the derived detection functions

Peak Picker. The peak picking algorithm of Bello is utilized [2]. It compromises the steps of normalization, low-pass-filtering, adaptive and fix thresholding and at last taking the local maxima as onsets. The parameters cutoff frequency f_c, M for the moving median filter were determined per detection function. The fix threshold parameter δ is the variable for the Receiver-Operating-Curve.

---

[1] https://www.jyu.fi/hum/laitokset/musiikki/en/research/coe/materials/mirtoolbox
[2] http://www.vamp-plugins.org/

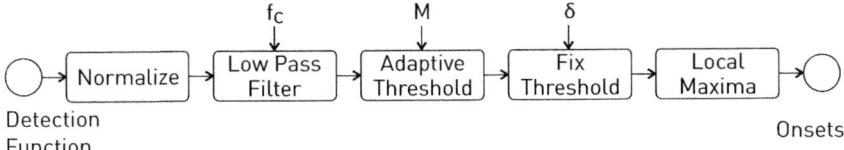

Detection
Function

Onsets

Fig. 4. Peak picker

4.3   Evaluation

The manually annotated labels are compared with the detected ones from the algorithms. A detected label is called true positive (TP) when there is a label in the reference within a time window of 50 ms either to the right or the left. If there is no matching reference onset it is a false positive (FP). Reference labels which do not match detected labels are false negative (FN). Bello uses Receiver Operating Curves to show the quality of the different algorithms in dependency of the threshold in the peak picking stage [2]. At the abscissa the False-Positive-Rate indicates the amount of falsely detected onsets within all detected onsets

$$\%FP = \frac{FP}{TP + FP} * 100 \tag{1}$$

and on the ordinate the True-Positive-Rate indicates the amount of correctly detected onsets at the ratio of all manually labeled onsets

$$\%TP = \frac{TP}{TP + FN} * 100. \tag{2}$$

The optimal trade-off between %TP and %FP is the closest point of the graph to the northwest point (northwestscore), which can be calculated as

$$nws = \sqrt{\left(\frac{FN}{TP + FN}\right)^2 + \left(\frac{FP}{TP + FP}\right)^2} \tag{3}$$

according to Collins [4].

4.4   Results

Music: The best results for musical signals are obtained with the spectral difference detection function leading to 86.41% true-positive-rate with 11.06% false-positive rate (see Table 2). Those results are quite encouraging with respect to further processing. As it can be seen in the ROC in Fig. 4.4 the detection functions rank from worst to best: MSE-BL, Klapuri and SVBello-SD.

Speech: The best results for speech are obtained with the MSE-BL detection function leading to 83.51% true-positive-rate with 30.61% false-positive-rate (see Table 3). A look on the data reveals that unvoiced parts are label as onsets an consecutive voiced parts like nasals (/m, n/) or approximants (/l, j, w/) followed

Table 2. *Music:* Best onset detection results for music signals (Bello2005: 1060 reference onsets)

df	#os	#TP	%TP	#FP	%FP	nws
MSE-BL	1208	788	74.33	420	34.76	0.4321
Klapuri	944	827	78.01	117	12.39	0.2523
SVBello-SD	1030	916	86.41	114	11.06	0.1752

by a vowel as two onsets due to the change of the energy in the signal. The used database Ma2010 has labels for the beginning of voiced parts of speech. This means that labeled unvoiced onsets and the second onset label of consecutive voiced parts are interpreted as false postive which explains the high FP rate. It should be mentioned here that the used algorithms are not specially adapted to the speech signal. To overcome the problems just mentioned additional features like ZCR rate would be a possible solution. Here also a ranking of the detection functions could be made according to Fig. 4.4 from worst to best: Klapuri, SVBello-SD and MSE-BL.

Comparing the results for music and speech shows that the same approach is in principle feasible. The ranking of the used detection functions varies between the different kinds of signals, showing that they have to be chosen and adapted according to the signal. Further research could apply methods used in speech

Table 3. *Speech:* Best onset detection results for speech (Ma2010: 825 reference onsets)

df	#os	#TP	%TP	#FP	%FP	nws
MSE-BL	993	689	83.51	304	30.61	0.3477
Klapuri	1306	610	73.93	696	53.29	0.5932
SVBello-SD	1047	638	77.33	409	39.06	0.4516

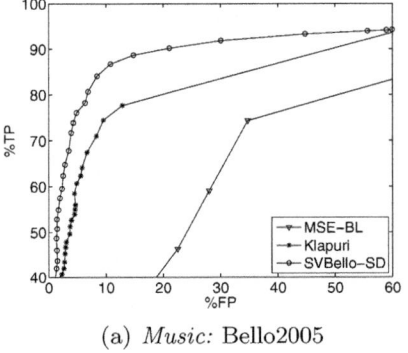

(a) *Music:* Bello2005

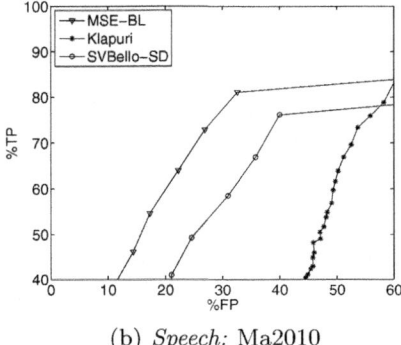

(b) *Speech:* Ma2010

Fig. 5. Receiver operating curves of onset detection varying the threshold of the peak picker

signal processing to musical signals. Every unvoiced and voiced part (including consecutive different voiced phonemes) should be used as analogy to musical onsets.

5   Conclusions

We sketched the actual situation of temporal information in ASR systems showing that there is room for improvements. Music has strong and more obvious rhythmic properties as speech. Music information retrieval research has adopted solutions from technical speech processing and maybe speech could benefit from rhythmical findings within the music domain. Therefore the rhythmic properties of both kinds of signals have been examined in Sect. 2, supplemented by literature review. Following those more theoretical points of view algorithms of onset detection have been applied. They showed that this common approach to speech and musical signals is inherently feasible.

A large number of practical tasks in music and speech processing will benefit from powerful rhythm detectors which are not yet completely available. They have to be optimized by the extension of the classical analysis-by-synthesis process to structures at the time scale. The Dresden UASR system is a hierarchical platform for analysis-by-synthesis experiments. It is the practical outcome of our investigation, to have prepared the UASR system for this purpose in both, speech and music.

References

1. Spiegelbild der Sprache - Neurokognition von Musik (May 2010),
   http://www.cbs.mpg.de/institute/foci/mirror
2. Bello, J.P., Daudet, L., Abdallah, S., Duxbury, C., Davies, M., Sandler, M.B.: A tutorial on onset detection in musical signals. IEEE Transactions on Speech and Audio Processing 13(5), 1035–1047 (2005)
3. Caruntu, A., Toderean, G., Nica, A.: Automatic silence/unvoiced/voiced classifcation of speech using a modified teager energy feature. In: WSEAS Int. Conf. on Dynamical Systems and Control, Venice, Italy, pp. 62–65 (2005)
4. Collins, N.: Towards Autonomous Agents for Live Computer Music: Realtime Machine Listening and Interactive Music Systems. PhD thesis, Centre for Science and Music, Faculty of Music, University of Cambridge (2006)
5. Cummins, F.: Rhythmic Coordination in English Speech: An Experimental Study. PhD thesis, Indiana University (1997)
6. Cushing, I.R., Dellwo, V.: The role of speech rhythm in attending to one of two simultaneous speakers. In: Speech Prosody, 5th International Conference, Chicago, Illinois (2010)
7. Dauer, R.M.: Stress-timing and syllable-timing reanalyzed. Journal of Phonetics 11, 51–62 (1983)
8. Dixon, S., Pampalk, E., Widmer, G.: Classification of dance music by periodicity patterns. In: ISMIR, 4th International Society for Music Information Retrieval Conference, Baltimore, USA, pp. 159–165 (2003)

9. Gouyon, F., Dixon, S.: A review of automatic rhythm description systems. Computer Music Journal 29(1), 34–35 (2005)
10. Gouyon, F., Dixon, S., Pampalk, E., Widmer, G.: Evaluating rhythmic descriptors for musical genre classification. In: AES, 25th International Conference, London, UK (June 2004)
11. Hübler, S., Wolff, M., Eichner, M.: Vergleich statistischer Klassifikatoren zur Ermittlung musikalischer Aspekte. In: Hoffmann, R. (ed.) Elektronische Sprachsignalverarbeitung. Tagungsband der 20. Konferenz, Dresden, 21. - 23. 9, of Studientexte zur Sprachkommunikation, Dresden, Germany, vol. 53, pp. 338–345 (September 2009)
12. Hirst, D.: The rhythm of text and the rhythm of utterances: from metrics to models. In: Interspeech, 10th Annual Conference of the International Speech Communication Association, Brighton, UK, pp. 1519–1522 (2009)
13. Hoffmann, R., Eichner, M., Wolff, M.: Analysis of verbal and nonverbal acoustic signals with the dresden UASR system. In: Esposito, A., Faundez-Zanuy, M., Keller, E., Marinaro, M. (eds.) COST Action 2102. LNCS (LNAI), vol. 4775, pp. 200–218. Springer, Heidelberg (2007)
14. Keller, E.: A phonetician's view of signal generation for speech synthesis. In: Vich, R. (ed.) Electronic Speech Signal Processing, 16th Conference, Prague. Studientexte zur Sprachkommunikation, vol. 36, pp. 13–20. TUDpress, Dresden (2005)
15. Keller, E.: Beats for individual timing variation. In: Esposito, A., Bratanic, M., Keller, E., Marinaro, M. (eds.) The Fundamentals of Verbal and Non-verbal Communication and the Biometric Issue, pp. 115–128. IOS Press, Amsterdam (2007)
16. Keller, E.: From sound to rhythm expectancy (Tutorial). 5o Convegno Nazionale AISV. Università de Zurigo, Switzerland (2009)
17. Kühne, M., Wolff, M., Eichner, M., Hoffmann, R.: Voice activation using prosodic features. In: Interspeech, 8th International Conference on Spoken Language Processing, Jeju, Korea, pp. 3001–3004 (2004)
18. Klapuri, A.: Sound onset detection by appliying psychoacoustic knowledge. In: ICASSP, Phoenix, USA, vol. 6, pp. 3089–3092 (March1999)
19. Kompe, R.: Prosody in Speech Understanding Systems. LNCS, vol. 1307. Springer, Heidelberg (1997)
20. Kotnik, B., Sendorek, P., Astrov, S., Koc, T., Ciloglu, T., Fernández, L.D., Banga, E.R., Höge, H., Kacic, Z.: Evaluation of voice activity and voicing detection. In: Interspeech, 9th Annual Conference of the International Speech Communication Association, Brisbane, Australia, pp. 1642–1645 (2008)
21. Krishna, A.G., Sreenivas, T.V.: Music instrument recognition: From isolated notes to solo phrases. In: ICASSP, pp. 265–268 (2004)
22. Lehiste, I.: Isochrony reconsidered. Journal of Phonetics 5, 253–263 (1977)
23. Lehrdal, F., Jackendoff, R.: The Generative Theory of Tonal Music. MIT Press, Cambridge (1983)
24. Leuschel, A., Docherty, G.J.: Prosodic assessment of dysarthria. In: Disorders of Motor Speech: Assessment, Treatment and Clinical Characterization, pp. 155–178. Paul H Brookes Publishing Co. Inc. (1996)
25. London, J.: Grove music online: Rhythm (April 2010),
http://www.grovemusic.com
26. Aniruddh Patel, D.: Language, music, syntax and the brain. Nature Neuroscience 6(7), 674–681 (2003)

27. Volín, J., Pollák, P.: The dynamic dimension of the global speech-rhythm attributes. In: Interspeech, 10th Annual Conference of the International Speech Communication Association, Brighton, UK, pp. 1543–1546 (2009)
28. Werner, S., Eichner, M., Wolff, M., Hoffmann, R.: Toward spontanuos speech synthesis - utilizing language model information in tts. IEEE Transactions on Speech and Audio Processing 12(4), 436–445 (2004)
29. Wolkowicz, J., Kesel, V.: Predicting development of research in music based on parallel with natural language processing. In: ISMIR, 11th International Society for Music Information Retrieval Conference, Utrecht, Netherlands, pp. 665–667 (2010)

The Ability of Children with Mild Learning Disabilities to Encode Emotions through Facial Expressions

Christiane El-Haddad and Yiannis Laouris

Cyprus Neuroscience & Technology Institute, Promitheos 5
1065 Nicosia, Cyprus
{Christiane,Laouris}@cnti.org.cy

Abstract. Children with limitations in their abilities to encode and decode emotions through corresponding facial expressions may be excluded from social and educational processes. Previous research has demonstrated that children with learning difficulties may suffer differentially in their ability to recognize and denominate facial expressions that correspond to the basic emotional states. This study evaluates the ability of children with mild learning difficulties to produce seven basic facial expressions (happiness, sadness, anger, afraid, disgusted, confidence, and surprise) in response to verbal commands. The evaluation was based on a subject's ability to communicate an emotional state correctly to his/her peers. The results show that their ability to produce a facial expression was affected in different degrees and that there exist correlations between the ability to perform certain facial expressions.

Keywords: Facial expressions, emotions, learning difficulties, multimodal, neuroscience.

1 Introduction

Human emotions are always accompanied by an orchestrated repertoire of facial (and body) expressions. Although emotional states constitute a most important aspect of human life, their systematic study and experiential teaching did not yet make it as an integral part of any school curriculum. As early as the eighties, it was proposed that individuals capable of interpreting and evaluating the interrelationship between their own emotional states and those of others tend to be favored in society [1]. Conversely, individuals with limitations in such abilities are more likely to be excluded [2]. In line with such findings, numerous early studies have reported that children with learning disabilities (LD) suffer also in skills related to their ability to recognize emotions. For example, Bachara [3] found relations between skills that involve empathy and learning difficulties whereas Dickstein & Warren [4] and Wong [5] reported difficulties in role taking. Both skills require the ability of children to recognize the emotions coded in certain facial expressions (i.e., to decode the emotion behind a certain facial expression). During the last decade, we have witnessed a growing interest and public debate concerning the value that emotional intelligence (EQ) plays on learning (see for example Goleman [6], [7] and Laouris [8] for reviews and applications and the NexusEQ Conference website [9] for references on international conferences). Many studies have

A. Esposito et al. (Eds.): COST 2102 Int. Training School 2010, LNCS 6456, pp. 387–402, 2011.

revealed how EQ is at least as important as other types of intelligence. Despite the overwhelming importance of such skills, studies that document the ability of young children, especially with mild LD, to recognize emotions behind facial expressions are limited. Even fewer studies have addressed possible relationships between the ability of children (with and without LD) to express emotions through production of facial expressions, and corresponding school performance. Several studies have indicated that children with LD, experience more social-emotional difficulties [10], [11], [12] but studies relating the scientific aspect with the implications for education are still unavailable.

Surviving at school requires sophisticated social skills; communication skills are key, accompanied, of course, with abilities such as independent work, the ability to work in a group and solve problems. For all these skills, children rely on their emotional intelligence, i.e., "being aware of our feelings and handling disruptive emotions well, empathizing with how others feel, and being skillful in handling our relationships" [7]. Elias and colleagues defined eight guidelines on what schools should teach, referring in the first two to academic learning in terms of understanding and using language, math and science to understand and improve the world we live in [13], [14]. They summarized the last six points as "character education, service learning, citizenship education, and emotional intelligence," and named them Social Emotional Learning (SEL). They argued that SEL "links academic knowledge with a set of skills important to success in schools, families, communities, workplaces and life in general." Subsequent research provided evidence that competencies in social emotional learning improved student's "social/emotional learning, readiness to learn, classroom behavior and academic performance" (see review in Payton et al [15].

A number of schools implement SEL programs (e.g., the State of Illinois). The Collaborative for Academic, Social, and Emotional Learning (CASEL[1]) "has identified a set of emotional-social skills that underlie effective performance of a wide range of social roles and life tasks" [13]; the first one being the ability to recognize (identify) and express (mimic) emotions. Research in the context of the Fast-Track project[2] showed that developing emotional skills improved classroom behavior of special needs students in frustration tolerance, assertive social skill, task orientation, peer skills, sharing, sociability and self-control."

In sum, studies have demonstrated that emotional intelligence (and SEL) is at least as important as other types of intelligence. And although even engineers involved in human computer intelligent interaction research admit that "the most natural way to display emotions is using facial expressions" [16], yet still little is known concerning the ability of young children, especially children with mild LD, to recognize emotions behind facial expressions. Even less, to mimic and/or produce facial expressions, which correspond to particular emotions.

1.1 Purpose and Goals of the Study

This study was designed to serve both social-educational as well as research purposes. Designed in the form of action research, it intended to provide opportunities to students

---

[1] www.casel.org
[2] www.fasttrackproject.org

with mild LD to develop a better understanding about emotions (non-verbal cues; facial expressions). A training session before the actual experiment and a group session following the experiment had as purpose to train their abilities to recognize and express emotions. We hypothesized that such training would help them to develop the necessary mental representations of emotional states that would bypass their possible language difficulties.

The first research goal was technical. We wanted to test whether we could use the average of all responses of a group of students with mild LD as our control (based on the idea of "collective wisdom"). We therefore devised a scheme to quantify the ability of children with mild LD to name facial expressions that correspond to specific emotions (denomination), as well as their ability to produce (mimic) requested facial expressions. Thus, the technical goal of the study was to investigate whether using one's peers' evaluations could serve as a control. The methodological assessment involved the evaluation of facial expressions produced by the subjects (on command) by their peers, as well as by independent adult expert evaluators. The ratings of the independent evaluators were used for validation of the methodological assessment.

The research goal was to test the following hypotheses: (1) the ability of a child with mild learning difficulties to encode an emotion using facial mimicry is invariant across different states (i.e., emotional states, see Methods). (2) A subject's ability to produce (on command) a facial expression, i.e., mimic a requested emotion is correlated with the same subject's ability to produce another facial expression. In addition to the above two hypotheses, although the sample was very small, the authors planned to explore for gender and age issues as well as for relations between a subject's ability to produce a facial expression and the subject's school performance as judged by their teachers. Preliminary results of this project have been presented in the 3rd International Multilingualism and Dyslexia Conference [17].

2 Methodology

2.1 Subjects

The sample of participants consisted of 18 K12 students, 9 males, 9 females, their ages ranging from 9 to 18 years (mean = 13.3, SD = ±2.6). They all attended Classes Orange, a private special education school in Lebanon, where the first author worked. The collection of the experimental data took place between February and April 2005 and their analysis was performed in June 2005.

Participants were asked if they would like to take part in an experiment, which involved recognizing and expressing emotions. It was explained to them that they would be videotaped and that they would subsequently watch the tapes of their peers and requested to evaluate their facial expressions. They were informed that they would participate in a subsequent workshop in which they would have the opportunity to share with classmates and researcher how easy or difficult had been to recognize emotions through facial expressions and to share their thoughts regarding the role that expression of emotions may play in their daily life. Parents' and teachers consent was not secured, however they were informed verbally by the headmistress and agreed to the experiments and videotaping as long as the showing of the tapes and usage of the data stayed within the circles of the scientific community. All participants of this experiment received support in terms of group and individual sessions for the development of their social skills as part of their regular school curriculum.

Before launching the actual experiment, the subjects participated in a session dedicated to a discussion about emotions and the role that emotions play in daily communication. This included also the engagement of the subjects in various experiential games that required them to mimic diverse facial expressions. The purpose of this introductory session was to ensure that all subjects had a basic understanding about the correspondence between a facial expression and an emotional state and that they were comfortable with the vocabulary used to describe different facial expressions associated with particular emotions.

Selection of emotions. Out of an infinite array of possible facial expressions that correspond to different emotions, we have chosen the six basic expressions discovered originally by Ekman [18], [19]. These have been selected also because it has been shown that they are expressed and interpreted in the same way by humans of any origin and do not depend on the cultural or ethnic background [20], [18] (refer to Discussion for debating). In addition to the six, we have chosen "Confident" for the experiments (see Table 1), because this is an emotional state that special needs students seldom feel. We therefore hypothesized that the subjects would have greater difficulty to express it.

Table 1. Emotional states selected for the experiments. In addition to the six universal states proposed originally by Ekman and Fnesen [18], the state of feeling "Confident" has been added. Each corresponding facial expression was coded using a number from 1 to 7. Subjects were given an oral command, e.g., "Happy" to produce one of these states.

Corresponding emotion	Coding
Happy	1
Sad	2
Angry	3
Afraid	4
Disgusted	5
Confident	6
Surprised	7

Experimental design. Eighteen sequences (i.e., one sequence to be used for each subject) each consisting of 15 numbers were generated using a random number generator. Each sequence contained the numbers 1-7 in random order, each one corresponding to a distinct emotional state as in Table 1. The number sequence was converted to a sequence of corresponding verbal commands that were used to request the subject to act (i.e., to mimic a particular state). It was ensured that the sequence included each state at least twice.

The subjects' performances in response to verbal commands requesting him/her to simulate a certain emotion were recorded using two cameras (Fig. 1) one placed straight in front and the other at an angle of 45 degrees at 2.5 meters from the subject set-up to record the head of the performing child.

The room was set up for filming to ensure normal lighting. Special provisions were taken to secure that no interruptions would take place and that no environmental noise could be heard. The subject sat on a pre-fixed chair and stared straight ahead towards the experimenter who was standing behind the first camera. The experimenter asked the subject to "produce" a particular emotional state by giving oral commands. The recording was continuous for the whole experiment in order to render the process as homogenous as possible. Isolation of video clips for each expression was completed off-line before the evaluation phase of the experiment.

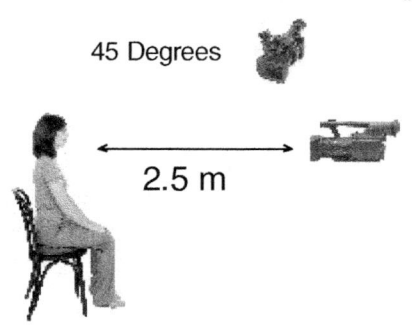

Fig. 1. Experimental setup

Measuring the ability to encode (i.e., perform) different facial expressions. The ability of one subject to "encode" a particular emotion into a facial expression was quantified based on the same subject's ability to communicate correctly the encoded emotion to his/her peers. We have hereby assumed that one's peers should be pretty good "readers" of one's emotions since they not only spend many hours together in school, but they also work together in exercises that engage experiential learning which involves learning to "observe" the emotions of others.

Upon completion of all experimental staging and recordings, the researchers edited the video to have short video clips of 5 s duration for each performance. All subjects (including the one acting) would view on film the fifteen facial expressions of a particular subject and record on an answer sheet their guess regarding the facial expression being displayed each time. The response would be counted as "correct" if their guess matched the command that the subject on film has received in order to perform the displayed facial expression. The number of correct recognitions for each expression was counted and it was expressed as percentage of the total number of presentations of the particular expression. For example, assuming subject A displayed the facial expression "Happy" two times, the 18 subjects would have to evaluate these expressions 36 times. If say 30 guesses of the evaluators' guesses were correct, then 83.3% (i.e., 30/36) was used as the normalized score of the ability of Subject A to encode the emotional state "Happy".

In order to search for correlations between a subject's ability to produce a facial expression and their corresponding school performance, their teachers were requested to provide ranking estimates for the participating students on a Likert scale 1-3 using (-) and (+) where appropriate (e.g., 2+). The judgments of two teachers, their headmistress, the speech therapist and their psychologist were used. The scores were converted to numerical values from 1 to 9 and normalized to 100%.

The External Evaluator's Control phase was analogous, but it involved "independent" evaluations of facial expressions by two different raters. The external evaluators were not only expected to "recognize" the displayed emotion but also to rate it on a Likert scale 1-5 regarding its quality. These scores were used for the external validation of the method.

The study was concluded with a final session, where all participants got together with the experimenter, viewed the film together, and expressed their difficulties or their ease at recognizing emotions behind their friends' facial expressions.

3   Results

The data included videoclips (with 2 cameras) of 18 subjects (9 male, 9 female) while producing a sequence of 15 facial expressions in response to verbal commands as described above. The picture shots in Fig. 2 document typical facial expressions produced by two subjects in response to corresponding "verbal commands." There was great variability in their ability to produce the requested facial expressions.

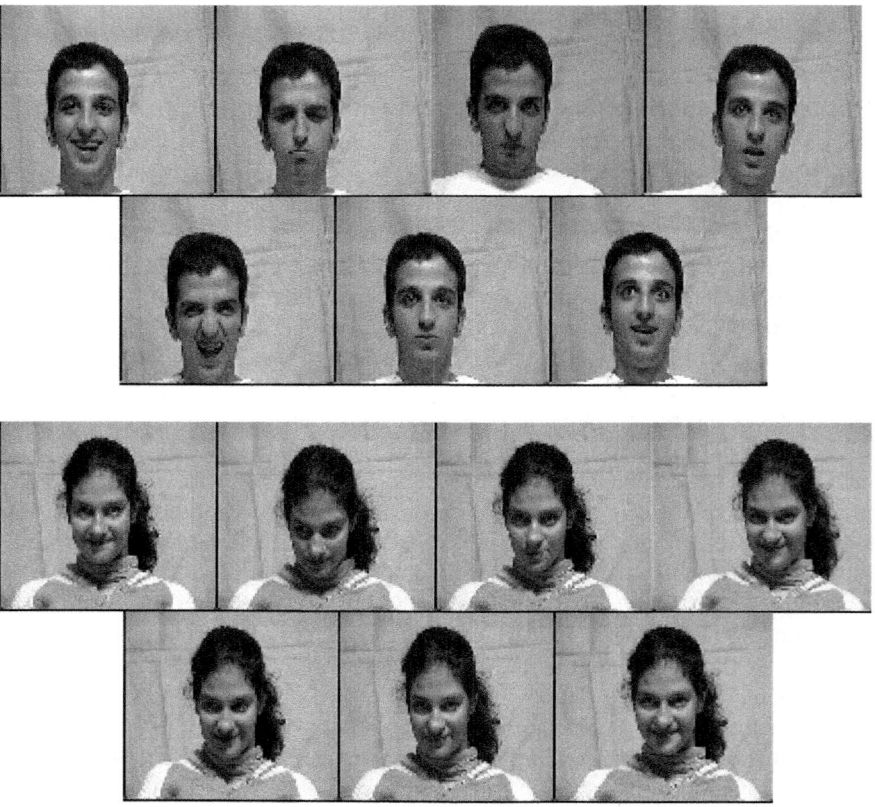

Fig. 2. Sample facial expressions by two of the subjects. Shown are facial expressions produced in response to the following verbal commands: Happy (*top left*), Sad (*top middle-left*), Angry (*top middle-right*), Afraid (*top right*), Disgusted (*bottom left*), Confident (*bottom middle*), and Surprised (*bottom right*). Note the differences between the abilities of the two children to express their emotions with the female finding it more difficult to distinguish between different facial expressions.

3.1 External Validation of the Assessment Methodology

The external evaluators were subjected to practically the same conditions as the students. They participated in a training session in which they viewed the pictures of facial affect (PoFA) from Ekmann (SET-METT test[3], ©Paul Ekman 1993). They viewed the film in the same way as the students, individually and rated the performances on paper. A short discussion took place after the viewing, where they were all astonished at the difficulty of the student to mimic facial expressions on command, they both use cues to guess emotions whenever hand or body movement viewable in the video. One of the evaluators was a Swiss, working in Lebanon for over 18 years. She discovered that Lebanese children put their head down when they were sad. Therefore, whenever she saw children "putting their head down, or looking down," she assessed it as "sad." Interestingly, she was correct most of the time.

3.2 Differential Ability to Produce the Basic States

The subjects were found to have different abilities in the production of the seven states. Fig. 3 reports the normalized averages for the 18 subjects. Specifically, participants

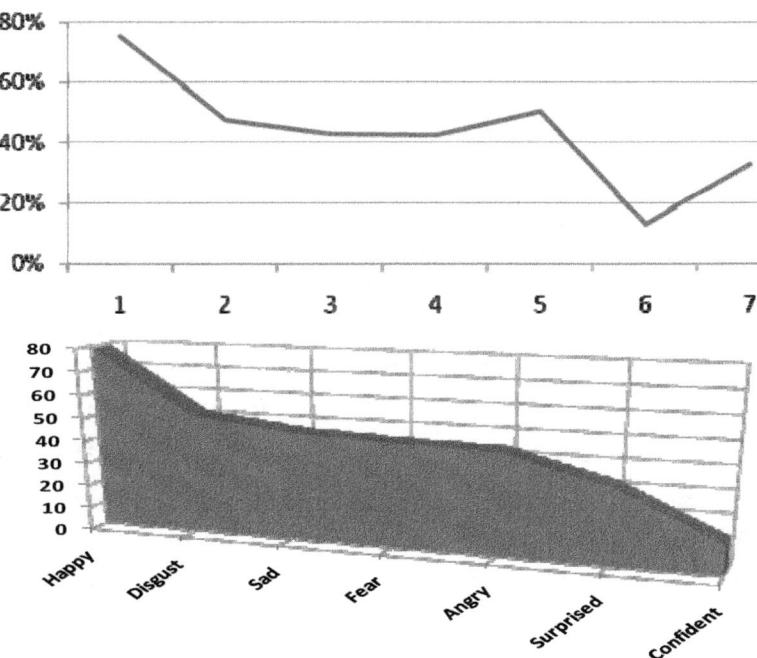

Fig. 3. Differential abilities of children to encode the seven basic emotions. The upper graph plots the normalized scores averaged for the 18 subjects for each skill. The numbers 1-7 on the x-axis correspond to happy, sad, angry, afraid, disgusted, confident and surprised. The lower graph plots the same data, but sorted in descending order. The ability to express the state "Happy" was significantly better than all other abilities ($p<0.001$). For other significant differences refer to text and Table 2.

---

[3] http://face.paulekman.com/productdetail.aspx?pid=1

were found able to produce the 'happy' state much easier than the "sad" (t(17)=5.838, p<.001), the 'angry' (t(17)=6.316, p<.001), the 'afraid' (t(17)=4.761, p<.001), the 'disgusted' (t(17)=5.017, p<.001), "confident" (t(17)=10.629, p<.001) and the 'surprised' states (t(17)=7.662, p<.001). Similarly, it was found that the participants are better able to produce the 'sad' state than the 'confident' state (t(17)=7.432, p<.001) and the 'surprised' state (t(17)=2.219, p<.05). For more details refer to Table 2.

Table 2. Columns report the means (μ), standard deviation (SD), standard mean errors (σM), Lower and Upper values, Student's t variable (t), Degree(s) of freedom (df) and the level of Significance using a 2-tailed t-test (2-t)

	μ	SD	σM	Lower	Upper	t	df	Sig. (2-t)
Happy – Sad	11.611	8.438	1.989	7.415	15.807	5.838	17	.000
Happy – Angry	14.444	9.703	2.287	9.619	19.270	6.316	17	.000
Happy – Afraid	13.722	12.227	2.882	7.642	19.803	4.761	17	.000
Happy – Disgusted	11.833	10.007	2.359	6.857	16.810	5.017	17	.000
Happy – Confident	25.222	10.068	2.373	20.216	30.229	10.629	17	.000
Happy – Surprised	17.500	9.691	2.284	12.681	22.319	7.662	17	.000
Sad – Angry	2.833	10.326	2.434	-2.301	7.968	1.164	17	.260
Sad – Afraid	2.111	8.324	1.962	-2.028	6.250	1.076	17	.297
Sad – Disgusted	.222	10.586	2.495	-5.042	5.487	.089	17	.930
Sad – Confident	13.611	7.770	1.831	9.747	17.475	7.432	17	.000
Sad – Surprised	5.889	11.261	2.654	.289	11.489	2.219	17	.040
Angry – Afraid	-.722	11.129	2.623	-6.257	4.812	-.275	17	.786
Angry – Disgusted	-2.611	6.980	1.645	-6.082	.860	-1.587	17	.131
Angry - Confident	10.778	9.124	2.150	6.241	15.315	5.012	17	.000
Angry - Surprised	3.056	11.461	2.701	-2.644	8.755	1.131	17	.274
Afraid – Disgusted	-1.889	11.066	2.608	-7.392	3.614	-.724	17	.479
Afraid – Confident	11.500	10.755	2.535	6.152	16.848	4.536	17	.000
Afraid – Surprised	3.778	10.167	2.396	-1.278	8.834	1.577	17	.133
Disgusted - Confident	13.389	9.325	2.198	8.752	18.026	6.092	17	.000
Disgusted - Surprised	5.667	12.054	2.841	-.328	11.661	1.995	17	.062
Confident - Surprised	-7.722	10.028	2.364	-12.709	-2.735	-3.267	17	.005

In sum, the results confirmed the first hypothesis for most of the states, i.e., "The ability of a child with mild learning difficulties to encode an emotion using facial mimicry is invariant across different states.

3.3 Inter-relations between Abilities

The next phase aimed to test the second hypothesis, i.e., whether a subject's ability to produce (on command) a facial expression, i.e., mimic a requested emotion is correlated with the same subject's ability to produce another facial expression. Table 3 documents correlations between states. The state "Happy" was positively correlated with the state "Sad", "Angry", "Disgust" and "Surprised". Furthermore, it was found that the ability to produce the "Sad" state was positively correlated with their ability to produce the "Fear" state (r=.552, p<.05). Likewise, the ability to produce the "Angry" state was positively correlated with the ability to produce "Disgust" state (r=.768, p<.01). Last, it was found that the ability to produce the "Disgust state was positively correlated with the ability to produce the "Confident" state (r=.513, p<.05).

Table 3. Differences between the group averages across different abilities. The state "Happy" is significantly different from the states "Sad", "Angry", "Disgust" and "Fear". Refer to the text for more discussion. The level of Significance was calculated using a 2-tailed t-test.

		Happy	Sad	Angry	Fear	Disgust	Confident	Surprised
Happy	Pearson Correlation	1	.561(*)	.475(*)	.178	.528(*)	.277	.472(*)
	Sig. (2-tailed)		.015	.046	.479	.024	.265	.048
Sad	Pearson Correlation		1	.291	.552(*)	.399	.446	.146
	Sig. (2-tailed)			.241	.017	.101	.064	.563
Angry	Pearson Correlation			1	.284	.768(**)	.368	.221
	Sig. (2-tailed)				.254	.000	.133	.378
Afraid	Pearson Correlation				1	.405	.119	.397
	Sig. (2-tailed)					.095	.639	.103
Disgusted	Pearson Correlation					1	.513(*)	.278
	Sig. (2-tailed)						.030	.263
Confident	Pearson Correlation						1	.213
	Sig. (2-tailed)							.396
Surprised	Pearson Correlation							1
	Sig. (2-tailed)							

3.4 Exploring for Age – Gender and School Performance Issues

In order to test whether the ability to produce facial expressions is correlated to age, the subjects were divided according to their age using a median split and their scores were compared using ANOVA. No significant differences were found. The scores of girls vs. boys were also compared using ANOVA; again no significant differences were found. In sum, the data do not provide support to the thesis that age and/or gender differences exist in the abilities of children with learning difficulties to express facial expressions. Similarly, no correlation was found between school performance as judged by their teachers and their ability to produce a facial expression.

4 Discussion

The ability of the subjects of this study to express facial expressions in response to verbal commands was far from ideal for all seven emotional states tested. It was close to 80% for the state "Happy," which means that when this emotional state was displayed by one subject, it was recognized 8 out of 10 times by his/her peers. "Disgust" was recognized about half of the times. For all other states, the peer-evaluators recognized less than half of the intended emotional states. Interestingly, the evaluations provided by the expert-evaluators were not significantly different from those of the peer-evaluators. This finding has also been considered as sufficient for the external validation of the assessment methodology (section 3.1).

The partial impairment of the encoding ability of the subjects is serious given that the ability to recognize emotions behind facial expressions develops already at a young age. Children at the age of 4 are normally able to recognize and name emotions when presented as pictures on the basis of corresponding expressive cues [21], [22], [23], [24], [25], [26], [27]. The observed partial impairment of the encoding ability may find origin at a number of levels of the neuronal processing pathways. First, it may well be that subjects fail to understand the meaning of the verbal command. This possibility has been ruled out by the methodological approach. All subjects participated in a preliminary session dedicated to a discussion about emotions and their role in communication. The purpose of this introductory session was to ensure that all subjects understood the correspondence between facial expressions and emotional states, and that they commanded the vocabulary used to describe the seven facial expressions that were used for the experiments. Second, because it is known that children with mild learning abilities experience less social interactions and have difficulty *recognizing* emotional states, we may hypothesize that such deprivation could lead to under-development of their respective ability to also *produce* facial expressions that correspond to emotions. It has been reported by various authors that socially excluded and shy children as well as socially anxious, depressed or abused children may show signs of such limitations [12], [28], [29], [30], [31]. This possibility cannot be addressed by the present study. Third, it is conceivable that children with any type of cognitive limitations may also suffer in other mental abilities in the context of a "general" regulatory factor [32] (see also Matzel et al, [33]. These issues are discussed below. Finally, it is likely that the abilities of peer-evaluators to recognize displayed emotions are underdeveloped as well; it is thinkable that a particular subject's ability to *act* appears low simply because her evaluator-peers fail to recognize her acting. This possibility has been anticipated. The study incorporated expert-evaluators' judgments in order to validate, or not, the judgments of peer-evaluators. It is therefore considered improbable, because the evaluations of the peer-evaluators were not significantly different from those of external professional evaluators. It is therefore concluded that for the purpose of this study, peers may serve as "good-enough" evaluators. The validation of their evaluations using external evaluators provides sufficient evidence to the authors' assumption (see Methodology) that one's peers are probably good "readers" of their displayed emotions. This is probably because they interact daily and for long periods with them. Irrespective of which of the above mechanisms may contribute to the observed impairment, the authors postulate that the subjects' inability to express emotions may influence their ability to communicate and socialize adequately with their teachers, parents and peers, which in turn may influence their learning and academic achievement.

This experimental study was set up to test two hypotheses. The first hypothesis was whether the ability of a child with mild learning difficulties to encode an emotion using facial mimicry is invariant across different states. The analysis has rejected this hypothesis. Children's abilities to produce a facial expression corresponding to an emotion are different for different expressions. The expression "Happy" is by far easier than all the others to mimic, whereas the expression "Confident" is by far the most difficult for this particular group. The first conclusion is compatible with previous literature and with the fact that also the ability to recognize the "Happy" emotion is a lot more developed in all children, including children with mild learning problems [30]. Their difficulty to produce the expression "Confident" is interesting, but not surprising. It has been postulated by the authors (see Methodology: Selection of emotions) that this ability would be affected, as children with learning problems also suffer quite often from reduced self-confidence. The second hypothesis, i.e., whether a subject's ability to produce a facial expression is correlated with the same subject's ability to produce another facial expression, has been supported by the experimental data. We have found significant correlations between the state "Happy" and all others, as well as between six additional pairs: Sad–Confident; Sad–Surprised; Angry–Confident; Afraid–Confident; Disgusted–Confident; Confident–Surprised.

4.1 Relations between Ability to En/Decode and Other Cognitive/Behavioral Skills

Children who were better at decoding non-verbal emotional information in faces and tones of voice were also found to be more popular and more likely to have higher academic achievement scores [34]. Studies, which compare behavioral abilities of LD children with behavioral abilities of their normally achieving peers, have found that the former groups exhibit also more behavioral difficulties. Such difficulties have often been considered secondary to cognitive correlates of their learning difficulty and have been mainly attributed to the impact of negative experiences common to most children with LD, such as the frustration of repeated school failure [35], [36], [37]. However, early research pointed out that the central processing deficiencies underlying cognitive, linguistic, and academic aspects of learning disorders may also underlie their social and emotional features [38]. It has also been suggested that human performance on diverse tests of intellect is impacted by a "general" regulatory factor that accounts for up to 50% of the variance between individuals on intelligence tests ([32], see also Matzel et al [33]. For example, the authors have also found significant correlations among a repertoire of non-verbal abilities such as the ability to navigate in space, the ability to categorize objects based on common attributes, short-term visual and auditory memory, discrimination etc. [39]. This finding has also been interpreted to point towards "shared cognitive structures" engaged in different tasks.

Socially anxious children reported significantly more often that they "saw" emotions when neutral faces were presented. Moreover, reaction times were longer. There was also "neither indication of enhanced ability to decode negative expressions, nor a specific tendency to interpret neutral or positive faces as negative" [40]. Analogous studies have shown that abused children were less skilled in decoding facial expressions and were rated less socially competent than non-abused [41].

Hess et al [42] investigated the influence of the physical intensity of emotional facial expressions and decoding accuracy for expressions of anger, disgust, sadness, and happiness. Their results revealed that the decoding accuracy varied largely linearly with the manipulated physical intensity of the expression for anger, disgust, and sadness. The subjects had reduced abilities to produce firm facial expressions. This impairment can partly explain the difficulty of their peer-evaluators as well as of the expert-evaluators to recognize correctly their expressions. Another study [43], assessed children on their ability to recognize and identify facial expressions of emotions either based on photographs presented requiring them to select the photo representing a particular emotion or by asking them to name the emotional state expressed in a facial photograph. The study found an age trend for both tasks: scores on the first task were significantly better, suggesting that recognition of an emotional state was less difficult than verbally identifying it. Again, the study reported here required children with mild learning difficulties to name the expressed emotion, which is a more difficult task. It is therefore possible that even when they don't evaluate a facial expression correctly, they might still react socially correctly on it!

In sum, the above studies indicate that the ability to recognize (and possibly to produce) facial expressions that correspond to emotions may be impaired in conjunction with other impairments that involve diverse cognitive circuits. Whatever the underlying mechanism, the learning is that, children with such difficulties may require more attention and probably individualized and tailored-made instruction.

4.2 Age and Gender Issues

Although a number of early studies provided circumstantial evidence to support a female advantage, i.e., females are generally better encoders and also more extraverted [1] (see studies on young children by Charlesworth & Kieutzer, [44] and an early study on infants by Field & Walden, [28]), the literature is not yet in definitive agreement. Unfortunately, this study cannot provide a reliable view either. Even though we did not find any correlation between gender and facial expression acting ability, the results suffer in two ways. First, the sample is small (only 18 subjects; 9 male, 9 female) and the ages are spread (9-18 ys). Second, the experiments were performed in a Lebanese school; where the culture could at times discourages girls from making eye contact with other people and expressing emotions.

4.3   The Ability to Encode/Decode Emotions and Its Neurophysiological Substrates

The present study does not provide direct insights as to underlying neurophysiological substrates of the observed behaviors. Therefore, the results are discussed within this limitation. Waller et al. [45] used intramuscular stimulation in humans and chimpanzees to simulate facial expressions and replicate the work of Duchene [46]. Several studies have correlated depression with a right hemisphere dysfunction [47]. Lenti et al [47] reported that, "Patients affected by Major Depressive Disorder recognized less fear in 6 fundamental emotions ... could indicate a subtle right hemisphere dysfunction in depressed children/adolescents." It would be interesting in future studies to explore the relationship between depression (due to intrinsic or environmental factors) and ability of children to recognize/produce emotions.

In addition, a neuro-biochemical study has revealed that very shy children may process some facial expressions differently [48]: Children with high indexes of shyness are at a heightened risk of developing social phobia. They analyzed the responses of 3rd and 4th grade school children (characterized as shy) to different emotional facial expressions showing them pictures of boys and girls with facial expressions that depicted joy, neutrality, and anger. They assessed responses through questionnaires as well as through neuro-chemical analyses and recordings of brain wave activity. They found that "the shyness-BI index and the presence of particular forms of the serotonin transporter promoter gene predicted smaller responses to overtly hostile and neutral facial expressions in certain regions of the brain." Again, future studies could explore these relations using standardized methods from the field of neuropsychology in order to enable better comparisons and discussion.

Another neuro-electro-physiological study may provide insights into the relations between abuse, event-related potentials (ERP) and ability to detect/produce emotions [49]. The investigation examined the effects of maltreatment during the first year of life on the neural correlates of processing facial expressions of emotion at 30 months of age. ERPs in response to children passively viewing standardized pictures of female models posing angry, happy, and neutral facial expressions were examined. The authors derived the following components: early negative (N150), early positive (P260), negative central (Nc), and positive slow wave (PSW). They found differences in these waveforms between a group of 35 maltreated and 24 normal treated children.

In sum, neurophysiological and neuro-chemical studies may not only reveal underlying mechanisms for the observed behaviors but they might also be used with regard to their implications for the design and evaluation of preventive interventions.

5   Conclusions and Future Studies

This present study has shown that children with mild learning difficulties suffer in their ability to produce facial expressions that correspond to the six basic emotions and even more the expression "Confident." Future studies may address underlying neurophysiological and neuro-chemical factors as well as focus on options for intervention and design of tailored-made curricula for children with such difficulties.

Acknowledgments. The authors would like to thank the headmistress of the Classes Orange School in Lebanon for providing access to the subjects and Mrs. Elena Aristodemou for helping with the statistical analysis. The work was partly supported by COST2102, by Cyber Kids and by Safer Internet Plus project "CyberEthics" through a grant given to the Cyprus Neuroscience & Technology Institute.

References

1. Buck, R.: The communication of emotion. Guilford Press, New York (1984)
2. Bandura, A.: Social foundations of thought and action: A social cognitive theory. Prentice-Hall, Englewood Cliffs (1986)
3. Bachara, G.H.: Empathy in learning disabled children. Perceptual and Motor Skills 43, 541–542 (1976)
4. Dickstein, E., Warren, D.: Role-Taking Deficits in Learning Disabled Children. Journal of Learning Disabilities 13, 33–37 (1980)
5. Wong, B.: Activating the inactive learner: Use of question/prompts to enhance comprehension and retention of implied information in learning disabled children. Council for Learning Disabilities 3, 29–37 (1980)
6. Goleman, D.: Emotional intelligence. Bantam Books, New York (1995)
7. Goleman, D.: Emotional Intelligence. Bantam, New York (2005)
8. Laouris, Y.: Innovative Education for the New Millenium, A Leap into the New Millenium. IMSC Nikias Max, Nicosia (1998)
9. NexusEQ Conferences, http://www.nexuseq.com
10. Bryan, T., Donohue, M., Pearl, R.: Learning disabled children's communicative competence on referential communication tasks. Journal of Pediatric Psychology, 6383–6393 (1981)
11. Bursuck, W.: A comparison of students with learning disabilities to lowachieving and higher achieving students on three dimensions of social competence. Journal of Learning Disabilities 22, 188–193 (1989)
12. Dimitrovsky, L., Spector, H., Levy-Shiff, R., Vakil, E.: Interpretation of Facial Expressions of Affect in Children with Learning Disabilities with Verbal or Nonverbal Deficits. Journal of Learning Disabilities 31, 286–292 (1998)
13. Elias, M.J., Zins, J.E., Weissberg, R.P., Frey, K.S., Greenberg, M.T., Haynes, N.M., Kessler, R., Schwab-Stone, M.E., Shriver, T.P.: Promoting social and emotional learning: Guidelines for educators. Association for Supervision and Curriculum Development, Alexandria, VA (1997)
14. Zins, J.E., Elias, M.E.: Social and Emotional Learning. In: Minke, G., Bear, K.M. (eds.) Children's Needs III. s.l. (2006),
    http://www.nasponline.org/educators/elias_zins.pdf
15. Payton, J., Weissburg, R.P., Durlak, J.A., Dminiki, A.B., Taylor, A.D., Schellinger, K.B., Pachan, M.: The positive impact of social and emotional learning from kindergarten to eighth-grade students: Findings from three scientific reviews. Collaborative for Academic, Social and Emotional Learning, Chicago (2008)
16. Cohen, I., Garg, A.H., Thomas, S.: Emotion Recognition using Multilevel-HMM. Colorado: NIPS Workshop on Affective Computing (2000),
    http://www.ifp.illinois.edu/~iracohen/publications/
    mlhmmemotions.pdf

17. El-Haddad, C., Laouris, Y.: Introducing the concept of "emotions" in school curricula; Technology-assisted recognition and mimicking of facial expressions in a team of elementary school children with mild learning disabilities. In: Limassol: 3rd International Multilingualism and Dyslexia Conference: Multilingual and Cross-Cultural Perspectives on Dyslexia (2005)
18. Ekman, P., Fnesen, W.V.: Constants across cultures in the face and emotion. Journal of Personality and Social Psychology 17, 124–129 (1971)
19. Ekman, P.: Basic Emotions. In: Dalgleish, T., Power, M. (eds.) Handbook of Cognition and Emotion. John Wiley & Sons, Ltd, Sussex (1999)
20. Ekman, P.: Universals and cultural differences in facial expressions of emotion. In: Cole, J. (ed.) Nebraska Symposium on Motivation. University Nebraska Press, Lincoln (1972)
21. Bullock, M., Russel, J.A.: Further evidence on pre-schooler's interpretation of facial expressions. International Journal of Behavioral Development 8, 15–38 (1985)
22. Cutting, A., Dunn, J.: Theory of mind, emotion understanding, language, and family background: Individual differences and interrelations. Child Development 70, 853–865 (1999)
23. Denham, S.: Social cognition, pro-social behavior, and emotion in preschoolers: Contextual validation. Child Development 57, 194–201 (1986)
24. Dunn, J., Brown, J., Beardsall, L.: Family talk about feeling states and children's later understanding of others' emotions. Developmental Psychology 27, 448–455 (1991)
25. Hughes, C., Dunn, J.: Understanding mind and emotion: Longitudinal associations with mental-state talk between young friends. Developmental Psychology 34, 1026–1037 (1998)
26. Pons, F., Harris, P.L., De Rosnay, M.: Emotion comprehension between 3 and 11 years: Developmental Periods and hierarchical organization. European Journal of Developmental Psychology 2, 127–152 (2004)
27. Rothenberg, B.: Children's social sensitivity and the relationship to interpersonal competence, intrapersonal comfort and intellectual level. Developmental Psychology 2, 335–350 (1970)
28. Field, T., Walden, T.: Production and perception of facial expressions m infancy and early childhood. In: Lipsttt, H., Reese, L. (eds.) Advances in child development, vol. 16. Academic Press, New York (1981)
29. Garitte, C.: La reconnaissance des expressions faciales chez des enfants de 8 ans d'âge réel et/ou mental processus cognitifs ou sociaux? A.N.A.E. 71, 42–52 (2003)
30. Holder, H.B., Kirkpatrick, S.W.: Interpretation of Emotion From Facial Expressions in Children With and Without Learning Disabilities. J. Learn. Disabil. 24, 170 (1991)
31. Pons, F., Lawson, J., Harris, P.L., De Rosnay, M.: Individual differences in children's emotion understanding: Effects of age and language. Scandinavian Journal of Psychology 44, 347–353 (2003)
32. Sternberg, R.J., Kaufman, J.C.: Human abilities. Annu. Rev. Psychol. 49, 479–502 (1998)
33. Matzel, L.D., Han, Y.R., Grossman, H., Karnik, M.S., Patel, D., Scott, N., Specht, S.M., Gandhi, C.C.: Individual Differences in the Expression of a "General" Learning Ability in Mice. The Journal of Neuroscience 23, 6423–6433 (2003)
34. Nowicki Jr., S., Duke, M.P.: The association of children's nonverbal decoding abilities with their popularity, locus of control, and academic achievement. The Journal of genetic psychology 153, 385–393 (1992)
35. Bruck, M.: The adult outcomes of children with learning disabilities. Annals of Dyslexia 37, 252–263 (1987)

36. Coleman, J.M.: Handiccaped labels and instructional segragation: Influences of children's self-concepts versus the perceptions of others. Learning Disability Quarterly 6, 3–11 (1983)
37. Swayze, M.C.: The self-concept development in young children. In: Yawkey, T.D. (ed.) The self-concept of the young child. Brigham Young University Press, Provo (1980)
38. Pearl, R.: Social cognitive factors in learning disabled children's social problems. In: Ceci, S.J. (ed.) Handbook of Cognitive, Social, and Neuropsychological Aspects of Learning Disabilities, vol. 2. Lawrence Erlbaum Associates Hillsdale, NJ (1987)
39. Laouris, Y., Aristodemou, E., Makris, P.: Prediction of Learning Abilities Based on a Cross-Modal Evaluation of Non-verbal Mental Attributes Using Video-Game-Like Interfaces. In: Esposito, A., Vích, R. (eds.) Cross-Modal Analysis of Speech, Gestures, Gaze and Facial Expressions. LNCS, vol. 5641, pp. 248–265. Springer, Heidelberg (2009)
40. Melfsen, S., Florin, I.: Do Socially Anxious Children Show Deficits in Classifying Facial Expressions of Emotions? Journal of Nonverbal Behavior 26, 109–126 (2002)
41. Camras, L.A., Grow, J.G., Ribordy, S.C.: Recognition of emotional expression by abused children. Journal of Clinical Child Psychology 12, 325–328 (1983)
42. Hess, U., Blairy, S., Kleck, R.E.: The Intensity of Emotional Facial Expressions and Decoding Accuracy. Behavioral Science 21, 241–257 (1997)
43. Harrigan, J.A.: The effects of task order on children's identification of facial expressions. Behavioral Science 8, 157–169 (1984)
44. Charlesworth, W.R., Kreutzer, M.A.: Facial expressions of infants and children. In: Ekman, P. (ed.) Darwin and facial expression. Academic Press, New York (1973)
45. Waller, B.M., Vick, S.J., Parr, L., Bard, K.M., Smith Pasqualini, M.C., Gothard, K.M., Fuglevard, A.J.: Intramascular electrical stimulation of facial muscles in humans and chimpanzees: Duchenne revisited and extended. Emotion 6, 367–382 (2006)
46. Duchenne de Boulogne, G.B.: The Mechanism of Human Facial Expression. In: Cuthbertson, R. (ed.) Cambridge University Press, New York (1990)
47. Lenti, C., Giacobbe, A., Pegna, C.: Recognition of emotional facial expressions in depressed children and adolescents. Percept Mot Skills 91, 227–236 (2000)
48. Battaglia, M., Ogliari, A., Zanoni, A., Citterio, A., Pozzoli, U., Giorda, R., Maffei, C., Marino, C.: Influence of the Serotonin Transporter Promoter Gene and Shyness on Children's Cerebral Responses to Facial Expressions. Arch. Gen. Psychiatry 62, 85–94 (2005)
49. Cicchetti, D., Curtis, W.J.: An event-related potential study of the processing of affective facial expressions in young children who experienced maltreatment during the first year of life. Development and psychopathology 17, 641–677 (2005)

Designing a Hungarian Multimodal Database –
Speech Recording and Annotation

Kinga Papay

University of Debrecen,
Egyetem ter 1, 4032 Debrecen, Hungary
kinga.papay@gmail.com
http://www.unideb.hu

Abstract. The Hungarian spontaneous speech recording and annotation subproject is being carried out by our Computational Linguistics research group and my PhD work at the University of Debrecen and is a part of a comprehensive multimodal human-machine interaction development project and multimodal (audio and video) database collection. The efficiency of speech recognition systems can be increased by proper acoustic preprocessing and by investigation of the suprasegmental characteristics of spontaneous speech. The research aims to contribute to the exact knowledge of prosody through the examination of spontaneous speech, with special regard to syntactic embeddings, insertions, iterations, hesitations and restarts, various kinds of emotions and discourse markers regarding Hungarian, the lack of a prosodically labelled, representative spontaneous speech database makes the development more difficult. The spontaneous multimodal database is being recorded via guided formal and informal conversations. During the conversation, several points are to be discussed in order to provoke longer monologues, including those phenomena of spontaneous speech, which are to be examined within our research. Designing a continuous spontaneous speech recognition system that is speaker-independent and is able to contribute to our theoretical assumptions, requires the construction of a speech database for which we need to take several personnel and technical aspects into account. The visual channel also needs to be annotated, which will enable us to examine and implement multimodal features as well.

Keywords: database planning, spontaneous speech, prosody research, multimodality.

1 Introduction

Marking, detecting or capturing the units of spontaneous speech are among the fundamental problems of automatic speech recognition [14], [17]. In addition to the fact that prosodic and other keys vary depending on text type, a further problematic point is that mapping relations between the prosodic realization and the syntactic structure of sentences are the subject of a linguistic debate [4], [7], [8], [15]. The efficiency of speech recognition systems can be increased by proper

A. Esposito et al. (Eds.): COST 2102 Int. Training School 2010, LNCS 6456, pp. 403–411, 2011.
© Springer-Verlag Berlin Heidelberg 2011

acoustic preprocessing and the investigation of the suprasegmental characteristics of spontaneous speech. The project is aimed at breaking down Hungarian spontaneous speech into intonational phrases (IPs), determining the prosodic boundaries and adapting the resulting information to the speech recognition engine. The research also aims to contribute to the exact knowledge of the overlaps between the verbal and nonverbal aspects of communicative events and prosodic features through the examination of spontaneous speech, with special regard to syntactic embeddings, insertions, iterations, hesitations and restarts, various kinds of emotions and discourse markers. Concerning Hungarian, because of the lack of a multimodal, functionally labelled, representative spontaneous speech database, the first step of the project is the database design, collection and annotation. The paper describes the design of the first Hungarian Multimodal Database: design of collection and annotation, personnel and technical aspects.

2   Material Design

2.1   Personnel Requirements - Database Speakers

The database aims to represent Hungarian university students and workers, therefore database speakers have to be the same kind of people with appropriate gender, age and birth place distribution. When recruiting candidates, the following distribution considerations are to be applied (the following considerations reflect standards imported from SpeechDat project descriptions): The total number of candidates taken, the number of male and female speakers must be in the range of 45-50%. This means that out of the ca 100 recruits, we need approximately 50 men and 50 women. The database is to represent university people, therefore the speakers are young adults (18-30 yrs old) and adults (over 30 yrs). Distribution according to age group should be 80% young adults and 20% adults. Considering the fact that only 100 speakers are to be recorded, the number of dialectal regions has to be limited to 6, while in order to get an adequate representation of the given dialect a minimum of 13 speakers per region have to be included. Regarding the dialectal distribution of Hungarian university students and workers, the 6 main cities that represent the 6 most prominent dialectal regions are Budapest, Debrecen, Miskolc, Szeged, Pecs and Gyor. 27% of the speakers should represent Budapest, 20% of the speakers should represent Debrecen and 13-13-13-13% of the speakers should represent Miskolc, Szeged, Pecs and Gyor. Participants selected have to be native speakers (speakers without foreign accent) and have to have the dialect/accent of the region, in addition every region should cover the gender and age distribution specified above. As for the video design, we have 5 degrees of skin, hair and eye colours: very light, light, intermediate, dark and very dark skin colours, blond, brown, black, red and grey/white hair colours, and blue, grey, green, brown and dark brown eye colours.

2.2   Technical Requirements - Studio Equipment

The research group is planning to use the studio of the Institute of English and American Studies at the University of Debrecen. The studio is already equipped with an adequate PC, recording software (Sound Forge Pro 10) and 2 far-talk cardioid microphones (Shure 16 A). This model has smooth, extended frequency response, which provides intelligibility and crispness of sound and high output condenser cartridge for high fidelity; the cardioid (unidirectional) pickup pattern suppresses feedback. The ideal position of the microphones is next to the individual speakers, not too close and not too far from each of them. We are going to record CD quality stereo wav files (with 44.1 kHz sampling frequency and 16 bit quantization). The studio has to be equipped with 1 HD camera (Sony HDRXR520VE) recording the agent and 2 HD as well as 2 web cameras (Logitech Webcam Pro 9000) directed at the speaker to record his/her face and hand gestures, and appropriate lights. All the cameras will record sound as well, synchronization should be managed using flash lights and beep sounds during the recordings. The file format of the HD cameras is mts, while the file format of the web cameras is jpg.

2.3   Database Contents

Each speaker is going to have 3 short tasks: First, the speaker reads out 20 phonetically rich sentences and 7 words (this is needed in the case of a continuous Speech Recognition Engine (SRE) to cover all the phoneme variations of the language and also to ease and prepare the speaker for the spontaneous dialogues) as well as embedded sentences (this is needed for us to be able to compare the prosodic manifestation of embeddings in read and in spontaneous speech). Second, we record the main part, the spontaneous dialogues regarding the differences between real and acted speech [11], we have decided not to record acted speech. The informal dialogues are designed to be about natural topics, mostly about university and other life experiences. The questions are also intend to provoke emotions. The agent should start the conversation with the less personal questions and progress towards the more personal topics. The transition from one question to the other should be as smooth as possible. Although the guided conversation contains a lot of dialogues, it should contain as many long stretches of speech from the speaker as possible; instead of yes/no questions, information seeking Wh-questions (why..., when..., what happened..., please tell me...) will be used. In order to provoke backchannels and more spontaneous interaction, during the informal conversation, the agent is going to tell his/her own stories (i.e. the agent will behave as an equal partner in the conversation). Third, the formal dialogues of the database will be produced via simulated job interviews where the agent is the interviewer and the speaker is the interviewee. When the recording process is over, the agent records speaker-related data (age, sex, dialectal region/city, identification number). Time demand per speaker is 30 minutes, out of which we record ca 4 minutes of reading and 26 minutes of dialogues.

3   Speech Annotation

Annotation means transcription of the utterance and some segmentation by using timestamps. For speech annotation, we examined the possible tools - see
a review in [13] - and finally decided to use the Praat speech analyser program [2]. Of the ca 100 speakers, 50 hours of audio and video material have
to be annotated. After examining other databases and annotation methods, or
prosodic analysis methods [1], [3], [5], [6], [22], [23], [24], we have created an
annotation method for our research purposes. Annotators must produce a ver-
batim (word-for-word) transcript of everything that is said within the file. The
words transcribed within each segment boundary must correspond exactly to the
timestamps that have been created by the segmentation, so that the audio file
is aligned with the transcript. The main role of the transcription is that all au-
dible sound events (speech and eventual noises) should be marked. In the Praat
program, speaker data is to be fixed in the beginning of the transcription lines
and is separated from the transcription with an asterisk *. The following types
of speaker data are to be fixed: speaker ID, sex of the speaker (male or female),
age group of the speaker (young adult/adult) and region of the speaker (Bu-
dapest/Debrecen/Miskolc/Szeged/Pecs/Gyor). For instance: 001FYDebrecen*.
The speech annotation process is simultaneous at five levels: three functional and
two transcription levels of the dialogue; segment units are clauses (see Fig. 1).

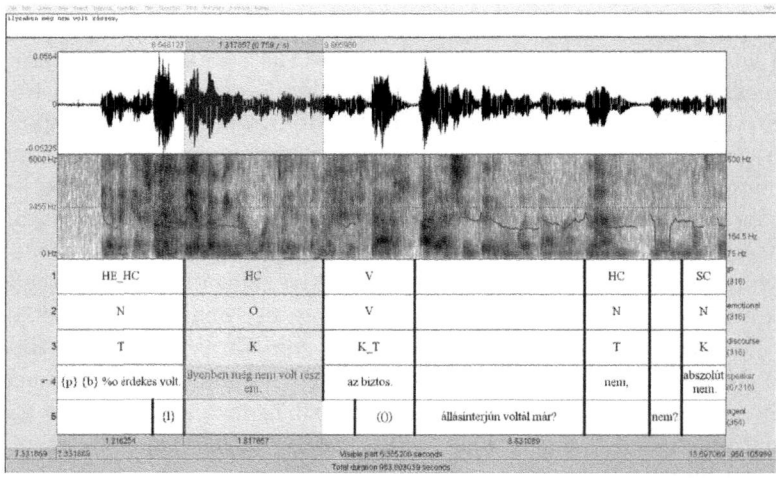

Fig. 1. Using Praat for a five-level speech annotation

The functional level has three sub-levels: intonational, emotional and discourse
phrase types. With the sound files and transcriptions of the intonational phrase
level and emotional level, the phrase detector program and the emotion recognizer of BME (Budapest University of Technology and Economics) Laboratory of
Speech Acoustics [18], [19], [20], [21] or [16] can be retrained and thus improved

to recognize the phrase boundaries and the emotions of spontaneous speech. Labels of the functional levels are abbreviations of intonational phrase types, emotional and cognitive state types and discourse phrase types (see Table 1).

Table 1. Summary of audio annotation levels and labels

Level 1: Intonational phrases (IP labels)	Level 2: Emotions (emotional labels)	Level 3: Diaogue turns (discourse labels)	Level 4: Transcription of speaker's speech (speaker text)	Level 5: Transcription of agent's speech (agent text)
HC (head clause)	N (neutral)	T (turn-take)	text + symbols	text + symbols
SC (subordinate clause)	S (sad)	G (turn-give)		
EM (embedding)	H (happy, laughing)	K (turn-keep)		
IN (insertion)	P (surprised)	B (backchannel)		
BC (backchannel)	R (recalling, thinking)			
HE (hesitation) + linking, e.g. HE_HC1	T (tensed)			
RE (restart) + linking	O (other)			
IT (iteration) + linking				
SL (silence) + linking	SL (silence)	SL (silence)		
V (overlapping speech)	V (overlapping speech)	Overlapping speech, e.g. K_T		

3.1 Labels of Intonational Phrase Types, Expressed Attitudes and Discourse Types

The categories of the Intonational Phrase (IP) level are established based on Hunyadi's [8], [9] research on embeddings, iterations and insertions. Keszler [10] also made some interesting remarks on the acoustic properties of insertions in the Hungarian language: the inserted clauses have lower fundamental frequency, flatter intonation and faster speech rate than the neighbouring ones. Abbreviations regarding intonational phrase type, emotional or cognitive state type and discourse phrase type are the following: Among the codes of intonational phrase types we distinguish head clause (HC), subordinate clause (SC), embedding (EM), insertion (IN) and backchannel (BC) labels. We also mark some phenomena which can occur *within* a clause type: hesitation (HE), restart (RE), iteration (IT), silence (SL) - we mark silence only if it exceeds 250 ms. A low line is to be used for linking the clause type in which the given phenomenon occurs. When some words in the clause are chopped off, and there are no restarts in the given clause, it is marked as HC-, SC-, etc. One clause can contain several phenomena, in this case each of them is separated by a low line (without spaces). Comparing to [12] there are some changes in the label categories on the IP level. Labels of expressed attitudes are: neutral (N), happy (H), sad (S), surprised (P), tensed (T), recalling or thinking (R) and other (O). In the case of overlapping speech, we use the label V on level 1 and level 2. Besides, we implement a discourse-level annotation using the following labels: turn-taking (T), turn-giving (G), backchannel (B), turn-keeping (K). In case of overlapping speech, annotators use the T/G/K/B_T/G/K/B convention's first part for the speaker, and second part for the agent.

3.2 Transcription Levels

We use two separate levels for the two participants of the discourse; level four is for the speaker (interviewee) and level five is for the agent (interviewer). In discourse, the speech transcription alternates between the two levels. As for the orthographic annotation, the following fields are to be considered: spelling, capitalization, punctuation, numbers, acronyms, spoken letters, disfluent speech (including hesitations, partial words, restarts and mispronounced words), noise (including speaker and external noises) and hard-to-understand sections. Regions of disfluent speech are particularly difficult to transcribe. Speakers may stumble over their words, repeat themselves, utter partial words, restart phrases or sentences, and use lots of hesitation sounds. Annotators must take particular care in sections of disfluent speech to transcribe exactly what is said, including all of the partial words, repetitions and filled pauses used by the speaker. Table 2 summarizes our solutions for how to mark the above mentioned speech phenomena.

Table 2. Summary of transcriptional level symbols

Condition	Markup	Example	Explanation
Numbers	spelled out	nyolcszázöt	Write out full text, not digits.
Punctuation	comma, question, explanation, period	, ? ! .	Do not use other symbols.
Acronyms	@	@MÁV, @DE-BTK	Letters in caps, no space between.
Spelling	~	~B ~M ~E	All with spaced caps.
Filled pause, pause	%	%o, %m, %s	Filled pauses limited to 2 items.
Partial words	--	termése~	Transcribe as much of the word as you hear. No spaces preceding/following the word!
Restart	< >	azt hi-- <azt> hiszem	Use it if speaker stops and restarts.
Mispronunciation	+	+pszichológus	Incorrect pronunciation. Note: non-standard, but correct pronunciations are to be accepted!
Speaker noise	{}	{b} - breath {c} - cough {l} - laugh {s} - sneeze {p} - lipsmack	Non-phoneme sounds produced by the speaker. Use only these 5 categories! Mark up only well audible speaker noises.
Instantaneous non-speaker noise	[ ] [b] – for beep sounds	mit [mondasz]?	Short intermittent noise. Mark up only well audible noises.
Semi-intelligible speech	((transcript))	itt van a ((szomszédban))	If you are uncertain about what is said.
Unintelligible speech	(( ))	(( ))	If you do not understand what is said.
Idiosyncratic words	*	*drrr	Made-up word.
Foreign word	[Language: text] [foreign]	[Hunglish: you tube-ról]	For foreign sentences, use only [foreign] and quarantine them by using timestamps.

3.3   Second Passing

Second passing is used as a quality control measure to ensure the accuracy of segmentation, transcription (including markup), and speaker identification. After the initial file has been fully segmented and transcribed, a new annotator listens to the entire recording while viewing the corresponding transcript, and makes adjustments to the timestamps or transcription as needed. Second passing entails a mix of manual and programmatic checks on the transcript files. Second pass annotators verify that each timestamp matches the corresponding transcript or label exactly. Annotators play each timestamp in turn and make sure that the audio, video transcript and labels for that segment are an exact match and make any necessary corrections. Annotators also check that the timestamp has been placed in a suitable location between phrases, sentences, or breaths and that the timestamp does not chop off the start or end of any word. During the transcript checking phase of second passing, annotators examine the transcript in detail, checking for accuracy, completeness and the consistent use of transcription conventions. Annotators pay particular attention to a handful of areas that are particularly difficult to transcribe, in particular unintelligible speech sections and areas of speaker disfluency. Any proper names whose spelling could not be verified during the initial transcription process are corrected and standardized within the file.

4   Future Steps

After the annotators have finished their work, within the framework of my PhD research, I will examine the intonational phrases of spontaneous speech, set up prosodic rules and test if it improves phrase boundary detection and the automatic recognition of spontaneous speech in general. Thus the analysis of the speech material is followed by the creation of prosodic rules, statistical modelling and their implementation to the HTK speech recognizer [25]. In case of statistical modelling, the suprasegmental feature vectors are extracted from the preprocessing of the speech files and the segmentation and the labelling data can be used in building prosodic models. The visual channel of these phenomena is also to be annotated so that we can examine and implement multimodal features as well.

Acknowledgments. The database construction is a part of the Theoretical fundamentals of human-computer interaction technologies project (TAMOP-4.2.2-08/1/2008-0009).

References

1. Beckman, M., Hirschberg, J., Pierrehumbert, J., Pitrelli, J., Price, P., Silverman, K., Ostendorf, M.: TOBI: A Standard Scheme for Labeling Prosody. In: Proceedings of the International Conference on Spoken Language, Banff, pp. 867–870 (1992),
   http://faculty.wcas.northwestern.edu/ jbp/publications/
   ToBI_standard.pdf

2. Boersma, P., Weenink, D.: Praat: Doing Phonetics by Computer 5.1.43 (2010), http://www.praat.org
3. Burkhardt, F., Paeschke, A., et al.: A Database of German Emotional Speech. In: Proc. Of Interspeech 2005, pp. 1517–1520 (2005)
4. Chomsky, N., Halle, M.: The Sound Pattern of English. Harper and Row, New York (1968)
5. Douglas-Cowie, E., Campbell, N., Cowie, R., Roach, P.: Emotional Speech: Towards a New Generation of Databases. Speech Communication 40, 33–60 (2003)
6. Hirschberg, J.: Pragmatics and Intonation. In: Horn, L.R., Ward, G. (eds.) The Handbook of Pragmatics. Blackwell Publishing, Oxford (2007)
7. Hunyadi, L.: Hungarian Sentence Prosody and Universal Grammar. Peter Lang, Frankfurt am Main (2002)
8. Hunyadi, L.: Grouping, the Cognitive Basis of Recursion in Language. In: Kertsz, A. (ed.) Argumentum, vol. 2, pp. 67–114. Kossuth University Press, Debrecen (2006)
9. Hunyadi, L.: Experimental Evidence for Recursion in Prosody. In: Benjamins, J., Diken, T., ten Vago, R. (eds.) Approaches to Hungarian, vol. 11, pp. 119–141 (2009)
10. Keszler, B.: Die grammatischen und satzphonetischen Eigenschaften der Parenthesen. In: Szende, T. (ed.) Proceedings of the Speech Research 89 International Conference. Notes on Hungarian Phonetics, vol. 21, pp. 355–358. MTA Linguistics Research Institute, Budapest (1989)
11. Kramber, E., Swerts, M., Wilting, J.: Real vs. Acted Emotional Speech. In: Proceedings of the Interspeech, pp. 805–808 (2006)
12. Papay, K.: The Prosodic Phrase Structure of Spontaneous Speech - Modelling and Application in Speech Recognition. In: Tanacs, A., Szauter, D., Vincze, V. (eds.) Proc. of the 6th Hungarian Computational Linguistics Conference, pp. 373–375. Szeged University Press, Szeged (2009)
13. Papay, K.: Experimental Methods in Speech Technology Research. In: Reference Works for Studying Linguistics. Tinta Press, Budapest (in press 2010)
14. Rabiner, L.: Fundamentals of Speech Recognition. Prentice Hall, Englewood Hills (1993)
15. Selkirk, E.O.: Phonology and Syntax: The Relation between Sound and Structure. MIT Press, Cambridge (1984)
16. Seppanen, T., Toivanen, J., Vayrynen, E.: Automatic Discrimination of Emotion from Spoken Finnish. Language and Speech 47(4), 383–412 (2004)
17. Szaszak, Gy., Vicsi, K.: Automatic Segmentation of Continuous Speech on Word Level Based on Suprasegmental Features. International Journal of Speech Technology 8(4), 363–370 (2005)
18. Szaszak, Gy., Vicsi, K.: Using Prosody for the Improvement of ASR: Sentence Modality Recognition. In: Interspeech 2008, Brisbane. ISCA Archive (2008), http://www.isca-speech.org/archive
19. Szaszak, Gy.: The Role of Suprasegmental Features in Automatic Speech Recognition. PhD thesis, BME TMIT, Budapest (2009)
20. Szaszak, Gy., Vicsi, K.: Using Prosody to Improve Automatic Speech Recognition. Speech Communication 52, 413–426 (2010)
21. Sztaho, D.: Speech Emotion Perception by Human and Machine. In: Esposito, A., Bourbakis, N.G., Avouris, N., Hatzilygeroudis, I. (eds.) HH and HM Interaction. LNCS (LNAI), vol. 5042, pp. 213–224. Springer, Heidelberg (2008)

22. Sztaho, D., Vicsi, K.: Problems of Automatic Emotion Recognitions in Spontaneous Speech; an Example for the Recognition in a Dispatcher Center. In: Proceedings of COST 2102 International Training School Caserta, Italy. Springer, Heidelberg (in press, 2010)
23. Varga, L.: The Unit of the Hungarian Intonation. In: Szathmari, I. (ed.) Annales Universitatis Scientiarum Budapestinensis de Rolando Etvs nominatae. Sectio Linguistica tomus, vol. 24, pp. 5–13. ELTE University Press, Budapest (2001)
24. Varga, L.: Intonation and Stress. Evidence from Hungarian. Palgrave Macmillan, Houndmills (2002)
25. Young, S., et al.: The HTK Book (for version 3.3). Cambridge University, Cambridge (2005)

Conveying Directional Gaze Cues to Support Remote Participation in Hybrid Meetings

Betsy van Dijk , Job Zwiers, Rieks op den Akker, Olga Kulyk, Hendri Hondorp,
Dennis Hofs, and Anton Nijholt

Human Media Interaction, University of Twente,
P.O. Box 217, 7500 AE Enschede,
The Netherlands
{bvdijk,zwiers,infrieks,o.kulyk,g.h.w.hondorp,
hofs,anijholt}@ewi.utwente.nl

Abstract. We study videoconferencing for meetings with some co-located participants and one remote participant. A standard Skype-like interface for the remote participant is compared to a more immersive 3D interface that conveys gaze directions in a natural way. Experimental results show the 3D interface is promising: all significant differences are in favor of 3D and according to the participants the 3D interface clearly supports selective gaze and selective listening. We found some significant differences in perceived quality of cooperation and organization, and on the opinions about other group members. No significant differences were found for perceived social presence of the remote participants, but we did measure differences in social presence for co-located participants. Measured gaze frequency and duration nor perceived turn-taking behavior did differ significantly.

Keywords: Hybrid meetings, videoconferencing, selective gaze, selective listening, social presence, group process, turn-taking, remote participation.

1 Introduction

Collaboration between physically dispersed teams has become very important in the last decades, in industry and in science. Because of this development much research has been done on systems for multiparty videoconferencing and many systems are on the market now. Videoconferencing systems such as Skype or Adobe Connect offer a 2D picture-in-picture interface on a single video screen. All the participants are seated facing the camera and are visible in separate video frames. These frames are combined at a central location and the output is broadcast to the participants. Added value of the use of such systems, as compared to phone conferences, is that both speech and facial expressions are communicated. However, due to this setup, such videoconferencing systems fail to support selective gaze and selective listening [13]. Participants cannot show in a natural way to whom they look and they are not aware of who is visually attending to them. Though these disadvantages of distributed meetings with only mediated communication are well-known (e.g., [13]), remote meetings are often used to avoid having to choose between traveling too much or meeting too little.

A. Esposito et al. (Eds.): COST 2102 Int. Training School 2010, LNCS 6456, pp. 412–428, 2011.
© Springer-Verlag Berlin Heidelberg 2011

In this paper we focus on hybrid meetings, where one remote person is connected to a meeting taking place in a meeting room. Hybrid meetings are interesting because both face-to-face interaction and mediated interaction occur in the same group [2]. Remote participants might, as a consequence of their isolation, feel different about the group, the process and the outcomes of the meeting [2]. This feeling will be strengthened if co-located meeting participants use the opportunity they have to form a cohesive subgroup, making the remote participant a marginal member of the group [2]. As Yankelovich put very aptly in [20]: *"If you have ever dialed-in to a meeting taking place in a conference room, you probably know what it feels like to be a second-class citizen"*. Hybrid meetings suffer from almost all problems of fully distributed meetings but the difference in user experience between the remote participants and the co-located participants results in many additional problems that mainly have to do with social presence [20], the feeling of being together with another. A few important problems of the remote participant are the inability to participate in informal conversations (important for forming relationships and trust) and difficulty to break into a conversation. The people in the meeting room tend to forget about the remote participant because the physical presence of the people in the room takes their attention [20]. These and other problems make it difficult for the remote participant to stay engaged and keep paying adequate attention.

In this paper, we examine the effects of two different user environments for videoconferencing. The environments aim to improve the user experience of a remote participant. We compare a *"standard"* *conventional video conferencing interface* with an interface where video streams were presented to remote participants in an *integrated 3D environment*. In the conventional interface, co-located meeting participants all look straight into their webcam and they are visible to the remote participant in separate video frames presented in a horizontal row and in random order on a classical large screen. In the meeting room the video image of the remote participant is projected on a large projection display at the head of the table. Such a multimodal interface already communicates both speech and facial expressions. However, non-verbal behavioral cues like gaze direction and selective listening are lacking. The integrated 3D interface aims to enhance the group process and social presence of the participants by conveying gaze directions of both co-located participants and the remote participant in a natural way. To accomplish this other camera positions are chosen (explained in Section 3) and the video images of the co-located participants are presented to the remote participant in a more immersive way: they appear to be sitting around a virtual table, in a location that is consistent with the real, physical, situation. The co-located participants are presented to the remote participant on the same classical screen that was used for the conventional interface.

Other research projects have focused on improvement of audio- or videoconferencing systems before, and often conveying gaze direction was an important part of the efforts (e.g., [14, 16, 20]). In contrast to these projects, where they built special systems that often were expensive, we used rather basic low cost equipment (cameras, normal computers, microphones, standard screens). Hence the environments are easy to realize and change once the software is available.

This research takes place in the context of the European Network of Excellence on Social Signal Processing (SSPNet) and the European Augmented Reality Multi-party Interaction project (AMI and its successor AMIDA). SSPNet focuses on recognition, interpretation and synthesis of non-verbal behavioral cues in data captured with sensors like microphones and cameras. The aim is to provide computers with the ability to sense and understand human social signals and to design computer systems capable of adapting and responding to these signals. AMIDA concentrates on multi-party interaction during meetings and aims to develop technologies that can provide live meeting support to remote and co-located meeting participants. Part of the work is capturing non-verbal meeting interactions (posture, gestures, head orientation) and to look at ways to transform these into a virtual reality representation of a meeting room and meeting participants [9]. The real-time display of, for instance, head orientations will not always display gaze direction accurately, but it allows a fairly realistic representation of the focus of attention of participants (e.g., looking at a speaker, addressing someone). Within AMIDA we developed a demonstrator system to support remote meeting participation [1]. This User Engagement and Floor Control (UEFC) demo uses, amongst others, automatic speech recognition, visual focus of attention recognition and addressee detection. It can automatically support (remote) participants in identifying (1) if they are being addressed and (2) who is speaking to whom. The graphical user interface of the UEFC demo presents an overview of the meeting room and separate video images of the faces of the other participants. Although the design of the interface was not the focus of [1], an important observation was that participants appreciated the overview and the separate images of faces but had difficulty establishing mutual gaze in remote interactions. The experimental user environments that are evaluated in this paper were inspired by the experiences with the UEFC demo and aim to improve mutual gaze in interactions.

This paper presents the effects of the two experimental environments on perceived social presence and perceived quality of the group process and satisfaction with the outcome. In addition, subjective data will be presented on the turn-taking process, recognition of gaze behavior (awareness of who is looking to whom) and usability of the environments, as well as preliminary results of the analysis of objective data on gaze behavior. The paper is organized as follows. Section 2 presents related work. In Section 3 we describe the design of the two experimental conditions in more detail and we present the hypotheses. Section 4 describes the methodology used in the user study we conducted and Section 5 gives the results, followed by a discussion of the results in Section 6. Finally, conclusions and future work can be found in Section 7.

2   Transmission of Gaze Behavior in Mediated Communication

Studies comparing mediated communication with face to face communication often point out the importance of non-verbal behavior (facial expressions, head nods, gaze and gestures) for turn-taking and for the transmission of social and affective information [17]. To be conveyed, non-verbal behavior depends on the presence of visual information. Hence it is to be expected that technologies that do not support visual information show impaired communication [19]. However, simply adding a video channel to the supporting technologies does not always result in improved mediated communication that resembles face to face communication more in the sense that it is more efficient. Whittaker [18, 19] argues we should identify the contributions of various communication behaviors (e.g., speech, gaze, gestures, backchannel feedback) in supporting core communication phenomena, such as turn-taking. If we can also specify how the affordances of various mediated communication technologies affect behaviors we will be able to predict more precisely how technologies affect communication [19]. Much research has been done to elucidate the role of gaze in mediating turn-taking behavior in face to face communication (e.g., [7]). One hypothesis that Whittaker [19] treats is that technologies that do not transmit gaze behavior properly will disrupt turn-taking.

Results of studies that investigated this hypothesis are mixed. Sellen [13] found no differences between an audio-only system and three different videoconferencing systems on measures of turn-taking behavior, such as duration of turns, turn frequencies, number of interruptions. Compared to face to face communication, both the audio-only system and all videoconferencing systems showed reduced ability of listeners to take the floor spontaneously (less interruptions) and speakers used more formal techniques to hand over the floor (e.g., naming a possible next speaker). However, subjective data gathered by questionnaires did show differences in perceived influence of the systems. Participants mentioned several benefits of video. Video was thought to: (a) lead to more natural and more interactive conversations; (b) help identify and discriminate among speakers and to help to generally keep track of the conversation; (c) allow one to determine whether others are paying attention; (d) may support selective gaze and selective listening; (e) make them feel more part of the group and less remote from the other participants.

Vertegaal [16] also argues that just adding video to increase the number of cues conveyed does not necessarily improve communication when it comes to regulation of conversations. He believes turn-taking problems with multiparty conferencing systems may be attributed to a lack of cues about other participants' attention. He developed a system, the GAZE Groupware System, which provides awareness about the participants' gaze direction. By conveying only gaze direction the system allowed meeting participants to establish who is talking or listening to whom without some of the drawbacks of videoconferencing systems.

Another study [6] studied the impact of adding spatial cues, such as individual views and gaze awareness, to videoconferencing systems. They found that the spatial interfaces scored higher than a standard 2D control interface on social presence and co-presence measures but lower on task performance because of higher mental load.

The porta-person [20] is a telepresence device designed to improve the user experience of remote participants in hybrid meetings. It was inspired by the Hydra system [14] that uses a set-up of separate video displays representing each remote participant in order to preserve the notion of physical location of participants. The porta-person device contains a display screen, a video camera, stereo speakers and microphones on a rotating platform. It takes video images of the room and the device can present a video image of the remote participant and his or her voice. The device also conveys gaze direction and is designed to enhance the sense of social presence of remote meeting participants. The first experiences with the system were positive but the system turned out to be far too expensive to run field trials on a bigger scale.

3   Experimental Conditions and Hypotheses

The present study was designed to examine the effects of two different videoconferencing environments. We compare a standard 2D videoconferencing interface with an interface where video streams were presented to remote participants in an integrated 3D environment. The main difference between these environments is that the integrated 3D environment aims to support selective gaze and selective listening. In that environment gaze behavior of participants is transmitted in such a way that it is visible to all the participants (including the remote participant) to whom they look and who is visually attending to them.

3.1   Standard 2D Videoconferencing Interface

In the condition with the standard 2D videoconferencing interface (STANDARD), the three co-located participants (LP1, LP2 and LP3) are presented to the remote participant (RP) in a way similar to the presentation in a Skype or Adobe Connect meeting: the co-located participants have a webcam right in front of them. The camera images are presented to the remote participant in separate video frames positioned in a horizontal row and in 'random' order. Consequently, view directions on the screen do not match the real view directions. The images were presented to the RP on a classical large (52") video screen, see Figure 1.

Fig. 1. Presentation of co-located participants to the remote participant in STANDARD

3.2   Integrated 3D Videoconferencing Interface

In the condition with the integrated 3D video conferencing interface (3D) the placement of the cameras is different. See Figure 2 for an overview of the room with the camera settings. If the co-located participants look to the screen with the remote participant they look into the camera. In this condition view directions on the screen of the RP match the real view directions as good as possible.

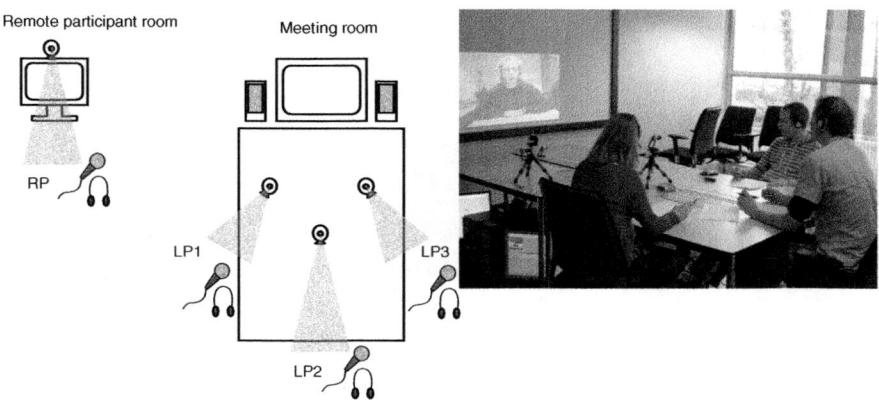

Fig. 2. Meeting room setting Integrated 3D version

Additionally the video images of the three co-located participants are presented to the remote participant in a more immersive representation around a virtual table, thus aiming to enhance the social presence of the remote participant. For this presentation we used the same video screen as was used in the other condition. Consequently the presentation was not really 3D but it offered the right perspective on the people in the meeting room. See Figure 3. Presentation of the remote participant in the meeting room was the same as in the other condition (see Figure 2, right picture).

3.3   Hypotheses

In both conditions we used the same cameras and the same screens for presentation of the video images. The quality of the images was good enough to capture non-verbal signals like facial expressions, eye movements and postures of participants in both conditions. However, recognition of gaze direction will be more difficult in STANDARD than in the 3D environment that was designed to reflect gaze directions in a natural way. Note that in STANDARD the co-located participants LP1 and LP3 look away from the camera when they look to the screen with the RP, hence in the perception of the RP they look away from him/her. Because of this, added to the fact that in STANDARD video images are presented to the RP in random order, we expect that in STANDARD (compared to 3D) the group process and turn-taking process will be impaired, resulting in lower scores on the group process questions and turn-taking, usability and recognition questions of the questionnaire described in section 4.4.

In addition, because in the 3D environment the co-located participants are presented to the remote participant in a more immersive way and they really seem to look at the remote participant when addressing him or her, the 3D condition is expected to establish a higher involvement of the remote participant in the group discussion (higher participation, a feeling of 'being there'). Hence, compared to STANDARD, the perceived social presence in the 3D condition is expected to be higher. The differences between STANDARD and 3D are expected to have more impact on the remote participants than on the participants in the meeting room.

Fig. 3. Remote participant room in the Integrated 3D version

4   User Study – Method

The two user environments for video-mediated hybrid meetings have been compared in a user study that measured the effects of the different environments on perceived social presence, satisfaction with the decision making process of the group and perceived turn-taking behavior and usability. In addition gaze behavior was observed. This section describes the setup of this study.

4.1   Participants and Experimental Design

Participants in the study were 40 young adults (5 women and 35 men) with ages ranging from 18 to 38 (most between 21 and 29). They were researchers (most PhD students) and students from the Computer Science department of the University of Twente who were not paid for their participation. They discussed in the hybrid meeting environment for the first time. Participants took part in hybrid small group meetings (10 groups with four participants in each group). Three participants of each group met in a common (instrumented) meeting room and one participant took part remotely, via a videoconferencing system.

Within-group design is chosen for this experimental study, which means that each group performed a task in each of the two conditions. The conditions were counterbalanced, hence 5 groups started with the standard 2D videoconferencing interface and the other 5 started with the integrated 3D interface.

The experiment took place in the Smart XP Lab at the University of Twente. All sessions were captured with 4 web-cameras (1 per participant), 3 ceiling-mounted video cameras in the meeting room and one camera in the remote participant's room, capturing the image on the video screen the RP saw.

4.2 Group Decision Tasks

Since decision making tasks require more coordination and group member interaction than many other tasks [1], the groups were given two decision making tasks on which to come to consensus. One task was to select one student (out of three) to admit into the university's undergraduate program. The other task was to select a location (out of three possible locations) for a new 24-hour supermarket. These tasks were taken from [3] and adapted in the sense that there was no demonstrably best answer. According to Stasser and Steward [15] this is a judgement task and the best the group can do is come to consensus. In this kind of tasks the decision process is not so much focusing on exchanging critical information and finding the truth. Instead the decision process "is more aptly characterized by egalitarian social combination schemes such as majority- or plurality-wins models" [15; pp. 432].

In a few additional adaptations to the tasks we followed [8]. Instead of receiving different hidden profiles, all group members had the same information about the student candidates and the possible locations. This was done to avoid participants looking at the paper description during the discussion. As our intention was to observe the visual attention we took away the paper descriptions during discussion. To initiate an engaging group discussion, the participants received different roles in the discussion: they had to defend different beliefs and values probably leading to different choices. E.g., for the student selection task one participant role emphasized intellectual ability while another role emphasized diversity in cultural backgrounds.

The tasks were counter-balanced within each condition and order of condition, to rule out influences of the tasks on the results.

4.3 Procedure

Participants were scheduled in groups of 4 on the basis of availability at certain times. In some groups participants knew each other, in other groups they did not and there were mixed groups as well. Participants met in a room next to the meeting room. They received a short introduction, only stating that they participated in a user study on videoconferencing support for group meetings and that they would engage in two group discussions, each followed by filling in a questionnaire. Then the remote participant was randomly chosen from the four participants in the group and brought to a separate room, while the three other group members entered the meeting room.

The group started with a warm-up discussion of 5 minutes about a topic they chose from a list of topics. During this discussion we checked if all the equipment functioned well. Then participants got 5 minutes time to independently read the first group decision task. They studied the available alternatives and their role in the discussion, and they were asked to make a preliminary choice. They were told in advance that the task descriptions would not be available during the discussion. Additional time was given on request. After the task descriptions were taken away, participants engaged in a discussion for 15 minutes. Two minutes before the end of the discussion time the experimenter warned the participants they only had two minutes left to come to a final decision which every team member can agree with. After the discussion all four participants went to the room where they met, to fill in a questionnaire. In the meantime settings in the meeting room and the remote participant room where prepared for the second part of the session.

When people returned in the meeting room (respectively the remote participant room) they received the second group decision task and followed the same procedure in the other condition: 5 minutes reading, handing in task descriptions, 15 minutes discussion - with a warning to come to consensus - and filling in a questionnaire in the other room. In the end there was a short post-interview with the group.

4.4 Measures

The questionnaire participants filled in after each group decision task consisted of several parts: a part to assess perceived group process (18 questions), a part with a social presence questionnaire (19 questions), and a part with 11 questions about usability, turn-taking and recognition of gaze direction and other non-verbal signals. All questions were rated on a 5-point Likert scale, where '1' meant 'Strongly disagree' and '5' meant 'Strongly agree'.

The group process part of the questionnaire consisted of 12 questions about perceived group process quality [10], 5 questions about satisfaction with the decision making process [11, 12] and one question about overall satisfaction with the final group decision [12].

In the social presence questionnaire we included parts of the validated social presence questionnaire of Harms and Biocca [5] and a few questions taken from Hauber et al. [6]. From Harms and Biocca we used 16 questions: the complete subscales Co-presence and Attention Allocation and a few items from the subscales Message Understanding and Perceived Behavioral Interdependence. We left out the subscales Perceived Emotional Interdependence and Perceived Affective Understanding because we expected these to be of less relevance in this meeting context. The three questions taken from Hauber et al. [6] were labelled Co-presence as well. We added them because they were formulated in relation to face-to-face contact (e.g., "sometimes it was just like being face-to-face with the RP/LPs" and "it sometimes felt as if the RP/LPs and I were in the same room") and hence were expected to be very relevant for our study. The co-presence questions of Harms and Biocca were formulated in terms of noticing each other (e.g., "The RP/LPs always noticed me" and "My presence was obvious to the RP/LPs"), which of course is also relevant.

The rest of the questions were about turn-taking, floor control and usability, taken from [6, 12] and a few questions we made for this study: about recognition of gaze direction and other non-verbal signals.

During the discussions visual focus of attention of the participants was observed and annotated real-time. Every observer monitored one of the participants and annotated who the participant was looking at. If the participant did not look at one of the other participants it was annotated the participant looked somewhere else.

5 Results

This section presents the results of the questionnaires, an analysis of the observed gaze behavior of the participants, and the results of the post-interviews.

5.1 Group Process and Satisfaction with the Outcome

We used exploratory factor analysis (principal component analysis with oblimin rotation) to find underlying dimensions in the data from the questionnaire part on perceived group process quality and satisfaction with the decision making process. Two questions about overall satisfaction with the process and the outcome were excluded from this analysis, as well as a question about trustworthiness of the group members. Because of their deviating form, these questions were studied separately. In the factor analysis the question "group members brought a variety of perspectives to bear on the tasks" loaded on a separate factor and will be treated separately as well.

The remaining questions loaded on three factors. The first factor contains 7 questions (e.g., "The general quality of the group members' contributions to group discussions was very good" and "The evaluation of arguments was very thorough") and was labelled Group process and contributions. The second factor contains 4 questions (e.g., "The group discussions were unorganized" and "There were disruptive conflicts") and was labelled Organization and cooperation. The third factor contains 3 questions (e.g., "People were friendly in my group" and "Comments reflected respect for one another") and was labelled Group members.

Cronbach Alpha tests were used to analyze the reliability of the subscales identified by the factor analysis for both the STANDARD and the 3D condition. For *Group process and contributions* the alpha reliabilities were .73 in 3D and .85 in STANDARD. *Organization and cooperation* had an alpha of .66 in 3D and .75 in STANDARD and the alphas of *Group member* were .65 (3D) and .89 (STANDARD). Hence reliabilities varied from reasonable (.65) to high (.89) [4].

We used Wilcoxon signed ranks tests (α=.05) to analyze the differences between the two experimental conditions on the three subscales and four questions of the group process part of the questionnaire. We did the tests for all participants (40 persons) and for the 10 remote participants (RP) and 30 co-located participants (LPs) separately. The results of the analyses are shown in Table 1.

As can be seen in Table 1, there were no factors or questions on which the STANDARD condition scored significantly higher than the 3D condition. 3D scored significantly better on Organization and cooperation. This effect is strong for the LPs (p < .01) and not significant for the remote participants. Here we have to keep in mind that the group of remote participants was only small (10 people) and hence finding statistically significant differences will only be possible if the differences are really consistent and quite large. We found a marginally significant difference in favor of 3D for Group member (all group members) and Group process and contribution (only RPs). Furthermore, to our surprise, with the RPs we found a significant difference, in favor of 3D, on satisfaction with the final decision. On the questions on trustworthiness of group members and satisfaction with the solution process there were no significant difference between the conditions.

Table 1. Differences between STANDARD and 3D on Group Process and Satisfaction with the Outcome. Columns "Best" shows the condition (3D or ST) that scored significantly higher.

Factor or question	All		RP		LPs	
	Best	Z	Best	Z	Best	Z
Group process and contribution			3D	-1.79[†]		
Organization and cooperation	3D	-2.37[*]			3D	-2.88[**]
Group members	3D	-1.80[†]				
Variety of perspectives					3D	-1.97[*]
Trustworthiness group members						
Satisfaction solution process						
Satisfaction final decision			3D	-1.98[*]		

[†] $p < 0.1$ [*] $p < 0.05$ [**] $p < 0.01$

5.2 Social Presence

Cronbach Alpha tests were used to find out if the subscales of Harms and Biocca and Hauber were reliable in both the STANDARD and the 3D condition. The results are shown in Tabel 2.

Table 2. Cronbach's Alphas for the social presence subscales of Harms and Biocca and the co-presence subscale of Hauber et al

Factor	3D	STANDARD
Co-Presence Harms and Biocca (6 items)	.76	.82
Attention Allocation (6 items)	.57	.51
Message Understanding (2 items)	.72	.70
Perceived Behavioral Interdependence (2 items)	.66	.73
Co-Presence Hauber et al. (3 items)	.79	.80

Except for Attention Allocation, all scales are reliable hence we decided to use the scales in the analyses. To study the differential effects of the two experimental conditions on social presence we again used the Wilcoxon signed rank test. The results are presented in Table 3. Because analyses for all participants (All) and for the remote participant (RP) did not show significant differences, these columns are left empty. During the interviews we noticed there was a difference in perceptions between the co-located participants LP2 that were in the position facing the screen with the remote participant and LP1 and LP3 that had to look to their left or right to see the remote participant. Hence we repeated the Wilcoxon tests for LP2 (10 persons) and LP1+LP3 (20 persons) separately as well.

Table 3. Differences between STANDARD and 3D on Social Presence. Columns "Best" shows the condition (3D or ST) that scored significantly higher.

Factor	All	RP	LPs		LP1+LP3		LP2
			Best	Z	Best	Z	
Co-Presence Harms and Biocca					3D	-2.04*	
Attention Allocation			3D	-1.66†	3D	-1.99*	
Message Understanding							
Perceived Behavioral Interdep.			3D	-1.80†	3D	-3.14**	
Co-Presence Hauber et al.							

† $p < 0.1$ * $p < 0.05$ ** $p < 0.01$

For "All participants" and for the "Remote Participant" and the participants on location 2 no significant differences between the conditions were found on any of the social presence subscales. Participants on locations 1 and 3, however, did perceive significant differences, all in favor of 3D, on three of the subscales of the social presence questionnaire of Harms and Biocca [5]: Co-presence, Attention Allocation and Perceived Behavioral Interdependance.

5.3 Turn-Taking, Usability, Recognition of Non-verbal Cues and Gaze Direction

The remaining questions on turn-taking, usability and recognition of non-verbal signals and gaze direction were analyzed separately because no reliable subscales could be identified. The questions and the results of Wilcoxon tests we used to analyze the differences between the experimental conditions can be found in Table 4.

No significant differences between the conditions were found for any of the turn-taking questions. The perceived effort it took to follow the discussion and ease of recognition of non-verbal signals did not differ significantly either. But very significant differences, again in favor of 3D, were found for all participants on the statements "I got the feeling that the other participants/the remote participant looked at me " and "It was clear to whom the other participants/the remote participants talked." Hence the participants clearly noticed the intended difference between the two conditions.

Table 4. Differences between STANDARD and 3D on Turn-taking, Usability, Recognition of Gaze direction and Non-verbal Cues. Columns "Best" shows the condition (3D or ST) that scored significantly higher.

Question	All		RP		LPs	
	Best	Z	Best	Z	Best	Z
I knew exactly when it was my turn to speak						
We were never talking over one another						
There was a lot of time when no-one spoke at all						
I could always clearly hear the voices of the other group members (LPs)			3D	$-1.89^{\dagger}$		
It was easy to take my speaker turn when I wished to do so						
It took me a lot of effort to follow the discussion						
I could recognize non-verbal signals of the RP/LPs easily						
I got the feeling that the RP/LPs looked at me	3D	-3.00^{**}	3D	-2.10^{*}	3D	-2.18^{*}
It was clear to whom the RP/LPs talked	3D	-3.49^{***}	3D	-2.26^{*}	3D	-2.63^{**}
The presentation of the RP/LPs on the screen was appealing	3D	$-1.90^{\dagger}$	3D	$-1.90^{\dagger}$		

$^{\dagger} p < 0.1$ $^{*} p < 0.05$ $^{**} p < 0.01$ $^{***} p < 0.001$

5.4 Visual Focus of Attention

To find out if there was a difference between the experimental conditions in the frequency and duration the co-located participants looked at the remote participant we used the annotations of the observers. For every participant in the discussions, we derived the number of times they looked at each of the other participants in the discussions. From the durations of each of these counted gaze acts we also derived how long (in seconds) the participant looked at each of the other participants during the whole discussion. Because there were small differences between the durations of the discussions, in the analyses we used variables that correct for duration of the discussion. Instead of using the number of times participant x looked at participant y during the discussion we used the number of times participant x would have looked at participant y if the discussion would have lasted an hour (relative number of times). Instead of using the total time participant x looked at participant y during the discussion we used the percentage of the discussion time participant x looked at participant y (percentage of time).

To find out if the two experimental conditions were different in how often and how long the co-located participants looked at the remote participant we used the paired t-test. The results are presented in Table 5.

No significant differences were found between the conditions in how often and how long the co-located participants looked at the remote participant. Similar analyses of the relative number of times and the percentage of time other participants in the discussion (LP1, LP2, LP3) were looked at yielded no significant differences between STANDARD and 3D either.

Table 5. Differences between STANDARD and 3D in Gaze Behavior

	STANDARD		3D		Results paired t-test		
	Mean	SD	Mean	SD	t	df	p
Relative number of times LPs looked at RP	191.4	95.7	188.7	72.4	.18	29	.86
Percentage of time LPs looked at RP	15.9	8.13	18.9	9.4	-1.54	29	.13

5.5 Group Interviews

The post-interviews with the groups were open-ended, starting with the question if they had a preference for one of the environments and, if so, what was the preferred environment and what were the reasons. Seven groups unanimously chose 3D as their favorite. In the three remaining groups only the remote participants had a deviating opinion: one of them said he had no preference, the other two preferred STANDARD. They did not like the 3D view with the virtual table and the backgrounds of the images that did not fit together very well. Most important reasons that were mentioned: 3D was more natural (mentioned by 7 groups), more intuitive (mentioned twice). Some groups added that 3D worked well: they really felt this was a good way to meet or to have a conversation. In 3D it was more clear who looked/talked to whom (5 times) and most remote participants said that in 3D it was clear when people looked at them and they could see if they had the attention of the others. A few remote participants said they had the idea they looked the others in the eyes. In STANDARD they had to find out first if they were addressed and if it was their turn to speak. Moreover, in STANDARD many remote participants did not know to whom the co-located participants talked. Four groups mentioned that in 3D the remote participant was more involved in the group and in two groups the co-located participants said that in STANDARD they paid less attention to the remote participant. Participants on locations 1 and 3 (LP1 and LP3) often mentioned the cameras in STANDARD were inconvenient – too close in front of them. Another thing often mentioned was that in STANDARD it was difficult to look at the remote participant on the screen and at the same time look in the camera. Only people who were aware of how the remote participant would probably see them mentioned this. Others reacted by saying they never thought about the fact that the remote participant would see them from the side if they looked at the image of the remote participant. Often participants LP2, the people right in front of the screen with the remote participant, said they did not notice much difference between 3D and STANDARD.

6 Discussion

The participants clearly noticed the intended difference between the two conditions. In 3D both the remote participants and the co-located participants stated they could better distinguish who was being addressed. In addition, many of the remote participants got the feeling the co-located participants looked at them and many of the co-located participants got the feeling the remote participant looked at them. As a result of this we would expect the remote participants to be more involved in the 3D meetings than in the STANDARD meetings. However, no significant differences were found for the *remote* participants on any of the social presence subscales, though mean scores were consistently higher in 3D. (Hence the differential effects, if any, were not strong enough to be significant for 10 participants.) The situation was different for the two local co-located participants LP1 and LP3 that were affected by the differences between the two interfaces: here we did measure significant differences in favor of 3D on the social presence subscales co-presence, attention allocation and perceived behavioral interdependence. This indicates, for instance, that in the 3D condition LP1 and LP3 felt more present to and felt more noticed by the remote group member and visa versa and they remained more focused on each other during interaction than in the STANDARD condition.

To our surprise, no significant differences between the conditions were found for any of the turn-taking questions and the perceived effort it took to follow the discussion did not differ either. Hence, though the participants could distinguish gaze directions better, that did not influence their perceived turn-taking behavior. The analysis we did on the observer annotations of visual focus of attention did not show any significant differences between STANDARD and 3D in how often or how long the co-located participants looked at the remote participant. If the 3D condition would resemble face-to-face communication more than the STANDARD condition we would have expected more attention for the remote participant in the 3D condition. It will be interesting to do more analyses on the behavioral data to see if objective measurements support the outcomes of the subjective measurements and for instance number of interruptions, the time no-one spoke at all, or participants started talking at the same time really did not differ between the conditions.

On the questionnaires measuring the perceived quality of the group process and the discussions, significant differences in favor of 3D were found on the organization of and cooperation in the meetings and on the opinions about the other group members. Trustworthiness of the group members did not differ between the conditions.

The results of the group interviews at the end of the user study mainly support the results of the questionnaires: overall 3D was preferred by most participants. Actually we did expect the differences between the conditions to be very clear for remote participants and not so clear for the co-located participants because for them the only difference between the conditions was the gaze behavior of the RP. But obviously the differences were clearly noticeable, especially for LP1 and LP3. The 3D environment was found to be more natural and intuitive and suitable to support remote meetings or conversations. Based on the interviews we would have expected to find differences in perceived turn-talking behavior. Possible explanation for the absence of these differences might be that the meeting participants thought that in STANDARD they succeeded to have equally fluent turn-taking behavior, despite the missing directional gaze cues. Further analyses of observational data should show if that was really the case or meeting participants are not really very conscious about their turn-taking behavior.

7 Conclusions

This study compared two user environments that aim to support remote participation in hybrid meeting. One environment, named STANDARD, is the control environment. It resembles a conventional video conferencing environment: co-located meeting participants all look straight into their webcam and their video images are presented to the remote participant in separate frames, presented in a horizontal row. This environment fails to support selective gaze and selective listening. The experimental environment, named integrated 3D or shortly 3D, is designed to convey gaze directions in a natural way. Results of the user study indicate that the 3D environment is promising: all differences that were significant were in favor of 3D and according to most participants the environment clearly supports selective gaze and selective listening in a natural way. Moreover, remote participants often mentioned they felt as if co-located participants looked at them. Nevertheless, on the social presence measures no significant differences between the two environments were found for remote participants, possibly because the number of groups and hence of remote participants was only 10. Another possible explanation was put forward by Hauber et al. [6]. In their study they did not find any significant results on social presence measures. They conclude that the social presence measure might not be sensible enough to find differences and suggest to add objective or physiological measurements. In our study we did find significantly higher scores for 3D on the social presence subscales co-presence, attention allocation, and perceived behavioral interdependence for co-located participants in locations 1 and 3, the locations where they had to look to their left or right to see the screen with the remote participant. In addition we found some significant differences on measures of perceived quality of group process. We did not find any significant differences between 3D and STANDARD in perceived turn-taking behavior. Considering the fact that in the interviews and the questionnaires the participants clearly stated that in 3D they could better distinguish who was being addressed, we intend to further analyze observational data (gaze annotations, video recordings) to find out if differences in turn-taking behavior occurred between the two environments.

Acknowledgments. The work reported in this paper is sponsored by the European IST Programme Project FP6-0033812 (AMIDA) and the European Community's Seventh Framework Programme (FP7/2007-2013) under grant agreement no. 231287 (SSPNet). This paper only reflects the authors views and funding agencies are not liable for any use that may be made of the information contained herein.

References

1. op den Akker, H.J.A., Hofs, D.H.W., Hondorp, G.H.W., op den Akker, H., Zwiers, J., Nijholt, A.: Supporting Engagement and Floor Control in Hybrid Meetings. In: Esposito, A., Vích, R. (eds.) Cross-Modal Analysis of Speech, Gestures, Gaze and Facial Expressions. LNCS, vol. 5641, pp. 276–290. Springer, Heidelberg (2009)

2. Burke, K., Aytes, K., Chidambaram, L., Johnson, J.: A Study of Partially Distributed Work Groups: The Impact of Media, Location, and Time on Perceptions and Performance. Small Group Research 30(4), 453–490 (1999)

3. DiMicco, J., Pandolfo, A., Bender, W.: Influencing Group Participation with a Shared Display. In: Proc. CSCW 2004, pp. 614–623. ACM Press, New York (2004)

4. Field, A.: Discovering Statistics Using SPSS, 3rd edn. Sage Publications Ltd, Thousand Oaks (2009)

5. Harms, C., Biocca, F.: Internal Consistency and Reliability of the Networked Minds Social Presence Measure. In: Alcaniz, M., Rey, B. (eds.) Seventh Annual International Workshop: Presence 2004, pp. 246–251. Universidad Politecnica de Valencia, Valencia (2004)

6. Hauber, J., Regenbrecht, H., Billinghurst, M., Cockburn, A.: Spatiality in videoconferencing: trade-offs between efficiency and social presence. In: Proc. CSCW 2006, pp. 413–422. ACM Press, New York (2006)

7. Kendon, A.: Some Functions of Gaze-Direction in Social Interaction. Acta Psychologica 26, 22–63 (1967)

8. Kulyk, O., Wang, C., Terken, J.: Real-Time Feedback Based on Nonverbal Behaviour to Enhance Social Dynamics in Small Group Meetings. In: Renals, S., Bengio, S. (eds.) MLMI 2005. LNCS, vol. 3869, pp. 150–161. Springer, Heidelberg (2006)

9. Nijholt, A., Rienks, R.J., Zwiers, J., Reidsma, D.: Online and Off-line Visualization of Meeting Information and Meeting Support. The Visual Computer 22(12), 965–976 (2006)

10. Olaniran, B.A.: A Model of Group Satisfaction in Computer Mediated Communication and Face-to-Face Meetings. Behaviour & Information Technology 15(1), 24–36 (1996)

11. Paul, S., Seetharaman, P., Ramamurthy, K.: User Satisfaction with System, Decision Process, and Outcome in GDSS Based Meeting: An Experimental Investigation. In: Proc. of the 37th Hawaii International Conference on System Sciences. IEEE Computer Society Press, Los Alamitos (2004)

12. Post, W., Elling, E., Cremers, A., Kraaij, W.: Experimental Comparison of Multimodal Meeting Browsers. In: Smith, M.J., Salvendy, G. (eds.) HCII 2007. LNCS, vol. 4558, pp. 118–127. Springer, Heidelberg (2007)

13. Sellen, A.J.: Remote Conversations: The Effects of Mediating Talk With Technology. Human–Computer Interaction 10, 401–444 (1995)

14. Sellen, A., Buxton, B., Arnott, J.: Using spatial cues to improve videoconferencing. In: Proc. CHI 1992, pp. 651–652. ACM Press, New York (1992)

15. Stasser, G., Stewart, D.: Discovery of Hidden Profiles by Decision-Making Groups: Solving a Problem Versus Making a Judgment. Journal of Personality and Social Psychology 63(3), 426–434 (1992)

16. Vertegaal, R.: The GAZE Groupware System: Mediating Joint Attention in Multiparty Communication and Collaboration. In: Proc. CHI 1999, pp. 294–301. ACM Press, New York (1999)

17. Vinciarelli, A., Pantic, M., Bourlard, H.: Social Signal Processing: Survey of an Emerging Domain. Image and Vision Computing 27(12), 1743–1759 (2009)

18. Whittaker, S.: Rethinking Video as a Technology for Interpersonal Communications: Theory and Design Implications. Intl. J. of Man-Machine Studies 42, 50–529 (1995)

19. Whittaker, S.: Theories and Methods in Mediated Communication. In: Handbook of Discourse Processes, Erlbaum, NJ, pp. 243–286 (2002)

20. Yankelovich, N., Simpson, N., Kaplan, J., Provino, J.: Porta-Person: Telepresence for the Connected Conference Room. In: Proc. CHI 2007, pp. 2789–2794. ACM Press, New York (2007)

Affect Recognition in Real Life Scenarios

Theodoros Kostoulas, Todor Ganchev, and Nikos Fakotakis

Wire Communications Laboratory, Department of Electrical and Computer Engineering
University of Patras, 26500 Rion-Patras, Greece
{tkost,tganchev,fakotaki}@wcl.ee.upatras.gr

Abstract. Affect awareness is important for improving human-computer inter-action, but also facilitates the detection of atypical behaviours, danger, or crisis situations in surveillance and in human behaviour monitoring applications. The present work aims at the detection and recognition of specific affective states, such as panic, anger, happiness in close to real-world conditions. The affect recognition scheme investigated here relies on an utterance-level audio parame-terization technique and a robust pattern recognition scheme based on the Gaus-sian Mixture Models with Universal Background Modelling (GMM-UBM) paradigm. We evaluate the applicability of the suggested architecture on the PROMETHEUS database, implemented in a number of indoor and outdoor conditions. The experimental results demonstrate the potential of the suggested architecture on the challenging task of affect recognition in real world condi-tions. However, further enhancement of the affect recognition performance would be needed before any deployment of practical applications.

Keywords: affect recognition, emotion recognition, real-world data.

1 Introduction

Recent research efforts towards enhancing human-machine interaction and towards the development of autonomous surveillance systems increased the demands of successful modeling of the human affective states/emotions [1]. Awareness of the affective state of a person can be of great assistance to detecting crisis and danger situations, to interpreting atypical human behaviours, as well as for the prediction of short-term human actions [1-3].

To this end, various approaches for affect/emotion recognition have been reported [4-6]. In [7] Callejas et al. studied the impact of contextual information for the anno-tation of emotions. They carried out experiments on a corpus extracted from the inter-action of humans with a spoken dialogue system. Their results show that both humans and machines are affected by the contextual information. In [8] Seppi et al. reported classification results with the use of acoustic and linguistic features, utilizing the FAU Aibo Emotion Corpus [9,10]. In [11], Brendel et al. describe research efforts towards emotion detection for monitoring an Artificial Agent by voice.

This work aims at the detection and recognition of specific affective/emotional states, such as panic, anger, happy that are important for improving human-computer interaction and for the detection of atypical behaviors, danger, or crisis situations. The affect recognition system is based on state of the art audio parameterization technique

A. Esposito et al. (Eds.): COST 2102 Int. Training School 2010, LNCS 6456, pp. 429–435, 2011.
© Springer-Verlag Berlin Heidelberg 2011

and GMM-UBM classifier. We perform evaluation of the proposed scheme in a number of real-world setups, such as smart home scenario and public areas surveillance (airport, ATM, etc) scenarios. All experiments were performed on the audio part of the PROMETHEUS multi-modal multi-sensor database [12,13]. This corpus contains both single-person and multi-person scenarios, recorded in uncontrolled indoor and outdoor environments.

The remainder of this work is organized as follows: In Section 2 we outline the architecture of our affect recognition system. Section 3 offers details about the audio part of the PROMETHEUS corpus that was used in the experimental evaluation. In Section 4 we discuss the results from the experimentations performed and Section 5 concludes the present work.

2   System Architecture

The block diagram of the GMM-UBM based affect recognition system is shown in Fig. 1. The upper part of the figure summarizes the training of the speaker-independent affect/emotion models, and the bottom part outlines the operational mode of the system.

As the Fig. 1 presents, during both the training and the operational phases, speech data are subject to parameterization. In the present work we make use of openSMILE speech parameterization toolkit [14], and compute a 384-dimensional feature vector for each input utterance following the procedure illustrated in Fig. 2. Specifically, 16 low level descriptors and their delta coefficients are initially computed. Next, twelve functionals are applied on sentence level [4].

During training (Fig.1), two types of data (labelled and unlabeled) are utilized for the creation of the affect/emotion models of interest. Specifically, the feature vectors computed from the unlabelled speech recordings, different from the speakers involved in the testing of the affect/emotion models, are utilized for the creation of a large Gaussian mixture model, which is referred to as Universal Background Model (UBM) [15,16]. This model is assumed to represent the general properties of speech, and thus, it does not represent accurately any of the affect/emotion categories of interest or the individual characteristics of the speakers whose speech was used in its creation. Next, a category-specific set of labelled speech recordings are used for deriving the models for each affect/emotion category of interest. This is done by the Bayesian adaptation technique also known as maximum a posteriori (MAP) adaption of the UBM [17]. During MAP adaptation we adapted only the means.

The affect/emotion models built during training are utilized in the operational phase for the classification of unlabeled speech recordings to one of the predefined affective/emotional categories. In brief, the feature vectors resulting from the speech parameterization stage are fed to the GMM classification stage, where the log-likelihoods for the input data belonging to each of the category-specific models are computed. A decision about the emotional content of the input utterance is made by applying a threshold on the log-likelihood ratio computed from the affect/emotion models built.

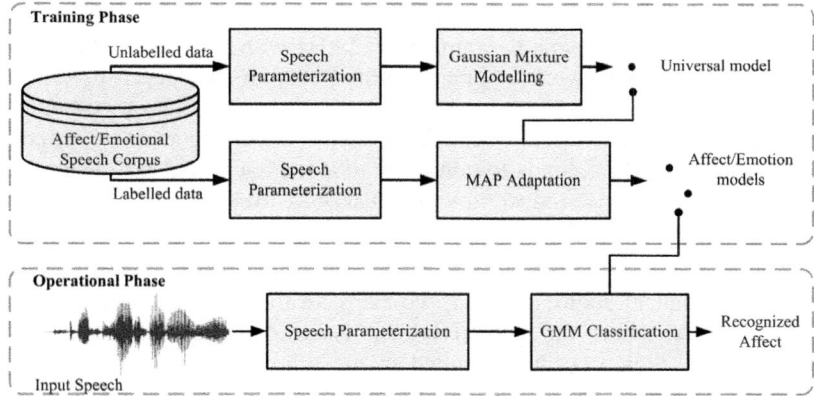

Fig. 1. Block diagram of the affect recognition system

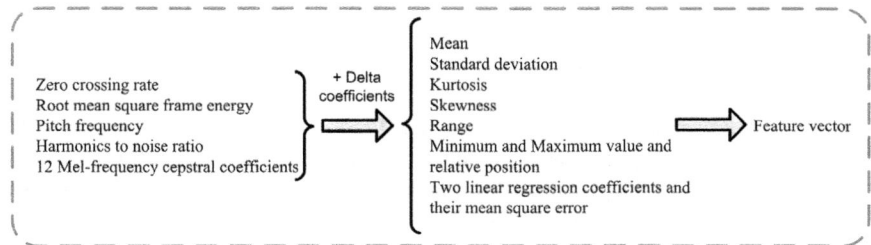

Fig. 2. Speech Parameterization

3   The PROMETHEUS Database

The multimodal PROMETHEUS database [12,13] was created in support of RTD activities aiming at the creation of a framework for monitoring and interpretation of human behaviours in unrestricted indoor and outdoor environments. The audio part of this database consists of four hours of recordings, representative for two application scenarios: smart-home (indoors, Greek spoken by native speakers) and public security – airport and ATM (outdoors, English spoken by non-native speakers). Each recording session is comprised of multiple action scenes concatenated in a single sequence, where each action scene is implemented a number of times by different actors. The indoor scenes were implemented by five skilled actors: three females and two males. In addition, twelve supernumerary actors (including one female) were involved in the outdoor scenes. The actors' age was in the range between 22 and 56 years with mean value of 33.8 years. In the following, we report results on the so-called *selected scenes*, which the PROMETHEUS consortium identified as the most interesting from application point of view. These thirty-two scenes with individual durations between 15 and 134 seconds have a cumulative length of approximately 30 minutes and represent typical multiple-person interaction episodes.

The audio, recorded with an 8-channel uniform linear array with spacing between the microphones of 0.1 meters, is sampled at 32 kHz with resolution 32-bits per sample. Since in the present work we are interested only in the speech portions of the signal, we downsampled the 8-channel audio to 8 kHz and resolution 16-bit, and next made use of a minimum variance beamformer with processing window of 0.064 seconds and overlap 0.032 seconds to convert it to a single-channel audio signal. Afterwards, we performed noise reduction with a band-pass Butterworth filter of order six, with low and high cut $f_{lo} = 250\,Hz$ and $f_{hi} = 3700\,Hz$, respectively.

The annotation of the PROMETHEUS selected scenes was performed on the band limited single-channel audio signal in two steps. In the first step, one annotator listened the selected scenes for indentifying the existing affective states based on his human intuition. This procedure resulted in the following affective states: {*panic, happy, angry, neutral*}. In the second step, another annotator was asked to segment the selected scenes into parts based on the perceived affective state.

The aforementioned steps resulted to 180 error-free single-person and multi-person utterances {*panic* (47), *happy* (11), *angry* (40), *neutral* (77), *rest* (5)}.

4   Experiments and Results

During the training phase, the LDC[1] Emotional Prosody Speech and Transcripts database (panic, happy, angry and neutral speech recordings) was utilized for the creation of the emotion models. The choice of the LDC corpus for building the emotion models resulted from the need of having sufficient amount of training data for each affective state, given the limited duration of speech recordings within the selected scenes. All experimentations were performed towards detecting the affective states/emotions of interest (panic, happy, angry) on the PROMETHEUS selected scenes.

In order to identify the most appropriate settings of the GMM model, we experimented with different number of mixture components, i.e. {1, 2, 4, 8}. The maximum number of iterations was set to 1000 and the training was terminated when the error between two subsequent iterations of the EM algorithm decreased with less than 10^{-5}. The impact of the number of mixtures to the performance of the affect recognition system and the optimal results obtained in terms of Equal Error Rate (EER) are shown in Fig. 3 (a) and Table 1 respectively.

In Fig. 3 (b) we present the DET (Detection Error Trade-off) curves that correspond to the three aforementioned experiments. The error rates for each affective state detector are reported in terms of false alarm probability and miss probability. The best accuracy is achieved for the detector of the affective state *angry*. This can be explained by the observation that *anger* is characterized by high level of activation and evaluation [18], which positions it further away from both *happy* and *panic* affective states in the feature space.

The results of the evaluation of the three aforementioned affect detectors conform to recent research on cross-corpora evaluations [19]. Affect recognition in emotionally coloured speech in uncontrolled indoor and outdoor environments is a challenging task, and the present stage of technology does not favour the development of practical applications, which heavily depend on robust affect/emotion detection. Thus, although some

---

[1] http://www.ldc.upenn.edu/Catalog/CatalogEntry.jsp?catalogId=LDC2002S28

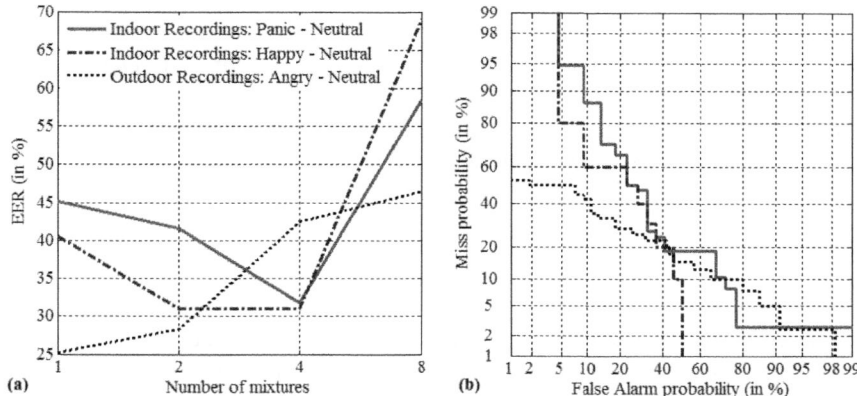

Fig. 3. (a) Impact of the number of mixtures to the performance of the affect detectors, **(b)** Optimal DET curves for the different setups and different affect/emotion detectors

Table 1. Performance of the affect/emotion detectors

Environment	Affect	Number of mixtures	EER
Indoor	Panic	4	31.70 %
Indoor	Happy	4	30.91 %
Outdoor	Angry	1	25.23 %

high-intensity emotional categories seem easier to recognize, further research efforts are needed for improving the affect/emotion detection accuracy in uncontrolled indoor and outdoor real-world environments.

5 Conclusion

We studied the capacity of a UBM-GMM based affect recognition system to deal with the challenges of real-world data and genuine formulations collected in uncontrolled environments. Furthermore, despite the mismatch between training and testing data (emotion's intensity, recording environment, spoken language), and the co-occurrence of more than one speakers in the testing data (multi-person recordings in the PRO-METHEUS selected scenes), the affect detectors offer reasonable EERs, which are close to state-of-art performance observed in laboratory conditions. Affect/emotion detection in uncontrolled real-life environments remains a challenging task and further research efforts are needed in this direction.

Potential directions for the improvement of the recognition performance are related to minimizing the mismatch between training and testing data, further developments towards extracting and exploiting linguistic features, and fusion of results from acoustic detectors with evidence from other modalities (vision, biodata, etc), which are resistant to acoustic interference.

Acknowledgment

The research reported was partially supported by the PROMETHEUS project (FP7-ICT-214901) "Prediction and interpretation of human behaviour based on probabilistic models and heterogeneous sensors", co-funded by the European Commission under the Seventh' Framework Programme.

References

1. Clavel, C., Devillers, L., Richard, G., Vasilexcu, I., Ehrette, T.: Detection and analysis of abnormal situations through fear type acoustic manifestations. In: Proc. of the IEEE International Conference on Acoustics, Speech and Signal Processing (ICASSP 2007), vol. 4, pp. 21–24 (2007)
2. Ntalampiras, S., Potamitis, I., Fakotakis, N.: An adaptive framework for acoustic monitoring of potential hazards. EURASIP Journal on Audio, Speech, and Music Processing 2009, article ID: 594103 (2009)
3. Clavel, C., Vasilescu, I., Devillers, L., Richard, G., Ehrette, T.: Fear-type emotion recognition for future audio-based surveillance systems. Speech Communication 50(6), 487–503 (2008)
4. Schuller, B., Steidl, S., Batliner, A.: The Interspeech 2009 Emotion Challenge. In: Proc. of Interspeech 2009, ISCA, Brighton, UK, pp. 312–315 (2009)
5. Kockmann, M., Burget, L., Cernocky, J.: Brno University of Technology System for Interspeech 2009 Emotion Challenge. In: Proc. of Interspeech 2009, ISCA, Brighton, UK, pp. 348–351 (2009)
6. Steidl, S., Schuller, B., Seppi, D., Batliner, A.: The Hinterland of Emotions: Facing the Open-Microphone Challenge. In: Proc. of 4th International HUMAINE Association Conference on Affective Computing and Intelligent Interaction (ACII 2009), vol. I, pp. 690–697 (2009)
7. Callejas, Z., Lopez-Cozar, R.: Influence of contextual information in emotion annotation for spoken dialogue systems. Speech Communication, 416–433 (2008)
8. Seppi, D., Batliner, A., Schuller, B., Steidl, S., Vogt, T., Wagner, J., Devillers, L., Vidrascu, L., Amir, N., Aharonson, V.: Patterns, prototypes, performance: classifying emotional user states. In: Proc. of Interspeech 2008, pp. 601–604 (2008)
9. Steidl, S.: Automatic classification of emotion-related user states in spontaneous children's speech. In: Studien zur Mustererkennung, Bd, 28. Logos Verlag, Berlin (2009) ISBN 978-3-8325-2145-5
10. Batliner, A., Steidl, S., Hacker, C., Nöth, E.: Private emotions vs. social interaction – a data-driven approach towards analysing emotion in speech. In: User Modeling and User-Adpated Interaction (umuai), vol. 18(1-2), pp. 175–206 (2008)
11. Brendel, M., Zaccarelli, R., Devillers, L.: Building a system for emotions detection from speech to control an affective avatar. In: Proc. of LREC 2010, pp. 2205–2210 (2010)
12. Ntalampiras, S., Arsić, D., Stiörmer, A., Ganchev, T., Potamitis, I., Fakotakis, N.: PROMETHEUS database: A multimodal corpus for research on modeling and interpreting human behavior. In: Proc. of the 16th International Conference on Digital Signal Processing (DSP 2009), Santorini, Greece (2009)
13. Ntalampiras, S., Ganchev, T., Potamitis, I., Fakotakis, N.: Heterogeneous sensor database in support of human behaviour analysis in unrestricted environments: The audio part. In: Valletta, Malta, Calzolari, N., et al. (eds.) Proc. of LREC 2010. ELRA, pp. 3006–3010 (2010) ISBN: 2-9517408-6-7

14. Eyben, F., Wollmer, M., Schuller, B.: openEAR – Introducing the Munich open-source emotion and affect recognition toolkit. In: Proc. of the 4th International HUMAINE Association Conference on Affective Computing and Intelligent Interaction 2009 (ACII 2009). IEEE, Amsterdam (2009)
15. Reynolds, D.A., Rose, R.C.: Robust text-independent speaker identification using Gaussian mixture speaker models. IEEE Transactions on Speech and Audio Processing 3, 72–83 (1995)
16. Dempster, A.P., Laird, N.M., Rubin, D.B.: Maximum likelihood from incomplete data via the EM algorithm. J. Roy. Stat. Soc. 39, 1–38 (1977)
17. Reynolds, D.A., Quatieri, T.F., Dunn, R.B.: Speaker verification using adapted Gaussian mixture models. Digital Signal Processing 10, 19–41 (2000)
18. Cowie, R., Douglas-Cowie, E., Tsapatsoulis, N., Votsis, G., Kollias, S., Fellenz, W., Taylor, J.G.: Emotion recognition in human-computer interaction. IEEE Signal Processing Magazine 18(1), 32–80 (2001)
19. Eyben, F., Batliner, A., Schuller, B., Seppi, D., Steidl, S.: Cross-corpus classification of realistic emotions – some pilot experiments. In: Proc. 3rd International Workshop on Emotion (satellite of LREC), Valletta, Malta, pp. 77–82 (2010)

Understanding Parent-Infant Behaviors Using Non-negative Matrix Factorization

Ammar Mahdhaoui and Mohamed Chetouani

Université Pierre & Marie Curie
Institut des Systèmes Intelligents et de Robotique
CNRS, UMR 7222, Paris, France
Ammar.Mahdhaoui@isir.upmc.fr, Mohamed.Chetouani@upmc.fr

Abstract. There are considerable differences among infants in the quality of interaction with their parents. These differences depend especially on the infants development which affects the parent behaviors. In our study we are interested on 3 groups of infants: typical development infants (TD), autistic infants (AD) and mental retardation infants (MR). In order to identify the groups of signs/behaviors that differentiate the development of the three groups of children we investigated a clustering method NMF (non-negative matrix factorization), an algorithm based on decomposition by parts that can reduce the dimension of interaction signs to a few number of interaction behaviors groups. Coupled with a statistical data representation $tf\text{-}idf$, usually used for document clustering and adapted to our work, NMF provides an efficient method for identification of distinct interaction groups. Forty-two infants and their parents were observed in this study. Parent-infant interactions were videotaped by one of the parents at home during the first two years age of child.

Keywords: Parent-infant interaction, Clustering, $tf\text{-}idf$, NMF, Autism.

1 Introduction

Parent-infant interaction has an important contribution to infant development, particularly during the first two years age of child. However, there are some developments and psychological pathologies that can affect the parent-infant interaction; one of these pervasive developmental disorders is autism.

Autism is a severe psychiatric syndrome characterized by the presence of abnormalities in reciprocal social interactions, abnormal patterns of communication, and a restricted, stereotyped, repetitive repertoire of behaviors, interests, and activities. Although it is a well-defined clinical syndrome after the second, and especially after the third, years of life, information on autism in the first two years of life is still lacking [1]. Home movies (movies recorded by parents during the first years of life, before diagnosis) and direct observation of infants at high

A. Esposito et al. (Eds.): COST 2102 Int. Training School 2010, LNCS 6456, pp. 436–447, 2011.

risk due to having an autistic sibling are the two most important sources of information for overcoming this problem. They have both described children with autism disorder (AD) during the first year of life (and also in the first part of the second year) as not displaying the rigid patterns described in older children [2]. In particular, from a clinical point of view, the autistic children can gaze at people, turn toward voices and express interests in communication as typically developing infants do. It is of seminal importance to have more insight into these social competencies and in which situations they preferentially emerge in infants who are developing autism. However, there are various signs that differentiate children with ASD from children with developmental delays. The autistic child characterized by less of a response to their name, less looking at others, lower eye contact quality and quantity, less positive facial expression and intersubjective behaviors (e.g., showing shared attention).

In our study, we focus on automatically characterization of the interaction quality of the different group of children by age with the goal to study further specific early signs in the interactive field. We studied home movies of the first 18 months of life of 42 infants categorized in 3 groups. Then, using a statistical representation of data and an automatic clustering technique, we performed a longitudinal analysis of the first 3 semesters and found significant results. These results are confirmed by the clinicians analysis.

The general view of the study is presented in Fig. 1. After data collection, all parent and infant behaviors are annotated. After that, an interaction database has been created by extracting all interaction sequences, parent behaviors and infant behaviors co-occuring, in a window of 3 seconds. Then, quantitative statistics have been performed to describe the interaction, and to assess emergence of language and social engagement by time and by group. Then we investigated a statistical method usually used for document analysis, tf-idf, to make a statistical representation of interaction data. This statistical characterization presents an input of the clustering algorithm.

This paper is organized as follows. Section 2 presents the longitudinal corpus and the annotation process. Section 3 presents the multimodal interaction database. Section 4 describes our method for statistical data representation and clustering. Experimental results of the proposed method are provided in section 5. In a last section, some concluding remarks and the direction of future works are presented.

2 Home Movies Corpus and Annotation

2.1 Corpus

The database used in our study contains 3 groups of children matched for gender and socio-economic status, with family home movies (HM) running for a minimum of 10 minutes for each of the 3 first semesters of life.

We selected 42 infants and their parents from the Pisa home movies database [3], with the following criteria: 15 children (10 male and 5 female) who will be diagnosed with autism disorder (AD), 12 children (7 male and 5 female) with

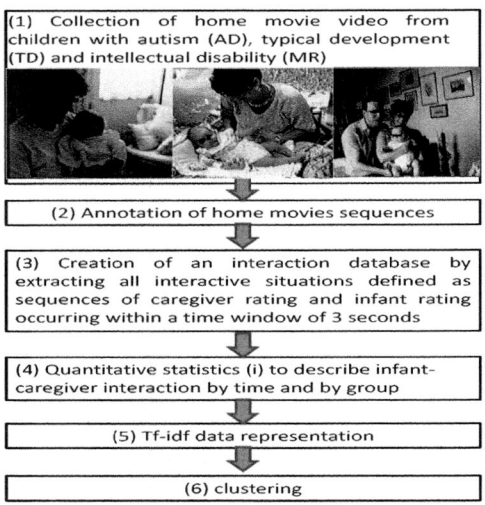

Fig. 1. Interaction analysis

Table 1. Number and duration (in min) of different scenes from the three semesters analyzed in the home movies database of the three group of children

	AD (15)	*MR* (12)	*TD* (15)	*AD* vs *MR*	*AD* vs *TD*	*MR* vs *TD*
				t-test (*p* value)		
Number *Semester 1*	162	100	164	.116	.163	.138
Duration *Semester 1*	258.5	148.5	237.3	.142	.759	.105
Number *Semester 2*	164	111	201	.639	.088	.079
Duration *Semester 2*	258.1	176.3	347.5	.863	.148	.278
Number *Semester 3*	127	90	120	.917	.747	.701
Duration *Semester 3*	212	194.5	194.5	.202	.474	.371

intellectual disability, mental retardation (MR), and 15 (9 male and 6 female) with a history of typical development (TD). All scenes showing a situation in which an interaction can occur (i.e. all scenes with an infant and an adult) were extracted. Table 1 shows the total number of scenes and their duration. Preliminary *t-test* analysis was used to verify that chosen video material was comparable across groups and for each range of age, in length and number of standard situations (table 1).

2.2   Annotation

After data collection, the annotation process is a fundamental task. The annotators used a computer-based coding system called Observer which is a complete manual event recorder, designed for collection, management and analysis of observational data. It was configured for the application of the Infant Caregiver

Table 2. Parent Behaviors

Behaviors	E/S	Discription
Regulation	State	The caregiver modulates the child's arousal and mood.
up/down		The caregiver may act to either excite or calm-down the child.
Caregiver's solicitation	Event	Within a sequence of interaction, the caregiver stimulates the child
vocalising/naming/gesturing/		requesting attention by vocalizing, naming, gesturing, touching him/her
touching/showing object/request		or showing him object

Behavior Scale to our video media file-material [4]. 4 coders were trained to use Observer 4.0, until they achieve a satisfactory agreement (Cohen's Kappa $\geq 0,7$) with an expert clinician in almost 6 matched sequences. The standard situations derived from the home movies of the 3 groups of children (AD, MR and TD) were mixed and each one was rated by one trained coder (blind to the group belonging). 25% of standard situations were randomized and rated by 2 coders independently, with a final inter-rater reliability, calculated directly by the Observer program, showing a satisfactory Cohen-mean value (0.75 to 0.77).

Table 2 and 3 are composed successively of items referring to the ability of the infant to engage in interactions and to caregiver's actions towards the infant. Behaviors are grouped into 4 independent classes (Table 4) created to allow the coders to focalize their attention selectively on one class:

- Infant Basic Behavior: composed of 6 simple items regarding social engagement.
- Infant Complex Behavior: composed of 10 items regarding a more complex level of social engagement (they can sometime overlap the previous, basic, level of description).
- Infant Vocalization: composed of 3 items regarding vocal activity towards the other.
- Caregiver Behavior: composed of 6 items describing caregiver's solicitation or stimulation toward the infant, to obtain his attention.

All target behaviors (table 4) can be described as Events which take an instant of time and only frequency of occurrence (rate) matters for an Event. Some of the behaviors can also be described as states which take a period of time, have a distinct start and an end; rate and duration matter for a State.

The clinical study [5] confirms that babies who have become autistic, particularly during the first six months of life, can display intersubjective behaviors; nevertheless, the duration of these behaviors, such as enjoying with people and maintaining social engagement, are reduced in infants with autism and the duration of syntony emerges as an item which significantly differentiates infant with autism from typical infants and mentally retarded infants.

3 Multi-modal Interaction

We first created a multimodal interaction database by extracting all interactive situations defined as sequences of parents rating and infant rating occurring

Table 3. Infant Behaviors

Behaviors	E/S	Discription
Looking at people/at object/around	State	The child directs his/her eyes towards an object, or a human face, or simply looks around.
Orienting toward people/object/name prompt	Event	The child assumes a spontaneous gaze direction towards a new sensory stimulation coming from a people/object or towards the person.
Gaze Following a person/an object/a gaze of a person	Event	The child shifts his gaze to follow the gaze or the trajectory of another person, or object.
Smiling at people/at object	Event	The child intentionally smiles at a person or at object.
Seeking contact with person/with object	Event	The child employs spontaneous and intentional movements to reach contact with a person or with an object.
Explorative activity with person/object	State	The child touches something to find out what it feels like. The exploring activity may be done by hands, mouth or other sensory-motor actions.
Enjoying with person/with object	State	The child finds pleasure and satisfaction experiencing a physical and/or visual contact with a person or with an object.
Sintony	State	The child shows a sintonic response to the other's mood; he/she shows signs of congruous expressions to affective environmental solicitations.
Anticipation of other's intention	Event	The child makes anticipatory movements predicting the other's action.
Communicative gestures	Event	The child displays use of social gestures.
Referential gaze	Event	The child shifts his/her gaze towards the caregiver to look for consultation in a specific situation.
Soliciting	Event	The child displays a verbal, vocal, or tactile action to attract the partner's attention or to elicit an other kind of response.
Accept Invitation	Event	The child's behavior is attuned to the other person's solicitation within 3 seconds from the start of stimulation.
Offering him/her self	Event	The child offers parts of his/her body to the other person.
Imitation	Event	The child repeats, after a short delay, another person's action.
Pointing comprehension/declarative/ requestive	Event	The child shifts his gaze towards the direction indicated by parent uses his her finger to indicate something in order to share an emotional experience
Maintaining social engagement	State	The child takes up an active role within a two-way interaction. The child interacts, vocalises and maintains turn taking.
Simple Vocalisation	Event	The child produces sounds towards people or objects.
Meaningful Vocalisation	Event	The child intentionally produces sounds with a stable semantic meaning
Crying	State	The child starts crying after a specific/non specific event.

Table 4. Parent and Infant Behaviors tags

Infant Basic Behaviors	tags	Infant Complex Behaviors	tags	infant Vocalizations	tags	Parent solicitation	tags
Looking People	B_lkp	ENJOYING*	C_ejx	simple	v_sim	REGULATION*,UP	G_reu
Looking object	B_lko	ENJOYING*,WITH PEOPLE	C_ejp	meaningful	v_mea	REGULATION*,DOWN	G_red
Looking around	B_lka	ENJOYING*,WITH OBJECT	C_ejo	CRYING	V_cry	request behavior	g_req
Explorative Act/Object	B_exo	SINTONY	C_snt			naming	g_nam
Contact People	b_ctp	SOCIAL ENGAGE	C_seg			touching	g_tou
Contact Object	b_cto	anticipation	c_ant			vocalising	g_voc
Orienting XXX	b_orx	comm. gestures	c_com			gesturing	g_ges
Orienting People	b_orp	referential gaze	c_ref			show object	g_sho
Orienting Object	b_oro	soliciting	c_sol			NULL (cg)	G_nul
Orienting to Name	b_orn	acc invitation	c_acc				
Gaze Follow Person	b_gfp	offering	c_off				
Gaze Follow Object	b_gfo	imitation	c_imi				
Smiling People	b_smp	pointing	c_poi				
Smiling Object	b_smo						

within a time window of 3 seconds. Moreover, all infant states (with a duration) that demonstrate synchrony, reciprocity, quality of interaction (called social behaviors): enjoying with people or object, syntony, social engagement were automatically integrated in the interaction database. Then, we performed quantitative statistics to describe the interaction, and to assess emergence of language and social engagement by time and by group.

After creation of the multimodal interaction database, we obtained $m = 176$ different interaction behaviors, Fig. 2, Fig. 3 and Fig. 4 show the 20 most frequent

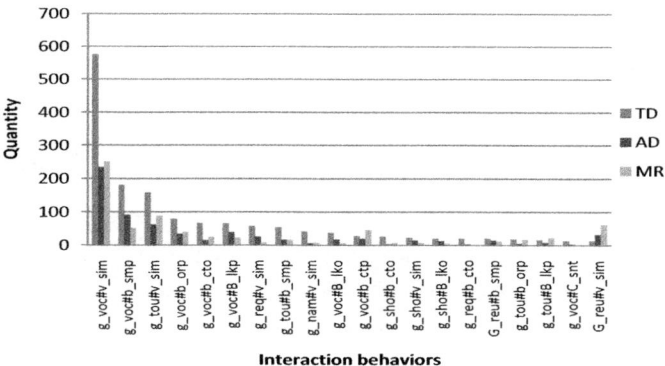

Fig. 2. 20 most frequent interaction behaviors in the first semester

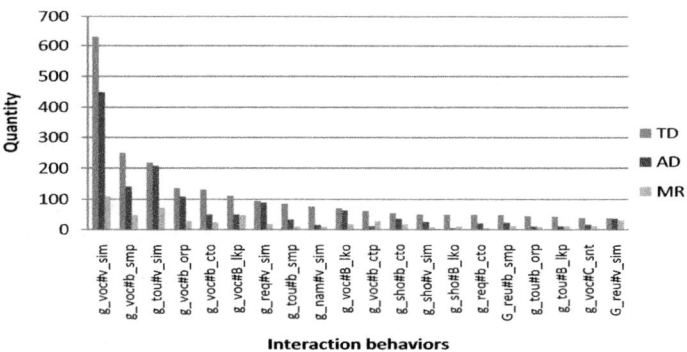

Fig. 3. 20 most frequent interaction behaviors in the second semester

interaction behaviors successively in the first, second and third semesters by group of infant (G_reu#V_sim means that regulation up, G_reu, produced by parent and the response of the child by a simple vocalization, V_sim, co-occuring in a time window of 3 seconds).

However, this quantitative representation of interaction behaviors is not always informative for grouping and distinguishing the different behaviors dyads. Therefore, we propose to compute a statistical characterization of data based on *tf-idf* (term frequency-inverse document frequency) representation.

4   Parent-infant Interaction Analysis

After data collection, data characterization process is the key problem for parent-infant interaction analysis to allow the automatic processing of this data. In this context, this section describes the usually adopted statistical representation method as *tf-idf* (term frequency-inverse document frequency), then the clustering method in order to extract the different groups of interaction behaviors.

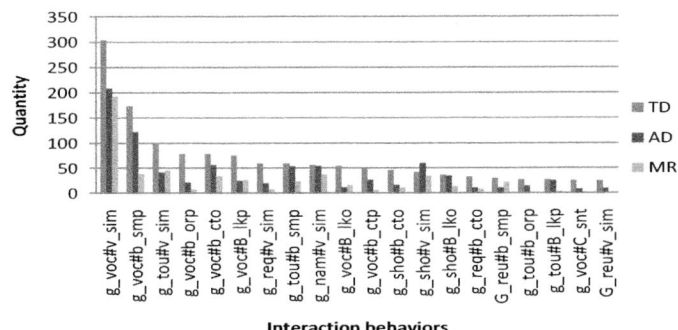

Fig. 4. 20 most frequent interaction behaviors in the third semester

4.1   Statistical Interaction Characterization

The first step in social signals analysis is to transform the scenes annotations into a representation suitable for the learning algorithm and the clustering task. This leads to an attribute value representation of interaction. A simple way to transform the annotations into a feature vector is using a statistical *tf-idf* representation which is widely used in information retrieval applications, where each feature is a single interaction behavior.

The *tf-idf* weight (term frequency-inverse document frequency) is evolved from IDF which is proposed by Sparck Jones [6] with the heuristic intuition that a query term which occurs in many documents is not a good discriminator, and should be given less weight than one which occurs in few documents. This weight is a statistical measure used to evaluate how important a word is to a document in a collection or corpus. The importance increases proportionally to the number of times a word appears in the document but is offset by the frequency of the word in the corpus. Variations of the *tf-idf* weighting scheme are often used by search engines as a central tool in scoring and ranking a document's relevance given a user query. One of the simplest ranking function is computed by summing the *tf-idf* for each query term; many more sophisticated ranking functions are variants of this simple model. Similar to the *tf-idf* normalization steps for document word matrices, a *tf-idf* procedure is applied to represent statistically the parent-infant interaction. We adapt this method for our interaction model problem. First, we simply count the number of times a given behavior appears by movie. Then, this count is usually normalized to prevent a bias towards longer movies (which may have a higher term count regardless of the actual importance of that term in the movie) to give a measure of the importance of the term t_i within the particular movie d_j. Thus we have the term frequency, defined as follows.

$$tf_{ij} = \frac{n_{ij}}{\sum_k n_{kj}} \tag{1}$$

where n_{ij} is the number of occurrences of the considered dyad of behavior (t_i) in the movie d_j, and the denominator is the sum of number of occurrences of all the dyads in the movie d_j.

The inverse document frequency is a measure of the general importance of the term (obtained by dividing the total number of movies by the number of movies containing the interaction behavior, and then taking the logarithm of that quotient).

$$idf_i = log\frac{|D|}{|\{d : t_i \in d\}|} \tag{2}$$

where $|D|$ is the total number of movies in the database and $|\{d : t_i \in d\}|$ is the number of movies where the interaction behavior t_i appears (that is $n_{ij} \neq 0$). Then, we calculate:

$$(tf - idf)_{ij} = tf_{ij} \times idf_i \tag{3}$$

4.2   Clustering

Non-Negative Matrix Factorization. Non-negative matrix factorization (NMF) has been studied under the name of positive matrix factorization [7] at the early stage. It is then popularized by the work of Lee and Seung and has been found lots of applications in text mining [8] [9]. Recent advancement of NMF has shown that it shares much similarity with K-means and spectral clustering methods, and is capable of producing good cluster capability [10]. However, NMF is more difficult algorithmically because of the non-negativity requirement but provides a more intuitive decomposition of the data.

Given a non-negative matrix X in size $n \times m$, NMF factorizes it into two non-negative matrices W and H (Fig. 5),

$$X = WH \tag{4}$$

where W is a $n \times k$ matrix and H is $k \times m$, while k is usually much smaller than both n and m. Define the loss as the square of the Euclidean distance between X and the reconstructed matrix $\overline{X} = WH$,

$$\min_{W \geq 0, H \geq 0}||X - \overline{X}||^2 = \sum_{i=1}^{n}\sum_{j=1}^{m}(X_{ij} - \overline{X}_{ij}) \tag{5}$$

The objective function can be iteratively reduced, or nonincreasing, via the following updating rules,

$$H = H.*(W^T X)./(W^T WH) \tag{6}$$

$$W = W.*(XH^T)./(WHH^T) \tag{7}$$

where $.*$ and $./$ denotes the element-wise multiplication and division between a pair of matrices, respectively.

The two matrices after factorization have the effect of indicating the cluster membership. The cluster membership c_i of the i-th interaction behavior is simply given by:

$$c_i = \underset{j}{argmax}W_{ij} \tag{8}$$

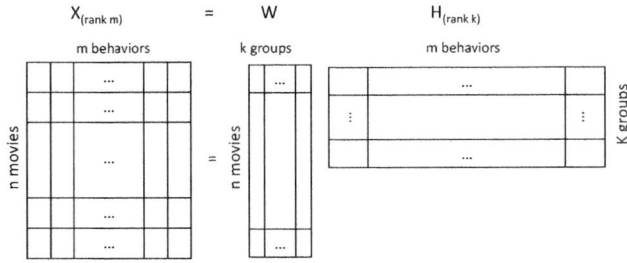

Fig. 5. A rank-k reduction of a behaviors of n movies and m behaviors is obtained by NMF, $X = WH$

where j is the label of the latent cluster of the interaction behaviors. Usually the number of latent clusters are a much smaller number than the total number of interaction behaviors.

In addition, the singular value decomposition (SVD) [11] was used we used to initialize the standard NMF algorithm. The initialization based on SVD enables NMF to perform better results compared to random initialization.

Model Selection. We computed NMF with different values of k (number of clusters). Then, for any rank k, NMF algorithm groups the samples into clusters. Therefore, we should determine the optimal k which decomposes the samples into 'meaningful' clusters. For this purpose we investigated 'Homogeneity-Separation' to optimize the number k of clusters, since that the standard definition of a good clustering is that of 'homogeneity and separation'. Every element in a cluster must be highly similar (homogeneous) to the other elements in the same cluster and highly dissimilar (separation) to elements outside its own cluster. In addition, there are typically interactions between homogeneity and separation - usually, high homogeneity is linked with low separation, and vice versa.

5   Experimental Results

Table 5 shows the best solutions of behavior signals clustering for the 'Homogeneity-Separation' method. To further illustrate the advantage of the proposed method, we compare our method with the k-means clustering method. In order to understand the developmental similarity of the different groups of children, we compared both mental retardation infants and autistic infant with typical developmental infants.

Therefore, to calculate the disagreement between the 3 groups of children, we used the value of the Normalized Mutual Information (NMI) as proposed in [12]. The normalized mutual information of two different clusterings measures the agreement between the two clusterings $\widehat{y}^1$ and $\widehat{y}^2$. Formally, the normalized mutual information of two clusterings $\widehat{y}^1$ and $\widehat{y}^2$ can be defined as:

Table 5. Number of obtained cluster by group of children

	Method	Typical	Autistic	Mental retardation
Semester 1	NMF	11	12	5
	K-means	12	8	7
Semester 2	NMF	14	8	11
	K-means	14	11	11
Semester 3	NMF	9	10	14
	K-means	12	12	10

$$NMI(\widehat{y}^1, \widehat{y}^2) = \frac{\sum_{i=1}^{k} \sum_{j=1}^{k} n_{i,j}^{1,2} log \left(\frac{n \times n_{i,j}^{1,2}}{n_i^1 \times n_j^2} \right)}{\sqrt{\left(\sum_{i=1}^{k} n_i^1 log \frac{n_i^1}{n} \right) \left(\sum_{j=1}^{k} n_j^2 log \frac{n_j^2}{n} \right)}} \qquad (9)$$

where n_i^1 is the number of behaviors assigned to the cluster label c_i in $\widehat{y}^1$, n_j^2 is the number of behaviors assigned to the cluster label c_j in $\widehat{y}^2$, and $n_{i,j}^{1,2}$ is the number of behaviors assigned to the cluster label c_i in $\widehat{y}^1$ and c_j in $\widehat{y}^2$.

Table 6 shows the normalized mutual information values between the clustering result of typical infants/autistic infants, typical infants/mental retardation infants and autistic infants/mental retardation infants. The results show that the behaviors similarity between typical development children and autistic children is quite similar to the correlation between typical development children and mental retardation children during the first semester of life. However, NMF performs better than K-means, since that we obtained similarity between TD/AD equals to 0.482 during the first semester and 0.438 using NMF clustering method compared to 0.343 for semester 1 and 0.240 for semester 2 using k-means clustering method. From the clinical observation, NMF provides better results, since that signs of autism are not very obvious during the first year of life, the same things by comparing mental retardation and typical development children.

Using NMF clustering method, TD groups and MR groups are more correlated than TD groups and AD groups during the second and the third semester of age. On the other hand, the mutual information between TD second semester and MR third semester is about 0.522 using NMF method which explains the mental retardation of MR children compared to TD children. However, the behaviors similarity between typical development children and autistic children decreases during the time from the first semester to the third semester which is explained by the development deviance of autistic children. This is the quality that most differentiates the symptoms of autism from those of mental retardation [13].

Several studies on early home movies [14] have revealed that, during first year, mental retardation and autistic infants are characterized by a reduced response to the infant's own name, a reduced quality of affect and a tendency to look less to others. However, these pre-autistic signs become more obvious for autistic children. These characteristics are confirmed by the results obtained using NMF clustering method. Table 6 shows that, during the two first semesters, AD groups

Table 6. Normalized mutual information between TD/AD, TD/MR et AD/MR

	Mthode	TD/AD	TD/MR	AD/MR
S1	NMF	0.482	0.491	0.473
	K-moyennes	0.343	0.301	0.485
S2	NMF	0.438	0.520	0.506
	K-moyennes	0.240	0.262	0.399
S3	NMF	0.372	0.456	0.465
	K-moyennes	0.273	0.219	0.416

are quiet similar to MR groups (semester 1: 0.473; semester 2: 0.506). However, we obtained similarity equal to 0.399 using K-means clustering method.

In addition, preliminary results show that, using NMF clustering method, the behaviors dyads initiated by G_reu, regulation up, are always grouped together for autistic children group. This result is motivated by the interaction quality of the autistic children, then the parents act always to excite the child and to attract his attention.

6   Conclusions

In this paper, we propose a statistical data characterization based on $tf\text{-}idf$ representation which allows the automatic processing of parent-infant interaction behaviors. In addition, we propose the use of clustering method NMF to reduce the dimensionality of human (Parent/infant) behaviors in order to understand parent-infant interaction and to analyze the quality of parent-infant interactive behavior of mental retardation and autistic infant compared to typical developmental infant. Experimental results show that the developmental similarity of TD and AD groups decrease during the time. In addition we notice that the development of mental retardation infants is shifted compared to the normal development (TD).

Parent-infant interaction understanding is a multidisciplinary problem in which automatic analysis of interactions behaviors and the social psychology research are complementary [15]. Therefore, the next step of this work is to analyze with more details the clustering results (the behaviors contained by each cluster) and to investigate clinical interpretations with our psychologist partners to understand the interaction quality of each group of children.

Acknowledgments

Thanks to Filippo Muratori and Fabio Apicella from Scientific Institute Stella Maris of University of Pisa, Italy, who have provided data; family home movies. We would also like to extend our thanks to David Cohen and his staff, Raquel Sofia Cassel and catherine Saint-Georges, from the Department of Child and

Adolescent Psychiatry, AP-HP, Groupe Hospitalier Pitié-Salpétrière, Université Pierre et Marie Curie, Paris France, for their collaboration and the manual database annotation and data analysis.

References

1. Stone, W., Coonrod, E., Ousley, O.: Brief report: Screening tool for autism in two-year-olds (stat): Development and preliminary data. Autism and Developmental Disorders 30(6), 607–612 (2000)
2. Saint-Georges, C., Cassel, R.S., Cohen, D., Chetouani, M., Laznik, M.C., Maestro, S.: What studies of family home movies can teach us about autistic infants: A literature review. Research in Autism Spectrum Disorders 4(3), 355–366 (2010)
3. Maestro, S., Muratori, F., Barbieri, F., Casella, C., Cattaneo, V., Cavallaro, M.: Early behavioral development in autistic children: The first 2 years of life through home movies. Psychopathology 34, 147–152 (2001)
4. Muratori, F., Apicella, F., Muratori, P., Maestro, S.: Intersubjective disruptions and caregiver-infant interaction in early autistic disorder. Research in Autism Spectrum Disorders, Corrected Proof (in Press 2010)
5. Muratori, F., Maestro, S.: Autism as a downstream effect of primary difficulties in intersubjectivity interacting with abnormal development of brain connectivity. Dialogical Science 2(1), 93–118 (2007)
6. Jones, K.S.: Idf term weighting and ir research lessons. Journal of Documentation 60(6), 521–523 (2004)
7. Pentti Paatero, U.: Positive matrix factorization: A nonnegative factor model with optimal utilization of error estimates of data values. Environmetrics 5(2), 111–126 (1994)
8. Lee, D., Seung, H.: Algorithms for non-negative matrix factorization. In: NIPS, pp. 556–562 (2000)
9. Xu, W., X., Liu, Gong, Y.: Document clustering based on non-negative matrix factorization. In: SIGIR, pp. 267–273 (2003)
10. Ding, C., he, X., Simon, H.: On the equivalence of nonnegative matrix factorization and spectral clustering. In: Fifth SIAM International Conference on Data Mining, pp. 606–610. SIAM, Philadelphia (2005)
11. Strang, G.: Introduction to Linear Algebra. Wellesley-Cambridge Press (2003)
12. Strehl, A., Ghosh, J.: Cluster ensembles - a knowledge reuse framework for combining multiple partitions. Machine Learning Research 3, 583–617 (2002)
13. Mays, R., Gillon, J.: Autism in young children: an update. Pediatric Health Care 7, 17–23 (1993)
14. Baranek, G.: Autism during infancy: a retrospective video analysis of sensory-motor and social behaviors at 9-12 months of age. Autism and Developmental Disorders 29, 213–224 (1999)
15. Vinciarelli, A., Pantic, M., Bourlard, H., Pentland, A.: Social signal processing: state-of-the-art and future perspectives of an emerging domain. In: ACM Multimedia, pp. 1061–1070 (2008)

Learning and Knowledge-Based Sentiment Analysis in Movie Review Key Excerpts

Björn Schuller[1] and Tobias Knaup[2]

[1] Institute for Human-Machine Communication
Technische Universität München, Germany
[2] Pingsta Inc., 1700 Seaport Boulevard, Redwood City, CA 94063, USA
{schuller}@tum.de

Abstract. We propose a data-driven approach based on back-off N-Grams and Support Vector Machines, which have recently become popular in the fields of sentiment and emotion recognition. In addition, we introduce a novel valence classifier based on linguistic analysis and the on-line knowledge sources ConceptNet, General Inquirer, and WordNet. As special benefit, this approach does not demand labeled training data. Moreover, we show how such knowledge sources can be leveraged to reduce out-of-vocabulary events in learning-based processing. To profit from both of the two generally different concepts and independent knowledge sources, we employ information fusion techniques to combine their strengths, which ultimately leads to better overall performance. Finally, we extend the data-driven classifier to solve a regression problem in order to obtain a more fine-grained resolution of valence.

Keywords: Sentiment Analysis, Emotion Recognition.

1 Introduction

Sentiment analysis has been studied for a number of different application domains: Among the most popular ones are product reviews [24,3,29,19,12,4], the stock market [2], hotels and travel destinations [24,19], and movie reviews [24,17,31]. While good results have been reported for product reviews, movie reviews seem to be more difficult to handle. In [24], a 66 % accuracy of valence estimation is reported for movie reviews, while up to 84 % are obtained for automobile reviews with the same method. The author explains this by a discrepancy between the semantic orientation of words that describe the elements of a movie (i. e., a scene, the plot), and its style or art. Obviously, movie reviews are exceptionally challenging for sentiment analysis. Motivated by these facts, the main goals of this chapter are: to introduce a novel approach to valence estimation that is based on on-line knowledge sources and linguistic methods, incorporate on-line knowledge sources into a machine learning approach, introduce an annotated database of over 100 k movie reviews collected from the review website Metacritic[1]—the largest to-date, experiment with both machine learning and

---

[1] http://www.metacritic.com

A. Esposito et al. (Eds.): COST 2102 Int. Training School 2010, LNCS 6456, pp. 448–472, 2011.

linguistic methods for the first time on a movie review database of that size, and—additionally—use Metacritic's fine-grained review scores as ground truth for a regression approach that leads to a higher resolution of valence prediction.

This remainder of this chapter is organized as follows: Section 2 introduces the Metacritic movie review corpus for analysis. Popular on-line knowledge sources are introduced in section 3. The on-line knowledge sources-based, syntax-driven algorithm we developed is described in section 4. It is evaluated in extensive experiments against data-driven modeling in section 5, and concluding remarks are given in section 6.

2   Metacritic – A Movie Review Database

To the best knowledge of the authors, the database that is described in this section is the largest movie review corpus to date. Several such corpora have been presented in the past, ranging in size from 120 to 2 000 reviews. Turney [24] collected 120 movie reviews from Epinions[2]. Zhuang et al. [31] selected 11 movies from the top 250 list of IMDB[3], and retrieved the first 100 reviews for each one of them. The data set contains a total of 16 k sentences and 260 k words. Probably the most widely used movie review database was introduced in [17]. In its initial version, 752 negative, and 1 301 positive reviews from the usenet newsgroup *rec. arts. movies. reviews* were used. Different versions have been released on the author's website[4], the current one containing 1 000 negative and 1 000 positive reviews.

Compared to these language resources, our Metacritic movie review corpus is significantly larger, containing a total of 102 622 reviews for 4 901 movies. Metacritic[5] is a website that compiles reviews for films, video/DVDs, books, music, television series, and computer games from various sources. An automated crawler was used to retrieve the HTML source of the webpages and store it for further processing. Because this chapter focuses on movies, only reviews from the film and video/DVD sections are included in the corpus that is described here. The web pages have been retrieved on January 8, 2009 between 12 p.m. and 2 p.m. CET. Reviews in Metacritic are available as excerpts of key sentences taken from the original text. The accumulated number of sentences is 133 394, and the total number of words in the database is 2 482 605. On average, a review has a length of 1.3 sentences, with a standard deviation of 0.6. Thus, Metacritic contains mostly short statements rather than long texts. The average length in words is 24.2, ranging between 1 and 104, with a standard deviation of 12.4 (cf. table 1). The vocabulary of the database has a size of 83 328 words. Looking at the breakdown of word classes, nouns (683 259) are the most frequent, followed by verbs (382 822), adjectives (244 825), and adverbs (174 152).

---

[2] http://www.epinions.com
[3] http://www.imdb.com
[4] http://www.cs.cornell.edu/people/pabo/movie-review-data/
[5] http://www.metacritic.com

Table 1. Size of Metacritic film and movie reviews. The minimum, maximum, average, and standard deviation (Std. Dev.) are given for each measure.

#	Minimum	Maximum	Average	Std. Dev.
Reviews per Movie	1	65	21.1	10.3
Word Count	1	104	24.2	12.4
Sentence Count	1	13	1.3	0.6

What makes Metacritic especially valuable is the fine-grained score value that accompanies every review. It is an integer score value ranging from 0 to 100, with higher scores indicating a better review. Metacritic scores are calculated from the original numeric rating scheme used by each source. Since the score is in most cases decided on by the author of the review, it can be considered very accurate. If no score is available from the author, though, it is assigned by a Metacritic staffer. Metacritic has its own classification schema that maps scores into three valence classes: positive/mixed/negative. Depending on the subject type, different mappings are used. The mapping for movies is shown in table 2.

Table 2. Mapping of score to valence class in Metacritic. Numbers apply to movies.

Score	Valence Class	# Reviews
81 – 100	positive	15 353
61 – 80	positive	38 766
40 – 60	mixed	32 586
20 – 39	negative	13 194
0 – 19	negative	2 723

This score and class label, and the huge number of reviews make Metacritic an ideal corpus for sentiment analysis: The accuracy of machine learning algorithms depends on the amount of available training data. Usually, a considerable amount of manual annotation work is required to build a corpus that is large enough to yield satisfying results. However, since the Metacritic score and class label can be directly used as ground truth for regression and classification respectively, no further annotation is needed.

The number of reviews in each class differs largely, as can be seen in table 3: There are about three times more positive reviews than negative reviews. Since machine learning techniques require a subset of the database to be used for training purposes, we chose to split the data into one set containing only reviews that have been released in odd years, and another set covering the even years. The resulting review subsets are of almost equal size: There are 49 698 instances in the 'odd' set, and 52 924 instances in the 'even' set.

The histogram of scores in figure 1 clearly shows that scores are not evenly distributed within each of the classes. Instead there are spikes for every score S that is a multiple of ten. For $S > 60$ (positive), there are also many bars

Table 3. Number and percentage of reviews in Metacritic falling into all, odd, and even years of release

# Reviews	All years	Odd years	Even years
Mixed	32 586 (31.75 %)	15 756 (31.70 %)	16 830 (31.80 %)
Positive	54 119 (52.74 %)	26 410 (53.14 %)	27 709 (52.36 %)
Negative	15 917 (15.51 %)	7 532 (15.16 %)	8 385 (15.84 %)

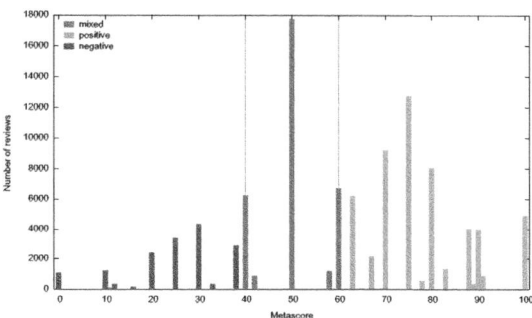

Fig. 1. Histogram of scores in the Metacritic database

in between, but especially for $40 \leq S \leq 60$ (mixed) there are almost only the bars at 40, 50, and 60. This is due to the fact that scores are converted from the original numerical rating schemas, and not all of these are as fine-grained as Metacritic, resulting in only a few values on the $0 - 100$ scale.

3   On-line Knowledge Sources

On-line knowledge sources in natural language processing are databases of linguistic knowledge that are publicly available on the Internet. They contain information about words, concepts, or phrases, as well as connections among them. The kind of connection can be of different nature, such as commonsense knowledge, or lexical relations. Most databases focus on one of these fields. Different representational schemes have been developed to provide the information in a suitable and efficient way. In semantic networks, words or concepts are represented as nodes in a graph, and relations are represented by named links [10]. Another form are annotated dictionaries, where properties of a term are stored as tags. Note that dictionaries usually do not contain relations between terms. In the rest of this section, we will introduce some well-known on-line knowledge sources that are used in this chapter.

ConceptNet is a semantic network which contains commonsense knowledge in a machine-readable format. The knowledge is added by non-specialized humans through a data acquisition interface[6]. A lot of effort has been put into making

---

[6] http://commons.media.mit.edu/en/

the interface capable of ruling out false claims and other mistakes [8]. As the name implies, ConceptNet is a network of concepts, such as *"actor"* or *"to watch a movie"*. The storage format does not contain syntactic category information and therefore has no support for word sense disambiguation. But since a concept can consist of an arbitrary amount of words, this can be overcome by formulating sufficiently specific concepts. Concepts are stored in a normalized format which aims at ignoring minor syntactic variations that do not affect the meaning of the concept. The following steps are used to normalize a concept [8]: remove punctuation, remove stop words, run each word through Porter's stemmer, alphabetize the stems, so that the order of words does not matter.

As mentioned earlier, ConceptNet focuses on concepts, rather than single words. Figure 2 (left) clearly shows that multi-word concepts (e. g., two, three, four words) form the largest part of the database, whereas single word concepts are significantly less common.

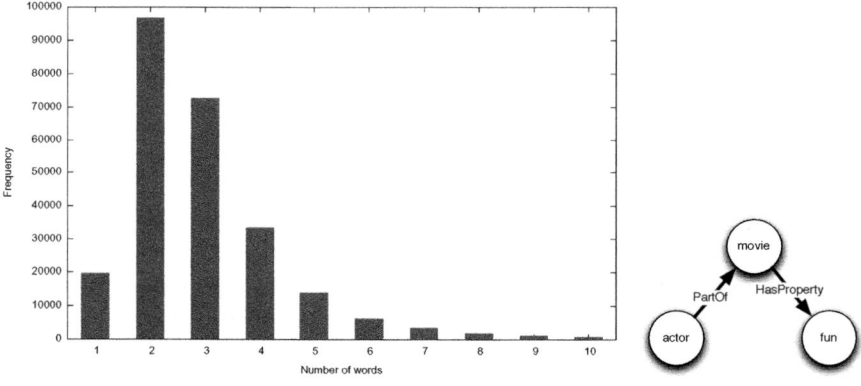

Fig. 2. The concept size in words and their occurrence frequency in ConceptNet 3 (left) and an example of concepts and relations found in ConceptNet 3 (right)

Concepts are interlinked by 21 different relations that encode the meaning of the connection between them. Relations are given intuitive names, e. g., `IsA` or `PartOf`. The unit of meaning representation is called a *predicate* in ConceptNet. An example of how predicates are stored in ConceptNet can be seen in figure 2 (right). Each predicate always consists of two concepts and one relation, e. g., *"actor"* `PartOf` *"movie"* (*"An actor is part of a movie"*). However, each concept can be part of many relations. In the example above, *"movie"* is also connected to *"fun"* by a `HasProperty` relation. To account for the fact that in the majority of cases predicates are not true if the order is changed (*"A movie is part of an actor"* does not make sense), relations are always unidirectional. They may also be negated to express that a certain statement is not true, such as *"A car cannot travel at the speed of light"*. Furthermore, each predicate has a score that represents its reliability. It defaults to 1 and can be increased/decreased by users. Predicates with zero or negative score are considered unreliable [8].

ConceptNet is available for download on the project homepage[7]. We use the snapshot from November 9, 2008 of the ConceptNet 3 database in the experiments reported in this chapter. This version comes with a total of 250 556 concepts, and 390 885 predicates for the English language.

General Inquirer [23] is a lexical database that uses tags to carry out its tasks. Each entry consists of the term and a number of tags denoting the presence of a specific property in the term. The two tags `Positiv` and `Negativ` express valence, hence they are the most interesting for our task. There are 1 915 terms in the `Positiv` category, and 2 291 in the `Negativ` counterpart. Examples are *"adore"*, *"master"*, *"intriguing"* for `Positiv`, and *"accident"*, *"lack"*, *"boring"* for `Negativ`. There is only partial support for part-of-speech information, to the extent that some terms have tags for different verb or adjective classes assigned. However, part-of-speech tags are not mandatory, and thus not all verbs or adjectives are tagged as such. General Inquirer also contains definitions and occurrence frequencies for most ambiguous words, which could be used to perform rudimentary word sense disambiguation.

WordNet is a database that organizes lexical concepts in sets of synonymous words, called *synsets*. Its design is inspired by current psycholinguistic and computational theories of human lexical memory [6]. Entries are strictly separated by syntactic category membership such as nouns, verbs, adjectives, and adverbs. Unlike ConceptNet, synsets are not linked by relations that express commonsense knowledge. They are rather connected by their lexical or semantic relatedness, such as *hyponymy* (one word being a specific instance of a more general word), *meronymy* (one word being a constituent part of another one), or *antonymy* (one word being the opposite of another). However, some of these relations are also found in ConceptNet, e. g., the complement of meronymy is `PartOf`.

4   Valence Estimation Using On-line Knowledge Sources

This section introduces the on-line knowledge sources-based approach to review valence estimation that has been developed during the work described in this chapter. Figure 3 shows the main building blocks of the algorithm. After preprocessing, two parallel steps extract words that convey sentiment information, as well as their targets – the words towards which the sentiment is expressed. This information is combined into expressions, which are in turn filtered in order to discard the irrelevant ones. A score value is obtained from the remaining expressions, which acts as the sole value upon which classification is performed. The remainder of this section gives a detailed description of each processing step.

Except for stemming (achieved by Porter's Snowball Stemmer [20]) and stopping, we used the implementations provided by OpenNLP[8]. The employed sentence detector utilizes a maximum entropy model to identify end of sentence characters. The Part-of-speech (POS) tagger used in our work is a stochastic

---

[7] http://conceptnet.media.mit.edu/

[8] http://opennlp.sourceforge.net/

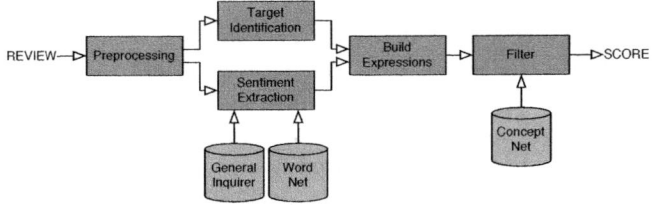

Fig. 3. Flowchart of the on-line knowledge sources-based approach

tagger based on maximum entropy. It supports the 48 word-level tags introduced by the Penn Treebank project [15]. Further, we use an English chunker: Each chunk is usually equal to a phrase in the syntax of a sentence, such as a noun phrase (NP), verb phrase (VP), or prepositional phrase (PP). The chunker is based on maximum entropy and the chunking model introduced in [22], which uses conditional random fields.

In order to transform the text into a suitable format for the main algorithm, some preprocessing steps are carried out. First, the text is split into sentences, which are in turn analyzed by a syntactic parser to label words and phrases with corresponding part-of-speech (POS) information. Since it is not necessary for our task to have comprehensive knowledge of the syntax, we employ a chunker only. An additional benefit of that is the flat structure produced by a chunker, which is better suited for the processing steps that follow.

As a unit of sentiment representation, we extract *ternary expressions (T-expressions)* on a per-sentence basis. T-expressions were introduced in [11] for automatic question answering tasks and have been adapted to product review classification in [29]. In the latter context, a T-expression has the following format: `<target, verb, source>`. Target refers to a feature term of the topic of the text, i.e., a movie in our case. The verb is selected from the same phrase in which the target occurs. If the verb does not convey sentiment information by itself, a sentiment source, which is typically an adverb, is extracted from the same phrase. Thus, the T-expression for the phrase *"a/DT well/RB written/VB story/NN"* is `<story, written, well>`. However, there are common situations where verbs are absent from a phrase, e.g., *"a/DT great/JJ movie/NN"*. Since a T-expression cannot be built in this case, we fall back to a second form, referred to as *binary expression (B-expression)* as suggested in [29]. A B-expression is simply a combination of an adjective and a target co-occurring in the text. Hence, the aforementioned utterance is represented by `<movie, great>`.

Target candidates are extracted from noun phrases (NP), based on the observation that feature terms are nouns. In [29], base noun phrase (BNP) patterns are applied successfully to extract sentiment about a given topic. A noun phrase needs to conform to one of these patterns in order to be considered for target identification. Patterns used are as follows: `NN; NN, NN; JJ, NN; NN, NN, NN; JJ, NN, NN; JJ, JJ, NN`. Before they are applied, words from POS classes that do not contribute to target identification are removed from the phrase. These are determiners, adverbs, and punctuation. All mentions of the personal pronoun *"it"* are regarded as referring directly to the topic of the text, and are also used as targets.

In the next step, the goal is to identify sentiment sources for each target, i. e., words that convey the actual affect information. In order to make sure that a given sentiment source is actually directed to the target in question, we need to restrict the search space. We accomplish this by finding 'border indicators' that appear between clauses or phrases within a sentence, and thus split it into units of statements. A sentiment source is only associated to a given target if they occur in the same section, i. e., there is no border indicator between them. Subordinating conjunctions, prepositional phrases, coordinating conjunctions, and punctuation such as commas or colons are used as border indicators.

We select all verbs and adjectives from the target section, and use General Inquirer to determine its valence v. A word u_i is assigned a valence $v(u_i) = 1$ if it has the General Inquirer tag `Positiv`, and a valence $v(u_i) = -1$ if it is tagged `Negativ`. In case a word is not found in General Inquirer, we use WordNet synsets to also lookup a word's synonyms, until a match is found. We refer to words for which a valence was found as 'sentiment words'. If a sentiment word is an adjective, a B-expression is built from it and stored in the result set. If it is a verb, its *siblings* (the words next to it within the same phrase) are first searched for sentiment adverbs. In case a match was found, we build a T-expression of the form `<target, verb, adverb>`. The adverb part is left out if no match was found. This step is also carried out for non-sentiment verbs, and a T-expression is generated if a sentiment adverb was found within its siblings. That way, phrases like *"a/DT beautifully/RB directed/VB movie/NN"*, with *"directed"* not being a sentiment verb, also yield an expression. Depending on the POS of the sentiment word, T-expressions and B-expressions are built.

We use the distance between the sentiment word and the target of an expression as a measure for its strength. It appears intuitive that words that occur closer together are more related. Many researchers have set a maximum distance between two words to decide whether or not they are related [16,25]. However, the experiments carried out in [30] showed that setting a maximum distance ('window size') actually degrades performance compared to not using it. Another approach that takes distance information into account was recently presented in [4]: Feature-opinion pairs similar to B-expressions are extracted, and the sentiment value of each pair is calculated using the multiplicative inverse of the distance between the two words. The results in that work also confirm that setting a maximum distance has a negative effect on performance.

Based on these findings, we use distance information for two purposes: First, for a given sentiment word, only the expression with the shortest distance between the sentiment word and its target is kept for further processing. The underlying assumption is that a sentiment word is in most cases directed at the target that it occurs closer to. That way we also lower the chance that a sentiment word is accidentally associated with an unrelated target. However, multiple expressions may exist for a given target, in order to catch all sentiment

words in sentences containing more than one. The sentence *"a/DT well/RB writ-ten/VB ,/, beautifully/RB directed/VB story/NN"* contains two sentiment adverbs: *"well"* and *"beautifully"*. Two corresponding T-expressions are extracted accordingly:
`<story, written, well>` and `<story, directed, beautifully>`.

Secondly, we also use the word distance to boost or lower the score of an expression by means of a decay function. The weighted score s of an expression that contains the target t_i and the sentiment source u_i is calculated according to the following equation:

$$s(u_i, t_i) = c \cdot v(u_i) \cdot \frac{1}{D(u_i, t_i)^e} \tag{1}$$

The valence of u_i, as taken from General Inquirer, is denoted by $v(u_i)$, and $D(u_i, t_i)$ is the distance of words between u_i and t_i. The decay function is similar to the one introduced in [4], as it is based on the multiplicative inverse of the distance, too. However, we added a constant factor c, and an exponent e to adjust and fine-tune the level of decay. Because

$$\frac{1}{D(u_i, t_i)^e} = 1 \tag{2}$$

holds for any e if $D(u_i, t_i) = 1$, i.e., u_i and t_i occur right next to each other, $c > 1$ effectively amplifies the valence in that case. On the other hand, c has little effect for $D(u_i, t_i) \gg 1$, which is the case for words that occur further apart and are therefore less related. By choosing $e > 1$, it is possible to let the valence decrease 'faster' for greater $D(u_i, t_i)$, thereby controlling the amount of influence of the word distance. In an analogous manner, $e < 1$ results in a 'slower' decrease of valence. We provide an evaluation for these parameters in our experiments in section 5.

4.1   Fallback Mechanisms

Due to the fact that it is not always possible to find an expression in a sentence, we rely on two fallback mechanisms that allow us to create pseudo expressions in case no real expression was found. The first mechanism is used if no target could be extracted from a sentence. In that case, we assume that the sentence is referring to the movie in question, and build pseudo B-expressions that have *"it"* as target. The search for sentiment words is extended to include verbs, adjectives, adverbs, and nouns. Since a real target is not available, we do not have word distance information for a pseudo expression. Therefore, the decay function cannot be applied, resulting in a score that is equal to the valence of the sentiment word that was extracted. Hence, this fallback mechanism is basically similar to keyword spotting. The second mechanism takes place if no target, and no sentiment words could be found in a sentence. Based on the observation that there are more than three times as many positive than negative reviews, the score of a sentence is set to $s = 1$ as a last resort. However, this case is rare, with only 1.9 % of the reviews in our test set not yielding any expressions. Failure to extract sentiment words can be caused by very short utterances, and the use of colloquial language: Colloquial terms are most likely not contained in general purpose dictionaries.

4.2 Filtering and Classification

The final step of our algorithm determines if the expressions that were found earlier are actually directed at the movie. We assume that an expression refers to the movie in question, if its target word is a feature of the term *"movie"*. Since we operate only in the movie domain, a manually assembled list of features could be used. However, building such a list can be a daunting task, and one of our intentions was to keep the algorithm domain-independent. Instead, we rely on ConceptNet to identify features. A drawback of this approach is that ConceptNet does not contain features specific to a given movie, as it has been designed to be a generic knowledge source. More precisely, it generally does not contain named entities such as names of actors, characters in the movie, or movie titles. Therefore, sentiment expressed against such named entities, e. g., "Al Pacino's performance was outstanding" are currently not extracted. We plan to overcome this issue by using an even larger scale encyclopedia that contains this kind of domain-specific knowledge for many different domains.

Assuming that the topic of a review (i. e., movie in our case) is known, feature terms can be selected by looking up the following predicates in ConceptNet: *feature* PartOf *"movie"*, *feature* AtLocation *"movie"*, and *"movie"* HasProperty *feature*. The features retrieved this way form the list against which expressions are checked. All expressions whose target is not contained in the feature list are filtered out. In case all expressions for a review would have to be dropped, filtering is not performed. This ensures that there is always at least one expression for each review.

In order to determine the final valence of a review, the accumulated score S of the n expressions it contains is calculated:

$$S = \sum_{i=1}^{n} s(u_i, t_i) \qquad (3)$$

The valence class V is chosen as follows:

$$V = \begin{cases} +1 & \text{if } S \geq 0 \\ -1 & \text{if } S < 0 \end{cases} \qquad (4)$$

The decision of including $S = 0$ in the positive class is simply motivated by the fact that there are more positive than negative reviews.

5 Evaluation

This section describes the experiments we conducted to assess the performance of the introduced approach in comparison to data-based learning by 'Bag of N-Grams' (BoNG) as extension over Bag of Words [9], i. e., constructing a vector space by one feature per N-Gram (rather than word) in the training by different normalizations of this N-Gram's frequency in the current review and assigning valence by Support Vector Machines (SVM) or Regression (SVR). Both methods have been optimized on binary classification into positive and negative reviews. Later on in this section, we study classification performance on all three classes, as well as regression performance on the full $0 - 100$ scale of scores that Metacritic provides. We will also investigate out of vocabulary resolution as well as ways of fusing information from both approaches to improve performance.

We rely on Metacritic's release year attribute to split the database (cf. table 3) into a training subset (odd years, 49 698 instances), and a test subset (even years, 52 924 instances). For parameter tuning, we simplify the task into a binary classification problem by dropping all instances of the *mixed* class from both the training (including development) and test data. The remaining data sets have 33 942 instances for training, and 36 094 instances for testing. In order to avoid overfitting, parameter tuning is performed using a development subset of the training data for validation. It is defined as every other odd year, starting at 1; or more precisely all years for which $(year - 1) \bmod 4 = 0$. There are 15 730 instances in the development set and the remaining 18 212 instances are used for training during development. Using this approach, we can eventually use the test set to evaluate the classifiers on unseen data.

As mentioned in section 2, there are a lot more positive than negative review instances in the database. This can be a problem when training a machine learning algorithm, because the resulting model would be biased towards the class that has more training instances. The recognition rate for the class with less instances would then be degraded. In order to avoid a biased model, we use down sampling without replacement to extract a subset of the training data set with a balanced class distribution. The resulting balanced training corpus has a size of 15 063 instances. The balanced subset that is used for training during development has 8 158 instances.

5.1   Parameter Tuning

Decay Function. We first carried out experiments to find the optimum parameters for the decay function as described. Various combinations of the two parameters c and e have been evaluated on the training data subset. The tested range is $c, e \in \{0.1, 0.2, ..., 1.0, 2.0\}$. First, we set $c = 1$ to determine the optimum value for e. Lowering e to values below 1 increased accuracy until a maximum was reached for $e = 0.1$ and $e = 0.2$. For all values of $e > 1$, accuracy decreased significantly [7]. Using $e = 0.1$, we determined the best setting for c. It turned out that setting c to values other than 1 had a negative effect on accuracy. Compared to the decay function used in [4], which is similar to $c = 1$ and $e = 1$, we were able to improve accuracy by 0.23 % for $c = 1$ and $e = 0.1$. Figure 4 shows a three-dimensional plot of the accuracy over the parameters c and e. The highest accuracy of 70.29 % for $c = 1.0$ and $e = 0.1$ is visible as a 'summit'. Significantly lower accuracy for $e > 1.0$ can be observed as a 'valley'. The 'ridge' indicates that $c = 1.0$ is the best setting for all values of e.

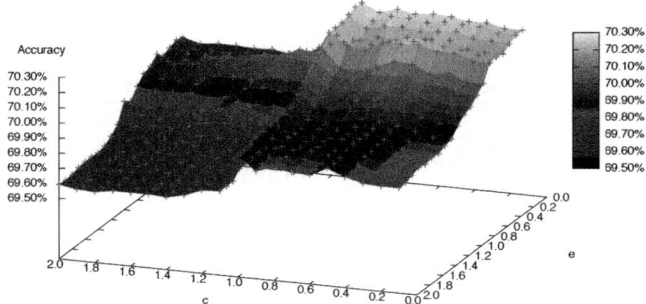

Fig. 4. Accuracy by different combinations of the decay function parameters c and e

Bag of N-Grams. For classification of the features we employ an implementation of the sequential minimal optimization algorithm described in [18] for training a support vector classifier using polynomial kernels [28].

With a size of over 83 k words, the vocabulary of the Metacritic database is large. After stemming is applied, over 62 k word stems remain. When using Bag of Words [9], this results in a feature space of the same size. If N-Grams are involved, the feature space can be significantly larger, depending on the minimum and maximum N-Gram lengths that are used. In order to make this problem computable, we need to take measures to reduce the dimensionality of the feature space. A minimum term frequency f_{min} can be employed to remove infrequent words. However, in [26] it is pointed out that low-frequency words are likely to be meaningful features for opinionated sentences. Since the valence of a review is determined by the opinions it contains, low-frequency words are indeed important for our task. Therefore, we use a gentle value of $f_{min} = 2$. With respect to this, we utilize a related method, *periodic pruning*, to carefully reduce the number of features without dropping potentially important ones. Periodic pruning divides the data set into chunks of configurable size, and is executed after such a chunk has been processed by the word or N-Gram tokenizer. Each feature that has only occurred once until this point is removed from the feature vector. If the chunk size is set high, the chances of discarding important features can be minimized. We chose to set it to 25 % of the data set.

Before the actual N-Gram parameters were evaluated, we determined the optimum settings for transformation and normalization. Table 4 gives the accuracy and F-measure obtained by each possible combination of methods. Simple N-Gram frequency (f_{ij}), term frequency transformation (TF), inverse document frequency transformation (IDF), and normalization (norm) are considered. The N-Gram parameters are set to $g_{min} = 1$ and $g_{max} = 3$, the setting that yields highest accuracy as we will show in the next section. Although the values do not differ much, normalization combined with TFIDF yields best results. Normalization increases performance in every case. IDF seems to benefit largely from normalization, as it only adds to performance significantly if values are normalized, too.

Table 4. Influence of transformations and normalization on Bag of N-Grams. Reported are overall accuracy and weighted F-measure.

Transformation	Accuracy	F-measure
f_{ij}	75.03 %	76.93 %
norm(f_{ij})	75.72 %	77.49 %
TF	75.44 %	77.30 %
norm(TF)	75.66 %	77.44 %
IDF	75.05 %	76.95 %
norm(IDF)	76.42 %	78.11 %
TFIDF	75.45 %	77.30 %
norm(TFIDF)	**77.14 %**	**78.57 %**

To investigate the influence of the N-Gram length, different combinations of g_{min} and g_{max} are tested. As shown in table 5, best accuracy is obtained for $g_{min} = 1$ and $g_{max} = 3$, and significantly decreases for $g_{min} > 1$. On the one hand, this is in line with the results reported in [3] for product reviews, where best performance was attained using trigrams. On the other hand, the same work reports that back-off N-Grams degrade performance, which we cannot confirm. Our results point out the importance of single words, which is emphasized further when looking at the composition of the feature space in case of the optimal settings. Only 12 % are taken by single words, whereas 52 % are bigrams, and 36 % are trigrams. This leads to the conclusion that despite their small contribution to the feature space, single words convey important valence information in the context of movie reviews in Metacritic. However, information about the context of a word, which is included by higher-order N-Grams, seems to be equally important. The largest feature space among our results has a dimensionality of 177 733 for $g_{min} = 1$ and $g_{max} = 5$. The smallest space for $g_{min} = 1$ and $g_{max} = 1$ has a size of 18 316 dimensions.

Table 5. Effect of the minimum and maximum N-Gram length g_{min} and g_{max} on the accuracy and weighted F-measure achieved by Bag of N-Grams

g_{min}	g_{max}	# Features	Accuracy	F-measure
1	1	18 316	74.58 %	76.43 %
1	2	96 152	75.95 %	77.70 %
1	**3**	**151 083**	**77.14 %**	**78.57 %**
1	4	171 438	76.41 %	78.03 %
1	5	177 733	76.92 %	78.46 %
2	2	77 840	66.72 %	69.53 %
2	3	132 780	66.54 %	69.38 %
2	4	153 146	69.62 %	72.07 %
2	5	159 465	71.66 %	73.73 %
3	3	54 968	71.59 %	73.43 %
3	4	75 418	72.33 %	74.05 %
3	5	81 911	72.61 %	74.29 %

In [17] it is reported that best movie review classification performance is obtained by using word presence information (as opposed to word frequency), and single words without stemming as features for SVM. Extensive experiments with different combinations of machine learning algorithms, N-Gram settings, stemming, and derived features such as part-of-speech and word position information are conducted in this work. Using the best reported combination, we obtain an accuracy of 76.51%, and an F-measure of 77.97% on our data. Comparing these values to our best results in table 5, the accuracy is 0.63% lower, and the F-measure is 0.60% lower when using the parameters suggested in [17].

5.2 Out of Vocabulary Resolution

If a given word is contained in the vocabulary of the test data set, but does not occur in the training vocabulary, we call it an *out of vocabulary* (OoV) word. Because these words are missing in the training set, a machine learning algorithm is unable to determine a numerical feature for them. Meaningful features are possibly lost due to this problem. Compared to the database vocabulary size of 83 328, the number of these out of vocabulary words is quite significant, adding up to 25 217, or 30.3% of the vocabulary. The number of OoV events, i.e., the number of occurrences of such words in all reviews, is 38 244. This amounts to only 3.0% of the total 1 288 384 words in the database (cf. table 6). The difference between the percentage of OoV vocabulary words and OoV events is likely caused by proper nouns, e.g., the title of a movie, or the name of its actors. Many of these words occur only in reviews for one single movie. Since the training and test data sets are obtained by separating movies released in odd years from those released in even years, all reviews for a given movie are contained in one set only. Therefore, these proper nouns are inevitably out of vocabulary.

Other forms of OoV can be reduced by utilizing a stemming algorithm. Because stemming treats all different forms of a word as one feature, OoVs resulting from a unique occurrence of a certain word form can be avoided. After stemming has been applied, the database vocabulary has a size of 62 212, and the OoV words account to 19 228. Surprisingly, the percentage of 30.9% is actually slightly higher than before. Looking at OoV events however, the number decreases to 29 482, or 2.3%, respecitvely, of all words.

Table 6. Number of OoV words and percentage of the vocabulary size, as well as number of OoV events and percentage of words in the database. Values are reported for no OoV resolution (baseline), stemming, and stemming with on-line knowledge sources-based (OKS) resolution.

# Words	Vocabulary	OoV words	OoV events
Baseline	83 328	25 217 (30.3%)	38 244 (3.0%)
Stemming	62 212	19 228 (30.9%)	29 482 (2.3%)
Stemming & OKS	62 212	14 123 (22.7%)	22 746 (1.8%)

In addition to stemming, OoVs can be resolved by replacing them with synonyms which are not OoV. We leverage the on-line knowledge sources ConceptNet and WordNet to find synonyms. If one of a word's synonyms does occur in the training vocabulary, it is used to replace every occurrence of the original word in the text. This step is carried out before N-Grams are assembled. We were able to substitute 5 105 vocabulary words and 6 736 OoV events using this method. Only 1.8 % of all words are still accounted as OoV, hence we were able to resolve 40.5 % of the initial OoV events using both stemming and synonym substitution.

Running the SVM classifier with both resolution methods enabled yields an accuracy gain of 0.04 %. Obviously, the resolved OoVs do not add a significant amount of important discriminating features. A possible cause is that the method of finding synonyms has a certain degree of inaccuracy. In fact, WordNet has no support for word sense disambiguation, and sometimes produces more noise than signal when used for finding similarities of meaning, according to [3]. Because a word can be part of multiple synsets, depending on its various meanings, they need to be equally considered. Therefore false correlations are very likely to be encountered. If in the worst case an OoV word is replaced by a false synonym which conveys a different sentiment, the overall accuracy suffers. Since this is a general shortcoming of WordNet, resolving it is beyond the scope of this chapter.

5.3 Bag of N-Grams vs. On-line Knowledge Sources

To compare the performance obtained by Bag of N-Grams to the approach based on on-line knowledge sources, we evaluated the algorithm described in section 4 on the same test data. The parameters for Bag of N-Grams are chosen as $g_{min} = 1$ and $g_{max} = 3$ to produce best results. Normalization and TFIDF transformation, as well as out of vocabulary resolution are used.

Results of the comparison between Bag of N-Grams and SVM (BoNG/SVM) and the on-line knowledge sources (OKS) based approach are shown in table 7. BoNG/SVM performs significantly better than OKS according to all reported measures. The accuracy of BoNG/SVM is 7.95 % higher than the accuracy of OKS. The largest gap between the two approaches is observed for the recall for

Table 7. Bag of N-Grams (BoNG) with SVM, Random Forests (RF), Naïve Bayes (NB), On-line Knowledge Sources (OKS), and Pointwise Mutual Information (PMI-IR) performance compared for two review classes (positive (+)/negative (-))

Measure	BoNG/SVM	BoNG/RF	BoNG/NB	OKS	PMI-IR
Accuracy	77.37 %	76.41 %	67.45 %	69.42 %	65.13 %
Weighted F-measure	78.77 %	77.94 %	69.12 %	70.29 %	65.91 %
Area under curve	0.777	0.852	0.643	0.644	0.605
$Precision_+$	92.18 %	92.12 %	82.78 %	81.92 %	78.54 %
$Precision_-$	50.84 %	49.52 %	35.69 %	36.70 %	28.11 %
$Recall_+$	77.07 %	75.76 %	72.73 %	77.21 %	75.09 %
$Recall_-$	78.39 %	78.58 %	50.01 %	43.67 %	32.19 %

negative reviews, which is 34.72 % lower for OKS. Obviously, negative reviews contain certain linguistic properties that are unaccounted for by this approach. A possible cause is the fact that our method does not detect if negation is involved in an expression it has extracted, assuming that negation is more common in negative reviews. Negation detection is a complex problem to solve [3,27], especially for syntax-driven approaches. BoNG solves this problem in an elegant way: By using N-Grams as features, a given term automatically results in a different feature if a negation word co-occurs within the neighbourhood range.

Interestingly, the precision for negative reviews is far below the precision for positive reviews in both approaches, meaning that they both tend to detect negative sentiment when it is actually positive. This confirms the hypothesis brought up in [24] that positive movie reviews may contain negative wording, e. g., to describe unpleasant scenes in a war or horror movie. To resolve this issue, domain specific knowledge of movie genres would be required.

Figure 5 (left) compares the receiver operating characteristic (ROC) of the two approaches. The values for BoNG were obtained by gradually shifting SVM's decision rule based on the distance to the class separating hyper plane. For OKS, the discrimination threshold d of the classifier was varied over the full range of scores observed for the test data. Scores range from 12.9 on the highest, to -7.6 on the lowest end. The step size between two consecutive thresholds was chosen to be 0.1. Some interesting values of d are highlighted in figure 5 (right). There are significant differences in the TPR and FPR between $d = 1.0$ and $d = 1.1$, as well as between $d = -0.9$ and $d = -1.0$. A score of ± 1.0 corresponds to a review that has only a single positive or negative expression. Obviously a large number of such reviews exists in the database, which explains these significant

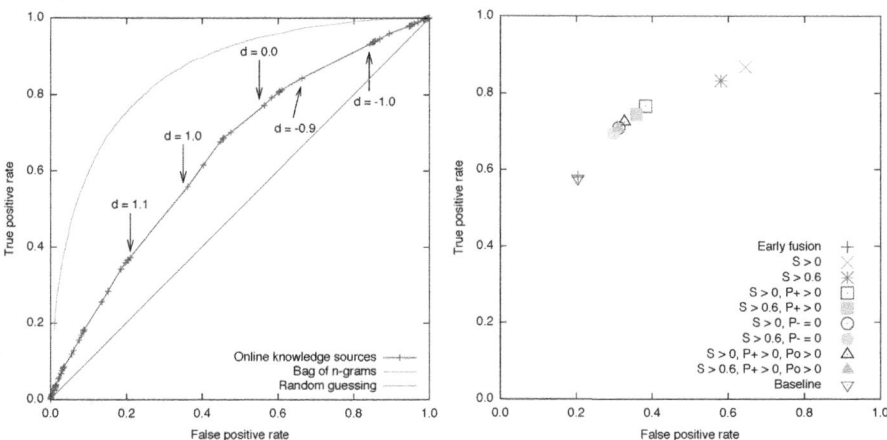

Fig. 5. ROC of OKS and BoNG/SVM for the two class problem (left). The discrimination threshold d is varied along the curve of OKS. The curve that results from random guessing is plotted for comparison. ROC for late fusion methods compared to the baseline without fusion (right). Values shown apply to the positive class.

differences. Also highlighted is $d = 0.0$, which is the discrimination threshold that was used in all experiments on the binary classification problem. The superior performance of BoNG is clearly visible in the graph, its ROC curve being more convex and closer to the upper left corner than the curve for OKS. In numerical terms, the area under curve for BoNG resembles 0.777, whereas the value for OKS is only 0.644. Also plotted is the ROC that results from randomly guessing on the class, which naturally has an area under curve of 0.5.

Since the two approaches are different in nature, we compared each of them to a more similar one. The key difference between them is that OKS is based on generally available knowledge sources, whereas BoNG is based on machine learning – usually employing data from the target domain. Therefore, we chose to compare OKS to the PMI-IR-based method described in [24], as it also incorporates data available on-line. The original algorithm uses the Altavista[9] search engine to get the number of matching web pages for a given query ("hits"), which is used as input data for the algorithm. We chose Yahoo![10] instead, as it provides a larger search index, more accurate hits numbers, and a fast API. The PMI-IR algorithm does not perform as good as OKS on our data set. It is able to achieve an accuracy of 65.13 %, which is 4.29 % short of OKS. PMI-IR and OKS both suffer from bad precision and recall for negative reviews. One of the reasons is that PMI-IR was not able to extract any phrases from 16 448 reviews in the test data set, which is 45.57 % of the instances. As a fallback, we assumed positive sentiment for these cases. The authors report an average of 29.13 phrases per movie review in their corpus. Since Metacritic reviews are very brief, it only extracted an average of 1.51 phrases per review on our data, not counting the reviews that did not yield any phrase.

Using the same N-Gram features, we compared the performance of the SVM classifier to other popular methods. We chose the simple yet widely used Naïve Bayes (e.g., [3]), as well as the more recent Random Forests [1] classifiers. We trained a forest with 100 trees, allowing infinite depth of the trees, as found to be optimal in a series of experiments on the development set. The number of features to consider for random feature selection was set to $F = int(log_2 M + 1)$, where M is the number of inputs [1]. BoNG/RF performs almost as good as BoNG/SVM, with an accuracy of 76.41 % only 0.96 % short of BoNG/SVM. BoNG/NB on the other hand falls back significantly, yielding only 67.45 % accuracy.

5.4   Error Analysis

Sentiment word detection yielded a total of 339 099 lookups, at a coverage of 65.72 %. With 4 206 words tagged either positive or negative, General Inquirer contains a relatively large amount of sentiment words. That said, one would expect a higher coverage rate. We suspect that the use of slang in the database, as well as the uncertainty involved in POS tagging are the main reasons for the low coverage rate. In the feature detection step, there were a total of 109 238

---

[9] http://www.altavista.com/

[10] http://www.yahoo.com/

feature lookups, at a coverage of 84.43 %. Obviously, the coverage of the on-line knowledge sources the algorithm is based on is problematic. We expect that performance of our algorithm will increase with future expansions of these data sources.

Another source of error are reviews that contain both positive and negative statements. Ideally, the algorithm would extract both statements, decide which one is stronger, and pick that one to determine the score. These cases are problematic, as the decision is not always obvious, even for a human being. In fact it is left to the author to decide on that. The following reviews taken from the corpus illustrate the problem.

"Completely ridiculous, but fun to look at." (Score: 25). This review contains a negative statement – "completely ridiculus"; and a positive one – "fun to look at". The author regards the negative one as being stronger, as he assigned a score of 25. The OKS algorithm correctly identifies "fun" and "ridiculous" as sentiment-bearing words, but also extracts "completely" as a positive word. Because it is not able to determine which statement is stronger, they are all equally considered, resulting in an overall score of 1.0 and leading to misclassification.

"Cheerful and easy to watch but surprisingly inept in the telling." (Score: 63). In this case, the algorithm is able to detect the sentiment correctly. It extracts two positive sentiment words – "easy" and "cheerful", and a negative one – "inept". This is in line with the expressed sentiment, and with the assigned score.

Another source of error are reviews that contain figurative or otherwise complex language. Because our approach is based only on shallow linguistic analysis, deeply buried meaning can often not be detected.

"Minimally plotted but beautifully atmospheric nightmare." (Score: 70). This review also contains a negative statement – "minimally plotted", as well as a positive one – "beautifully atmospheric nightmare". The words used in these two statements are problematic for the algorithm. From the first one, it extracts the verb "to plot", which has ambiguous meanings. Since there is no support for word sense disambiguation in General Inquirer, it is seen as a negative sentiment word. The second statement is problematic because of its use of figurative language. The true meaning cannot be detected by the algorithm – it yields a positive expression for "beautiful", and a negative expression for "nightmare". This results in an overall score of 0 for this statement. Because the first statement produced a negative score, the review is misclassified.

"Exploding on the screen in a riot of movement, music and color." (Score: 90). This review uses negative sentiment bearing words ("exploding", "riot") to express a positive opinion. The algorithm extracted only "exploding", putting this review in the negative class.

"The influence of Danish filmmaker Lars von Trier looms heavily over the whole film." (Score: 75). This review uses the verb "to loom" in order to express that the movie is dark, for which Lars von Trier is known. Lacking this background information, the algorithm only sees a negative sentiment word, which leads to misclassification.

"The less said the better." (Score: 25). Here, the algorithm only extracts the word "better" as a positive sentiment word. Again, shallow linguistic analysis cannot extract the true meaning of the sentence.

5.5   Estimating Mixed Sentiment

Until now, our evaluation has been carried out on a prototypical two class problem. However, the Metacritic database contains a third class for mixed or average reviews (see table 2). We skipped this class for parameter optimization in order to simplify the problem to a binary classification task, and because mixed or neutral reviews are especially hard to estimate [25,5], just as non-prototypical sentiment in general [21]. Both our approaches do not perform subjectivity/objectivity classification, which is widely used to distinguish neutral reviews from opinionated (positive/negative) ones. But still we were able to gain results by making only minor modifications to the algorithms. For the data-driven approach, the three class problem is modeled as a series of binary classification problems which are solved in the same way as before by SVM. For the syntax-driven approach, the decision function in (4) has to be replaced by one that supports three classes. The solution is to break down the three class problem into two binary classification problems. For the first classifier, the negative and mixed classes are treated as one class, and distinguished from the positive class. The second classifier distinguishes between negative and mixed/positive merged into one class. In order to obtain the best possible overall performance, we evaluate each classifier separately and observe two classification thresholds τ_+ and τ_-. The thresholds can then be combined into a valence decision function

$$V = \begin{cases} +1 & \text{if} & S > \tau_+ \\ 0 & \text{if} & \tau_- \leq S \leq \tau_+ \\ -1 & \text{if} & S < \tau_- \end{cases} \qquad (5)$$

that distinguishes between all three classes. Because of $\tau_- < \tau_+$, we effectively allow a range of values around $S = 0$ to be associated to the mixed class. We observed the average weighted F-measure for optimizing the two binary classifiers on the validation data set. The highest values were obtained by setting $\tau_+ = 0.6$ for the first classifier, and $\tau_- = -1.9$ for the second. The performance of the resulting ternary classifier is shown in table 8, next to the performance of the BoNG ternary classifier. Both classifiers have been evaluated on the test data set.

Both approaches show significantly lower performance compared to the two class problem. BoNG accuracy drops by 23.66 % to 53.71 %, and OKS accuracy is decreased by 20.04 % to 49.38 %. Better values are achieved by the BoNG approach for most measures. Only the recall for positive reviews is higher when OKS is used, with 68.43 % compared to 57.62 % for BoNG. OKS, however, suffers from a low recall for negative instances. BoNG recall values are more balanced between the three classes, ranging from 43.91 % for mixed, up to 60.43 % for negative reviews.

Table 8. Bag of N-Grams (BoNG) and On-line Knowledge Sources (OKS) performance compared for three review classes (positive (+)/mixed (0)/negative (-)). The OKS classification thresholds are $\tau_+ = 0.6$, and $\tau_- = -1.9$.

Measure	BoNG	OKS
Accuracy	**53.71 %**	49.38 %
Weighted F-measure	**55.04 %**	47.19 %
$Precision_+$	**75.66 %**	58.82 %
$Precision_0$	**42.92 %**	35.74 %
$Precision_-$	**34.70 %**	28.71 %
$Recall_+$	57.62 %	**68.43 %**
$Recall_0$	**43.91 %**	37.32 %
$Recall_-$	**60.43 %**	10.66 %

5.6   Information Fusion

The evaluation of the two approaches on three review classes has shown that none of them performs always better than the other. Obviously, each method has advantages in certain areas, but disadvantages in other areas. By combining them into one classifier, the disadvantages may be alleviated. All experiments in this section again use the parameters which yielded best results earlier. The N-Gram settings are chosen as $g_{min} = 1$ and $g_{max} = 3$; normalization and TFIDF transformation, as well as out of vocabulary resolution are used.

Early fusion takes place at the feature level, before the machine learning algorithm is run, thus preserving utmost knowledge prior to the final decision process. This is known to be in particular advantageous if the information is highly correlated, as given here [14]. In our case, we can simply add the score produced by OKS to the BoNG feature vector, and then run SVM on the extended vector. The influence of the OKS score on the class decision is relatively low in this case, since it 'competes' with the numerous other components of the feature vector, which are generated by BoNG. The performance achieved by early fusion is given in table 9. Compared to the baseline values, i.e., the BoNG results given in table 8, accuracy increased slightly by 0.13 % to 53.84 %. There is an improvement in the recall for positive and negative reviews, however, only at the cost of a worsened recall for the mixed class.

In contrast to early fusion, late such combines the output of different methods on a semantic layer [14]. Each approach determines a numerical or boolean result, and the results are, e.g., arithmetically or logically combined to make the final decision on a class. This allows for selectively switching between the involved methods based on their performance characteristics, in order to obtain best overall performance. From the results presented earlier we know that the BoNG approach has better performance than OKS in almost all measures. However, OKS has a much better recall of positive reviews, if all three review classes are considered. The idea arises to improve overall recognition of positive reviews by relying on OKS, while basing the decision for other classes on BoNG only.

SVM are able to provide a prediction value for each class based on the distance to the separating hyperplane, on which the final classification is based. The prediction values for each class will be denoted as P_- (negative), P_0 (mixed), and P_+ (positive). Each value determines how much evidence the classifier has for the corresponding class. The range for these values is $0 \leq P \leq 1$, where 0 stands for weakest, and 1 stands for strongest evidence. Together with the score S produced by OKS, we can set conditions under which the classifier votes for the positive class. If the conditions are not met, SVM's initial vote is used to determine the class. The different conditions we evaluated, and the resulting performance, are shown in table 9. Regarding the OKS score, we examined both $S > 0$, and $S > 0.6$, the latter being the positive discrimination threshold τ_+ we determined earlier. For SVM we investigated evidence for the positive class being present ($P_+ > 0$), no evidence for the negative class ($P_- = 0$), and evidence for both the mixed and positive classes ($P_+ > 0$, $P_0 > 0$).

Table 9. Early and late fusion methods for the three review classes (positive (+)/mixed (0)/negative (-)) compared to the baseline (no fusion) with the conditions for the OKS score S, and the SVM predictions P_-, P_0, P_+ under which the classifier votes for the positive class are given

	Accuracy	$Recall_-$	$Recall_0$	$Recall_+$
Baseline	53.71 %	60.43 %	**43.91 %**	57.62 %
Early fusion	53.84 %	**60.67 %**	43.65 %	57.96 %
Late fusion				
$S > 0$	55.93 %	32.65 %	16.83 %	**86.72 %**
$S > 0.6$	55.95 %	37.04 %	20.60 %	83.14 %
$S > 0$, $P_+ > 0$	**57.77 %**	51.64 %	29.74 %	76.64 %
$S > 0.6$, $P_+ > 0$	57.37 %	52.74 %	31.56 %	74.45 %
$S > 0$, $P_- = 0$	56.19 %	60.43 %	29.74 %	70.98 %
$S > 0.6$, $P_- = 0$	55.99 %	60.43 %	31.56 %	69.49 %
$S > 0$, $P_+ > 0$, $P_0 > 0$	56.83 %	59.14 %	29.74 %	72.58 %
$S > 0.6$, $P_+ > 0$, $P_0 > 0$	56.54 %	59.25 %	31.56 %	70.89 %

All late fusion methods are significantly better in a one-tailed test at the 0.1 % level and can therefore be considered a true improvement. Early fusion improvement over the baseline is not significant and therefore can be considered as not to improve performance.

At first glance it is not obvious which combination of late fusion parameters has the best overall performance. On the one hand, best accuracy is obtained by $S > 0$ and $P_+ > 0$. On the other hand this configuration shows a low recall rate for positive and negative reviews at the same time. The most balanced recall over all three classes is obtained by the baseline and early fusion methods, however, they also produce a low accuracy of 53.71 % and 53.84 %, respectively. In order to have better measures for comparison, we rely on an ROC graph. The true positive rates (TPR) over the false positive rates (FPR) for all combinations from table 9 are plotted in figure 5 (right). The baseline and early fusion methods produce points towards the left part of the graph, and can therefore be regarded as 'conservative' classifiers. They have the lowest FPR, at the cost of the lowest TPR. Using only the OKS score produces 'liberal' classifiers, with points close to the top right corner of the graph. The TPR is the highest among the evaluated methods, but the FPR significantly increases as well. All combinations which are using values from both approaches, produce points between these extreme cases. Judging from the ROC graph only, best performance is obtained for the conditions $S > 0.6$, $P_+ > 0$, $P_0 > 0$ since its point in the graph appears closest to the top left corner.

5.7   Review Score Prediction

In order to distinguish even between reviews within a class, we next use Support Vector Regression to estimate the score value of reviews on its scale of $0 - 100$. Since SVR uses the same vector space representation as SVM, the best settings we determined earlier for Bag of N-Grams are used. Normalization and TFIDF transformation, as well as out of vocabulary resolution are also employed again. N-Gram parameters are chosen to be the optimum values $g_{min} = 1$ and $g_{max} = 3$. A radial basis function kernel with the variance parameter set to $\gamma = 0.01$ is further chosen based on findings from the development set. In order to evaluate the performance, two values are observed: The *correlation coefficient*, and the *mean absolute error*. We achieve a correlation coefficient of 0.57, and a mean absolute error of 14.1 on the test data. Occurring deviations from the actual scores may be owed to the fact that the score value is not evenly distributed within the data set (see figure 1).

When interpreting these results, one should keep in mind that the ground truth itself is likely to be partly inaccurate: The reviews in Metacritic are written by both professional and non-professional writers, and usually only the author of a review gets to decide on its score. It has been reported that multiple persons often disagree on which sentiment is expressed in a given review, or through a given word [17,3]. Methods that rely heavily on on-line knowledge sources are additionally impacted, because they suffer from the same inaccuracy of judgement. ConceptNet tries to overcome the problem by letting users vote on the reliability of predicates.

6   Conclusion and Outlook

Different evolution steps of on-line knowledge sources have been used, from annotated dictionaries (General Inquirer, 1966) to comprehensive semantic networks (ConceptNet, 2003). Two approaches suitable for valence estimation of movie reviews have been presented. However, the proposed methods are generic in nature and do not rely on domain-specific features. The on-line knowledge sources-based approach leverages linguistic methods, dictionaries, and semantic networks to estimate valence, and tries to resemble the way that humans understand text. Its special benefit is that it does not require any training. The data-driven approach is based on Bag of N-Grams and Support Vector Machines. On-line knowledge sources have been utilized to improve performance of this approach by resolving out of vocabulary events. While we were able to resolve 40.5 % of these events, the accuracy gain was only 0.04 %. Both methods have been optimized on a subset of Metacritic containing only positive and negative reviews. We were able to achieve 77.37 % accuracy with the data-driven approach, and 69.42 % with the on-line knowledge sources approach. Early fusion was applied, but could not improve the accuracy. Both our approaches show significant performance gains compared to previous state of the art methods. We later extended the problem to three valence classes by estimating mixed reviews as well. The data-driven approach was able to achieve 53.71 %, whereas the on-line knowledge sources approach achieved 49.38 %. The latter showed very unbalanced recall for the three classes, with 68.43 % recall for positive reviews. We were able to improve accuracy up to 57.77 % using late fusion. The method that showed the best compromise between the true positive and false positive rates has an accuracy of 56.54 %. The data-driven approach has been extended by Support Vector Regression. To evaluate this approach, we observed the correlation coefficient between the actual and the predicted score, which was 0.57. The mean absolute error was 14.1 on Metacritic's 0 – 100 scale of scores.

Based on these observations, we propose the following future improvements: We are seeking to improve performance of the on-line knowledge sources-based approach by incorporating more specific term categories from General Inquirer. [13] have shown that ConceptNet can serve as a source of sentiment information as well. It could complement General Inquirer for that purpose. Furthermore, multi-word terms or even full statements could be extracted and looked up in ConceptNet. Together with named entity recognition, other on-line knowledge sources as Wikipedia will allow us to detect for example names of actors or characters in a movie, and use them as additional features. In order to further improve out of vocabulary resolution, more WordNet relations, e. g., *antonymy* (opposite meaning), or *hypernymy* (more general meaning) could be considered. Our method currently does not resolve out of vocabulary N-Grams. By adding a second substitution step after N-Grams have been assembled, this can be done as well. Finally, Metacritic's further review bodies dealing with music and video games can be considered for according experiments.

References

1. Breiman, L.: Random forests. Machine Learning 45(1), 5–32 (2001)
2. Das, S.R., Chen, M.Y.: Yahoo! for amazon: Sentiment parsing from small talk on the web. In: Proceedings of the 8th Asia Pacific Finance Association Annual Conference (2001)
3. Dave, K., Lawrence, S., Pennock, D.M.: Mining the peanut gallery: opinion extraction and semantic classification of product reviews. In: Proceedings of the 12th international conference on World Wide Web, pp. 519–528. ACM, Budapest (2003)
4. Ding, X., Liu, B., Yu, P.S.: A holistic lexicon-based approach to opinion mining. In: WSDM 2008: Proceedings of the International Conference on Web Search and Web Data Mining, pp. 231–240. ACM, New York (2008)

5. Esuli, A., Sebastiani, F.: Determining term subjectivity and term orientation for opinion mining. In: Proceedings of the 11th Conference of the European Chapter of the Association for Computational Linguistics (EACL 2006), Trento, Italy (2006)
6. Fellbaum, C.: Wordnet: An Electronic Lexical Database. MIT Press, Cambridge (1998)
7. Gillick, L., Cox, S.J.: Some statistical issues in the comparison of speech recognition algorithms. In: Proceedings of the International Conference on Audio Speech and Signal Processing (ICASSP), vol. I, pp. 23–26. Glasgow, Scotland (1989)
8. Havasi, C., Speer, R., Alonso, J.: Conceptnet 3: a flexible, multilingual semantic network for common sense knowledge. In: Recent Advances in Natural Language Processing. Borovets, Bulgaria (September 2007)
9. Joachims, T.: Text categorization with support vector machines: learning with many relevant features. In: Nédellec, C., Rouveirol, C. (eds.) ECML 1998. LNCS, vol. 1398, pp. 137–142. Springer, Heidelberg (1998)
10. Jurafsky, D., Martin, J.H.: Speech and Language Processing. Prentice-Hall, Englewood Cliffs (2000)
11. Katz, B.: From sentence processing to information access on the world wide web. In: Proceedings of the AAAI Spring Symposium on Natural Language Processing for the World Wide Web, pp. 77–86 (1997)
12. Liu, B., Hu, M., Cheng, J.: Opinion observer: analyzing and comparing opinions on the web. In: WWW 2005: Proceedings of the 14th International Conference on World Wide Web, pp. 342–351. ACM, New York (2005)
13. Liu, H., Lieberman, H., Selker, T.: A model of textual affect sensing using real-world knowledge. In: IUI 2003: Proceedings of the 8th International Conference on Intelligent User Interfaces, pp. 125–132. ACM, New York (2003)
14. Lizhong, W., Oviatt, S., Cohen, P.R.: Multimodal integration – a statistical view. IEEE Transactions on Multimedia 1, 334–341 (1999)
15. Marcus, M., Marcinkiewicz, M., Santorini, B.: Building a large annotated corpus of english: the Penn Treebank. Computational Linguistics 19(2), 313–330 (1993)
16. Morinaga, S., Yamanishi, K., Tateishi, K., Fukushima, T.: Mining product reputations on the web. In: KDD 2002: Proceedings of the Eighth ACM SIGKDD International Conference on Knowledge Discovery and Data Mining, pp. 341–349. ACM, New York (2002)
17. Pang, B., Lee, L., Vaithyanathan, S.: Thumbs up?: sentiment classification using machine learning techniques. In: Proceedings of EMNLP 2002, Morristown, NJ, USA. Association for Computational Linguistics, pp. 79–86 (2002)
18. Platt, J.C.: Fast training of support vector machines using sequential minimal optimization, pp. 185–208. MIT Press, Cambridge (1999)
19. Popescu, A., Etzioni, O.: Extracting product features and opinions from reviews. In: Proceedings of the conference on Human Language Technology and Empirical Methods in Natural Language Processing. Association for Computational Linguistics, Morristown, NJ, USA, pp. 339–346 (2005)
20. Porter, M.F.: An algorithm for suffix stripping. Program 14(3), 130–137 (1980)
21. Schuller, B., Steidl, S., Batliner, A.: The interspeech 2009 emotion challenge. In: Proceedings of the Interspeech, Brighton, UK, pp. 312–315 (2009)
22. Sha, F., Pereira, F.: Shallow parsing with conditional random fields. In: NAACL 2003: Proceedings of the 2003 Conference of the North American Chapter of the Association for Computational Linguistics on Human Language Technology. Association for Computational Linguistics, Morristown, NJ, USA, pp. 134–141 (2003)

23. Stone, P., Kirsh, J., Associates, C.C.: The General Inquirer: A Computer Approach to Content Analysis. MIT Press, Cambridge (1966)
24. Turney, P.D.: Thumbs up or thumbs down? semantic orientation applied to unsupervised classification of reviews. In: Proceedings of the 40th Annual Meeting of the Association for Computational Linguistics (ACL), Philadelphia, pp. 417–424 (July 2002)
25. Turney, P.D., Littman, M.L.: Measuring praise and criticism: Inference of semantic orientation from association. ACM Transactions on Information Systems 21(4), 315–346 (2003)
26. Wiebe, J., Wilson, T., Bell, M.: Identifying collocations for recognizing opinions. In: Proceedings of the ACL 2001 Workshop on Collocation: Computational Extraction, Analysis, and Exploitation, pp. 24–31 (2001)
27. Wilson, T., Wiebe, J., Hoffmann, P.: Recognizing contextual polarity in phrase-level sentiment analysis. In: HLT 2005: Proceedings of the Conference on Human Language Technology and Empirical Methods in Natural Language Processing. Association for Computational Linguistics, Morristown, NJ, USA, pp. 347–354 (2005)
28. Witten, I.H., Frank, E.: Data Mining: Practical machine learning tools and techniques, 2nd edn. Morgan Kaufmann, San Francisco (2005)
29. Yi, J., Nasukawa, T., Bunescu, R., Niblack, W.: Sentiment analyzer: extracting sentiments about a given topic using natural language processing techniques. In: Proceedings of the Third IEEE International Conference on Data Mining, pp. 427–434 (November 2003)
30. Zhang, M., Ye, X.: A generation model to unify topic relevance and lexicon-based sentiment for opinion retrieval. In: SIGIR '08: Proceedings of the 31st annual international ACM SIGIR conference on Research and development in information retrieval, pp. 411–418. ACM, New York (2008)
31. Zhuang, L., Jing, F., Zhu, X.Y.: Movie review mining and summarization. In: Proceedings of the 15th ACM International Conference on Information and Knowledge Management (CIKM 2006), pp. 43–50. ACM, New York (2006)

Author Index